PLAYFAIR
FOOTBALL
ANNUAL 1989-90

PLAYFAIR FOOTBALL ANNUAL 1989-90

EDITED BY JACK ROLLIN

Macdonald
Queen Anne Press

A Queen Anne Press BOOK

© Queen Anne Press 1989

First published in Great Britain in 1989 by
Queen Anne Press, a division of
Macdonald & Co (Publishers) Ltd
6th Floor, Headway House
66–73 Shoe Lane
London EC4P 4AB

A member of Maxwell Pergamon Publishing Corporation plc

Jacket photograph: Colorsport

British Library Cataloguing in Publication Data

Playfair football annual_____1989–90
  1. Soccer_____Periodicals
  796.334′05   GV942
  ISBN 0-356-17846-3

Typeset by Selectmove Ltd, London
Reproduced, printed and bound in Great Britain
by Cox & Wyman Ltd, Reading

CONTENTS

Non-League Football

Information and Records

Editorial

The Hillsborough disaster in which 95 innocent Liverpool supporters died and nearly 200 were injured, was the most tragic event in the history of sport in this country. It would be a lasting memorial to those who lost their lives if attitudes inside and outside the game could be changed for the better as a result of this dreadful occurrence. Alas this seems unlikely, at least in the short term.

Nearly 30 years of gradually declining behaviour has left both interested and disinterested parties in entrenched positions. People who could not care less about the game – though they are still in a minority according to Research Services Ltd – are simply appalled by the mention of football nowadays. The Government considers, rightly or wrongly, that the game's authorities are not taking sufficient responsibility for controlling the hooligan element and intends to impose its unpopular identity card scheme.

The genuine fan objects to being herded along under a police escort whenever he wants to visit an away ground. There he is enclosed behind a fence. The police look upon the younger supporters with suspicion because it is from this age group that the hooligans have emerged. Moreover by far the largest proportion of those attending matches come from the 15–24 age group, something in the region of one four in fact.

Oddly enough the age group that retains the highest level of interest, aside from the young, is that of pensioners, though they have only an eighth as much interest is actually attending games, for a variety of reasons, not all of them obvious. Many older supporters are put off by the general level of aggression which can be shown by young people at matches. Much of this over-the-top behaviour is caused by drinking. Again, a recent survey produced the frightening statistic that 77 per cent of 15 year olds are drinking up to half the accepted level of 21 units per week of alcohol – the quantity regarded as safe for one's health.

But none of us can escape blame for the situation in which football finds itself. It is no excuse to say that we live in a violent society and hooliganism has nothing to do with the game. The media has fostered partisanship and the notion that winning is all important. Would-be troublemakers are only too ready to prove themselves better than their rivals.

Lack of parental control and the erosion of discipline at home and in schools requires a re-education programme which could take a generation to have an effect. Questioning authority on the football field is a sure way of finding yourself in the referee's black book with a yellow card flashing before your eyes, so why should bad behaviour be tolerated off the field?

In the wake of Hillsborough there was an immediate call for all-seater stadiums. This would certainly help spectator control inside grounds but not attend to the problem outside. Installing more flexible fencing arrangements is another idea which received approval.

At the end of the domestic season the World Youth Cup was held in Scotland. The host nation reached the final before losing on penalties to Saudi Arabia. The general opinion was that the entire tournament was a huge success. Moreover it made the game family entertainment once more. Those who reported on the tournament and were young enough not to have had experience of watching football in happier times were pleasantly surprised. Indeed, they considered this to be an occasion when the image of the game improved dramatically. The word 'dignity' was even used.

There was probably little in this competition to interest the die-hard troublemaker. Contrast this with the behaviour of supporters going to the England v Poland game at Wembley early in June. The kick-off had to be delayed because of the late arrival of spectators. The latecomers arrived by public transport and many of them were the worse for drink. Fortunately the number of Polish supporters present was minimal and there was no confrontation. Overall, the police thought the afternoon went well enough without serious trouble, but only because they expect to face problems of a more violent nature when large football crowds are brought together.

Getting clubs involved with the community is to be recommended and already much progress has been made in this direction. The factions likely to present problems can be squeezed out by replacing them with fans who want to be involved in a more responsible way. These are youngsters from families who either support the game themselves or who approve of their children being associated with football. This way, we might begin to isolate the hooligan.

At present the wilful troublemaker or the one influenced by others can thrive. Football may not be able to alter society, but it can play a significant role in influencing the cultivation of a different type of spectator. This has to be an ideal for the future, otherwise the game will simply lurch from one crisis to another. Family enclosures should not be pockets of harmonic resistance to the terrace louts nosily chanting obscenities. The balance must swing the other way and then the atmosphere might improve to such an extent that the areas where violence could erupt inside and outside the ground start to shrink.

While off-the-field activities tended to take maximum attention, the race for the League Championship could not have been more exciting. The title was decided in the last minute of the last League game and saw Arsenal wrest the prize from Liverpool at Anfield. Arsenal needed to win by at least a two goal margin. They took the lead early in the second half and scored a dramatic second goal in the dying seconds through Michael Thomas. It was an awful anti-climax for Liverpool who had appeared sure of achieving their second League and Cup double in three years. Arsenal had frittered away chances of piling up the points at Highbury when they collected just one point from a possible six and their prospects at Anfield seemed bleak.

Overall attendances at Barclays League matches improved for the third season in succession, rising to 18.4 million. This is the first time since WWII that there has been an increase for three seasons in a row, though the total is modest enough compared with 40 years and even 20 years ago.

Though Arsenal were champions and Liverpool became the closest of runners-up, having scored fewer goals despite having the same goal difference, so-called non-Super League teams acquitted themselves well enough. At no time in the season did they have less than five in the top half of the table. Norwich City looked good enough at times to be champions themselves until falling away towards the later stages, while Millwall surprised even themselves with their sound start which also tapered away only at the end.

Norwich eventually finished fourth behind the often equally attractive Nottingham Forest. In fifth place Derby County for whom veteran England goalkeeper Peter Shilton kept an excellent defence and also beat the Bobby Moore record of 108 caps for his country.

Coventry City and Queen's Park Rangers were the other two 'unfashionable' teams to finish in the top half. In the second half of the season Tottenham Hotspur became the most improved side and during the close season signed Gary Lineker from Barcelona for £1.5 million.

Although the First Division's programme was reduced to 380 matches, the overall number of games played in the League itself increased to 2,036 the highest figure in the history of the competition. All divisions showed increased average attendances, the Third Division gaining most, largely through the support given to Wolverhampton Wanderers, regularly watched by five figure crowds.

Taking success and failure on a geographical level, it is interesting to note areas which produced celebration and others revealing depression. London, naturally, with the League champions Arsenal at their head, could be well satisfied if at the same time feeling sad at the fall of West Ham from the top of the echelon.

The departure of the Hammers was offset by the addition of two teams from the Second Division in the form of Chelsea – returning after just a season below – and Crystal Palace who finished third and then succeeded in the play-offs. Another triumph for the capital was the promotion to Division Three of Leyton Orient, again through the play-offs after they had finished sixth in the Fourth Division.

That once hot-bed of the game, the North East, suffered two further blows with the relegation from the First Division of Middlesbrough and Newcastle United, the former going down after just one season back at the top. Darlington lost their League status completely at the foot of Division Four.

The North West could look to another excellent playing season at Liverpool while promotion came for Manchester City as runners-up in Division Two. Another Merseyside triumph came in the shape of Tranmere Rovers who finished second in Division Four.

Yorkshire had two promotion spots to please them. Sheffield United followed on the heels of Wolves in the Third Division while Rotherham United bounced straight back by winning the championship of Division Four.

But the depressed Midlands showed few signs of lifting itself out of the doldrums. Shrewsbury, Birmingham and Walsall made it an unhappy trio descending to Division Three. But there was brighter news from the Potteries with Port Vale slipping into Division Two via the play-offs and Crewe Alexandra gaining promotion from Division Four. In the north Midlands Chesterfield found themselves relegated to Division Four after a near miss the previous season.

The South East also suffered a treble disappointment with the loss of Southend, Gillingham and Aldershot to the Fourth Division, though the gain of Maidstone United from the GM Vauxhall Conference was welcomed in that part of the world.

Finally Spurs manager Terry Venables sold England striker Chris Waddle to Marseille for a British record £4.5 million. The drift abroad shows no sign of diminishing. At home the close season had its usual hints of the top clubs wanting more money from television and rumours of a Super League on one hand and even a return to 22 clubs in the First Division on the other. Football as usual is not sure where it is heading.

FOOTBALL LEAGUE CLUBS AND THEIR PLAYERS

ALDERSHOT   DIV. 4

Anderson, Darren I.
Barnes, David
Brown, Kevan B.
Burvill, Glen
Claridge, Stephen E.

Devereux, James A.
Holsgrove, Paul
Lange, Anthony S.
McDonald, Ian C.
Phillips, Ian A.

Puckett, David C.
Randall, Adrian J.
Smith, Colin R.
Stewart, Ian
Wignall, Steven L.

Leagues Appearances: Anderson, Darren I. 22(11); Barnes, David 39; Berry, Stephen A. 12; Brown, Kevan 27(1); Burvill, Glen 42; Chandler, Ian 5(4); Claridge, Stephen E. 37; Coombs, Paul A. 1; Devereux, James A. −(1); Hewitt, Daren P. −(2); Holsgrove, Paul −(1); Lange, Anthony S. 45; McDonald, Ian C. 43; Mazzon, Giorgio 18(10); Osgood, Stephen 1; Phillips, Ian A. 30; Puckett, David C. 21; Randall, Adrian J. 37; Riley, Glyn 22(7); Ring, Michael P. 8(6); Smith, Colin R. 45; Stewart, Ian 21(1); Wignall, Steven L. 30(2).
League Goals (48): Puckett 11 (3 pens), Claridge 9, Burvill 7, McDonald 6 (1 pen), Anderson 2, Chandler 2, Randall 2, Ring 2, Smith 2, Barnes 1, Mazzon 1, Wignall 1, own goals 2.
Littlewoods Cup (0)
FA Cup (4): McDonald 2 (1 pen), Claridge 1, Randall 1.
Ground: Recreation Ground, High St., Aldershot GU11 1TW (0252–20211)
Nearest station: Aldershot
Manager: Len Walker **Secretary:** J. Pollard
Colours: Plain red shirts with blue trim; blue shorts
Record home gate: 19,138 v Carlisle, January 1970 (FA Cup)
Honours: Nil

ARSENAL   DIV. 1

Adams, Tony A.
Ampadu, Kwame
Bould, Stephen A.
Caesar, Gus C.
Campbell, Kevin J.
Carstairs, James
Connelly, Dean
Davis, Paul V.
Dixon, Lee M.
Francis, Lee C.
Groves, Perry

Hannigan, Al J.
Hayes, Martin
Hillier, David
Lee, Raymond M.
Lukic, Jovan
McKeown, Gary J.
Marriott, Andrew
Marwood, Brian
Merson, Paul C.
Miller, Alan J.
Mockler, Andrew J.

Morrow, Stephen J.
O'Leary, David A.
Quinn, Niall J.
Richardson, Kevin,
Rocastle, David
Scully, Patrick J.
Smith, Alan M.
Thomas, Michael L.
Wilmot, Rhys J.
Winterburn, Nigel

League Appearances: Adams, Tony A. 36; Bould, Stephen A. 26(4); Caesar, Gus C. 2; Davis, Paul V. 11(1); Dixon, Lee M. 31(2); Groves, Perry 6(15); Hayes, Martin 3(14); Lukic, Jovan 38; Marwood, Brian 31; Merson, Paul C. 29(8); O'Leary, David A. 26; Quinn, Niall J. 2(1); Richardson, Kevin 32(2); Rocastle, David 38; Smith, Alan M. 36; Thomas, Michael L. 33(4); Winterburn, Nigel 38.

8

League Goals (73): Smith 23, Merson 10, Marwood 9 (2 pens), Thomas 7, Rocastle 6, Adams 4, Groves 4, Winterburn 3, Bould 2, Davis 1, Dixon 1, Hayes 1, Quinn 1, Richardson 1.
Littlewoods Cup (7): Merson 2, Smith 2, Marwood 1, Rocastle 1, Winterburn 1.
FA Cup (2): Merson 2.
Ground: Arsenal Stadium, Avenell Road, N5 1BU (01–226 0304)
Nearest stations: Arsenal (Piccadilly Line), Drayton Park (British Rail) or Finsbury Park (BR, Piccadilly Line or Victoria Line)
Manager: George Graham **Secretary:** Ken Friar
Colours: Red shirts, with white sleeves; white shorts
Record home gate: 73,295 v Sunderland, March 1935 (League)
Honours – Champions: Division 1: 1930–1, 1932–3, 1933–4, 1934–5, 1937–8, 1947–8, 1952–3, 1970–71, 1988–9
FA Cup winners: 1929–30, 1935–6, 1949–50, 1970–71, 1978–9
League Cup winners: 1986–7
Fairs Cup winners: 1969–70

ASTON VILLA   DIV. 1

Birch, Paul	Gray, Stuart	Ormonroyd, Ian
Butler, Lee S.	Keown, Martin R.	Platt, David
Callaghan, Nigel	Lillis, Mark A.	Price, Christopher J.
Cowans, Gordon S.	McInally, Alan	Simms, Steven F.
Daley, Anthony M.	Mountfield, Derek N.	Spink, Nigel P.
Gage, Kevin W.	Olney, Ian D.	Williams, Gareth J.
Gallacher, Bernard		

League Appearances: Birch, Paul 6(6); Butler, Lee S. 4; Callaghan, Nigel 15(1); Cowans, Gordon S. 32(1); Daley, Anthony M. 25(4); Duffy, Darrell G. 1; Evans, Allan 26(1); Gage, Kevin W. 27(1); Gallacher, Bernard 3(1); Gray, Andrew A. 15(3); Gray, Stuart 35; Hunt, David 1; Keown, Martin R. 32(2); Lillis, Mark A. 2; McInally, Alan 32(1); Mountfield, Derek N. 22(2); Olney, Ian D. 8(7); Ormondroyd, Ian 9(3); Platt, David 38; Price, Christopher J. 36; Sims, Steven F.12; Spink, Nigel P. 34; Thompson, Garry L. 2(3); Williams, Gareth J. 1.
League Goals (45): McInally 14, Platt 7, Daley 5, Gray, S. 4(1 pen), Gray, A. 3, Gage 3, Cowans 2, Olney 2, Callaghan 1, Mountfield 1, Ormondroyd 1, own goals 2.
Littlewoods Cup (17): Platt 6, McInally 4, Gage 3, Daley 1, Gray, A. 1, Mountfield 1, Olney 1.
FA Cup (3): Gage 1, McInally 1, Platt 1.
Ground: Villa Park, Birmingham B6 6HE (021–327 6604)
Nearest station: Witton and Aston
Manager: Graham Taylor **Secretary:** Steven Stride
Colours: Claret and blue shirts; white shorts
Record home gate: 76,588 v Derby, March 1946 (FA Cup)
Honours – Champions: Division 1: 1893–4, 1895–6, 1896–7, 1898–9, 1899–1900, 1909–10, 1980–81; Division 2: 1937–8, 1959–60; Division 3: 1971–2
FA Cup winners: 1886–7, 1894–5, 1896–7, 1904–5, 1912–13, 1919–20, 1956–7. (Seven wins joint record with Spurs)
League Cup winners: 1960–61, 1974–5, 1976–7
European Cup winners: 1981–2

BARNSLEY   DIV. 2

Agnew, Stephen M.
Baker, Clive E.
Broddle, Julian R.
Clarke, Michael D.
Cooper, Stephen B.
Cross, Paul
Currie, David N.
Dobbin, James

Foreman, Darren
Futcher, Paul
Joyce, Joseph P.
Lowndes, Stephen R.
MacDonald, John
McGugan, Paul J.
Marshall, Colin
Rees, Anthony A.

Robinson, Mark J.
Rolph, Darren G.
Ross, David
Shotton, Malcolm
Thomas, David G.
Tiler, Carl
Wardle, Ian S.

League Appearances: Agnew, Stephen M. 35(4); Baker, Clive E. 46; Beresford, John 27; Broddle, Julian R. 34(4); Clarke, Michael D. 3; Cooper, Stephen B. 28(7); Currie, David N. 41; Dobbin, James 36(5); Foreman, Darren −(5); Futcher, Paul 41; Joyce, Joseph P. 45; Lowndes, Stephen R. 30(3); MacDonald, John 28(4); McGugan, Paul J. 19(1); Marshall, Colin −(1); Rees, Anthony A. 15(2); Robinson, Mark J. 15(3); Shotton, Malcolm 35(2); Thomas, David G. 24; Tiler, Carl 4.

Leagues Goals (66): Currie 16 (8 pens), Agnew 6, Cooper 6, Lowndes 6, Dobbin 5 (1 pen), MacDonald 5, Shotton 5, Broddle 3, Robinson 2, Thomas 2, Beresford 1, McGugan 1, Rees 1, own goals 7.

Littlewoods Cup (1): Currie 1.

FA Cup (9): Currie 3, Agnew 2, MacDonald 2, Cooper 1, Thomas 1.

Ground: Oakwell, Grove Street, Barnsley S71 1ET (0226–295353)

Nearest station: Barnsley

Manager: Allan Clarke **Secretary:** Michael Spinks

Colours: Red shirts; white shorts

Record home gate: 40,255 v Stoke 1936 (FA Cup)

Honours – Champions: Division 3 North: 1933–4, 1938–9, 1954–5

FA Cup winners: 1911–12

BIRMINGHAM CITY   DIV. 3

Ashley, Kevin M.
Atkins, Ian L.
Bird, Adrian L.
Burton, Michael J.
Childs, Gary P.C.
Clarkson, Ian S.
Frain, John W.

Hansbury, Roger
Hopkins, Robert A.
Langley, Kevin J.
Morris, Ronald
Overson, Vincent D.
Peer, Dean
Richards, Carroll L.

Roberts, Brian L.F.
Robinson, Colin R.
Sturridge, Simon A.
Tait, Paul R.
Thomas, Martin R.
Yates, Mark J.

League Appearances: Ashley, Kevin M. 15; Atkins, Ian L. 40; Bird, Adrian 11(1); Bremner, Desmond G. 28(1); Burton, Michael J. −(4); Childs, Gary P.C. 16(7); Clarkson, Ian S. 9; Fox, Matthew C. 3; Frain, John W. 28; Godden, Anthony L. 7; Hansbury, Roger 3; Hopkins, Robert A. 9; Langley, Kevin J. 34(2); Morris, Ronald 3(7); Overson, Vincent D. 41; Peer, Dean 15(2); Ranson, Raymond 17; Richards, Carroll L. 18(1); Roberts, Brian L.F. 41; Robinson, Colin R. 31(2); Sturridge, Simon A. 13(8); Tait, Paul R. 6(4); Thomas, Martin R. 36; Trewick, John 10(1); Whitton, Stephen P. 23; Wigley, Steven 33; Yates, Mark J. 16(4)

League Goals (31): Robinson 5, Whitton 5 (1 pen), Atkins 3 (1 pen), Frain 3,

10

Sturridge 3, Yates 3, Langley 2, Richards 2, Bremner 1, Childs 1, Peer 1, Wigley 1, own goal 1.
Littlewoods Cup (3): Bird 1, Whitton 1, own goal 1.
FA Cup (0)
Ground: St Andrews, Birmingham B9 4NH (021–772 0101 and 2689)
Nearest station: Birmingham, New Street
Manager: Dave Mackay **Secretary:** H.J. Westmancoat FFA, MBIM.
Colours: Blue shirts with white trim; white shorts
Record home gate: 66,844 v Everton, February 1939 (FA Cup)
Honours – Champions: Division 2: 1892–3, 1920–21, 1947–8, 1954–5
League Cup winners: 1962–3

BLACKBURN ROVERS   DIV. 2

Atkins, Mark N.	Gennoe, Terence W.	Mail, David
Collier, Darren	Hendry, Edward C.J.	May, David
Dawson, Alistair J.	Hildersley, Ronald	Millar, John
Diamond, Anthony J.	Hill, Keith J.	Reid, Nicholas S.
Finnigan, Anthony	Johnrose, Leonard	Sellars, Scott
Garner, Simon	Kennedy, Andrew J.	Sulley, Christopher S.
Gayle, Howard A.		

League Appearances: Ainscow, Alan 6(9); Atkins, Mark N. 46; Byrne, David S. 4; Collier, Darren 1; Curry, Sean P. 1(6); Dawson, Alistair J. 3(3); Diamond, Anthony J. 1(10); Finnigan, Anthony 13(4); Garner, Simon 43(1); Gayle, Howard A. 45; Gennoe, Terence W. 43; Hendry, Edward C.J. 38; Hildersley, Ronald 23(2); Hill, Keith J. 13(2); Kennedy, Andrew J. 23(2); Mail, David 40; May, David 1; Millar, John 37(1); Miller, Ian 21(10); O'Keefe, James V. 2; Reid, Nicholas S. 37; Sellars, Scott 46; Sulley, Christopher S. 19
League Goals (73): Garner 20, Gayle 19 (8 pens), Kennedy 10, Hendry 7, Atkins 6, Hildersley 4, Sellars 2, Diamond 1, Hill 1, Reid 1, own goals 2.
Littlewoods Cup (7): Garner 2, Sellars 2, Atkins 1, Gayle 1, own goal 1.
FA Cup (3): Finnigan 1, Garner 1, Hildersley 1.
Ground: Ewood Park, Nuttall Street, Blackburn BB2 4JF (0254–55432)
Nearest station: Blackburn
Manager: Donald Mackay **Secretary:** John W. Howarth F.A.A.I.
Colours: Shirts: blue and white halves; white shorts
Record home gate: 61,783 v Bolton Wanderers, March 1929 (FA Cup)
Honours – Champions: Division 1: 1911–12, 1913–14; Division 2: 1938–9; Division 3: 1974–5
FA Cup winners: 1883–4, 1884–5, 1885–6, 1889–90, 1890–91, 1927–8
Full Members' Cup winners: 1986–7

BLACKPOOL   DIV. 3

Bradshaw, Mark	Deary, John S.	Morgan, Stephen A.
Burgess, David J.	Elliott, Shaun	Rooney, Simon A.
Burns, Steven A.	Garner, Andrew	Taylor, Peter M.R.
Coughlin, Russell	Gore, Ian G.	Thompson,
Cunningham, Anthony E.	Madden, Craig A.	Christopher D.
Davies, Michael J.	Matthews, Neil P.	Wright, Alan G.

League Appearances: Burgess, David J. 46; Coughlin, Russell 42(1); Cunningham, Anthony E. 31; Davies, Michael J. 25(5); Deary, John S. 35(2); Elliott, Shaun 41; Garner, Andrew 41(1); Gore, Ian G. 19(2); Kelly, Gary A. 5; Madden, Craig A. 20(7); Matthews, Neil P. 10(4); Methven, Colin J. 41(1); Morgan, Stephen A. 43(1); O'Keefe, James V. 6; Rooney, Simon A. −(1); Siddall, Barry 35; Taylor, Peter M.R. 8(1); Thompson, Christopher D. 25(11); Walsh, Michael C. 6(3); Walwyn, Keith I. 13(17); Wright, Alan G. 14(2).
League Goals (56): Garner 11 (1 pen), Thompson 8, Cunningham 7, Coughlin 5 (4 pens), Deary 5, Madden 4, Morgan 3, Taylor 3, Walwyn 3, Davies 2, Matthews 1, Methven 1, own goals 3.
Littlewoods Cup (7): Garner 2, Coughlin 1, Cunningham 1, Deary 1, Morgan 1, Taylor 1 (pen).
FA Cup (5): Cunningham 2, Garner 2, Deary 1.
Ground: Bloomfield Road, Blackpool FY1 6JJ (0253–404331)
Nearest station: Blackpool North
Manager: Jimmy Mullen **Secretary:** D. Johnson
Colours: Tangerine shirts with white collar and cuffs; tangerine shorts
Record home gate: 38,098 v Wolves, April 1952 (League)
Honours – Champions: Division 2: 1929–30
FA Cup winners: 1952–3
Anglo–Italian Cup winners: 1971

BOLTON WANDERERS   DIV. 3

Brookman, Nicholas A.
Brown, Gary M.
Brown, Philip
Came, Mark R.
Chandler, Jeffrey G.
Cowdrill, Barry J.
Crombie, Dean M.

Darby, Julian T.
Felgate, David W.
Gray, Gareth
Henshaw, Gary
Hughes, Paul
Jeffrey, Michael R.
Morgan, Trevor J.

Neal, Philip G.
Savage, Robert J.
Stevens, Ian D.
Storer, Stuart J.
Thomas, John W.
Thompson, Stephen J.
Winstanley, Mark A.

League Appearances: Barnes, Peter S. 2(1); Brookman, Nicholas A. 20(5); Brown, Philip 46; Came, Mark R. 2; Chandler, Jeffrey G. 16(4); Cowdrill, Barry J. 38; Crombie, Dean M. 28(3); Darby, Julian T. 44; Elliott, Stephen B. 3; Felgate, David W. 46; Henshaw, Gary 16(5); Jeffrey, Michael R. 7(2); Jemson, Nigel B. 4(1); Keeley, Glenn M. 20; Morgan, Trevor J. 34(5); Neal, Philip G. 3(5); Savage, Robert J. 37(1); Stevens, Ian D. 15(6); Storer, Stuart J. 10(13); Thomas, John W. 28(1); Thompson, Stephen J. 43; Winstanley, Mark A. 44.
League Goals (58): Morgan 10, Thomas 9, Thompson 9 (3 pens), Savage 6, Darby 5, Stevens 5, Brookman 4, Brown 4, Chandler 2, Henshaw 2, Storer 2.
Littlewoods Cup (2): Cowdrill 1, Darby 1.
FA Cup (4): Darby 1, Keeley 1, Stevens 1, Storer 1.
Ground: Burnden Park, Manchester Rd., Bolton BL3 2QR (0204–389200)
Player/Manager: Phil Neal **Secretary:** Des McBain, F.A.A.I.
Nearest station: Bolton
Colours: White shirts; navy blue shorts
Record home gate: 69,912 v Manchester City, February 1933 (FA Cup)
Honours – Champions: Division 2: 1908–9, 1977–8; Division 3: 1972–3
FA Cup winners: 1922–3, 1925–6, 1928–9, 1957–8
Sherpa Van Trophy winners: 1988–9

AFC BOURNEMOUTH   DIV. 2

Aylott, Trevor K.C.
Barnes, David O.
Bishop, Ian W.
Blissett, Luther L.
Bond, Kevin J.
Brooks, Shaun
Close, Shaun C.

Coleman, David H.
Holmes, Matthew J.
Morrell, Paul D.P.
Mundee, Denny W.J.
Newson, Mark J.
O'Connor, Mark A.

O'Driscoll, Sean M.
Peyton, Gerald J.
Pulis, Anthony R.
Shearer, Peter A.
Teale, Shaun
Williams, William J.

League Appearances: Aylott, Trevor K.C. 39(1); Barnes, David O. 10; Bishop, Ian W. 44; Blissett, Luther L. 30; Bond, Kevin J. 27; Brooks, Shaun 29(7); Clarke, Colin J. 3(1); Close, Shaun C. 13(10); Coleman, David H. 6(3); Cooke, Richard E. 11(4); Holmes, Matthew J. 4; Morrell, Paul D.P. 44; Mundee, Denny W.J. 1(1); Newson, Mark J. 40; O'Connor, Mark A. 29(4); O'Driscoll, Sean M. 38(3); Peyton, Gerald J. 39; Puckett, David C. 2(2); Pulis, Anthony R. 10; Richards, Carroll L. 8; Shearer, Peter A. 4; Smeulders, John 7; Teale, Shaun 19(1); Whitlock, Mark 12(1); Williams, William J. 37.

League Goals (53): Blissett 19 (3 pens), Newson 7, Aylott 6, Brooks 3, Cooke 3, Bishop 2, Clarke 2, Close 2, O'Connor 2, Williams 2, Bond 1, Coleman 1, Holmes 1, Shearer 1, own goal 1.

Littlewoods Cup (2): Aylott 1, Cooke 1.

FA Cup (8): Blissett 2 (1 pen), Aylott 1, Cooke 1, Morrell 1, Newson 1, own goals 2

Ground: Dean Court, Bournemouth, Dorset BH7 7AF (0202–35381)

Nearest station: Bournemouth

Manager: Harry Redknapp **Secretary:** Brian Tiler

Colours: All red

Record home gate: 28,799 v Manchester United, March 1957 (FA Cup)

Honours – Champions: Division 3: 1986–7 **Associate Members Cup winners** 1983–4

BRADFORD CITY   DIV. 2

Abbott, Gregory S.
Campbell, David A.
Chapman, Gary A.
Costello, Peter
Duxbury, Lee E.
Ellis, Mark E.
Evans, David G.

Evans, Mark
Goddard, Karl E.
Graham, James
Jackson, Peter A.
Jewell, Paul
Leonard, Mark A.
Mitchell, Charles B.

Oliver, Gavin R.
Palin, Leigh G.
Quinn, James M.
Sinnott, Lee
Thomas, Andrew M.
Tinnion, Brian
Tomlinson, Paul

League Appearances: Abbott, Gregory S. 23(5); Banks, Ian F. 26(4); Campbell, David A. 12; Chapman, Gary A. 1(1); Costello, Peter 3(5); Duxbury, Lee E. −(1); Ellis, Mark E. 4(1); Evans, David G. 33(1); Evans, Mark 3; Goddard, Karl E. 18(5); Graham, James (1); Jackson, Peter A. 30(2); Jewell, Paul 22(17); Kennedy, Michael F. 30; Leonard, Mark A. 40(4); Litchfield, Peter 5; Mitchell, Charles B. 44(1); Oliver, Gavin R. 38(1); Ormondroyd, Ian 25; Palin, Leigh G. 28(2); Quinn, James M. 12; Sinnott, Lee 42; Thomas, Andrew M. 15(8); Tinnion, Brian 14; Tomlinson, Paul 38.

League Goals (52): Quinn 8, Leonard 7, Thomas 5 (1 pen), Abbott 4 (2 pens),

Jewell 4, Ormondroyd 4, Palin 4 (1 pen), Banks 3, Jackson 3, Costello 2, Sinnott 2, Campbell 1, Ellis 1, Kennedy 1, Mitchell 1, Oliver 1, Tinnion 1 (pen).
Littlewoods Cup (8): Banks 3, Leonard 2, Jewell 1, Ormondroyd 1, Palin 1.
FA Cup (2): Leonard 1, Mitchell 1.
Ground: Valley Parade, Bradford BD8 7DY (0274–306062)
Nearest station: Bradford Exchange
Manager: Terry Yorath **Secretary:** T.F. Newman
Colours: Claret and amber striped shirts; black shorts
Record home gate: 39,146 v Burnley, March 1911 (FA Cup)
Honours – Champions: Division 2: 1907–8, Division 3: 1984–5; Division 3 North: 1928–9
FA Cup winners: 1910–11 (first holders of present trophy)

BRENTFORD   DIV. 3

Ansah, Andrew
Bates, Jamie
Birch, Paul A.
Blissett, Gary P.
Buttigieg, John
Cadette, Richard R.

Cockram, Allan C.
Evans, Terence, W.
Feeley, Andrew J.
Godfrey, Kevin
Jones, Keith A.

Millen, Keith
Parks, Anthony
Ratcliffe, Simon
Smillie, Neil
Stanislaus, Roger E.P.

League Appearances: Ansah, Andrew 3(4); Bates, Jamie 31(5); Birch, Paul A. –(2); Blissett, Gary P. 35(1); Booker, Robert 5(3); Buttigieg, John 12(6); Cadette, Richard R. 31(1); Cockram, Allan C. 31(6); Driscoll, Andrew –(1); Evans, Terence W. 45; Feeley, Andrew J. 30(3); Gayle, Marcus A. –(3); Godfrey, Kevin 24(5); Holdsworth, Dean C. 2(5); Jones, Keith A. 40; Lee, Colin 1(1); Millen, Keith 36; Parks, Anthony 33; Pearce, Graham 11(7); Perryman, Stephen J. 2(3); Purdie, Jon 5(1); Ratcliffe, Simon 7(2); Roberts, Jeremy 5; Sealy, Anthony J. 11(1); Sinton, Andrew 31; Smeulders, John 8; Smillie, Neil 25(3); Stanislaus, Roger E.P. 42(1).
League Goals (66): Cadette 12, Sinton 9 (4 pens), Godfrey 8, Cockram 7 (2 pens), Blissett 6, Evans 5, Sealy 4, Jones 3, Millen 3, Ansah 2, Smillie 2, Bates 1, Holdsworth 1, Ratcliffe 1, Stanislaus 1, own goal 1.
Littlewoods Cup (8): Blissett 2, Cadette 2, Sinton 2, Jones 1, Stanislaus 1.
FA Cup (12): Blissett 4, Cockram 2, Jones 2, Cadette 1, Evans 1, Sinton 1, Smillie 1.
Ground: Griffin Park, Braemar Road, Brentford TW8 0NT (01–847 2511/3)
Nearest stations: Brentford (BR) or South Ealing (Piccadilly line)
Manager: Steve Perryman **Secretary:** Polly Kates
Colours: Red and white striped shirts; black shorts.
Record home gate: 39,626 v Preston North End, March 1968 (FA Cup)
Honours – Champions: Division 2: 1934–5; Division 3 South: 1932–3; Division 4: 1962–3.

BRIGHTON & HOVE ALBION DIV. 2

Bissett, Nicholas
Bremner, Kevin J.
Chapman, Ian R.
Chivers, Gary P.S.
Codner, Robert A.G.
Crumplin, John L.
Curbishley, Llewellyn C.
Digweed, Perry M.

Dineen, Jack A.
Dublin, Keith B.L.
Gatting, Steven P.
Isaac, Robert C.
Keeley, John H.
McCarthy, Paul J.
May, Lawrence C.
Nelson, Garry P.

Owers, Adrian R.
Penney, Steven A.
Robinson, John R.C.
Stemp, Wayne D.
Trusson, Michael S.
Wilkins, Dean M.
Wood, Paul A.

League Appearances: Armstrong, Gerard J. 3(2); Bissett, Nicholas 16; Bremner, Kevin J. 41; Brown, Kevan 2(1); Chapman, Ian R. 18(1); Chivers, Gary P.S. 46; Codner, Robert A.G. 22(6); Cooper, Geoffrey V. 2(3); Coles, David A. 1; Crumplin, John L. 7(5); Curbishley, Llewellyn C. 32(5); Digweed, Perry M. 1; Dublin, Keith B.L. 43; Fearon, Ronald T. 7; Gatting, Steven P. 29; Isaac, Robert C. 9; Keeley, John H. 37; May, Lawrence C. 24; Nelson, Garry P. 46; Owers, Adrian R. 21(3); Penney, Steven A. 9(1); Trusson, Michael S. 21(1); Wilkins, Dean M. 42(1); Wood, Paul A. 27(8)
League Goals (57): Bremner 15, Nelson 15, Chivers 6, Curbishley 6 (4 pens), Gatting 3, May 3, Owers 2, Armstrong 1, Codner 1, Penney 1, Wilkins 1, Wood 1, own goals 2.
Littlewoods Cup (0)
FA Cup (1): Curbishley 1 (pen)
Ground: Goldstone Ground, Old Shoreham Road, Hove, Sussex BN3 7DE (0273–739535)
Nearest station: Hove
Manager: Barry Lloyd **Secretary:** Steve Rooke
Colours: Blue and white striped shirts; white shorts
Record home gate: 36,747 v Fulham, December 1958 (League)
Honours – Champions: Division 3 South: 1957–8; Division 3: 1971–2; Division 4: 1964–5

BRISTOL CITY DIV. 3

Bailey, John A.
Bromage, Russel
Dent, Nicholas
Eaton, Jason C.
Galliers, Steven
Gavin, Mark W.
Hawkins, Nigel S.

Honor, Christian R.
Humphries, Glenn
Jordan, Joseph
Leaning, Andrew J.
Llewellyn, Andrew
McClaren, Stephen
McQuilter, Ronald

Mardon, Paul J.
Newman, Robert N.
Pender, John P.
Taylor, Robert
Turner, Robert P.
Walsh, Alan
Waugh, Keith

League Appearances: Bailey, John A. 35; Bromage, Russel 13; Caldwell, Anthony 1; Carter, Timothy D. 3; Dolan, Eamonn J. 3; Eaton, Jason C. −(2); Fitzpatrick, Paul J. −(1); Galliers, Steven 30(3); Gavin, Mark W. 26(3); Hawkins, Nigel S. 7(10); Honor, Christian R. 24(2); Humphries, Glenn 20(2); Jordan, Joseph 2(7); Leaning, Andrew J. 6; Llewellyn, Andrew 13(3); McClaren, Stephen 44(1); McGarvey, Scott T. 20(6); Mardon, Paul J. 13(7); Milne, Ralph 10(1); Newman, Robert N. 46; Pender, John P. 45; Shepherd, Anthony 2(1); Shutt, Carl S. 21(3); Stanley, Gary E. 8(2); Taylor, Robert 12; Turner, Robert P. 19; Walsh, Alan 46; Waugh, Keith 37.

League Goals (53): Walsh 11 (1 pen), McGarvey 9, Taylor 8, Newman 6 (3 pens), Turner 6, Gavin 3, Hawkins 2, Milne 2, Bromage 1, Jordan 1, Llewellyn 1, McClaren 1, Pender 1, Shutt 1.
Littlewoods Cup (15): Shutt 4, Walsh 4, Milne 3, Hawkins 1, McClaren 1, Mardon 1, Newman 1 (pen).
FA Cup (7): Shutt 4, McGarvey 1, Newman 1 (pen), Walsh 1.
Ground: Ashton Gate, Bristol BS3 2EJ (0272–632812)
Nearest station: Bristol Temple Meads
Manager: Joe Jordan **Secretary** Miss J. Harrison
Colours: Red shirts; white shorts
Record home gate: 43,335 v Preston, February 1935 (FA Cup)
Honours – Champions: Division 2: 1905–6; Division 3 South: 1922–3, 1926–7, 1954–5. **Freight Rover Trophy winners:** 1985–6

BRISTOL ROVERS   DIV. 3

Alexander, Ian
Clark, William R.
Holloway, Ian S.
Jones, Vaughan
McClean, Christian A.
Martyn, Anthony N.

Mehew, David S.
Nixon, Paul
Penrice, Gary K.
Purnell, Phillip
Reece, Andrew J.

Stapleton, Simon J.
Twentyman, Geoffrey
White, Devon W.
Willmott, Ian M.
Yates, Steven

League Appearances: Alexander, Ian 42; Bailey, Dennis L. 17; Clark, William R. 10(1); Dryden, Richard –(1); Hazel, Ian 3; Hibbitt, Kenneth –(1); Holloway, Ian
S. 44; Jones, Vaughan 45; McClean, Christian A. 16(12); Martyn, Anthony N. 46; Mehew, David S. 31; Nixon, Paul –(1); Penrice, Gary K. 43; Purnell, Phillip 35(2);
Reece, Andrew J. 42; Smith, Paul S. 14(2); Stapleton, Simon J. 4(1); Twentyman, Geoffrey 46; Viney, Keith B. 2(1); White, Devon W. 31(9); Yates, Steven 35.
League Goals (67): Penrice 20, Bailey 9, Mehew 7, Purnell 7, Reece 7, Holloway 6 (2 pens), White 5, Jones 2 (1 pen), McClean 2, Smith 1, Twentyman 1.
Littlewoods Cup (0)
FA Cup (4): Holloway 1 (pen), Jones 1, Penrice 1, Reece 1.
Ground: Twerton Park, Bath, Avon BA2 1DB (offices: 0272–352508)
Nearest station: Bath Spa
Manager: Gerry Francis **Secretary:** R.C. Twyford
Colours: Blue and white quartered shirts; white shorts
Record home gate: 38,472 v Preston, January 1960 (FA Cup)
Honours – Champions: Division 3 South: 1952–3

BURNLEY   DIV. 4

Atkinson, Paul G.
Comstive, Paul T.
Davis Steven P.
Deakin, Raymond J.
Farrell, Andrew J.
Gardner, Steven G.

Grewcock, Neil
Hardy, Jason P.
Heggarty, James P.
McGrory, Shaun P.
Measham, Ian
Monington, Mark D.

O'Connell, Brendan
Oghani, George
Pearce, Christopher L.
Rowell, Gary
White, Eric W.
Williams, David P.

League Appearances: Atkinson, Paul G. 13(1); Britton, Ian 36(1); Comstive, Paul T. 37(1); Daniel, Peter W. 14; Davis, Steven P. 37; Deakin, Raymond J. 14; Farrell Andrew J. 35(1); Gardner, Stephen G. 44; Grewcock, Neil 12(1); Hardy, Jason P. 16(1); Hooper, Stuart R.J. −(1); Hoskin, James A. 2(3); James, Leighton 14(4); Jones, David 4; McGrory, Shaun P. 12(7); Measham, Ian 30; Miller, David B. 4; Monington, Mark D. 6(2); Morley, Anthony 5; O'Connell, Brendan 42(1); Oghani, George 37; Pearce, Christopher L. 39; Rowell, Gary 8(10); Taylor, Steven J. −(3); White, Eric W. 30(5); Williams, David P. 7; Zelem, Peter R. 8(1).

League Goals (52): O'Connell 13, Comstive 9 (3 pens), Oghani 7, White 5 (1 pen), Farrell 4, Britton 3, James 3 (3 pens), Atkinson 1, Grewcock 1, Hardy 1, McGrory 1, Measham 1, Monington 1, Rowell 1, Zelem 1.

Littlewoods Cup (6): O'Connell 3, Comstive 2 (2 pens), Oghani 1.

FA Cup (0).

Ground: Turf Moor, Brunshaw Road, Burnley BB10 4BX (0282–27777)

Nearest station: Burnley Central

Manager: Frank Casper **Secretary:** R. Bradshaw

Colours: Claret shirts; white shorts

Record home gate: 54,775 v Huddersfield, February 1924 (FA Cup)

Honours – Champions: Division 1: 1920–21, 1959–60; Division 2: 1897–8, 1972–3; Division 3: 1981–2

FA Cup winners: 1913–14

BURY   DIV. 3

Atkin, Paul A.
Bishop, Charles
Brotherston, Noel
Clements, Kenneth H.
Elliott, Stephen B.

Farnworth, Simon
Greenwood, Nigel P.
Hill, Andrew
Hoyland, Jamie W.
Lee, David

McIlroy, Samuel B.
Parkinson, Philip J.
Pashley, Terence
Robinson, Spencer L.
Valentine, Peter

League Appearances: Atkin, Paul A. −(1); Bishop, Charles 37(1); Brotherston, Noel 2; Clements, Kenneth H. 43(1); Eli, Roger −(2); Elliott, Stephen B. 31; Entwistle, Wayne P. −(2); Farnworth, Simon 45; Fazackerley, Derek W. 7(7); Godden, Anthony L. 1; Greenwood, Nigel P. 10(13); Higgins, Mark N. 5; Hill, Andrew 43; Hoyland, Jamie W. 46; Hulme, Kevin 3(2); Jones, David −(1); Lee, David 45; Leonard, Gary A. 4(5); McIlroy, Samuel B. 45; Parkinson, Philip J. 36(3); Pashley, Terence 23(2); Robinson, Spencer L. 43; Valentine, Peter 29(1); Wassall, Darren P. 7; Windridge, David H. 1.

League Goals (55): Robinson 20 (7 pens), Elliott 11, Hoyland 9, Lee 4, Bishop 3, McIlroy 2, Greenwood 1, Leonard 1, Pashley 1, Valentine 1, Wassall 1, own goal 1.

Littlewoods Cup (6): Hoyland 2, Robinson 2 (1 pen), Entwistle 1, Lee 1.

FA Cup (1): Parkinson 1.

Ground: Gigg Lane, Bury BL9 9HR (061–764 4881/2)

Nearest station: Bury Metro Interchange

Manager: Martin Dobson **Secretary:** John Heap

Colours: White shirts; navy blue shorts

Record home gate: 35,000 v Bolton, January 1960 (FA Cup)

Honours – Champions: Division 2: 1894–5; Division 3: 1960–61

FA Cup winners: 1899–1900, 1902–3

CAMBRIDGE UNITED   DIV. 4

Bailie, Colin J.
Beck, John A.
Chapple, Philip R.
Clayton, Gary

Croft, Brian G.A.
Daish, Liam S.
Dennis, John A.
Dublin, Dion

Kimble, Alan F.
Ryan, Laurie J.
Taylor, John P.
Vaughan, John

League Appearances: Allen, Gregory F. 4; Anderson, Douglas E. 8; Bailie, Colin J. 23; Bastock, Paul A. 2; Beck, John A. 35(5); Bull, Gary W. 4(6); Byrne, David S. 4; Chapple, Philip R. 46; Clayton, Gary 45(1); Croft, Brian G.A. 12(5); Daish, Liam S. 28; Dearden, Kevin C. 15; Dennis, John A. 18; Dublin, Dion 12(9); Hamilton, Ian R. 14(1); Holmes, Michael A. 7(4); Howard, Mark E. −(2); Kimble, Alan F. 45; Leadbitter, Christopher J. 27(4); Poole, Gary 1; Reilly, George G. 20; Ryan, Laurie J. 34(5); Smith, Lyndsey J. 18; Taylor, John P. 34(6); Turner, Paul E. 21(1); Vaughan, John 29.
League Goals (71): Ryan 12, Taylor 12, Reilly 7, Dublin 6, Kimble 6 (5 pens), Leadbitter 6, Beck 4, Smith 4 (3 Pens), Chapple 3, Dennis 3, Anderson 2, Croft 2, Bailie 1, Bull 1, Clayton 1, own goal 1.
Littlewoods Cup (2): Clayton 1, Ryan 1.
FA Cup (5): Croft 2, Reilly 2, Chapple 1.
Ground: Abbey Stadium, Newmarket Road, Cambridge CB5 8LL (0223–241237)
Nearest station: Cambridge
Manager: Chris Turner **Secretary:** R. Johnson
Colours: Yellow and black shirts; yellow and black shorts
Record home gate: 14,000 v Chelsea (friendly), May 1970
Honours – Champions: Division 4: 1976–7

CARDIFF CITY   DIV. 3

Abraham, Gareth J.
Bater, Philip T.
Boyle, Terence D.J.
Curtis, Alan T.
Fry, Christopher D.
Gilligan, James M.
Gummer, Jason C.

Kelly, Mark D.
Lynex, Stephen C.
Morgan, Jonathan P.
Perry, Jason
Platnauer, Nicholas R.
Roberts, Jonathan W.

Rodgerson, Ian
Tupling, Stephen
Walsh, Ian P.
Wheeler, Paul
Wimbleton, Paul P.
Wood, George

League Appearances: Abraham, Gareth J. 31; Bartlett, Kevin 18(4); Bater, Philip T. 27(9); Boyle, Terence D.J. 34(2); Curtis, Alan T. 34(1); Fry, Christopher D. 5(4); Gibbins, Roger 9(3); Gilligan, James M. 46; Gummer, Jason C. 9(2); Haig, Richard N. −(1); Holmes, Matthew J. −(1); Kelly, Mark D. 24(4); Ketteridge, Stephen J. 6; Lynex, Stephen C. 34(2); McDermott, Brian J. 4(2); Morgan, Jonathan P. 13(6); Platnauer, Nicholas R. 39; Roberts, Jonathan W. 1; Rodgerson, Ian 39(1); Stevenson, Nigel C.A. 31(1); Tupling, Stephen 3(1); Walsh, Ian P. 4(7); Wheeler, Paul 15(12); Wimbleton, Paul P. 35(1); Wood, George 45.
League Goals (44): Gilligan 15 (1 pen), Bartlett 9, Curtis 4, Walsh 4, Abraham 2, Boyle 2, Ketteridge 2, Platnauer 2, Gummer 1, McDermott 1, Stevenson 1, Wheeler 1.
Littlewoods Cup (3): Bartlett 1, Curtis 1, Wheeler 1.
FA Cup (8): Gilligan 3, Lynex 2, Bartlett 1, Tupling 1, Wimbleton 1 (pen).

Ground: Ninian Park, Sloper Road, Cardiff CF1 8SX (0222–398636)
Nearest stations: Cardiff Central and Queens Street
Manager: Frank Burrows **Secretary:** Eddie Harrison
Colours: Blue shirts; white shorts
Record home gate: 61,655 Wales v England, October 1961 (Club record); 57,893 v Arsenal Division 1: 22 April, 1953
Honours – Champions: Division 3 South: 1946–7
FA Cup winners: 1926–7

CARLISLE UNITED   DIV. 4

Dalziel, Ian
Fitzpatrick, Paul J.
Fyfe, Tony
Gorman, Paul A.
Graham, Michael A.
Halpin, John
Hampton, Peter J.

Harkness, Steven
Hetherington, Robert B.
Jeffels, Simon
McCafferey, Aidan
McKellar, David
Marshall, Gary

Ogley, Mark A.
Poudlock, Paul
Robertson, James
Saddington, Nigel J.
Sendall, Richard A.
Walsh, Derek

League Appearances: Butler, Martin 1; Clark, Jonathan 8; Dalziel, Ian 42; Fitzpatrick, Paul J. 32; Fyfe, Tony 17(8); Gorman, Paul A. 43; Graham, Michael A. 44; Halpin, John 33; Harkness, Steven 12(1); Hetherington, Robert B. 29(10); Jeffels, Simon 28(1); McKellar, David 34; Marshall, Gary 18(3); Nuttell, Michael J. 1(2); Ogley, Mark A. 26; Proudlock, Paul 10; Prudhoe, Mark 12; Robertson, James 5(2); Saddington, Nigel J. 40; Sendall, Richard A. 22(7); Stephens, Arthur 15(3); Stonehouse, Kevin –(3); Walsh, Derek 34(1).
League Goals (53): Hetherington 11, Halpin 7, Gorman 6 (1 pen), Sendall 6, Saddington 4, Fyfe 4, Proudlock 3, Walsh 3, Graham 2, Marshall 2, Clark 1, Dalziel 1, Stephens 1, own goals 2.
Littlewoods Cup (1): Gorman 1 (pen).
FA Cup (6): Fitzpatrick 1, Gorman 1, Halpin 1, Saddington 1, Walsh 1, own goal 1.
Ground: Brunton Park, Warwick Road, Carlisle CA1 1LL (0228–26237)
Nearest station: Carlisle Citadel
Manager: Clive Middlemass **Secretary:** Miss Alison Moore
Colours: Blue shirts; white shorts
Record home gate: 27,500 v Birmingham, January 1957 (FA Cup) and v Middlesbrough, February 1970 (FA Cup)
Honours – Champions: Division 3: 1964–5

CHARLTON ATHLETIC   DIV. 1

Bacon, Paul D.
Bennett, Michael R.
Bolder, Robert J.
Caton, Thomas S.
Crooks, Garth A.
Gritt, Stephen J.
Humphrey, John
Jones, Andrew M.

Leaburn, Carl W.
Lee, Robert M.
MacKenzie, Stephen
Minto, Scott C.
Mortimer, Paul
Pates, Colin G.
Peake, Andrew M.

Pitcher, Darren E.J.
Reid, Mark
Shirtliff, Peter A.
Smart, Marcus J.
Walsh, Colin D.
Watson, Gordon W.G.
Williams, Paul A.

League Appearances: Bennett, Michael R. 11; Bolder, Robert J. 38; Campbell, David A. 5(4); Caton, Thomas 13; Crooks, Garth A. 10(4); Gritt, Stephen J. 22; Humphrey, John 38; Jones, Andrew M. 2(7); Leaburn, Carl W. 29(3); Lee, Robert M. 25(6); MacKenzie, Stephen 35(1); Miller, Paul R. 5; Minto, Scott C. 1(2); Mortimer, Paul 30(3); Pates, Colin G. 20(1); Peake, Andrew M. 29(2); Reid, Mark 36; Shirtliff, Peter A. 33(1); Stuart, Mark R. 4; Walsh, Colin D. 2(3); Williams, Paul A. 30(2).

League Goals (44): Williams 13, Lee 5, Mortimer 5, Jones 4, MacKenzie 3, Crooks 2, Gritt 2, Leaburn 2, Shirtliff 2, Caton 1, Humphrey 1, Peake 1, Reid 1 (pen), own goals 2.

Littlewoods Cup (4): Williams 2, Jones 1, Reid 1 (pen).

FA Cup (4): Williams 2, Crooks 1, Lee 1.

Ground: Selhurst Park, London SE25 6PH (01–771 6321)
Nearest stations: Selhurst, Norwood Junction and Thornton Heath
Manager: Lennie Lawrence **Secretary:** Miss Anne Payne
Colours: Red shirts; white shorts
Record home gate: 75,031 v Aston Villa, February 1938 (FA Cup)
Honours – Champions: Division 3 South: 1928–9, 1934–5
FA Cup winners: 1946–7

CHELSEA   DIV. 1

Beasant, David J.
Beattie, Stephen D.
Bumstead, John
Clarke, Stephen
Cundy, Jason V.
Dixon, Kerry M.
Dodds, William
Dorigo, Anthony R.

Durie, Gordon S.
Freestone, Roger
Hall, Gareth D.
Hazard, Michael
Hitchcock, Kevin J.
Lee, David J.
Le Saux, Graeme P.
McAllister, Kevin

McLaughlin, Joseph
Mitchell, David S.
Monkou, Kenneth J.
Nicholas, Peter
Roberts Graham P.
West, Colin W.
Wilson, Clive
Wilson, Kevin J.

League Appearances: Beasant, David J. 22; Bumstead, John 27(2); Clarke, Stephen 36; Dixon, Kerry M. 39; Dodds, William −(2); Dorigo, Anthony R. 40; Durie, Gordon S. 32; Freestone, Roger 21; Hall, Gareth D. 17(5); Hazard, Michael 4; Hitchcock, Kevin J. 3; Lee, David J. 12(8); Le Saux, Graeme P. −(1); McAllister, Kevin 28(8); McLaughlin, Joseph 31; Mitchell David S. 6; Monkou, Kenneth J. −(2); Nicholas, Peter 39; Pates, Colin G. 10; Roberts, Graham P. 46; Wilson, Clive 29(3); Wilson, Kevin J. 43(3); Wood, Darren T. 21(1).

League Goals (96): Dixon 25, Durie 17, Roberts 15 (12 pens), Wilson K. 13, Dorigo 6, McAllister 6, Lee 4, Wilson C. 3, Bumstead 2, Nicholas 1, Pates 1, Wood 1, own goals 2.

Littlewoods Cup (3): Dixon 1, Wilson K 1, own goal 1.
FA Cup (0)
Ground: Stamford Bridge, Fulham Road, London SW6 1HS (01–385 5545)
Nearest station: Fulham Broadway (District Line)
Manager: Bobby Campbell **Secretary:** Janet Wayth
Colours: All royal blue
Record home gate: 82,905 v Arsenal, October 1935 (League)
Honours – Champions: Division 1: 1954–5; Division 2: 1983–4, 1988–9
FA Cup winners: 1969–70
League Cup winners: 1964–5
European Cup Winners' Cup winners: 1970–71 **Full Members Cup winners:**
1985–6

CHESTER CITY   DIV. 3

Abel, Graham
Barrow, Graham
Butler, Barry
Dale, Carl
Farrelly, Steven

Graham, Milton M.
Hinnigan, Joseph P.
Jakub, Yanek
Lane, Martin J.
Lightfoot, Christopher

Lundon, Sean
O'Keefe, Eamon
Stewart, William I.
Woodthorpe, Colin

League Appearances; Abel, Graham 40; Barrow, Graham 35; Benjamin, Ian T.
18(4); Bennett, Gary M. 2(5); Butler, Barry 34(1); Dale, Carl 38(3); Glenn,
David A. 17(1); Graham, Milton M. 20(4); Hawtin, Craig S. 3; Hinnigan, Joseph
P. 38(1); Jakub, Yanek 42; Johnson, Stephen A. 35(3); Kelly, Anthony G. 5;
Lane, Martin J. 23; Lightfoot, Christopher 31(5); Lundon, Sean 5(1); Newhouse,
Aidan R. 14(11); O'Keefe, Eamon 11(3); Painter, Peter 5(3); Stewart, William I.
46; Woodthorpe, Colin 44.
League goals (64): Dale 22, Johnson 10 (1 pen), Lightfoot 7, O'Keefe 4 (3 pens),
Abel 3, Barrow 3, Woodthorpe 3, Benjamin 2, Hinnigan 2, Newhouse 2, Graham
1, Hawtin 1, Jakub 1, Painter 1, own goals 2.
Littlewoods cup (3): Barrow 1, Lightfoot 1, own goal 1.
FA Cup (2): Benjamin 1, Dale 1
Ground: The Stadium, Sealand Road, Chester CH1 4LW (0244–371376 and
371809)
Nearest station: Chester
Manager: Harry McNally **Secretary:** J.A. Eckersley
Colours: Royal blue shirts; white shorts
Record home gate: 20,500 v Chelsea, January 1952 (FA Cup)
Honours: Nil

CHESTERFIELD   DIV. 4

Alleyne, Robert A.
Arnott, Kevin W.
Astbury, Michael J.
Bloomer, Robert
Brien, Anthony J.
Eley, Kevin

Henderson, Michael R.
Hewitt, James R.
Leonard, Michael C.
Morris, Andrew D.
Prindiville, Steven A.
Rogers, Lee J.

Rolph, Andrew J.P.
Shaw, Adrian
Slack, Trevor C.
Thompson, Nigel D.
Waller, David H.
Wood, Darren

League Appearances: Alleyne, Robert A. 22(8); Arnott, Kevin W. 32(4); Astbury, Michael J. 8; Bloomer, Robert 41(3); Brien, Anthony J. 29; Brown, James G. 12; Cherry, Steven R. 10; Dempsey, Mark J. 3; Eley, Kevin 38(2); Gormley, Edward J. 4; Henderson, Michael R. 10(1); Hewitt, James R. 39(1); Hoole, David 6(7); Hunter, Leslie 6; Leonard, Michael C. 16; McDonald, Gavin 5(7); McGeeney, Patrick 10(1); Morris, Andrew D. 42; Prindiville, Steven A. 43; Rogers, Lee J. 22(2); Rolph, Andrew J.P. 4(8); Shaw, Adrian, 24(1); Slack, Trevor C. 21; Thompson, Nigel D. 5(1); Waller, David H. 35(1); Wood, Darren 19(3).

League Goals (51): Waller 18, Bloomer 10 (6 pens), Morris 9, Alleyne 3, Brien 1, Hewitt 1, Rolph 1, Shaw 1, Prindiville 1, McDonald 1, Wood 1, own goals 4.

Littlewoods Cup (3): Morris 2, Waller 1.

FA Cup (2): Morris 2

Ground: Recreation Ground, Chesterfield S40 4SX (0246–209765)

Nearest station: Chesterfield

Manager: Paul Hart **Secretary:** R.F. Pepper

Colours: Royal blue shirts; white shorts

Record home gate: 30,968 v Newcastle United, April 1939 (League)

Honours – Champions: Division 3 North: 1930–31, 1935–6; Division 4: 1969–70, 1984–5

COLCHESTER UNITED   DIV. 4

Allinson, Ian J.R.
Bennett, Gary
Daniels, Scott
English, Antony K.
Hetzke, Stephen E.R.
Hicks, Stuart J.

Hill, Colin F.
Hunter, Lee
Radford, Mark
Rooke, Rodney
Scott, Robert

Stafford, Clive A.
Taylor, Leslie
Walsh, Mario M.
Walton, Mark A.
Wilkins, Richard J.

League Appearances: Allinson, Ian J.R. 24(4); Barnett, David K. 19(1); Bedford, Kevin E. 24(2); Bennett, Gary 6(3); Cartwright, Stephen R. 10; Chatterton Nicholas J. 1(1); Coleman, Philip 6(4); Coombe, Mark A. 3; Daniels, Scott 18(8); English, Antony K. 36; Grenfell, Stephen J. 5(1); Hedman, Rudi 17; Hetzke, Stephen E.R. 22(2); Hicks, Stuart J. 34(3); Hill, Colin F. 42(2); Hunter, Lee 4(4); Kelly, Anthony G. 13; McAlister, Thomas G. 20; McGee, Paul 3; Pollard, Kelly J. –(2); Radford, Mark 16(14); Scott, Robert 12; Stafford, Clive A. 16; Swindlehurst, David 12; Taylor, Leslie 14(2); Tempest, Dale M. 25(8); Walsh, Mario M. 25(2); Walton, Mark A. 23; Warner, John 7(8); White, Eric W. 10; Wilkins, Richard J. 39(1).

League Goals (60): Walsh 10, English 8, Allinson 7 (1 pen), Wilkins 7, Swindlehurst 6, (1 pen), Tempest 6, Scott 5, Hetzke 2, Kelly 2, Warner 3, Bennett 1, Hedman 1, Pollard 1, Radford 1.

Littlewoods Cup (0)

FA Cup (12): Walsh 3, Hedman 2, Wilkins 2, Allinson 1(pen), Hetzke 1, Hicks 1, Hill 1, own goal 1

Ground: Layer Road, Colchester CO2 7JJ (0206–574042)

Nearest station: Colchester North (2 miles)

Manager: Jock Wallace **Secretary:** Dee Elwood

Colours: Sky blue and white striped shirts; sky blue shorts

Record home gate: 19,072 v Reading, November 1948 (FA Cup)

Honours: Nil

COVENTRY CITY   DIV. 1

Bannister, Gary
Borrows, Brian
Clark, Howard W.
Dobson, Anthony J.
Downs, Gregory
Emerson, Dean
Greenman, Christopher
Gynn, Michael

Kiely, Dean L.
Kilcline, Brian
Livingstone, Stephen
McGrath, Lloyd A.
McGuire, Douglas J.
Ogrizovic, Steven
Peake, Trevor

Phillips, David O.
Regis, Cyrille
Rodger, Graham
Sedgley, Stephen P.
Smith, David
Speedie, David R.
Thompson, Keith A.

League Appearances: Bannister, Gary 22(2); Bennettt, David A. 5(2); Borrows, Brian 38; Clark, Howard W.4(5); Dobson, Anthony J. 16; Downs, Gregory 20(2); Emerson, Dean 18; Gynn, Michael 8; Houchen, Keith M. 10(3); Kilcline, Brian 33; Livingstone, Stephen 1; McGrath, Lloyd A. 6(2); Ogrizovic, Stephen 38; Peake, Trevor 32; Phillips, David O. 22(4); Regis, Cyrille 34; Rodger, Graham 8; Sedgley, Stephen P. 31; Smith, David 34(1); Speedie, David R. 36; Thompson, Keith A. 2(7).
League Goals (47): Speedie 14, Bannister 8, Regis 7, Kilcline 4 (3 pens), Smith 3, Houchen 2, Phillips 2, Borrows 1, Clark 1, Gynn 1, Rodger 1, Sedgley 1, Thompson 1, own goal 1.
Littlewoods Cup (9): Gynn 3, Bannister 2, Downs 1, Kilcline 1 (pen), Sedgley 1, Speedie 1.
FA Cup (1): Phillips 1.
Ground: Highfield Road Stadium, King Richard Street, Coventry CV2 4FW (0203–257171)
Nearest station: Coventry
Team manager: John Sillett **Secretary:** G.P. Hover
Colours: All sky blue
Record home gate: 51,455 v Wolverhampton, April 1967 (League)
Honours – Champions: Division 2: 1966–7; Division 3: 1963–4; Division 3 South: 1935–6
FA Cup winners: 1986–7

CREWE ALEXANDRA   DIV. 3

Billing, Peter G.
Callaghan, Aaron J.
Clayton, Paul S.
Cutler, Christopher P.
Edwards, Paul R.
Edwards, Robert

Fishenden, Paul A.
Gardiner, Mark C.
Greygoose, Dean
Jasper, Dale W.
Jones, Robert

Milligan, Terence J.
Murphy, Aidan J.
Sussex, Andrew R.
Swain, Kenneth
Walters, Steven

League Appearances: Billing, Peter G. 36(1); Callaghan, Aaron J. 39(2); Clayton, Paul S. 20; Cronin, Denis 12(3); Cutler, Christopher P. 2(1); Doyle, Maurice 3(1); Edwards, Paul 10; Edwards, Paul R. 45; Edwards, Robert –(4); Elliott, Lee 1; Fishenden, Paul A. 46; Gage, Wakeley A.J. 6(8); Gardiner, Mark C. 37(1); Goodison, Christopher W. 24(1); Greygoose, Dean 36; Harrison, Wayne 3; Hignett, Graig J. 1; Jasper, Dale W. 38(1); Jones, Robert 12(7); Macowat, Ian S. 25(5); Morton, Neil –(5); Murphy Aidan J. 31(4); Sussex, Andrew R. 16(9); Swain, Kenneth 40(1); Wakenshaw, Robert A. 1(1); Walters, Steven 19(3); Wilkinson, Mark S. 3(2).

League Goals (67): Fishenden 16 (1 pen), Gardiner 10, Clayton 6, Murphy 5, Callaghan 4, Edwards P.R. 4, Sussex 4, Cronin 2, Cutler 2, Doyle 2, Wilkinson 2, Billing 1, Goodison 1, Harrison 1, Jones 1, Jasper 1, Macowat 1, Walters 1, own goals 3.

Littlewoods Cup (2): Fishenden 1, Sussex 1.

FA Cup (10): Fishenden 3, Gardiner 2, Murphy 2, Cronin 1, Edwards 1, own goal 1.

Ground: Gresty Road, Crewe CW2 6EB (0270–213014)

Nearest station: Crewe

Manager: Dario Grady **Secretary:** Mrs G.C. Palin

Colours: Red shirts; white shorts

Record home gate: 20,000 v Tottenham, January 1960 (FA Cup)

Honours: Nil

CRYSTAL PALACE   DIV. 1

Bailey, Dennis
Barber, Phillip A.
Bright, Mark A.
Burke, David I.
Dyer, Alexander C.
Harris, Mark A.
Hedman, Rudolph G.
Hone, Mark J.
Hopkins, Jeffrey
Locke, Adam S.

McGoldrick, Edward J.P.
Madden, David J.
Nebbeling, Gavin M.
Newman, Richard A.
O'Reilly, Gary M.
Pardew, Alan S.
Parkin, Brian
Pemberton, John M.
Pennyfather, Glenn J.

Powell, Christopher G.R.
Salako, John A.
Shaw, Richard E.
Southgate, Gareth
Stevens, David K.
Suckling, Perry J.
Thomas, Geoffrey R.
Whyte, David A.
Wright, Ian E.

League Appearances: Barber, Phillip A. 44(2); Bright, Mark A. 46; Burke, David I. 38(1); Dyer, Alexander C. 6(1); Harris, Mark A. –(2); Hedman, Rudolph G. 1(4); Hone, Mark J. 1; Hopkins, Jeffrey 43; McGoldrick, Eddie J.P. 20(1); Madden, David J. 17(2); Nebbeling, Gavin M. 14; O'Reilly, Gary M. 32; Pardew, Alan S. 43(2); Parkin, Brian 19; Pemberton, John M. 42; Pennyfather, Glenn J. 13(2); Powell, Christopher G.R. 2(1); Redfearn, Neil D. 15; Salako, John A. 12(16); Shaw, Richard E. 8(6); Suckling, Perry J. 27; Thomas, Geoffrey R. 22; Wright, Ian E. 41(1)

League Goals (71): Wright 24 (2 pens), Bright 20 (2 pens), Barber 6, Madden 5 (4 pens), Thomas 5, Dyer 2, O'Reilly 2, Redfearn 2 (1 pen), Nebbeling 1, Pardew 1, Pemberton 1, own goals 2.

Littlewoods Cup (5): Bright 1, Pardew 1, Thomas 1, Wright 1, own goal 1.

FA Cup (0)

Ground: Selhurst Park, SE25 6PU (01–653 4462)

Nearest stations: Selhurst, Norwood Junction or Thornton Heath

Manager: Steve Coppell **Secretary:** Alan J. Leather

Colours: Red and blue shirts; red shorts

Record home gate: 51,801 v Burnley, May 1979 (League)

Honours – Champions: Division 2: 1978–9; Division 3 South: 1920–21

DARLINGTON   GMV CONF

Anderson, Dale
Batch, Nigel A.
Emson, Paul
Granger, Keith W.

Hine, Mark
Hyde, Gary S.
McJannet, William L.
Prudhoe, Mark

Robinson, Neil
Stephens, Arthur
Willis, James A.
Worthington, Gary L.

League Appearances: Anderson, Dale 4(6); Batch, Nigel A. 30; Bonnyman, Philip 11(1); Caizley, Kevin 8(4); Clayton, Paul S. 9(1); Dyson, Paul I. 12; Emson, Paul 27(7); Gidman, John 13; Hine, Mark 38(2); Hyde, Gary S. 31(5); McAndrew, Anthony 11; McAughtrie, David 19(1); MacDonald, Garry 35(6); McJannet, William L. 26; Moore, David 25(5); Morgan, Gary 38; Prudhoe, Mark 12; Robinson, Michael A. –(1); Robinson, Neil 36(2); Rodwell, James R. 1; Shearer, David J. 6(1); Smallwood, Neil 4; Smith, Alan D. 10(5); Stephens Arthur 10; Stonehouse, Kevin 21(8); Willis, James A. 41; Willis, Paul E. 1(1); Worthington, Gary L. 27(4).
League Goals (53): Worthington 12 (1 pen), Stonehouse 7 (1 pen), Emson 5, MacDonald 5, Stephens 4, Dyson 3, Hyde 3, Bonnyman 2 (2 pens), Hine 2, Willis J. 2, Caizley 1, Gidman 1, McJannet 1, Moore 1, Morgan 1, Robinson N. 1, Willis P. 1, own goal 1.
Littlewoods Cup: (5): Clayton 1, Hine 1, Hyde 1, MacDonald 1, Moore 1.
FA Cup (1): Own goal 1.
Ground: Feethams Ground, Darlington DL1 5JB (0325–465097 and 467712)
Nearest station: Darlington
Manager: Brian Little **Secretary:** Brian Anderson
Colours: All white
Record home gate: 21,023 v Bolton, November 1960 (League Cup)
Honours – Champions: Division 3 North: 1924–5

DERBY COUNTY   DIV. 1

Blades, Paul A.	Gregory, John C.	Pickering, Nicholas
Briscoe, Robert D.	Hayward, Steven L.	Ramage, Craig D.
Chiedozie, John O.	Hebberd, Trevor N.	Sage, Melvyn
Cross, Stephen C.	Hindmarch, Robert	Saunders, Dean N.
Davidson, Jonathan S.	Kavanagh, Jason C.	Shilton, Peter L.
Forsyth, Michael E.	McCord, Brian J.	Sleeuwenhoek, Kris
Francis, Kevin M.D.	McMinn, Kevin C.	Taylor, Martin J.
Gee, Phillip J.	Micklewhite, Gary	Taylor, Stephen M.
Goddard, Paul	Patterson, Mark	Williams, David G.
Green, Scott P.	Penney, David W.	Wright, Mark

League Appearances: Blades, Paul A. 38; Chiedozie, John O. 2; Callaghan, Nigel 18; Cross, Stephen C. 7(12); Forsyth, Michael E. 38; Gee, Phillips J. 8(4); Goddard, Paul 31; Hebberd, Trevor N. 37; Hindmarch, Robert 25; McMinn, Kevin C. 32; Micklewhite, Gary 19(7); Patterson, Mark 1; Penney, David W. 3(6); Pickering, Nicholas 5(3); Sage, Melvyn 16; Saunders, Dean N. 30; Shilton, Peter L. 38; Williams, David G. 37; Wright, Mark 33.
League Goals (40): Saunders 14 (2 pens), Goddard 7, Hebberd 5, McMinn 4, Micklewhite 3, Callaghan 2 (1 pen), Blades 1, Gee 1, Sage 1, Williams 1, Wright 1.
Littlewoods Cup: (3): Hebberd 2, Penney 1.
FA Cup (4): Callaghan 1, Hebberd 1, McMinn 1, Micklewhite 1.
Ground: The Baseball Ground, Shaftesbury Crescent, Derby DE3 8NB (0332–40105)
Nearest station: Derby
Manager: Arthur Cox **Secretary:** M.J. Dunford
Colours: White shirts; black shorts
Record home gate: 41,826 v Tottenham, September 1969 (League)
Honours – Champions: Division 1: 1971–2, 1974–5; Division 2: 1911–12, 1914–15, 1968–9, 1986–7; Division 3 North: 1956–7
FA Cup winners: 1945–6

DONCASTER ROVERS　　　　　　　DIV. 4

Ashurst, Jack
Brevett, Rufus E.
Brockie, Vincent
Daly, Gerard A.

Douglas, Colin F.
Gaughan, Steven E.
Hall, Mark
Raffell, Stephen C.

Rankine, Simon M.
Robinson, Leslie
Samways, Mark
Turnbull, Lee M.

League Appearances: Ashurst, Jack 30; Beattie, Stuart R. 17; Brevett, Rufus E. 22(1); Brockie, Vincent 23; Daly, Gerard A. 37(2); Dobson, Paul 22(2); Douglas, Colin F. 46; Gaughan, Steven E. 22(12); Gorman, Paul M. −(9); Hall, Mark 1; Jones, Gary 9(8); Kimble, Garry L. 26(5); Malcolm, Paul A. 34; Peckett, Andrew R. −(7); Powell, Clifford G. 4; Raffell, Stephen C. 11(2); Rankine, Simon M. 46; Raven, Paul 35; Robinson, Leslie 43; Robinson, Ronald 27(2); Samways, Mark 12; Stewart, Robert A. 1; Trotter, Michael 3; Turnbull, Lee M. 31(1); Ward, Anthony 4.

League Goals (49): Rankine 11, Dobson 10 (4 pens), Daly 4 (1 pen), Robinson R. 4, Turnbull 4, Robinson L. 3 (2 pens), Brockie 2 (2 pens), Gaughan 2, Douglas 2, Jones 2, Ashurst 1, Beattie 1, Gorman 1, Raven 1, own goal 1.

Littlewoods Cup (1): Rankine 1.

FA Cup (3): Dobson 2, Daly 1.

Ground: Belle Vue Ground, Doncaster DN4 5HT (0302–539441)

Nearest station: Doncaster

Manager: Billy Bremner **Secretary:** Mrs K.J. Oldale

Colours: White shirts with red trim; red shorts

Record home gate: 37,149 v Hull City, October 1948 (League)

Honours – Champions: Division 3 North: 1934–5, 1946–7, 1949–50; Division 4: 1965–6, 1968–9

EVERTON　　　　　　　DIV. 1

Adams, Neil J.
Bracewell, Paul W.
Clarke, Wayne
Cottee, Anthony R.
Ebbrell, John K.
Jones, Philip A.
Kearton, Jason
McCall, Stuart M.

McDonald, Neil R.
Nevin, Patrick K.F.
Pointon, Neil G.
Powell, Gary
Ratcliffe, Kevin
Sharp, Graeme M.
Sheedy, Kevin M.
Snodin, Ian

Southall, Neville
Steven, Trevor M.
Stowell, Michael
Van Den Hauwe, Patrick
Watson, David
Wilson, Ian W.
Wright, Mark A.
Youds, Edward P.

League Appearances: Bracewell, Paul W. 20; Clarke, Wayne 12(8); Cottee, Antony R. 35(1); Ebbrell, John K. 1(3); Heath, Adrian P. 6(1); McCall, Stuart M. 29(4); McDonald, Neil R. 22(3); Nevin, Patrick K.F. 20(5); Pointon, Neil G. 20(3) Ratcliffe, Kevin 30; Reid, Peter 16(2); Sharp, Graeme M. 26; Sheedy, Kevin M. 24(2); Snodin, Ian 23; Southall, Neville 38; Steven, Trevor M. 29; Van Den Hauwe, Patrick W.R. 24(1); Watson, David 32; Wilson, Ian W. 11(7).

League Goals (50): Cottee 13, Sheedy 8 (1 pen), Sharp 7 (1 pen), Steven 6 (2 pens), Clarke 3 (1 pen), Watson 3, Bracewell 2, Heath 2, Nevin 2, Reid 1, McDonald 1, Wilson 1, own goal 1.

Littlewoods Cup (9): Cottee 2, Sharp 2, Steven 2 (2 pens), McCall 1, McDonald 1, Watson 1.

FA Cup (12): Sheedy 4 (2 pens), McCall 3, Sharp 3, Nevin 2.

Ground: Goodison Park, Liverpool L4 4EL (051–521 2020)

Nearest station: Liverpool Lime Street

Manager: Colin Harvey **Secretary:** Jim Greenwood

Colours: Royal blue shirts; white shorts

Record home gate: 78,299 v Liverpool, September 1948 (League)
Honours – Champions: Division 1: 1890–91, 1914–15, 1927–8, 1931–2, 1938–9, 1962–3, 1969–70, 1984–5, 1986–7; Division 2: 1930–31
FA Cup winners: 1905–6, 1932–3, 1965–6, 1983–4
European Cup winners Cup winners: 1984–5

EXETER CITY   DIV. 4

Batty, Paul W.
Benjamin, Ian T.
Burgher, Symon G.
Dryden, Richard A.
Harrower, Steven G.

Hiley, Scott P.
McDermott, Brian J.
Neville, Steven F.
Rogers, Lee

Rowbotham, Darren
Taylor, Shaun
Walter, David W.
Young, Richard A.

League Appearances: Banks, Christopher R. 43(2); Batty, Paul W. 15; Benjamin, Ian T. 20; Cooper, Richard D. 25(4); Dryden, Richard A. 21; Gwinnett, Melvyn L. 17; Harris, Carl S. 11(5); Harris, Jamie 1(4); Harrower, Steven G. 18; Heath, Herbert G. 3(2); Hiley, Scott P. 36(1); Jones, Mark 5; Langley, Thomas W. 14(7); McDermott, Brian J. 19; Miller, Kevin 3; Neville, Steven F. 38; Parker, Martin T. −(1); Roberts, Paul 3; Rogers, Lee 45; Rowbotham, Darren 45; Smith, Keith 2(13); Taylor, Shaun 46; Tupling, Stephen 8(1); Viney, Keith B. 3; Vinnicombe, Christopher 21(4); Walter, David W. 26; Withey, Graham A. 5(2); Young, Richard A. 13(1)
League Goals (65): Rowbotham 20 (6 pens), Neville 14 (3 pens), Taylor 6, Hiley 5, Young 4, Benjamin 3, Langley 2, Smith 2, Withey 2, Banks 1, Batty 1, Cooper 1, Harris C. 1, McDermott 1, Tupling 1, own goal 1.
Littlewoods Cup (0)
FA Cup (1): Rowbotham 1.
Ground: St James' Park, Exeter, Devon EX4 6PX (0392–54073)
Nearest stations: Exeter Central or St David's
Manager: Terry Cooper **Secretary:** M. Holladay
Colours: Red and white vertical striped shirts; black shorts with white stripes
Record home gate: 20,984 v Sunderland, March 1931 (FA Cup)
Honours: Nil

FULHAM   DIV. 3

Achampong, Kenneth
Barnett, Gary L.
Batty, Laurence
Cole, Michael W.
Davies, Gordon J.
Donnellan, Leo J.
Eckhardt, Jeffrey E.
Elkins, Gary

Gordon, Colin K.
Gore, Shaun M.
Greaves, Steven R.
Howes, Jason R.
Langley, Richard J.
Lewington, Raymond
Marshall, John P.
Mauge, Ronald C.

Rougvie, Douglas
Sayer, Andrew C.
Scott, Peter R.
Skinner, Justin
Stannard, James
Thomas, Glen A.
Walker, Clive
Wilson, Robert J.

League Appearances: Barnett, Gary L. 28; Batty, Laurence 1; Cawley, Peter 3(2); Cole, Michael W. 35(1); Davies, Gordon J. 29(5); Donnellan, Leo J. −(4); Eckhardt, Jeffrey E. 43; Elkins, Gary 20(2); Gordon, Colin K. 12(5); Gore, Shaun M. 6; Hoddy, Kevin R. −(2); Kerrins, Wayne M. 3(1); Langley, Richard J. 19; Marshall, John P. 39(2); Mauge, Ronald C. 12(1); Peters, Gary 7(2); Rougvie, Douglas 18; Sayer, Andrew C. 19(9); Scott, Peter R. 34(3); Skinner, Justin 34(4); Stannard, James 45; Thomas, Glen A. 38(2); Walker, Clive 36(2); Wilson, Robert J. 25(2).

League Goals (69): Davies 14, Sayer 10, Skinner 8 (5 pens), Walker 8, Marshall 7, Barnett 5, Cole 3, Scott 3, Eckhardt 2, Gordon 2, Peters 2, Elkins 1, Rougvie 1, Thomas 1, Wilson 1, own goal 1.
Littlewoods Cup (2): Sayer 1, Skinner 1 (pen).
FA Cup (0)
Ground: Craven Cottage, Stevenage Road, Fulham SW6 6HH (01–736 6561)
Nearest stations: Putney Bridge (District) or Hammersmith (Metropolitan, District and Piccadilly)
Manager: Ray Lewington **Secretary** Mrs Yvonne Haines
Colours: White shirts with black trim; black shorts
Record home gate: 49,335 v Millwall, October 1938 (League)
Honours – Champions: Division 2: 1948–9; Division 3 South: 1931–2.

GILLINGHAM   DIV. 4

Clarke, Brian R.	Joseph, Francis	Peacock, Gavin K.
Docker, Ian	Kite, Philip D.	Perry, Andrew
Gavin, Patrick J.	Lovell, Stephen J.	Smith, David A.
Haines, Ivan	Manuel, William A.J.	Walker, Alan
Haylock, Paul	O'Shea, Timothy J.	Williams Jerry S.
Hillyard, Ronald W.		

League Appearances: Beadle, Peter C. 1(1); Burley, George E. 46; Clarke, Brian R. 10; Cooper, Mark D. 14(4); Docker, Ian 32(3); Eeles, Anthony G. 3; Gavin, Patrick J. 13; Guscott, Lindon –(2); Haines, Ivan 10(2); Haylock, Paul 28(3); Hillyard, Ronald W. 19; Joseph, Francis 10(5); Kite, Philip D. 27; Lillis, Jason W. 12(10); Lovell, Stephen J. 38(1); Manuel, William A.J. 13(4); O'Shea, Timothy J. 17; Peacock, Gavin K. 43(1); Pearson, Richard 2(1); Perry, Andrew 8(5); Quow, Trevor 16(4); Reeves, Alan 18; Shipley, George M. 12(2); Smith, David A. 40(2); Stimson, Mark 18; Walford, Stephen J. 4; Walker, Alan 22; Weatherly, Colin M. 14(3); West, Garry 9(1); Williams, Jerry S. 7(6).
League Goals (47): Lovell 14 (3 pens), Peacock 9 (1 pen), Gavin 7, Cooper 3, Lillis 3, Burley 2, Smith 2, Joseph 1, Manuel 1, Quow 1, Shipley 1, Walker 1, West 1, own goal 1.
Littlewoods Cup (6): Lillis 2, Lovell 2, Quow 1 (pen), Walker 1.
FA Cup (3): Lovell 1, Quow 1, Smith 1.
Ground: Priestfield Stadium, Gillingham, Kent ME7 4DD (0634–51854 and 576828)
Nearest station: Gillingham
Manager: Damien Richardson **Secretary:** Barry Bright
Colours: Blue shirts with white trim; white shorts with blue trim
Record home gate: 23,001 v Queen's Park Rangers, January 1948 (FA Cup)
Honours – Champions: Division 4: 1963–4

GRIMSBY TOWN   DIV. 4

Agnew, Paul	Lever, Mark	Sherwood, Stephen
Alexander, Keith	McDermott, John	Stephenson, Geoffrey
Cockerill, John	O'Kelly, Richard F.	Stoutt, Stephen P.
Cunnington, Shaun G.	Reece, Paul J.	Tillson, Andrew
Gilbert, David J.	Saunders, Steven J.	Watson, Thomas R.
Jobling, Kevin A.		

League Appearances: Agnew, Paul 32(2); Alexander, Keith 42(2); Banton, Dale C. 3(5); Caldwell, Anthony 2(1); Cockerill, John 24(5); Cunnington, Shaun G. 44; Dixon, Andrew 4(1); Gilbert, David J. 11; Grocock, Christopher R. 4(7); Jobling, Kevin A. 31(1); Lever, Mark 37; McDermott, John 36(2); North, Marc V. 27(2); O'Kelly, Richard F. 38(1); Reece, Paul J. 14; Saunders, Steven J. 36(5); Sherwood, Stephen 32; Smaller, Paul A. −(1); Stephenson, Geoffrey 12(2); Stoutt, Stephen P. 2; Tillson, Andrew 44(1); Watson, Thomas R. 12(9); Williams, Thomas E. 19.

League Goals (65): Alexander 14, O'Kelly 10, Saunders 10, Cockerill 6, North 6, Jobling 4 (1 pen), Watson 4 (3 pens), Gilbert 3, Lever 2, Tillson 2, Banton 1, Cunnington 1, McDermott 1, Stoutt 1.

Littlewoods Cup (0)

FA Cup (10): North 4, Cunnington 2, Alexander 1, Cockerill 1, Jobling 1, own goal 1.

Ground: Blundell Park, Cleethorpes, DN35 7PY (0472–697111)

Nearest stations: Cleethorpes or Grimsby Town

Manager: Alan Buckley **Secretary:** I. Fleming

Colours: Black and white striped shirts; black shorts

Record home gate: 31,657 v Wolverhampton, February 1937 (FA Cup)

Honours – Champions: Division 2: 1900–1, 1933–4; Division 3 North: 1925–6, 1955–6; Division 3: 1979–80; Division 4: 1971–2

HALIFAX TOWN   DIV. 4

Allison, Wayne
Barr, William J.
Bramhall, John
Fleming, Paul
Hedworth, Christopher

Horner, Philip M.
McPhillips, Terence
Martin, Dean
Matthews, Neil

Richardson, Nicholas
Robinson, David A.
Watson, Andrew
Whitehead, Philip M.

League Appearances: Allison, Wayne 41; Barr, Robert A. 4; Barr, William J. 42(1); Blain, Colin A.16(4); Bramhall, John 39; Broadbent, Graham 2(10); Donnelly, Paul A. −(1); Fleming, Craig −(1); Fleming, Paul 22(1); Harrison, Francis N. 13; Hedworth, Christopher 11; Henry, Liburd A. 1(4); Horner, Philip M. 36(2); Logan, David 3; McPhillips, Terence 37(4); Martin, Dean 32; Matthews, Michael 15; Matthews, Neil 32(2); Paterson, Toby L. −(1); Pullan, Christopher 5; Richardson, Lee J. 22(3); Richardson, Nicholas 4(3); Robinson, David A. 30; Roche, Patrick J. 25; Sinclair, Ronald M. 10; Smith, Gareth −(1); Watson, Andrew 42(3); Whitehead, Alan 10(1); Whitehead, Philip M. 11; Willis, Paul 1(3).

League Goals (69): McPhillips 22 (5 pens), Allison 15, Matthews N. 7, Watson 5, Barr W. 4, Bramhall 3, Horner 3, Broadbent 2, Martin 2 (1 pen), Matthews M. 1, Pullan 1, Richardson, Lee J. 1, Robinson 1, Whitehead A. 1, own goal 1.

Littlewoods Cup (3): Allison 1, McPhillips 1, Watson 1,

FA Cup (7): Barr W. 2, Allison 2, Bramhall 1, McPhillips 1, Watson 1.

Ground: The Shay, Halifax HX1 2YS (0422–53423)

Nearest station: Halifax

Manager: Bill Ayre **Secretary:** Mrs A. Pettifor

Colours: Royal blue shirts with white trim; white shorts with blue trim

Record home gate: 36,885 v Tottenham, February 1953 (FA Cup)

Honours: Nil

HARTLEPOOL UNITED   DIV. 4

Allon, Joseph B.   Grayson, Simon D.   Ogden, Paul
Atkinson, Patrick D. Honour, Brian   Smith, Anthony
Baker, David P.   McKinnon, Robert   Stokes, Wayne D.
Borthwick, John   Moverley, Robert   Tinkler, John
Dalton, Paul   Nobbs, Alan K.   Toman, James A.
Doig, Russell

League Appearances: Allon, Joseph B. 21; Atkinson, Patrick D. 6(7); Baker, David P. 39(1); Barrass, Anthony 1(2); Barratt, Anthony 31(1); Borthwick, John 14(5); Dalton, Paul 17; Dixon, Kevin L. 14; Doig, Russell 11(8); Grayson, Simon D. 36(5); Haigh, Paul 10(1); Hepple, John A. 1(1); Honour, Brian 34; Locker, Stephen −(1); McAndrew, Anthony 4; McKellar, David 5; McKinnon, Robert 46; Moverley, Robert 23; Muggleton, Carl D. 8; Nobbs, Alan K. 17(1); Norton, Paul 5; Ogden, Paul 7(3); Plaskett, Stephen C. 12; Smith, Anthony 19; Stokes, Wayne D. 37; Tinkler, John 38; Toman, James A. 45; Tunks, Roy W. 5.
League Goals (50): Grayson 12, Baker 7 (4 pens), Toman 6, Allon 4, Dixon 4 (2 pens), Atkinson 3, Tinkler 3, Dalton 2, McKinnon 2, Smith 2, Barratt 1, Borthwick 1, Doig 1, Honour 1, Stokes 1.
Littlewoods Cup (2): Dixon 1 (pen), own goal 1.
FA Cup (7): Allon 2, Baker 1 (pen), Borthwick 1, Honour 1, Smith 1, Toman 1.
Ground: Victoria Ground, Clarence Road, Hartlepool TS24 8BZ (ground 0429–272584; office 0429–222077)
Nearest station: Hartlepool
Manager: Bobby Moncur **Secretary:** M. Kirby
Colours: All blue
Record home gate: 17,426 v Manchester United, January 1957 (FA Cup)
Honours: Nil

HEREFORD UNITED   DIV. 4

Benbow, Ian R.   Jones, Richard J.   Pejic, Melvyn
Bowyer, Ian   McLoughlin, Paul B.   Rose, Kevin P.
Devine, Steven B.   Narbett, Jonathan V.   Stant, Phillip R.
Elliott, Anthony R.   Peacock, Darren   Tester, Paul L.
Jones, Mark A.W.

League Appearances: Benbow, Ian R. 27(7); Bowyer, Ian 5(4); Bradley, Russell 12; Campbell, Michael J. 1; Crane, Andrew D. 30(2); Devine, Steven B. 40(1); Elliott, Anthony R. 23; Jones, Mark A.W. 41; Jones Richard J. 38; Lamb, Alan 9(1); McLoughlin, Paul B. 44(1); Maddy, Paul M. 21(6); Mardenborough, Stephen A. 20(7); Narbett, Jonathan V. 35(1); Peacock, Darren 6(2); Pejic, Melvyn 16(2); Rose, Kevin P. 23; Stant Phillip R. 40(1); Stevens, Gary M. 30(3); Tester, Paul L. 40(4); Williams, Robert J. 5.
League Goals (66): Stant 28 (4 pens), McLoughlin 13, Narbett 7, Tester 6, Pejic 3, Stevens 3 (1 pen), Lamb 2, Bradley 1, Benbow 1, Jones R. 1, Maddy 1.
Littlewoods Cup (2): Stant 1, Tester 1.
FA Cup (0)
Ground: Edgar Street, Hereford HR4 9JU (0432–276666)
Nearest station: Heréford
Player/Manager: Ian Bowyer **Secretary:** D.H. Vaughan

HUDDERSFIELD TOWN   DIV. 3

Bent, Junior A.	Kirkham, Paul	O'Regan, Kieran
Bray, Ian M.	Marsden, Christopher	Shelton, Richard M.
Byrne, Michael	Martin, Lee B.	Smith, Mark C.
Cecere, Michele J.	Maskell, Craig D.	Trevitt, Simon
Duggan, Andrew J.	May, Andrew M.	Tucker, Gordon
Hardwick Steven	Mitchell, Graham L.	Winter, Julian
Hutchings, Christopher	O'Doherty, Kenneth B.	

League Appearances: Barham, Mark F. 1; Bent, Junior A. 14(8); Brown, Malcolm 1; Byrne, Michael 29(8); Cecere, Michele J. 28(3); Duggan, Andrew G. 14; France, Michael P. 2(1); Hardwick, Steven 46; Holmes, Michael A. 3(4); Hutchings, Christopher 41; McInerney, Ian 5(5); Marsden, Christopher 10(4); Maskell, Craig D. 46; May, Andrew M. 45; Mitchell, Graham L. 33(1); O'Doherty, Kenneth B. 37; O'Regan, Kieran 36; Shotton, Malcolm 2; Smith, Mark C. 17(3); Trevitt, Simon 35(4); Tucker, Gordon 11(1); Ward, Peter 1(3); Winter, Julian 35; Withe, Peter 14(12).

League Goals (63): Maskell 28 (5 pens), Byrne 7, Bent 5, Hutchings 5, Cecere 4, Duggan 2, May 2, O'Regan 2, Smith 2, Winter 2, McInerney 1, Marsden 1, O'Doherty 1, Shotton 1.

Littlewoods Cup (4): Maskell 2, Mitchell 1, Trevitt 1.

FA Cup (6): Bent 1, Maskell 1, May 1, O'Regan 1, Withe 1, own goal 1.

Ground: Kirklees Stadium, Leeds Road, Huddersfield
HD1 6PE (0484–420335/6)

Nearest station: Huddersfield

Manager: Eoin Hand **Secretary:** G.S. Binns

Colours: Blue and white striped shirts; white shorts

Record home gate: 67,037 v Arsenal, February 1932 (FA Cup)

Honours – Champions: Division 1: 1923–4, 1924–5, 1925–6; Division 2: 1969–70; Division 4: 1979–80

FA Cup winners: 1921–2

HULL CITY   DIV. 2

Askew, William	Jenkinson, Leigh	Roberts, Gareth W.
Brown, Nicholas L.	Jobson, Richard I.	Smith, Michael K.
Buckley, Neil A.	Kelly, Gavin J.	Swan, Peter H.
Daniel, Raymond C.	McParland, Ian J.	Terry, Steve G.
De Mange, Kenneth	Moore, John	Thompson Leslie
Edwards, Keith	Murray, Malcolm	Warren, Lee A.
Hesford, Iain	Payton, Andrew P.	Whitehurst, William
Jacobs, Wayne G.		

League Appearances: Askew, William 16; Bell, Douglas 4; Brown, Nicholas L. 13; Buckley, Neil A. 13; Calvert, Mark R. 5; Daniel, Raymond C. 23; De Mange, Kenneth J.P.P. 19(13); Dyer, Alexander C. 15; Edwards, Keith 44; Hesford, Iain

22; Hotte, Timothy A. −(1); Jacobs, Wayne G. 33; Jenkinson, Leigh 6(5); Jobson, Richard I. 46; Kelly, Gavin J. 3; McParland, Ian J. 11; Moore, John 11(3); Mudd, Paul A. 1; Murray, Malcolm 6(2); Norman, Anthony J. 21; Palmer, Charles A. 17(1); Payton, Andrew P. 18(10); Roberts, Gareth W. 35; Saville, Andrew V. 14(6); Skipper, Peter D. 3; Smith, Michael K. 9(3); Swan, Peter H. 11; Terry, Steve G. 33; Thomspson, Leslie 6(1); Warren, Lee A. 27(1); Whitehurst, William 21.
League Goals (52): Edwards 26 (5 pens), Whitehurst 5, Payton 4 (1 pen), Roberts 3, Dyer 2, Daniel 1, De Mange 1, Jobson 1, McParland 1, Moore 1, Palmer 1, Saville 1, Smith 1, Swan 1, Terry 1, own goals 2.
Littlewoods Cup (1): Edwards 1.
FA Cup (6): Edwards 3, Whitehurst 2, Brown 1.
Ground: Boothferry Park, Hull HU4 6EU (0482–51119)
Nearest stations: Hull or Boothferry Park Halt
Manager: Colin Appleton **Secretary:** Kevin Adamson
Colours: Amber shirts; black shorts
Record home gate: 55,019 v Manchester United, February 1949 (FA Cup)
Honours – Champions: Division 3 North: 1932–3, 1948–9; Division 3: 1965–6

IPSWICH TOWN   DIV. 2

Atkinson, Dalian R.	Harbey, Graham K.	Milton, Simon C.
Bernal, Andrew	Hill, David M.	Redford, Ian P.
Cheetham, Michael M.	Humes, Anthony	Stockwell, Michael T.
D'Avray, Jean M.	Johnson, Gavin	Wark, John
Dozzell, Jason A.W.	Kiwomya, Christopher M.	Woods, Neil S.
Fearon, Ronald T.	Linighan, David	Yallop, Frank W.
Forrest, Craig L.	Lowe, David A.	Zondervan, Romeo
Gregory, David S.		

League Appearances: Atkinson, Dalian R. 33(1); Baltacha, Sergei P. 19(1); Cheetham, Michael M. 1(2); D'Avray, Jean M. 24(8); Dozzell, Jason A.W. 29; Fearon, Ronald T. 18; Forrest, Craig L. 28; Gregory, David S. −(2); Harbey, Graham K. 19(4); Hill, David M. 35(1); Humes, Anthony 26; Johnson, Gavin 4; Juryeff, Ian M. −(2); Kiwomya, Christopher M. 16(10); Linighan, David 40(1); Lowe, David A. 30(2); Milton, Simon C. 25(10); O'Donnell, Christopher 1(1); Redford, Ian P. 22(2); Stockwell, Michael T. 20(3); Wark, John 41; Woods, Neil S. −(1); Yallop, Frank W. 38(2); Zondervan, Romeo 37.
League Goals (71): Wark 13 (7 pens), Dozzell 11, Atkinson 10, Milton 10, Lowe 6, D'Avray 3, Humes 3, Zondervan 3, Kiwomya 2, Linighan 2, Redford 2, Stockwell 2, Yallop 2, Baltacha 1, own goal 1.
Littlewoods Cup (7): Atkinson 3, Stockwell 2, Dozzell 1, Lowe 1.
FA Cup (0)
Ground: Portman Road, Ipswich IP1 2DA (0473–219211)
Nearest station: Ipswich
Manager: John Duncan **Secretary:** D.C. Rose
Colours: Royal blue shirts; white shorts
Record home gate: 38,010 v Leeds United, March 1975 (FA Cup)
Honours – Champions: Division 1: 1961–2; Division 2: 1960–61, 1967–8; Division 3 South: 1953–4, 1956–7
FA Cup winners: 1977–8
UEFA Cup winners: 1980–81

LEEDS UNITED   DIV. 2

Aizlewood, Mark   Haddock, Peter M.   Shutt, Carl S.
Aspin, Neil   Hilaire, Vincent M.   Sinclair, Ronald M.
Baird, Ian J.   Kerr, Dylan   Snodin, Glynn
Batty, David   Maguire, Peter J.   Speed, Gary A.
Blake, Noel L.G.   Noteman, Kevin S.   Stiles, John C.
Davison, Robert   Ormsby, Brendon T.C.   Strachan, Gordon D.
Day, Mervyn R.   Parsley, Neil   Whitlow, Michael
Edwards, Neil R.   Pearson, John S.   Williams, Andrew
Fairclough, Courtney H. Rennie, David   Williams, Gary
Grayson, Simon N.   Sheridan, John J.

League Appearances: Adams, Michael R. 15(1); Aizlewood, Mark 34(4); And-
rews, Ian E. 1; Ashurst, Jack 6(1); Aspin, Neil 31(2); Baird, Ian J. 43; Batty,
David 25(5); Blake, Noel L.G. 44; Davison, Robert 37(2); Day, Mervyn R.
45; Fairclough, Courtney H. 11; Haddock, Peter M. 8(4); Hilaire, Vincent M.
42; Kerr, Dylan 1(2); Mumby, Peter −(1); Ormsby, Brendon T.C. 1; Pearson,
John S. 6(27); Rennie, David 30(3); Sheridan, John J. 38(2); Shutt, Carl S. 3;
Snodin, Glynn 33(2); Speed, Gary A. 1; Stiles, John C. 4(6); Strachan, Gordon
D. 11; Swan, Peter H. 1; Taylor, Robert 2(4); Whitlow, Michael 18(2); Williams,
Andrew 7(11); Williams, Gary 8.
League Goals (59): Davison 14, Baird 10, Sheridan 7 (6 pens), Hilaire 6, Blake 4,
Shutt 4, Aizlewood 3, Snodin 3, Strachan 3 (1 pen), Adams 1, Pearson 1, Rennie
1, Whitlow 1, Williams A. 1.
Littlewoods Cup (5): Baird 1, Davison 1, Hilaire 1, Pearson 1, Sheridan 1 (pen).
FA Cup (2): Baird 2.
Ground: Elland Road, Leeds LS11 0ES (0532–716037)
Nearest station: Leeds
Manager: Howard Wilkinson **Secretary:** D.J. Dowse
Colours: All white
Record home gate: 57,892 v Sunderland, March 1967 (FA Cup)
Honours – Champions: Division 1: 1968–9, 1973–4; Division 2: 1923–4, 1963–4
FA Cup winners: 1971–2
League Cup winners: 1967–8
European Fairs Cup winners: 1967–8, 1970–71

LEICESTER CITY   DIV. 2

Baraclough, Ian R.   Mills, Gary R.   Ramsey, Paul
Brown, Grant A.   Morgan, Simon C.   Rantanen, Jari J.
Cross, Nicholas J.R.   Muggleton, Carl D.   Reid, Paul R.
Groves, Paul   Newell, Michael C.   Smith, Richard G.
Hodge, Martin J.   North, Marc V.   Spearing, Anthony
Kennedy, Michael F.   O'Connor, Paul D.   Walsh, Stephen
Kitson, Paul   Paris, Alan D.   Wilkinson, Stephen J.
McAllister, Gary   Puttnam, David   Williams, Darren
Mauchlen, Alister H.

League Appearances: Brien, Anthony J. 1; Brown, Grant A. 12; Charles, Gary
A. 5(3); Cooper, Paul D. 24; Cross, Nicholas J.R. 37(4); Eccles, Peter 1; Groves,
Paul 7(8); Hodge, Martin J. 19; Kennedy, Michael F. 9; McAllister, Gary 46;

Mauchlen, Alister H. 38; Mills, Gary R. 13; Morgan, Simon C. 30(2); Muggleton, Carl D. 3; Newell, Michael C. 45; North, Mark V. 1(7); Paris, Alan D. 37; Puttnam, David 2(1); Quinn, James M. 13(18); Ramsey, Paul 22; Reid, Paul R. 43(2); Russell, Martin C. 6(4); Spearing, Anthony 36; Turner, Philip 14(2); Walsh, Stephen 30; Weir, Peter R. 8(2); Wilkinson, Stephen J. −(1); Williams, Darren 4(2).

League Goals (56): Newell 13 (1 pen), McAllister 11 (1 pen), Cross 9, Quinn 6, Reid 6, Mauchlen 3, Turner 2, Walsh 2, North 1, Paris 1, Williams 1, own goal 1.

Littlewoods Cup (9): Newell 2, Reid 2, Cross 1, Groves 1, McAllister 1 (pen), Mauchlen 1, Walsh 1.

FA Cup (0).

Ground: City Stadium, Filbert Street, Leicester LE2 7FL (0533–555000)

Nearest station: London Road, Leicester

Manager: David Pleat **General Secretary:** A.K. Bennett

Colours: Blue shirts; white shorts

Record home gate: 47,298 v Tottenham Hotspur, February 1928 (FA Cup)

Honours − Champions: Division 2: 1924–5, 1936–7, 1953–4, 1956–7, 1970–71, 1979–80

League Cup winners: 1963–4

LEYTON ORIENT   DIV. 3

Baker, Stephen
Carter, Darren S.
Castle, Stephen C.
Comfort, Alan
Cooper, Mark D.
Corner, David E.
Day, Keith
Dickenson, Kevin J.

Gill, Jeremy M.
Hales, Kevin P.
Harvey, Lee D.
Heald, Paul A.
Howard, Terry
Hull, Alan E.
Juryeff, Ian M.

Ketteridge, Stephen J.
Marks, Michael D.
Nugent, Kevin P.
Sitton, John E.
Smalley, John D.
Ward, Paul T.
Wells, Peter A.

League Appearances: Baker, Stephen 46; Campbell, Kevin 16; Carter, Darren S. −(1); Castle, Stephen C. 22(2); Comfort, Alan 44; Cooper, Mark D. 10(4); Corner, David E. 4; Day, Keith 45; Dickenson, Kevin J. 38(1); Hales, Kevin P. 35; Harvey, Lee D. 25(4); Heald, Paul A. 28; Howard, Terry 46; Hull, Alan E. 12(5); Jones, David −(2); Juryeff, Ian M. 28(1); Kerrins, Wayne M. 3; Ketteridge, Stephen J. 5; Nugent, Kevin P. 2(1); O'Shea, Timothy J. 7(2); Shinners, Paul 4(2); Sitton, John E. 37; Smalley, Mark A. 3(1); Ward, Paul T. 28; Wells, Peter A. 18.

League Goals (86): Comfort 19, Campbell 9, Hales 9 (3 pens), Juryeff 9, Castle 6, Harvey 6, Howard 5, Hull 5, Cooper 4, Sitton 4, Baker 3, Day 2, Dickenson 1, Ketteridge 1, O'Shea 1, Ward 1, own goal 1.

Littlewoods Cup (5): Juryeff 2, Comfort 1, Hales 1 (pen), Hull 1.

FA Cup (3): Juryeff 2, Ward 1.

Ground: Leyton Stadium, Brisbane Road, Leyton, E10 5NE (01–539 2223/4)

Nearest station: Leyton (Central Line)

Manager: Frank Clark **Secretary:** Miss C. Stokes

Colours: Red shirts; white shorts

Record home gate: 34,345 v West Ham United, January 1964 (FA Cup)

Honours − Champions: Division 3: 1969–70; Division 3 South: 1955–6

LINCOLN CITY   DIV. 4

Bowling, Ian	Davis, Darren J.	Schofield, John D.
Bressington, Graham	Dunkley, Malcolm	Sertori, Mark A.
Brown, Philip J.	Hobson, Gordon	Smith, Paul M.
Casey, Paul	James, Anthony C.	Wiatt, Michael H.
Clarke, David A.	Matthewson, Trevor	Wallington, Francis M.
Cook, Mark R.	Nicholson, Shane M.	

League Appearances: Bowling, Ian 8; Bressington, Graham 30; Brown, Philip J. 31(7); Casey, Paul 6(2); Clarke, David A. 33(3); Cook, Mark R. 1; Cumming, Robert 29; Davis, Darren J. 37(1); Dunkley, Malcolm 9(2); Evans, Andrew C. 42; Franklin, Neil J. −(1); Gamble, Simon W. 15(7); Hobson, Gordon 32; James, Anthony C. 23(5); McGinley, John 15(5); Matthewson, Trevor 43; Nicholson, Shane M. 32(2); Ranshaw, Richard W.G. −(1); Schofield, John D. 29; Scott, Christopher 4; Sertori, Mark A. 22(4); Smith, Paul M. 27(1); Wallington, Francis M. 38.
League Goals (64): Hobson 14 (3 pens), Smith 10, Cumming 5 (1 pen), Gamble 5 (1 pen), Clarke 4 (1 pen), Dunkley 4, Sertori 4, Brown 3, Davis 2, Evans 2, McGinley 2, Matthewson 2, Schofield 2, Bressington 1, Nicholson 1, own goals 3.
Littlewoods Cup (5): Brown 1, Clarke 1, Gamble 1, Hobson 1, own goal 1.
FA Cup (2): Davis 1, Sertori 1.
Ground; Sincil Bank, Lincoln LN5 8LD (0522–22224 and 510263)
Nearest stations: Lincoln Central and St Mark's
Manager: Colin Murphy **Secretary:** G.R. Davey
Colours: Red and white striped shirts; black shorts
Record home gate: 23,196 v Derby, November 1967 (League Cup)
Honours – Champions: Division 3 North: 1931–2, 1947–8, 1951–2; Division 4: 1975–6

LIVERPOOL   DIV. 1

Ablett, Gary I.	Grobbelaar, Bruce D.	Molby, Jan
Aldridge, John W.	Hansen, Alan D.	Nichol, Stephen
Barnes, John C.B.	Harrison, Wayne	Rush, Ian J.
Beardsley, Peter A.	Hooper, Michael D.	Smyth, John M.
Boyd, Charles M.	Houghton, Raymond J.	Staunton, Stephen
Brack, Mark	Johnston, Craig P.	Tanner, Nicholas
Burrows, David	Jones, Barry	Venison, Barry
Carroll, John, G.M.	McMahon, Stephen	Watson, Alexander F.
Collins, David D.	Magilton, James	Whelan, Ronald A.
Gillespie, Gary T.	Marsh, Michael A.	

League Appearances: Ablett, Gary I. 34(1); Aldridge, John W. 31(4); Barnes, John C.B. 33; Beardsley, Peter A. 33(4); Burrows, David 16(5); Gillespie, Gary T. 15; Grobbelaar, Bruce D. 21; Hansen, Alan D. 6; Hooper, Michael D. 17; Houghton, Raymond J. 38; MacDonald, Kevin D. 3; McMahon, Stephen 28(1); Marsh, Michael A. −(1); Molby, Jan 12(1); Nicol, Stephen 38; Rush, Ian J. 16(8); Spackman, Nigel J. 8(4); Staunton, Stephen 17(4); Venison, Barry 14(1); Watson, Alexander F. 1(1); Whelan, Ronald A. 37.
League Goals (65): Aldridge 21 (4 pens), Beardsley 10, Barnes 8, Houghton 7, Rush 7, Whelan 4, McMahon 3, Molby 2 (2 pens), Nicol 2, Gillespie 1.
Littlewoods Cup (8): Aldridge 2 (1 pen), Barnes 2, Gillespie 1, McMahon 1, Molby 1 (pen), Rush 1.

FA Cup (18): Aldridge 6, Barnes 3, McMahon 3, Rush 3, Beardsley 2, own goal 1.
Ground: Anfield Road, Liverpool L4 0TH (051–263 2361)
Nearest station: All stations Liverpool
Player/Manager: Kenny Dalglish MBE Chief Executive/Secretary: P.B. Robinson
Colours: All red
Record home gate: 61,905 v Wolverhampton, February 1952 (FA Cup)
Honours – Champions: Division 1: 1900–1, 1905–6, 1921–2, 1922–3, 1946–7, 1963–4, 1965–6, 1972–3, 1975–6, 1976–7, 1978–9, 1979–80, 1981–2, 1982–3, 1983–4, 1985–6, 1987–8; (record 17 titles); Division 2: 1893–4, 1895–6, 1904–5, 1961–2
FA Cup winners: 1964–5, 1973–4, 1985–6, 1988–9
League Cup winners: 1980–81
Milk Cup winners: 1981–2, 1982–3, 1983–4
European Champions Cup winners: 1976–7, 1977–8, 1980–81, 1983–4
UEFA Cup winners: 1972–3, 1975–6
Super Cup winners: 1977

LUTON TOWN   DIV. 1

Beaumont, David A.	Harford, Michael G.	Poutch, Neil A.
Black, Kingsley	Harvey, Richard G.	Preece, David W.
Breacker, Timothy S.	Hill, Ricky A.	Rees, Jason
Chamberlain, Alec F.R.	James, Julian C.	Salton, Darren B.
Cobb, Gary E.	Johnson, Marvin A.	Scott, Ian
Cooke, Richard E.	Johnson, Robert S.	Sealey, Leslie J.
Dowie, Iain	McDonough, Darron K.	Telfer, Paul N.
Dreyer, John B.	Meade, Raphael J.	Tighe, Aaron P.
Farrell, Sean P.	O'Brien, Michael T.	Wegerle, Roy C.
Foster, Stephen B.	O'Sullivan, Michael A.	Williams, Steven C.
Gillard, Kenneth J.	Petterson, Andrew K.	Wilson, Daniel
Gray, Robert P.		

League Appearances: Allinson, Ian J.R. 1(4); Beaumont, David A. 15; Black, Kingsley 36(1); Breacker, Timothy S. 19(3); Chamberlain, Alex F.R. 6; Cooke, Richard E. –(6); Donaghy, Malachy 6; Dowie, Iain 1(7); Dreyer, John B. 16(2); Foster, Stephen B. 36; Grimes, Augustine A. 12; Harford, Michael G. 33; Harvey, Richard G. 11(1); Hill, Ricky A. 33; James, Julian C. 1; Johnson, Marvin A. 16; Johnson, Robert S. 19(2); McDonough, Darron K. 9(1); Meade, Raphael J. 2(2); Oldfield, David C. 15(6); Preece, David W. 26; Sealey, Leslie J. 32; Wegerle, Roy C. 26(4); Williams, Steven C. 10; Wilson, Daniel 37.
League Goals (42): Wilson 9 (4 pens), Black 8, Wegerle 8, Harford 7, Foster 3, Hill 3, Dreyer 1, Oldfield 1, own goals 2.
Littlewoods Cup (16): Harford 4, Wegerle 4, Hill 3, Oldfield 2, Wilson 2 (1 pen), Johnson 1.
FA Cup (2): Black 1, Wilson 1 (pen).
Ground: 70–72 Kenilworth Road, Luton LU1 1DH (0582–411622)
Nearest station: Luton
Manager: Ray Harford General Secretary: William J. Tomlins
Colours: White shirts with navy V-neck; navy shorts
Record home gate: 30,069 v Blackpool, March 1959 (FA Cup)
Honours – Champion: Division 2: 1981–2; Division 3 South: 1936–7; Division 4: 1967–8
Littlewoods Cup winners: 1987–8

MAIDSTONE UNITED   DIV. 4

Ground: Watling Street, Dartford, Kent DA2 6EN (0622) 54403.
Nearest station: Dartford
Record attendance: (at The Stadium, London Road, Maidstone) 10,591 v
Charlton FA Cup January 1979.
Manager: Keith Peacock.
Secretary: Mike Mercer.
Colours: Amber shirts, black shorts, black stockings with gold trim.
Honours: Nil.

MANCHESTER CITY   DIV. 1

Beckford, Jason N.	Gayle, Brian W.	Morley, Trevor W.
Biggins, Wayne	Gleghorn, Nigel W.	Moulden, Paul A.
Bradshaw, Carl	Hinchcliffe, Andrew G.	Oldfield, David C.
Brightwell, David J.	Hughes, Michael E.	Redmond, Stephen
Brightwell, Ian	Lake, Paul A.	Scott, Ian
Cooper, Paul D.	McNab, Neil	Seagraves, Mark
Deehan, John M.	Megson, Gary J.	White, David
Dibble, Andrew	Milner, Andrew J.	Wilson, Darren A.

League Appearances: Beckford, Jason N. 2(1); Biggins, Wayne 29(3); Bradshaw,
Carl 1(4); Brightwell, Ian 24(2); Cooper, Paul D. 8; Dibble, Andrew 38; Gayle,
Brian W. 41; Gleghorn, Nigel W. 25(7); Hinchcliffe, Andrew G. 37(2); Hughes,
Michael E. 1; Lake, Paul A. 37(1); McNab, Neil 42, Megson, Gary J. 22; Morley,
Trevor W. 39(1); Moulden, Paul A. 29(7); Oldfield, David C. 8(3); Redmond,
Stephen 46; Scott, Ian 1; Seagraves, Mark 21(2); Simpson, Paul D. 1; Taggart,
Gerald P. 9(2); Varadi, Imre 1(2); White, David 44(1); Williams, William R.
–(1).
League Goals (77): Moulden 13, Morley 12, Biggins 9, Brightwell 6, Gleghorn
6, White 6, Hinchcliffe 5 (3 pens), McNab 5 (4 pens), Gayle 3, Lake 3, Oldfield
3, Beckford 1, Megson 1, Redmond 1, Taggart 1, own goals 2.
Littlewoods Cup (12): Moulden 4, Gleghorn 2, White 2, Biggins 1, Lake 1, McNab
1 (pen), Morley 1.
FA Cup (2): Gleghorn 1, McNab 1 (pen).
Ground: Maine Road, Moss Side, Manchester M14 7WN (061–226 1191/3)
Nearest station: Manchester Piccadilly
Manager: Jimmy Frizzell **Secretary:** J.B. Halford
Colours: Sky blue shirts; white shorts
Record home gate: 84,569 v Stoke City, March 1934 (FA Cup)
Honours – Champions: Division 1: 1936–7, 1967–8; Division 2: 1898–9, 1902–3,
1909–10, 1927–8, 1946–7, 1965–6
FA Cup winners: 1903–4, 1933–4, 1955–6, 1968–9
League Cup winners: 1969–70, 1975–6
European Cup Winners' Cup winners: 1969–70

MANCHESTER UNITED   DIV. 1

Anderson, Vivian A.
Beardsmore, Russell P.
Blackmore, Clayton G.
Brazil, Derek M.
Bruce, Stephen R.
Bullimore, Wayne A.
Donaghy, Malachy M.
Duxbury, Michael
Garton, William F.
Gibson, Colin J.

Gill, Anthony G.D.
Goater, Leonard S.
Graham, Deiniol W.T.
Hesletine, Wayne A.
Hughes, Leslie M.
Leighton, James
McClair, Brian J.
McGrath, Paul
Maiorana, Giuliano

Martin, Lee A.
Milne, Ralph
Robins, Mark G.
Robson, Bryan
Sharpe, Lee S.
Walsh, Gary
Whiteside, Norman
Wilson, David G.
Wratten, Paul

League Appearances: Anderson, Vivian A. 5(1); Beardsmore, Russell P. 17(6); Blackmore, Clayton G. 26(2); Brazil, Derek M. −(1); Bruce, Stephen R. 38; Davenport, Peter 7(1); Donaghy, Malachy M. 30; Duxbury, Michael 16(2); Garton, Williams F. 13(1); Gibson, Colin J. 1(1); Gill, Anthony G.D. 4(5); Hughes, Leslie M. 38; Leighton, James 38; McClair, Brian J. 38; McGrath, Paul 18(2); Maiorana, Giuliano 2(4); Martin, Lee A. 20(4); Milne, Ralph 19(3); O'Brien, Liam F. 1(2); Olsen, Jesper 6(4); Robins, Mark G. 1(9); Robson, Bryan 34; Sharpe, Lee S. 19(3); Strachan, Gordon D. 21; Whiteside, Norman 6; Wilson, David G. −(4).
League Goals (45): Hughes 14, McClair 10, Robson 4, Blackmore 3, Milne 3, Beardsmore 2, Bruce 2, Davenport 2, Gill 1, McGrath 1, Martin 1, Strachan 1, own goal 1.
Littlewoods Cup (7): McClair 3, Robson 2, Bruce 1, Davenport 1.
FA Cup (11): McClair 3 (1 pen), Hughes 2, Robson 2, Bruce 1, Gill 1, Graham 1, own goal 1.
Ground: Old Trafford, Manchester M16 0RA (061–872 1661/3)
Nearest station: All stations Manchester
Manager: Alex Ferguson **Secretary:** K.R. Merrett
Colours: Red shirts; white shorts
Record home gate: 76,962 FA Cup semi-final (Wolverhampton v Grimsby Town), March 1939; **club:** 70,504 v Aston Villa, December 1920 (League)
Honours – Champions: Division 1: 1907–8, 1910–11, 1951–2, 1955–6, 1956–7, 1964–5, 1966–7; Division 2: 1935–6, 1974–5
FA Cup winners: 1908–9, 1947–8, 1962–3, 1976–7, 1982–3, 1984–5
European Champions Cup winners: 1967–8

MANSFIELD TOWN   DIV. 3

Beasley, Andrew
Cassells, Keith B.
Charles, Stephen
Christie, Trevor
Coleman, Simon
Cox, Brian R.
Foster, George W.

Hathaway, Ian A.
Hodges, David
Kearney, Mark J.
Kent, Kevin J.
Kenworthy, Anthony D.
Leishman, Graham

Lowery, Anthony W.
McKernon, Craig A.
Owen, Gordon
Place, Mark
Ryan, John B.
Stringfellow, Ian R.

League Appearances: Anderson, Nicholas J. 1; Beasley, Andrew 6; Cassells, Keith B. 36(1); Chambers, Stephen 3(2); Charles, Stephen 45(1); Christie, Trevor 12; Coleman, Simon 45; Cox, Brian R. 39; Foster, George W. 42; Garner, Paul 1(2); Graham, Michael A. 1; Gray, Kevin J. 1; Hathaway, Ian 4(8); Hodges, David 38(2); Kearney, Mark J. 44(1); Kent, Kevin J. 36(3); Kenworthy, Anthony D. 19(1); Leishman, Graham 6(6); Lowery, Anthony W. 11(1); McKernon, Craig A. 42; Owen, Gordon 39(2); Pearcey, Jason 1; Place, Mark 11(3); Ryan, John B. 23(7); Stringfellow, Ian R. −(8); Williams, Steven 1(2).
League Goals (48): Cassells 14, Charles 7 (1 pen), Coleman 5, Kent 5, Owen 5, Hodges 4, Kearney 2, Christie 1, Hathaway 1, Leishman 1, Stringfellow 1, own goals 2.
Littlewoods Cup (1): Hodges 1.
FA Cup (2): Kearney 1, Kent 1.
Ground: Field Mill, Quarry Lane, Mansfield, Nottingham NG18 5DA (0623–23567)
Nearest station: Mansfield, Alfreton Parkway
Manager: George Foster **Secretary:** J.D. Eaton
Colours: Amber shirts with blue stripe on side; amber shorts with blue stripe down side
Record home gate: 24,657 v Nottingham Forest, January 1953 (FA Cup)
Honours – Champions: Division 3: 1976–7; Division 4: 1974–5
Freight Rover Trophy winners: 1986–7

MIDDLESBROUGH   DIV. 2

Agnew, Garry H.	Gill, Gary	Parkinson, Gary A.
Barham, Mark	Hamilton, Gary J.	Pears, Stephen
Brennan, Mark R.	Kernaghan, Alan N.	Poole, Kevin
Burke, Mark S.	Kerr, Paul	Proctor, Mark G.
Coddington, Matthew J.	McGee, Owen E.	Ripley, Stuart E.
Cooper, Colin T.	Mohan, Nicholas	Slaven, Bernard
Davenport, Peter	Mowbray, Anthony M.	Trotter, Michael
Fletcher, Andrew M.	Pallister, Gary A.	

League Appearances: Barham, Mark 3(1); Brennan, Mark R. 25; Burke, Mark S. 21(8); Cooper, Colin T. 35; Davenport, Peter 23(1); Gill, Gary 6(2); Glover, Dean V. 8(4); Hamilton, Gary J. 35(1); Kernaghan, Alan N. 5(18); Kerr, Paul 18(2); Mohan, Nicholas 5(1); Mowbray, Anthony M.37; Pallister, Gary A. 37; Parkinson, Gary A. 36; Pears, Stephen 26; Poole, Kevin 12; Proctor, Mark G. 10; Proudlock, Paul −(1); Ripley, Stuart E. 36; Senior, Trevor J. 4; Slaven, Bernard 36(1).
League Goals (44): Slaven 15, Burke 5, Davenport 4, Ripley 4, Brennan 3, Hamilton 3, Mowbray 3, Cooper 2, Parkinson 2 (2 pens), Glover 1 (pen), Kerr 1, Pallister 1.
Littlewoods Cup (0)
FA Cup (1): Slaven 1.
Ground: Ayresome Park, Middlesbrough TS1 4PB (0642–819659)
Nearest station: Middlesbrough
Manager: Bruce Rioch **Secretary:** Tom Hughes
Colours: Red shirts; white shorts
Record home gate: 53,596 v Newcastle United, December 1949 (League)
Honours – Champions: Division 2: 1926–7, 1928–9, 1973–4

MILLWALL   DIV. 1

Anthrobus, Stephen A.
Babb, Philip A.
Branagan, Keith G.
Briley, Leslie
Carter, James W.C.
Cascarino, Anthony G.
Coleman, Nicholas
Dawes, Ian R.
Dowson, Alan P.

Horne, Brian S.
Horrix, Dean V.
Hurlock, Terence A.
Lawrence, George R.
McLeary, Alan T.
Magill, Manus P.
Morgan, Darren J.
O'Callaghan, Kevin
Reid, Wesley A.

Salman, Danis M.M.
Sheringham, Edward P.
Sparham, Sean R.
Stephenson, Paul
Stevens, Keith H.
Thompson, David
Torpey, Stephen D.J.
Treacy, Darren P.
Wood, Stephen A.

League Appearances: Anthrobus, Stephen A. 3; Briley, Leslie 31; Carter, James W.C. 14(6); Cascarino, Anthony G. 38; Dawes, Ian R. 27(3); Horne, Brian S. 38; Horrix, Dean V. 5(3); Hurlock, Terence A. 34; Lawrence, George, R. 10(1); McLeary, Alan T. 38; Morgan, Darren J. 7(1); O'Callaghan, Kevin 34; Reid, Wesley A. 1; Ruddock, Neil −(2); Salman, Danis M.M. 11(8); Sheringham, Edward P. 33; Sparham, Sean R. 10(2); Stephenson, Paul 11(1); Stevens, Keith H. 22(1); Thompson, David 13(2); Treacy, Darren P. 3; Wood, Stephen A. 35.
League Goals (47): Cascarino 13, Sheringham 11, Carter 5, O'Callaghan 5 (1 pen), Hurlock 3, Briley 2, Dawes 1, McLeary 1, Ruddock 1, Salman 1, Stephenson 1, Thompson 1, own goals 2.
Littlewoods Cup (7): Sheringham 3, Ruddock 2, Ruddock 1, Salman 1.
FA Cup (3): Carter 1, Cascarino 1, Sheringham 1.
Ground: The Den, Cold Blow Lane, London SE14 5RH (01–639 3143/4)
Nearest stations: New Cross or New Cross Gate (SR and Metropolitan line)
Manager: John Docherty **Secretary:** G.I.S. Hortop
Colours: Royal blue shirts; white shorts
Record home gate: 48,672 v Derby County, February 1937 (FA Cup)
Honours – Champions: Division 2: 1987–8; Division 3 South: 1927–8, 1937–8; Division 4: 1961–2

NEWCASTLE UNITED   DIV. 2

Anderson, John
Brazil, Gary N.
Brock, Kevin S.
Carter, Graeme
Chapman, Craig
Da Silva, Francisco E.L.
  Mirandinha
Gill, Mark P.
Gourlay, Archibald M.

Hendrie, John G.
Kelly, Gary A.
Kristensen, Bjorn
Lormor, Anthony
McDonald, Robert R.
O'Brien, Liam F.
O'Neill, Michael A.
Pingel, Frank

Ranson, Raymond
Robinson, David J.
Roche, David
Sansom, Kenneth
Scott, Kevin W.
Sweeney, Paul
Thorn, Andrew
Wright, Thomas J.

League Appearances: Anderson, John 21; Beasant, David 20; Bogie, Ian 3(3); Brazil, Gary N. 3(4); Brock, Kevin S. 21; Cornwell, John A. 8(1); Craig, Albert H. −(1); Da Silva, Francisco E.L. Mirandinha 22(6); Gourlay, Archibald M. −(1); Hendrie, John J. 34; Howey, Stephen N. −(1); Jackson, Darren 13(2); Jackson, Peter A. 1; Kelly, Gary A. 9; Kristensen, Bjorn 4(1); Lormor, Anthony 3; McCreery, David 36; McDonald, Robert R. 6(4); O'Brien, Liam F. 17(3); O'Neill, Michael A. 17(10); Payne, Lee J. 6(1); Pingel, Frank 13(1); Ranson, Raymond 13(1); Robertson, John G. 7(5); Robinson, David J. −(1); Roeder, Glenn V. 18; Roche, David −(2); Sansom, Kenneth 20; Scott, Kevin W. 29; Stephenson, Paul 7(1); Sweeney, Paul 6(2); Thorn, Andrew 26; Tinnion, Brian

12(1); Wharton, Kenneth 14(4); Wright, Thomas J. 9.
League Goals (32): Mirandinha 9 (4 pens), Hendrie 4, O'Brien 4, O'Neill 3, Brock 2, Jackson D. 2, Anderson 1, Lormor 1, McDonald 1, Pingel 1, Ranson 1, Thorn 1, Tinnion 1, own goal 1.
Littlewoods Cup (2): Hendrie 1, Mirandinha 1.
FA Cup (2): Brock 1, Mirandinha 1 (pen).
Ground: St James' Park, Newcastle-upon-Tyne NE1 4ST (Tyneside 091–2328361)
Nearest station: Newcastle Central (BR) or St James' Park (Metro)
Manager: Jim Smith **Secretary:** R. Cushing
Colours: Black and white vertically striped shirts; black shorts
Record home gate: 68,386 v Chelsea, September 1930 (League)
Honours – Champions: Division 1: 1904–5, 1906–7, 1908–9, 1926–7; Division 2: 1964–5
FA Cup winners: 1909–10, 1923–4, 1931–2, 1950–1, 1951–2, 1954–5
European Fairs Cup winners: 1968–9
Anglo–Italian Cup winners: 1973

NORTHAMPTON TOWN   DIV. 3

Adcock, Anthony C.
Berry, Stephen A.
Bodley, Michael J.
Collins, Darren
Culpin, Paul
Donald, Warren R.

Donegal, Glenville
Gleasure, Peter
McPherson, Keith A.
Quow, Trevor S.
Sandeman, Bradley R.

Singleton, Martin D.
Thomas, Dean R.
Wilcox, Russell
Williams, Wayne
Wilson, Paul A.

League Appearances: Adcock, Anthony C. 46; Anderson, Douglas E. 4(1); Berry, Stephen A. 34; Blair, Andrew 1(2); Bodley, Michael J. 20; Cobb, Gary E. 1; Collins, Darren 4(4); Craig, Albert H. 2; Culpin, Paul 33(6); Donald, Warren R. 37; Donegal, Glenville 4(5); Flexney, Paul 12; Garwood, Jason 5(1); Gilbert, David J. 34; Gleasure, Peter 46; Johnson, Ian 2(1); Longhurst, David J. 1(1); McGoldrick, Edward J.P. 22; McPherson, Keith A. 41; Preece, Andrew P. –(1); Quow, Trevor 17(1); Reed, Graham 8; Sandeman, Bradley R. 8(14); Singleton, Martin D. 11; Thomas, Dean R. 43; Wilcox, Russell 11; Williams, Wayne 26; Wilson, Paul A. 33(6).
League Goals (66): Adcock 17, Culpin 13, Thomas 9, Gilbert 7 (2 pens), Berry 3, Donegal 2, McGoldrick 2, McPherson 2, Sandeman 2, Craig 1, Donald 1, Quow 1, Singleton 1, Wilcox 1, Williams 1, Wilson 1, own goals 2.
Littlewoods Cup (7): Adcock 2, Culpin 2, Gilbert 1 (pen), Singleton 1, Wilson 1.
FA Cup (1): Berry 1.
Ground: County Ground, Abington Avenue, Northampton NN1 4PS (0604–721103)
Nearest station: Northampton
Manager: Graham Carr **Secretary:** Dr John Evans
Colours: Claret shirts with white shoulders; white shorts
Record home gate: 24,523 v Fulham, April 1966 (League)
Honours – Champions: Division 3: 1962–3; Division 4: 1986–7

NORWICH CITY   DIV. 1

Allen, Malcolm
Bowen, Mark R.
Butterworth, Ian S.
Coney, Dean H.
Cook, Paul A.
Crook, Ian S.
Culverhouse, Ian B.

Fleck, Robert
Flynn, Michael A.
Fox, Ruel A.
Gordon, Dale A.
Goss, Jeremy
Gunn, Bryan
Linighan, Andrew

Phelan, Michael C.
Putney, Trevor A.
Reeves, Alan
Rosario, Robert M.
Sheffield, Jonathan
Taylor, Alan D.
Townsend, Andrew D.

League Appearances: Allen, Malcolm 15(8); Bowen Mark R. 35; Butterworth, Ian S. 35(2); Coney, Dean H. 6(2); Cook, Paul A. 3(1); Crook, Ian S. 19(7); Culverhouse, Ian B. 38; Fleck, Robert 29(4); Fox, Ruel A. 1(3); Gordon, Dale A. 38; Gunn, Bryan 37; Linighan, Andrew 37; Phelan, Michael C. 36(1); Putney, Trevor A. 31(2); Rosario, Robert M. 25(2); Sheffield, Jonathan 1; Taylor, Alan D. 1(3); Townsend, Andrew D. 31(5).

League Goals (48): Fleck 10, Allen 5, Gordon 5, Townsend 5, Linighan 4, Putney 4, Rosario 4, Bowen 2, Butterworth 2, Phelan 2, Coney 1, Crook 1, Taylor 1, own goals 2.

Littlewoods Cup (5): Rosario 2, Crook 1, Fleck 1, Gordon 1.

FA Cup (17): Allen 7 (1 pen), Fleck 4, Gordon 2, Townsend 2, Putney 1, own goal 1.

Ground: Carrow Road Stadium, Norwich NR1 1JE (0603–612131)

Nearest station: Norwich Thorpe

Manager: Dave Stringer **Secretary:** A.R.W. Neville

Colours: Yellow shirts with green trim; green shorts with yellow trim

Record home gate: 43,984 v Leicester, March 1963 (FA Cup)

Honours – Champions: Division 2: 1971–2, 1985–6; Division 3 South: 1933–4

League Cup winners: 1961–2

Milk Cup winners: 1984–5

NOTTINGHAM FOREST   DIV. 1

Boardman, Craig G.
Bradley, Russell
Carr, Franz A.
Chapman, Lee R.
Charles, Gary A.
Chettle, Stephen
Clark, Martin J.
Clough, Nigel H.
Crosby, Gary
Crossley, Mark G.
Danzey, Michael J.
Dyche, Sean M.

Fleming, James G.
Foster, Colin J.
Gaynor, Thomas
Glover, Edward L.
Hodge, Stephen B.
Hurst, Mark D.
Jemson, Nigel B.
Lamb, Alan
Laws, Brian
McLoughlin, Steven R.G.
Parker, Garry S.

Pearce, Stuart
Rice, Brian
Sharpe, Kevin R.
Starbuck, Philip M.
Stone, Steven B.
Sutton, Stephen J.
Walker, Desmond S.
Wassall, Darren P.
Webb, Neil J.
Williams, Brett
Wilson, Terry

League Appearances: Carr, Franz A. 18(5); Chapman, Lee R. 30; Charles, Gary A. 1; Chettle, Stephen 23(5); Clough, Nigel H. 36; Crosby, Gary 11(2); Crossley, Mark G. 2; Foster, Colin J. 17(1); Gaynor, Thomas 16(3); Hodge, Stephen B. 33(1); Laws, Brian 20(2); Parker, Garry S. 22; Pearce, Stuart 36; Rice, Brian 19(1); Starbuck, Philip M. 2(5); Walker, Desmond S. 34; Webb, Neil J. 36; Williams, Brett 2; Wilson, Terry 24(3).

League Goals (64): Clough 14 (4 pens), Chapman 8, Hodge 7, Parker 7, Pearce

6, Webb 6, Gaynor 4, Carr 3, Chettle 2, Foster 2, Laws 1, Rice 1, Wilson 1, own goals 2.
Littlewoods Cup (25): Clough 7 (2 pens), Chapman 5, Gaynor 4, Hodge 2, Webb 2, Crosby 1, Foster 1, Parker 1, Pearce 1, own goal 1.
FA Cup (10): Chapman 3, Parker 2, Webb 2, Gaynor 1, Laws 1, own goal 1.
Ground: City Ground, Pavilion Road, Nottingham NG2 5FJ (0602–822202)
Nearest Station: Nottingham Midland
Manager: Brian Clough **Secretary:** K. Smales
Colours: Red shirts; white shorts
Record home gate: 49,945 v Manchester United, October, 1967 (League)
Honours – Champions: Division 1: 1977–8; Division 2: 1906–7, 1921–2; Division 3 South: 1950–1
FA Cup winners: 1897–8, 1958–9
League Cup winners: 1977–8, 1978–9
Littlewoods Cup winners: 1988–9
Simod Cup winners: 1988–9
Super Cup winners: 1979–80
European Champions Cup winners: 1978–9,1979–80

NOTTS COUNTY   DIV. 3

Barnes, Paul L.
Cherry, Steven R.
Davison, Aidan J.
Dolan, Kenneth P.
Draper, Mark A.
Fairclough, Wayne R.
Johnson, Thomas

Kevan, David J.
Law, Nicholas
Lund, Gary J.
Machin, Scott, J.L.
McStay, William
Norton, David W.
O'Riordan, Donald J.

Palmer, Charles A.
Pike, Geoffrey A.
Snook, Edward K.G.
Thorpe, Adrian
Turner, Philip
Withe, Christopher
Yates, Dean R.

League Appearances: Barnes, P.L. 11(4); Birtles, Garry 19(1); Cherry, Steven R. 18; Davison, Aidan J. 1; Draper, Mark A. 16(4); Fairclough, Wayne R. 14(6); Johnson, Thomas 6(4); Kevan, David J. 16(2); Law, Nicholas 42(2); Leonard, Michael C. 27; Lund, Gary J. 37(5); McParland, Ian J. 19(4); McStay, William 27(6); Mills, Gary R. 29; Norton, David W. 8; O'Riordan, Donald J. 40(3); Palmer, Charles A. 11; Pike, Geoffrey A. 34(2); Rimmer, Stuart A. 3(1); Thorpe, Adrian 26(10); Turner, Philip 16; Withe, Christopher 45; Yates, Dean R. 41.
League Goals (64): Lund 8, Barnes 7, McParland 6, (2 pens), Yates 6, Johnson 4, Law 4 (2 pens), Thorpe 4, Draper 3, Mills 3 (1 pen), O'Riordan 3, Pike 3 (1 pen), Birtles 2, Kevan 2, Rimmer 2, Turner 2, McStay 1, Withe 1, own goals 3.
Littlewoods Cup (7): McParland 3, Birtles 1, Mills 1, Pike 1, Thorpe 1.
FA Cup (2): Pike 1 Thorpe 1.
Ground: Meadow Lane, Nottingham NG2 3HJ (0602–861155)
Nearest station: Nottingham
Manager: Neil Warnock **Secretary:** N.E. Hook, M.Inst.M.
Colours: Black and white striped shirts; black shorts
Record home gate: 47,310 v York, March 1955 (FA Cup)
Honours – Champions: Division 2: 1896–7, 1913–14, 1922–3; Division 3 South: 1930–31, 1949–50; Division 4: 1970–71
FA Cup winners: 1893–4

OLDHAM ATHLETIC   DIV. 2

Barlow, Andrew J.   Holden, Andrew I.   Rhodes, Andrew C.
Barrett, Earl D.   Irwin, Denis J.   Richie, Andrew T.
Blundell, Christopher K.   Kelly, John   Skipper, Peter D.
Bunn, Frankie S.   McGarvey, Scott T.   Stewart, Mark A.
Donachie, William   Marshall, Ian P.   Warhurst, Paul
Hallworth, Jonathan G.   Milligan, Michael J.   Williams, Gary A.
Hartford, Richard A.   Palmer, Roger N.   Wright, Thomas E.
Henry, Nicholas I.

League Appearances: Adams, Neil J. 9; Barlow, Andrew J. 14(1); Barrett, Earl
D. 44; Blundell, Christopher K. 2; Bramwell, Steven −(1); Bunn, Frankie S.
26(2); Cecere, Michele 9(4); Donachie, William 4(5); Flynn, Michael A. 8(1);
Gayle, Andrew K. −(1); Hallworth, Jonathon G. 16; Hartford, Richard A.
3(4); Henry, Nicholas I. 14(4); Holden, Andrew I. 13; Irwin, Denis J. 40(1);
Kelly, John 41(1); Kelly, Norman −(1); Litchfield, Peter 3; Marshall, Ian P. 41;
Milligan, Michael J. 39; Morgan Stephen J. 1; Palmer, Roger N. 46; Philliskirk,
Anthony 3(7); Rhodes, Andrew C. 27; Ritchie, Andrew T. 30(1); Skipper, Peter
D. 27; Warhurst, Paul 2(2); Williams, Gary A. 2(4); Wright, Thomas E. 42(1).
League Goals (75): Palmer 15, Ritchie 14 (3 pens), Bunn 12, Wright 7, Kelly 6,
Milligan 6, Holden 4, Marshall 4, Cecere 2, Irwin 2, Philliskirk 1, Skipper 1,
Williams 1.
Littlewoods Cup (5): Ritchie 2, Bunn 1, Philliskirk 1, Williams 1.
FA Cup (1): Milligan 1.
Ground: Boundary Park, Oldham OL1 2PA (061–624 4972)
Nearest station: Oldham, Werneth and Oldham Mumps
Manager: Joe Royle **Secretary:** P.M. Hough
Colours: All blue with red trim
Record home gate: 47,671 v Sheffield Wednesday, January 1930 (FA Cup)
Honours – Champions: Division 3 North: 1952–3; Division 3: 1973–4

OXFORD UNITED   DIV. 2

Bardsley, David J.   Hill, Richard W.   Phillips, James N.
Beauchamp, Joseph D.   Hucker, Peter I.   Phillips, Leslie M.
Durnin, John   Judge, Alan G.   Reck, Sean M.
Evans, Ceri L.   Kee, Paul V.   Rhoades–Brown, Peter
Ford, Michael P.   Lewis, Michael   Shelton, Gary
Foyle, Martin J.   McDonnell, Matthew T.   Simpson, Paul D.
Greenall, Colin A.   Mustoe, Robbie   Slatter, Neil J.
Heath, Phillip A.   Nogan, Lee M.   Smart, Garry
Hewitson, Mark

League Appearances: Bardsley, David J. 37; Beauchamp, Joseph D. −(1);
Briggs, Gary 15; Durnin, John 19; Evans, Ceri L. 4: Ford, Michael P.
6(4); Foyle, Martin J. 40; Greenall, Colin A. 40; Heath, Phillip A. 8(8);
Hill, Richard W. 33(6); Hucker, Peter I. 26; Judge, Alan G. 20; Leworthy,
David J. 3(9); Lewis, Michael 36; Mustoe, Robbie 28(5); Nogan, Lee M.
2(1); Phillips, James N. 45; Phillips, Leslie M. 25(1); Purdie, Jon 5(6);
Reck, Sean M. 6; Rhoades–Brown, Peter 5(2); Saunders, Dean N. 10;
Shelton, Gary 28(5); Simpson, Paul D. 24(1); Slatter, Neil J. 25; Smart,
Gary 16(1).

League Goals (62): Foyle 14, Hill 10, Simpson 8, Bardsley 6 (2 pens), Phillips J. 4, Saunders 4, Durnin 3, Mustoe 3, Phillips L. 3, Greenall 2 (1 pen), Briggs 1, Ford 1, Heath 1, Leworthy 1, Shelton 1.
Littlewoods Cup (2): Saunders 2.
FA Cup (3): Hill 3.
Ground: Manor Ground, Beech Road, Headington, Oxford OX3 7RS (0865–61503)
Nearest station: Oxford
Manager: Brian Horton **Secretary:**
Colours: Gold shirts with navy blue sleeves; navy shorts
Record home gate: 22,730 v Preston, February 1964 (FA Cup)
Honours – Champions: Division 2: 1984–5; Division 3: 1967–8, 1983–4
Milk Cup winners: 1985–6

PETERBOROUGH UNITED   DIV. 4

Andrews, Gary M.
Butterworth, Garry J.
Collins, Stephen M.
Crichton, Paul A.
Cusack, Nicholas J.
Goldsmith, Craig S.W.

Gunn, Brynley C.
Halsall, Michael
Harle, David
Longhurst, David J.
Luke, Noel E.

McElhinney, Gerard
Nuttell, Michael J.
Oakes, Keith B.
Osborne, Steven C.
Sterling, Worrell R.

League Appearances: Andrews, Gary M. 33; Butterworth, Garry J. 6(2); Carr, Ashley −(1); Collins, Stephen M. 28(6); Crichton, Paul A. 31; Cusack, Nicholas J. 44; Genovese, Domenico 7(8); Goldsmith, Craig S.W. 34(6); Gooding, Michael C. 3; Gunn, Brynley C. 46; Halsall, Michael 42; Harle, David 7; Langan, David 18(1); Longhurst, David J. 37; Luke, Noel E. 45; McElhinney, Gerard M.A. 33; Madrick, Carl J. 3(5); Neenan, Joseph P. 15; Oakes, Keith B. 41; Osborne, Steven C. 3(6); Philpott, Lee 1(?); Pollard, Gary 8, Sterling, Worrell R. 12; Swindlehurst, David 4; Walsh, Colin D. 5.
League Goals (52): Cusack 10, Gunn 7 (6 pens), Longhurst 7, Goldsmith 6, Oakes 5, Gooding 3 (1 pen), Luke 3, Sterling 3, Collins 1, Genovese 1, Halsall 1, McElhinney 1, Osborne 1, Swindlehurst 1, Walsh 1, own goal 1.
Littlewoods Cup (5): Cusack 1, Genovese 1, Goldsmith 1, Gunn 1 (pen), Oakes 1.
FA Cup (6): Longhurst 3, Cusack 1, Halsall 1, own goal 1.
Ground: London Road Ground, Peterborough PE2 8AL (0733–63947)
Nearest station: Peterborough
Manager: Mick Jones **Secretary:** A.V. Blades
Colours: Blue shirts; white shorts
Record home gate: 30,096 v Swansea, February 1965 (FA Cup)
Honours – Champions: Division 4: 1960–61, 1973–4

PLYMOUTH ARGYLE

DIV. 2

Anderson, Douglas E.
Brimacombe, John
Brown, Kenneth J.
Burrows, Adrian M.
Byrne, David S.
Campbell, Gregory R.
Casey, Stuart R.
Cooper, Leigh V.

Garner, Darren J.
Hodges, Kevin
McCarthy, Sean C.
Marker, Nicholas R.T.
Morrison, Andrew C.
Penhaligon, Garry
Pickard, Owen
Plummer, Calvin A.

Rowbotham, Jason
Smith, Mark C.
Stuart, Mark R.N.
Summerfield, Kevin
Tynan, Thomas E.
Uzzell, John E.
Whiston, Peter

League Appearances: Barlow, Martin D. –(1); Brimacombe, John 24; Brown, Kenneth J. 39; Burrows, Adrian M. 43; Byrne, David S. 13; Campbell, David A. 1; Campbell, Gregory R. 6(7); Cherry, Steven R. 15; Cooper, Leigh V. 15; Evans, Stewart J. 1(2); Garner, Darren J. 1; Hodges, Kevin 23(8); McCarthy, Sean C. 37(1); Marker, Nicholas R.T. 42(1); Matthews, John M. 29(1); Miller, Alan J. 13; Morrison Andrew C. 2; Penhaligon, Garry 1; Pickard, Owen 1(1); Plummer, Calvin A. 17(6); Rowbotham, Jason 5; Smith, Mark C. 35; Stuart, Mark R.N. 32; Summerfield, Kevin 17(3); Tynan, Thomas E. 46; Uzzell, John E. 30(3); Whiston, Peter 1(1); Wilmot, Rhys J. 17.

League Goals (55): Tynan 24 (4 pens), McCarthy 8, Marker 6, Stuart 5, Campbell 3, Summerfield 2, Brimacombe 1, Brown 1, Burrows 1, Byrne 1, Hodges 1, Plummer 1, own goal 1.

Littlewoods Cup (9): McCarthy 4, Marker 2, Smith 1, Summerfield 1, Tynan 1.

FA Cup (3): McCarthy 1, Summerfield 1, Tynan 1.

Ground: Home Park, Plymouth, Devon PL2 1BQ (0752–52561)

Nearest station: Plymouth North Road

Manager: Ken Brown **Secretary:** Graham Little

Colours: Green shirts; black shorts

Record home gate: 43,596 v Aston Villa, October 1936 (League)

Honours – Champions: Division 3 South: 1929–30, 1951–2; Division 3: 1958–9

PORT VALE

DIV. 2

Atkinson, Paul
Beckford, Darren
Davies, Steven E.
Earle, Robert
Finney, Kevin
Ford, Gary
Futcher, Ronald

Glover, Dean V.
Grew, Mark S.
Hughes, Darren J.
Jeffers, John J.
Millar, Paul W.
Mills, Simon A.
Porter, Andrew M.

Riley, David S.
Sheppard, Glen
Simpson, Wayne W.
Walker, Raymond
Webb, Alan R.
West, Gary
Wood, Trevor J.

League Appearances: Atkinson, Paul 4; Beckford, Darren 41(1); Earle, Robert 44; Finney, Kevin 5(9); Ford, Gary 21(1); Futcher, Ronald 39(2); Glover, Dean V. 22; Grew, Mark 37; Harper, Steven J. –(7); Hazell, Robert J. 17; Hughes, Darren J. 44; Jeffers, John J. 11(4); Jepson, Ronald 1(1); Jones, Andrew M. 8(9); Mills, Simon A. 43; Porter, Andrew M. 12(2); Riley, David S. 39(1); Sproson, Philip J. 20; Stowell, Michael 7; Walker, Raymond 43; Webb, Alan R. 35(2); West, Gary 11(3); Wood, Trevor J. 2.

46

League Goals (78): Beckford 20 (1 pen), Futcher 17 (3 pens), Earle 13, Ford 7, Walker 5, Atkinson 3 (2 pens), Jones 3, Riley 3, Sproson 2, Finney 1, Porter 1, West 1, own goals 2.
Littlewoods Cup (5): Earle 2, Sproson 2, Futcher 1 (pen).
FA Cup (5): Earle 1, Futcher 1, Riley 1, Sproson 1, Webb 1.
Ground: Vale Park, Hamil Road, Burslem, Stoke-on-Trent ST6 1AW (0782-814134)
Nearest stations: Longport, and Stoke-on-Trent
Manager: John Rudge **Secretary:** D.E. Barber J.P. AMITD
Colours: White shirts with black trim; black shorts
Record home gate: 50,000 v Aston Villa, February 1960 (FA Cup)
Honours – Champions: Division 3 North: 1929–30, 1953–4; Division 4: 1958–9

PORTSMOUTH   DIV. 2

Aspinall, Warren	Gosling, Lee J.	Neill, Warren A.
Ball, Kevin A.	Gosney, Andrew R.	Powell, Darryl A.
Beresford, John	Hardyman, Paul G.	Quinn, Michael
Chamberlain, Mark V.	Hogg, Graeme J.	Ross, Michael P.
Connor, Terence F.	Kelly, Mark J.	Russell, Lee
Darby, Lee A.	Knight, Alan E.	Sandford, Lee R.
Fillery, Michael C.	Kuhl, Martin	Symons, Christopher J.
Gale, Shaun M.	Maguire, Gavin T.	Wigley, Steven

League Appearances: Aspinall, Warren 36(4); Awford, Andrew T. 3(1); Ball, Kevin 14; Beresford, John 1(1); Chamberlain, Mark V. 28; Connor, Terence F. 14; Dillon, Kevin P. 24(5); Fillery, Michael C. 14(3); Gilbert, William A. 9(3); Gosney, Andrew R. 14; Hardyman, Paul G. 23(2); Hogg, Graeme J. 41; Horne, Barry 30(11); Kelly, Mark J. 15(13); Knight, Alan E. 32; Kuhl, Martin 31(1); Maguire, Gavin T. 18; Moncur, John F. 7; Moran, Paul 3; Neill, Warren A. 43; Powell, Darryl A. 2(1); Quinn, Michael 36(3); Ross, Michael P. −(1); Russell, Lee −(2); Sandford, Lee R. 28(3); Symons, Christopher J. 2; Whitehead, Clive R. 27(5); Wigley, Steven 11.
League Goals (53): Quinn 18 (2 pens), Aspinall 11 (5 pens), Chamberlain 6, Connor 5, Horne 4, Fillery 2, Ball 1, Hardyman 1, Hogg 1, Kelly 1, Kuhl 1, own goals 2.
Littlewoods Cup (3): Aspinall 1, Connor 1, Quinn 1.
FA Cup (1): Quinn 1.
Ground: Fratton Park, Frogmore Road, Portsmouth PO4 8RA (0705–734129)
Nearest stations: Fratton, Portsmouth and Southsea
Manager: John Gregory **Secretary:** W.J.B. Davis
Colours: Blue shirts; white shorts
Record home gate: 51,385 v Derby County, February 1949 (FA Cup)
Honours – Champions: Division 1: 1948–9, 1949–50; Division 3 South; 1923–4; Division 3: 1961–2, 1982–3
FA Cup Winners: 1938–9

PRESTON NORTH END   DIV. 3

Allen, Shaun A.   Jones, Alexander   Philliskirk, Anthony
Atkins, Robert G.   Joyce, Warren G.   Rathbone, Michael J.
Bennett, Michael   Kelly, Alan T.   Swann, Gary
Bogie, Ian   McAteer, Andrew W.   Tunks, Roy W.
Chapman, Leslie   Maloney, Paul M.   Walker, Gary J.
Ellis, Anthony J.   Miller, David B.   Williams, Neil J.F
Harper, Steven J.   Mooney, Brian J.   Wrightson, Jeffrey G.
Hughes, Adrian F.S.   Patterson, Mark A.

League Appearances: Allardyce, Samuel 13 (1); Atkins, Robert G. 39; Bogie, Ian 9(4); Brazil, Gary N. 23(2); Brown, David J. 23; Ellis, Anthony J. 43(2); Fitzpatrick, Paul J. 2; Harper, Steven J. 2(3); Hughes, Adrian F.S. 22(1); Jemson, Nigel B. 6(3); Jones, Alexander 29(1); Joyce, Warren G. 35(5); McAteer, Andrew W. 11(2); Miller, David B. 9(3); Mooney, Brian J. 38(2); Patterson, Mark A. 42; Philliskirk, Anthony 13(1); Rathbone, Michael J. 32(2); Swann, Gary 16(2); Tunks, Roy W. 23; Williams, Neil J.F. 40(1); Wrightson, Jeffrey G. 36(2).
League Goals (79): Ellis 19, Patterson 15 (4 pens), Brazil 9 (3 pens), Joyce 9, Mooney 6, Philliskirk 6, Jemson 2, Rathbone 2, Swann 2, Williams N. 2, Bogie 1, Hughes 1, McAteer 1, own goals 4.
Littlewoods Cup (1): Brazil 1.
FA Cup (1): Atkins 1.
Ground: Deepdale, Preston PR1 6RU (0772–795919)
Nearest station: Preston
Manager: John McGrath **Secretary** D.J. Allan
Colours: All white
Record home gate: 42,584 v Arsenal, April 1938 (League)
Honours – Champions: Division 1: 1888–9, 1889–90; Division 2: 1903–4, 1912–13, 1950–51; Division 3: 1970–71
FA Cup winners: 1888–9, 1937–8

QUEEN'S PARK RANGERS   DIV. 1

Allen, Bradley J.   Fereday, Wayne   Maddix, Daniel S.
Allen, Martin J.   Francis, Trevor J.   Parker, Paul A.
Barker, Simon   Gray, Andrew A.   Pizanti, David
Channing, Justin A.   Herrera, Roberto   Reid, Peter
Clarke, Colin J.   Johns, Nicholas P.   Roberts, Anthony M.
Costello, Gregory J.P.   Kerslake, David   Seaman, David A.
Dennis, Mark E.   Kingsmore, Kevin L.   Sinton, Andrew
Doyle, Maurice   Law, Brian J.   Spackman, Nigel J.
Falco, Mark P.   Lynch, Stephen M.   Stein, Earl M.S.
Ferdinand, Leslie   McDonald, Alan

League Appearances: Allen, Bradley J. –(1); Allen, Martin J. 26(2); Ardiles, Osvaldo C. 4(4); Barker, Simon 21(4); Brock, Kevin S. 12(2); Channing, Justin A. 9; Clarke, Colin J. 12; Coney, Dean H. 11(5); Dennis, Mark E. 16(1); Falco, Mark P. 22(5); Fereday, Wayne 29(2); Fleming, Mark J. 1; Francis, Trebor J. 19; Gray, Andrew A. 11; Herrera, Roberto –(2); Johns, Nicholas P. 3; Kerslake, David 11(10); Law, Brian J. 6; McDonald, Alan 27(3); Maddix, Daniel S. 28(5);

Maguire, Gavin T. 7(1); Parker, Paul A. 36; Pizanti, David 13(2); Reid, Peter 14; Seaman, David A. 35; Sinton, Andrew 10; Spackman, Nigel J. 16; Stein, Earl M.S. 19(12).

League Goals (43): Falco 12 (2 pens), Francis 7 (1 pen), Clarke 5, Allen M. 4, Stein 4, Sinton 3, Gray 2, Maddix 2, Barker 1, Channing 1, Reid 1, Spackman 1.

Littlewoods Cup (12): Francis 3, Stein 3, Falco 2, Allen M. 1, Fereday 1, Kerslake 1, Maddix 1.

FA Cup (2): McDonald 1, Stein 1.

Ground: Rangers Stadium, South Africa Road, Shepherds Bush, W12 7PA (01–743 0262)

Nearest stations: Shepherds Bush (Metropolitan and Central lines); White City (Central line)

Manager: Trevor Francis **Secretary:** R.J. Phillips F.A.A.I.

Colours: Blue and white hooped shirts; white shorts

Record home gate: 35,353 v Leeds United, April 1974 (League)

Honours – Champions: Division 2: 1982–3; Division 3: 1966–7; Division 3 South: 1947–8

League Cup winners: 1966–7

READING   DIV. 3

Bashir, Naseem
Beavon, Michael S.
Burns, Phillip M.
Chatterley, Adrian P.
Conroy, Michael K.
Elsey, Karl W.
Francis, Stephen S.
Gernon, Frederick A.J.

Gilkes, Michael E.
Hicks, Martin
Jones, Linden
King, Andrew J.
Knight, Keith
Mitchell, Colin
Moran, Stephen J.
Newman, Domenyk E.

Payne, Lee J.
Phillips, Gary C.
Richardson, Steven E.
Senior, Trevor J.
Tait, Michael P.
Whitlock, Mark
Williams, Adrian

League Appearances: Beavon, Michael S. 37(2); Conroy, Michael K. 9(4); Curle, Keith 10; Elsey, Karl W. 41(3); Francis, Stephen S. 22; Franklin, Paul L. 14(2); Gernon, Frederick A.J. 18(4); Gilkes, Michael E. 46; Gordon, Colin K. 3(1); Hicks, Martin 45; Jones, Linden 27(2); King, Andrew J. –(1); Knight, Keith 25(4); Moran, Stephen J. 23(11); Payne, Lee J. 15; Phillips, Gary C. 24; Richardson, Steven E. 38(1); Senior, Trevor J. 37; Tait, Michael P. 36; Taylor, Leslie 12(2); Taylor, Scott D. –(3); Whitehurst, William 2; Whitlock, Mark 16(1); Williams, Adrian 6(2).

League Goals (68): Senior 16 (1 pen), Beavon 9 (6 Pens), Gilkes 9, Knight 7, Conroy 4, Moran 4, Tait 4, Elsey 3, Hicks 3, Jones 3, Payne 3, Whitehurst 2, Gordon 1.

Littlewoods Cup (6): Moran 2, Tait 2, Beavon 1 (pen), Jones 1.

FA Cup (12): Senior 4, Elsey 2, Taylor 2, Franklin 1, Gernon 1, Moran 1, own goal 1.

Ground: Elm Park, Norfolk Road, Reading RG3 2EF (0734–507878)

Nearest station: Reading

Manager: Ian Branfoot **Secretary:** Miss A. Meek

Colours: Sky blue shirts with white centre panel; sky blue shorts

Record home gate: 33,042 v Brentford, February 1927 (FA Cup)

Honours – Champions: Division 3: 1985–6; Division 3 South: 1925–6; Division 4: 1978–9

Simod Cup winners: 1987–8

ROCHDALE   DIV. 4

Beaumont, Christopher P. O'Shaughnessy, Stephen   Walling, Dean A.
Edmonds, Neil A.   Smart, Jason   Welch, Keith J.
Frain, David   Taylor, Steven J.

League Appearances: Alford, Carl P. −(4); Armitage, Andrew M. 33(3); Beaumont, Christopher P. 31(3); Brown, Malcolm 11; Copeland, Simon D. 27(1); Edmonds, Neil A. 34(5); Fothergill, Ashley G. 8(1); Frain, David 42; Harris, Carl S. 9(1); Jones, Paul 14; Lomax, Geoffrey W. 26(1); Lucketti, Christopher J. 1; McIntyre, Joseph G. 2(2); Mellish, Stuart M. 12(3); Mycock, David C. 10(1); O'Shaughnessy, Stephen 38(3); Reid, Shaun 17(1); Roberts, William J. 1; Smart, Jason 41(1); Smith, Mark C. 26(1); Sutton, David 28; Taylor, Steven J. 16(1); Walling, Dean A. 26(8); Welch, Keith J. 46; Windridge, David H. 5; Wood, Paul A. 2(3).
League Goals (56): Frain 12 (3 pens), Edmunds 8, Beaumont 7, Smith 7, O'Shaughnessy 6, Taylor 4, Walling 3, Jones 2, Reid 2, Sutton 2, Harris 1, Mellish 1, own goal 1.
Littlewoods Cup (4): O'Shaughnessy 2, Beaumont 1, Reid 1 (pen).
FA Cup (4): Beaumont 1, Edmonds 1, Frain 1, Reid 1 (pen).
Ground: Spotland, Sandy Lane, Rochdale OL11 5DS (0706–44648/9)
Nearest station: Rochdale
Manager: Terry Dolan **Secretary:** Ms Jacqueline Armstrong
Colours: All royal blue
Record home gate: 24,231 v Notts County, December 1949 (FA Cup)
Honours – Champions: Nil

ROTHERHAM UNITED   DIV. 3

Barnsley, Andrew   Haycock, Thomas P.   O'Hanlon, Kelham G.
Buckley, John W.   Hazel, Desmond L.   Pepper, Nigel C.
Crosby, Philip A.   Heard, Timothy P.   Russell, William M.
Dempsey, Mark J.   Johnson, Nigel M.   Scott, Martin
Evans, Stewart J.   Mendonca, Clive P.   Thompson, Simon L.
Goodwin, Shaun L.   Mercer, William   Williamson, Robert
Grealish, Anthony P.

League Appearances: Ash, Mark C. 1; Barnsley, Andrew 27; Buckley, John W. 19(17); Crosby, Philip A. 36(1); Dempsey, Mark J. 24(3); Evans, Stewart J. 19(6); Goodwin, Shaun L. 33(8); Grealish, Anthony P. 36(3); Green, John R. 21; Haycock, Thomas P. 27(6); Hazel, Desmond L. 39(3); Heard, Timothy P. 28(2); Johnson, Nigel M. 26; Mendonca, Clive P. 5(5); O'Hanlon, Kelham G. 46; Pepper, Nigel C. 1(1); Russell, William M. 44; Scott, Martin 18(1); Thompson, Simon L. −(1); Williams, Andrew 15; Williamson, Robert 41(1).
League Goals (76): Williamson 27 (7 pens), Evan 6, Hazel 6, Buckley 5, Goodwin 4, Haycock 4, Heard 4, Grealish 3, Williams 3, Crosby 2, Johnson 2, Russell 2, Dempsey 1, Green 1, Mendonca 1, Scott 1, own goals 4.
Littlewoods Cup (2): Grealish 1, own goal 1.
FA Cup (5): Dempsey 1 (pen), Grealish 1, Green 1, Williamson 1 (pen), own goal 1.
Ground: Millmoor, Rotherham S60 1HR (0709–562434)

Nearest station: Rotherham
Manager: Billy McEwan **Secretary:** N. Darnhill
Colours: Red shirts; white shorts
Record home gate: 25,000 v Sheffield United, December 1952 and Sheffield Wednesday, January 1952 (League)
Honours – Champions: Division 3: 1980–81; Division 3 North: 1950–51; Division 4: 1988–9

SCARBOROUGH   DIV. 4

Adams, Stephen	Graham, Thomas	Richards, Stephen C.
Bennyworth, Ian R.	Ironside, Ian	Russell, Martin C.
Blackwell, Kevin P.	Kamara, Alan	Short, Christian M.
Brook, Gary	Morris, Colin	Short, Jonathan C.
Cook, Mitchell C.	Norris, Stephen M.	Thompson, Neil
Dobson, Paul	Olsson, Paul	

League Appearances: Adams, Stephen 8(12); Bennyworth, Ian R. 35; Blackwell, Kevin P. 15; Brook, Gary 44; Brotherston, Noel 5; Charlton, Kevin 3; Cook, Mitchell C. 33(10); Dobson, Paul 18; Graham, Thomas 40(3); Ironside, Ian 28; Kamara, Alan 44; McJannet, William L. −(3); Matthews, Michael 7; Mell, Stewart A. 1(4); Morris, Colin 20(3); Norris, Stephen M. 27 (4); Olsson, Paul 25(7); Outhart, Anthony −(1); Richards, Stephen C. 42; Russell, Martin C. 20; Short, Christian M. 2; Short, Jonathan C. 41(1); Thompson, Leslie 2(1); Thompson, Neil 46.
League Goals (67): Brook 12, Norris 9, Thompson N. 9 (2 pens), Cook 5 (2 pens), Dobson 5, Short (Craig) 5, Graham 4, Olsson 4, Adams 3, Morris 3, Bennyworth 2, Russell 2, Kamara 1, Matthews 1, Richard 1, Thomson L. 1.
Littlewoods Cup (10): Cook 4 (2 pens), Norris 2, Brook 1, Graham 1, Richards 1, Thompson 1.
FA Cup (2): Brook 1, Cook 1.
Ground: The Athletic Ground, Seamer Road, Scarborough Y012 4HF (0723–375094)
Nearest station: Scarborough
Manager: Colin Morris **General Manager/Secretary:** Michael Dooley
Colours: All red
Record home gate: 11,130 v Luton T., January 1938 (FA Cup)
Honours: Nil

SCUNTHORPE UNITED   DIV. 4

Cowling, David R.	Hodkinson, Andrew J.	Nicol, Paul J.
Daws, Anthony	Lister, Stephen H.	Smalley, Paul T.
Flounders, Andrew J.	Longden, David P.	Stevenson, Andrew J.
Hamilton, Ian R.	Musselwhite, Paul S.	Taylor, Kevin

League Appearances: Brown, Anthony J. 29(3); Brown, David J. 5; Cork, David 8(7); Cotton, Perry −(1); Cowling, David R. 38(1); Daws, Anthony 45(1); Flounders, Andrew J. 45(1); Hamilton, Ian R. 25(2); Harle, David 18; Hodkinson, Andrew J. 38(3); Lister, Stephen H. 34; Longden, David P. 39 (2); Money, Richard 5(1); Musselwhite, Paul S. 41; Nicol, Paul J. 20(3); Richardson,

Ian P. 2(7); Rumble, Paul 8; Shearer, David J. 1; Smalley, Paul T. 39; Stevenson, Andrew J. 23(3); Taylor, Kevin 39(2); Winter, Julian 4.

League Goals (77): Daws 24, Flounders 16, Lister 9 (1 pen), Hodkinson 8, Taylor 8 (3 pens), Brown 2, Cowling 2, Harle 2 (2 pens), Hamilton 1, Nicol 1, Richardson 1, Rumble 1, Smalley 1, own goal 1.

Littlewoods Cup (12): Flounders 4, Daws 3, Harle 1 (pen), Hodkinson 1, Lister 1, Stevenson 1, Taylor 1;

FA Cup (1): Harle 1 (pen).

Ground: Glanford Park, Scunthorpe DN15 7RH (0724–848077)

Nearest station: Scunthorpe

Manager: Mick Buxton **Secretary:** A.D. Rowing

Colours: All claret and blue

Record home gate: 23,935 v Portsmouth, January 1954 (FA Cup)

Honours – Champions: Division 3 North: 1957–8

SHEFFIELD UNITED   DIV. 2

Agana, Patrick A.O.
Benstead, Graham M.
Booker, Robert
Bryson, James I.C.
Carr, Darren
Deane, Brian C.
Dickinson, Martin J.

Downes, Christopher B.
Duffield, Peter
Francis, John A.
Gannon, James P.
Pike, Martin R.
Powell, Clifford J.
Roberts, Alan

Smith, Brian
Stancliffe, Paul I.
Thompson, Steven P.
Todd, Mark K.
Tracey, Simon P.
Webster, Simon P.
Wilder, Christopher J.

League Appearances: Agana, Patrick A.O. 44(2); Barnsley, Andrew 1(2); Benstead, Graham M. 39; Booker, Robert 26; Bryson, James I.C. 36(1); Carr, Darren 9(1); Deane, Brian C. 43; Dickinson, Martin J. −(1); Downes, Christopher B. 2; Duffield, Peter 25(13); Francis, John A. 3(19); Gannon, John S. 8(8); Joseph, Francis 5(8); Moore, John 4(1); Pike, Martin R. 45; Powell, Clifford G. 2(2); Roberts, Alan 25(4); Ryan, Vaughan W. 2(1); Smith, Brian 34(1); Stancliffe, Paul I. 42; Thompson, Steven P. 20; Todd, Mark K. 39; Tracey, Simon P. 7; Webster, Simon P. 12; Whitehouse, Dane L. 3(2); Wilder, Christopher J. 29; Williams, Paul A. 1(1).

League Goals (93): Agana 24, Deane 22, Duffield 11 (5 pen), Bryson 8, Pike 5, Todd 4, Joseph 3, Stancliffe 3, Booker 2, Roberts 2, Webster 2, Carr 1, Francis 1, Gannon 1, Thompson 1, Wilder 1, own goals 2.

Littlewoods Cup (9): Deane 3, Agana 2, Duffield 2, Bryson 1, Stancliffe 1.

FA Cup (14): Deane 5, Agana 3, Bryson 2, Duffield 1, Stancliffe 1, Todd 1, own goal 1.

Ground: Bramall Lane, Sheffield S2 4SU (0742–738955)

Nearest station: Sheffield

Manager: Dave Bassett **Secretary:** D. Capper

Colours: Red and white striped shirts; black shorts

Record home gate: 68,287 v Leeds, February 1936 (FA Cup)

Honours – Champions: Division 1: 1897–8; Division 2: 1952–3; Division 4: 1981–2

FA Cup winners: 1898–9, 1901–2, 1914–15, 1924–5

SHEFFIELD WEDNESDAY   DIV. 1

Barrick, Dean
Bennett, David
Beresford, Marlon
Cam, Scott H.
Cranson, Ian
Fee, Gregory
Galvin, Anthony
Gregory, Anthony G.
Haigh, Kevin

Harper, Alan
Hirst, David E.
Hodgson, David J.
Hyde, Graham
Jonsson, Sigurdur
Knight, Ian J.
McCall, Stephen H.
Madden, Lawrence D.
Palmer, Carlton L.

Pearson, Nigel G.
Pressman, Kevin P.
Reeves, David
Rostron, John W.
Turner, Christopher R.
Varadi, Imre
Whitton, Stephen P.
Wood Darren T.
Worthington, Nigel

League Appearances: Barrick, Dean 8; Bennett, David 10; Bradshaw, Carl 1(2); Cranson, Ian 25(1); Fee, Gregory 8; Galvin, Anthony 9(9); Gregory, Anthony G. 1(2); Harper, Alan 23 (1); Hirst, David E. 28(4); Hodgson, David J. 6(5); Jonsson, Sigurdur 25 (3); Knight, Ian J. 2; McCall, Stephen H. 2; Madden, Lawrence D. 27; Megson, Gary J. 16(2); Palmer, Carlton L. 13; Pearson, Nigel G. 37; Pressman, Kevin P. 9; Proctor, Mark G. 24; Reeves, David 8(9); Rostron John W. 7; Sterland, Melvyn 22; Turner, Christopher R. 29; Varadi, Imre 14(6); West, Colin 17(3); Whitton, Stephen P. 12; Wood, Darren T. 7(1); Worthington, Nigel 28.
League Goals (34): Hirst 7, Sterland 6, Varadi 3, Whitton 3, Barrick 2, Pearson 2, Proctor 2, Reeves 2, Galvin 1, Hodgson 1, Jonsson 1, Megson 1, Palmer 1, West 1, own goal 1.
Littlewoods Cup (3): Hirst 1, Reeves 1, Varadi 1.
FA Cup (6): Varadi 2, Hirst 1, Hodgson 1, Jonsson 1, Proctor 1.
Ground: Hillsborough, Sheffield S6 1SW (0742–343123, box office 343122)
Nearest station: Sheffield
Manager: Ron Atkinson **Secretary:** R.H. Chester F.A.A I
Colours: Blue and white striped shirts; black shorts
Record home gate: 72,841 v Manchester City, February 1934 (FA Cup)
Honours – Champions: Division 1: 1902–3, 1903–4, 1928–9, 1929–30; Division 2: 1899–1900, 1925–6, 1951–2, 1955–6, 1958–9
FA Cup winners: 1895–6, 1906–7, 1934–5

SHREWSBURY TOWN   DIV. 3

Bell, Douglas
Brown, Michael A.
Finley, Alan
Green, Richard E.
Griffiths, Carl B.
Hughes, Kenneth D.
Irvine, Alan J.

Kasule, Victor
Kelly, Anthony G.
McGinlay, John
McNally, Bernard A.
Melrose, James M.
Moyes, David W.
Perks, Stephen J.

Pittman, Stephen
Pratley, Richard G.
Priest, Phillip
Thomas, Michael R.
Williams, Brian
Worseley, Graeme

League Appearances: Bell, Douglas 25(1); Brown, Michael A. 35(5); Finley, Alan 32(2); Geddis, David 7(2); Green, Richard E. 37(2); Green, Ronald R. 17; Griffin, Colin R. –(1); Griffiths, Carl B. 17(11); Hughes, Kenneth D. 7; Irvine, Alan J. 29(2); Kasule, Victor 12(9); Kelly, Anthony G. 19(1); McGinlay, John 14(2); McNally, Bernard A. 21(1); Melrose, James M. 16(5); Moyes, David W. 28(5); Osbourne, Calvert G. J. 3(4); Perks, Stephen J. 22;

53

Pittman, Stephen 11(1); Pratley, Richard G. 26(2); Priest, Phillip 26(2); Rougvie, Douglas 20(1); Steele, Timothy W. 6(9); Thomas, Michael R. 40; Williams, Brian 20(3); Williams, Wayne 10; Worsley, Graeme 6.

League Goals (40): Griffiths 6, Irvine 5, Kelly 5 (1 pen), McGinley 5, Green (Richard) 3, Rougvie 3, McInally 2 (1 pen), Melrose 2, Bell 1 (pen), Finley 1, Geddis 1, Kasule 1, Moyes 1, Priest 1, Steele 1, Thomas 1, Williams B. 1.

Littlewoods Cup (2): Brown 1, Melrose 1.

FA Cup (0)

Ground: Gay Meadow, Shrewsbury SY2 6AB (0743–60111)

Nearest station: Shrewsbury

Manager: Ian McNeill **Secretary:** M.J. Starkey

Colours: White shirts with blue trim; blue shorts

Record home gate: 18,917 v Walsall, April 1961 (League)

Honours – Champions: Division 3: 1978–9

SOUTHAMPTON   DIV. 1

Adams, Michael R.	Dodd, Jason R.	Osman, Russell C.
Baker, Graham	Flowers, Timothy D.	Radford, Dean
Banger, Nicholas L.	Forrest, Gerald	Rideout, Paul D.
Benali, Francis V.	Horne, Barry	Ruddock, Neil.
Blake, Mark C.	Kenna, Jeffrey J.	Shearer, Alan
Burridge, John	Le Tissier, Matthew P.	Statham, Derek J.
Case, James R.	Luscombe, Lee J.	Wallace, David L.
Cockerill, Glenn	Maddison, Neil S.	Wallace, Raymond G.
Cook, Andrew C.	Masters, Paul J.	Wallace, Rodney S.
Davis, Stephen M.	Moore, Kevin T.	Webb, Jamieson

League Appearances: Adams, Michael R. 8; Baker, Graham 20(1); Benali, Francis V. 3(4); Blake, Mark C. 3; Burridge, John 31; Case, James R. 34; Clarke, Colin J. 9; Cockerill, Glenn 33(1); Cook, Andrew C. 2(1); Flowers, Timothy D. 7; Forrest, Gerald 15(2); Horne, Barry 11; Le Tissier, Matthew P. 21(7); Maddison, Neil S. 3(2); Moore, Kevin T. 25; Osman, Russell C. 36; Rideout, Paul D. 20(4); Ruddock, Neil 13; Shearer, Alan 8(2); Statham, Derek J. 26; Wallace, David L. 27(4); Wallace, Raymond G. 25(1); Wallace, Rodney S. 38.

League Goals (52): Wallace (Rod) 12, Le Tissier 9, Cockerill 6, Rideout 6, Wallace D. 5, Baker 4, Moore 3, Ruddock 3 (1 pen), Maddison 2, Statham 2 (2 pens).

Littlewoods Cup (11): Baker 2, Cockerill 2, Le Tissier 2, Wallace (Rod) 2, Case 1, Moore 1, Rideout 1.

FA Cup (2): Forrest 1, Statham 1 (pen).

Ground: The Dell, Milton Road, Southampton SO9 4XX (0703–220505)

Nearest station: Southampton

Manager: Chris Nicholl **Secretary:** B.P. Truscott

Colours: Red and white striped shirts; black shorts

Record home gate: 31,044 v Manchester United, October 1969 (League)

Honours – Champions: Division 3 South: 1921–2; Division 3: 1959–60

FA Cup winners: 1975–6

SOUTHEND UNITED DIV. 4

Bennett, Gary M.
Brush, Paul
Butler, Peter J.
Clark, Paul P.
Crown, David I.
Edinburgh, Justin

Johnson, Peter E.
Ling, Martin
McDonough, Roy
Martin, David
Newell, Paul C.

Roberts, Paul
Sansome, Paul E.
Smith, Nicolas L.
Tilson, Stephen B.
Westley, Shane L.M.

League Appearances: Bennett, Gary M. 16(1); Brush, Paul 28; Butler, Peter J. 34(1); Clark, Paul P. 16; Crown, David I. 44; Edinburgh, Justin 14(1); Edwards, Andrew D. 1; Hall, Derek R. 38(2); Johnson, Peter E. 43; Jones, Matthew L. −(1); Ling, Martin 42(2); McDonough, Roy 36(4); Martin, David 34(3); Matthews, David 1(5); Newell, Paul C. 2; O'Shea, Daniel E. 19(1); Prior, Spencer J. 14; Roberts, Paul 23; Robinson, Martin J. 12(7); Sansome, Paul E. 44; Smith, Nicholas L. 7(4); Tilson, Stephen B. 10(6); Westley, Shane L.M. 28; Young, Richard A. −(2).
Leagues Goals (56): Crown 25 (5 pens), Ling 6, Robinson 6, McDonough 5, Hall 3, Bennett 2, Butler 2, Tilson 2, Martin 1, O'Shea 1, Prior 1, own goals 2.
Littlewoods Cup (4): Ling 2, Crown 1, own goal 1.
FA Cup (1): Ling 1.
Ground: Roots Hall Ground, Victoria Avenue, Southend SS2 6NQ (0702 340707)
Nearest stations: Pittlewell or Southend Central
Manager: David Webb **Secretary:** R.J. Osborne
Colours: Blue shirts; yellow shorts with blue trim
Record home gate: 31,033 v Liverpool, January 1979 (FA Cup)
Honours – Champions: Division 4: 1980–81

STOCKPORT COUNTY DIV. 4

Angell, Brett
Bullock, Steven
Butler, Brian F.
Caldwell, Antony
Colville, Robert J.
Cooke, John

Gorton, Andrew W.
Hancock, Antony E.
Hart, Nigel
Howard, Mark E.
Leonard, Gary A.

Logan, David
Matthews, Michael
Payne, Mark R.C.
Thorpe, Andrew
Williams, William R.

League Appearances: Angell, Brett, 17(9); Batch, Nigel A. 12; Bullock, Steven 13(9); Butler, Brian F. 32; Caldwell, Anthony 23(1); Colville Robert J. 27(4); Cooke, John 31(3); Coyle, Anthony 23; Dooner, Gary J. 1; Gorton, Andrew W. 34; Hancock, Anthony E. 12(10); Hart, Nigel 37(1); Hartford, Richard A. 12(2); Hendrie, Paul 11; Howard, Mark E. 10(6); Leonard, Gary A. 11; Logan, David 35; McKenzie Ian E. 10(7); Matthews, Michael 19; Payne, Mark R.C. 20(2); Pickering, Michael J. 7(1); Scott, Ian R. 8(1); Stapleton John R. 1; Thorpe, Andrew 41; Williams, William R. 35; Wylde, Rodger J. 24(2).
League Goals: (54): Wylde 12 (1 pen), Colville 6, Cooke 6 (1 pen), Angell 5, Caldwell 5 (1 pen), Hancock 5, Coyle 3, Butler 2, Hart 2, Howard 2, Williams 2 (1 pen), Leonard 1, Matthews 1, Payne 1, own goal 1.
Littlewood Cup (1): Wylde 1 (pen)
FA Cup (1): Colville 1.

Ground: Edgeley Park, Stockport SK3 9DD (061–480 8888)
Nearest station: Stockport
Manager: Danny Bergara **Secretary:** T.R. McCreery F.A.A.I.
Colours: White shirts: royal blue shorts
Record home gate: 27,833 v Liverpool, February 1950 (FA Cup)
Honours – Champions: Division 3 North: 1921–2, 1936–7; Division 4: 1966–7

STOKE CITY   DIV. 2

Bamber, John D.	Fowler, Lee E.	Kamara, Christopher
Barrett, Scott	Fox, Peter D.	Morgan, Nicholas
Beagrie, Peter S.	Hackett, Gary S.	Parkin, Stephen J.
Beeston, Carl F.	Hemming, Christopher	Saunder, Carl S.
Berry, George F. St.J.	Henry, Anthony	Shaw, Graham P.
Butler, John E.	Higgins, Mark N.	Stainrod, Simon A.
Carr, Clifford P.	Holmes, Andrew J.	Ware, Paul D.

League Appearances: Bamber, John D. 23; Barrett, Scott 17; Beagrie, Peter S. 41; Beeston, Carl F. 22(1); Berry, George F.S. 32(1); Butler, John E. 25; Carr, Clifford P. 40(11); Ford, Tony 27; Fox, Peter D. 29; Gidman, John 7(3); Hackett, Gary S. 45(1); Hemming, Christopher A.J. 4; Henry, Anthony 37(3); Higgins, Mark N. 33; Kamara, Christopher 38; Morgan, Nicholas 11(7); Parkin, Stephen J. 4; Saunders, Carl S. 27(6); Shaw, Graham P. 19(9); Stainrod, Simon A. 16; Ware, Paul D. 9(2).
League Goals (57): Beagrie 7, Bamber 6, Henry 6, Hackett 5, Morgan 5, Shaw 5, Berry 4 (3 pens), Kamara 4, Stainrod 4, Beeston 2, Saunders 2, Butler 1, Carr 1, Higgins 1, Ware 1, own goals 3.
Littlewoods Cup (3): Kamara 1, Morgan 1, Stainrod 1 (pen).
FA Cup (5): Bamber 2, Beagrie 1, Berry 1, Shaw 1.
Ground: Victoria Ground, Stoke-on-Trent ST4 4EG (0782–413511)
Nearest station: Stoke-on-Trent
Player/Manager: Mick Mills **Secretary:** M.J. Potts
Colours: Red and white striped shirts; white shorts
Record home gate: 51,380 v Arsenal, March 1937 (League)
Honours – Champions: Division 2: 1932–3, 1962–3; Division 3 North: 1926–7
League Cup winners: 1971–2

SUNDERLAND   DIV. 2

Agboola, Reuben O.F.	Gabbiadini, Ricardo	Lemon, Paul A.
Armstrong, Gordon I.	Gates, Eric L.	Lynch, Thomas
Bennett, Gary E.	Hauser, Thomas	MacPhail, John
Carter, Timothy D.	Hawke, Warren R.	Norman, Anthony J.
Cornforth, John M.	Hay, Alan B.	Ord, Richard J.
Cullen, Anthony	Heathcote, Michael	Owers, Gary
Doyle, Stephen C.	Kay, John	Pascoe, Colin J.
Gabbiadini, Marco		

League Appearances: Agboola, Reuben O.F. 25(4); Armstrong, Gordon I. 45; Atkinson, Paul 2(1); Barnes, Peter S. 1; Bennett, Gary E. 37(3); Carter, Timothy D. 2; Cornforth, John M. 10(5); Cullen, Anthony 3(4); Doyle, Stephen C. 35; Gabbiadini, Marco 35(1); Gates, Eric L. 27(10); Gray, Francis T. 36(4); Hauser, Thomas 6(7); Hawke, Warren R. 1(3); Hay, Alan B. 1; Hesford, Iain 20; Kay John 11; Lemon, Paul A. 12(6); Lynch, Thomas 4; MacPhail, John 45; Norman, Anthony 24; Ogilvie, Gary F. −(1); Ord, Richard J. 31(3); Owers, Gary 36(2); Pascoe, Colin J. 39; Wharton, Sean R. 1; Whitehurst, William 17; Williams, Paul L. −(1).
League Goals (60): Gabbiadini, Marco 18 (2 pcns), Pascoe 10, Armstrong 8, Gates 4, MacPhail 4 (3 pens), Bennett 3, Owers 3, Whitehurst 3, Hauser 2, Doyle 1, Lemon 1, Ord 1, own goals 2.
Littlewoods Cup (5): Gabbiadini, Marco 3, Pascoe 2.
FA Cup (1): Ord 1.
Ground: Roker Park, Grantham Road, Sunderland SR6 9 SW (091–5140332)
Nearest stations: Sunderland or Seaburn.
Manager: Denis Smith **Secretary:** G. Davidson F.C.A.
Colours: Red and white striped shirts; black shorts
Records home gate: 75,118 v Derby, March 1933 (FA Cup)
Honours – Champions: Division 1: 1891–2, 1892–3, 1894–5, 1901–2, 1912–13, 1935–6; Division 2: 1975–6; Division 3: 1987–8
FA Cup winners: 1936–7, 1972–3

SWANSEA CITY   DIV. 3

Bracey, Lee M.I.
Coleman, Christopher P.
D'Auria, David A.
Davies, Alan
Hough, David J.
James, Robert M.

Jones, Lee
Knill, Alan R.
Legg, Andrew
Lewis, Dudley K.
Melville, Andrew R.
Phillips, Stewart G.

Raynor, Paul J.
Thornber, Stephen J.
Toshack, Jon C.
Trick, Desmond
Wade, Bryan A.

League Appearances: Allon, Joseph 1(1); Bodak, Peter J. 16(6); Bracey, Lee M.I. 30; Coleman, Christopher P. 43; D'Auria David A. 9(5); Davey, Simon 3; Davies, Alan 42; Holdsworth, Dean C. 4(1); Hough, David J. 30(10); Hutchison, Thomas 42(2); James, Robert M. 38(3); Knill, Alan R. 43; Legg, Andrew 6; Lewis, Dudley K. 40; Love, Ian J. 7(7); Melville, Andrew R. 44(1); Phillips Stewart G. 4(2); Puckett, David C. 7(1); Raynor, Paul J. 23(3); Thornber, Stephen J. 27(4); Wade, Bryan A. 17(8); West, Colin W. 14; Wilmot, Rhys J. 16.
League Goals (51): Melville 10, James 9 (4 pens), Davies 5, Raynor 5, Bodak 4, Wade 4, Hutchison 3, Puckett 3, West 3, D'Auria 2, Knill 2, Holdsworth 1.
Littlewoods Cup (1): Thornber 1.
FA Cup (6): Melville 2, Wade 2, Coleman 1, Hutchison 1.
Ground: Vetch Field, Swansea SA1 3SU (0792–474114)
Nearest station: Swansea
Manager: Ian Evans **Secretary:** George Taylor
Colours: All white
Record home gate: 32,796 v Arsenal, February 1968 (FA Cup)
Honours – Champions: Division 3 South: 1924–5, 1948–9

SWINDON TOWN   DIV. 2

Barnard, Leigh K.
Barnett, David P.
Bodin, Paul J.
Calderwood, Colin
Casserly, Dean S.
Cornwell, John A.
Coyne, Peter D.
Digby, Fraser C.
Fleming, Curtis

Foley, Steven
Geddis, David
Gittens, Jon
Hammond, Nicholas D.
Henry, Charles A.
Hockaday, David
Jones, Mark
Jones, Tom
King, Philip G.

MacLaren, Ross
McLoughlin, Alan F.
Parkin, Timothy J.
Reynolds, James A.
Shearer, Duncan N.
Simpson, Fitzroy
Tomlinson, Neil R.
Viveash, Adrian L.
White, Stephen J.

League Appearances: Barnard, Leigh K. 1(1); Barnes, David O. 17; Bodin, Paul J. 15(1); Calderwood, Colin 43; Cornwell, John A. 5(1); Coyne, Peter D. −(1); Digby, Fraser C. 46; Foley, Steven 40; Geddis, David 8(2); Gittens, Jon 29; Henry, Charles A. 13(9); Hockaday, David 44; Jones, Tom 40; King, Philip G. 34(3); MacLaren, Ross 37; McLoughlin, Alan F. 25(1); Parkin, Timothy J. 32; Shearer, Duncan N. 33(3); Simpson, Fitzroy 3(4); White, Stephen J. 41(2).
League Goals (68): Shearer 14, White 13, Foley 8, Jones 6 (1 pen), Calderwood 4, MacLaren 4 (2 pens), Barnes 3, Geddis 3, Henry 3, McLoughlin 3, King 2, Bodin 1, Gittens 1, Parkin 1, own goals 2.
Littlewoods Cup (1): Shearer 1.
FA Cup (3): Foley 2, Shearer 1.
Ground: County Ground, Swindon SN1 2ED (0793–22118 and 36170)
Nearest station: Swindon
Manager: Ossie Ardiles **Secretary:** D.G. King
Colours: All red
Record home gate: 32,000 v Arsenal, January 1972 (FA Cup)
Honours – Champions: Division 4: 1985–6; **League Cup winners:** 1968–9
Anglo-Italian Cup winners: 1970

TORQUAY UNITED   DIV. 4

Airey, Carl
Bastow, Ian J.
Coombe, Mark A.
Edwards, Dean S.
Elliott, Matthew S.
Hirons, Paul T.
Holmes, Paul

Joyce, Sean W.
Lloyd, Philip R.
Loram, Mark J.
Love, Ian J.
McNichol, James A.
Morrison, John
Pugh, Daral J.

Smith, James
Smith, Paul S.
Thompson, Richard J.
Underhill, Phillip A.
Veysey, Kenneth J.
Weston, Ian P.

League Appearances: Airey, Carl 10(7); Bastow, Ian J. 1(1); Code, David A. 32(3); Coombe, Mark A. 8; Crichton, Paul A. 13; Davies, Andrew J. 3; Dawkins, Derek A. 6(6); Edwards, Dean S. 30(10); Elliott, Matthew S. 13; Gibbins, Roger G. 20(1); Gummer, Jason C. 7; Haslegrave, Sean M. 1(1); Hirons, Paul T. 1(4); Holmes, Paul 19(6); Joyce, Sean W. 27(3); Kelly, Thomas J. 43(1); Leyden, Darren 7(2); Lloyd, Phillip R. 46; Loram, Mark J. 33(4); Love, Ian J. 8(1); McNichol, James A. 36; Morrison, John 13(5); Pugh, Daral J. 26(3); Smith, James 26(8); Smith, Paul S. 8(3); Thompson, Richard J. 11(4); Tupling, Stephen 1(2); Veysey, Kenneth J. 25; Weston, Ian P. 32(5).
League Goals (45): Edwards 8, Lloyd 4, Smith J. 4 (1 pen), Loram 4, McNichol 4, Thompson 4, Airey 3, Gibbins 3, Joyce 3, Elliott 2, Weston 2, Cole 1, Gummer

1, Smith P. 1, own goal 1.
Littlewood Cup (1): Dawkins 1.
FA Cup (8): Loram 2, Smith J. 2, Edwards 1, Joyce 1, McNichol 1, Thompson 1.
Ground: Plainmoor, Torquay, Devon TQ1 3PS (0803–38666/7)
Nearest stations: Torquay or Torre
Manager: Cyril Knowles **Secretary:** D.F. Turner
Colours: All white with yellow and blue trim
Record home gate; 21,908 v Huddersfield, January 1955 (FA Cup)
Honours: Nil

TOTTENHAM HOTSPUR   DIV. 1

Allen, Paul K.
Amar, Mohamed A. Nayim
Bergsson, Gudni
Butters, Guy
Dearden, Kevin C.
Fenwick, Terence W.
Gascoigne, Paul J.
Gilzean, Ian R.
Gormley, Edward J.
Gray, Philip
Guthrie, Peter J.

Howells, David
Howells, Gareth J.
Hughton, Christopher
Johnston, Richard W.
McDonald, David H.
Mabbutt, Gary V.
Mimms, Robert A.
Moncur, John F.
Moran, Paul
Murray, Shaun
Polston, Andrew A.

Polston, John D.
Robson, Mark A.
Samways, Vincent
Statham, Brian
Stevens, Gary A.
Stewart, Paul A.
Stimson, Mark
Thomas, Mitchell A.
Thorstvedt, Erik
Waddle, Christopher R.
Walsh, Paul A.

League Appearances: Allen, Paul K. 35(2); Amar, Mohamed A. (Nayim) 8(3); Bergsson, Gudni 8; Butters, Guy 27(2); Fairclough, Courtney H. 20; Fenwick, Terence W. 34; Gascoigne, Paul J. 31(1); Gray, Philip −(1); Howells, David 12(15); Hughton, Christopher W.G. 20(1); Mabbutt, Gary V. 38; Mimms, Robert A. 20; Moncur, John F. −(1); Moran, Paul 4(4); Polston, John D. −(3); Robson, Mark A. 3(2); Samways, Vincent 12(7); Statham, Brian 6; Stevens, Gary A. 5; Stewart, Paul A. 29(1); Stimson, Mark −(1); Thomas, Mitchell A. 22(3); Thorstvedt, Erik 18; Waddle, Christopher R. 38, Walsh, Paul A. 28(5).
League Goals (60): Waddle 14, Stewart 12, Fenwick 8 (6 pens), Gascoigne 6, Walsh 6, Howells 3, Samways 3, Nayim 2, Allen 1, Butters 1, Fairclough 1, Mabbutt 1, Thomas 1, own goal 1.
Littlewoods Cup (6): Fenwick 1 (pen), Gascoigne 1, Samways 1, Stewart 1, Thomas 1, own goal 1.
FA Cup (0)
Ground: White Hart Lane, 748 High Road, Tottenham, N17 0AP (01–808 8080)
Nearest station: White Hart Lane (BR), Northumberland Park (BR), or Seven Sisters (Victoria Lane) thence by bus
Manager: Terry Venables **Secretary:** Peter Barnes
Colours: White shirts; navy blue shorts
Record home gate: 75,038 v Sunderland, March 1938 (FA Cup)
Honours – Champions: Division 1: 1950–51, 1960–61; Division 2: 1919–20, 1949–50

FA Cup winners: 1900–1, 1920–21, 1960–61, 1961–2, 1966–7, 1980–81, 1981–2. (Seven wins joint record with Aston Villa)
League Cup winners: 1970–71, 1972–3
European Cup Winners' Cup winners: 1962–3
UEFA Cup winners: 1971–2, 1983–4

TRANMERE ROVERS   DIV. 3

Bishop, Edward M.
Collings, Paul W.
Garnett, Shaun M.
Harvey, James
Higgins, David A.
Hughes, Mark

McCarrick, Mark B.
McKenna, Kenneth M.
Malkin, Christopher G.
Martindale, David
Morrissey, John J.
Muir, Ian J.

Mungall, Steven H.
Nixon, Eric W.
Smith, John
Steel, William J.
Thomas, Tony
Vickers, Stephen H.

League Appearances: Bishop, Edward M. 26(9); Collings, Paul W. 1; Harvey, James 42; Higgins, David A. 43; Hughes, Mark 37; McCarrick, Mark B. 42; McKenna, Kenneth M. −(1); Malkin, Christopher G. 6(14); Martindale, David 20(12); Moore, Ronald D. 10; Morrissey, John J. 42; Muir, Ian J. 46; Mungall, Steven H. 42; Murray, Edward J. −(7); Nixon, Eric W. 45; Smith, John 1(1); Steel, William J. 44; Thomas, Tony 8(1); Vickers, Stephen H. 46; Williams, Gary 5(3).
League Goals (62): Muir 21 (4 pens), Bishop 8, Steel 7, Harvey 4, Malkin 4, Morrissey 4, McCarrick 3, Vickers 3, Thomas 2, Higgins 1, Hughes 1, Martindale 1, Mungall 1, own goals 2.
Littlewoods Cup (4): Muir 2, Bishop 1, Hughes 1.
FA Cup (8): Muir 5 (1 pen), Steels 1, Vickers 1, own goal 1.
Ground: Prenton Park, Birkenhead, L42 9PN (051–608 4194/3677)
Nearest stations: Central Station Birkenhead and Rock Ferry
Player/Manager: John King **Secretary:** C.N. Wilson F.A.A.I.
Colours: All white
Record home gate: 24,424 v Stoke, February 1972 (FA Cup)
Honours – Champions: Division 3 North: 1937–8

WALSALL   DIV. 3

Banton, Dale G.
Barber, Frederick
Bertschin, Keith E.
Dornan, Andrew
Forbes, Graeme S.A.
Goldsmith, Martin
Goodwin, Mark A.
Green, Ronald R.

Hart, Peter O.
Hawker, Philip N.
Jones, Mark
Jones, Paul A.
McIlhargey, Stephen
Marsh, Christopher J.
Mower, Kenneth M.
Naughton, William B.S.

Pritchard, Howard K.
Rees, Mark
Rimmer, Stuart A.
Saville, Andrew V.
Shakespeare, Craig R.
Taylor, Alexander
Taylor, Robert M.

League Appearances: Banton, Dale G. 9(1); Barber, Frederick 44; Bertschin, Keith E. 11(9); Callaghan, William T. 2; Christie, Trevor 26(2); Dornan, Andrew 26; Forbes, Graeme S.A. 45; Goldsmith, Martin −(2); Goodwin, Mark A. 30(2); Green, Ronald R. 2; Hart, Peter O. 26(1); Hawker, Philip N. 23(3); Jones, Paul A. 13(3); Marsh, Christopher J. 3(10); Mower, Kenneth M. 28 (1); Naughton, William B.S. 31(4); Pritchard, Howard K. 36(5); Rees, Mark 16(9); Rimmer, Stuart A. 20; Saville, Andrew V. 12; Shakespeare, Craig R. 45; Smith, Dean 15; Taylor, Alexander 13; Taylor, Robert M. 30(4).
League Goals (41): Rimmer 8, Naughton 7 (3 pens), Pritchard 6, Saville 4,

Shakespeare 3, Taylor A. 3, Christie 2 (1 pen), Hawker 2, Callaghan 1, Forbes 1, Rees 1, Taylor M. 1, own goals 2.
Littlewoods Cup (6): Shakespeare 2, Forbes 1, Goodwin 1, Hawker 1, Taylor A. 1.
FA Cup (1): Pritchard 1.
Ground: Fellows Park, Walsall WS2 9DB (0922–22791)
Nearest station: Walsall or Bescott then 15 min walk
Manager: John Barnwell **Secretary:** K.R. Whalley
Colours: Red shirts; white shorts
Record home gate: 25,453 v Newcastle, August 1961 (League)
Honours – Champions: Division 4: 1959–60

WATFORD   DIV. 2

Ashby, Barry J.	Holdsworth, David G.	Redfearn, Neil D.
Coton, Anthony P.	Holdsworth, Dean C.	Rees, Melvyn J.
Drysdale, Jason	Jackett, Kenneth F.	Richardson, Lee J.
Falconer, William	James, David	Roberts, Iwan W.
Gardener, Martin	McClelland, John	Sherwood, Timothy A.
Gibbs, Nigel J.	Miller, Paul R.	Soloman, Jason R.
Gunn, Andrew C.	Morris, Mark J.	Thomas, Roderick C.
Henry, Liburd A.	Naylor, Dominic J.	Thompson, Garry L.
Hodges, Glyn P.	Porter, Gary M.	Wilkinson, Paul
Holden, Richard W.	Pullan, Christopher J.	

League Appearances: Bamber, John D. 16(2); Blissett, Luther L. 3; Coton, Anthony P. 46; Falconer, William 30(3); Gibbs, Nigel J. 46; Henry, Liburd A. 1; Hodges, Glyn P. 25(2); Holden, Richard W. 32; Holdsworth, David G. 27(6); Holdsworth, Dean C. 2(8); Jackett, Kenneth F. 39(3); McClelland, John 43; Miller, Paul R. 20; Morris, Mark J. 2; Porter, Gary M. 40(2); Pullan, Christopher J. 1; Redfearn Neil D. 12; Richardson, Lee J. 9; Rimmer, Stuart A. 1; Roberts, Iwan W. 11(11); Rostron, John W. 7; Sherwood, Tim A. 14(5); Sterling, Worrell R. 3; Thomas, Roderick C. 15(3); Thompson, Garry L. 17(4); Wilkinson, Paul 44(1).
League Goals (74): Wilkinson 19, Porter 10 (3 pens), Thompson 7, Holden 6, Roberts 6, Falconer 5, Hodges 5, Bamber 3, Holdsworth (Dean) 2, Redfearn 2, Sherwood 2, Thomas 2, Blissett 1, Gibbs 1, Holdsworth (David) 1, Miller 1, own goal 1.
Littlewoods Cup (3): Bamber 1, Rimmer 1, Wilkinson 1.
FA Cup (5): Redfearn 3 (1 pen), Holden 1, own goal 1.
Ground: Vicarage Road Stadium, Watford WD1 8ER (0923–30933)
Nearest stations: Watford Junction, Watford High Street or Watford Stadium Halt
Manager: Steve Harrison **Chief Executive:** E. Plumley F.A.A.I.
Colours: Yellow shirts with black and red trim; black shorts
Records home gate: 34,099 v Manchester United, February 1969 (FA Cup)
Honours – Champions: Division 3: 1968–9; Division 4: 1977–8

WEST BROMWICH ALBION   DIV. 2

Albiston, Arthur R.
Anderson, Colin R.
Banks, Ian F.
Bartlett, Kevin F.
Bennett, Martyn
Bradley, Darren M.
Bradshaw, Paul W.

Dobbins, Lionel W.
Ford, Tony
Goodman, Donald R.
Hodson, Simeon P.
Naylor, Stuart W.
North, Stacey S.
Paskin, William J.

Raven, Paul D.
Robinson, Ronald
Robson, Gary
Rogers, Darren J.
Talbot, Brian E.
West, Colin
Whyte, Christopher A.

League Appearances: Albiston, Arthur R. 43; Anderson, Colin R. 42; Banks, Ian F. 2(2); Bartlett, Kevin F. 10(7); Bradley, Darren M. 23(3); Bradshaw, Paul W. 2; Burrows, David 7(2); Cartwright, Neil A. −(1); Cork, David 1(3); Dobbins, Lionel W. 12(4); Durnin, John 5; Dyson, Paul I. 3; Ford, Tony 11; Goodman, Donald R. 30(6); Gray, Andrew M. 2(1); Hodson, Simeon P. 9; Hopkins, Robert A. 28(1); Naylor, Stuart W. 44; North, Stacey S. 46; Palmer, Carlton L. 26; Paskin, William J. 14(1); Phillips, Stewart G. 5;Raven Paul D. 3; Rice, Brian 2; Robinson, Ronald 1; Robson, Gary 36(2); Talbot, Brian E. 39; Walford, Stephen J. 3(1); West, Colin 17; Whyte, Christopher A. 40.
League Goals (65): Goodman 15, Robson 8, West 8, Anderson 6 (2 pens), Hopkins 5, Paskin 5, Bartlett 3, Whyte 3, Albiston 2, Durnin 2, Phillips 2, Talbot 2, Dyson 1, Ford 1, own goals 2.
Littlewoods Cup (2): Gray 1 (pen), Palmer 1.
FA Cup (1): Anderson 1.
Ground: The Hawthorns, West Bromwich B71 4LF (021–525 8888)
Nearest stations: Smethwick Rolfe Street or Birmingham New Street
Manager: Brian Talbot **Secretary:** G.H. Dimbleby, M.B.I.M.
Colours: Navy blue and white striped shirts; navy blue shorts
Record home gate: 64,815 v Arsenal, March 1937 (FA Cup)
Honours – Champions: Division 1: 1919–20; Division 2: 1901–2, 1910–11
FA Cup winners: 1887–8, 1891–2, 1930–31, 1953–4, 1967–8
League Cup winners: 1965–6

WEST HAM UNITED   DIV. 2

Brady, William L.
Dickens, Alan W.
Dicks, Julian A.
Dolan, Eammon J.
Gale, Anthony P.
Harwood, Christopher T.
Hilton, Paul
Ince, Paul E.C.
Keen, Kevin I.
Kelly, David T.A.

Kelly, Paul, M.
King, Adam
Livett, Simon R.
McAvennie, Francis
McKnight, Allen
McMenemy, Paul C.
McQueen, Thomas F.
Martin, Alvin E.
Parkes, Philip B.F.

Parris, George M.R.
Pearson, Andrew J.
Potts, Steven J.
Robson, Stewart I.
Rosenior, Leroy D.G.
Slater, Stuart I.
Stewart, Raymond S.
Strodder, Gary J.
Ward, Mark W.

League Appearances: Brady, William L. 21(1); Devonshire, Alan E. 14(6); Dickens, Alan W. 34(3); Dicks, Julian A. 34; Gale, Anthony P. 31; Hilton Paul 9(2); Ince, Paul E.C. 31(1); Keen, Kevin I. 16(8); Kelly, David T.A. 21(4); McAlister, Thomas G. 2; McAvennie, Francis 8(1); McKnight, Allen 23; McQueen, Thomas F. −(2); Martin, Alvin E. 27; Parkes, Philip B.F. 13; Parris, George M.R. 23(4);

Potts, Steven J. 23(5); Robson, Stewart I. 6; Rosenior, Leroy D.G. 26(2); Slater,
Stuart I. 16(2); Stewart, Raymond S. 5(1); Strodder, Gary J. 4(3); Ward, Mark
W. 30.
League Goals (37): Rosenior 7, Kelly 6, Dickens 5, Brady 3 (2 pens), Ince 3,
Keen 3 (1 pen), Dicks 2, Stewart 2 (2 pens), Ward 2, Martin 1, Parris 1, Slater
1, own goal 1.
Littlewoods Cup (16): Kelly 4, Ince 3, Martin 2, Rosenior 2, Dickens 1, Gale 1,
Keen 1, Stewart 1 (pen), own goal 1.
FA Cup (6): Rosenior 2, Dickens 1, Ince 1, Slater 1, own goal 1.
Ground: Boleyn Ground, Green Street, Upton Park E13 9AZ (01–472 2740)
Nearest station: Upton Park (District line)
Manager: Lou Macari **Chief Executive Secretary:** T.M. Finn
Colours: Claret shirts with blue trim; white shorts
Record home gate: 42,322 v Tottenham, October 1970 (League)
Honours – Champions: Division 2: 1957–8, 1980–81
FA Cup winners: 1963–4, 1974–5, 1979–80
European Cup Winners' Cup winners: 1964–5

WIGAN ATHLETIC   DIV. 3

Adkins, Nigel H.	Hilditch, Mark	Pilling, Andrew J.
Ainscow, Andrew P.	Hughes, Philip	Rimmer, Neill
Atherton, Peter	Johnson, Alan K.	Senior, Stephen
Beesley, Paul	Page, Donald R.	Tankard, Allen J.
Crompton, Jonathon D.	Parkinson, Joseph S.	Thompson, David S.
Griffiths, Bryan	Patterson, Darren J.	Woods, Raymond G.

League Appearances: Adkins, Nigel H. 30; Ainscow, Andrew P. 5(2); Atherton,
Peter 38(2); Beesley, Paul 44; Butler, John E. 20; Diamond, Antony J. 6;
Entwistle, Wayne P. 24(5); Fallon, Shaun 1; Griffiths, Bryan 29; Hamilton,
David 13(4); Hemming, Christopher A. J. 4; Hilditch, Mark 23(2); Holden,
Andrew I. 23; Hughes, Philip 16; Jones, Paul B. 4(4); McEwan, Stanley 3(3);
Page, Donald R. 13(2); Parkinson, Joseph S. 8(4); Pilling, Andrew J. 38(1);
Ramage, Craig D. 10; Rimmer, Neill 24(1); Russell, Colin 8; Senior, Stephen
44; Tankard, Allen J. 31(2); Thompson, David S. 42; Wilson, Andrew W. –(1);
Woods, Raymond G. 5(3).
League Goals (55): Griffiths 8 (1 pen), Thompson 7, Entwistle 6, Butler 3, Hilditch
3, Rimmer 3 (1 pen), Russell 3, Beesley 2, Diamond 2, Hamilton 2, Page 2, Pilling
2, Ramage 2, Senior 2, Atherton 1, Holden 1, Johnson 1, Parkinson 1, Tankard
1, own goals 3.
Littlewoods Cup (0)
FA Cup (0)
Ground: Springfield Park, Wigan WN6 7BA (0942–44433)
Nearest stations: Wigan Wallgate and Wigan North West
Manager: Bryan Hamilton **Secretary:** Mrs L.M. Fillingham
Colours: White shirts with royal blue trim; royal blue shorts
Record home gate: 27,500 v Hereford United, December 1953 (FA Cup)
Honours: Nil
Freight Rover Trophy winners: 1984–5

WIMBLEDON   DIV. 1

Blackwell, Dean R.   Gayle, John   Phelan, Terry M.
Brooke, Garry J.   Gibson, Terence B.   Quamina, Mark E.
Clement, Andrew D.   Goodyear, Clive   Ryan, Vaughan W.
Cork, Alan G.   Jones, Vincent   Sanchez, Lawrence P.
Cotterill, Stephen   Joseph, Roger A.   Scales, John R.
Curle, Keith   Kruszynski Zbigniew   Segers, Johannes C.A.
Fairweather, Carlton   McAllister, Brian   Sullivan, Neil
Fashanu, John   McGee, Paul   Wise, Dennis F.
Fiore, Mark J.   Miller Paul   Young, Eric

League Appearances: Brooke, Garry J. 5(5); Cawley, Peter 1; Clement, Andrew
D. 9(2); Cork, Alan G. 9(16); Cotterill, Stephen (4); Curle, Keith 16(2);
Fairweather, Carlton 23(3); Fashanu, John 30; Fiore, Mark J. 1; Gayle, John
2; Gibson, Terence B. 17; Green, Ronald R. 4; Hazel, Ian 1; Jones, Vincent 31;
Joseph, Roger A. 30(1); Kruszynski, Zbigniew 13(3); McGee, Paul 1; Miller, Paul
A. 17(1); Phelan, Terry M. 27(2); Quamina, Mark E. 1; Ryan, Vaughan W. 4(1);
Sanchez, Lawrence P. 34(2); Scales, John R. 36(2); Segers, Johannes C.A. 33;
Tracey, Simon P. 1; Turner, Robert P. 2(4); Wise, Dennis F. 37; Young, Eric
33(2).
League Goals (50): Fashanu 12 (4 pens), Gibson 5, Miller 5 (1 pen), Sanchez 5,
Scales 5, Wise 5 (l pen), Fairweather 3, Jones 3, Cork 2, Cotterill 1, McGee 1,
Young 1, own goals 2.
Littlewoods Cup (4): Fashanu 2, Fairweather 1, Gibson 1.
FA Cup (5): Fashanu 1, Gibson 1, Jones 1, Phelan 1, Wise 1.
Ground: Plough Lane Ground, Durnsford Road, Wimbledon, SW19 (01–946
6311)
Nearest stations: Wimbledon or Haydons Road (BR) Wimbledon Park (District)
Manager: Bobby Gould **Secretary:** Adrian Cook
Colours: All blue with yellow trim
Record home gate: 18,000 v HMS Victory, 1934–5 (FA Amateur Cup)
Honours – Champions: Division 4: 1982–3
FA Cup winners: 1987–8

WOLVERHAMPTON WANDERERS   DIV. 2

Bartram, Vincent L.   Downing, Keith G.   Robinson, Phillip J.
Bellamy, Gary   Gooding, Michael C.   Steele, Timothy W.
Bennett, Thomas M.   Kelly, Robert A.   Streete, Floyd A.
Bull, Stephen G.   Kendall, Mark   Thompson, Andrew R.
Chard, Philip J.   Mutch, Andrew   Vaughan, Nigel M.
Clarke, Nicholas J.   Robertson, Alistair   Venus, Mark
Dennison, Robert

League Appearances: Bellamy, Gary 43; Bennett, Thomas M. – (2); Bull, Stephen
G. 45; Chard, Philip J. 14(5); Clarke, Nicholas J. 8; Dennison, Robert 41(2);
Downing. Keith G. 25(7); Gallagher, Jackie C. 4(4); Gooding, Michael C. 30(1);
Hansbury, Roger 3; Kelly, Robert A. – (2); Kendall, Mark 36; Mutch, Andrew
45; Robertson, Alistair 30; Robinson, Phillip J. 23(7); Steele, Timothy W. 7(4);
Stowell, Michael 7; Streete, Floyd A. 38; Thompson, Andrew R. 46; Vaughan,

64

Nigel M. 30(2); Venus, Mark 31(4).
League Goals (96): Bull 37, Mutch 21, Dennison 8, Thompson 6 (5 pens), Streete 5, Gooding 4, Vaughan 4, Chard 3 (1 pen), Robinson 3, Bellamy 1, Downing 1, Gallagher 1, Steele 1, own goal 1.
Littlewoods Cup (3): Bull 2, Dennison 1.
FA Cup (0)
Ground: Molineux Grounds, Wolverhampton WV1 4QR (0902–712181)
Nearest station: Wolverhampton
Manager: Graham Turner **Secretary:**K.D. Pearson A.C.I.S.
Colours: Gold shirts; black shorts
Record home gate: 61,315 v Liverpool, February 1939 (FA Cup)
Honours – Champions: Division 1: 1953–4, 1957–8, 1958–9; Division 2: 1931–2, 1976–7; Division 3 North: 1923–4; Division 3: 1988–9; Division 4: 1987–8
FA Cup winners: 1892–3, 1907–8, 1948–9, 1959–60
League Cup winners: 1973–4, 1979–80
Sherpa Van Trophy winners: 1987–8

WREXHAM   DIV. 4

Armstrong, Christopher
Beaumont, Nigel
Bowden, Jon L.
Buxton, Stephen C.
Cooper, Graham
Flynn, Brian
Hunter, Geoffrey

Jones, Joseph P.
Kearns, Oliver A.
Lee, Anthony S.
Morris, Mark
Preece, Roger
Russell, Kevin J.

Salathiel, David N.
Salmon, Michael B.
Thackeray, Andrew J.
Williams, Michael
Wrench Mark N.
Wright, Darren J.

League Appearances: Beaumont, Nigel 20(1); Bowden, Jon L. 41(1); Buxton, Stephen C. 25(5); Carter, Michael 6(7); Cooper, Graham 29(7); Filson, Robert M. –(1); Flynn, Brian 38(3); Hunter, Geoffrey 36(2); Jones, Joseph P. 41; Jones, Paul A. 5; Kearns, Oliver A. 10(7); Lane, Martin J. 6; Morris, Mark 3; Preece, Roger 23(8); Raynor, Paul J. 6; Russell, Kevin J. 46; Salathiel, David N. 34(1); Salmon, Michael B. 43; Taylor, Jason S. –(1); Thackeray, Andrew J. 27(8); Williams, Michael 27; Wrench, Mark N. 3(1); Wright, Darren J. 37.
League Goals (77): Russell 22 (5 pens), Cooper 11, Bowden 10, Jones 8, Preece 5, Buxton 4, Hunter 4, Kearns 4, Wright 3, Thackeray 2, Carter 1, Flynn 1, own goals 2.
Littlewoods Cup (3): Buxton 2, Cooper 1.
FA Cup (4): Kearns 2, Bowden 1, Cooper 1.
Ground: The Racecourse, Mold Road, Wrexham LL1 2AN (0978–262129)
Nearest station: Wrexham General
Manager: Dixie McNeil **Secretary:** S. Gandy
Colours: Red shirts; white shorts
Record home gate: 34,445 v Manchester United, January 1957 (FA Cup)
Honours – Champions: Division 3: 1977–8

YORK CITY   DIV. 4

Barratt, Anthony   Greenough, Richard A.   Marples, Christopher
Bradshaw Darren S.   Helliwell, Ian   Reid, Shaun
Canham, Anthony   Himsworth, Gary P.   Smith, Kevan
Dixon, Kevin L.   Howlett, Gary P.   Spooner, Stephen A.
Dunn, Iain G.W.   McMillan, Lyndon A.   Tutill, Stephen A.
Endersby, Scott A.G

League Appearances: Banton, Dale C. 11; Barratt. Anthony 12; Bradshaw, Darren S. 34; Branagan, James P. 13(1); Butler, Martin 9(3); Canham, Anthony 40(1); Clegg, Tony 3(1); Dixon, Kevin L. 18(1); Dunn, Iain G.W. 18(8); Eli, Roger 3(1); Endersby, Scott A.G. 1; Fazackerley, Derek W. 16; Greenough, Richard A. 26; Hall, Wayne −(2); Hay, Alan B. 1; Helliwell, Ian 41; Himsworth, Gary P. 30(2); Hotte, Timothy A. 1(1); Howlett, Gary P. 20(3); Hurlstone, Gary 1(1); Johnson, Paul 44; McMillan, Lyndon A. −(2); Marples, Christopher 45; Morris, Neil A. 3(1); Reid, Shaun 24; Shaw, Adrian 5; Smith, Kevan 30(1); Spooner, Stephen A. 31; Tutill, Stephen A. 21(1); Wilson, Philip 5(5).
League Goals (62): Helliwell 11, Canham 9, Dunn 6, Smith 5, Spooner 5 (2 pens), Banton 4 (2 pens), Dixon 4, Howlett 4, Butler 3, Bradshaw 2, Himsworth 2, Reid 2, Eli 1, Greenough 1, Johnson 1, Tutill 1, Wilson 1.
Littlewoods Cup (0)
FA Cup (0)
Ground: Bootham Crescent, York YO3 7AQ (0904–624447)
Nearest station: York
Manager: John Bird **Secretary:** Keith Usher
Colours: Red shirts, navy blue shorts
Record home gate: 28,123 v Huddersfield, March 1938 (FA Cup)
Honours – Champions: Division 4: 1983–4

BARCLAYS LEAGUE – DIVISION 1

Home \ Away	Arsenal	Aston Villa	Charlton Ath	Coventry C	Derby Co	Everton	Liverpool	Luton T	Manchester U	Middlesbrough	Millwall	Newcastle U	Norwich C	Nottingham F	QPR	Sheffield W	Southampton	Tottenham H	West Ham U	Wimbledon
Arsenal	—	3-2	4-0	2-2	2-1	3-1	1-1	2-0	1-2	1-0	2-1	1-0	5-0	2-2	2-2	2-1	2-2	2-0	2-1	2-2
Aston Villa	0-3	—	2-2	2-1	1-1	0-1	1-1	1-1	0-2	2-2	2-2	4-0	1-0	1-0	1-0	1-0	2-1	1-2	1-1	1-0
Charlton Ath	2-3	2-2	—	3-0	2-2	1-2	0-3	3-0	0-0	2-1	3-0	2-0	2-2	1-2	2-1	3-0	2-1	2-2	1-0	0-0
Coventry C	2-1	2-1	1-2	—	4-1	1-2	1-0	0-1	1-0	4-0	2-0	3-2	1-1	2-3	3-0	5-0	2-1	1-1	1-2	1-1
Derby Co	1-3	1-1	2-1	1-2	—	1-0	1-0	4-1	2-2	1-0	1-0	2-2	0-1	2-1	1-2	1-1	1-1	3-0	1-1	4-1
Everton	0-2	1-0	1-2	1-1	3-1	—	1-0	1-1	1-1	2-1	1-1	4-0	4-0	0-1	2-0	0-0	4-1	1-0	1-1	1-2
Liverpool	1-1	1-1	0-3	2-1	1-0	0-1	—	5-0	1-0	1-0	1-2	2-1	0-1	1-1	3-0	1-1	3-2	1-1	2-0	2-1
Luton T	1-1	1-0	2-0	0-1	2-1	1-0	0-1	—	1-2	2-1	1-0	4-0	1-1	1-0	1-0	2-0	1-0	6-1	0-1	1-1
Manchester U	1-1	2-0	3-0	0-1	0-0	1-2	3-1	2-0	—	1-0	3-0	0-0	2-1	0-1	0-0	1-0	2-2	1-0	2-0	1-1
Middlesbrough	0-1	3-3	1-0	0-0	1-0	2-3	0-0	1-0	1-0	—	4-2	3-0	1-0	2-1	2-2	1-0	4-0	0-0	1-2	1-1
Millwall	0-2	2-2	3-0	3-3	1-1	2-1	1-1	1-2	0-0	4-2	—	2-1	0-1	3-0	3-1	2-1	2-1	2-0	0-0	1-0
Newcastle U	0-1	2-2	2-0	3-0	0-2	4-0	2-1	4-0	0-0	3-0	0-1	—	1-1	0-2	2-1	1-0	2-2	2-2	0-0	1-4
Norwich C	0-0	3-1	2-2	1-1	1-1	0-1	1-1	1-0	2-1	3-3	2-0	1-1	—	3-2	2-2	1-1	0-2	2-1	2-2	0-2
Nottingham F	1-4	1-1	1-0	2-2	2-1	1-0	2-0	3-2	2-0	4-2	2-1	2-1	2-1	—	1-1	2-3	0-1	1-2	1-2	3-1
QPR	0-0	1-0	0-1	1-1	1-0	3-0	0-0	0-2	3-2	2-1	1-0	2-0	1-0	2-1	—	0-1	2-1	2-2	0-0	1-0
Sheffield W	1-3	0-1	2-0	2-0	0-0	1-1	2-1	1-1	1-0	2-0	1-0	2-1	1-1	0-1	1-1	—	1-2	0-0	0-0	1-0
Southampton	2-3	1-0	1-0	2-2	1-1	1-2	1-1	2-1	2-2	0-2	1-2	0-2	3-3	2-3	0-2	1-1	—	1-2	0-2	1-1
Tottenham H	2-3	2-1	1-2	1-1	1-1	1-0	1-1	2-1	2-0	0-0	0-0	2-0	2-1	1-2	2-2	0-0	2-1	—	0-2	2-2
West Ham U	1-4	1-1	1-1	1-0	1-1	1-1	2-0	1-0	3-1	2-1	2-3	0-0	2-2	1-2	0-0	0-0	0-2	1-2	—	0-1
Wimbledon	1-5	1-0	0-0	1-1	4-1	1-2	1-2	1-1	1-1	1-1	1-0	1-4	0-2	3-1	1-0	1-0	2-1	1-2	0-1	—

1988–89 RESULTS

Final results season 1988–89

First Division	Home						Away						
	P	W	D	L	F	A	W	D	L	F	A	GD	Pts
Arsenal	38	10	6	3	35	19	12	4	3	38	17	+37	76
Liverpool	38	11	5	3	33	11	11	5	3	32	17	+37	76
Nottingham F	38	8	7	4	31	16	9	6	4	33	27	+21	64
Norwich C	38	8	7	4	23	20	9	4	6	25	25	+3	62
Derby Co	38	9	3	7	23	18	8	4	7	17	20	+2	58
Tottenham H	38	8	6	5	31	24	7	6	6	29	22	+14	57
Coventry C	38	9	4	6	28	23	5	9	5	19	19	+5	55
Everton	38	10	7	2	33	18	4	5	10	11	27	+5	54
QPR	38	9	5	5	23	16	5	6	8	20	21	+6	53
Millwall	38	10	3	6	27	21	4	8	7	20	31	−5	53
Manchester U	38	10	5	4	27	13	3	7	9	18	22	+10	51
Wimbledon	38	10	3	6	30	19	4	6	9	20	27	+4	51
Southampton	38	6	7	6	25	26	4	8	7	27	40	−14	45
Charlton Ath	38	6	7	6	25	24	4	5	10	19	34	−14	42
Sheffield W	38	6	6	7	21	25	4	6	9	13	26	−17	42
Luton T	38	8	6	5	32	21	2	5	12	10	31	−10	41
Aston Villa	38	7	6	6	25	22	2	7	10	20	34	−11	40
Middlesbrough	38	6	7	6	28	30	3	5	11	16	31	−17	39
West Ham U	38	3	6	10	19	30	7	2	10	18	32	−25	38
Newcastle U	38	3	6	10	19	28	4	4	11	13	35	−31	31

Leading goalscorers
Goals listed in following order: League, Littlewoods Cup, FA Cup, total.

Division 1: Alan Smith (Arsenal) **23**, 2, 0, 25; John Aldridge (Liverpool) **21**, 2, 5, 28; Dean Saunders (Derby Co) **18**, 2, 0, 20 *(inc. 4 League, 2 Littlewoods Cup for Oxford U)*; Bernie Slaven (Middlesbrough) **15**, 0, 1, 16; Nigel Clough (Nottingham F) **14**, 7, 0, 21; Mark Hughes (Manchester U) **14**, 0, 2, 16; Alan McInally (Aston Villa) **14**, 4, 1, 19; David Speedie (Coventry C) **14**, 1, 0, 15; Chris Waddle (Tottenham H) **14**, 0, 0, 14; Tony Cascarino (Millwall) **13**, 0, 1, 14; Tony Cottee (Everton) **13**, 2, 0, 15; Paul Williams (Charlton Ath) **13**, 2, 2, 17; Mark Falco (QPR) **12**, 3, 0, 15; John Fashanu (Wimbledon) **12**, 2, 1, 15; Teddy Sheringham (Millwall) **11**, 3, 1, 15; Rod Wallace (Southampton) **11**, 2, 0, 13; Peter Beardsley (Liverpool) **10**, 2, 0, 12; Robert Fleck (Norwich C) **10**, 1, 4, 15; Brian McClair (Manchester U) **10**, 3, 3, 16; Paul Merson (Arsenal) **10**, 2, 2, 14.

BARCLAYS LEAGUE – DIVISION II

	WBA	Watford	Walsall	Swindon T	Sunderland	Stoke C	Shrewsbury	Portsmouth	Plymouth Arg	Oxford U	Oldham Ath	Manchester C	Leicester C	Leeds U	Ipswich T	Hull C	Crystal Palace	Chelsea	Brighton & HA	Bradford C	Bournemouth	Blackburn R	Birmingham C	Barnsley
Barnsley	2-1	2-2	1-0	1-2	3-0	1-0	1-2	1-0	3-1	2-0	4-3	1-2	3-0	2-2	2-0	0-2	1-1	1-1	2-2	0-0	5-2	0-1	0-0	—
Birmingham C	1-2	2-3	1-0	1-0	3-2	0-1	1-1	0-0	0-1	0-3	0-1	0-2	2-3	0-0	2-0	1-1	1-1	1-1	1-2	2-1	0-1	2-0	—	3-5
Blackburn R	2-1	1-1	2-1	2-0	1-0	3-1	2-1	1-0	1-2	1-1	2-2	0-0	2-1	2-0	1-0	1-1	5-1	1-0	2-1	2-3	1-0	—	3-0	2-1
Bournemouth	2-0	0-1	2-1	0-3	1-0	0-1	0-1	1-0	0-0	2-0	2-0	1-1	1-1	0-0	1-2	5-1	0-1	2-2	2-1	2-3	—	1-1	2-2	3-2
Bradford C	0-1	0-1	2-1	2-2	0-1	1-0	3-1	2-1	3-0	1-1	2-0	0-1	1-1	1-1	0-3	1-1	0-1	0-1	0-1	—	0-1	1-1	2-2	1-2
Brighton & HA	1-0	2-2	2-2	3-2	3-0	2-0	1-3	0-1	2-2	0-2	2-0	1-1	2-4	2-1	0-3	2-1	2-2	2-3	—	2-0	2-3	1-1	4-1	0-1
Chelsea	0-1	0-1	4-0	1-1	1-0	1-1	2-0	1-0	4-0	1-2	2-1	1-0	2-0	2-0	3-0	2-1	1-2	—	2-3	1-3	2-3	1-1	4-1	0-1
Crystal Palace	1-0	0-3	3-1	2-1	0-0	1-4	3-0	1-2	2-0	1-0	2-1	2-4	4-2	0-2	4-0	1-1	—	2-2	2-3	2-1	4-3	2-1	4-0	1-1
Hull C	1-1	2-2	3-1	1-2	0-2	1-0	0-2	2-1	2-0	2-2	1-1	1-0	2-0	0-1	1-2	—	2-2	0-1	2-3	1-1	3-1	2-1	1-0	0-0
Ipswich T	2-1	3-1	1-0	3-3	2-1	2-1	2-3	1-1	5-3	2-1	2-1	1-0	1-1	1-2	—	4-1	1-1	3-0	2-3	2-1	4-1	2-1	4-0	2-0
Leeds U	2-1	3-0	2-0	1-1	2-0	0-1	2-1	0-1	—	1-2	2-2	2-0	3-0	1-0	2-2	2-0	2-1	1-0	3-0	2-1	4-0	2-0	4-0	2-0
Leicester C	1-1	0-1	3-1	2-0	0-0	2-2	2-1	3-0	1-0	3-0	1-1	2-4	—	1-2	4-3	4-1	2-1	2-0	2-1	1-1	1-1	2-1	3-1	2-3
Manchester C	1-0	0-1	3-1	1-1	3-2	1-4	1-2	2-1	2-0	2-0	2-1	—	2-1	1-0	1-2	2-1	1-2	1-2	3-2	1-1	2-0	4-0	2-0	1-2
Oldham Ath	3-1	1-0	2-3	4-0	2-0	2-2	1-1	5-2	2-2	2-0	—	1-0	3-0	2-2	1-1	2-1	1-1	1-1	3-0	1-1	3-3	3-2	3-0	1-1
Oxford U	1-1	1-1	1-0	1-1	1-0	1-0	2-1	0-1	2-2	—	1-2	1-3	1-1	1-2	1-1	2-2	0-2	1-0	2-1	3-1	1-0	1-1	3-0	0-1
Plymouth Arg	1-0	1-0	2-2	0-3	1-1	2-1	3-0	5-3	—	1-1	3-1	3-0	1-1	3-0	4-0	4-1	2-2	2-0	2-2	1-1	1-1	4-3	0-1	1-2
Portsmouth	3-0	1-0	2-2	0-1	2-1	2-0	2-0	—	2-2	1-0	0-1	2-1	2-0	2-0	4-0	2-0	2-2	2-0	3-0	1-1	1-1	4-0	2-1	3-0
Shrewsbury T	1-1	1-1	2-2	3-3	2-2	2-2	—	2-2	2-2	2-1	2-2	2-1	1-1	2-1	1-1	2-4	0-1	0-1	1-2	1-0	1-1	1-1	0-1	2-3
Stoke C	1-0	2-0	2-0	2-2	2-1	—	3-0	2-0	2-0	2-2	0-1	1-0	1-1	3-0	1-0	1-3	2-1	0-2	0-1	1-1	1-1	1-1	1-0	1-0
Sunderland	3-1	3-1	2-2	1-1	—	1-0	2-0	0-1	2-2	3-1	1-2	0-1	1-1	2-0	4-0	4-1	2-1	2-3	1-1	3-1	4-3	1-1	2-2	2-3
Swindon T	1-1	1-0	2-1	—	2-0	1-0	2-1	1-0	2-0	1-0	0-2	2-1	2-0	2-2	2-0	2-0	2-1	2-2	3-0	2-1	4-1	2-1	1-0	0-0
Walsall	1-1	2-1	—	0-3	1-0	2-1	2-1	1-0	2-1	3-1	1-0	3-1	2-1	2-0	2-0	1-1	1-0	1-3	2-1	0-1	0-1	0-1	3-0	1-3
Watford	2-2	—	1-0	1-2	2-0	1-1	0-1	0-0	1-0	2-1	1-0	2-1	2-2	2-2	1-1	3-1	1-1	1-1	1-2	0-1	0-0	2-2	0-1	4-0
WBA	—	0-1	0-0	3-1	1-0	0-0	1-0	1-1	2-2	1-2	3-1	1-0	1-1	2-1	1-2	2-0	5-3	2-3	1-0	2-0	0-0	1-1	1-1	1-1

70

1988–89 RESULTS

Final results season 1988–89

Second Division	Home						Away						
	P	W	D	L	F	A	W	D	L	F	A	GD	Pts
Chelsea	46	15	6	2	50	25	14	6	3	46	25	+46	99
Manchester C	46	12	8	3	48	28	11	5	7	29	25	+24	82
Crystal Palace	46	15	6	2	42	17	8	6	9	29	32	+22	81
Watford	46	14	5	4	41	18	8	7	8	33	30	+26	78
Blackburn R	46	16	4	3	50	22	6	7	10	24	37	+15	77
Swindon T	46	13	8	2	35	15	7	8	8	33	38	+15	76
Barnsley	46	12	8	3	37	21	8	6	9	29	37	+8	74
Ipswich T	46	13	3	7	42	23	9	4	10	29	38	+10	73
WBA	46	13	7	3	43	18	5	11	7	22	23	+24	72
Leeds U	46	12	6	5	34	20	5	10	8	25	30	+9	67
Sunderland	46	12	8	3	40	23	4	7	12	20	37	0	63
Bournemouth	46	13	3	7	32	20	5	5	13	21	42	−9	62
Stoke C	46	10	9	4	33	25	5	5	13	24	47	−15	59
Bradford C	46	8	11	4	29	22	5	6	12	23	37	−7	56
Leicester C	46	11	6	6	31	20	2	10	11	25	43	−7	55
Oldham Ath	46	9	10	4	49	32	2	11	10	26	40	+3	54
Oxford U	46	11	6	6	40	34	3	6	14	22	36	−8	54
Plymouth Arg	46	11	4	8	35	22	3	8	12	20	44	−11	54
Brighton & HA	46	11	5	7	36	24	3	4	16	21	42	−9	51
Portsmouth	46	10	6	7	33	21	3	6	14	20	41	−9	51
Hull C	46	7	9	7	31	25	4	5	14	21	43	−16	47
Shrewsbury T	46	4	11	8	25	31	4	7	12	15	36	−27	42
Birmingham C	46	6	4	13	21	33	2	7	14	10	43	−45	35
Walsall	46	3	10	10	27	42	2	6	15	14	38	−39	31

PLAY-OFFS (*all matches two legs*): Semi-finals – Swindon T 1,0, Crystal Palace 0,2; Blackburn R 0,1, Watford 0,1 (*Blackburn R won on away goals aet*); Final – Blackburn R 3,0, Crystal Palace 1,3 (*aet*). **Crystal Palace promoted to First Division**.

Leading goalscorers
Goals listed in following order: League, Littlewoods Cup, FA Cup, total.

Division 2: Keith Edwards (Hull C) **26**, 1, 3, 30; Kerry Dixon (Chelsea) **25**, 1, 0, 26; Tommy Tynan (Plymouth Arg) **24**, 1, 1, 26; Ian Wright (Crystal Palace) **24**, 1, 0, 25; Mark Bright (Crystal Palace) **20**, 1, 0, 21; Simon Garner (Blackburn R) **20**, 2, 1, 23; Luther Blissett (Bournemouth) **19**, 2, 0, 21; Howard Gayle (Blackburn R) **19**, 1, 0, 20; Paul Wilkinson (Watford) **19**, 0, 0, 19; Marco Gabbiadini (Sunderland) **18**, 3, 0, 21; Mike Quinn (Portsmouth) **18**, 1, 1, 20; Gordon Durie (Chelsea) **17**, 0, 0, 17; David Currie (Barnsley) **16**, 1, 3, 20; Kevin Bremner (Brighton & HA) **15**, 0, 0, 15; Don Goodman (WBA) **15**, 0, 0, 15; Garry Nelson (Brighton & HA) **15**, 0, 0, 15; Roger Palmer (Oldham Ath) **15**, 0, 0, 15; Graham Roberts (Chelsea) **15**, 0, 0, 15.

BARCLAYS LEAGUE DIVISION III

Home \ Away	Wolverhampton W	Wigan Ath	Swansea C	Southend U	Sheffield U	Reading	Preston NE	Port Vale	Notts Co	Northampton T	Mansfield T	Huddersfield T	Gillingham	Fulham	Chesterfield	Chester C	Cardiff C	Bury	Bristol R	Bristol C	Brentford	Bolton W	Blackpool	Aldershot
Aldershot	1-2	0-2	1-1	2-2	0-1	0-3	1-1	1-3	2-3	1-0	3-1	1-1	0-2	1-2	2-0	1-1	1-1	4-2	1-3	0-2	0-0	0-3	1-0	—
Blackpool	2-2	1-2	0-1	3-2	1-2	1-1	2-0	3-1	0-1	3-1	0-1	0-1	2-1	1-2	2-0	1-1	0-1	2-2	2-1	2-2	0-2	2-0	—	1-0
Bolton W	0-1	1-1	0-1	2-0	2-0	1-2	0-1	1-1	3-3	2-0	3-3	3-0	2-0	3-2	2-0	1-1	4-1	1-5	2-1	2-0	4-1	—	2-0	1-0
Brentford	2-1	1-1	1-0	0-2	1-1	1-2	2-1	2-1	0-1	1-1	2-3	1-2	1-0	1-0	2-0	2-1	2-0	2-2	2-2	2-0	—	3-2	4-2	2-1
Bristol C	2-1	1-1	1-0	1-1	3-2	0-2	0-1	3-0	2-1	0-1	0-0	3-1	2-0	1-5	2-0	0-1	2-2	2-1	2-1	—	1-1	2-0	2-0	1-1
Bristol R	0-1	1-2	0-1	2-1	2-2	1-3	2-1	2-1	2-1	1-0	3-0	0-6	1-0	3-2	0-1	1-2	0-2	2-1	—	0-3	1-2	2-0	2-1	1-2
Bury	0-3	3-1	1-3	0-3	1-0	2-1	1-3	0-0	0-0	1-2	3-0	2-1	3-2	2-1	0-1	2-0	1-2	—	2-1	1-1	1-0	0-1	0-0	4-0
Cardiff C	3-1	2-0	2-0	1-1	0-1	3-4	3-3	1-0	0-1	1-2	0-3	1-1	3-1	2-1	1-1	1-2	—	2-1	2-2	2-0	1-2	1-0	0-2	3-2
Chester C	1-1	1-1	0-1	1-1	3-2	1-1	1-2	2-2	1-0	1-2	3-0	2-1	2-2	2-1	0-1	—	1-2	0-1	2-3	1-1	1-2	1-1	0-2	2-1
Chesterfield	2-0	1-1	2-0	1-1	2-1	2-1	1-3	0-1	0-1	2-0	2-0	0-2	2-2	4-1	—	1-1	3-1	4-0	0-2	4-0	0-1	0-3	1-2	1-0
Fulham	1-2	1-3	3-2	1-5	3-1	2-1	2-1	1-1	2-1	1-1	3-1	1-0	2-1	—	1-1	2-1	1-0	3-0	1-1	1-0	0-0	1-1	2-0	1-2
Gillingham	0-1	4-1	1-0	2-0	2-0	1-0	1-0	3-1	1-2	—	1-1	1-1	1-2	2-1	0-1	1-4	2-1	2-1	3-2	0-6	1-1	0-1	2-1	1-1
Huddersfield T	2-1	1-1	3-1	6-1	5-0	3-0	3-1	2-1	1-2	2-0	—	1-0	1-2	3-0	2-0	1-1	2-1	3-1	2-1	3-1	2-0	1-2	0-0	0-1
Mansfield T	0-1	1-1	0-1	2-0	0-1	0-1	0-1	3-0	1-2	—	2-1	2-1	2-1	2-1	0-1	2-1	1-2	1-1	0-4	1-1	1-2	3-1	6-2	0-2
Northampton T	5-1	1-2	2-0	3-1	1-1	1-0	1-2	1-2	0-1	1-1	1-0	—	1-2	2-1	1-0	1-0	0-1	1-1	4-0	0-0	1-0	2-1	1-1	3-2
Notts Co	2-3	0-1	3-3	0-1	1-0	1-0	1-0	3-1	2-1	1-2	—	1-0	0-3	1-2	2-1	0-0	1-2	3-1	2-0	—	1-0	2-0	2-0	0-0
Port Vale	2-2	3-2	1-1	1-1	0-1	0-0	3-1	2-2	1-0	0-1	3-1	—	1-3	2-0	0-1	0-2	3-3	—	—	—	—	—	—	—
Preston NE	2-1	0-1	1-0	1-1	0-1	0-1	3-1	1-3	1-2	0-3	0-1	1-1	—	2-1	3-1	1-1	1-1	0-0	—	—	—	—	—	—
Reading	1-1	2-1	3-2	2-1	1-2	0-2	2-4	2-1	0-2	2-1	0-3	3-0	2-1	—	1-0	2-0	2-0	2-1	—	—	—	—	—	—
Sheffield U	1-2	2-0	2-1	2-0	1-2	0-3	2-1	2-1	3-1	1-2	1-1	3-3	2-0	—	2-1	2-2	2-1	2-2	—	—	—	—	—	—
Southend U	2-2	3-0	0-0	2-1	1-1	2-1	2-1	1-0	1-1	2-2	2-1	2-0	4-2	—	2-0	3-0	—	—	—	—	—	—	—	—
Swansea C	1-0	1-1	2-0	1-0	2-1	1-0	2-2	2-0	2-1	0-0	1-0	2-1	1-0	2-0	2-1	0-2	—	1-1	—	—	—	—	—	—
Wigan Ath	1-1	2-0	1-1	1-1	2-1	1-2	1-0	1-1	1-1	1-0	1-1	1-2	2-2	0-3	1-2	1-1	—	2-1	—	—	—	—	—	—
Wolverhampton W	—	2-1	1-1	3-0	0-1	3-1	1-1	1-3	2-3	1-0	3-1	1-1	0-3	3-2	0-2	3-1	2-1	1-1	—	—	—	—	—	—

72

1988–89 RESULTS

Final results season 1988–89

Third Division	Home					Away							
	P	W	D	L	F	A	W	D	L	F	A	GD	Pts
Wolverhampton W	46	18	4	1	61	19	8	10	5	35	30	+47	92
Sheffield U	46	16	3	4	57	21	9	6	8	36	33	+39	84
Port Vale	45	15	3	5	46	21	9	9	5	32	27	+30	84
Fulham	46	12	7	4	42	28	10	2	11	27	39	+2	75
Bristol R	46	9	11	3	34	21	10	6	7	33	30	+16	74
Preston NE............	46	14	7	2	56	31	5	8	10	23	29	+19	72
Brentford	46	14	5	4	36	21	4	9	10	30	40	+5	68
Chester C..............	46	12	6	5	38	18	7	5	11	26	43	+3	68
Notts Co	46	11	7	5	37	22	7	6	10	27	32	+10	67
Bolton W	46	12	8	3	42	23	4	8	11	16	31	+4	64
Bristol C...............	46	10	3	10	32	25	8	6	9	21	30	−2	63
Swansea C.............	46	11	8	4	33	22	4	8	11	18	31	−2	61
Bury	46	11	7	5	27	22	5	6	12	28	45	−12	61
Huddersfield T	46	10	8	5	35	25	7	1	15	28	48	−10	60
Mansfield T	46	10	8	5	32	22	4	9	10	16	30	−4	59
Cardiff C...............	46	10	9	4	30	16	4	6	13	14	40	−12	57
Wigan Ath	46	9	5	9	28	22	5	9	9	27	31	+2	56
Reading	46	10	6	7	37	29	5	5	13	31	43	−4	56
Blackpool	46	10	6	7	36	29	4	7	12	20	30	−3	54
Northampton T	46	11	2	10	41	34	5	4	14	25	42	−10	54
Southend U	46	10	9	4	33	26	3	6	14	23	49	−19	54
Chesterfield	46	9	5	9	35	35	5	2	16	16	51	−35	49
Gillingham	46	7	3	13	25	32	5	1	17	22	49	−34	40
Aldershot	46	7	6	10	29	29	1	7	15	19	49	−30	37

PLAY–OFFS (*all matches two legs*): Semi-finals – Bristol R 1, 4, Fulham 0, 0; Preston NE 1, 1, Port Vale 1, 3; Final – Bristol R 1, 0, Port Vale 1, 1. **Port Vale promoted to Second Division**.

Leading goalscorers
Goals listed in following order: League, Littlewood Cup, FA Cup, total.

Division 3: Steve Bull (Wolverhampton W) **37**, 2, 0, 39; Craig Maskell (Huddersfield T) **28**, 2, 1, 31; David Crown (Southend U) **25**, 1, 0, 26; Tony Agana (Sheffield U) **23**, 2, 3, 28; Carl Dale (Chester C) **22**, 0, 1, 23; Brian Deane (Sheffield U) **22**, 3, 5, 30; Andy Mutch (Wolverhampton W) **21**, 0, 0, 21; Darren Beckford (Port Vale) **20**, 0, 0, 20; Gary Penrice (Bristol R) **20**, 0, 1, 21; Liam Robinson (Bury) **20**, 1, 0, 21; Tony Ellis (Preston NE) **19**, 0, 0, 19; David Waller (Chesterfield) **18**, 1, 0, 19; Ron Futcher (Port Vale) **17**, 1, 1, 19; David Gilbert (Northampton T) **17**, 1, 0, 18; Trevor Senior (Reading) **16**, 0, 4, 20; Jimmy Gilligan (Cardiff C) **15**, 0, 4, 19; Mark Patterson (Preston NE) **15** 0, 0, 15; Keith Cassells (Mansfield T) **14**, 0, 0, 14; Gordon Davies (Fulham) **14**, 0, 0, 14; Steve Lovell (Gillingham) **14**, 2, 1, 17.

BARCLAYS LEAGUE – DIVISION IV

	Burnley	Cambridge U	Carlisle U	Colchester U	Crewe Alex	Darlington	Doncaster R	Exeter C	Grimsby T	Halifax T	Hartlepool U	Hereford U	Leyton Orient	Lincoln C	Peterborough U	Rochdale	Rotherham U	Scarborough	Scunthorpe U	Stockport Co	Torquay U	Tranmere R	Wrexham	York C
Burnley	—	2-0	0-0	4-0	1-1	1-0	3-0	1-0	2-2	0-0	2-2	3-3	2-2	1-4	2-2	2-0	3-1	1-0	2-1	1-0	2-0	4-2	1-3	6-0
Cambridge U	2-1	—	1-0	2-0	1-1	1-2	0-3	2-0	0-2	2-2	2-1	3-1	2-2	2-3	1-2	3-1	0-1	1-0	2-1	1-1	3-1	2-1	1-3	1-0
Carlisle U	0-0	1-1	—	1-2	1-1	2-2	0-1	0-3	0-0	3-3	0-0	1-1	1-0	2-3	2-2	3-1	1-0	0-2	0-0	1-1	3-1	2-1	1-2	0-2
Colchester U	4-0	1-2	1-0	—	2-1	2-0	1-0	0-0	0-2	3-2	1-0	1-0	1-0	2-0	2-1	1-2	2-0	3-1	2-1	1-1	1-0	2-3	2-1	1-1
Crewe Alex	1-1	2-1	1-1	2-1	—	1-0	0-0	0-1	0-3	1-2	0-1	0-2	0-1	0-1	0-0	4-4	2-2	1-2	2-2	2-2	0-1	1-0	0-0	2-2
Darlington	1-1	3-0	2-0	1-1	2-2	—	1-0	1-0	2-1	0-0	3-2	2-1	1-0	1-0	3-2	3-1	1-0	1-2	3-2	5-0	1-1	2-0	3-3	2-2
Doncaster R	3-0	0-3	1-2	0-2	1-3	—	3-0	0-0	2-0	2-0	1-1	1-3	3-0	2-0	3-0	2-0	2-1	2-0	1-2	3-2	1-1	1-1	—	2-2
Exeter C	3-0	2-0	0-0	4-1	2-1	—	0-3	—	2-0	2-0	1-0	2-0	0-1	2-1	2-0	4-0	1-0	2-0	1-0	2-0	4-0	3-0	3-1	2-0
Grimsby T	1-0	2-0	0-3	0-2	2-1	1-1	—	2-1	—	2-0	3-0	0-0	5-2	2-2	0-0	2-0	1-0	2-1	1-1	2-2	1-1	3-2	1-2	0-3
Halifax T	2-2	0-2	4-0	0-3	0-0	4-2	0-1	2-2	2-1	—	2-0	3-0	2-1	1-0	3-0	0-0	2-1	2-0	3-0	0-2	0-0	0-2	3-1	5-3
Hartlepool U	2-2	0-0	0-0	2-0	0-0	0-0	3-0	1-2	2-1	2-2	—	2-1	3-0	3-1	0-0	4-0	4-0	2-1	0-0	3-0	2-0	4-3	2-3
Hereford U	3-3	3-0	1-1	0-2	1-1	3-1	2-1	1-2	1-2	—	1-0	3-0	2-2	2-0	6-0	2-1	2-0	3-1	1-2	1-0	1-1	1-1	4-1
Leyton Orient	2-2	2-0	1-0	1-0	1-3	1-0	2-2	2-0	1-1	—	1-0	5-0	3-1	4-0	3-2	2-0	3-0	3-0	3-1	0-1
Lincoln C	1-4	2-1	1-3	2-1	2-1	0-1	1-0	0-3	2-1	2-1	—	1-2	2-0	1-0	1-0	1-0	1-0	3-0	2-1
Peterborough U	1-1	2-2	2-1	2-2	2-3	3-0	5-0	2-1	2-1	—	0-1	3-2	1-0	1-0	1-1	1-1	1-5
Rochdale	2-0	1-0	3-1	1-2	1-1	5-1	1-1	4-4	3-1	1-0	—	1-3	3-0	3-0	1-0	1-3	3-3
Rotherham U	1-1	2-0	1-1	1-0	0-0	1-1	1-1	1-1	3-1	0-2	1-0	—	1-0	0-0	1-2	0-1	1-1
Scarborough	0-2	1-1	1-1	1-1	1-0	1-2	3-1	2-3	3-3	2-2	4-1	1-2	—	0-3	2-1	1-1	0-0
Scunthorpe U	0-3	0-3	2-2	2-3	3-2	3-2	5-0	2-1	1-1	2-3	3-0	—	1-2	2-2	2-0	0-2
Stockport Co	1-0	1-1	1-1	1-4	2-2	2-2	2-2	2-2	1-2	0-1	1-1	1-1	—	1-2	2-0	2-0
Torquay U	1-0	3-2	2-2	2-0	0-3	1-0	2-0	3-1	1-1	3-1	3-1	1-0	5-2	3-0	—	3-0	1-1
Tranmere R	2-2	1-1	2-3	1-2	0-1	0-3	0-0	2-2	0-9	1-0	1-2	2-3	0-1	0-0	2-1	—	2-1
Wrexham	1-3	2-0	2-1	2-2	2-1	0-2	4-0	1-3	0-3	4-3	1-0	2-2	0-3	2-1	1-0	—	1-0
York C	6-0	1-0	0-2	1-1	2-2	2-2	2-0	0-1	2-0	4-1	0-1	2-0	0-1	0-3	2-2	3-2	0-1	1-1	2-1	—

1988–89 RESULTS
Final results season 1988–89

Fourth Division		Home					Away						
	P	W	D	L	F	A	W	D	L	F	A	GD	Pts
Rotherdam U	46	13	6	4	44	18	9	10	4	32	17	+41	82
Tranmere R	46	15	6	2	34	13	6	11	6	28	30	+19	80
Crewe Alex	46	13	7	3	42	24	8	8	7	25	24	+19	78
Scunthorpe U	46	11	9	3	40	22	10	5	8	37	35	+20	77
Scarborough	46	12	7	4	33	23	9	7	7	34	29	+15	77
Leyton Orient	46	16	2	5	61	19	5	10	8	25	31	+36	75
Wrexham	46	12	7	4	44	28	7	7	9	33	35	+14	71
Cambridge U	46	13	7	3	45	25	5	7	11	26	37	+9	68
Grimsby T	46	11	9	3	33	18	6	6	11	32	41	+6	66
Lincoln C	46	12	6	5	39	26	6	4	13	25	34	+4	64
York C	46	10	8	5	43	27	7	5	11	19	36	−1	64
Carlisle U	46	9	6	8	26	25	6	9	8	27	27	+1	60
Exeter C	46	14	4	5	46	23	4	2	17	19	45	−3	60
Torquay U	46	15	2	6	32	23	2	6	15	13	37	−15	59
Hereford U	46	11	8	4	40	27	3	8	12	26	45	−6	58
Burnley	46	12	6	5	35	20	2	7	14	17	41	−9	55
Peterborough U	46	10	3	10	29	32	4	9	10	23	42	−22	54
Rochdale	46	10	10	3	32	26	3	4	16	24	56	−26	53
Hartlepool U	46	10	6	7	33	33	4	4	13	17	45	−28	52
Stockport Co	46	8	10	5	31	20	2	11	10	23	32	+2	51
Halifax T	46	10	7	6	42	27	3	4	16	27	48	−6	50
Colchester U	46	8	7	8	35	30	4	7	12	25	48	−18	50
Doncaster R	46	9	6	8	32	32	4	4	15	17	46	−29	49
Darlington	46	3	12	8	28	38	5	6	12	25	38	−23	42

PLAY–OFFS (*all matches two legs*): Semi-finals – Leyton Orient 2,0, Scarborough 0,1; Wrexham 3,2, Scunthorpe U 1,0; Final – Wrexham 0,1, Leyton Orient 0,2. **Leyton Orient promoted to Division Three.**

Leading goalscorers
Goals listed in following order: League, Littlewoods Cup, FA Cup, total.

Division 4: Phil Stant (Hereford U) **28**, 1, 0, 29; Tony Daws (Scunthorpe U) **24**, 3, 0, 27; Terry McPhillips (Halifax T) **22**, 1, 1, 24; Kevin Russell (Wrexham) **22**, 0, 0, 22; Ian Muir (Tranmere R) **21**, 2, 5, 28; Darran Rowbotham (Exeter C) **20**, 0, 1, 21; Alan Comfort (Leyton Orient) **19**, 1, 0, 20; Paul Fishenden (Crewe Alex) **16**, 1, 3, 20; Wayne Allison (Halifax T) **15**, 1, 2, 18; Andy Flounders (Scunthorpe U) **15**, 4, 0, 19; Keith Alexander (Grimsby T) **14**, 0, 1, 15; Gordon Hobson (Lincoln C) **14**, 1, 0, 15; Steve Neville (Exeter C) **14**, 0, 0, 14; Paul McLoughlin (Hereford U) **13**, 0, 0, 13; Brendan O'Connell (Burnley) **13**, 3, 0, 16.

LEAGUE CHAMPIONSHIP HONOURS

*Won on goal average. †Won on goal difference.
No championships during WWI and WWII.*

First Division

	First	Pt	Second	Pt	Third	Pt
1888–9 *a*	Preston NE	40	Aston Villa	29	Wolverhampton	28
1889–90	Preston NE	33	Everton	31	Blackburn R	27
1890–1	Everton	29	Preston NE	27	Wolverhampton ⎤ Notts Co ⎦	26
1891–2 *b*	Sunderland	42	Preston NE	37	Bolton W	36
1892–3 *c*	Sunderland	48	Preston NE	37	Everton	36
1893–4	Aston Villa	44	Sunderland	38	Derby Co	36
1894–5	Sunderland	47	Everton	42	Aston Villa	39
1895–6	Aston Villa	45	Derby Co	41	Everton	39
1896–7	Aston Villa	47	Sheffield U	36	Derby Co	36
1897–8	Sheffield U	42	Sunderland	37	Wolverhampton W	35
1898–9 *d*	Aston Villa	45	Liverpool	43	Burnley	39
1899–1900	Aston Villa	50	Sheffield U	48	Sunderland	41
1900–1	Liverpool	45	Sunderland	43	Notts Co	40
1901–2	Sunderland	44	Everton	41	Newcastle U	37
1902–3	Sheffield W	42	Aston Villa	41	Sunderland	41
1903–4	Sheffield W	47	Manchester C	44	Everton	43
1904–5	Newcastle U	48	Everton	47	Manchester C	46
1905–6 *e*	Liverpool	51	Preston NE	47	Sheffield W	44
1906–7	Newcastle U	51	Bristol C	48	Everton	45
1907–8	Manchester U	52	Aston Villa	43	Manchester C	43
1908–9	Newcastle U	53	Everton	46	Sunderland	44
1909–10	Aston Villa	53	Liverpool	48	Blackburn R	45
1910–11	Manchester U	52	Aston Villa	51	Sunderland	45
1911–12	Blackburn R	49	Everton	46	Newcastle U	44
1912–13	Sunderland	54	Aston Villa	50	Sheffield W	49
1913–14	Blackburn	51	Aston Villa	44	Middlesbrough	43
1914–15	Everton	46	Oldham Ath	45	Blackburn R	43
1919–20 *f*	WBA	60	Burnley	51	Chelsea	49
1920–1	Burnley	59	Manchester C	54	Bolton W	55
1921–2	Liverpool	57	Tottenham H	51	Burnley	49
1922–3	Liverpool	60	Sunderland	54	Huddersfield T	53
1923–4	*Huddersfield T	57	Cardiff C	57	Sunderland	43
1924–5	Huddersfield T	58	WBA	56	Bolton W.	55
1925–6	Huddersfield T	57	Arsenal	52	Sunderland	48
1926–7	Newcastle U	56	Huddersfield T	51	Sunderland	49
1927–8	Everton	53	Huddersfield T	51	Leicester C	48
1928–9	Sheffield W	52	Leicester C	51	Aston Villa	50
1929–30	Sheffield W	60	Derby Co	50	Manchester C	47
1930–1	Arsenal	66	Aston Villa	59	Sheffield W	52
1931–2	Everton	56	Arsenal	54	Sheffield W	50
1932–3	Arsenal	58	Aston Villa	54	Sheffield W	51
1933–4	Arsenal	59	Huddersfield T	56	Tottenham H	49
1934–5	Arsenal	58	Sunderland	54	Sheffield W	49
1935–6	Sunderland	56	Derby Co	48	Huddersfield T	48
1936–7	Manchester C	57	Charlton Ath	54	Arsenal	52
1937–8	Arsenal	52	Wolverhampton W	51	Preston NE	49
1938–9	Everton	59	Wolverhampton W	55	Charlton Ath	50
1946–7	Liverpool	57	Manchester U	56	Wolverhampton W	56
1947–8	Arsenal	59	Manchester U	52	Burnley	52

76

1948–9	Portsmouth	58	Manchester U	53	Derby Co	53
1949–50	*Portsmouth	53	Wolverhampton W	53	Sunderland	52
1950–1	Tottenham H	60	Manchester U	56	Blackpool	50
1951–2	Manchester U	57	Tottenham H	53	Arsenal	53
1952–3	*Arsenal	54	Preston NE	54	Wolverhampton W	51
1953–4	Wolverhampton W	57	WBA	53	Huddersfield T	51
1954–5	Chelsea	52	Wolverhampton W	48	Portsmouth	48
1955–6	Manchester U	60	Blackpool	49	Wolverhampton W	49
1956–7	Manchester U	64	Tottenham H	56	Preston NE	56
1957–8	Wolverhampton W	64	Preston NE	59	Tottenham H	51
1958–9	Wolverhampton W	61	Manchester U	55	Arsenal	50
1959–60	Burnley	55	Wolverhampton W	54	Tottenham H	53
1960–1	Tottenham H	66	Sheffield W	58	Wolverhampton W	57
1961–2	Ipswich T	56	Burnley	53	Tottenham H	52
1962–3	Everton	61	Tottenham H	55	Burnley	54
1963–4	Liverpool	57	Manchester U	53	Everton	52
1964–5	*Manchester U	61	Leeds U	61	Chelsea	56
1965–6	Liverpool	61	Leeds U	55	Burnley	55
1966–7	Manchester U	60	Nottingham F	56	Tottenham H	56
1967–8	Manchester C	58	Manchester U	56	Liverpool	55
1968–9	Leeds U	67	Liverpool	61	Everton	57
1969–70	Everton	66	Leeds U	57	Chelsea	55
1970–1	Arsenal	65	Leeds U	64	Tottenham H	52
1971–2	Derby Co	58	Leeds U	57	Liverpool	57
1972–3	Liverpool	60	Arsenal	57	Leeds U	53
1973–4	Leeds U	62	Liverpool	57	Derby Co	48
1974–5	Derby Co	53	Liverpool	51	Ipswich T	51
1975–6	Liverpool	60	QPR	59	Manchester U	56
1976–7	Liverpool	57	Manchester C	56	Ipswich T	52
1977–8	Nottingham F	64	Liverpool	57	Everton	55
1978–9	Liverpool	68	Nottingham F	60	WBA	59
1979–80	Liverpool	60	Manchester U	58	Ipswich T	53
1980–1	Aston Villa	60	Ipswich T	56	Arsenal	53
1981–2 g	Liverpool	87	Ipswich T	83	Manchester U	78
1982–3	Liverpool	82	Watford	71	Manchester U	70
1983–4	Liverpool	80	Southampton	77	Nottingham F	74
1984–5	Everton	90	Liverpool	77	Tottenham H	77
1985–6	Liverpool	88	Everton	86	West Ham U	84
1986–7	Everton	86	Liverpool	77	Tottenham H	71
1987–8 h	Liverpool	90	Manchester U	81	Nottingham F	73
1988–9 i†	Arsenal	76	Liverpool	76	Nottingham F	64

Maximum points: *a*, 44; *b*, 56; *c*, 60; *d*, 58; *e*, 76; *f*, 84; *g*, 126; *h*, 120; *i*, 114

Second Division

1892–3 a	Small Heath	36	Sheffield U	35	Darwen	30
1893–4 b	Liverpool	50	Small Heath	42	Notts Co	39
1894–5 c	Bury	48	Notts Co	39	Newton Heath	38
1895–6	*Liverpool	46	Manchester C	46	Grimsby T	42
1896–7	Notts Co	42	Newton Heath	39	Grimsby T	38
1897–8	Burnley	48	Newcastle	45	Manchester C	39
1898–9 d	Manchester C	51	Glossop NE	46	Leicester Fosse	45
1899–1900	Sheffield W	54	Bolton W	52	Small Heath	46
1900–1	Grimsby T	49	Small Heath	48	Burnley	44
1901–2	WBA	55	Middlesbrough	51	Preston NE	42
1902–3	Manchester C	54	Small Heath	51	W'lwich Arsenal	48
1903–4	Preston NE	50	W'lwich Arsenal	49	Manchester U	48
1904–5	Liverpool	58	Bolton W	56	Manchester U	53
1905–6 e	Bristol C	66	Manchester U	62	Chelsea	53
1906–7	Nottingham F	60	Chelsea	57	Leicester Fosse	48
1907–8	Bradford C	54	Leicester Fosse	52	Oldham	50
1908–9	Bolton W	52	Tottenham H	51	WBA	51

1909–10	Manchester C.......54	Oldham Ath 53	Hull C 53
1910–11	WBA.................53	Bolton W 51	Chelsea...............49
1911–12	*Derby Co 54	Chelsea 54	Burnley...............52
1912–13	Preston NE..........53	Burnley...............50	Birmingham 46
1913–14	Notts Co 53	Bradford 49	W'lwich Arsenal ...49
1914–15	Derby Co 53	Preston NE...........50	Barnsley..............47
1919–20 f	Tottenham H 70	Huddersfield T 64	Birmingham C 56
1920–1	*Birmingham 58	Cardiff C 58	Bristol C 51
1921–2	Nottingham F........56	Stoke C...............52	Barnsley..............52
1922–3	Notts Co 53	West Ham U.........51	Leicester C 51
1923–4	Leeds U 54	Bury 51	Derby Co 51
1924–5	Leicester C 59	Manchester U 57	Derby Co 55
1925–6	Sheffield W...........60	Derby Co 57	Chelsea...............52
1926–7	Middlesbrough 62	Portsmouth 54	Manchester C........54
1927–8	Manchester C........59	Leeds U 57	Chelsea...............54
1928–9	Middlesbrough 55	Grimsby T 53	Bradford C 48
1929–30	Blackpool.............58	Chelsea 55	Oldham Ath 53
1930–1	Everton................61	WBA.................55	Tottenham H 51
1931–2	Wolverhampton W56	Leeds U 54	Stoke C...............52
1932–3	Stoke C...............56	Tottenham H 55	Fulham...............50
1933–4	Grimsby 59	Preston NE...........52	Bolton W 51
1934–5	Brentford 61	Bolton W 56	West Ham U.........56
1935–6	Manchester U 56	Charlton Ath 55	Sheffield U 52
1936–7	Leicester C 56	Blackpool.............55	Bury 52
1937–8	Aston Villa 57	Manchester U 53	Sheffield U 53
1938–9	Blackburn R 55	Sheffield U 54	Sheffield W...........53
1946–7	Manchester C........62	Burnley...............58	Birmingham 55
1947–8	Birmingham 59	Newcastle U 56	Southampton........52
1948–9	Fulham...............57	WBA.................56	Southampton........55
1949–50	Tottenham H 61	Sheffield W...........52	Sheffield U 52
1950–1	Preston NE...........57	Manchester C........52	Cardiff C 50
1951–2	Sheffield W...........53	Cardiff C 51	Birmingham C 51
1952–3	Sheffield U 60	Huddersfield T 58	Luton T 52
1953–4	*Leicester C 56	Everton................56	Blackburn R 55
1954–5	*Birmingham C........54	Luton 54	Rotherham U.........54
1955–6	Sheffield W...........55	Leeds U 52	Liverpool 48
1956–7	Leicester C 61	Nottingham F........54	Liverpool 53
1957–8	West Ham U.........57	Blackburn R 56	Charlton Ath 55
1958–9	Sheffield W...........62	Fulham 60	Sheffield U 53
1959–60	Aston Villa 59	Cardiff C 58	Liverpool 50
1960–1	Ipswich T 59	Sheffield U 58	Liverpool 52
1961–2	Liverpool 62	Leyton O 54	Sunderland 53
1962–3	Stoke C...............53	Chelsea 52	Sunderland 52
1963–4	Leeds U 63	Sunderland 61	Preston NE...........56
1964–5	Newcastle U 57	Northampton T 56	Bolton W 50
1965–6	Manchester C........59	Southampton.........54	Coventry C 53
1966–7	Coventry C 59	Wolverhampton W58	Carlisle U 52
1967–8	Ipswich T 59	QPR..................58	Blackpool.............58
1968–9	Derby Co 63	Crystal P 56	Charlton Ath 50
1969–70	Huddersfield T 60	Blackpool.............53	Leicester C 51
1970–1	Leicester C 59	Sheffield U 56	Cardiff C 53
1971–2	Norwich C 57	Birmingham C.......56	Millwall...............55
1972–3	Burnley................62	QPR..................61	Aston Villa 50
1973–4	Middlesbrough 65	Luton 50	Carlisle 49
1974–5	Manchester U 61	Aston Villa 58	Norwich C............53
1975–6	Sunderland 56	Bristol C 53	WBA.................53
1976–7	Wolverhampton W57	Chelsea 55	Nottingham F........52
1977–8	Bolton W 58	Southampton........57	Tottenham H 56
1978–9	Crystal P 57	Brighton & HA 56	Stoke C...............56
1979–80	Leicester C 55	Sunderland 54	Birmingham C.......53
1980–1	West Ham U.........66	Notts Co 53	Swansea C............50

78

1981–2 g	Luton T 88	Watford 80	Norwich C 71
1982–3	QPR......................85	Wolverhampton W 75	Leicester C 70
1983–4 †	Chelsea.................88	Sheffield W...........88	Newcastle U 80
1984–5	Oxford U 84	Birmingham C......82	Manchester C.......74
1985–6	Norwich C............84	Charlton Ath 77	Wimbledon 76
1986–7	Derby Co 84	Portsmouth 78	Oldham Ath 75
1987–8 h	Millwall................82	Aston Villa 78	Middlesbrough 78
1988–9 i	Chelsea.................99	Manchester C........82	Crystal P 81

Maximum points: *a*, 44; *b*, 56; *c*, 60; *d*, 58; *e*,76; *f*,84; *g*,126; *h*,132; *i* 138

Third Division

1958–9 a	Plymouth A 62	Hull C 61	Brentford 57
1959–60	Southampton........61	Norwich C............59	Shrewsbury 52
1960–1	Bury.....................68	Walsall.................62	QPR......................60
1961–2	Portsmouth 65	Grimsby T 62	Bournemouth 59
1962–3	Northampton T 62	Swindon T 58	Port Vale 54
1963–4	*Coventry C...........60	Crystal P 60	Watford 58
1964–5	Carlisle U.............60	Bristol C 59	Mansfield T 59
1965–6	Hull C 69	Millwall................65	QPR......................57
1966–7	QPR......................67	Middlesbrough 55	Watford 54
1967–8	Oxford U 57	Bury....................56	Shrewsbury T 55
1968–9	*Watford 64	Swindon T 64	Luton T 61
1969–70	Orient...................62	Luton T 60	Bristol R 56
1970–1	Preston NE...........61	Fulham 60	Halifax.................56
1971–2	Aston Villa 70	Brighton & HA 65	Bournemouth 62
1972–3	Bolton W 61	Notts Co 57	BLackburn R 55
1973–4	Oldham Ath ....:62	Bristol R 61	York C 61
1974–5	Blackburn R 60	Plymouth Arg 59	Charlton Ath 55
1975–6	Hereford U...........63	Cardiff C..............57	Millwall................56
1976–7	Mansfield T 64	Brighton & HA 61	Crystal P 59
1977–8	Wrexham 61	Cambridge U 58	Preston NE...........56
1978–9	Shrewsbury T 61	Watford 60	Swansea C.............60
1979–80	Grimsby T 62	Blackburn R 59	Sheffield W...........58
1980–1	Rotherham U........61	Barnsley...............59	Charlton Ath 59
1981–2 b	Burnley................80	Carlisle U.............80	Fulham 78
1982–3	Portsmouth 91	Cardiff C..............86	Huddersfield T 82
1983–4	Oxford U 95	Wimbledon 87	Sheffield U 83
1984–5	Bradford C 94	Millwall................90	Hull C 87
1985–6	Reading 94	Plymouth Arg 87	Derby Co 84
1986–7	Bournemouth 97	Midlesbrough 94	Swindon T 87
1987–8	Sunderland 93	Brighton & HA 84	Walsall..................82
1988–9	Wolverhampton W 92	†Sheffield U 84	Port Vale 84

Maximum points *a* 92; *b* 138

Third Division (Southern Section)

1920–1 a	Crystal P 59	Southampton........54	QPR......................53
1921–2	*Southampton.......61	Plymouth Arg 61	Portsmouth 53
1922–3	Bristol C 59	Plymouth Arg 53	Swansea 53
1923–4	Portsmouth 59	Plymouth Arg 55	Millwall................54
1924–5	Swansea C............57	Plymouth Arg 56	Bristol C 53
1925–6	Reading 57	Plymouth Arg 56	Millwall................53
1926–7	Bristol C 62	Plymouth Arg 60	Millwall................56
1927–8	Millwall................65	Northampton T 55	Plymouth Arg 53
1928–9	Charlton Ath 54	Crystal P 54	Northampton T 52
1929–30	Plymouth Arg 68	Brentford 61	QPR......................51
1930–1	Notts Co 59	Crystal P 51	Brentford 50
1931–2	Fulham 57	Reading 55	Southend U 53
1932–3	Brentford 62	Exeter 58	Norwich C 57
1933–4	Norwich C............61	Coventry C...........54	Reading 54
1934–5	Charlton Ath 61	Reading 53	Coventry C...........51
1935–6	Coventry C...........57	Luton T 56	Reading 54

Year			Year			Year		
1936–7	Luton T	58	Notts Co	56	Brighton & HA	53
1937–8	Millwall	56	Bristol C	55	QPR	53
1938–9	Newport C	55	Crystal P	52	Brighton & HA	49
1946–7	Cardiff	66	QPR	57	Bristol C	51
1947–8	QPR	61	Bournemouth	57	Walsall	51
1948–9	Swansea	62	Reading	55	Bournemouth	52
1949–50	Notts Co	58	Northampton T	51	Southend U	51
1950–1 *b*	Nottingham F	70	Norwich C	64	Reading	57
1951–2	Plymouth Arg	66	Reading	61	Norwich C	61
1952–3	Bristol R	64	Northampton T	62	Millwall	62
1953–4	Ipswich T	64	Brighton & HA	61	Bristol C	56
1954–5	Bristol C	70	Leyton O	61	Southampton	59
1955–6	Leyton O	66	Brighton & HA	65	Ipswich T	64
1956–7	*Ipswich T	59	Torquay U	59	Colchester U	58
1957–8	Brighton & HA	60	Brentford	58	Plymouth Arg	58

Maximum points: *a*, 84; *b* 92

Third Division (Northern Section)

1921–2 *a*	Stockport C	56	Darlington	50	Grimsby	50
1922–3	Nelson	51	Bradford	47	Walsall	46
1923–4 *b*	Wolverhampton W	63	Rochdale	62	Chesterfield	54
1924–5	Darlington	58	Nelson	53	New Brighton	53
1925–6	Grimsby T	61	Bradford	60	Rochdale	59
1926–7	Stoke C	63	Rochdale	58	Bradford	55
1927–8	Bradford	63	Lincoln C	55	Stockport C	54
1928–9	Bradford C	63	Stockport C	62	Wrexham	52
1929–30	Port Vale	67	Stockport C	63	Darlington	50
1930–1	Chesterfield	58	Lincoln C	57	Wrexham	54
1931–2 *c*	*Lincoln C	57	Gateshead	57	Chester	50
1932–3 *b*	Hull C	59	Wrexham	57	Stockport C	54
1933–4	Barnsley	62	Chesterfield	61	Stockport C	59
1934–5	Doncaster R	57	Halifax T	55	Chester	54
1935–6	Chesterfield	60	Chester	55	Tranmere R	55
1936–7	Stockport C	60	Lincoln C	57	Chester	53
1937–8	Tranmere R	56	Doncaster R	54	Hull C	53
1938–9	Barnsley	67	Doncaster R	56	Bradford C	52
1946–7	Doncaster R	72	Rotherham U	64	Chester	56
1947–8	Lincoln C	60	Rotherham U	59	Wrexham	50
1948–9	Hull C	65	Rotherham U	62	Doncaster R	50
1949–50	Doncaster R	55	Gateshead	53	Rochdale U	51
1950–1 *d*	Rotherham U	71	Mansfield T	64	Carlisle U	62
1951–2	Lincoln C	69	Grimsby T	66	Stockport C	59
1952–3	Oldham Ath	59	Port Vale	58	Wrexham	56
1953–4	Port Vale	69	Barnsley	58	Scunthorpe	57
1954–5	Barnsley	65	Accrington S	61	Scunthorpe	58
1955–6	Grimsby T	68	Derby Co	63	Accrington S	59
1956–7	Derby Co	63	Hartlepool	59	Accrington S	58
1957–8	Scunthorpe U	66	Accrington S	59	Bradford C	57

Maximum points: *a*, 70; *b*, 84; *c*, 80; *d*, 90.

Fourth Division

1958–9 *a*	Port Vale	64	Coventry C	60	York C	60
1959–60	Walsall	65	Notts Co	60	Torquay	60
1960–1	Peterborough	66	Crystal P	64	Northampton T	60
1961–2	Millwall	56	Colchester U	55	Wrexham	53
1962–3	Brentford	62	Oldham Ath	59	Crewe Alex	59
1963–4	*Gillingham U	60	Carlisle U	60	Workington T	59
1964–5	Brighton & HA	63	Millwall	62	York C	62
1965–6	*Doncaster R	59	Darlington	59	Torquay	58
1966–7	Stockport C	64	Southport C	59	Barrow	59
1967–8	Luton T	66	Barnsley	61	Hartlepool	60

1968–9	Doncaster R	59	Halifax T	57	Rochdale	56
1969–70	Chesterfield	64	Wrexham	61	Swansea T	60
1970–1	Notts Co	69	Bournemouth	60	Oldham Ath	59
1971–2	Grimsby T	63	Southend U	60	Brentford	59
1972–3	Southport	62	Hereford U	58	Cambridge U	57
1973–4	Peterborough U	65	Gillingham	62	Colchester U	60
1974–5	Mansfield T	68	Shrewsbury T	62	Rotherham U	59
1975–6	Lincoln C	74	Northampton T	68	Reading	60
1976–7	Cambridge U	65	Exeter C	62	Colchester	59
1977–8	Watford	71	Southend U	60	Swansea C	56
1978–9	Reading	65	Grimsby T	61	Wimbledon	61
1979–80	Huddersfield T	66	Walsall	64	Newport Co	61
1980–1	Southend U	67	Lincoln C	65	Doncaster R	56
1981–2 b	Sheffield U	96	Bradford C	91	Wigan Ath	91
1982–3	Wimbledon	98	Hull C	90	Port Vale	88
1983–4	York C	101	Doncaster R	85	Reading	82
1984–5	Chesterfield	91	Blackpool	86	Darlington	85
1985–6	Swindon T	102	Chester C	84	Mansfield T	81
1986–7	Northampton T	99	Preston NE	90	Southend U	80
1987–8	Wolverhampton W	90	Cardiff	85	Bolton W	78
1988–9	Rotherham U	82	Tranmere R	80	Crewe Alex	78

Maximum points *a*, 92; *b*, 138

RELEGATED CLUBS

(Since inception of automatic promotion and relegation in 1898–9)
*Relegated after play–offs

Season	Division I to Division II	Division II to Division III
1988–9	Middlesbrough, West Ham U, Newcastle U	Shrewsbury T, Birmingham C, Walsall
1987–8	Oxford U, Watford, Portsmouth, Chelsea*	Huddersfield T, Reading, Sheffield U*
1986–7	Leicester C, Manchester C, Aston Villa	Sunderland*, Grimsby T, Brighton & HA
1985–6	Ipswich T, Birmingham C, WBA	Carlisle U, Middlesbrough, Fulham
1984–5	Norwich C, Sunderland Stoke C	Notts Co, Cardiff C, Wolverhampton W
1983–4	Birmingham C, Notts Co, Wolverhampton W	Derby Co, Swansea C, Cambridge U
1982–3	Manchester C, Swansea C, Brighton & HA	Rotherham U, Burnley, Bolton W
1981–2	Leeds U, Middlesbrough, Wolverhampton W	Cardiff, Wrexham, Orient
1980–1	Norwich C, Leicester C, Crystal P	Preston NE, Bristol C, Bristol R
1979–80	Bristol C, Derby Co, Bolton W	Fulham, Burnley, Charlton Ath
1978–9	QPR, Birmingham, Chelsea	Sheffield U, Millwall, Blackburn

1977–8	West Ham, Newcastle, Leicester	Blackpool, Mansfield, Hull C
1976–7	Sunderland, Stoke, Tottenham	Carlisle, Plymouth, Hereford
1975–6	Wolves, Burnley, Sheffield U	Oxford, York, Portsmouth
1974–5	Luton, Chelsea, Carlisle	Millwall, Cardiff, Sheff. W
1973–4	So'ton, Man. U, Norwich	C. Palace, Preston, Swindon
1972–3	Crystal P and WBA	Huddersfield and Brighton
1971–2	Huddersfield and Nottingham F	Charlton and Watford
1970–1	Burnley and Blackpool	Blackburn and Bolton
1969–70	Sunderland and Sheffield W	Aston Villa and Preston
1968–9	Leicester and QPR	Bury and Fulham
1967–8	Sheffield U and Fulham	Rotherham and Plymouth
1966–7	Aston Villa and Blackpool	Northampton and Bury
1965–6	Blackburn and Northampton	Leyton O and Middlesbrough
1964–5	Birmingham and W'hampton	Swindon and Swansea
1963–4	Bolton and Ipswich	Grimsby and Scunthorpe
1962–3	Manchester C and Leyton O	Walsall and Luton
1961–2	Cardiff and Chelsea	Bristol R and Brighton
1960–1	Newcastle and Preston	Portsmouth and Lincoln
1959–60	Leeds and Luton	Hull and Bristol C
1958–9	Aston V and Portsmouth	Grimsby and Barnsley
1957–8	Sunderland and Sheffield W	Notts Co and Doncaster
1956–7	Cardiff and Charlton	Bury and Port Vale
1955–6	Huddersfield and Sheffield U	Plymouth and Hull
1954–5	Leicester and Sheffield W	Ipswich and Derby
1953–4	Middlesbrough and Liverpool	Brentford and Oldham
1952–3	Stoke and Derby	Southampton and Barnsley
1951–2	Fulham and Huddersfield	Coventry and QPR
1950–1	Sheffield W and Everton	Chesterfield and Grimsby
1949–50	Manchester C and Birmingham	Plymouth and Bradford
1948–9	Preston and Sheffield U	Lincoln and Nottingham F
1947–8	Blackburn and Grimsby	Doncaster and Millwall
1946–7	Brentford and Leeds	Swansea and Newport
1938–9	Birmingham and Leicester	Norwich and Tranmere
1937–8	Manchester C and WBA	Barnsley and Stockport
1936–7	Manchester U and Sheffield W	Doncaster and Bradford C
1935–6	Aston Villa and Blackburn	Port Vale and Hull
1934–5	Leicester and Tottenham	Oldham and Notts Co
1933–4	Newcastle and Sheffield U	Millwall and Lincoln
1932–3	Bolton and Blackpool	Chesterfield and Charlton
1931–2	Grimsby and West Ham	Barnsley and Bristol City
1930–1	Leeds and Manchester U	Reading and Cardiff
1929–30	Burnley and Everton	Hull and Notts Co
1928–9	Bury and Cardiff	Port Vale and Clapton O
1927–8	Tottenham and Middlesbrough	Fulham and South Shields
1926–7	Leeds and WBA	Darlington and Bradford C
1925–6	Manchester C and Notts Co	Stoke and Stockport
1924–5	Preston and Nottingham F	Crystal Palace and Coventry
1923–4	Chelsea and Middlesbrough	Nelson and Bristol City
1922–3	Stoke and Oldham	Rotherham and W'hampton
1921–2	Bradford C and Manchester U	Bradford and Bristol City
1920–1	Derby Co and Bradford	Stockport
1919–20	Notts Co and Sheffield W	
1916–18	*During the War the Football League competition was suspended.*	
	Previously the clubs relegated from Div. I to Div. II were:	
1914–15	Tottenham and Chelsea	
1913–14	Preston NE and Derby Co	
1912–13	Notts Co and Woolwich Arsenal	
1911–12	Preston NE and Bury	
1910–11	Bristol City and Nottingham F	
1909–10	Bolton W and Chelsea	
1908–9	Manchester C and Leicester Fosse	

1907–8	Bolton W and Birmingham
1906–7	Derby Co and Stoke
1905–6	Nottingham F and Wolverhampton W
1904–5	*League extended.* Bury and Notts Co, two bottom clubs in First Division, re-elected.
1903–4	Liverpool and West Bromwich Albion
1902–3	Grimsby and Bolton
1901–2	Small Heath and Manchester C
1900–1	Preston NE and West Bromwich
1899–1900	Burnley and Glossop
1898–9	Bolton and Sheffield Wednesday

Season	Relegation from Division III to Division IV
1988–9	Southend U, Chesterfield, Gillingham, Aldershot
1987–8	Doncaster R, York C, Grimsby T, Rotherham U*
1986–7	Bolton W*, Carlisle U, Darlington, Newport Co
1985–6	Lincoln C, Cardiff C, Wolverhampton W, Swansea C
1984–5	Burnley, Orient, Preston NE, Cambridge U
1983–4	Scunthorpe U, Southend U, Port Vale, Exeter C
1982–3	Reading, Doncaster R, Wrexham, Chesterfield
1981–2	Wimbledon, Swindon T, Bristol C, Chester
1980–1	Sheffield U, Colchester U, Hull C, Blackpool
1979–80	Bury, Southend U, Mansfield T and Wimbledon
1978–9	Peterborough, Walsall, Tranmere and Lincoln
1977–8	Port Vale, Bradford, Hereford and Portsmouth
1976–7	Reading, Northampton, Grimsby and York
1975–6	Aldershot, Colchester, Southend U, and Halifax T
1974–5	Bournemouth, Tranmere, Watford and Huddersfield
1973–4	Cambridge, Shrewsbury, Southport and Rochdale
1972–3	Rotherham, Brentford, Swansea and Scunthorpe
1971–2	Mansfield, Barnsley, Bradford C and Torquay
1970–1	Reading, Bury, Doncaster and Gillingham
1969–70	Bournemouth, Southport, Barrow and Stockport
1968–9	Northampton, Hartlepool, Crewe and Oldham
1967–8	Grimsby, Colchester, Scunthorpe and Peterborough†
1966–7	Swansea, Darlington, Workington and Doncaster
1965–6	Southend, Exeter, Brentford, and York
1964–5	Luton, Port Vale, Colchester and Barnsley
1963–4	Millwall, Crewe, Wrexham and Notts Co
1962–3	Bradford, Brighton, Carlisle and Halifax
1961–2	Torquay, Lincoln, Brentford and Newport
1960–1	Tranmere, Bradford C, Colchester and Chesterfield
1959–60	York, Mansfield, Wrexham and Accrington
1958–9	Stockport, Doncaster, Notts Co and Rochdale

†*Expelled to Fourth Division by League*

APPLICATION FOR RE-ELECTION TO THIRD DIVISION UNTIL 1957–58

Seven times: Walsall
Six: Exeter, Halifax, Newport
Five: Accrington, Barrow, Gillingham, New Brighton, Southport
Four: Norwich, Rochdale
Three: Crewe, Crystal P, Darlington, Hartlepool, Merthyr T, Swindon
Two: Aberdare Ath, Aldershot, Ashington, Bournemouth, Brentford, Chester, Colchester, Millwall, Durham C, Nelson, Queen's Park Rangers, Rotherham, Southend, Tranmere, Watford, Workington

One: Bradford, Bradford C, Brighton, Bristol R, Cardiff, Carlisle, Charlton, Gateshead, Grimsby, Mansfield, Shrewsbury, Thames, Torquay, York

APPLICATION FOR RE-ELECTION TO FOURTH DIVISION UNTIL 1985–86

Eleven times: Hartlepool
Seven: Crewe
Six: Barrow, Halifax T, Rochdale, Southport and York
Five: Chester C, Darlington, Lincoln, Stockport Co and Workington
Four: Bradford, Newport Co and Northampton T
Three: Doncaster R and Hereford U
Two: Bradford C, Exeter C, Oldham, Scunthorpe and Torquay U
One: Aldershot, Blackpool, Cambridge U, Colchester, Gateshead, Grimsby, Port Vale, Preston NE, Swansea C, Tranmere R, and Wrexham.

Gateshead not re-elected, their place being taken by Peterborough in the 1960–1 season.
Accrington resigned March 1962, and Oxford U elected to replace them in 1962–3 season.
Bradford not re-elected, their place being taken by Cambridge U in the 1970–1 season.
Barrow not re-elected, their place being taken by Hereford U in the 1972–3 season.
Workington not re-elected, their place being taken by Wimbledon in the 1977–8 season.
Southport not re-elected, their place being taken by Wigan in the 1978–9 season.
LEAGUE STATUS FROM 1986–87
1986–7 *Relegated*: Lincoln C *Promoted*: Scarborough
1987–8 *Relegated*: Newport C *Promoted*: Lincoln C
1988–9 *Relegated*: Darlington *Promoted*: Maidstone U
PROMOTED AFTER PLAY–OFFS
1986–7 Aldershot, Div 4 to Div 3.
1987–8 Swansea C, Div 4 to Div 3.
1988–9 Leyton Orient, Div 4 to Div 3

LEAGUE TITLE WINS

League Division I 17 Liverpool; 9 Arsenal, Everton; 7 Aston Villa, Manchester U; 6 Sunderland; 4 Newcastle, Sheffield Wednesday; 3 Huddersfield, Wolves; 2 Blackburn R, Burnley, Derby Co, Leeds, Manchester C, Portsmouth, Preston NE, Tottenham; 1 Chelsea, Ipswich, Nottingham F, Sheffield U, West Bromwich Albion.

League Division II 6 Manchester C, Leicester; 5 Sheffield Wednesday; 4 *Birmingham, Derby Co, Liverpool; 3 Middlesbrough, Notts Co, Preston; 2 Aston Villa, Bolton, Burnley, Chelsea, Grimsby, Ipswich, Leeds, Manchester U, Norwich C, Nottingham F, Stoke, Tottenham, West Bromwich, West Ham U, Wolverhampton W; 1 Blackburn R, Blackpool, Bradford C, Brentford, Bristol C, Bury, Coventry, Crystal P, Everton, Fulham, Huddersfield, Luton, Millwall, Newcastle, Oxford U, QPR, Sheffield U, Sunderland. *Once as Small Heath.*

League Division III 2 Oxford U, Portsmouth; 1 Aston Villa, Blackburn R, Bolton, Bournemouth, Bradford C, Burnley, Bury, Carlisle, Coventry, Grimsby T, Hereford U, Hull, Mansfield, Northampton, Oldham Ath, Orient, Plymouth, Preston NE, Queen's Park Rangers, Reading, Rotherham U, Shrewsbury T, Southampton, Sunderland, Watford, Wolverhampton W, Wrexham.

League Division IV 2 Chesterfield, Doncaster R, Peterborough U; 1 Brentford, Brighton, Cambridge, Gillingham, Grimsby, Huddersfield T, Lincoln C, Luton, Mansfield T, Millwall, Northampton T, Notts Co, Port Vale, Reading, Rotherham U, Sheffield U, Southend U, Southport, Swindon T, Walsall, Watford, Wimbledon, Wolverhampton W, York C.

To 1957–58
Division III (South): 3 Bristol C; 2 Charlton, Ipswich, Millwall, Notts Co, Plymouth, Swansea; 1 Brentford, Bringhton, Bristol R, Cardiff, Coventry, Crystal P, Fulham, Leyton Orient, Luton, Newport, Nottingham F, Norwich, Portsmouth, Queen's Park Rangers, Reading, Southampton.
Division III (North): 3 Barnsley, Doncaster, Lincoln; 2 Chesterfield, Grimsby, Hull, Port Vale, Stockport; 1 Bradford, Bradford C, Darlington, Derby, Nelson, Oldham, Rotherham, Scunthorpe, Stoke, Tranmere, Wolverhampton.

BARCLAYS LEAGUE ATTENDANCES 1988–89

For the first time since the war, League attendances increased for the third successive season. The increase was half a million up on the 1987–88 figure. Liverpool maintained their lead as the best supported club, attracting an average of 38,574 per game compared with Manchester United's 36,488. Close behind came champions Arsenal with 35,595. Second Division runners-up Manchester City proved the biggest draw in producing an average of 23,500, while Third Division champions Wolverhampton Wanderers led the way in their section with 14,392. Wolves thus became the first club to win the championship of all four divisions of the League. Despite a disappointing season in the Fourth Division, Burnley averaged 7,062 at home games. All four divisions showed increases in comparison with 1987–88, even though the First Division was reduced to 20 clubs.

Division: this season's total, average, last season.

Division One: 7,809,993, ave. 20,552 (8,094,571, ave. 19,272)
Division Two: 5,887,805, ave. 10,666 (5,341,599, ave. 10,555)
Division Three: 3,035,327, ave. 5,498 (2,751,275, ave. 4,984)
Division Four: 1,791,067, ave. 3,244 (1,772,287, ave. 3,210)
Total: 18,464,192, ave. 9,068 (17,959,732, ave. 8,847)

TOTAL LEAGUE ATTENDANCES SINCE 1946–47

Season	Matches	Total	Season	Matches	Total
1946–47	1848	35,604,606	1968–69	2028	29,382,172
1947–48	1848	40,259,130	1969–70	2028	29,600,972
1948–49	1848	41,271,414	1970–71	2028	28,194,146
1949–50	1848	40,517,865	1971–72	2028	28,700,729
1950–51	2028	39,584,967	1972–73	2028	25,448,642
1951–52	2028	39,015,866	1973–74	2027	24,982,203
1952–53	2028	37,149,966	1974–75	2028	25,577,977
1953–54	2028	36,174,590	1975–76	2028	24,896,053
1954–55	2028	34,133,103	1976–77	2028	26,182,800
1955–56	2028	33,150,809	1977–78	2028	25,392,872
1956–57	2028	32,744,405	1978–79	2028	24,540,627
1957–58	2028	33,562,208	1979–80	2028	24,623,975
1958–59	2028	33,610,985	1980–81	2028	21,907,569
1959–60	2028	32,538,611	1981–82	2028	20,006,961
1960–61	2028	28,619,754	1982–83	2028	18,766,158
1961–62	2015	27,979,902	1983–84	2028	18,358,631
1962–63	2028	28,885,852	1984–85	2028	17,849,835
1963–64	2028	28,535,022	1985–86	2028	16,488,577
1964–65	2028	27,641,168	1986–87	2028	17,379,218
1965–66	2028	27,206,980	1987–88	2030	17,959,732
1966–67	2028	28,902,596	1988–89	2036	18,464,192
1967–68	2028	30,107,298			

ALL-SEATER STADIA PROJECTION DIVISION ONE (1989–90)

A *Current capacity* B *Present standing capacity;* C *present seated capacity;* D *projected all-seated capacity;* E *average attendance season 1988–89;* F *no of times attendance exceeded average;* G *no of times attendance exceeded projected all-seated capacity.*

	A	B	C	D	E	F	G
Arsenal	57,000	39,800	17,200	38,925	35,595	10	5
Aston Villa	48,100	32,095	16,005	33,657	23,310	8	1
Charlton Ath	38,366	26,858	11,508	26,280	9,398	6	0
Chelsea	43,900	23,300	20,600	33,415	15,731	11	0
Coventry C	29,800	11,304	18,496	24,713	16,040	9	0
Crystal Palace	38,366	26,858	11,508	26,280	10,655	8	0
Derby Co	26,500	16,278	10,222	19,175	17,536	7	5
Everton	50,271	23,800	26,471	39,561	27,765	8	2
Liverpool	45,628	23,100	22,328	35,233	38,574	12	16
Luton T	14,470	7,660	6,510	11,023	9,504	8	2
Manchester C	51,993	26,155	25,238	40,223	23,500	6	0
Manchester U	56,385	30,699	25,686	42,570	36,488	11	3
Millwall	25,850	22,650	3,200	15,675	15,416	8	9
Norwich C	26,812	15,587	11,225	19,798	16,785	7	5
Nottingham F	35,367	20,358	15,009	26,206	20,785	8	1
QPR	27,330	12,000	15,330	21,930	12,281	8	0
Sheffield W	54,324	31,000	23,334	40,374	20,037	6	0
Southampton	25,175	16,000	9,175	17,975	15,590	7	3
Tottenham H	34,258	18,650	15,608	25,866	24,467	10	9
Wimbledon	16,000	14,000	2,000	9,700	7,824	9	5
Total:	**745,895**			**548,579**			

ALL-SEATER STADIA PROJECTION DIVISION TWO (1989–90)

	A	B	C	D	E	F	G
AFC Bournemouth	12,038	8,000	4,038	8,438	8,087	12	10
Barnsley	36,987	34,700	2,287	21,372	7,215	8	0
Blackburn R	21,956	19,300	2,656	13,271	8,891	9	1
Bradford C	15,519	10,937	4,582	10,597	10,524	12	12
Brighton & HA	29,026	24,272	4,754	18,104	9,048	11	0
Hull C	19,797	13,752	6,040	13,606	6,666	9	0
Ipswich T	37,345	23,177	14,168	26,915	15,333	2	0
Leeds U	39,133	21,244	17,889	29,573	21,811	11	3
Leicester C	31,057	15,200	15,857	24,217	10,694	9	0
Middlesbrough	30,647	21,080	9,567	21,161	19,999	8	6
Newcastle U	37,703	26,290	11,413	25,873	22,921	7	4
Oldham Ath	21,949	18,950	2,999	10,423	7,204	6	2
Oxford U	14,006	8,063	5,943	10,378	6,352	9	0
Plymouth Arg	28,000	24,741	3,259	16,867	8,628	7	0
Port Vale	18,640	14,340	4,300	12,187	6,731	6	5
Portsmouth	29,664	22,988	6,676	19,319	10,201	12	0
Sheffield U	44,010	30,413	13,597	30,324	12,222	9	0
Stoke C	35,812	24,500	11,312	24,787	9,817	9	0
Sunderland	37,775	28,750	9,025	24,837	14,878	10	0
Swindon T	19,652	14,590	5,062	13,088	8,687	11	0
Watford	26,956	20,050	6,906	17,932	12,292	10	0
WBA	35,000	23,000	12,000	24,650	12,757	10	0
West Ham U	35,556	26,816	8,740	23,488	20,738	7	5
Wolverhampton W	28,051	18,551	9,500	19,703	14,392	10	3
Total:	686,279			460,480			

ALL-SEATER STADIA PROJECTION DIVISION THREE (1989–90)

	A	B	C	D	E	F	G
Birmingham C	38,408	29,040	9,368	25,340	6,265	9	0
Blackpool	12,696	9,500	3,196	8,421	4,276	6	0
Bolton W	29,000	21,000	8,000	19,550	5,528	7	2
Brentford	12,100	9,183	2,917	7,968	5,681	9	0
Bristol C	30,868	23,452	7,416	20,315	8,120	8	10
Bristol R	8,844	8,186	658	5,160	5,259	10	0
Bury	8,000	5,300	2,700	5,615	3,367	9	1
Cardiff C	39,545	34,000	5,545	24,245	4,384	8	0
Chester C	8,474	5,640	2,834	5,936	3,055	10	0
Crewe Alex	5,900	4,800	1,100	3,740	3,296	8	6
Fulham	19,400	11,860	7,540	14,063	4,938	7	0
Huddersfield T	31,010	25,221	5,789	19,660	5,821	7	0
Leyton Orient	26,500	19,328	7,172	17,802	3,793	12	2
Mansfield T	12,298	8,850	3,448	8,316	4,005	8	0
Northampton T	11,000	10,658	342	6,204	3,918	8	0
Notts Co	24,077	20,200	3,877	14,987	5,675	8	3
Preston NE	16,500	13,200	3,300	10,560	7,737	9	1
Reading	13,500	11,547	1,953	8,304	5,105	9	0
Rotherham U	17,913	14,506	3,407	11,385	5,063	9	0
Shrewsbury T	16,000	12,000	4,000	10,660	4,706	7	0
Swansea C	18,165	15,000	3,165	11,415	4,896	9	0
Tranmere R	18,500	14,700	3,800	11,885	5,331	8	1
Walsall	16,018	14,660	1,358	9,421	6,108	12	0
Wigan Ath	12,500	11,400	1,100	7,370	3,151	6	0
Total:	447,216			288,262			

ALL-SEATER STADIA PROJECTION DIVISION FOUR (1989–90)

	A	B	C	D	E	F	G
Aldershot	12,000	11,200	1,800	7,960	2,609	8	0
Burnley	20,961	14,200	6,761	14,571	7,062	11	0
Cambridge U	12,500	9,104	3,396	8,403	2,653	11	0
Carlisle U	18,506	16,344	2,162	11,153	3,176	5	1
Chesterfield	12,838	10,200	2,638	8,248	3,717	7	4
Colchester U	6,500	5,416	1,084	4,063	2,893	11	0
Doncaster R	8,259	7,000	1,259	5,109	2,158	10	0
Exeter C	9,230	7,622	1,608	5,800	2,679	9	0
Gillingham	10,482	9,257	1,225	6,316	3,676	9	0
Grimsby T	20,876	15,844	5,021	13,735	4,302	9	1
Halifax T	5,675	3,930	1,745	3,906	1,946	9	0
Hartlepool U	6,650	5,150	1,500	4,332	2,048	9	1
Hereford U	16,119	13,815	2,304	9,902	2,132	7	0
Lincoln C	9,477	7,448	2,029	6,125	3,887	6	1
Maidstone U	4,948	4,228	720	3,045	1,037	10	0
Peterborough U	17,440	14,000	3,440	11,140	3,264	11	0
Rochdale	12,000	11,350	650	6,892	1,968	10	0
Scarborough	11,000	10,200	800	6,410	2,961	8	0
Scunthorpe U	11,260	6,466	4,800	8,356	4,547	8	0
Southend U	12,753	10,102	2,651	7,708	3,699	11	1
Stockport Co	7,200	4,700	2,500	5,085	2,792	8	0
Torquay U	4,999	3,549	1,450	3,402	2,349	11	1
Wrexham	22,426	17,400	5,026	14,596	2,636	9	0
York C	14,109	11,050	3,059	9,135	2,613	10	0
Total:	276,215			185,390			

TRANSFER TRAIL
1988–89 Transfers involving First Division Clubs
(from May 1988 to May 1989)

May 1988
23 Cook, Paul A. – Wigan Ath to Norwich C
31 Maskell, Craig D. – Southampton to Huddersfield T

June 1988
13 Beasant, David – Wimbledon to Newcastle U
13 Bould, Stephen A. – Stoke C to Arsenal
27 Dreyer, John B. – Oxford U to Luton T
17 Hendrie, John G. – Bradford C to Newcastle U
 1 Leighton, James – Aberdeen to Manchester U
15 McCall, Stuart M. – Bradford C to Everton
 6 Mountfield, Derek N. – Everton to Aston Villa
17 Osman, Russell C. – Leicester C to Southampton
 1 Price, Christopher J. – Blackburn Rovers to Aston Villa
29 Ruddock, Neil – Tottenham H to Millwall
10 Sharpe, Lee S. – Torquay U to Manchester U
21 Stewart, Paul A. – Manchester C to Tottenham H
23 Thomas, Andrew M. – Newcastle U to Bradford C

Temporary transfer
13 Neal, Dean J. – Southend U to Queen's Park Rangers

July 1988
20 Barker, Simon – Blackburn Rovers to Queen's Park Rangers
19 Benstead, Graham M. – Norwich C to Sheffield U
15 Biggins, Wayne – Norwich C to Manchester C
27 Chamberlain, Alec F.R. – Everton to Luton T
 1 Dibble, Andrew – Luton T to Manchester C
 5 Drinkell, Kevin S. – Norwich C to Rangers FC
18 Gascoigne, Paul J. – Newcastle U to Tottenham H
 6 Gayle, Brian W. – Wimbledon to Manchester C
 6 Harper, Alan – Everton to Sheffield Wednesday
13 Hazel, Desmond I. – Sheffield Wednesday to Rotherham U
 7 Laws Brian – Middlesbrough to Nottingham F
26 McKnight, Allen – Celtic to West Ham U
28 Neill, Warren A. – Queen's Park Rangers to Portsmouth
13 Nevin, Patrick K.F. – Chelsea to Everton
12 Spearing, Anthony – Norwich C to Leicester C
19 Stevens, Michael G. – Everton to Rangers
 8 Tanner, Nicholas – Bristol Rovers to Liverpool
14 Thompson, Steven P. – Charlton Ath to Leicester C
27 Wegerle, Roy C. – Chelsea to Luton T

August 1988
12 Allen, Malcolm – Watford to Norwich C
26 Aspinall, Warren – Aston Villa to Portsmouth
16 Bond, Kevin J. – Southampton to AFC Bournemouth
 2 Chamberlain, Mark V. – Sheffield Wednesday to Portsmouth
 2 Cottee, Antony R. – West Ham U to Everton
26 Dawes, Ian R. – Queen's Park Rangers to Millwall
26 Garner, Andrew – Derby Co to Blackpool
 4 Gleghorn, Nigel W. – Ipswich T to Manchester C

2 Goddard, Paul – Newcastle U to Derby Co
17 Hebberd, Trevor N. – Oxford U to Derby Co
31 Hodge, Martin J. – Sheffield Wednesday to Leicester C
17 Hodge, Stephen B. – Tottenham H to Nottingham F
25 Hogg, Graeme J. – Manchester U to Portsmouth
25 Joseph, Roger – Brentford to Wimbledon
1 Kelly, David T. – Walsall to West Ham U
25 Lewis, Michael – Derby Co to Oxford U
4 Maclaren, Ross – Derby Co to Swindon T
3 McDonald, Neil R. – Newcastle U to Everton
19 McGuire, Douglas J. – Celtic to Coventry C
24 Norton, David W. – Aston Villa to Notts Co
24 Parks, Anthony – Tottenham H to Brentford
25 Pickering, Nicholas – Coventry C to Derby Co
25 Sayer, Andrew C. – Wimbledon to Fulham
26 Stein, Earl M.S. – Luton T to Queen's Park Rangers
1 Thorn, Andrew – Wimbledon to Newcastle U
31 Townsend, Andrew D. – Southampton to Norwich C
25 Wallington, Francis M. – Derby Co to Lincoln C
16 Wilkinson, Paul – Nottingham F to Watford
5 Williams, Steven C. – Arsenal to Luton T

Temporary transfers
25 Crichton, Paul A. – Nottingham F to Torquay U
26 Hodge, Martin J. – Sheffield Wednesday to Leicester C
24 Strain, John E. – West Ham U to Falkirk
11 Walsh, Gary – Manchester U to Airdrieonians
31 Walsh, Gary – Airdrieonians to Manchester U (Tr. back)
26 Wilmot, Rhys – Arsenal to Swansea C

September 1988
15 Hobson, Gordon – Southampton to Lincoln C
15 Jackson, Peter A. – Newcastle U to Bradford C
30 May, Lawrence C. – Sheffield Wednesday to Brighton & HA
28 Segers, Johannes C.A. – Nottingham F to Wimbledon
12 Turner, Christopher R. – Manchester U to Sheffield Wednesday
30 Varadi, Imre – Manchester C to Sheffield Wednesday

Temporary transfers
8 Byrne, David S. – Millwall to Cambridge U
29 Crichton, Paul A. – Nottingham F to Torquay U
30 Green, Ronald R. – Wimbledon to Shrewsbury T
8 Plummer, Calvin A. – Nottingham F to Plymouth Arg

October 1988
20 Angell, Brett – Derby Co to Stockport Co
20 Burrows, David – West Bromwich Albion to Liverpool
6 Cooper, Neale J. – Aston Villa to Rangers
21 Curle, Keith – Reading to Wimbledon
28 Donaghy, Malachy – Luton T to Manchester U
13 Miller, Paul R. – Charlton Ath to Watford
26 Pates, Colin G. – Chelsea to Charlton Ath
20 Plummer, Calvin A. – Nottingham F to Plymouth Arg
28 Saunders, Dean N. – Oxford U to Derby Co
14 Senior, Trevor – Middlesbrough to Reading
19 Tracey, Simon P. – Wimbledon to Sheffield U

Temporary transfers
13 Cobb, Gary E. – Luton T to Northampton T

20 Durnin, John – Liverpool to West Bromwich Albion
21 Hucker, Peter I. – Oxford U to Manchester U
 7 Kelly, Gary A. – Newcastle U to Blackpool
 6 Lane, Martin J. – Coventry C to Wrexham
13 Pates, Colin G. – Chelsea to Charlton Ath
21 Stowell, Michael – Everton to Port Vale
 3 Thomas, Martin R. – Newcastle U to Birmingham C

November 1988
 2 Barham, Mark – Huddersfield T to Middlesbrough
18 Caton, Thomas – Oxford U to Charlton Ath
 3 Crichton, Paul A. – Nottingham F to Peterborough U
 3 Davenport, Peter – Manchester U to Middlesbrough
17 Milne Ralph – Bristol C to Manchester U
15 O'Brien, Liam F. – Manchester U to Newcastle U
10 Stephenson, Paul – Newcastle U to Millwall
 4 Stuart, Mark R. – Charlton Ath to Plymouth Arg
 2 Thomas, Martin R. – Newcastle U to Birmingham C

Temporary transfers
13 Bradley, Russell – Nottingham F to Hereford U
14 Fensome, Andrew B. – Norwich C to Newcastle U
24 Gormley, Edward J. – Tottemham H to Chesterfield
14 Lormor, Anthony – Newcastle U to Norwich C
25 MacDonald, Kevin D. – Liverpool to Rangers
24 Miller, Alan J. – Arsenal to Plymouth Arg
19 Trotter, Michael – Middlesbrough to Doncaster Rovers

December 1988
14 Allinson, Ian J.R. – Luton T to Colchester U
 8 Brock, Kevin S. – Queen's Park Rangers to Newcastle U
31 Cornwell, John A. – Newcastle U to Swindon T
22 Flynn, Michael A. – Oldham Ath to Norwich C
16 Jackson, Darren – Newcastle U to Dundee U
23 Ranson, Raymond – Birmingham C to Newcastle U
 9 Robertson, John G. – Newcastle U to Heart of Midlothian
24 Sansom, Kenneth G. – Arsenal to Newcastle U
24 Thompson, Garry L. – Aston Villa to Watford

Temporary transfers
14 Cawler, Peter – Wimbledon to Fulham
 1 Clarke, Colin J. – Southampton to AFC Bournemouth
23 Guthrie, Peter J. – Tottenham H to Charlton Ath
 9 Harrison, Wayne – Liverpool to Crewe Alex
11 Jeffers, John J. – Liverpool to Port Vale
23 Jemson, Nigel B. – Nottingham F to Bolton W
 6 O'Donnell, James A. – Manchester U to Charlton Ath
30 Petterson, Andrew K. – Luton T to Swindon T
14 Stowell, Michael – Port Vale to Everton (Tr. back)
 7 Walford, Stephen J. – West Ham U to Gillingham
24 Ward, Anthony – Everton to Doncaster Rovers

January 1989
14 Beasant, David – Newcastle U to Chelsea
20 Beaumont, David A. – Dundee U to Luton T
13 Lane, Martin J. – Coventry C to Chester C
 4 Maguire, Gavin T. – Queen's Park Rangers to Portsmouth
12 Megson, Gary J. – Sheffield Wednesday to Manchester C
13 Ratcliffe, Simon – Norwich C to Brentford

13 Rostron, John W. – Watford to Sheffield Wednesday
27 Turner, Robert P. – Wimbledon to Bristol C
20 Wood, Darren T. – Chelsea to Sheffield Wednesday

Temporary transfers
14 Achampong, Kenneth – Fulham to West Ham U
11 Adams, Neil J. – Everton to Oldham Ath
16 Campbell, Kevin – Arsenal to Leyton Orient
26 Craig, Albert H. – Newcastle U to Northampton T
10 Holsgrove, Paul – Aldershot to Wimbledon
11 Moran, Paul – Tottenham H to Portsmouth
13 Pitcher, Darren E.J. – Charlton Ath to Galway U
12 Rice, Brian – Nottingham F to West Bromwich Albion
11 Ryan, Vaughan W. – Wimbledon to Sheffield U
19 Stimson, Mark – Tottenham H to Gillingham

February 1989
9 Bogie, Ian – Newcastle U to Preston N E
9 Brazil, Gary N. – Preston N E to Newcastle U
2 Callaghan, Nigel – Derby Co to Aston Villa
20 Clark, Martin J. – Clyde to Nottingham F
10 Durnin, John – Liverpool to Oxford U
3 Glover, Dean V. – Middlesbrough to Port Vale
2 Gray, Andrew A. – Aston Villa to Queen's Park Rangers
10 Manuel, William A.J. – Tottenham H to Gillingham
2 Ormondroyd, Ian – Bradford C to Aston Villa
23 Palmer, Carlton L. – West Bromwich Albion to Sheffield Wednesday
9 Reid, Peter – Everton to Queen's Park Rangers
13 Ruddock, Neil – Millwall to Southampton
2 Spackman, Nigel J. – Liverpool to Queen's Park Rangers
24 West, Colin – Sheffield Wednesday to West Bromwich Albion

Temporary transfers
23 Byrne, David S. – Millwall to Blackburn Rovers
9 Dolan, Eamonn J. – West Ham U to Bristol C
23 Gannon, John S. – Wimbledon to Sheffield U
15 Gormley, Edward J. – Tottenham H to Motherwell
16 Green, Ronald R. – Wimbledon to Manchester C
27 Hazel, Ian – Wimbledon to Bristol Rovers
1 Hucker, Peter I. – Oxford U to Manchester U
9 Hucker, Peter I. – Manchester U to Oxford U (Tr. back)
3 Jeffers, John – Port Vale to Liverpool (Tr. back)
2 Jones, Andrew M. – Charlton Ath to Port Vale
1 McAlister, Thomas G. – West Ham U to Colchester U
16 Mercer, William – Liverpool to Rotherham U
20 Miller, Alan J. – Plymouth Arg to Arsenal (Tr. back)
16 Ramage, Craig D. – Derby Co to Wigan Ath
9 Reeves, Alan – Norwich C to Gillingham
20 Tighe, Aaron P. – Luton T to Leicester C
2 Walsh, Colin D. – Charlton Ath to Peterborough U
23 Wilmot, Rhys J. – Arsenal to Plymouth Arg
3 Young, Richard A. – Southend U to Wimbledon

March 1989
14 Adams, Michael, R. – Leeds U to Southampton
23 Bennett, David – Coventry C to Sheffield Wednesday
16 Byrne, David S. – Millwall to Plymouth Arg
17 Campbell, David A. – Charlton Ath to Bradford C

94

9 Clarke, Colin J. – Southampton to Queen's Park Rangers
20 Coney, Dean H. – Queen's Park Rangers to Norwich C
23 Cooke, Richard E – AFC Bournemouth to Luton T
23 Green, Ronald R. – Wimbledon to Walsall
22 Horne, Barry – Portsmouth to Southampton
29 Houchen, Keith M. – Coventry C to Hibernian
23 Jeffers, John J. – Liverpool to Port Vale
23 McAvennie, Francis – Celtic to West Ham U
3 McGee, Paul – Colchester U to Wimbledon
21 Meade, Raphael J. – Dundee U to Luton T
24 Mercer, William – Liverpool to Rotherham U
14 Oldfield, David C. – Luton T to Manchester C
10 Payne, Lee J. – Newcastle U to Reading
23 Proctor, Mark G. – Sheffield Wednesday to Middlesbrough
23 Proudlock, Paul – Middlesbrough to Carlisle U
23 Sinton, Andrew – Brentford to Queen's Park Rangers
3 Sterland, Melvyn – Sheffield Wednesday to Rangers
23 Strachan, Gordon D. – Manchester U to Leeds U
22 Sweeney, Paul – Raith Rovers to Newcastle U
9 Tinnion, Brian – Newcastle U to Bradford C
3 Whitton, Stephen P. – Birmingham C to Sheffield Wednesday

Temporary transfers
21 Bradley, Russell – Nottingham F to Hereford U
15 Byrne, David S. – Blackburn Rovers to Millwall (Tr. back)
9 Campbell, David A. – Charlton Ath to Plymouth Arg
17 Campbell, David A. – Plymouth Arg to Charlton Ath (Tr. back)
16 Charles, Gary A. – Nottingham F to Leicester C
4 Dalton, Paul – Manchester U to Hartlepool U
9 Dearden, Kevin C. – Tottenham H to Cambridge U
23 Elliott, Matthew S. – Charlton Ath to Torquay U
23 Fairclough, Courtney H. – Tottenham H to Leeds U
23 Godden, Anthony L. – Birmingham C to Sheffield Wednesday
16 Gormley, Edward J. – Motherwell to Tottenham H (Tr. back)
22 Hamilton, Lindsay – Rangers to Charlton Ath
15 Jemson, Nigel B. – Nottingham F to Preston NE
21 Lamb, Alan – Nottingham F to Hereford U
22 Moncur, John F. – Tottenham H to Portsmouth
21 O'Donnell, James A. – Manchester U to Swindon T
17 Stowell, Michael – Everton to Wolverhampton W
3 Walford, Stephen J. – West Ham U to West Bromwich Albion
2 Wassall, Darren P. – Nottingham F to Bury

April 1989
21 Doyle, Maurice – Crewe Alex to Queen's Park Rangers
18 Elliott, Matthew S. – Charlton Ath to Torquay U
4 Fairclough, Courtney H. – Tottenham H to Leeds U

Temporary transfers
13 Hutchinson, Simon – Manchester U to Sheffield Wednesday
21 Stowell, Michael – Wolverhampton W to Everton (Tr. back)

May 1989
5 Dalton, Paul – Manchester U to Hartlepool U

Temporary transfers
2 Esqulant, Daniel J. – Arsenal to Charlton Ath
11 Hamilton, Lindsay – Charlton Ath to Rangers (Tr. back)
2 Jones, Andrew M. – Port Vale to Charlton Ath (Tr. back)

Merseyside United at Wembley

Merseyside had the FA Cup final it wanted and Liverpool achieved the victory the club had desperately sought once it decided to end the mourning for the Hillsborough tragedy, beating Everton 3–2 after extra time. Fittingly perhaps, on a hot humid emotionally charged afternoon, the game was as late stirring itself as the city had been in laying aside its grief. The period of extra time made the event memorable as a match, but the occasion was marred by pitch invasions which seem inevitable at grounds without fences.

For many, the FA Cup – if not the season itself – had ended at 3.06 p.m. on 15 April in Sheffield. Before that, Liverpool had started out on the road to Wembley in confident enough mood, winning 3–0 at Carlisle, while Everton needed a replay to despatch West Bromwich Albion. Liverpool then picked off Millwall at The Den at a time when the Londoners were in full flight. Yet again Everton had to take advantage of a second attempt before convincingly beating Plymouth 4–0. Hull proved a different proposition for Liverpool despite losing a goal to John Barnes after 15 minutes. In fact they recovered to lead 2–1 at the interval only for John Aldridge to strike early in the second half. Coincidentally Graeme Sharp's goal also came after a quarter of an hour, so ensuring Everton's win at Barnsley.

In the sixth round, Liverpool's class finally destroyed Brentford while Everton winkled out a goal against Wimbledon through Stuart McCall just on the hour to earn Merseyside places in the semi-final. But Everton's game with Norwich at White Hart Lane was overshadowed by the Hillsborough disaster. Again one goal was enough for them to qualify for a final that might not even have been played.

Liverpool probably found the return to competitive football more difficult than their experience against a disappointing Nottingham Forest, who were unable to recapture the free-flowing style that had epitomised their season. Liverpool won 3–1 and duly took their place against Everton at Wembley.

It took Liverpool just four minutes to strike after a finely weighted through ball from Steve Nicol which Steve McMahon curled into the path of John Aldridge, who happily erased the memory of his penalty miss at the same end a year earlier.

For the rest of normal time, Everton had the possession but their pedestrian approach rarely tested a complacent Liverpool, whose more direct thrusts always threatened danger. Then in the 58th minute, Everton brought on Stuart McCall for Paul Bracewell and the substitution transformed the Goodison Park side. It was appropriate that McCall should equalise in the dying seconds, snapping up a rebound when Bruce Grobbelaar failed to hold on to the ball.

Liverpool manager Kenny Dalglish wisely reshuffled the left side of his defence for extra time, bringing on Barry Venison for Steve Staunton and switching Nicol to left-back. Moreover with Ian Rush already on for the tiring Aldridge, Liverpool looked much better equipped to turn the game. Indeed Rush collected a flighted pass from Nicol, turned and drove in from seven yards with only six minutes of the extra period played. But Everton and McCall were not finished. The red-headed midfield player equalised six minutes later with a volley on the edge of the penalty area. Back came Liverpool and Rush, delightfully nudging a cross from Barnes with a flick of his head in the 105th minute, put the game beyond Everton.

McCall and Rush became the first substitutes to score twice in the final and Rush overhauled Dixie Dean's record of 19 goals in Merseyside derbies. A world-wide television audience of 500 million watched a game which produced ground receipts of a record £1.6 million.

Liverpool: Grobbelaar; Ablett, Staunton (Venison), Nicol, Whelan, Hansen, Beardsley, Aldridge (Rush), Houghton, Barnes, McMahon

Everton: Southall; McDonald, Van Den Hauwe, Ratcliffe, Watson, Bracewell (McCall), Nevin, Steven, Sharp, Cottee, Sheedy (Wilson)

Referee: J. Worrall (Warrington)

FA CUP 1988–89

First Round

Aldershot	1	Hayes	0
Altrincham	3	Lincoln C	2
Bath	2	Grays	0
Blackpool	2	Scunthorpe U	1
Bognor	2	Exeter C	1
Bolton W	0 3	Chesterfield	0 2
Brentford	2	Halesowen	0
Bristol C	3	Southend U	1
Bristol R	3	Fisher	0
Burnley	0	Chester C	2
Cardiff C	3	Hereford U	0
Dagenham	0	Sutton	4
Darlington	1	Notts Co	2
Doncaster R	0 2	Brandon	0 1
Enfield	1 2 1	Leyton Orient	1 2 0
Frickley	0	Northwich	2
Fulham	0	Colchester U	1
Gillingham	3 0	Peterborough U	3 1
Grimsby T	1	Wolverhampton W	0
Guisborough	0	Bury (at Middlesbrough)	1
Halifax T	1	York C	0
Hartlepool U	2	Wigan Ath	0
Huddersfield T	1 4	Rochdale	1 3
Kettering	2	Dartford	1
Mansfield T	1 1	Sheffield U	1 2
Newport Co	1	Maidstone U	2
Preston NE	1 0	Tranmere R	1 3
Reading	4	Hendon	2
Rotherham U	3	Barrow	1
Runcorn	2 3	Wrexham	2 2
Scarborough	2	Stockport Co	1
Southport	0	Port Vale	2
Stafford	2 2	Crewe Alex	2 3
Swansea C	3	Northampton T	1
Telford	1 1	Carlisle U	1 4
Torquay U	2 3	Farcham	2 2
Waterlooville	1	Aylesbury	4
Welling	3	Bromsgrove	0
Woking	1	Cambridge U	4
Yeovil	3	Merthyr	2

Second Round

Aldershot	1 0 2 0	Bristol C	1 0 2 1
Altrincham	0	Halifax T	3
Aylesbury	0	Sutton	1
Bath	0 2	Welling	0 3
Blackpool	3	Bury	0
Bognor	0	Cambridge U	1
Bolton W	1	Port Vale	2
Colchester U	2 3	Swansea C	2 1
Doncaster R	1	Sheffield U	3
Enfield	1	Cardiff C	4
Grimsby T	3	Rotherham U	2

97

Hartlepool U	1	Notts Co	0
Huddersfield T	1	Chester C	0
Kettering	2	Bristol R	1
Northwich	1	Tranmere R	2
Peterborough U	0 2	Brentford	0 3
Reading	1 2	Maidstone U	1 1
Runcorn	0	Crewe Alex	3
Scarborough	0	Carlisle U	1
Yeovil	1 0	Torquay U	1 1

Third Round

Barnsley	4	Chelsea	0
Birmingham C	0	Wimbledon	1
Blackpool	0	Bournemouth	1
Bradford C	1	Tottenham H	0
Brighton & HA	1	Leeds U	2
Cardiff C	1	Hull C	2
Carlisle U	0	Liverpool	3
Charlton Ath	2	Oldham Ath	1
Crewe Alex	2	Aston Villa	3
Derby Co	1 2	Southampton	1 1
Hartlepool U	1	Bristol C	0
Huddersfield T	0	Sheffield U	1
Kettering	1 3	Halifax T	1 2
Manchester C	1	Leicester C	0
Manchester U	0 2 3	QPR	0 2 0
Middlesbrough	1	Grimsby T	2
Millwall	3	Luton T	2
Newcastle U	0 2 0 0	Watford	0 2 0 1
Nottingham F	3	Ipswich T	0
Plymouth Arg	2	Cambridge U	0
Port Vale	1	Norwich C	3
Portsmouth	1 0	Swindon T	1 2
Sheffield W	5	Torquay U	1
Shrewsbury T	0	Colchester U	3
Stoke C	1	Crystal Palace	0
Sunderland	1 0	Oxford U	1 2
Sutton	2	Coventry C	1
Tranmere R	1 1	Reading	1 2
Walsall	1 0	Brentford	1 1
Welling	0	Blackburn R	1
WBA	1 0	Everton	1 1
West Ham U	2 1	Arsenal	2 0

Fourth Round

Aston Villa	0	Wimbledon	1
Blackburn R	2	Sheffield W	1
Bradford C	1	Hull C	2
Brentford	3	Manchester C	1
Charlton Ath	2	Kettering	1
Grimsby T	1 2	Reading	1 1
Hartlepool U	1 2	Bournemouth	1 5
Manchester U	4	Oxford U	0
Millwall	0	Liverpool	2
Norwich C	8	Sutton	0
Nottingham F	2	Leeds U	0

Plymouth Arg	1 0	Everton	1 4
Sheffield U	3 2	Colchester U	3 0
Stoke C	3 1	Barnsley	3 2
Swindon T	0 0	West Ham U	0 1
Watford	2	Derby Co	1

Fifth Round

Barnsley	0	Everton	1
Blackburn R	0	Brentford	2
Bournemouth	1 0	Manchester U	1 1
Charlton Ath	0	West Ham U	1
Hull C	2	Liverpool	3
Norwich C	3	Sheffield U	2
Watford	0	Nottingham F	3
Wimbledon	3	Grimsby T	1

Sixth Round

Everton	1	Wimbledon	0
Liverpool	4	Brentford	0
Manchester U	0	Nottingham F	1
West Ham U	0 1	Norwich C	0 3

Semi-finals

Everton	1	Norwich C	0
(at White Hart Lane)			
Liverpool	0 3	Nottingham F	0 1
(game abandoned at Hillsborough; rescheduled at Old Trafford)			

Final at Wembley, 20 May 1989, att. 82,800
Liverpool (1) 3 (*Aldridge, Rush 2*), Everton (0) 2 (*McCall 2*) (*aet; 90 mins 1–1*).

PAST FA CUP FINALS

Details of some goalscorers are not available for the early years

1872	The Wanderers	1	Royal Engineers	0
	Betts		
1873	The Wanderers	2	Oxford University	0
	Kinnaird, Wollaston		
1874	Oxford University	2	Royal Engineers	0
	Mackarness, Patton		
1875	Royal Engineers	1	Old Etonians	1*
	Unknown		*Bonsor*
	Royal Engineers	2	Old Etonians	0
	Scorers in replay: Renny-Tailyour, Stafford		
1876	The Wanderers	1	Old Etonians	1*
	Edwards		*Bonsor*
	The Wanderers	3	Old Etonians	0
	Wollaston, Hughes 2		
1877	The Wanderers	2	Oxford University	1*
	Kenrick, Heron		*Kinnaird (og)*
1878	The Wanderers	3	Royal Engineers	1
	Kenrick 2, unknown		*Unknown*

1879	Old Etonians 1	Clapham Rovers 0	
	Clerke		
1880	Clapham Rovers 1	Oxford University 0	
	Lloyd-Jones		
1881	Old Carthusians................. 3	Old Etonians 0	
	Page, Wynard, Tod		
1882	Old Etonians 1	Blackburn Rovers 0	
	Anderson		
1883	Blackburn Olympic 2	Old Etonians 1*	
	Costley, Mathews	*Goodhart*	
1884	Blackburn Rovers 2	Queen's Park 1	
	Forrest, Brown	*Christie*	
1885	Blackburn Rovers 2	Queen's Park 0	
	Forrest, Brown		
1886	Blackburn Rovers 0	West Bromwich Albion 0	
	Blackburn Rovers 2	West Bromwich Albion 0	
	Brown, Sowerbutts		
1887	Aston Villa........................ 2	West Bromwich Albion 0	
	Hunter, Hodgetts		
1888	West Bromwich Albion 2	Preston NE...................... 1	
	Woodall, Bayliss	*Goodall*	
1889	Preston NE........................ 3	Wolverhampton W............. 0	
	Ross, Dewhurst, Thomson		
1890	Blackburn Rovers 6	Sheffield Wednesday 1	
	Dewar, Lofthouse,	*Bennett*	
	John Southworth, Townley 3		
1891	Blackburn Rovers 3	Notts Co 1	
	Dewar, John Southworth	*Oswald*	
	Townley		
1892	West Bromwich Albion 3	Aston Villa....................... 0	
	Reynolds, Nicholls, Geddes		
1893	Wolverhampton W.............. 1	Everton 0	
	Allen		
1894	Notts Co 4	Bolton W 1	
	Watson, Logan 3	*Cassidy*	
1895	Aston Villa........................ 1	West Bromwich Albion 0	
	Chatt		
1896	Sheffield Wednesday 2	Wolverhampton W............. 1	
	Spiksley	*Black*	
1897	Aston Villa........................ 3	Everton 2	
	Crabtree, Campell, Weldon	*Boyle, Bell*	
1898	Nottingham F..................... 3	Derby Co 1	
	McPherson, Capes 2	*Bloomer*	
1899	Sheffield U 4	Derby Co 1	
	Bennett, Beers, Almond, Priest	*Boag*	
1900	Bury................................ 4	Southampton 0	
	Wood, McLuckie 2, Plant		
1901	Tottenham H 2	Sheffield U 2	
	Brown	*Bennett, Priest*	
	Tottenham H 3	Sheffield U 1	
	Cameron, Smith, Brown	*Priest*	
1902	Sheffield U 1	Southampton 1	
	Common	*Wood*	
	Sheffield U 2	Southampton 1	
	Hedley, Barnes	*Brown*	
1903	Bury................................ 6	Derby Co 0	
	Wood, Sagar, Ross, Plant,		
	Leeming 2		
1904	Manchester C..................... 1	Bolton W 0	
	Meredith		

1905	Aston Villa	2	Newcastle U	0
	Hampton			
1906	Everton	1	Newcastle U	0
	Young			
1907	Sheffield Wednesday	2	Everton	1
	Stewart, Simpson		*Sharp*	
1908	Wolverhampton W	3	Newcastle U	1
	Hunt, Harrison, Hedley		*Howie*	
1909	Manchester U	1	Bristol C	0
	A. Turnbull			
1910	Newcastle U	1	Barnsley	1
	Rutherford		*Tuffnell*	
	Newcastle U	2	Barnsley	0
	Shepherd (1 pen)			
1911	Bradford C	0	Newcastle U	0
	Bradford C	1	Newcastle U	0
	Spiers			
1912	Barnsley	0	West Bromwich Albion	0
	Barnsley	1	West Bromwich Albion	0*
	Tuffnell			
1913	Aston Villa	1	Sunderland	0
	Barber			
1914	Burnley	1	Liverpool	0
	Freeman			
1915	Sheffield U	3	Chelsea	0
	Simmons, Fazackerley, Kitchen			
1920	Aston Villa	1	Huddersfield T	0*
	Kirton			
1921	Tottenham H	1	Wolverhampton W	0
	Dimmock			
1922	Huddersfield T	1	Preston NE	0
	Smith (pen)			
1923	Bolton W	2	West Ham U	0
	Jack, J.R. Smith			
1924	Newcastle U	2	Aston Villa	0
	Harris, Seymour			
1925	Sheffield U	1	Cardiff C	0
	Tunstall			
1926	Bolton W	1	Manchester C	0
	Jack			
1927	Cardiff C	1	Arsenal	0
	Ferguson			
1928	Blackburn Rovers	3	Huddersfield T	1
	Roscamp 2, McLean		*A. Jackson*	
1929	Bolton W	2	Portsmouth	0
	Butler, Blackmore			
1930	Arsenal	2	Huddersfield Town	0
	Lambert, James			
1931	West Bromwich Albion	2	Birmingham C	1
	W.G. Richardson		*Bradford*	
1932	Newcastle U	2	Arsenal	1
	Allen		*John*	
1933	Everton	3	Manchester C	0
	Dunn, Dean, Stein			
1934	Manchester C	2	Portsmouth	1
	Tilson		*Rutherford*	
1935	Sheffield Wednesday	4	West Bromwich Albion	2
	Hooper, Palethorpe, Rimmer 2		*Sandford, Boyes*	
1936	Arsenal	1	Sheffield U	0
	Drake			

1937	Sunderland 3	Preston NE..................1
	Carter, Gurney, Burbanks	*F. O'Donnell*
1938	Preston NE..................1	Huddersfield T 0*
	Mutch (pen)	
1939	Portsmouth..................4	Wolverhampton W............1
	Anderson, Barlow, Parker 2	*Dorsett*
1946	Derby Co 4	Charlton Ath 1*
	H. Turner (og), Stamps 2,	*H. Turner*
	Doherty	
1947	Charlton Ath 1	Burnley......................0*
	Duffy	
1948	Manchester U 4	Blackpool....................2
	Anderson, Rowley 2, Pearson	*Shimwell (pen), Mortensen*
1949	Wolverhampton W............3	Leicester C 1
	Smyth, Pye 2	*Griffiths*
1950	Arsenal.......................2	Liverpool 0
	Lewis	
1951	Newcastle....................2	Blackpool....................0
	Milburn	
1952	Newcastle....................1	Arsenal......................0
	G. Robledo	
1953	Blackpool.....................4	Bolton W 3
	Mortensen 3, Perry	*Bell, Moir, Lofthouse*
1954	West Bromwich Albion 3	Preston NE..................2
	Griffin, Allen 2	*Wayman, Morrison*
1955	Newcastle U 3	Manchester C..................1
	Milburn, Hannah, Mitchell	*Johnstone*
1956	Manchester C..................3	Birmingham C..................1
	Johnstone, Hayes, Dyson	*Kinsey*
1957	Aston Villa.....................2	Manchester U 1
	McParland	*T. Taylor*
1958	Bolton W 2	Manchester U 0
	Lofthouse	
1959	Nottingham F..................2	Luton T 1
	Dwight, Wilson	*Pacey*
1960	Wolverhampton W............3	Blackburn Rovers 0
	Deeley 2, McGrath (og)	
1961	Tottenham H 2	Leicester C 0
	Smith, Dyson	
1962	Tottenham H 3	Burnley......................1
	Blanchflower (pen), Smith,	*Robson*
	Greaves	
1963	Manchester U 3	Leicester C 1
	Herd 2, Law	*Keyworth*
1964	West Ham U 3	Preston N E..................2
	Boyce, Hurst, Sissons	*Dawson, Holden*
1965	Liverpool 2	Leeds U......................1*
	Hunt, St John	*Bremner*
1966	Everton.......................3	Sheffield Wednesday 2
	Trebilcock 2, Temple	*McCalliog, Ford*
1967	Tottenham H 2	Chelsea......................1
	Robertson, Saul	*Tambling*
1968	West Bromwich Albion 1	Everton 0*
	Astle	
1969	Manchester C..................1	Leicester C 0
	Young	
1970	Chelsea.......................2	Leeds U......................2*
	Houseman, Hutchinson	*Charlton, Jones*
	Chelsea.......................2	Leeds U......................1*
	Webb, Osgood	*Jones*

1971	Arsenal	2	Liverpool	1*
	Kelly, George		*Heighway*	
1972	Leeds U	1	Arsenal	0
	Clarke			
1973	Sunderland	1	Leeds U	0
	Porterfield			
1974	Liverpool	3	Newcastle U	0
	Keegan 2, Heighway			
1975	West Ham U	2	Fulham	0
	A. Taylor			
1976	Southampton	1	Manchester U	0
	Stokes			
1977	Manchester U	2	Liverpool	1
	Pearson, J. Greenhoff		*Case*	
1978	Ipswich T	1	Arsenal	0
	Osborne			
1979	Arsenal	3	Manchester U	2
	Talbot, Stapleton, Sunderland		*McQueen, McIlroy*	
1980	West Ham U	1	Arsenal	0
	Brooking			
1981	Tottenham H	1	Manchester C	1*
	Hutchison (og)		*Hutchison*	
	Tottenham H	3	Manchester C	2
	Crooks, Villa 2		*Mackenzie, Reeves (pen)*	
1982	Tottenham H	1	QPR	1*
	Hoddle		*Fenwick*	
	Tottenham H	1	QPR	0
	Hoddle (pen)			
1983	Manchester U	2	Brighton & HA	2*
	Stapleton, Wilkins		*Smith, Stevens*	
	Manchester U	4	Brighton & HA	0
	Robson 2, Whiteside, Muhren (pen)			
1984	Everton	2	Watford	0
	Sharp, Gray			
1985	Manchester U	1	Everton	0*
	Whiteside			
1986	Liverpool	3	Everton	1
	Rush 2, Johnston		*Lineker*	
1987	Coventry C	3	Tottenham H	2*
	Bennett, Houchen, Mabbutt(og)		*C. Allen, Kilcline (og)*	
1988	Wimbledon	1	Liverpool	0
	Sanchez			

After extra time

103

FA CUP WINNERS SINCE 1871

Aston Villa	7	Barnsley	1
Tottenham Hotspur	7	Blackburn Olympic	1
Blackburn Rovers	6	Blackpool	1
Manchester United	6	Bradford City	1
Newcastle United	6	Burnley	1
Arsenal	5	Cardiff City	1
Wanderers	5	Charlton Athletic	1
West Bromwich Albion	5	Chelsea	1
Bolton Wanderers	4	Clapham Rovers	1
Everton	4	Coventry City	1
Liverpool	4	Leeds United	1
Manchester City	4	Derby County	1
Sheffield United	4	Huddersfield Town	1
Wolverhampton Wanderers	4	Ipswich Town	1
Sheffield Wednesday	3	Notts County	1
West Ham United	3	Old Carthusians	1
Bury	2	Oxford University	1
Nottingham Forest	2	Portsmouth	1
Old Etonians	2	Royal Engineers	1
Preston North End	2	Southampton	1
Sunderland	2	Wimbledon	1

APPEARANCES IN FA CUP FINAL

Arsenal	11	Chelsea	3
Everton	11	Southampton	3
Newcastle United	11	Portsmouth	3
Manchester United	10	Sunderland	3
West Bromwich Albion	10	Barnsley	2
Aston Villa	9	Birmingham City	2
Liverpool	9	Cardiff City	2
Blackburn Rovers	8	Bury	2
Manchester City	8	Charlton Athletic	2
Tottenham Hotspur	8	Clapham Rovers	2
Wolverhampton Wanderers	8	Nottingham Forest	2
Bolton Wanderers	7	Notts County	2
Preston North End	7	Queen's Park (Glasgow)	2
Old Etonians	6	Blackburn Olympic	1
Sheffield United	6	Bradford City	1
Huddersfield Town	5	Brighton & Hove Albion	1
Sheffield Wednesday	5	Bristol City	1
Wanderers	5	Coventry City	1
Derby Country	4	Fulham	1
Leeds United	4	Ipswich Town	1
Leicester City	4	Luton Town	1
Oxford University	4	Old Carthusians	1
Royal Engineers	4	Queen's Park Rangers	1
West Ham United	4	Watford	1
Blackpool	3	Wimbledon	1
Burnley	3		

LITTLEWOODS CHALLENGE CUP 1988–89
Forest's second half fire sweeps Luton aside

For the second year in succession the holders of the Cup were beaten by the challengers, when Nottingham Forest recovered from being behind at half-time to overhaul Luton Town 3–1, in a final of thoughtful, entertaining football.

Both teams had problems on the way, though Luton had slightly more to contend with than Forest who began by taking ten goals off Chester City without reply: six at home, four away. Meanwhile Luton found themselves held at Kenilworth Road in a 1–1 draw by Fourth Division Burnley, before scoring the only goal in the second leg at Turf Moor.

Luton gave a far more impressive performance at Leeds in the third round, winning by two clear goals, while Forest just edged out Coventry 3–2 at the City Ground. Then in the fourth round Forest were held to a goalless draw at Leicester in contrast to Luton who beat Manchester City 3–1 at home.

Leicester caused Forest a few problems at the City Ground in the replay before going down 2–1, but they displayed their most fluent form in the quarter-final with Queen's Park Rangers. Lee Chapman scored four times in Forest's 5–2 win. However it was at this stage that Luton stuttered against Southampton. Though Ricky Hill opened the scoring for Luton in the 71st minute, Glenn Cockerill earned the Saints a replay with the equaliser eight minutes later, leaving the Hatters with a tough task at The Dell. There, Luton scraped through after extra time by the odd goal in three to earn the right to meet West Ham in the semi-final.

Forest's opponents were Third Division Bristol City, who proved more difficult than anticipated. Only an own goal at the City Ground saved Forest from the embarrassment of losing in a 1–1 draw, while at Ashton Gate the Third Division side restricted Forest to a single goal in driving rain.

In contrast, Luton moved into the final without trouble following up their 3–0 first leg win at Upton Park with two more goals without reply at home. And it must be said that at Wembley they deserved their first half lead from Mick Harford's headed goal after 35 minutes.

Chapman had previously had a goal disallowed for offside – a marginal decision as it happened – but it was an incident involving the Forest striker and Luton goalkeeper Les Sealey which might have sown the seeds of trouble later on. Sealey managed to gather the ball after a scramble in front of his goal while Chapman tried to winkle it from his grasp. The goalkeeper reacted angrily and had to be restrained.

After the interval, probably following a pep talk from Brian Clough, Forest played with more urgency, but it was a reckless dash from goal by Sealey ending in Steve Hodge being up-ended in the penalty area that turned the game in the 54th minute.

Clough junior tucked the spot-kick away nicely, though there was no outward reaction from his father on the bench. But it was largely one-way traffic from here on with the static Luton rearguard under constant pressure.

Tommy Gaynor on the right wing crossed for Neil Webb to score from ten yards with Luton half-heartedly appealing for offside after 68 minutes. The winger varied his approach eight minutes later squaring the ball across the penalty box for Nigel Clough to sweep the ball in from 16 yards.

Luton Town: Sealey; Breacker, Grimes (McDonough), Preece, Foster,

Beaumont, Wilson, Wegerle, Harford, Hill, Black
Nottingham Forest: Sutton; Laws, Pearce, Walker, Wilson, Hodge, Gaynor, Webb, Clough, Chapman, Parker
Referee: R. Milford (Bristol). Att: 76,130

LITTLEWOODS CHALLENGE CUP 1988–89

First round (*2 legs*)

Bolton W	1 1	Chester C	0 3
Bournemouth	1 0	Bristol R	0 0
Bristol C	1 1	Exeter C	0 0
Bury	2 2*	Wrexham	1 2
Cambridge U	1 1	Gillingham	2 3
Cardiff C	0 2	Swansea C	1 0
Carlisle U	1 0	Blackpool	1 3
Colchester U	0 0	Northampton T	0 5
Crewe Alex	1 1	Lincoln C	1 2
Doncaster R	1 0	Darlington	1 2
Fulham	2 0	Brentford	2 1
Grimsby T	0 0	Rotherham U	1 1
Hartlepool U	2 0	Sheffield U	2 2*
Hereford U	0 2	Plymouth Arg	3 3
Leyton Orient	2 0	Aldershot	0 0
Notts Co	5 0	Mansfield T	0 1
Port Vale	3 1	Chesterfield	2 1
Rochdale	3 1	Burnley	3 2
Scarborough	1 2**	Halifax T	1 2
Scunthorpe U	3 2*	Huddersfield T	2 2
Shrewsbury T	2 0	Walsall	2 3
Southend U	2 1	Brighton & HA	0 0
Stockport Co	0 1	Tranmere R	1 1
Torquay U	0 1	Reading	1 3
WBA	0 2	Peterborough U	3 0
Wigan Ath	0 0	Preston NE	0 1
Wolverhampton W	3 0	Birmingham C	2 1**
York C	0 0	Sunderland	0 4

Second Round (*2 legs*)

Barnsley	0 1	Wimbledon	2 0
Birmingham C	0 0	Aston Villa	2 5
Blackburn R	3 3	Brentford	1 4
Blackpool	2 1**	Sheffield W	0 3
Bournemouth	0 1	Coventry C	4 3
Darlington	2 0	Oldham Ath	0 4*
Derby Co	1 2	Southend U	0 1
Everton	3 2	Bury	0 2
Hull C	1 0	Arsenal	2 3
Leicester C	4 2	Watford	1 2
Leyton Orient	1 2†	Stoke C	2 1

Lincoln C	1 1	Southampton	1 3
Liverpool	1 3	Walsall	0 1
Luton T	1 1	Burnley	1 0
Manchester C	1 6	Plymouth Arg	0 3
Middlesbrough	0 0	Tranmere R	0 1
Millwall	3 3	Gilingham	0 1
Northampton T	1 1	Charlton Ath	1 2
Norwich C	2 3	Preston NE	0 0
Nottingham F	6 4	Chester C	0 0
Notts Co	1 1	Tottenham H	1 2
Oxford U	2 0	Bristol C	4 2
Peterborough	1 1	Leeds U	2 3
Port Vale	1 0	Ipswich T	0 3
Portsmouth	2 1	Scarborough	2 3
QPR	3 4	Cardiff C	0 1
Reading	1 1	Bradford C	1 2*
Rotherham U	0 0	Manchester U	1 5
Scunthorpe U	4 2	Chelsea	1 2
Sheffield U	3 0	Newcastle U	0 2
Sunderland	0 1	West Ham U	3 2
Swindon T	1 0	Crystal Palace	2 2

Third Round

Aston Villa	3	Millwall	1
Bradford C	1 1	Scunthorpe U	0 1
Bristol C	4	Crystal Palace	1
Everton	2 1	Oldham Ath	0 1
Ipswich T	2	Leyton Orient	0
Leeds U	0	Luton T	2
Leicester C	2	Norwich C	0
Liverpool	2 0* 1	Arsenal	1 0 1
Manchester C	4	Sheffield U	2
Nottingham F	3	Coventry C	2
QPR	2	Charlton Ath	1
Scarborough	0 2	Southampton	1 2
Tottenham H	2* 0	Blackburn R	1 0
Tranmere R	1	Blackpool	0
West Ham U	5	Derby Co	0
Wimbledon	2	Manchester U	1

Fourth Round

Aston Villa	6	Ipswich T	2
Bradford C	3	Everton	1
Bristol	1	Tranmere R	0
Leicester C	1 0	Nottingham F	2 0
Luton T	3	Manchester C	1
QPR	1 0	Wimbledon	0 0
Southampton	2	Tottenham H	1
West Ham U	4	Liverpool	1

Fifth Round

Bradford C	0	Bristol C	1
Luton T	2* 1	Southampton	1 1
Nottingham F	5	QPR	2
West Ham U	2	Aston Villa	1

Semi-finals(*2 legs*)

Nottingham F	1 1	Bristol C	1 0
West Ham U	0 0	Luton T	3 2

Final at Wembley, 9 April 1989, att. 76,130
Nottingham F (0)3 (*Clough 2 (1 pen), Webb*), Luton T (1)1 (*Harford*)

*After extra time   †Won on penalties   **Won on away goals

PAST LEAGUE CUP FINALS

Played as two legs up to 1966

1961	Rotherham U	2	Aston Villa	0
	Webster, Kirkman			
	Aston Villa	3	Rotherham U	0*
	O'Neill, Burrows, McParland			
1962	Rochdale	0	Norwich C	3
			Lythgoe 2, Punton	
	Norwich C	1	Rochdale	0
	Hill			
1963	Birmingham C	3	Aston Villa	1
	Leek 2, Bloomfield		*Thomson*	
	Aston Villa	0	Birmingham C	0
1964	Stoke C	1	Leicester C	1
	Bebbington		*Gibson*	
	Leicester C	3	Stoke C	2
	Stringfellow, Gibson, Riley		*Viollet, Kinnell*	
1965	Chelsea	3	Leicester C	2
	Tambling, Venables (pen), McCreadie		*Appleton, Goodfellow*	
	Leicester C	0	Chelsea	0
1966	West Ham U	2	WBA	1
	Moore, Byrne		*Astle*	
	WBA	4	West Ham U	1
	Kaye, Brown, Clark, Williams		*Peters*	
1967	QPR	3	WBA	2
	Morgan R., Marsh, Lazarus		*Clark C.*	
1968	Leeds U	1	Arsenal	0
	Cooper			
1969	Swindon T	3	Arsenal	1
	Smart, Rogers 2		*Gould*	
1970	Manchester C	2	WBA	1
	Doyle, Pardoe		*Astle*	
1971	Tottenham Hotspur	2	Aston Villa	0
	Chivers			
1972	Chelsea	1	Stoke C	2
	Osgood		*Conroy, Eastham*	

1973	Tottenham Hotspur	1	Norwich C	0
	Coates			
1974	Wolverhampton W	2	Manchester C	1
	Hibbitt, Richards		Bell	
1975	Aston Villa	1	Norwich C	0
	Graydon			
1976	Manchester C	2	Newcastle U	1
	Barnes, Tueart		Gowling	
1977	Aston Villa	0	Everton	0
Replay	Aston Villa	1	Everton	1*
	Kenyon (og)		Latchford	
Replay	Aston Villa	3	Everton	2*
	Little 2, Nicholl		Latchford, Lyons	
1978	Nottingham F	0	Liverpool	0*
Replay	Nottingham F	1	Liverpool	0
	Robertson (pen)			
1979	Nottingham F	3	Southampton	2
	Birtles 2, Woodcock		Peach, Holmes	
1980	Wolverhampton W	1	Nottingham F	0
	Gray			
1981	Liverpool	1	West Ham U	1*
	Kennedy, A		Stewart (pen)	
Replay	Liverpool	2	West Ham U	1
	Dalglish, Hansen		Goddard	
1982	Liverpool	3	Tottenham	1*
	Whelan 2, Rush		Archibald	
1983	Liverpool	2	Manchester U	1*
	Kennedy, Whelan		Whiteside	
1984	Liverpool	0	Everton	0*
Replay	Liverpool	1	Everton	0
	Souness			
1985	Norwich C	1	Sunderland	0
	Chisholm (og)			
1986	Oxford U	3	QPR	0
	Hebberd, Houghton, Charles			
1987	Arsenal	2	Liverpool	1
	Nicholas		Rush	
1988	Luton T	3	Arsenal	2
	Stein, B. 2, Wilson		Hayes, Smith	

*After extra time

SIMOD CUP 1988-89

(formerly Full Members' Cup)

Forty of 44 eligible members from Divisions One and Two entered the competition.
Eight of these were seeded through to the third round by virtue of last season's final
positions in the League. Unfortunately for them, Reading's relegation to the Third
Division meant they were unable to defend their title. Seeded: Coventry C, Everton,
Luton T, Newcastle U, Nottingham F, QPR, Sheffield W, Wimbledon.

First Round
Aston Villa 6, Birmingham C 0
Blackburn R 3, Manchester C 2*
Bradford C 3, Brighton & HA 1
Charlton Ath 9, Sunderland 1
Chelsea 6, Plymouth Arg 2
Crystal Palace 4, Walsall 2
Derby C 1, Bournemouth 0
Leeds U 3, Shrewsbury T 1
Middlesbrough 1, Oldham Ath 0
Millwall 1, Barnsley 1*†
Norwich C 2, Swindon T 1
Oxford U 2, Ipswich T 3
Portsmouth 2, Hull C 1
Southampton 3, Stoke C 0
Watford 2, Leicester C 0*
West Ham U 5, WBA 2

Second Round
Blackburn R 2, Sunderland 1
Bradford C 2, Chelsea 3
Derby Co 2, Aston Villa 1
Ipswich T 1, Norwich C 0
Middlesbrough 2, Portsmouth 1
Millwall 2, Leeds U 0
Southampton 1, Crystal Palace 2
Watford 1, West Ham U 1*†

Third Round
Chelsea 1, Nottingham F 4*
Crystal Palace 4, Luton T 1
Everton 2, Millwall 0
Ipswich T 1, Blackburn R 0
Middlesbrough 1, Coventry C 0
Sheffield W 0, QPR 1*
Watford 2, Newcastle U 1
Wimbledon 0, Derby Co 0*

Quarter-finals
Ipswich T 1, Nottingham F 3
Middlesbrough 2, Crystal Palace 3
Watford 1, QPR 1*†
Wimbledon 1, Everton 2

Semi-finals
Everton 1, QPR 0
Nottingham F 3, Crystal Palace 1

Final at Wembley 30 April 1989, att. 46,604
Nottingham F (1) 4 *(Parker 2, Chapman 2)* Everton (1) 3 *aet (Cottee 2, Sharp)*

*After extra time   †Won on penalties

Season	Venue	Winners	Runners-up	Score
1985–86	Wembley	Chelsea	Manchester C	5–4
1986–87	Wembley	Blackburn R	Charlton Ath	1–0

Simod Cup

1987–88	Wembley	Reading	Luton T	4–1

Associate Members' Cup

Season	Venue	Winners	Runners-up	Score
1981–82[1]	Grimsby	Grimsby T	Wimbledon	3–2
1982–83[2]	Lincoln	Millwall	Lincoln C	3–2
1983–84	Hull	Bournemouth	Hull C	2–1
1984–85[3]	Wembley	Wigan Ath	Brentford	3–1
1985–86[3]	Wembley	Bristol C	Bolton W	3–0
1986–87[3]	Wembley	Mansfield T	Bristol C	1–1*
		Mansfield won 6–5 on penalties		
1987–88[4]	Wembley	Wolverhampton Wanderers	Burnley	2–0

[1] *Known as Football League Group Cup* *After extra time
[2] *Football League Trophy* [3] *Freight Rover Trophy* [4] *Sherpa Van Trophy*

SHERPA VAN TROPHY 1988–89

(formerly Freight Rover Trophy)

In the preliminary round, the teams were divided into 16 groups of three. The top two teams in each group qualified for the First Round, the team finishing first in the group being drawn at home. Teams in italics qualified.

Northern Area

Preliminary Round

Bury 1, Bolton W 0
Bolton W 1, Preston NE 0
Preston NE 4, Bury 0

Wigan Ath 1, *Blackpool* 2
Blackpool 2 Rochdale 0
Rochdale 0, *Wigan Ath* 2

Tranmere R 2, Stockport Co 0
Stockport Co 1, *Crewe Alex* 1
Crewe Alex 1, *Tranmere R* 1

Chester C 1, *Wrexham* 2
Wrexham 1, *Sheffield U* 1
Sheffield U 2, Chester C 2

York C 0, *Burnley* 2
Burnley 3, Hartlepool U 0
Hartlepool U 0, *York C* 2

Scunthorpe U 1, *Halifax T* 2
Halifax T 1, *Huddersfield T* 0
Huddersfield T 1, Scunthorpe U 0

Southern Area

Fulham 0, *Brentford* 2
Brentford 2, *Gillingham* 0
Gillingham 2, Fulham 1

Leyton Orient 1, *Reading* 1
Reading 5, Aldershot 2
Aldershot 1, *Leyton Orient* 3

Cardiff C 2, Swansea C 0
Swansea C 1, *Torquay U* 0
Torquay U 3, *Cardiff C* 1

Bristol R 1, *Bristol C* 0
Bristol C 2, Exeter C 0
Exeter C 1, *Bristol R* 1

Northampton T 1, *Cambridge U* 1
Cambridge U 2, Peterborough U 2
Peterborough U 0, *Northampton T* 2

Southend U 2, Lincoln C 1
Lincoln C 1, *Colchester U* 2
Colchester U 2, *Southend U* 1

Doncaster R 1, *Grimsby T* 1
Grimsby T 1, *Rotherham U* 0
Rotherham U 2, Doncaster R 1

Darlington 3, Carlisle U 2
Carlisle U 1, *Scarborough* 1
Scarborough 4, *Darlington* 0

Port Vale 1, *Hereford U* 1
Hereford U 2, *Wolverhampton W* 2
Wolverhampton W 5, Port Vale 1

Mansfield T 1, *Notts Co* 1
Notts Co 1, *Chesterfield* 1
Chesterfield 2, Mansfield T 1

First Round
Blackpool 4, Rotherham U 3
Burnley 1, Crewe Alex 1*†
Grimsby T 1, Huddersfield T 3
Halifax T 3, Darlington 0
Preston NE 0, Bolton W 1
Scarborough 3, York C 1
Tranmere R 0, Wigan Ath 1
Wrexham 2, Sheffield U 1

Bristol R 2, Cardiff C 1
Brentford 2, Notts Co 0
Chesterfield 4, Cambridge U 2
Colchester U 3, Leyton Orient 1
Northampton T 2, Southend U 1*
Reading 2, Hereford U 3
Torquay U 3, Gillingham 0
Wolverhampton W 3, Bristol C 0

Quarter-finals
Bolton W 3, Wrexham 1*
Halifax T 0, Blackpool 2
Huddersfield T 1, Scarborough 2
Wigan Ath 0, Crewe Alex 1

Bristol R 0, Torquay U 1
Chesterfield 0, Brentford 1
Colchester U 0, Hereford U 1
Wolverhampton W 3, Northampton T 1*

Semi-finals
Blackpool 1, Scarborough 0*
Crewe Alex 1, Bolton W 2*

Brentford 0, Torquay U 1
Hereford U 0, Wolverhampton W 2

Regional finals (*2 legs*)
Bolton W 1, Blackpool 0
Blackpool 1, Bolton W 1*

Torquay U 1, Wolverhampton W 2
Wolverhampton W 0, Torquay U 2

Final at Wembley 28 May 1989, att. 46,513
Bolton W (1)4 *(Darby, Chandler, Crombie, Morgan)* Torquay U (1)1 *(Edwards)*
**After extra time*   †*Won on penalties*

FA CHARITY SHIELD 1927–88

1927	Cardiff C	2	Corinthians	1
1928	Everton	2	Blackburn R	1
1929	Professionals	3	Amateurs	0
1930	Arsenal	2	Sheffield W	1
1931	Arsenal	1	WBA	0
1932	Everton	5	Newcastle U	3
1933	Arsenal	3	Everton	0
1934	Arsenal	4	Manchester C	0
1935	Sheffield W	1	Arsenal	0
1936	Sunderland	2	Arsenal	1
1937	Manchester C	2	Sunderland	0
1938	Arsenal	2	Preston NE	1
1948	Arsenal	4	Manchester U	3
1949	Portsmouth	1	Wolverhampton W	1*
1950	World Cup Team	4	Canadian Touring Team	2
1951	Tottenham H	2	Newcastle U	1
1952	Manchester U	4	Newcastle U	2
1953	Arsenal	3	Blackpool	1

1954	Wolverhampton W	4	WBA	4*
1955	Chelsea	3	Newcastle U	0
1956	Manchester U	1	Manchester C	0
1957	Manchester U	4	Aston Villa	0
1958	Bolton W	4	Wolverhampton W	1
1959	Wolverhampton W	3	Nottingham F	1
1960	Burnley	2	Wolverhampton W	2
1961	Tottenham H	3	FA X1	2
1962	Tottenham H	5	Ipswich T	1
1963	Everton	4	Manchester U	0
1964	Liverpool	2	West Ham U	2*
1965	Manchester U	2	Liverpool	2*
1966	Liverpool	1	Everton	0
1967	Manchester U	3	Tottenham H	3*
1968	Manchester C	6	WBA	1
1969	Leeds U	2	Manchester C	1
1970	Everton	2	Chelsea	1
1971	Leicester C	1	Liverpool	0
1972	Manchester C	1	Aston Villa	0
1973	Burnley	1	Manchester C	0
1974	Liverpool	1†	Leeds U	1
1975	Derby Co	2	West Ham U	0
1976	Liverpool	1	Southampton	0
1977	Liverpool	0	Manchester U	0*
1978	Nottingham F	5	Ipswich T	0
1979	Liverpool	3	Arsenal	1
1980	Liverpool	1	West Ham U	0
1981	Aston Villa	2	Tottenham H	2*
1982	Liverpool	1	Tottenham H	0
1983	Manchester U	2	Liverpool	0
1984	Everton	1	Liverpool	0
1985	Everton	2	Manchester U	0
1986	Everton	1	Liverpool	1*
1987	Everton	1	Coventry C	0

FA CHARITY SHIELD 1988
Liverpool (1) 2, Wimbledon (1) 1
Final at Wembley, 20 August 1988, att. 54,000

Liverpool: Grobbelaar; Gillespie, Venison, Ablett, Whelan, Watson, Beardsley, Aldridge, Houghton, Barnes, McMahon
Wimbledon: Tracey; Scales (Clement), Phelan, Ryan, Young, Cawley, Gibson, Fairweather, Fashanu (Turner), Sanchez, Wise
Scorers: Aldridge (Liverpool) 2; Fashanu (Wimbledon)
Referee: J.E. Martin (Alton)

Each club retained shield for six months.   †*Won on Penalties.*

SCOTTISH CLUBS

ABERDEEN   PREM. DIV.

Ground: Pittodrie Stadium, Aberdeen AB2 1QH (0224–632328)
Colours: All red with white trim.
Year formed: 1903. **Managers:** Alex Smith and Jocky Scott.
League appearances: Bett, J. 31; Connor, R. 36; Dodds, D. 17(6); Grant, B. 22(4); Gray, S. 4; Hewitt, J. 21(6); Irvine, B. 21(6); Jess, E. 1(1); McKimmie, S. 35; McLeish, A. 34; MacLeod, A. 1; Mason, P. 21(7); Miller, W. 21; Nicholas, C. 28(1); Robertson, C. 2(2); Robertson, D. 23; Robertson, I. 7; Simpson, N. 16; Snelders, T. 36; Van der Ark, W. 4(4); Watson, G. (4); Wright, P. 15(8).
Goals – League (51): Nicholas 16, Wright 6, Bett 5 (4 pens), Connor 4, Dodds 4, Mason 4, Hewitt 3, Irvine 2, Van der Ark 2, Grant 1, Miller 1, Robertson C. 1, own goals 2.
Skol Cup (12): Bett 3, Dodds 3, Hewitt 2, Miller 2, Grant 1, Nicholas 1.
Scottish Cup (5): Wright 2, Connor 1, Grant 1, Nicholas 1.

AIRDRIEONIANS   DIV.1

Ground: Broomfield Park, Gartlea Road, Airdrie ML6 9JL (02364–62067)
Colours: White shirts with red diamond, white shorts.
Year formed: 1878. **Manager:** Jim Bone.
League appearances: Balfour, E. (1); Black, T. 37; Butler, J. 6(10); Campbell, C. 32(4); Conn, S. 31; Curran, P. 1; Grant, D. 39; Lawrence, A. 7; Lawrie, D. 15(8); Lindsay, C. 9(4); MacCabe, D. 5; MacDonald, I. 36; Macdonald, K. 36; McKenna, T. (1); McKeown, B. 37; McKeown, D. 1(4); MacKinnon, D. 27; McLeod, G. 9; McPhee, I. 27; Martin, J. 36; Moore, V. 6(3); Nelson, M. 19(4); Ogilvie, G. 8; Shirkie, S. (2); Thomson, W. 2(5); Walsh, G. 3.
Goals – League (66): Macdonald, K. 22 (9 pens), Campbell 14, Conn 8, Black 4, MacDonald, I. 3, McPhee 3, Grant 2, Lawrence 2, Lawrie 2, Curran 1, MacKinnon 1, McLeod 1, own goals 3.
Skol Cup (0)
Scottish Cup (0)

ALBION ROVERS   DIV.1

Ground: Cliftonhill Stadium, Main Street, Coatbridge ML5 9XX (0236–32350)
Colours: Yellow shirts with red and white trim, red shorts with yellow stripes.
Year formed: 1882. **Manager:** David Provan.
League appearances: Ashcroft, I. 6; Bishop, J. 15(7); Cadden, S. 36; Chapman, J. 33(2); Clark, R. 37; Cormack, D. 2; Cougan, C. 12(8); Diver, D. 5(7); Edgar, D. 9(4); Fairlie, B. 1(2); Graham, A. 38(1); Granger, C. 29(5); Houston, D. 3; McCulloch, R. 37; McDonald, D. 28(7); McGowan, M. 36; McKenzie, P. 18; Oliver, M. 39; Rodgers, A. 3(1); Teevan, P. 34(2); Verlaque, D. 1(3); Watson, E. 7(7).
Goals – League (65): Chapman 15 (6 pens), Graham 15, Teevan 11, Cadden 5, Bishop 3, Cougan 3, Diver 3, Granger 3, McGowan 3, McKenzie 2 (1 pen), Watson 1, own goal 1.
Skol Cup (2): Chapman 1 (pen), Rodgers 1.
Scottish Cup (3): Diver 1, McDonald 1, McGowan 1.

ALLOA   DIV.1

Ground: Recreation Park, Alloa FK10 1RR (0259–722695)
Colours: Gold shirts with black trim, black shorts.
Year formed: 1883. **Manager** George Able.
League appearances: Bateman, A. 12(10); Blackie, W. 16(2); Conlin, L. 2(1); Gibson, J. 38; Haggart, L. 31(4); Henderson, A. 3(1); Lamont, P. 15(15); Lee, I. 30; Lee,

R. 29(6); Lowrie, R. 39; Lytwyn, C. 36(1); McCallum, M. 15(2); McCulloch, K. 37; McGurn, J. 4(1); Millen, A. 38; Ramsay, S. 27(4); Robertson, R. 22(1); Rodgers, A. 11(9); Rutherford, P. 7; Shiels, M. 2; Smith, A. 13(10); Smith, S. 1(2); Spence, T. 1.
Goals – League (66): Lytwyn 23 (2 pens), Lamont 9, McCallum 7, Blackie 4, Gibson 4, Smith A. 4, McCulloch 3, Millen 3 (1 pen), Bateman 2, Lee I. 2, Ramsay 2, Rodgers 1, Rutherford 1, Smith S. 1.
Skol Cup (2): Lytwyn 1, Rutherford 1 (pen).
Scottish Cup (13): Smith A. 5, Lytwyn 3, Gibson 2, Lamont 2, Ramsay 1.

ARBROATH   DIV.2

Ground: Gayfield Park, Arbroath DD11 1QB (0241–72157)
Colours: Marron shirts, white shorts.
Year formed: 1878. **Manager:** John Young.
League appearances: Anderson, P. 28; Anderson, R. 1; Balfour, D. 2; Bennett, M. 12; Brand, R. 16(11); Cosgrove, R. 11; Dewar, G. 33(3); Farnan, C. 6(1); Fleming, J. 27(1); Florence, S. 3; Forrest, R. 23(6); Fotheringham, J. 36(2); Hamilton, J. 17; Jack, P. 23(2); Jackson, D. 21; Kerr, B. 17(9); Logan, A. 1; McAlpine, H. 10; McEwan, G. 22; McGuiness, S. 6; McKenna, A. 1(3); Mitchell, B. 25; O'Brian, J. 1; Richardson, A. 28(1); Smith, R. 3(4); Stewart, I. 31(1); Tindal, K. 19(5); Todd, D. 6(4).
Goals – League (56): Fotheringham 11, Forrest 7, Stewart 6, Brand 5, Jack 5 (1 pen), Bennett 4, Kerr 4, Mitchell 4, Richardson 4 (2 pens), Dewar 3, Anderson P. 2, own goal 1.
Skol Cup (1): Forrest 1.
Scottish Cup (0)

AYR UNITED   DIV.1

Ground: Somerset Park, Ayr KA8 9NB (0292–263435)
Colours: White shirts with black trim, black shorts.
Year formed: 1910. **Manager:** Ally MacLeod
League appearances: Brown, R. 10(3); Cowell, J. 21(9); Evans, S. 37(1); Furphy, W. 34; Gilmour, G. (1); Hughes, J. 23(1); Kennedy, D. 13(3); Love, J. 21(3); McAllister, I. 22; McCann, J. 23; McCathie, N. 2; McCracken, D. (1); McIntyre, S. 19(7); McKenzie, P. (3); Ross, B. 12(2); Scott, R. 18(2); Shaw, G. 1(1); Sludden, J. 39; Templeton, H. 33; Tracey, K. 2; Walker, T. 32; Watson, G. 39; Welsh, P. 2(1); Wilson, K. 26(4).
Goals – League (56): Templeton 17 (5 pens), Sludden 15, Walker 13, McIntyre 3 (1 pen), Cowell 2, Love 2, Evans 1, Kennedy 1, McAllister 1, Wilson 1.
Skol Cup (1): Templeton 1.
Scottish Cup (1): Templeton 1.

BERWICK RANGERS   DIV.2

Ground: Shielfield Park, Berwick-on-Tweed TD15, 2EF (0289–307424)
Colours: Black and gold striped shirts, black shorts.
Year formed: 1881. **Manager:** Jim Jefferies.
League appearances: Ainslie, G. 2; Bickmore, S. 11(8); Cairns, M. 4; Callachan, R. 31; Cameron, M. 3(2); Cass, M. 23(1); Cavanagh, P. 1(1); Davidson, G. 13(1); Donaldson, B. 12; Douglas, H. 9; Fleming, J. 6(1); Graham, T. 8(8); Hughes, J. 27; Leetion, P. 5; Leitch, G. 26(6); Locke, S. 26; McLaren, P. 10(3); Marshall, B. 11(5); Muir, L. 33; Neil, M. 2(6); Neilson, D. 17; Oliver, N. 39; Porteous, S. 18(11); Renton, P. 3(1); Shell, K. 10(1); Sloan, S. 26; Smith, G. 4; Tait, G. 9(1); Thorpe, B. 33; Watson, S. 6; Wood, K. 1(1).
Goals – League (50): Hughes 10, Thorpe 8 (2 pens), Cass 7, Porteous 7, Callachan 4 (1 pen), Sloan 4, Ainslie 2, Douglas 2, Bickmore 1, Graham 1, Leetion 1, Locke 1, Marshall 1, Tait 1.
Skol Cup (0)
Scottish Cup (2): Hughes 1, Sloan 1.

BRECHIN CITY

Ground: Glebe Park, Brechin DD9 6BJ (03562–2856)
Colours: All red.
Year formed: 1906. **Manager:** John Ritchie
League appearances: Adam, C. 29; Brash, A. 9; Brown, R. 38(1); Buckley, G. 15(13); Candlish, C. 30; Frith, J. 4; Gallacher, W. 7; Gillespie, S. 5(4); Hamilton, R. 12(6); Healey, C. 8(2); Hill, H. 22(3); Inglish, J. 11(1); Kennedy, A. (1); Lawrie, D. 39; Lees, G. 25(14); Paterson, I.A. 32(6); Paterson, I.G. 19; Ritchie, P. 18; Scott, D. 31; Sexton, P. 4; Stevens, G. 21; Taylor, K. 2(3); Wardell, S. 21(6); Watt, D. 8; Wilkie, S. 19(3).
Goals – League (58): Adam 15 (2 pens), Lees 10, Paterson I.A. 10, Ritchie 7, Wardell 4, Brown 3, Buckley 2, Candlish 2 (1 pen), Candlish 2 (1 pen), Frith 1, Inglis 1, Paterson I.G. 1, Scott 1, Sexton 1.
Skol Cup (3): Adam 1, Buckley 1, Lees 1.
Scottish Cup (3): Adam 2, Scott 1.

CELTIC

Ground: Celtic Park, Glasgow G40 3RE (041–554 2710 and 556 2611)
Colours: Green and white hooped shirts, white shorts.
Year formed: 1888. **Manager:** Billy McNeill.
League appearances: Aitken, R. 32; Andrews, I. 5; Archdeacon, O. 2(8); Baillie, A. 8(1); Bonner, P. 26; Burns, T. 30(2); Coyne, T. 4(3); Elliot, D. 2(2); Fulton, S. 1(2); Grant, P. 20(1); McAvennie, F. 23; McCahill, S. 4(1); McCarrison, D. (1); McCarthy, M. 26; McGhee, M. 28(1); McStay, P. 33; Mathie, A. (1); Miller, J. 16(6); Morris, C. 33; Rogan, A. 34; Rough, A. 5; Stark, W. 22(3); Traynor, J. 3(1); Walker, A. 19(3); Whyte, D. 20(2).
Goals – League (66): McGhee 16, McAvennie 12, Stark 9, Miller 8 (1 pen), Walker 8 (1 pen), McStay 5, Morris 3, Burns 2, McCarrison 1, Rogan 1, own goal 1.
Skol Cup (11): Walker 4, McAvennie 3, Burns 2, Archdeacon 1, Stark 1.
Scottish Cup (12): Burns 3, McGhee 2, Walker 2, Aitken 1 (pen), McAvennie 1, McCarthy 1, Miller 1, Stark 1.

CLYDE

Ground: Firhill Park, Glasgow G20 7AL (041–946 9000)
Colours: White shirts with red trim, black shorts.
Year formed: 1878. **Manager:** John Clark.
League appearances: Anderson, N. 9; Atkins, D. 29; Callaghan, W. 6; Clark, M. 25; Cowan, T. 16; Devlin, J. 15(1); Donnelly, R. 12(2); Fairlie, J. 7; Knox, K. 33(1); McCabe, G. 25(1); McFarlane, R. 31; McGlashan, C. 37; McGuiness, B. 6(1); Mackin, A. 7; Mailer, J. 22(8); Millar, S. 10(8); Napier, C. 14; Nolan, M. 15(8); Quinn, P. 3(4); Quinn, S. 2(7); Reid, W. 8; Rooney, J. 17(1); Ross, S. 10; Speirs, C. 18; Tait, T. 27(4); Tracey, P. 1; Willock, A. 24(5).
Goals – League (40): McGlashan 16 (6 pens), Mailer 5, Tait 3, Clark 2, Cowan 2, Donnelly 2, McCabe 2, Fairlie 1, Knox 1, McGuiness 1, Millar 1, Rooney 1, Speirs 1, Willock 1, own goal 1.
Skol Cup (0)
Scottish Cup (1): Mailer

CLYDEBANK

Ground: Kilbowie Park, Clydebank G81 2PB (041–952 2887)
Colours: White with red band, white shorts.
Year formed: 1965. **Manager:** John Steedman.
League appearances: Auld, S. 33; Brodie, C. 6; Bryce, T. 38; Caffrey, H. 3(9); Campbell, K. 1; Charnley, J. 3; Coyle, O. 36; Davies, J. 38; Dickson, J. 29(2); Eadie,

K. 34; Gallacher, J. 33; Harvey, P. 19(10); Hughes, J. 9(5); Lindsay, C. 2; McGurn, G. 8(1); Maher, J. 11; Murdoch, S. 6(4); Rodger, J. 16(1); Spence, T. 29; Sweeney, S. 14(5); Treanor, M. 27; Wright, B. 34(1).
Goals – League (80): Eadie 21 (1 pen), Bryce 16, Coyle 16 (1 pen), Treanor 5 (4 pens), Auld 4, Spence 4 (1 pen), Davies 3, Rodger 3, Wright 2, Caffrey 1, Charnley 1, Harvey 1, Hughes 1, Lindsay 1, own goal 1.
Skol Cup (2): Charnley 1, Eadie 1.
Scottish Cup (3): Coyle 1, Eadie 1, Treanor 1 (pen).

COWDENBEATH   DIV.2

Ground: Central Park, Cowdenbeath KY4 9EY (0383–511205)
Colours: Royal blue shirts with white stripes, white shorts.
Year formed: 1881. **Manager:** John Brownlie.
League appearances: Allan, R. 36; Baillie, R. 18(8); Burnside, S. 16(3); Callaghan, W. 2; Docherty, S. 5(1); Douglas, H. 20(2); Ferguson, E. 10; Grant, R. 7(1); Hepburn, K. (2); Herd, W. 3; Hoggan, K. 18(4); Kerr, G. 34(1); Leetion, P. (5); McConville, J. 5(1); McElwee, K. 1; McGonigal, A. 25(1); McGovern, D. 36; Mackenzie, A. 10(9); Main, A. 3; Malone, G. 35; Muir, L. 2; Muir, S. (2); Rae, J. 5; Redpath, A. 21(6); Reid, J. 15(6); Scott, C. 5(1); Spence, T. 2; Taylor, D. 14; Watt, D. 30(2); Wright, J. 15(1); Yardley, K. 7(2); Yardley, M. 3(3); Young, D. 26(1).
Goals – League (48): McGonigal 8 (2 pens), Mackenzie 6, Ferguson 5, Malone 5 (1 pen), Reid 5, McGovern 4, Redpath 4, Callaghan 3, Grant 2, Hoggan 2, Docherty 1, Taylor 1, Yardley M. 1, Young 1.
Skol Cup (0)
Scottish Cup (3): Kerr 1, MacKenzie 1, Young 1.

DUMBARTON   DIV.2

Ground: Boghead Park, Dumbarton G82 2JA (0389–62569 and 67864)
Colours: Gold with white band, black shorts.
Year formed: 1872. **Manager:** James George.
League appearances: Blackie, W. 5(4); Cairney, P. 28; Cairns, W. 9(2); Callan, D. 4(1); Coyle, O. 3; Cranmer, C. 7; Dickie, G. 11; Docherty, R. 31(1); Douglas, C. (11); Doyle, G. 16(5); Doyle, J. 11(3); Duncan, G. 14(4); Elliott, G. 8(4); English, D. (1); Fulton, D. 7; Gow, S. 16(4); McCahill, S. 21; McDougall, I. 4(1); McGowan, P. 34; MacIver, S. 27; McKinlay, I. 1; McQuade, A. 18; McQuade, J. 26(8); Martin, D. 8; Robertson, S. 24(3); Rooney, B. 4; Quinn, P. 15; Spence, C. 19; Stevenson, H. 16; Strachan, H. 23; Wharton, P. 19.
Goals – League (45): MacIver 13, Docherty 7 (4 pens), McQuade J. 5, Quinn 4, Spence 3, Duncan 2, Robertson 2, Rooney 2, Cairney 1, Douglas 1, Doyle J. 1 (pen), McCahill 1, McGowan 1, McQuade A. 1, Wharton 1.
Skol Cup (1): McQuade J. 1.
Scottish Cup (8): MacIver 3, Cairney 2, McQuade J. 2, McGowan 1.

DUNDEE   PREM.DIV.

Ground: Dens Park, Dundee DD1 7JY (0382–826104)
Colours: Dark blue shirts with red and white trim, white shorts.
Year formed: 1893. **Manager:** Gordon Wallace.
League appearances: Angus, I. 12(3); Campbell, D. 6(2); Campbell, S. 18(6); Carson, T. 2; Chisholm, G. 33(1); Coyne, T. 26; Craib, M. 2(2); Craig, A. 6; Forsyth, S. 33; Frail, S. 21(2); Geddes, R. 34; Harvey, G. 11(9); Hendry, J. (2); Holt, J. 10(1); Kirkwood, W. 10(2); Lawrence, A. 8(2); McBride, J. 13(4); McGeachie, G. 6; Mckinlay, T. 18; Mennie, V. (4); Rafferty, S. 26(6); Saunders, W. 30; Shannon, R. 29; Smith, J. 7; Wright, K. 35.

Goals – League (34): Coyne 9, Wright 8, Chisholm 4, Harvey 4 (1 pen), Craig 2, McBride 2, Campbell D. 1, Frail 1, Rafferty 1, Saunders 1, Shannon 1.
Skol Cup (8): Harvey 3, Wright 2, Lawrence 1, McGeachie 1, Rafferty 1.
Scottish Cup (1): Angus 1.

DUNDEE UNITED   PREM.DIV.

Ground: Tannadice Park, Dundee DD3 7JW (0382–826289)
Colours: Tangerine shirts with black trim, black shorts.
Year formed: 1909 as Dundee Hibernians, Dundee United from 1923.
Manager: Jim McLean.
League appearances: Adam, C. 4(2); Beaumont, D. 12(6); Bowman, D. 21(8); Clark, J. 17(3); Cleland, A. 7(2); Curran, H. 3(3); Connolly, P. 2; French, H. 12(6); Gallacher, K. 29(2); Hegarty, P. 27(2); Irvine, J.A. 6(1); Jackson, D. 1; Krivokapic, M. 18(6); McGinnis, G. 7(4); McInally, J. 29; McKinlay, W. 29(1); McKinnon, R. 1; McLeod, G. 1; McLeod, J. (3); McPhee, I. 1(1); Malpas, M. 36; Meade, R. 8(3); Narey, D. 33; O'Neil, J. (1); Paatelainen, M. 33; Preston, A. 8(1); Redford, I. 9; Sturrock, P. 5(5); Thomson, W. 36; Welsh, B. 1.
Goals – League (44): Paatelainen 10 (2 pens), Gallacher 9, Meade 4, French 3, Clark 2, Redford 2, Beaumont 1, Bowman 1, Hegarty 1, Irvine 1, Krivokapic 1, McInally 1, McKinlay 1, McPhee 1, Malpas 1, Preston 1, Sturrock 1, own goals 3.
Skol Cup (7): Paatelainen 3, Gallacher 2, Meade 1, Redford 1.
Scottish Cup (7): Paatelainen 4 (2 pens), Bowman 1, Gallacher 1, Meade 1.

DUNFERMLINE ATHLETIC   PREM.DIV.

Ground: East End Park, Dunfermline KY12 7RB (0383–724295)
Colours: Black and white striped shirts, black shorts.
Year formed: 1885. **Manager:** Jim Leishman.
League appearances: Beedie, S. 22 (1); Burns, H. 13(2); Callaghan, W. (4); Davidson, G. (1); Farningham, R. 13; Feenie, M. 2; Gallagher, E. 4(3); Holt, J. 13; Irons, D. 36; Jack, R. 34(2); McCathie, N. 19(1); Morrison, S. 6(10); Riddell, G. 21(1); Robertson, C. 13; Robertson, D. 27(2); Sharp, R. 8(1); Smith, M. 18(5); Smith, P. 35; Smith, R. 32(1); Smith T. 18(5); Speirs, G. 2(2); Tierney, G. 18; Watson, J. 31(4); Westwater, I. 39; Williamson, A. 5(1).
Goals – League (60): Jack 18 (1 pen), Watson 14, Robertson C. 5, Smith P. 5, Smith T. 5, Beedie 2, Irons 2, Gallagher 1, Holt 1, McCathie 1, Robertson G. 1, Smith M. 1, Smith R. 1, Tierney 1, own goals 2.
Skol Cup (4): Watson 2, Irons 1, Smith T. 1.
Scottish Cup (1): Smith, T. 1.

EAST FIFE   DIV.2

Ground: Bayview Park, Methil, Fife KY8 3AG (0333–26323)
Colours: Black and gold striped shirts, black shorts.
Year formed: 1903. **Manager:** Gavin Murray.
League appearances: Banner, A. 9; Bardsley, A. 8(1); Bell, G. 12(2); Brown, W. 7; Charles, R. 30; Collins, N. 1(1); Connor, T. 38(1); Deas, B. 13(3); Fairley, G. 3(4); Gallacher, W. 22(1); Graham, D. 1(1); Hall, A. 27(3); Harrow, A. 24(8); Hope, D. 23(11); Hunter, P. 33; Kirkwood, D. 5; McCafferty, T. 32; McGonigal, A. 2(4); McIlhone, S. (9); McLaren, J. 20; McNaughton, B. 17(3); Mitchell, A. 18; Ogston, F. (2); Perry, J. 6; Pittman, S. 25; Reid, G. 37; Scott, C. 16(3); Thorpe, J. (4).
Goals – League (56): Hunter 9, Pittman 8 (3 pens), McNaughton 7, Hope 5, Gallacher 4 (2 pens), Mitchell 4, Connor 3, McGonigal 3, Bardsley 2, Deas 2, Harrow 2, Kirkwood 2, Brown 1, Fairley 1, Perry 1, own goals 2.
Skol Cup (1): Hunter 1.
Scottish Cup (5): Bardsley 1, Hope 1, Hunter 1, Mitchell 1, Pittman 1.

EAST STIRLING   DIV.2

Ground: Firs Park, Falkirk FK2 7AY (0324–23583)
Colours: White shirts with black band, black shorts.
Year formed: 1881. **Manager:** J. David Connell.
League appearances: Drew, D. 18, Feeney, P. 21(8); Gilchrist, A. 19(1), Grant, A. 36;
Hamill, K. (1); Hamilton, L. 1; Harvey, G. 9(5); Irvine, J. 11(1); Kelly, C. 36; Kelly, K.
3(4); Kelly, P. 8(4); Lauchlan, G. 13(14); McCann, H. 2; McEntegart, T. 13; McGraw,
A. 4(2); McIntosh, G. 1(1); McLeod, B. 3; McNeill, W. 33(3); Main, A. 2; O'Brien, P.
15(6); Peters, A. 10; Purdie, B. 19; Russell, G. 38; Scott, R. 12(4); Walker, P. 1; Ward,
T. 6(1); Wilcox, D. 39; Wilcox, G. 5(10); Wilson, C. 33; Woods, J. 16; Yardley, K. 2.
Goals – League (54): McNeill 16, Feeney 5, Wilcox D. 5 (2 pens), Wilson 5, Grant A. 4,
Irvine 4, Lauchlan 3, McEntegart 3, Harvey 2, Scott 2, O'Brien 1, Ward 1, Wilcox G. 1,
Woods 1, Yardley 1.
Skol Cup (0)
Scottish Cup (2): Wilcox D. 1, Wilson 1.

FALKIRK   DIV.1

Ground: Brockville Park, Falkirk FK1 5AX (0324–24121)
Colours: Dark blue shirts with white trim, white shorts.
Year formed: 1876. **Manager:** Jim Duffy.
League appearances: Baptie, C. 24(4); Brannigan, K. 5(2); Burgess, S. 37; Gallacher,
J. 9(7); Hetherston, P. 26(5); Holmes, J. 38; Houston, P. 19(14); McCall, A. (1);
McGivern, S. 30(4); McIntyre, B. 3; McLarty, W. (1); McNair, C. 29(4); McVeigh,
J. 2(1); McWilliams, D. 28; Manley, R. 35; Marshall, G. 39; Melvin, M. (1); Mennie,
V. 4(3); Mooney, M. 1(5); Nicol, A. 38; Rae, A. 34(3); Romaines, S. 2(2); Rutherford,
P. 24(4); Smith, G. 2(1); Stewart, R. (2).
Goals – League (71): Rae 12, McWilliams 11 (1 pen), Burgess 10 (6 pens), Rutherford
9, McGivern 8, Gallacher 5, McNair 4, Hetherston 3, Houston 3, Baptie 2, Manley 1,
Mennie 1, own goals 2.
Skol Cup (2): Burgess 1 (pen), Rae 1.
Scottish Cup (2): Burgess 1 (pen), Rutherford 1.

FORFAR ATHLETIC   DIV.1

Ground: Station Park, Forfar, Angus DD8 3BT (0307–63576)
Colours: Sky blue shirts, white shorts.
Year formed: 1885. **Manager:** Henry Hall.
League appearances: Bennett, M. (1); Bennett, W. 28(2); Brazil, A. 15(2); Brewster,
C. 35(2); Brown, W. 17(4); Clark, J. 29(8); Clarke, S. 16(2); Grant, B. 6(5); Hamill,
A. 37(1); Hutton, G. 3(1); Kennedy, S. 31; Lorimer, R. 36(1); McNaughton, B. 8(2);
Moffat, J. 8; Morris, R. 32(1); Morton, J. 37; Ormond, J. 13(7); Smith, P. 29(3);
Taylor, S. 3(4); Ward, K. 30(5); Whyte, G. 16(4); Winter, G. (1).
Goals – League (52): Ward 12 (1 pen), Brewster 9, Brown 5, Ormond 5, Clark J. 4,
McNaughton 4, Lorimer 3, Clarke S. 2, Grant 2, Whyte 2, Bennett W. 1, Hamill 1,
Morton 1, own goal 1.
Skol Cup (0)
Scottish Cup (3): Brewster 1, Clark J. 1, Ward 1.

HAMILTON ACADEMICAL   DIV. 1

Ground: Douglas Park, Hamilton ML3 0DF (0698–286103)
Colours: Red and white hooped shirts, white shorts.
Year formed: 1875. **Manager:** Jim Dempsey.
League appearances: Andrews, G. (1); Archer, S. 7(1); Charnley, J. 8(6); Collins, G.
10(1); Fairlie, J. 20; Ferguson, A. 30; Fraser, A. 2(6); Frith, J. (2); Gallagher, E. 12(2);

Gordon, S. 21(3); Harris, C. 27(1); Jamieson, W. 34; Kerr, J. 8(1); McCabe, G. 7(1); McDonald, P. 27(7); McKee, K. 36; McNaught, J. 3; Martin, P. 20(1); Miller, C.F. 20(1); Morrison, S. 8(1); Napier, C. 19(1); Nelson, M. 2(5); Prentice, A. 9; Roseburgh, D. 26(1); Rough, A. 6; Scott, G. 4(5); Speirs, C. 3(3); Weir, J. 27(2).

Goals – League (19): Gordon 5, Harris 5 (2 pens), Fairlie 3, Gallagher 3, Archer 1, Jamieson 1, McNaught 1.

Skol Cup (6): Fairlie 2, Collins 1, McDonald 1, McNaught 1, own goal 1.

Scottish Cup (0)

HEART OF MIDLOTHIAN   PREM. DIV

Ground: Tynecastle Park, Gorgie Road, Edinburgh EH11 2NL (031–337 6132)
Colours: Maroon shirts, white shorts.
Year formed: 1874. **Manager:** Alex MacDonald.
League appearances: Bannon, E. 23(7); Berry, N. 32; Black, K. 33; Clark, A. 1(1); Colquhoun, J. 34(2); Crabbe, S. 1; Ferguson, I. 23(6); Foster, W. 8(1); Galloway, M. 30(1); Gavin, M. (2); Jardine, I. 2(13); Kidd, W. 20; Levein, C. 8(1); Mackay, G. 29; McKinlay, T. 17; McLaren, A. 11(1); McPherson, D. 32; Moore, A. 5(7); Murray, M. 8; Robertson, J. 8(7); Smith, H. 36; Sandison, J. 11(3); Whittaker, B.24.
Goals – League (35): Colquhoun 5, Ferguson 5, McPherson 4, Robertson 4 (1 pen), Bannon 2, Galloway 2, Mackay 2, Moore 2, Berry 1, Black 1, Clark 1, Foster 1 (pen), Jardine 1, McKinlay 1, McLaren 1, own goals 2.
Skol Cup (11): Ferguson 5 (1 pen), Mackay 2, Black 1, Colqhoun 1, Jardine 1, Murray 1.
Scottish Cup (7): Bannon 2, Colquhoun 2, Galloway 1, McPherson 1, own goal 1.

HIBERNIAN   PREM. DIV.

Ground: Easter Road Stadium, Edinburgh EH7 5QG (031–661 2159)
Colours: Green shirts with white sleeves and collar, white shorts.
Year formed: 1875. **Manager:** Alex Miller.
League appearances: Archibald, S. 31; Collins, J. 35; Evans, G. 32(3); Fellenger, D. (2); Findlay, W. 2(1); Goram, A. 36; Houchen, K. 7; Hunter, G. 33; Kane, P. 35; Lennon, D. (1); McBride, J. 4; McCluskey, G. 4(12); McGinlay, P. (2); McIntyre, T. 16(1); May, E. 13(12); Milne, C. 18(1); Mitchell, G. 20; Orr, N. 33, Rae, G. 32; Sneddon, A. 26; Tortolano, J. 15(10); Watson, A. (1); Weir, M. 4(3)
Goals – League (37): Archibald 13, Evans 5, Kane 5, McCluskey 3 (1 pen), Collins 2, Houchen 2, McIntyre 2, May 2, Findlay 1, Hunter 1, Rae 1.
Skol Cup (6): Kane 3, Archibald 2, Evans 1.
Scottish Cup (5): Collins 2, Archibald 1, Kane 1, May 1.

KILMARNOCK   DIV.2

Ground: Rugby Park, Kilmarnock KA1 2DP (0563–25184)
Colours: Blue and white hooped shirts, blue shorts.
Year formed: 1869. **Manager:** Jim Fleeting.
League appearances: Bourke, J. 2; Brannigan, K. 15; Callaghan, T. 11; Cook, D. 8(4); Cuthbertson, S. (1); Davidson. F. 26; Faulds, G. 13(1); Flexney, P. 18; Gilmour, J. 14(2); Harkness, C. 26(7); Hughes, M. 3; Lindsay, A. 2(8); McConville, R. 7(3); McCulloch, A. 39; McDonald, T. 12(2); MacFarlane, D. 19(4); McGuire, J. 11(2); McInnes, I. (2); McLaughlin, M. 14(6); McLean, S. 29(3); McQueen, E. 4; Marshall, S. 21(3), Martin, P. 11; Millar, G. 12(2); Montgomerie, R. 31; Reilly, R. 17; Robertson, A. 12; Speirs, G. 4(1); Stewart, A. 7; Walker, David, 1(5); Walker, Derek 9(7); Watters, W. 20; Wylde, G. 11.
Goals – League (47): Watters 12, Harkness 5, McGuire 4, Cook 3, Gilmour 3 (1 pen), MacFarlane 3, Faulds 2, McLaughlin 2, Montgomerie 2, Reilly 2, Brannigan 1, Cuthbertson 1, McDonald 1, McInnes 1, Marshall 1, Martin 1, Stewart 1, Walker

(Derek) 1, Wylde 1.
Skol Cup (1): Gilmour 1 (pen).
Scottish Cup (2): Davidson 1, Speirs 1.

MEADOWBANK THISTLE   DIV.1

Ground: Meadowbank Stadium, Edinburgh EH7 6AE (031–661 5351)
Colours: Amber with black trim, black shorts.
Year formed: 1943 as Ferranti Thistle, Meadowbank Thistle from 1974.
Manager: Terry Christie.
League appearances: Armstrong, G. 39; Boyd, W. 38; Conroy, D. 4; Forrest, R. 7; Hendrie, T. 19(5); Inglis, J. 10(2); Irvine, N. 22(6); Lawrence, A. 3; Logan, S. 39; McCormack, J.T. 26; McGachie, J. 15(3); McQueen, J. 39: Park, D. 5(12); Perry, J. 15; Prentice, A. 21(1); Reilly, R. 8(4); Roseburgh, D. 10; Scott, G. 16(3); Sprott, A. 38; Tierney, G. 18; Walker, D. 6(5); Williamson, S. 31(3).
Goals – League (45): Roseburgh 6, McGachie 5, Sprott 5, Armstrong 4 (2 pens), Lawrence 4, Scott 4, Logan 3, Boyd 2, Forrest 2, Park 2, Perry 2, Prentice 2, Inglis 1, McCormack 1, Reilly 1, Williamson 1.
Skol Cup (2): Irvine 1, Prentice 1.
Scottish Cup (2): Lawrence 1, Logan 1.

MONTROSE   DIV.2

Ground: Links Park, Montrose DD10 8QD (0674–73200)
Colours: Blue with white trim, white shorts.
Year formed: 1879. **Manager:** Ian Stewart.
League appearances: Allan, M. 18(4); Barr, L. 10(8); Brown, K. 33; Brown, S. 4(13); Duffy, A. 15(1); Forbes, N. 34(5); Halley, K. 14; King, S. 12(2); Larter, D. 39; Lees, D. (1); Lyons, A. 36; Mackay, H. 18(17); McGlashan, J. 33(2); McLelland, C. 16; Maver, C. 35(2); Morrison, B. 28; Murray, G. 35(3); Paterson, D. 37; Powell, D. 7(9); Robertson, G. 2(6); Wrack, P. 2(1); Wright, F. 1.
Goals – League (54): Murray 21, Maver 9, Lyons 8 (6 pens), Mackay 6, Forbes 2, McGlashan 2, Brown S. 1, Duffy 1, Morrison 1, Paterson 1, Powell 1, own goal 1.
Skol Cup (1): Paterson 1.
Scottish Cup (5):Murray 2, Lyons 1, Mackay 1, Maver 1.

MORTON   DIV.1

Ground: Cappielow Park, Greenock PA15 2TY (0475–23571)
Colours: Blue and white hooped shirts, white shorts.
Year formed: 1874. **Manager:** Allan McGraw.
League appearances: Alexander, R. 31; Boag, James 1(6); Boag, John 27; Brown, C. (1); Clinging, I. 35(3); Collins, D. 35; Deeney, M. 3(3); Fowler, J. 18(5); Hunter, J. 35; Kelly, G. 1; MacDonald, R. 26; McGeachy, A. 4(6); McGraw, M. (1); McInnes, D. 24(5); McNeil, J. 10(5); Mahood, A. (1); O'Hara, A. 21(2); Pickering, M. 22(2); Reid, B. 2; Roberts, P. 14(2); Robertson, D. 11(9); Robertson, J. 10(6); Ronald, G. 25(2); Spencer, J. 4; Strain, B. 2; Turner, T. 29(2); Wylie, D. 39;
Goals–League (46): Alexander 11, Turner 10 (4 pens), Clinging 7, Roberts 3, Robertson J. 3, MacDonald 2, Robertson D. 2, Collins 1, Deeney 1, Fowler 1, McInnes 1, McNeil 1, Pickering 1, Ronald 1, Spencer 1.
Skol Cup (3): Alexander 2, McNeil 1.
Scottish Cup (6): Robertson D. 2, Turner 2, Alexander 1, Boag (John) 1.

MOTHERWELL   PREM.DIV.

Ground: Fir Park, Motherwell ML1 2QN (0698–61437)
Colours: Amber shirts with claret band, claret shorts.
Year formed: 1886. **Manager:** Tommy McLean.

League appearances: Arnott, D. 8(6); Boyd, T. 31(5); Bryce, S. 3(6); Cowan, S. 12(7); Dolan, J. 3(2); Duncan, C. 17; Farningham, R. 17(1); Gahagan, J. 10(4); Griffin, J. 1; Kennedy, A. 1; Kinnaird, P. 24; Kirk, S. 32(1); McAdam, T. 28; McBride, M. 10(6); MacCabe, D. 12(1); McCart, C. 25(1); McKeown, K. 2; Mair, G. 6(6); Maxwell, A. 17; O'Neill, C. 19; Paterson, C. 33; Philliben, J. 17(2); Russell, R. 28(3); Shanks, D. 2(2); Smith, P. 3(1); Wishart, F. 35.

Goals – League (35): Kirk 14 (1 pen), Russell 5, Farningham 3, Cowan 2, Gahagan 2, O'Neill 2 (2 pens), Arnott 1, Boyd 1, McAdam 1, McBride 1, Paterson 1, Wishart 1, own goal 1.

Skol Cup (2): Farningham 1, Kirk 1 (pen).

Scottish Cup (4): Kirk 3 (1 pen), Bryce 1.

PARTICK THISTLE   DIV.1

Ground: Firhill Park, Glasgow G20 7AL (041–946 2673)
Colours: Amber shirts with red trim, red shorts.
Year formed: 1876. **Manager:** John Lambie.
League appearances: Abercromby, W. 9(1); Brough, J. 16; Charnley, J. 14; Collins, G. 22; Dempsey, J. 30(4); Dinnie, A. 31; Docherty, P. 22; Elliott, T. (2); Flood, J. 33(2); Gallagher, B. 11(2); Gallagher, E. 3; Grant, A. 8(6); Kelly, P. 15(7); Kerr, J. 25(1); Law, R. 33; McCoy, G. 30(3); McDonald, I. 3(1); McGee, B. 3(1); McGhie, W. 9; McGinley, J. 1(4); McGuire, W. 3(1); MacLean, A. 10; Maher, P. (1); Mitchell, J. 35; Murdoch, A. 13; Peebles, G. 12; Purdie, B. 8; Spittal, J. 2(2); Thomson, I. 17(8); Watson, K. (1); Workman, J. 11(2).
Goals – League (57): McCoy 19 (1 pen), Flood 8, Kelly 5, Mitchell 5, Charnley 4 (1 pen), Gallagher E. 2 (1 pen), Kerr 2 (1 pen), Thomson 2, Collins 1, Dempsey 1, Dinnie 1, Gallagher B. 1, Grant 1, McGuire 1, Peebles 1, Purdie 1, own goals 2.
Skol Cup (0)
Scottish Cup (3): McCoy 2, Mitchell 1.

QUEEN OF THE SOUTH   DIV.2

Ground: Palmerston Park, Dumfries DG2 9BA (0387–54853)
Colours: Royal blue shirts, white shorts.
Year formed: 1919. **Manager:** William McLaren.
League appearances: Bain, A. 15; Clark, G. 1; Cook, D. 13(1); Cunningham, W. 8; Dawson, L. 1(2); Docherty, D. 12(1); Doherty, J. 11(6); Ferguson, R. 28; Fraser, G. 32; Gamble, J. 11(2); Gray, W. 12(3); Hetherington, K. 31; Holland, B. 3; Hughes, J. 9; Johnston, G. 24(5); McBride, J. 2; McCulloch, J. 4(2); McDonald, T. 14(1); McGuire, J. 16; Mackin, A. 11; McQueen, A. (2); Martin, D. 3; Mills, D. 28(2); Moore, S. 17(3); Olabode, J. 3; Reid, W. 24(1); Robertson, S. 4(1); Shanks, M. 26(3); Sim, W. 21(3); Sinclair, J. 16(1); Sloan, T. 13(2); Stewart, R. 8(1); Telfer, G. 9(16).
Goals – League (38): Fraser 7 (2 pens), Reid 5 (4 pens), Moore 4 (1 pen), Cook 3, Mills 3, Sloan 3, Doherty 2, Gamble 2, Olabode 2, Telfer 2, Bain 1, Hetherington 1, Hughes 1, McGuire 1, Robertson 1.
Skol Cup (1): Doherty 1.
Scottish Cup (5): McGuire 2, Hetherington 1, McDonald 1, Sloan 1.

QUEEN'S PARK   DIV.2

Ground: Hampden Park, Glasgow G42 9BA (041–632 1275)
Colours: Black and white hooped shirts, white shorts.
Year formed: 1876. **Coach:** Eddie Hunter.
League appearances: Armstrong, P. 28(4); Boyle, J. 39; Brown, I. 4(8); Caven, R. 27; Crooks, G. 34(3); Elder, G. 35; Elliot, D. 12(7); Flannigan, M. 2; Hendry, M. 28(4); Jack, S. 1; Lennox, G. 24(4); McEntegart, S. 2(3); McGregor, S. (1); McLaughlin, P. 34; McLean, P. 36(3); McLean, S. 3; McNamee, P. 25; Monaghan, M. 39; Morton, C. 13(10); O'Brien, P. 22(9); Rodden, J. 21(6).
Goals – League (50): Hendry 9, Crooks 8, Caven 5, Rodden 5, Boyle 4 (3 pens), O'Brien

122

4, McNamee 3, Armstrong 2, Brown 2, Elliot 2, Lennox 2 (2 pens), McLean P. 2, McEntegart 1 (pen), McLaughlin 1.
Skol Cup (1): Lennox 1.
Scottish Cup (5): Brown 2, Elliott 2, McLaughlin 1.

RAITH ROVERS   DIV.1

Ground: Stark's Park, Pratt Street, Kirkcaldy KY1 1SA (0592–263514)
Colours: All royal blue with white trim.
Year formed: 1883. **Manager:** Frank Connor.
League appearances: Archibald, E. 5(1); Arthur, G. 39; Brash, A. 13; Buchanan, N. 1(1); Burn, P. 2(1); Coyle, R. 36; Dalziel, G. 34(2); Dennis, S. 9(1); Ferguson, E. 6(2); Ferguson I. 19(9); Fraser, C. 23; Gibson, I. 37; Glennie, R. 16; Logan, A. 16(9); McStay, J. 37; Marshall, J. 11(9); Murray, D. 38; Nelson, M. 8(1); Romaines, S. 14(11); Simpson, S. 29(5); Spence, W. (2); Strachan, A. 4(4); Sweeney, P. 28; Wright, J. 4(4).
Goals – League (50): Dalziel 11, Logan 6, Gibson 5, McStay 5 (5 pens), Ferguson I. 4, Fraser 3 (1 pen), Simpson 3, Brash 2, Murray 2, Nelson 2, Sweeney 2, Coyle 1, Marshall 1, Strachan 1, Wright 1, own goal 1.
Skol Cup (1): Dalziel 1 (pen).
Scottish Cup (1): Dalziel 1.

RANGERS   PREM.DIV.

Ground: Ibrox Stadium, Glasgow G51 2XD (041–427 5232)
Colours: Royal blue shirts, white shorts.
Year formed: 1873. **Player Manager:** Graeme Souness.
League appearances: (62): Brown, J. 29; Butcher, T. 34; Cooper, D. 9(14); Cooper, N. 11(3); Cowan, T. 3(1); Drinkell, K. 32; Durrant, I. 8; Ferguson, D. 12(4); Ferguson, I. 30; Gough, R. 35; Gray, A. 3(10); Kirkwood, D. 2; McCall, I. 2(3); McCoist, A. 18(1); MacDonald, K. 2(1); McSwegan, S. (1); Munro, S. 21(1); Nicholl, J. 1; Nisbet, S. 5(2); Robertson, A. 1(1); Souness, G. (6); Stevens, G. 35; Sterland, M. 7(2); Walker, N. 12; Walters, M. 30(1); Wilkins, R. 30(1); Woods, C. 24.
Goals – League (62): Drinkell 12, McCoist 9, Walters 8 (3 pens), Ferguson I. 6, Gray 5, Gough 4, Sterland 3, Butcher 2, Durrant 2 (1 pen), Ferguson D. 2, Munro 2, Brown 1, Cooper D. 1 (pen), Cooper N. 1, McCall 1, Nisbet 1, Stevens 1, Wilkins 1.
Skol Cup (19): Walters 5, McCoist 4 (2 pens), Drinkell 2, Ferguson I. 2, Durrant 1, Ferguson D. 1, Gough 1, Nisbet 1, Wilkins 1, own goal 1.
Scottish Cup (19): Drinkell 5, McCoist 5 (1 pen), Walters 3, Brown 2, Ferguson I. 2, Stevens 1, own goal 1.

ST JOHNSTONE   DIV.1

Ground: McDiarmid Park, Crieff Road, Perth PU1 25J (0738–26961)
Colours: Royal blue shirts with white trim, blue shorts.
Year formed: 1884. **Manager:** Alex Totten.
League appearances: Balavage, J. 39; Barron, D. 38; Cherry, P. 36(3); Coyle, T. 24(6); Grant, R. 28; Heddle, I. 35(1); Irvine, J. 8(9); Jenkins, G. 24(9); Johnston, S. 21(9); McKillop, A. 3; McVicar, D. 28; Maher, G. 2(1); Martin, D. 1(2); Maskrey, S. 31; Murray, M. 1; Newbigging, W. 1; Nicolson, K. 3; Sorbie, S. 24(11); Smith, M. 7(5); Spence, W. 1(8); Thompson, G. 30; Thomson, K. 34; Treanor, M. 3; Watters, W. 7(7).
Goals – League (51): Maskrey 12, Jenkins 9, Sorbie 7, Grant 5, Watters 4 (1 pen), Johnston 3, McVicar 3 (2 pens), Cherry 2, Coyle 2 (1 pen), Heddle 2, own goals 2.
Skol Cup (0)
Scottish Cup (9): Maskrey 4, Coyle 1 (pen), Grant 1, Heddle 1, Jenkins 1, Sorbie 1.

ST MIRREN PREM.DIV.

Ground: St Mirren Park, Paisley PA3 2EJ (041–889 2558 and 840 1337)
Colours: White shirts with black vertical stripes, black shorts.
Year formed: 1877. **Manager:** Tony Fitzpatrick
League appearances: Cameron, I. 23(3); Chalmers, P. 33; Cooper, N. 30; Davies, W. 26(1); Dawson, R. 9; Fitzpatrick, A. (1); Fridge, L. 15; Galloway, S. 2(2); Godfrey, P. 27; Hamilton, B. 23; Hamilton, D. 2; Kinnaird, P. 2(4); Lambert, P. 8(8); McDowall, K. 4(5); McGarvey, F. 18(13); McIntosh, M. 1(1); McWalter, M. 21(10); McWhirter, N. 1(3); Martin, B. 34; Money, C. 21; Shaw, G. 8(2); Walker, K. 13(1); Weir, P. 15(1); Wilson, T. 30(1); Winnie, D. 30.
Goals – League (39): Chalmers 11, Weir 6 (4 pens), McWalter 5, Davies 4, Cameron 2, Lambert 2, McGarvey 2, Martin 2, Godfrey 1, Hamilton B. 1, Shaw 1, Walker 1, own goal 1.
Skol Cup (4): Cameron 1, Chalmers 1, Hamilton B. 1, McGarvey 1.
Scottish Cup (1): Weir 1 (pen).

STENHOUSEMUIR DIV.2

Ground: Ochilview Park, Stenhousemuir FK5 5QL (0324–562992)
Colours: Maroon shirts with white trim, white shorts.
Year formed: 1884. **Manager:** James Meakin.
League appearances: Barrie, S. 9(5); Beaton, D. 36; Bell, A. 13(3); Buchanan, G. (1); Cairney, H. 36; Clark, R. 5; Clouston, B. 13(1); Condie, T. 36(3); Elliott, A. 16(7); Erwin, H. 36; Gavin, S. 7; Gillen, J. 21; Hamill, S. 13(3); Keith, A. 6; Kennedy, D. 1; Loppas, C. 4(5); McBride, A. (2); McCafferty, T. 16(2); McConville, R. (1); McDonald, A. 1; McDonald, S. 1; McIntosh, G. 2(7); McKay, J. 1; McKenna, T. 1(1); Maitland, A. 2(2); Moore, C. 6(6); Pelosi, J. 2; Philliben, R. 23(1); Robertson, S. 33; Robinson, B. 21(4); Sexton, P. 31(1); Sharp, R. 5; Sinclair, D. 1; Speirs, A. 1; Walker, C. 29(1); Walker, D. 1.
Goals – League (44): Walker C. 9, Beaton 6 (2 pens), Sexton 6, Erwin 5 (1 pen), Condie 4, Bell 3, Elliott 2, Loppas 2, Cairney 1, Gavin 1, McDonald S. 1, McIntosh 1, Moore 1, Robinson 1, own goal 1.
Skol Cup (3): Sexton 2, McCafferty 1.
Scottish Cup (4): Erwin 2 (1 pen), Beaton 1, Sexton 1.

STIRLING ALBION DIV.2

Ground: Annfield Stadium, Stirling FK8 2UE (0786–50399)
Colours: All red.
Year formed: 1945. **Manager:** Jim Fleeting.
League appearances: Atchison, T. 18(2); Brogan, J. 30(5); Conway, M. 4(1); George, D. 31(2); Gibson, A. 4(8); Gibson, C. 39; Gilmour, J. 12(2); Given, J. 33(2); Graham, A. 34; Hughes, M. 16(2); Kemp, B. 32(2); McConville, R. 8(3); McKeown, K. 5; McTeague, G. 28; Maxwell, S. 16(7); Miller, R. 1(5); Mitchell, C. 28(4); Moore, V. 14; Sinclair, J. 2; Smith, G. 3; Tennant, S. 33(3); Thompson, D. 20(2); Walsh, M. 2(10); Wilson, K. 16(3).
Goals – League (64): Gibson C. 18, Brogan 15, George 5, Kemp 5, Moore 4 (1 pen), Thompson 4, Given 2 (1 pen), Hughes 2, Tennant 2, Conway 1, Gibson A. 1, Gilmour 1, McTeague 1, Mitchell 1, Walsh 1, own goal 1.
Skol Cup (5): Brogan 2, Gibson C. 1, Kemp 1, Thompson 1.
Scottish Cup (2): Brogan 2.

Ground: Stair Park, Stranraer DG9 8BS (0776–3271)
Colours: Royal blue shirts, white shorts.
Year formed: 1870. **Manager:** Alex McAnespie.
League appearances: Armour, N. 24; Arthur, J. 7(5); Cuthbertson, S. 9(4); Day, R. (1); Doherty, J. 7; Donnelly, J. 16(1); Duffy, B. 39; Ewing, A. 10(8); Frye, J.F. 9(11); Gallagher, A. 18(4); Hay, G. 35(1); Henderson, D. 32(3); Houston, H. 5(4); Lindsay, C. 7; Lloyd, D. 31(4); Lowe, L. 22(5); McCutcheon, D. 31; McDonald, I. 4; McInnes, I. 26(3); McIntyre, B. 4; McMillan, G. 22(9); McNiven, J. 31(2); McQueen, E. 8; Rogers, J. 5; Spittal, I. 9; Watt, N. 18(2).
Goals – League (59): Lloyd 11, McCutcheon 9 (7 pens), McMillan 8, Henderson 7, Frye 5, McInnes 4, Arthur 3, Cuthbertson 3, Doherty 2, McNiven 2, Donnelly 1, Lindsay 1, McIntyre 1 (1 pen), McQueen 1, Watt 1.
Skol Cup (2): McCutcheon 1 (pen), McMillan 1.
Scottish Cup (6): Ewing 2, McMillan 2, Lloyd 1, McInnes 1.

B & Q SCOTTISH LEAGUE
PREMIER DIVISION RESULTS 1988–89

Note: *In the Scottish League Divisions I and II, the teams play each other twice and after a draw made at the beginning of the season, half of the fixtures are repeated once.*

Home \ Away	Aberdeen	Celtic	Dundee	Dundee U	Hamilton Acad	Hearts	Hibernian	Motherwell	Rangers	St Mirren
St Mirren	1-1	1-1	0-1	1-0	2-2	1-0	2-0	2-0	2-1	—
Rangers	2-1	3-1	0-2	1-1	1-1	0-2	1-2	0-1	—	1-2
Motherwell	2-0	1-1	1-1	1-1	0-2	2-0	0-2	—	2-0	0-2
Hibernian	0-2	0-1	2-1	1-1	3-3	1-1	—	1-0	0-0	0-1
Hearts	0-0	0-1	1-1	0-0	1-0	—	0-0	2-1	3-0	1-1
Hamilton Acad	1-0	2-0	2-0	0-1	—	2-0	0-1	1-0	3-0	2-0
Dundee U	1-0	0-0	0-1	—	0-0	0-0	1-2	1-2	0-2	1-1
Dundee	0-0	2-1	—	2-0	1-0	1-1	1-1	1-0	2-1	0-1
Celtic	2-0	—	0-0	0-2	0-0	0-1	1-1	1-2	1-1	2-1
Aberdeen	—	0-0	1-2	2-1	0-2	1-0	1-2	1-2	0-0	1-3

126

B & Q SCOTTISH LEAGUE DIVISION 1 RESULTS 1988–89

	1	2	3	4	5	6	7	8	9	10	11	12	13	14
Airdrieonians (1)	—	2-1	1-1 / 1-1	1-1 / 1-1	0-2	2-0 / 3-0	0-3 / 2-1	5-1	0-0	1-1 / 2-1	5-1	3-0 / 3-1	3-1	1-0 / 1-1
Ayr U (2)	1-4 / 3-1	—	1-1	3-2 / 2-4	2-2 / 1-2	3-4	2-1	4-1 / 2-1	2-2 / 3-2	3-1 / 0-1	1-3	1-1	1-1 / 2-2	2-1
Clyde (3)	0-0	4-2 / 1-0	—	0-5 / 1-0	1-1	1-2	1-1 / 1-1	0-2	1-2	0-1 / 2-1	1-0 / 0-0	3-1 / 2-1	0-1	2-4 / 2-0
Clydebank (4)	3-3 / 4-1	5-1 / 3-2	3-2	—	2-1 / 0-1	2-2 / 0-1	2-2	2-2 / 3-2	2-1	1-1	3-2 / 4-2	4-2 / 3-0	3-1	2-0 / 2-2
Dunfermline Ath (5)	1-0 / 1-1	5-1	3-0 / 1-1	2-2	—	3-0	2-0	3-0 / 0-0	2-1 / 1-1	1-0 / 1-0	4-2	4-2	0-1 / 3-0	2-0
Falkirk (6)	0-0 / 2-0	1-0 / 2-0	0-0 / 3-1	3-1	4-0	—	1-2	2-0	3-0 / 0-0	0-1 / 1-0	0-1	2-0 / 7-1	3-1 / 3-0	1-0 / 1-1
Forfar Ath (7)	1-1	1-2 / 0-0	2-1	2-4 / 1-2	2-1 / 0-1	0-0 / 2-2	—	2-2	1-0 / 2-1	0-1 / 0-0	3-2	2-2	1-0 / 1-2	1-1 / 1-1
Kilmarnock (8)	0-3 / 1-1	2-0 / 0-0	1-2 / 0-0	1-0	1-2	0-2 / 2-2	2-1 / 2-2	—	1-0	3-4	0-1 / 0-0	2-1	1-0 / 1-2	0-3
Meadowbank Th (9)	3-2 / 3-1	1-2	3-2 / 2-0	0-0 / 1-1	0-1	1-5 / 2-2	1-1	0-2 / 1-2	—	2-1	0-2	1-2	2-1 / 1-3	1-1 / 2-1
Morton (10)	0-2	2-0	0-2	1-0 / 1-0	1-0	1-3 / 2-1	1-1	2-2 / 3-0	2-0 / 0-2	—	1-0 / 1-1	1-0 / 0-1	0-1 / 0-1	2-0
Partick Th (11)	0-2 / 1-0	2-2 / 4-1	0-0	1-1	1-0 / 0-0	1-3 / 2-1	1-2 / 4-1	0-1 / 2-1	1-1 / 2-1	1-4	—	2-1 / 2-1	0-1 / 0-1	2-0
Queen of the S (12)	2-4	0-2 / 1-2	3-3	0-3	0-0 / 0-2	0-3	2-2 / 2-3	2-2 / 0-6	0-1 / 1-2	2-3 / 1-1	1-4 / 2-4	—	0-1	1-1
Raith R (13)	1-2 / 1-1	0-0	0-0 / 2-0	1-3 / 3-0	1-3	1-3	2-1 / 2-3	0-0 / 1-0	1-0	5-3 / 1-1	2-1 / 4-1	2-1 / 1-1	—	1-1 / 0-2
St Johnstone (14)	2-1	2-0 / 0-1	0-0	2-0	0-1	2-1 / 0-1	2-0 / 2-2	0-0	4-2 / 0-1	2-1	3-1 / 1-1	2-1 / 3-1	3-1 / 3-1	—

127

B & Q SCOTTISH LEAGUE DIVISION II RESULTS 1988–89

	1	2	3	4	5	6	7	8	9	10	11	12	13	14
Albion R (1)	—	3-2	3-1 2-2	3-1 2-1	1-1	3-1 2-1	2-1 2-0	2-0 1-2	1-0	2-1 2-2	1-1	1-0	1-0	3-0 2-2
Alloa (2)	3-1 2-0	—	3-3 3-0	2-1	2-2	2-1 2-1	2-0	2-1	2-2	1-0 3-3	0-0	1-2 4-0	3-2 4-0	1-1
Arbroath (3)	0-3	2-2	—	1-2 0-3bz	1-2	0-1	1-1 1-3	2-1	3-3 2-2	0-0	2-2	5-1 2-1	2-1 0-4	1-0 4-3
Berwick R (4)	2-1	1-1 1-0	0-3	—	4-4	0-1 0-0	1-0	1-3 1-3	0-5 2-0	1-2 1-1	0-2 1-1	0-2 2-0	0-0 2-2	0-1
Brechin C (5)	0-2 2-1	2-1 1-2	1-0 3-4	2-0 0-2	—	1-0	1-1	1-2	2-2	1-1	2-0	3-1 1-1	2-3	2-2
Cowdenbeath (6)	1-1	1-1	1-1 1-1	3-3 0-2	3-3 0-2	—	2-0 1-1	1-1	2-1	2-6	2-2 3-1	2-0 2-1	1-1	1-0 1-1
Dumbarton (7)	1-0	1-1 0-2	1-4	2-2 0-4	0-0 1-0	3-0	—	3-1 4-0	3-0	3-2 2-0	0-3 1-0	0-2 2-0	1-2	0-2
East Fife (8)	1-2	2-1 2-0	0-0	2-2 1-1	1-0 1-0	4-1 1-0	1-1	—	2-2	1-1 1-4	2-2	2-1 1-1	2-0 3-0	1-2 1-0
East Stirling (9)	3-4 0-1	2-1 2-0	0-3	3-2	4-3 1-1	1-0 0-2	0-1 1-0	2-2 4-2	—	1-0	2-1 2-1	0-3	2-2	1-2
Montrose (10)	1-0	1-0	0-1 1-1	2-1	0-2 1-0	1-0 0-2	1-1	2-2	0-1 2-1	—	1-1	3-1	3-2 0-6	4-2 1-0
Queen's Park (11)	0-0 3-2	0-2 0-2	2-0 1-1	2-0	1-1 1-2	0-2 2-1	2-1	1-0 1-2	0-0	2-0 2-2	—	1-1	2-0	4-3
Stenhousemuir (12)	2-3 1-2	2-0	0-0	3-2 2-0	0-2 1-3	0-0	3-1	1-1	1-1 1-0	0-1 2-3	0-0 1-1	—	1-1 2-4	3-4 2-0
Stirling A (13)	4-2 0-0	3-1	1-1	2-1	2-2 0-0	2-3 0-1	1-1 3-1	3-1	1-0 2-1	2-0	3-2 0-0	2-0	—	0-3
Stranraer (14)	3-1	2-2 1-4	0-1	2-2 1-2	0-1 2-1	2-0	2-2 1-1	2-2	1-2 0-0	1-0	3-1 3-3	2-1	1-1 1-4	—

128

B & Q SCOTTISH LEAGUE
FINAL TABLES 1988–89

Premier Division

		Home			Goals		Away			Goals			
	P	W	D	L	F	A	W	D	L	F	A	GD	Pts
Rangers	36	15	1	2	39	11	11	3	4	23	15	+36	56
Aberdeen	36	10	7	1	26	10	8	7	3	25	15	+26	50
Celtic...................	36	13	1	4	35	18	8	3	7	31	26	+22	46
Dundee U.............	36	6	8	4	20	16	10	4	4	24	10	+18	44
Hibernian U..........	36	8	4	6	20	16	5	5	8	17	20	+1	35
Hearts	36	7	6	5	22	17	2	7	9	13	25	−7	31
St Mirren	36	5	6	7	17	19	6	1	11	22	36	−16	29
Dundee	36	8	4	6	22	21	1	6	11	12	27	−14	28
Motherwell	36	5	7	6	21	21	2	6	10	14	23	−9	27
Hamilton Acad	36	5	0	13	9	42	1	2	15	10	34	−57	14

First Division

		Home			Goals		Away			Goals			
	P	W	D	L	F	A	W	D	L	F	A	GD	Pts
Dunfermline Ath....	39	13	5	2	37	17	9	5	5	23	19	+24	54
Falkirk.................	39	13	3	3	38	10	9	5	6	33	27	+34	52
Clydebank	39	12	6	2	50	29	6	6	7	30	26	+25	48
Airdrieonians........	39	11	6	2	36	16	6	7	7	30	28	+22	47
Morton	39	8	5	6	20	20	8	4	8	26	26	0	41
St Johnstone	39	11	4	4	30	16	3	8	9	21	26	+9	40
Raith Rovers	39	8	6	6	29	25	7	4	8	21	27	−2	40
Partick Th	39	7	6	6	26	24	6	5	9	31	34	−1	37
Forfar Ath............	39	6	9	5	24	24	4	7	8	28	32	−4	36
Meadowbank Th	39	8	4	7	26	26	5	6	9	19	24	−5	36
Ayr U..................	39	8	6	6	39	37	5	3	11	17	35	−16	35
Clyde..................	39	7	6	7	23	26	2	10	7	17	26	−12	34
Kilmarnock...........	39	5	7	7	19	25	5	7	8	28	35	−13	34
*Q of S	39	1	6	13	20	47	1	2	16	18	52	−61	10

Second Division

		Home			Goals		Away			Goals			
	P	W	D	L	F	A	W	D	L	F	A	GD	Pts
Albion R..............	39	14	5	1	39	19	7	3	9	26	29	+17	50
Alloa....................	39	12	6	1	42	20	5	5	10	24	28	+18	45
Brechin C.............	39	8	5	6	27	24	7	8	5	31	25	+9	43
Stirling A	39	10	6	3	31	20	5	6	9	33	35	+9	42
East Fife	39	9	8	3	30	20	5	5	9	25	34	+1	41
Montrose	39	10	4	5	25	25	5	7	8	29	30	−1	41
Queen's Park	39	8	7	4	26	20	2	11	7	24	29	+1	38
*Cowdenbeath........	39	6	11	2	30	27	7	3	10	18	25	−4	38
E. Stirling	39	10	3	7	31	31	3	8	8	23	27	−4	37
Arbroath..............	39	5	6	9	29	40	6	9	4	27	23	−7	37
Stranraer..............	39	6	8	6	30	31	6	4	9	28	32	−5	36
Dumbarton	39	10	2	8	28	27	2	8	9	17	28	−10	34
Berwick R............	39	5	7	7	18	26	5	6	9	32	33	−9	33
Stenhousemuir	39	6	8	6	27	24	3	3	13	17	35	−15	29

*2 points deducted for breach of rules

SCOTTISH LEAGUE HONOURS LIST

Premier Division (maximum points: *a*, 72; *b*, 88)

	First	Pt	*Second*	Pt	*Third*	Pt
1975–76 *a*	Rangers	54	Celtic	48	Hibernian	43
1976–77 *a*	Celtic	55	Rangers	46	Aberdeen	43
1977–78 *a*	Rangers	55	Aberdeen	53	Dundee U	40
1978–79 *a*	Celtic	48	Rangers	45	Dundee U	44
1979–80 *a*	Aberdeen	48	Celtic	47	St Mirren	42
1980–81 *a*	Celtic	56	Aberdeen	49	Rangers	44
1981–82 *a*	Celtic	55	Aberdeen	53	Rangers	43
1982–83 *a*	Dundee U	56	Celtic	55	Aberdeen	55
1983–84 *a*	Aberdeen	57	Celtic	50	Dundee U	47
1984–85 *a*	Aberdeen	59	Celtic	52	Dundee U	47
1985–86 *a*	Celtic	50	Hearts	50	Dundee U	47
1986–87 *b*	Rangers	69	Celtic	63	Dundee U	60
1987–88 *b*	Celtic	72	Hearts	62	Rangers	60
1988–89 *a*	Rangers	56	Aberdeen	50	Celtic	46

First Division (maximum points: *a*, 52; *b*, 78; *c*, 88)

	First	Pt	*Second*	Pt	*Third*	Pt
1975–76 *a*	Partick Th	41	Kilmarnock	35	Montrose	30
1976–77 *b*	St Mirren	62	Clydebank	58	Dundee	51
1977–78 *b**	Morton	58	Hearts	58	Dundee	57
1978–79 *b*	Dundee	55	*Kilmarnock	54	Clydebank	54
1979–80 *b*	Hearts	53	Airdrieonians	51	Ayr U	44
1980–81 *b*	Hibernian	57	Dundee	52	St Johnstone	51
1981–82 *b*	Motherwell	61	Kilmarnock	51	Hearts	50
1982–83 *b*	St Johnstone	55	Hearts	54	Clydebank	50
1983–84 *b*	Morton	54	Dumbarton	51	Partick Th	46
1984–85 *b*	Motherwell	50	Clydebank	48	Falkirk	45
1985–86 *b*	Hamilton Acad.	56	Falkirk	45	Kilmarnock	44
1986–87 *c*	Morton	57	Dunfermline Ath	56	Dumbarton	53
1987–88 *c*	Hamilton Acad.	56	Meadowbank Th	52	Clydebank	49
1988–89 *b*	Dunfermline Ath	54	Falkirk	52	Clydebank	48

Second Division (maximum points: *a*, 52; *b*, 78)

	First	Pt	*Second*	Pt	*Third*	Pt
1975–76 *a**	Clydebank	40	Raith Rovers	40	Alloa	35
1976–77 *b*	Stirling Albion	55	Alloa	51	Dunfermline Ath.	50
1977–78 *b**	Clyde	53	Raith Rovers	53	Dunfermline Ath.	48
1978–79 *b*	Berwick	54	Dunfermline Ath.	52	Falkirk	50
1979–80 *b*	Falkirk	50	E. Stirlingshire	49	Forfar Ath	46
1980–81 *b*	Queen's Park	50	Q of S	46	Cowdenbeath	45
1981–82 *b*	Clyde	59	*Alloa	50	Arbroath	50
1982–83 *b*	Brechin	55	Meadowbank Th.	54	Arbroath	49
1983–84 *b*	Forfar Ath	63	E. Fife	47	Berwick Rangers	43
1984–85 *b*	Montrose	53	Alloa	50	Dunfermline Ath.	49
1985–86 *b*	Dunfermline Ath.	57	Q of the S	55	Meadowbank Th	49
1986–87 *b*	Meadowbank Th.	55	*Raith Rovers	52	Stirling Albion	52
1987–88 *b*	Ayr U	61	St Johnstone	59	Queen's Park	51
1988–89 *b*	Albion R	50	Alloa	45	Brechin C	43

First Division to 1974–75 (maximum points: a, 36; b, 44; c,40; d, 52; e, 60; f, 68; g, 76; h, 84; j, 60)

	First	Pt	Second	Pt	Third	Pt
1890–91 *a*	Dumbarton	29	Rangers	29	Celtic	24
1891–92 *b*	Dumbarton	37	Celtic	35	Hearts	30
1892–93 *a*	Celtic	29	Rangers	28	St Mirren	23
1893–94	Celtic	29	Hearts	26	St Bernards	22
1894–95	Hearts	31	Celtic	26	Rangers	21
1895–96	Celtic	30	Rangers	26	Hibernian	24
1896–97	Hearts	28	Hibernian	26	Rangers	25
1897–98	Celtic	33	Rangers	29	Hibernian	22
1898–99	Rangers	36	Hearts	26	Celtic	24
1899–1900	Rangers	32	Celtic	25	Hibernian	24
1900–1 *c*	Rangers	35	Celtic	29	Hibernian	25
1901–2 *a*	Rangers	28	Celtic	26	Hearts	22
1902–3 *b*	Hibernian	37	Dundee	31	Rangers	29
1903–4	Third Lanark	43	Hearts	39	*Rangers	38
1904–5 *d*	Celtic	41	Rangers	41	Third Lanark	35
1905–6 *e*	Celtic	49	Hearts	43	Airdrieonians	38
1906–7 *f*	Celtic	55	Dundee	48	Rangers	45
1907–8	Celtic	55	Falkirk	51	Rangers	50
1908–9	Celtic	51	Dundee	50	Clyde	48
1909–10	Celtic	54	Falkirk	52	Rangers	46
1910–11	Rangers	52	Aberdeen	48	Falkirk	44
1911–12	Rangers	51	Celtic	45	Clyde	42
1912–13	Rangers	53	Celtic	49	*Hearts	41
1913–14 *g*	Celtic	65	Rangers	59	*Hearts	54
1914–15 *g*	Celtic	65	Hearts	61	Rangers	50
1916–17 *g*	Celtic	64	Morton	54	Rangers	53
1917–18 *f*	Rangers	56	Celtic	55	Kilmarnock	43
1918–19	Celtic	58	Rangers	57	Morton	47
1919–20 *h*	Rangers	71	Celtic	68	Motherwell	57
1920–21	Rangers	76	Celtic	66	Hearts	56
1921–22	Celtic	67	Rangers	66	Raith Rovers	56
1922–23 *g*	Rangers	55	Airdrieonians	50	Celtic	46
1923–24	Rangers	59	Airdrieonians	50	Celtic	41
1924–25	Rangers	60	Airdrieonians	57	Hibernian	52
1925–26	Celtic	58	*Airdrieonians	50	Hearts	50
1926–27	Rangers	56	Motherwell	51	Celtic	49
1927–28	Rangers	60	*Celtic	55	Motherwell	55
1928–29	Rangers	67	Celtic	51	Motherwell	50
1929–30	Rangers	60	Motherwell	55	Aberdeen	53
1930–31	Rangers	60	Celtic	58	Motherwell	56
1931–32	Motherwell	66	Rangers	61	Celtic	48
1932–33	Rangers	62	Motherwell	59	Hearts	50
1933–34	Rangers	66	Motherwell	62	Celtic	47
1934–35	Rangers	55	Celtic	52	Hearts	50
1935–36	Celtic	66	*Rangers	61	Aberdeen	61
1936–37	Rangers	61	Aberdeen	54	Celtic	52
1937–38	Celtic	61	Hearts	58	Rangers	49
1938–39	Rangers	59	Celtic	48	Aberdeen	46
1946–47 *f*	Rangers	46	Hibernian	44	Aberdeen	39
1947–48 *j*	Hibernian	48	Rangers	46	Partick Th	36
1948–49	Rangers	46	Dundee	45	Hibernian	39
1949–50	Rangers	50	Hibernian	49	Hearts	43
1950–51	Hibernian	48	*Rangers	38	Dundee	38
1951–52	Hibernian	45	Rangers	41	E. Fife	37

1952–53	*Rangers	43	Hibernian	43	E. Fife	39
1953–54	Celtic	43	Hearts	38	Partick Th	35
1954–55	Aberdeen	49	Celtic	46	Rangers	41
1955–56 f	Rangers	52	Aberdeen	46	*Hearts	45
1956–57	Rangers	55	Hearts	53	Kilmarnock	42
1957–58	Hearts	62	Rangers	49	Celtic	46
1958–59	Rangers	50	Hearts	48	Motherwell	44
1959–60	Hearts	54	Kilmarnock	50	*Rangers	42
1960–61	Rangers	51	Kilmarnock	50	Third Lanark	42
1961–62	Dundee	54	Rangers	51	Celtic	46
1962–63	Rangers	57	Kilmarnock	48	Partick Th	46
1963–64	Rangers	55	Kilmarnock	49	*Celtic	47
1964–65 *	Kilmarnock	50	Hearts	50	Dunfermline Ath	49
1965–66	Celtic	57	Rangers	55	Kilmarnock	45
1966–67	Celtic	58	Rangers	55	Clyde	46
1967–68	Celtic	63	Rangers	61	Hibernian	45
1968–69	Celtic	54	Rangers	49	Dunfermline Ath	45
1969–70	Celtic	57	Rangers	45	Hibernian	44
1970–71	Celtic	56	Aberdeen	54	St Johnstone	44
1971–72	Celtic	60	Aberdeen	50	Rangers	44
1972–73	Celtic	57	Rangers	56	Hibernian	45
1973–74	Celtic	53	Hibernian	49	Rangers	48
1974–75	Rangers	56	Hibernian	49	Celtic	45

Second Division to 1974–75 from 1921–22 (maximum points: *a*, 76; *b*, 72; *c*, 68; *d*, 52; *e*, 60)

	First	Pt	Second	Pt	Third	Pt
1921–22 a†	*Alloa	60	Cowdenbeath	47	Armadale	45
1922–23 a	Queen's Park	57	Clydebank	**50	St Johnstone	**45
1923–24 a	St Johnstone	56	Cowdenbeath	55	Bathgate	44
1924–25 a	Dundee U	50	Clydebank	48	Clyde	47
1925–26 a	Dunfermline Ath	59	Clyde	53	Ayr U	52
1926–27 a	Bo'ness	56	Raith Rovers	49	Clydebank	45
1927–28 a	Ayr U	54	Third Lanark	45	King's Park	44
1928–29 b	Dundee U	51	Morton	50	Arbroath	47
1929–30 a*	Leith Ath	57	E. Fife	57	Albion Rovers	54
1930–31 a	Third Lanark	61	Dundee U	50	Dunfermline Ath	47
1931–32 a*	E. Stirling	55	St Johnstone	55	*Raith Rovers	46
1932–33 c	Hibernian	54	QofS	49	Dunfermline Ath	47
1933–34 c	Albion Rovers	45	*Dunfermline Ath	44	Arbroath	44
1934–35 c	Third Lanark	52	Arbroath	50	St Bernard's	47
1935–36 c	Falkirk	59	St Mirren	52	Morton	48
1936–37 c	Ayr U	54	Morton	51	St Bernard's	48
1937–38 c	Raith Rovers	59	Albion Rovers	48	Airdrieonians	47
1938–39 c	Cowdenbeath	60	*Alloa	48	E. Fife	48
1946–47 d	Dundee	45	Airdrieonians	42	E. Fife	31
1947–48 e	E. Fife	53	Albion Rovers	42	Hamilton Acad	40
1948–49 e*	Raith Rovers	42	Stirling Albion	42	*Airdrieonians	41
1949–50 e	Morton	47	Airdrieonians	44	*St Johnstone	36
1950–51 e*	QofS	45	Stirling Albion	45	*Ayr U	36
1951–52 e	Clyde	44	Falkirk	43	Ayr U	39
1952–53 e	Stirling Albion	44	Hamilton Acad	43	Queen's Park	37
1953–54 e	Motherwell	45	Kilmarnock	42	*Third Lanark	36
1954–55 e	Airdrieonians	46	Dunfermline Ath	42	Hamilton Acad	39
1955–56 b	Queen's Park	54	Ayr U	51	St Johnstone	49
1956–57 b	Clyde	64	Third Lanark	51	Cowdenbeath	45

132

1957–58	b	Stirling Albion	55	Dunfermline Ath	53	Arbroath	47
1958–59	b	Ayr U	60	Arbroath	51	Stenhousemuir	46
1959–60	b	St Johnstone	53	Dundee U	50	Q of S	49
1960–61	b	Stirling Albion	55	Falkirk	54	Stenhousemuir	50
1961–62	b	Clyde	54	Q of S	53	Morton	44
1962–63	b	St Johnstone	55	E. Stirling	49	Morton	48
1963–64	b	Morton	67	Cylde	53	Arbroath	46
1964–65	b	Stirling Albion	59	Hamilton Acad	50	Q of S	45
1965–66	b	Ayr U	53	Airdrieonians	50	Q of S	49
1966–67	b	Morton	69	Raith Rovers	58	Arbroath	57
1967–68	b	St Mirren	62	Arbroath	53	E. Fife	40
1968–69	b	Motherwell	64	Ayr U	53	*E. Fife	47
1969–70	b	Falkirk	56	Cowdenbeath	55	Q of S	50
1970–71	b	Partick Th	56	E. Fife	51	Arbroath	46
1971–72	b*	Dumbarton	52	Arbroath	52	Stirling Albion	50
1972–73	b	Clyde	56	Dunfermline Ath	52	*Raith Rovers	47
1973–74	b	Airdrieonians	60	Kilmarnock	59	Hamilton Acad	55
1974–75	b	Falkirk	54	*Q of S.	53	Montrose	53

*On goal average/difference. † Held jointly after indecisive play-off. ‡ Won on deciding match. †† Held jointly. ** Two points deducted for fielding ineligible player. *† Only one club promoted. Competition suspended 1940–45.

RELEGATED CLUBS

From Premier Division

1975–76	Dundee, St Johnstone	1984–85	Dumbarton, Morton
1976–77	Hearts, Kilmarnock	1985–86	*No relegation due to*
1977–78	Ayr U, Clydebank		*League reorganisation*
1978–79	Hearts, Motherwell	1986–87	Clidebank, Hamilton
1979–80	Dundee, Hibernian		Acad
1980–81	Kilmarnock, Hearts	1987–88	Falkirk, Dunfermline Ath,
1981–82	Partick Th. Airdrieonians		Morton
1982–83	Morton, Kilmarnock	1988–89	Hamilton Acad
1983–84	St Johnstone, Motherwell		

From First Division

1975–76	Dunfermline Ath, Clyde	1982–83	Dunfermline Ath, Queen's Park
1976–77	Raith R, Falkirk	1983–84	Raith R., Alloa
1977–78	Alloa, E. Fife	1984–85	Meadowbank Th,
1978–79	Montrose, Q of S		St Johnstone
1979–80	Arbroath, Clyde	1985–86	Ayr U, Alloa
1980–81	Stirling A, Berwick R	1986–87	Brechin City, Montrose
1981–82	E. Stirling, Q of S	1987–88	E. Fife, Dumbarton
		1988–89	Kilmarnock Q of S.

Relegated from First Division to 1973–74

1921–22	*Queen's Park,	1953–54	Airdrieonians,
	Dumbarton, Clydebank		Hamilton Acad
1922–23	Albion R, Alloa	1954–55	*No clubs relegated*
1923–24	Clyde, Clydebank	1955–56	Stirling A, Clyde
1924–25	Third Lanark, Ayr U	1956–57	Dunfermline Ath,
1925–26	Raith R, Clydebank		Ayr U

1926–27	Morton, Dundee U	1950–51	Clyde, Falkirk
1927–28	Dunfermline Ath, Bo'ness	1951–52	Morton, Stirling A
		1952–53	Motherwell, Third Lanark
1928–29	Third Lanark, Raith R,		
1929–30	St Johnstone, Dundee U	1957–58	E. Fife, Queen's Park
		1958–59	Q of S, Falkirk
1930–31	Hibernian, E. Fife	1959–60	Arbroath, Stirling A
1931–32	Dundee U, Leith Ath	1960–61	Ayr U, Clyde
1932–33	Morton, E. Stirling	1961–62	St Johnstone, Stirling A
1933–34	Third Lanark, Cowdenbeath	1962–63	Clyde, Raith R
		1963–64	Q of S, E. Stirling
1934–35	St Mirren, Falkirk	1964–65	Airdrieonians, Third Lanark
1935–36	Airdrieonians, Ayr U		
1936–37	Dunfermline Ath, Albion R	1965–66	Morton, Hamilton Acad
		1966–67	St Mirren, Ayr U
1937–38	Dundee, Morton	1967–68	Motherwell, Stirling A
1938–39	Queen's Park, Raith R	1968–69	Falkirk, Arbroath
1946–47	Kilmarnock, Hamilton Acad	1969–70	Raith R, Partick Th
		1970–71	St Mirren, Cowdenbeath
1947–48	Airdrieonians, Queen's Park	1971–72	Clyde, Dunfermline Ath
		1972–73	Kilmarnock, Airdrieonians
1948–49	Morton, Albion R		
1949–50	Q of S, Stirling A	1973–74	E. Fife, Falkirk
		1974–75	*League reorganised at end of season*

*Season 1921–22 – only 1 club promoted, 3 clubs relegated.

Scottish League
Leading scorers 1988–89
Listed in order of League goals. Columns indicate League, Skol Cup, Scottish Cup.

Premier Division

Mark McGhee (Celtic)	16	0	2	18
Charlie Nicholas (Aberdeen)	16	1	1	18
Steve Kirk (Motherwell)	14	1	3	18
Steve Archibald (Hibernian)	13	2	1	16
Kevin Drinkell (Rangers)	12	2	5	19
Frank McAvennie (Celtic)	12	3	1	16

Division I

Ken Macdonald (Airdrie)	22	0	0	22
Ken Eadie (Clydebank)	21	1	1	23
Gerry McCoy (Partick Th)	19	0	2	21
Ross Jack (Dunfermline Ath)	18	0	0	18
Henry Templeton (Ayr U)	17	1	1	19

Division 2

Charlie Lytwyn (Alloa)	23	1	3	27
Gary Murray (Montrose)	21	0	2	23
Charlie Gibson (Stirling A)	18	1	0	19
Jimmy Chapman (Albion R)	15	1	0	16
Alastair Graham (Albion R)	15	0	0	15

Scottish League and Cup honours
Championship wins
39 – Rangers (including one shared); 35 – Celtic; 4 – Aberdeen, Hearts, Hibernian; 2 –
Dumbarton (including one shared); 1 – Dundee, Dundee U, Kilmarnock, Motherwell,
Third Lanark.

Scottish FA Cup
29 – Celtic; 24 – Rangers; 10 – Queen's Park; 6 – Aberdeen; 5 – Hearts; 3 – Clyde,
St Mirren, Vale of Leven; 2 – Dunfermline Ath, Falkirk, Hibernian, Kilmarnock,
Renton, Third Lanark; 1 – Airdrieonians, Dumbarton, Dundee, East Fife, Morton,
Motherwell, Partick Th, St Bernard's.

Scottish League/Skol Cup
15 – Rangers; 9 – Celtic; 4 – Aberdeen, Hearts; 3 – Dundee, East Fife; 2 – Dundee U; 1
– Hibernian, Motherwell, Partick Th.

SCOTTISH CUP 1988–89

First Round

Berwick R	1	Alloa	1
Replay: Alloa	2	Berwick R	1
E. Fife	4	Spartans	1
E. Stirling	1	Gala Fairydean	0
Inverness Th	0	Dumbarton	0
Replay: Dumbarton	2	Inverness Th	1
Montrose	2	Arbroath	0
Stranraer	2	Stirling	2
Replay: Stirling	0	Stranraer	1

Second Round

Annan	1	Queen's Park	5
Coldstream	1	Albion	1
Replay: Albion	1	Coldstream	0
Cowdenbeath	1	Stenhousemuir	1
Replay: Stenhousemuir	3	Cowdenbeath	2
E. Stirling	1	Montrose	2
Elgin	2	Dumbarton	2
Replay: Dumbarton	4	Elgin	0
Forres Mech	1	Alloa	1
Replay: Alloa	2	Forres Mech	1
Inverness Cal	1	Brechin	1
Replay: Brechin	2	Inverness Cal	1
Stranraer	2	East Fife	1

Third Round

Alloa	3	Albion	1
Celtic	2	Dumbarton	0
Clydebank	2	Montrose	1
Dundee	1	Dundee U	2
Dunfermline Ath	0	Aberdeen	0
Replay: Aberdeen	3	Dunfermline Ath	1
Falkirk	1	Motherwell	1
Replay: Motherwell	2	Falkirk	1
Forfar Ath	1	Clyde	1
Replay: Clyde	0	Forfar Ath	1
Hearts	4	Ayr U	1
Hibernian	1	Brechin	0
Meadowbank Th	2	Hamilton Acad	0
Morton	0	Airdrieonians	0
Replay: Airdrieonians	0	Morton	1
Partick Th	0	St Mirren	0
Replay: St Mirren	1	Partick Th	3
Q of S	2	Kilmarnock	2
Replay: Kilmarnock	0	Q of S	1
Queen's Park	0	Stranraer	0
Replay: Stranraer	1	Queen's Park	0
Raith	1	Rangers	1
Replay: Rangers	3	Raith	0
St Johnstone	2	Stenhousemuir	0

Fourth Round

Aberdeen	1	Dundee U	1
Replay: Dundee U	1	Aberdeen	1
Second Replay: Dundee U	1	Aberdeen	0
Celtic	4	Clydebank	1
Hearts	2	Partick Th	0
Hibernian	2	Motherwell	1
Meadowbank	0	Morton	1
Q of S	0	Alloa	0
Replay: Alloa	4	Q of S	1
Rangers	8	Stranraer	0
St Johnstone	2	Forfar Ath	1

Fifth Round

Celtic	2	Hearts	1
Hibernian	1	Alloa	0
Morton	2	St Johnstone	2
Replay: St Johnstone	3	Morton	2
Rangers	2	Dundee U	2
Replay: Dundee U	0	Rangers	1

Semi-finals

Celtic	3	Hibernian	1
Rangers	0	St Johnstone	0
Replay: St Johnstone	0	Rangers	4

Final at Hampden Park, 20 May 1989, att. 72,069
Celtic (1) 1 (*Miller*), Rangers (0) 0

SCOTTISH CUP PAST FINALS

1874	Queen's Park	2	Clydesdale	0
1875	Queen's Park	3	Renton	0
1876	Queen's Park	1 2	Third Lanark	1 0
1877	Vale of Leven	0 1 3	Rangers	0 1 2
1878	Vale of Leven	1	Third Lanark	0
1879	Vale of Leven	1	Rangers	1
	Vale of Leven awarded cup, Rangers did not appear for replay			
1880	Queen's Park	3	Thornliebank	0
1881	Queen's Park	2 3	Dumbarton	1 1
	Replayed because of protest			
1882	Queen's Park	2 4	Dumbarton	2 1
1883	Dumbarton	2 2	Vale of Leven	2 1
1884	*Queen's Park awarded cup when Vale of Leven did not appear for the final*			
1885	Renton	0 3	Vale of Leven	0 1
1886	Queen's Park	3	Renton	1
1887	Hibernian	2	Dumbarton	1
1888	Renton	6	Cambuslang	1
1889	Third Lanark	3 2	Celtic	0 1
	Replayed because of protest			
1890	Queen's Park	1 2	Vale of Leven	1 1
1891	Hearts	1	Dumbarton	0
1892	Celtic	1 5	Queen's Park	0 1
	Replayed because of protest			

1893	Queen's Park	2	Celtic	1
1894	Rangers	3	Celtic	1
1895	St Bernards	2	Renton	1
1896	Hearts	3	Hibernian	1
1897	Rangers	5	Dumbarton	1
1898	Rangers	2	Kilmarnock	0
1899	Celtic	2	Rangers	0
1900	Celtic	4	Queen's Park	3
1901	Hearts	4	Celtic	3
1902	Hibernian	1	Celtic	0
1903	Rangers	1 0 2	Hearts	1 0 0
1904	Celtic	3	Rangers	2
1905	Third Lanark	0 3	Rangers	0 1
1906	Hearts	1	Third Lanark	0
1907	Celtic	3	Hearts	0
1908	Celtic	5	St Mirren	1
1909	*After two drawn games between Celtic and Rangers, 2–2, 1–1, there was a riot and the cup was withheld*			
1910	Dundee	2 0 2	Clyde	2 0 1
1911	Celtic	0 2	Hamilton	0 0
1912	Celtic	2	Clyde	0
1913	Falkirk	2	Raith Rovers	0
1914	Celtic	0 4	Hibernian	0 1
1920	Kilmarnock	3	Albion Rovers	2
1921	Partick Th	1	Rangers	0
1922	Morton	1	Rangers	0
1923	Celtic	1	Hibernian	0
1924	Airdrieonians	2	Hibernian	0
1925	Celtic	2	Dundee	1
1926	St Mirren	2	Celtic	0
1927	Celtic	3	East Fife	1
1928	Rangers	4	Celtic	0
1929	Kilmarnock	2	Rangers	0
1930	Rangers	0 2	Partick Th	0 1
1931	Celtic	2 4	Motherwell	2 2
1932	Rangers	1 3	Kilmarnock	1 0
1933	Celtic	1	Motherwell	0
1934	Rangers	5	St Mirren	0
1935	Rangers	2	Hamilton Acad	1
1936	Rangers	1	Third Lanark	0
1937	Celtic	2	Aberdeen	1
1938	East Fife	1 4	Kilmarnock	1 2
1939	Clyde	4	Motherwell	0
1947	Aberdeen	2	Hibernian	1
1948	Rangers	1 1	Morton	1 0
1949	Rangers	4	Clyde	1
1950	Rangers	3	East Fife	0
1951	Celtic	1	Motherwell	0
1952	Motherwell	4	Dundee	0
1953	Rangers	1 1	Aberdeen	1 0
1954	Celtic	2	Aberdeen	1
1955	Clyde	1 1	Celtic	1 0
1956	Hearts	3	Celtic	1
1957	Falkirk	1 2	Kilmarnock	1 1
1958	Clyde	1	Hibernian	0
1959	St Mirren	3	Aberdeen	1
1960	Rangers	2	Kilmarnock	0

1961	Dunfermline Ath	0 2	Celtic	0 0
1962	Rangers	2	St Mirren	0
1963	Rangers	1 3	Celtic	1 0
1964	Rangers	3	Dundee	1
1965	Celtic	3	Dunfermline Ath	2
1966	Rangers	0 1	Celtic	0 0
1967	Celtic	2	Aberdeen	0
1968	Dunfermline Ath	3	Hearts	1
1969	Celtic	4	Rangers	0
1970	Aberdeen	3	Celtic	1
1971	Celtic	1 2	Rangers	1 1
1972	Celtic	6	Hibernian	1
1973	Rangers	3	Celtic	2
1974	Celtic	3	Dundee U	0
1975	Celtic	3	Airdrieonians	1
1976	Rangers	3	Hearts	1
1977	Celtic	1	Rangers	0
1978	Rangers	2	Aberdeen	1
1979	Rangers	0 0 3	Hibernian	0 0 2
1980	Celtic	1	Rangers	0
1981	Rangers	0 4	Dundee U	0 1
1982	Aberdeen	4	Rangers	1
1983	Aberdeen	1	Rangers	0
1984	Aberdeen	2	Celtic	1
1985	Celtic	2	Dundee U	1
1986	Aberdeen	3	Hearts	0
1987	St Mirren	1	Dundee U	0
1988	Celtic	2	Dundee U	1

SKOL (SCOTTISH LEAGUE) CUP 1988–89

First Round
Alloa 2, Stirling 4
Brechin 3, Montrose 1
Cowdenbeath 0 Albion 9*†
E. Stirling 0, Arbroath 1
Queen's Park 1, Stranraer 2
Stenhousemuir 3, Berwick 0

Second Round
Aberdeen 4, Arbroath 0
Airdrie 0, Motherwell 1*
Albion 2, Hamilton 4
Brechin 0, Morton 2
Celtic 4, Ayr 1
Clyde 0, Rnagers 3
Clydebank 2, Stenhousemuir 0
Dunbarton 1, St Mirren 3*
Dundee 5, Q of S 1
East Fife 1, Dunfermline 1I†
Falkirk 1 Raith 1*†
Hearts 5, St Johnstone 0
Hibernian 4, Stranraer 0
Kilmarnock 1, Forfar 0
Meadowbank 2, Stirling 1
Partick 0, Dundee U 2*

Third Round
Celtic 7, Hamilton 2
Dundee 2, Falkirk 1
Dunfermline 2, Motherwell 1
Hibernian 1, Kilmarnock 0
Meadowbank 0, Hearts 2
Morton 1, Aberdeen 2
Rangers 6, Clydebank 0
St Mirren 1, Dundee U 3

Quarter-finals
Dundee U 2, Celtic 0
Dunfermline 1, Hearts 4
Hibernian 1, Aberdeen 2*
Rangers 4, Dundee 1

Semi-finals
Aberdeen 2, Dundee U 0
(at Dens Park)
Rangers 3, Hearts 0
(at Hampden Park)

Final at Hampden Park, 23 October, att. 72,122
Aberdeen (1)2 (*Dodds 2*), Rangers (1)3 (*McCoist 2 (P pen), I. Ferguson*)

After extra time   †Won on penalties

PAST SCOTTISH LEAGUE CUP FINALS

1946–47	Rangers	4	Aberdeen	0
1947–48	East Fife	0 4	Falkirk	0 1
1948–49	Rangers	2	Raith Rovers	0
1949–50	East Fife	3	Dunfermline	0
1950–51	Motherwell	3	Hibernian	0
1951–52	Dundee	3	Rangers	2
1952–53	Dundee	2	Kilmarnock	0
1953–54	East Fife	3	Partick Thistle	2
1954–55	Hearts	4	Motherwell	2
1955–56	Aberdeen	2	St Mirren	1
1956–57	Celtic	0 3	Partick Thistle	0 0
1957–58	Celtic	7	Rangers	1
1958–59	Hearts	5	Partick Rangers	1
1959–60	Hearts	2	Third Lanark	1
1960–61	Rangers	2	Kilmarnock	0
1961–62	Rangers	1 3	Hearts	1 1
1962–63	Hearts	1	Kilmarnock	0
1963–64	Rangers	5	Morton	0
1964–65	Rangers	2	Celtic	1
1965–66	Celtic	2	Rangers	1
1966–67	Celtic	1	Rangers	0
1967–68	Celtic	5	Dundee	3
1968–69	Celtic	6	Hibernian	2
1969–70	Celtic	1	St Johnstone	0
1970–71	Rangers	1	Celtic	0
1971–72	Partick Thistle	4	Celtic	1
1972–73	Hibernian	2	Celtic	1
1973–74	Dundee	1	Celtic	0
1974–75	Celtic	6	Hibernian	3
1975–76	Rangers	1	Celtic	0
1976–77	Aberdeen	2	Celtic	1
1977–78	Rangers	2	Celtic	1
1978–79	Rangers	2	Aberdeen	1
1979–80	Aberdeen	0 0	Dundee U.	0 3
1980–81	Dundee	0	Dundee U.	3
1981–82	Rangers	2	Dundee U.	1
1982–83	Celtic	2	Rangers	1
1983–84	Rangers	3	Celtic	2
1984–85	Rangers	1	Dundee U	0
1985–86	Aberdeen	3	Hibernian	0
1986–87	Rangers	2	Celtic	1
1987–88	Rangers	3	Aberdeen	3

After extra time   †Won on penalties

EUROPEAN SUPER CUP

1972	Ajax	3 3	Glasgow Rangers	1 2
1973	Ajax	0 6	AC Milan	1 0
1974	Not contested			
1975	Dynamo Kiev	1 2	Bayern Munich	0 0
1976	Anderlecht	4 1	Bayern Munich	1 2
1977	Liverpool	1 6	SV Hamburg	1 0
1978	Anderlecht	1 3	Liverpool	1 2
1979	Nottingham Forest	1 1	Barcelona	0 1
1980	Nottingham Forest	2 0	Valencia**	1 1
1981	Not contested			
1982	Aston Villa	0 3	Barcelona	1 0
1983	SV Hamburg	0 0	Aberdeen	0 2
1984	Juventus	2	Liverpool	0
1985	Not contested due to UEFA ban on English clubs.			
1986	Steaua Bucharest	1	Dynamo Kiev	0
1987	FC Porto	1 1	Ajax	0 0
1988	Mechelen	30	PSV Eindhoven	0 1

**Won on away goals*

WORLD CLUB CHAMPIONSHIP

Played annually up to 1974 between the winners of the European Cup and the winners of the South American Champions Cup – known as the Copa Libertadores de America. Revived in February 1981 (for the calendar year 1980), but played on a single match basis on a neutral ground.

Year	Winners	Runners-up	Score
1960	Real Madrid	Penarol	0–0, 5–1
1961	Penarol (Uruguay)	Benfica	0–1, 5–0, 2–1
1962	Santos (Brazil)	Benfica	3–2, 5–2
1963	Santos	AC Milan	2–4, 4–2, 1–0
1964	Inter-Milan	Independiente	0–1, 2–0, 1–0
1965	Inter-Milan	Independiente	3–0, 0–0
1966	Penarol	Real Madrid	2–0, 2–0
1967	Racing Club (Argentina)	Celtic	0–1, 2–1, 1–0
1968	Estudiantes (Argentina)	Manchester United	1–0, 1–1
1969	AC Milan	Estudiantes	3–0, 1–2
1970	Feyenoord	Estudiantes	2–2, 1–0
1971	Nacional (Uruguay)	Panathinaikos	1–1, 2–1
1972	Ajax	Independiente	1–1, 3–0
1973	Independiente (Argentina)	Juventus	1–0
1974	Atletico Madrid	Independiente	0–1, 2–0
1980	Nacional	Nottingham Forest	1–0 (in Tokyo)
1981	Flamengo (Brazil)	Liverpool	3–0 (in Tokyo)
1982	Penarol	Aston Villa	2–0 (in Tokyo)
1983	Greimo Porto Alegre (Brazil)	SV Hamburg	2–1 (in Tokyo)
1984	Independiente	Liverpool	1–0 (in Tokyo)
1985	Juventus	Argentinos Juniors	2–2 (in Tokyo)
	Juventus won 4–2 penalties		
1986	River Plate (Argentina)	Steaua Bucharest	1–0 (in Tokyo)
1987	FC Porto*	Penarol	2–1 (in Tokyo)
1988	Nacional*	PSV Eindhoven	2–2 (in Tokyo)
	Nacional won 7–6 on penalties.		

After extra time

REPUBLIC OF IRELAND

	P	W	D	L	F	A	Pts
Derry City	33	24	5	4	70	20	53
Dundalk	33	20	11	2	55	27	51
Limerick	33	18	9	6	57	37	45
St Patrick's	33	16	11	6	40	19	43
Bohemians	33	12	6	15	40	43	30
Athlone Town	33	11	7	15	30	33	29
Shamrock Rovers	33	8	13	12	34	42	29
Cork City	33	8	10	15	29	36	26
Shelbourne	33	8	10	15	26	40	26
Galway U	33	8	9	16	34	56	25
Cobh Ramblers	33	6	9	18	29	54	21
Waterford	33	6	6	21	21	58	18

Cup final: Derry City 1, Cork City 0 (*after 0–0 draw*)
Scorer: Healy. Att. 10,800

IRISH LEAGUE

	P	W	D	L	F	A	Pts
Linfield	26	21	2	3	58	19	65
Glentoran	26	17	4	5	60	29	55
Coleraine	26	15	5	6	42	23	50
Bangor	26	12	9	5	42	30	45
Glenavon	26	13	5	8	47	34	44
Portadown	26	10	9	7	39	19	39
Cliftonville	26	9	9	8	42	31	36
Carrick	26	11	3	12	29	40	36
Ballymena	26	6	11	9	33	41	29
Larne	26	6	10	10	38	38	28
Newry	26	7	5	14	33	43	26
Crusaders	26	5	5	16	22	47	20
Ards	26	4	6	16	25	54	18
Distillery	26	3	3	20	20	73	12

Irish Cup final at The Oval, 6 May 1989, att. 5,000
Ballymena Utd 1, Larne 0. *Scorer: Hardy*

ABACUS WELSH LEAGUE

National Division

	P	W	D	L	F	A	W	D	L	F	A	Pts
			Home						Away			
Barry T	32	15	1	0	59	9	13	3	0	37	11	88
Aberystwyth	32	11	4	1	41	16	13	0	3	44	21	76
Haverfordwest	32	11	3	2	43	13	8	3	5	28	19	63
Ebbw Vale	32	9	0	7	32	27	9	2	5	28	20	56
Brecon Corries	32	9	2	5	30	24	7	5	4	24	20	55
Bridgend T	32	7	4	5	23	23	7	3	6	26	23	49
Abergavenny	32	9	3	4	30	20	4	5	7	22	33	47
Ton Pentre	32	6	0	10	28	27	7	4	5	23	21	43
Pembroke	32	6	4	6	18	19	5	3	8	20	22	40
Maesteg Park	32	3	5	8	15	22	7	1	8	24	26	36
Briton Ferry	32	6	1	9	22	24	4	5	7	23	34	36
Port Talbot	32	6	4	6	20	24	4	2	10	18	40	36
AFC Cardiff	32	3	4	9	18	36	5	6	5	19	24	34
Cwmbran T	32	4	3	9	20	30	5	3	8	23	29	33
Pontllanfraith	32	3	4	9	24	34	4	1	11	15	37	26
Caerleon	32	3	5	8	20	36	3	2	11	20	32	25
Milford	32	4	2	10	17	28	3	1	12	20	48	24

Premier Division

	P	W	D	L	F	A	W	D	L	F	A	Pts
			Home						Away			
Afan Lido	34	12	5	0	33	9	11	2	4	37	20	76
Sully	34	10	5	2	53	20	12	3	2	43	21	74
Ammanford	34	13	1	3	39	15	9	6	2	33	21	73
Cardiff Corries	34	9	3	5	30	12	8	5	4	34	24	59
Panteg	34	11	2	4	38	23	4	8	5	26	26	55
Ferndale	34	9	4	4	35	17	7	1	9	18	28	53
Llanelli	34	9	2	6	39	30	5	5	7	35	45	49
Clydach	34	7	3	7	24	24	8	1	8	24	30	46*
Newport YMCA	34	7	3	7	21	22	5	4	8	22	31	43
Llanwern	34	6	6	5	30	29	4	4	9	20	30	40
B.P.	34	7	5	5	23	22	3	4	10	14	27	39
Morriston	34	5	6	6	34	33	5	2	10	15	28	38
Tonyrefail	34	3	6	8	18	23	7	2	8	22	30	38
Blaenrhondda	34	5	5	7	22	32	3	8	6	25	36	37
Trelewis	34	7	4	6	29	21	2	4	11	18	41	35
Merthyr Tydfil	34	6	4	7	29	29	3	2	12	19	34	33
S W Police	34	4	5	8	28	41	3	5	9	23	42	31
Abercynon	34	5	2	10	27	38	1	5	11	12	38	25

Division One

	P	W	D	L	F	A	W	D	L	F	A	Pts
			Home						Away			
Garw	34	12	3	2	40	19	11	3	3	38	13	75
Ynysybwl	34	9	4	4	39	23	12	2	3	43	20	69
Seven Sisters	34	11	4	2	56	24	8	6	3	33	24	67
Pontyclun	34	12	3	2	34	23	6	7	4	23	16	64
Carmarthen	34	12	3	2	37	18	7	3	7	25	20	63
Treharris	34	11	2	4	37	18	7	2	8	28	32	58
Aberaman	34	8	4	5	29	22	7	5	5	36	21	54
Caldicot	34	9	4	4	19	13	7	2	8	20	19	54
Skewen	34	7	4	6	26	19	7	5	5	32	31	51
Pontlottyn	34	.11	1	5	28	19	5	2	10	21	34	51
Taffs Well	34	8	3	6	35	25	7	2	8	31	29	50
Tondu Robins	34	5	7	5	27	23	4	7	6	30	26	41
Blaenavon	34	4	6	7	22	45	4	5	8	23	41	35
Caerau	34	7	5	5	24	20	1	5	11	15	35	34
South Glam Inst	34	5	3	9	18	32	4	3	10	22	42	33
Pontardawe	34	3	4	10	23	34	3	4	10	17	32	26
Tynte R	34	3	2	12	22	37	1	2	14	18	45	16
Blaina	34	1	4	12	19	52	1	1	15	11	55	11

*3 pts deducted
Welsh Cup final: Swansea C (1) 5, Kidderminster (0) 0
Scorers: Wade, James, Raynor, Hutchison, Thornber. Att: 5,100

WINNERS OF EUROPEAN CUP COMPETITIONS

COUNTRY	EUROPEAN CUP
Albania	17 Nentori
Austria	Rapid Vienna
Belgium	FC Brugge
Bulgaria	Vitosha
Cyprus	Pezoporikos
Czechoslovakia	Sparta Prague
Denmark	Brondby
Finland	HJK Helsinki
France	Monaco
East Germany	Dynamo Berlin
West Germany	Werder Bremen
Greece	Larissa
Holland	PSV Eindhoven
Hungary	Honved
Iceland	Valur
Italy	AC Milan
Rep of Ireland	Dundalk
N. Ireland	Glentoran
Luxembourg	Jeunesse Esch
Malta	Hamrun
Norway	Moss
Poland	Gornik Zabrze
Portugal	FC Porto
Rumania	Steaua
Scotland	Celtic
Spain	Real Madrid
Sweden	Gothenburg
Switzerland	Neuchatel Xamax
Turkey	Galatasaray
USSR	Moscow Spartak
Wales	—
Yugoslavia	Red Star Belgrade

COUNTRY	CUP WINNERS' CUP
Albania	Flamurtari
Austria	Kremser
Belgium	Anderlecht, Mechelen
Bulgaria	CFKA Sredets
Cyprus	Omonia
Czechoslovakia	Inter
Denmark	Aarhus
Finland	Kuusysi
France	Metz
East Germany	Carl Zeiss Jena
West Germany	Eintracht Frankfurt
Greece	Panathinaikos
Holland	Roda
Hungary	Bekescsaba
Iceland	Fram
Italy	Sampdoria
Rep of Ireland	Derry City
N. Ireland	Glenavon
Luxembourg	Avenir Beggen
Malta	Floriana
Norway	Bryne
Poland	Lech Poznan
Portugal	Vitoria Guimaraes
Rumania	Dinamo Bucharest
Scotland	Dundee U
Spain	Barcelona
Sweden	Norrkoping
Switzerland	Grasshoppers
Turkey	Sakaryaspor
USSR	Metallist
Wales	Cardiff City
Yugoslavia	Borac

COUNTRY	UEFA CUP
Albania	—
Austria	FK Austria, Vienna Sturm Graz
Belgium	Antwerp, Waregem, Liege
Bulgaria	Slavia, Trakia
Cyprus	Apoel
Czechoslovakia	Dukla, Dunajska
Denmark	Ikast
Finland	TPS Turku
France	Bordeaux, Montpellier
East Germany	Dynamo Dresden, Leipzig
West Germany	Bayern Munich, Stuttgart, Cologne, Leverkusen, Nuremberg
Greece	PAOK, AEK Athens
Holland	Groningen, Ajax
Hungary	Ujpest Dozsa, Tatabanya
Iceland	Akranes
Italy	Juventus, Napoli, Internazionale, Roma
Rep of Ireland	St Patrick's
N. Ireland	Linfield
Luxembourg	Union
Malta	Sliema
Norway	Molde
Poland	Legia Warsaw, Katowice
Portugal	Belenenses, Benfica, Sporting
Rumania	Otelul, Victoria
Scotland	Aberdeen, Hearts, Rangers
Spain	Real Sociedad, Bilbao, Atletico Madrid
Sweden	Brage, Malmo, Osters
Switzerland	Aarau, Servette
Turkey	Besiktas
USSR	Dnepr, Torpedo Moscow, Minsk, Jalguiris
Wales	—
Yugoslavia	Velez Mostar, Dinamo Zagreb, Partizan

EUROPEAN CUP COMPETITIONS 1988–89

Italian double but no treble

Italian clubs were hoping for a clean sweep in the three European competitions but had to be content with AC Milan winning the European Cup and Napoli taking the UEFA Cup. Sampdoria found themselves beaten in the Cup Winners' Cup.

AC Milan gave a vintage display against the Rumanian Army club side, Steaua Bucharest, with their Dutch trio of Frank Rijkaard, Marco Van Basten and Ruud Gullit in outstanding form. Gullit had just returned from a number of weeks out of action with cartilage problems.

There was a Dutch flavour about Barcelona's victory against Sampdoria, coach Johan Cruyff masterminding the Spaniards' success. Gary Lineker continued in his unusual role on the right wing, as Cruyff had preferred to use Julio Salinas in the middle all season.

Napoli's captain Diego Maradona gave inspirational performances in the games with Stuttgart, turning an early lead by the Germans in the first leg into a 2–1 win and keeping his team slightly more relaxed in the return game where Stuttgart equalised only in the last minute.

EUROPEAN CUP 1988–89

First Round, first leg

PSV Eindhoven (*holders*) – Bye

Brugge	(0)1	Brondby	(0)0
Dundalk	(0)0	Red Star Belgarde	(0)5
Dynamo Berlin	(1)3	Werder Bremen	(0)0
Gornik Zabrze	(2)3	Jeunesse D'Esch	(0)0
Hamrun Spartans	(0)2	Nentori	(1)1
Honved	(1)1	Celtic	(0)0
Larissa	(1)2	Neuchatel Xamax	(0)1
Moscow Spartak	(0)2	Glentoran	(0)0
Pezoporikos	(1)1	IFK Gothenburg	(1)2
FC Porto	(2)3	HJK Helsinki	(0)0
Rapid Vienna	(1)2	Galatasaray	(0)1
Real Madrid	(3)3	Moss	(0)0
Sparta Prague	(1)1	Steaua Bucharest	(2)5
Valur Reykjavik	(0)1	Monaco	(0)0
Vitosha	(0)0	AC Milan	(1)2

First Round, second leg

Brondby	(1)2	Brugge	(0)1
Celtic	(1)4	Honved	(0)0
Galatasaray	(0)2	Rapid Vienna	(0)0
Glentoran	(0)1	Moscow Spartak	(0)1
IFK Gothenburg	(4)5	Pezoporikos	(1)1
HJK Helsinki	(0)2	FC Porto	(0)0
Jeunesse D'Esch	(1)1	Gornik Zabrze	(2)4
AC Milan	(3)5	Vitosha	(1)2
Monaco	(2)2	Valur Reykjavik	(0)0

Moss	(0)0	Real Madrid	(1)1
Nentori	(0)2	Hamrun Spartans	(0)0
Neuchatel Xamax	(0)2	Larissa	(0)1
Red Star Belgrade	(1)3	Dundalk	(0)0
Steaua Bucharest	(1)2	Sparta Prague	(1)2
Werder Bremen	(1)5	Dynamo Berlin	(0)0

Second Round, first leg

Brugge	(0)1	Monaco	(0)0
Celtic	(0)0	Werder Bremen	(0)1
Gornik Zabrze	(0)0	Real Madrid	(0)1
AC Milan	(0)1	Red Star Belgrade	(0)1
Nentori	(0)0	IFK Gothenburg	(2)3
Neuchatel Xamax	(0)3	Galatasaray	(0)0
PSV Eindhoven	(3)5	FC Porto	(0)0
Steaua Bucharest	(1)3	Moscow Spartak	(0)0

Second Round, second leg

Galatasaray	(1)5	Neuchatel Xamaz	(0)0
IFK Gothenburg	(1)1	Nentori	(0)0
Monaco	(5)6	Brugge	(0)1
FC Porto	(1)2	PSV Eindhoven	(0)0
Real Madrid	(1)3	Gornik Zabrze	(1)2
Red Star Belgrade	(0)1	AC Milan	(0)0
(abandoned 61 mins – fog)			
Red Star Belgrade	(1)1	AC Milan	(1)1
(AC Milan won 4–2 on penalties)			
Spartak Moscow	(1)1	Steaua Bucharest	(1)2
Werder Bremen	(0)0	Celtic	(0)0

Quarter-finals, first leg

IFK Gothenburg	(0)1	Steaua Bucharest	(0)0
Monaco	(0)0	Galatasaray	(1)1
PSV Eindhoven	(0)1	Real Madrid	(1)1
Werder Bremen	(0)0	AC Milan	(0)0

Quarter-finals, second leg

Galatasaray	(0)1	Monaco	(0)1
AC Milan	(1)1	Werder Bremen	(0)0
Real Madrid	(0)2	PSV Eindhoven (aet)	(0)1
Steaua Bucharest	(3)5	IFK Gothenburg	(0)1

Semi-finals, first leg

Real Madrid	(1)1	AC Milan	(0)1
Steaua Bucharest	(2)4	Galatasaray	(0)0

Semi-finals, second leg

AC Milan	(3)5	Real Madrid	(0)0
Galatasaray	(1)1	Steaua Bucharest	(1)1

Final at Barcelona, 24 May 1989, att. 97,000

AC Milan	(3)4	Steaua Bucharest	(0)0

AC Milan:Galli G; Tassotti, Baresi, Costacurta (Galli F), Maldini, Colombo, Rijkaard, Donadoni, Ancelotti, Gullit (Virdis), Van Basten. Scorers: *Gullit 2, Van Basten 2*.
Steaua Bucharest: Lung; Petrescu, Iovan, Bumbescu, Ungureanu, Stoica, Minea, Hagi, Rotariu (Balint), Lacatus, Piturca
Referee: Tritschler (West Germany)

EUROPEAN CUP WINNERS' CUP 1988–89

Preliminary round

Bekescsaba	(3)3	Bryne	(0)0
Bryne	(1)2	Bekescsaba	(1)1

First Round, first leg

Borac Banjaluka	(1)2	Metallist Kharkov	(0)0
Carl Zeiss Jena	(1)5	FC Krems	(0)0
Derry	(0)0	Cardiff C	(0)0
Dinamo Bucharest	(1)3	Kuusysi Lahti	(0)0
Flamurtari	(1)2	Lech Poznan	(1)3
Floriana	(0)0	Dundee U	(0)0
Fram Reykjavik	(0)0	Barcelona	(1)2
Glenavon	(1)1	AGF Aarhus	(1)4
Grasshoppers	(0)0	Eintracht Frankfurt	(0)0
Inter Bratislava	(1)2	CFKA Sredets	(2)3
Mechelen	(0)5	Avenir Beggen	(0)0
Metz	(0)1	RSC Anderlecht	(2)3
Norrkoping	(1)2	Sampdoria	(0)1
Omonia Nicosia	(0)0	Panathinaikos	(1)1
Roda JC Kerkrade	(1)2	Vitoria Guimaraes	(0)0
Sakaryaspor	(1)2	Bekescsaba	(0)0

First Round, second leg

AGF Aarhus	(1)3	Glenavon	(0)1
RSC Anderlecht	(0)2	Metz	(0)0
Avenir Beggen	(0)1	Mechelen	(1)3
Barcelona	(2)5	Fram Reykavik	(0)0
Bekescsaba	(0)1	Sakaryaspor	(0)0
CFKA Sredets	(5)5	Inter Bratislava	(0)0
Cardiff C	(1)4	Derry	(0)0
Dundee U	(0)1	Floriana	(0)0
Eintracht Frankfurt	(1)1	Grasshoppers	(0)0
Krems	(1)1	Carl Zeiss Jena	(0)0
Kuusysi Lahti	(0)0	Dinamo Bucharest	(2)3
Lech Poznan	(1)1	Flamurtari	(0)0
Metallist Kharkov	(1)4	Borac Banjaluka	(0)0
Panathinaikos	(0)2	Omonia Nicosia	(0)0
Sampdoria	(1)2	Norrkoping	(0)0
Vitoria Guimaraes	(1)1	Roda JC Kerkrade	(0)0

Second Round, first leg

Barcelona	(1)1	Lech Poznan	(0)1
CFKA Sredets	(1)2	Panathinaikos	(0)0
Cardiff C	(1)1	AGF Aarhus	(1)2
Carl Zeiss Jena	(1)1	Sampdoria	(1)1
Dundee U	(0)0	Dinamo Bucharest	(0)1
Eintracht Frankfurt	(3)3	Sakaryaspor	(0)1
Mechelen	(0)1	RSC Anderlecht	(0)0
Roda JC Kerkrade	(1)1	Metallist Kharkov	(0)0

Second Round, second leg

AGF Aarhus	(2)4	Cardiff C	(0)0
RSC Anderlecht	(0)0	Mechelen	(1)2
Dinamo Bucharest	(0)1	Dundee U	(0)1
Lech Poznan	(1)1	Barcelona	(1)1
(Barcelona won 5–4 on penalties)			
Metallist Kharkov	(0)0	Roda JC Kerkrade	(0)0
Panathinaikos	(0)0	CFKA Sredets	(0)1
Sakaryaspor	(0)0	Eintracht Frankfurt	(0)3
Sampdoria	(1)3	Carl Zeiss Jena	(0)1

Quarter-finals, first leg

AGF Aarhus	(0)0	Barcelona	(0)1
CFKA Sredets	(1)2	Roda JC Kerkrade	(0)1
Dinamo Bucharest	(1)1	Sampdoria	(0)1
Eintracht Frankfurst	(0)0	Mechelen	(0)0

Quarter-finals, second leg

Barcelona	(0)0	AGF Aarhus	(0)0
Mechelen	(0)1	Eintracht Frankfurt	(0)0
Roda JC Kerkdrade	(1)2	CFKA Sredets	(0)1
Sampdoria	(0)0	Dinamo Bucharest	(0)0

Semi-finals, first leg

Barcelona	(2)4	CFKA Sredets	(1)2
Mechelen	(1)2	Sampdoria	(0)1

Semi finals, second leg

CFKA Sredets	(0)1	Barcelona	(1)2
Sampdoria	(0)3	Mechelen	(0)0

Final at Berne, 10 May 1989, att. 45,000
Barcelona (1)2   Sampdoria (0)0

Barcelona: Zubizarreta; Aloisio, Alesanco, Milla (Soler), Urbano, Amor, Lineker, Eusebio, Julio Salinas, Roberto, Beguiristain (Rekarte). Scorers: *Salinas, Rekarte*
Sampdoria: Pagliuca; Mannini (S. Pellegrini), Salsano, Pari, Lanna, L.Pellegrini (Bonomi), Victor, Cerezo, Vialli, Mancini, Dossena.
Referee: Courtney (England)

UEFA CUP 1988–89

First Round, first leg

AEK Athens	(1)1	Athletic Bilbao	(0)0
Aarau	(0)0	Lokomotiv Leipzig	(2)3
Aberdeen	(0)0	Dynamo Dresden	(0)0
Akranes	(0)0	Ujpest Dozsa	(0)0
Antwerp	(2)2	Cologne	(1)4
Bayer Leverkusen	(0)0	Belenenses	(0)1
Bayern Munich	(2)3	Legia Warsaw	(0)1
Besiktas	(0)1	Dinamo Zagreb	(0)0
Dnepr	(0)1	Bordeaux	(1)1
Groningen	(1)1	Atletico Madrid	(0)0
Inter Milan	(1)2	Brage	(0)1
Malmo	(1)2	Moscow Torpedo	(0)0
Molde	(0)0	Waregem	(0)0
Montpellier	(0)0	Benfica	(2)3
Napoli	(0)1	PAOK Salonika	(0)0
Oesters Vaxjo	(0)2	Dunajska Streda	(0)0
Otelul Galati	(0)1	Juventus	(0)0
Partizan Belgrade	(2)5	Slavia Sofia	(0)0
Rangers	(0)1	GKS Katowice	(0)0
Real Sociedad	(1)2	Dukla Prague	(1)1
Roma	(0)1	Nuremburg	(1)2
St Patrick's Athletic	(0)0	Hearts	(2)2
Servette	(0)1	Sturm Graz	(0)0
Sporting Lisbon	(3)4	Ajax Amsterdam	(1)2
Sliema Wanderers	(0)0	Victoria Bucharest	(1)2
Stuttgard	(0)2	Tatabanya	(0)0
TPs Turun	(0)0	Linfield	(0)0
Trakia Plovdiv	(0)1	Dynamo Minsk	(1)2
Union Sportive Luxembourg	(1)1	FC Liege	(2)7
Velez Mostar	(1)1	APOEL Nicosia	(0)0
Vienna	(1)1	Ikast	(0)0
Zhalgiris Vilnius	(0)2	FK Austria	(0)0

First Round, second leg

APOEL Nicosia	(1)2	Velez Mostar	(1)5
Ajax Amsterdam	(0)1	Sporting Lisbon	(1)2
Athletic Bilbao	(2)2	AEK Athens	(0)0
Atletico Madrid	(1)2	Groningen	(1)1
(*Groningen won on away goals*)			
Belenenses	(0)1	Bayer Leverkusen	(0)0
Benfica	(1)3	Montpellier	(0)1
Bordeaux	(0)2	Dnepr	(1)1
Brage	(0)1	Inter Milan	(1)2
Cologne	(2)2	Antwerp	(1)1
Dinamo Zagreb	(1)2	Besiktas	(0)0
Dukla Prague	(1)3	Real Sociedad	(0)2
(*Real won on away goals*)			
Dunajska Streda	(4)6	Oesters Vaxjo	(0)0
Dynamo Dresden	(1)2	Aberdeen	(0)0
FK Austria	(4)5	Zhalgiris Vilnius	(1)2

153

GKS Katowice	(1)2	Rangers	(2)4
Hearts	(1)2	St Patrick's Athletic	(0)0
Ikast	(0)2	Vienna	(1)1

(Vienna won on away goals.)

Juventus	(3)5	Otelul Galati	(0)0
Legia Warsaw	(1)3	Bayern Munich	(4)7
FC Liege	(2)4	Union Sportive Luxembourg	(0)0
Linfield	(0)1	TPs Turun	(1)1

(TPs won on away goals)

Lokomotiv Leipzig	(2)4	Aarau	(0)0
Dynamo Minsk	(0)0	Trakia Plovdiv	(0)0
Moscow Torpedo	(1)2	Malmo	(0)1
Nuremberg	(1)1	Roma	(2)3
PAOK Salonika	(0)1	Napoli	(1)1
Slavia Sofia	(0)0	Partizan Belgrade	(0)5
Sturm Graz	(0)0	Servette	(0)0
Tatabanya	(0)2	Stuttgart	(0)1
Ujpest Dozsa	(0)2	Akranes	(0)1
Victoria Bucharest	(5)6	Sliema Wanderers	(0)1
Waregem	(1)5	Molde	(0)1

Second Round, first leg

Bayern Munich	(1)3	Dunajska Streda	(0)1
Cologne	(0)2	Rangers	(0)0
Dinamo Zagreb	(0)1	Stuttgart	(1)3
Dynamo Dresden	(3)4	Waregem	(0)1
Groningen	(1)2	Servette	(0)0
Hearts	(0)0	FK Austria	(0)0
Juventus	(3)5	Athletic Bilbao	(1)1
FC Liege	(0)2	Benfica	(0)1
Lokomotiv Leipzig	(0)1	Napoli	(0)1
Malmo	(0)0	Inter Milan	(0)1
Dynamo Minsk	(1)2	Victoria Bucharest	(0)1
Partizan Belgrade	(2)4	Roma	(1)2
Sporting Lisbon	(1)1	Real Sociedad	(1)2
Ujpest Dozsa	(0)0	Bordeaux	(1)1
Velez Mostar	(0)0	Belenenses	(0)0
Vienna	(1)2	TPs Turun	(1)1

Second Round, second leg

Athletic Bilbao	(0)3	Juventus	(1)2
Belenenses	(0)0	Velez Mostar	(0)0

(Velez won 4–3 on penalties)

Bordeaux	(0)1	Ujpest Dozsa	(0)0
Benfica	(0)1	FC Liege	(1)1
Dunajska Streda	(0)0	Bayern Munich	(2)2
FK Austria	(0)0	Hearts	(0)1
Inter Milan	(1)1	Malmo	(0)1
Napoli	(1)2	Lokomotiv Leipzig	(0)0
Rangers	(0)1	Cologne	(0)1
Real Sociedad	(0)0	Sporting Lisbon	(0)0
Roma	(1)2	Partizan Belgrade	(0)0

(Roma won on away goals)

Servette .... (1)1	Groningen .... (0)1
Stuttgart .... (0)1	Dinamo Zagreb..................... (0)1
TPs Turun .... (0)1	Vienna................................... (0)0
(TPs won on away goals)	
Victoria Bucharest .... (0)1	Dynamo Minsk .... (0)0
Waregem .... (0)2	Dynamo Dresden .... (0)1

Third Round, first leg

Bayern Munich .... (0)0	Inter Milan............................ (0)2
Bordeaux .... (0)0	Napoli .... (1)1
Dynamo Dresden .... (1)2	Roma .... (0)0
Groningen.............................. (0)1	Stuttgart .... (3)3
Hearts .... (1)3	Velez Mostar .... (0)0
FC Liege................................ (0)0	Juventus .... (1)1
Real Sociedad........................ (0)1	Cologne .... (0)0
Victoria Bucharest .... (1)1	TPs Turun .... (0)0

Third Round, second leg

Cologne .... (2)2	Real Sociedad........................ (1)2
Inter Milan............................ (1)1	Bayern Munich .... (3)3
(Bayern won on away goals)	
Juventus .... (1)1	FC Liege................................ (0)0
Napoli .... (0)0	Bordeaux .... (0)0
Roma .... (0)0	Dynamo Dresden .... (0)2
Stuttgart .... (1)2	Groningen.............................. (0)0
TPs Turun .... (1)3	Victoria Bucharest .... (2)2
(Victoria won on away goals)	
Velez Mostar .... (1)2	Hearts .... (0)1

Quarter-finals, first leg

Hearts .... (0)1	Bayern Munich .... (0)0
Juventus .... (2)2	Napoli .... (0)0
Stuttgart .... (1)1	Real Sociedad........................ (0)0
Victoria Bucharest .... (0)1	Dynamo Dresden .... (1)1

Quarter-finals, second leg

Bayern Munich .... (1)2	Hearts .... (0)0
Dynamo Dresden .... (0)4	Victoria Bucharest .... (0)0
Real Sociedad........................ (1)1	Stuttgart .... (0)0
Napoli .... (1)3	Juventus .... (0)0

Semi-finals, first leg

Napoli .... (1)2	Bayern Munich .... (0)0
Stuttgart .... (0)1	Dynamo Dresden .... (0)0

Semi-finals, second leg

Bayern Munich .... (0)2	Napoli .... (0)2
Dynamo Dresden .... (0)1	Stuttgart .... (0)1

Final (*2 legs*) 3 May and 17 May
Napoli   (0)2   Stuttgart   (1)1 att. 83,000

Napoli: Giuliani; Corradini (Crippa), Renica, Ferrara, De Napoli, Alemao, Fusi, Francini, Careca, Maradona, Carnevale. **Scorers**: *Maradona (pen), Careca*
Stuttgart: Immel; Buchwald, Schmaler N., Allgower, Hartmann, Schafer, Katanec, Sigurvinsson, Schroder, Walter (Zietsch), Gaudino. **Scorer**: *Gaudino*
Referee: Germanakos (Greece)
Stuttgart (1)3, Napoli (2)3 att. 67,000
Stuttgart: Immel; Schmaler N., Allgower, Schafer, Schroder, Hartmann, Katanec, Sigurvinsson, Klinsmann, Walter (Schmaler O.), Gaudino. **Scorers**: *Klinsmann, De Napoli (og), Schmaler O.*
Napoli: Giuliani; Corrandini, Renica, Ferrara, De Napoli, Alemao (Carannante), Fusi, Francini, Careca (Bigliardi), Maradona, Carnevale.
Scorers: *Alemao, Ferrara, Careca*
Referee: Sanchez (Spain)

EUROPEAN CUP PAST FINALS

1956	Real Madrid	4	Stade de Rheims	3
1957	Real Madrid	2	Fiorentina	0
1958	Real Madrid	3	AC Milan	2*
1959	Real Madrid	2	Stade de Rheims	0
1960	Real Madrid	7	Eintracht Frankfurt	3
1961	SL Benfica	3	Barcelona	2
1962	SL Benfica	5	Real Madrid	3
1963	AC Milan	2	SL Benfica	1
1964	Inter Milan	3	Real Madrid	1
1965	Inter Milan	1	SL Benfica	0
1966	Real Madrid	2	Partizan Belgrade	1
1967	Celtic	2	Inter Milan	1
1968	Manchester U	4	SL Benfica	1
1969	AC Milan	4	Ajax Amsterdam	1
1970	Feyenoord	2	Celtic	1*
1971	Ajax Amsterdam	2	Panathinaikos	0
1972	Ajax Amsterdam	2	Inter Milan	0
1973	Ajax Amsterdam	1	Juventus	0
1974	Bayern Munich	1 4	Atletico Madrid	1 0
1975	Bayern Munich	2	Leeds U	0
1976	Bayern Munich	1	St Etienne	0
1977	Liverpool	3	Borussia Moenchengladbach	1
1978	Liverpool	1	FC Bruges	0
1979	Nottingham F	1	Malmö	0
1980	Nottingham F	1	SV Hamburg	0
1981	Liverpool	1	Real Madrid	0
1982	Aston Villa	1	Bayern Munich	0
1983	SV Hamburg	1	Juventus	0
1984	Liverpool†	1	AS Roma	1
1985	Juventus	1	Liverpool	0
1986	Steaua Bucharest†	0	Barcelona	0
1987	FC Porto	2	Bayern	1
1988	PSV Eindhoven†	0	Benfica	0

EUROPEAN CUP-WINNERS' CUP PAST FINALS

1961	Fiorentina	4	Rangers	1†
1962	Atletico Madrid	1 3	Fiorentina	1 0
1963	Tottenham Hotspur	5	Atletico Madrid	1
1964	Sporting Lisbon	3 1	MTK Budapest	3 0
1965	West Ham U	2	Munich 1860	0
1966	Borussia Dortmund	2	Liverpool	1*
1967	Bayern Munich	1	Rangers	0*
1968	AC Milan	2	SV Hamburg	0
1969	Slovan Bratislava	3	Barcelona	2
1970	Manchester C	2	Gornik Zabrze	1
1971	Chelsea	1 2	Real Madrid	1 1
1972	Rangers	3	Dynamo Moscow	2
1973	AC Milan	1	Leeds U	0
1974	FC Magdeburg	2	AC Milan	0
1975	Dynamo Kiev	3	Ferencvaros	0
1976	RSC Anderlecht	4	West Ham U	2
1977	SV Hamburg	2	Anderlecht	0
1978	RSC Anderlecht	4	Austria Vienna	0
1979	Barcelona	4	Fortuna Dusseldorf	3
1980	Valencia†	0	Arsenal	0
1981	Dinamo Tbilisi	2	Carl Zeiss Jena	1
1982	Barcelona	2	Standard Liege	1
1983	Aberdeen	2	Real Madrid	1
1984	Juventus	2	FC Porto	1
1985	Everton	3	Rapid Vienna	1
1986	Dynamo Kiev	3	Atletico Madrid	0
1987	Ajax Amsterdam	1	Lokomotiv Leipzig	0
1988	Mechelen	1	Ajax Amsterdam	0

FAIRS CUP FINALS

1958	Barcelona	8	London	2††
1960	Barcelona	4	Birmingham C	1††
1961	AS Roma	4	Birmingham C	2††
1962	Valencia	7	Barcelona	3††
1963	Valencia	4	Dynamo Zagreb	1††
1964	Real Zaragoza	2	Valencia	1
1965	Ferencvaros	1	Juventus	0
1966	Barcelona	4	Real Zaragoza	3††
1967	Dynamo Zagreb	2	Leeds U	0††
1968	Leeds U	1	Ferencvaros	0††
1969	Newcastle U	6	Ujpest Dozsa	2††
1970	Arsenal	4	Anderlecht	3††
1971	Leeds U	3**	Juventus	3††

UEFA CUP PAST FINALS

1972	Tottenham Hotspur	2 1	Wolverhampton W	1 1
1973	Liverpool	3 0	Borussia Moenchengladbach	0 2
1974	Feyenoord	2 2	Tottenham H	2 0
1975	Borussia Moenchengladbach	0 5	Twente Enschede	0 1
1976	Liverpool	3 1	FC Bruges	2 1
1977	Juventus**	1 1	Athletic Bilbao	0 2
1978	PSV Eindhoven	0 3	SEC Bastia	0 0
1979	Borussia Moenchengladbach	1 1	Red Star Belgrade	1 0
1980	Borussia Moenchengladbach	3 0	Eintracht Frankfurt**	2 1
1981	Ipswich T.	3 2	AZ 67 Alkmaar	0 4
1982	IFK Gothenburg	1 3	SV Hamburg	0 0
1983	RSC Anderlecht	1 1	Benfica	0 1
1984	Tottenham H †	1 1	RSC Anderlecht	1 1
1985	Real Madrid	3 0	Videoton	0 1
1986	Real Madrid	5 0	Cologne	1 2
1987	IFK Gothenburg	1 1	Dundee U	0 1
1988	Bayer Leverkusen †	0 3	Espanol	0 3

*After extra time   **Won on away goals   †Won on penalties   ††Aggregate score*

WORLD CUP REVIEW

There have been varying experiences for the five countries of the British Isles competing in the qualifying competition for the 1990 World Cup. England and Scotland have made good progress towards reaching the finals in Italy, closely followed by the Republic of Ireland. But for Wales and Northern Ireland, hopes have been dashed.

Elsewhere in Europe, Rumania and Denmark have emerged as the chief challengers in Group One, while the USSR appears the strongest in Group Three. Holland and West Germany lead Group Four while Spain heads the competitive Group Six. In Group Seven, Belgium, Czechoslovakia and Portugal all lay claim to qualifying.

England's record during the 1988–89 season was impressive on paper in both World Cup and friendlies. In ten matches they remained unbeaten, but face a couple of stiffer tests in Poland and Sweden when the new season restarts.

While the Scots have taken Group Five by storm, the biggest disappointment in this section has been the demise of France. Mo Johnston, who plays football with the French club Nantes, established a record for one of the four home countries in the World Cup by scoring in four successive ties.

With the South American zone tied up with the South American Championships in July, and the complicated matter of African and Asian areas still being clarified, Oceania's comparatively small entry, though well spread out geographically, has provided a definite answer. Israel, forced to play there because of political reasons, accomplished the feat of finishing above both Australia and New Zealand to earn the right to meet the winners of South America's Group Two for a place in the finals!

FIFA's remaining zone, North and Central America, has given the USA its best chance of reaching the finals since 1950 when, as every Englishman knows to his chagrin, a motley assembly of players from several countries gave the Americans a 1–0 win over England. Costa Rica, Guatemala and El Salvador pose threats to the Yanks, though there are two qualifiers from this part of the world, not including Mexico, who were banned from competing by FIFA because of irregularities involving a youth international squad.

Italy, the host nation, is spared the qualifying competition with a free passage to the finals, but after the worst ever season for off-the-field hooliganism there are serious worries for next summer. Towards the end of the Italian domestic programme, players considered striking in protest at the violence. Problems inside the grounds have been minor, but in city centres and along routes to and from stadia, there has been an escalation of that affliction which, these days, seems universal to one degree or another.

FIFA WORLD CUP 1990

EUROPE
Group 1 *(Denmark, Bulgaria, Rumania, Greece)*

19 October, Sofia, att. 52,000
BULGARIA (1) 1 *(Kolev 31)*
RUMANIA (1) 3 *(Mateut 25, Camataru 79, 89)*
Bulgaria: Mikhailov; Nikolov, Rankov, Vasev (Kiryakov 55), Iliev, Stoichkov, Sadkov, Yordanov, Getov, Alexandrov (Kolev 30), Penev
Rumania: Lung; Iovan, Andone, Belodedici, Rotariu, Mateut (Klein 55), Sabau, Hagi, Popescu, Lacatus (Vaiscovici 66), Camataru

19 October, Athens, att. 45,000
GREECE (1) 1 *(Mitropoulos 41)*
DENMARK (0) 1 *(Povlsen 56)*
Greece: Talikariadis; Hatziathanasiu, Manolas, Mavridis, Kolomitrousis, Skartados (Karapialis 74), Tsalouhidis, Bonovas, Mitropoulos (Georgamlis 56), Saravakos, Anastopoulos
Denmark: Schmeichel; Heintze, Nielsen I., Olsen L., Sivebaek (Kristensen 46), Bartram, Helt, Jensen J., Povlsen, Laudrup, Brylle (Elstrup 75)

2 November, Copenhagen, att. 34,600
DENMARK (1) 1 *(Elstrup 8)*
BULGARIA (1) 1 *(Sadkov 38)*
Denmark: Schmeichel; Olsen L., Sivebaek, Nielsen K., Kristensen, Heintze (Brylle 76), Helt (Bartram 65), Jensen J., Laudrup, Elstrup, Povlsen
Bulgaria: Valov; Iliev, Kiryakov, Dochev, Ivanov, Penev, Sadkov, Kirov, Yordanov (Rakov 86), Stoichkov (Balkov 88), Bezinski

2 November, Bucharest, att. 22,500
RUMANIA (2) 3 *(Mateut 26, Hagi 40 (pen), Sabau 84)*
GREECE (0) 0
Rumania: Lung; Iovan, Belodedici, Andone, Ungureanu, Popescu, Hagi, Sabau (Klein 85), Mateut, Lacatus (Vaiscovici 77), Camataru
Greece: Talikariadis; Hatziathanasiu, Kolomitrousis, Manolas, Mavridis, Tsalouhidis, Saravakos, Bonovas, Anastopoulos, Mitropoulos (Kutulas 46), Tsiantakis (Nioblias 68)

26 April, Athens, att. 30,000
GREECE (0) 0
RUMANIA (0) 0
Greece: Economopoulos; Apostolakis, Hatziathanasiu, Manolas, Mavridis, Tsalouhidis, Saravakos, Papadopoulos (Bonovas 65), Samaras, Savidis, Tsiantakis
Rumania: Lung; Iovan, Bumbescu, Klein, Rednic, Mateut, Lucescu, Sabau, Camataru (Vaiscovici 89), Hagi, Jupescu (Dumitrescu 78)

26 April, Sofia, att. 45,000
BULGARIA (0) 0
DENMARK (1) 2 *(Povlsen 41, Laudrup B. 89)*
Bulgaria: Valov (Donev 55); Kiryakov, Dochev, Bezinski, Iliev, Rakov, Kirov, Sadkov (Simeonov 46), Stoichkov, Mikhtarski, Getov
Denmark: Schmeichel; Heintze, Nielsen K., Olsen L., Sivebaek, Larsen J., Olsen M. (Vilfort 74), Jensen J. (Helt 84), Bartram, Povlsen, Laudrup B.

17 May, Copenhagen, att. 38,500
DENMARK (1) 7 *(Laudrup B. 24, Bartram 47, Nielsen K. 55, Povlsen 56, Vilfort 79, Andersen H. 85, Laudrup M. 89 (pen))*
GREECE (1) 1 *(Samaras 39)*
Denmark: Schmeichel; Sivebaek (Vilfort 30), Olsen L., Nielsen K., Larsen J., Bartram (Andersen H.), Olsen M., Jensen J., Laudrup M., Povlsen, Laudrup B.
Greece: Economopoulos; Hatziathanasiu, Mavridis, Manolas, Apostolakis, Tsalouhidis, Tsiantakis, Mitropoulos (Kalitzakis 50), Papadopoulos, Saravakos, Samaras

17 May, Bucharest, att. 20,000
RUMANIA (1) 1 *(Popescu 35)*
BULGARIA (0) 0
Rumania: Stelea; Iovan, Bumbescu, Rednic (Balint 64), Mateut, Sabau (Dumitrescu 85), Popescu, Rotariu, Hagi, Lacatus, Camataru
Bulgaria: Valov (Donev 46); Dochev, Ivanov, Vasev, Mladenov D., Tinchev, Kestadinov E., Stoichkov, Mladenov S., Bakalov, Balekov

	P	W	D	L	F	A	Pts
Rumania	4	3	1	0	7	1	7
Denmark	4	2	2	0	11	3	6
Greece	4	0	2	2	2	11	2
Bulgaria	4	0	1	3	2	7	1

Remaining fixtures: 11.10.89 Bulgaria v Greece, Denmark v Rumania; 15.11.89 Greece v Bulgaria, Rumania v Denmark

Group 2 *(England, Poland, Sweden, Albania)*

19 October, Wembley, att. 65,628
ENGLAND (0) 0
SWEDEN (0) 0
England: Shilton; Stevens, Pearce, Webb, Adams (Walker 64), Butcher, Robson, Beardsley, Waddle, Lineker, Barnes (Cottee 79)
Sweden: Ravelli T.; Nilsson R. (Schiller 77), Hysen, Larsson P., Ljung, Thern, Stromberg, Prytz, Nilsson J., Holmqvist (Ekstrom 63), Pettersson

19 October, Chorzow, att. 30,000
POLAND (0) 1 *(Warzycha K. 78)*
ALBANIA (0) 0
Poland: Wandzik; Warzycha R., Wojcicki, Lukasik, Wdowczyk, Matysik (Ziober 46), Warzycha K., Urban, Furtok (Komornicki 73), Rudy, Smolarek
Albania: Mersini; Alimehmeti, Josa, Hodja, Gega, Jera, Shehu (Stoia 70), Lekbello, Millo, Minga, Demollari

5 November, Tirana, att. 11,500
ALBANIA (1) 1 *(Shehu 33)*
SWEDEN (0) 2 *(Holmqvist 68, Ekstrom 71)*
Albania: Mersini; Alimehmeti, Hodja, Lekbello, Stoia, Josa, Gega, Demollari, Millo, Shehu, Minga
Sweden: Ravelli T., Nilsson R., Larsson P., Hysen, Ljung, Thern, Prytz (Holmqvist 66), Stromberg, Nilsson J., Pettersson, Ekstrom

8 March, Tirana, att. 30,000
ALBANIA (0) 0
ENGLAND (1) 2 *(Barnes 16, Robson 63)*
Albania: Mersini; Zmijani, Josa, Hodja, Gega, Jera, Shehu, Lekbello, Millo (Majaci 75), Minga, Demollari
England: Shilton; Stevens, Pearce, Webb, Walker, Butcher, Robson, Rocastle, Waddle (Beardsley 79), Lineker (Smith 79), Barnes

26 April, Wembley, att. 60,602
ENGLAND (2) 5 *(Lineker 5, Beardsley 12, 64, Waddle 72, Gascoigne 88)*
ALBANIA (0) 0
England: Shilton; Stevens (Parker 77), Pearce, Webb, Walker, Butcher, Robson, Rocastle (Gascoigne 67), Beardsley, Lineker, Waddle
Albania: Nallbani; Zmijani, Bubeqi, Hodja, Gega, Jera, Shehu, Lekbello, Millo, Hasanpapa (Noga 31), Demollari

7 May, Stockholm, att. 35,021
SWEDEN (0) 2 *(Ljung 76, Larsson N. 89)*
POLAND (0) 1 *(Tarasiewicz 86)*
Sweden: Ravelli T.; Nilsson R., Lonn (Ravelli A. 80), Ljung, Schiller, Limpar, Prytz, Thern, Nilsson J. (Larsson N. 58), Ekstrom, Magnusson
Poland: Bako; Soczynski, Lukasik, Wojcicki, Wdowczyk (Tarasiewicz 15), Prusik, Matysik, Urban, Dziekanowski (Kosecki 60), Furtok, Warzycha K.

3 June, Wembley, att. 69,203
ENGLAND (1) 3 *(Lineker 24, Barnes 69, Webb 82)*
POLAND (0) 0
England: Shilton; Stevens, Pearce, Webb, Walker, Butcher, Robson, Waddle (Rocastle 75), Beardsley (Smith 75), Lineker, Barnes
Poland: Bako; Wijas, Wojcicki, Wdowczyk, Lukasik, Matysik, Prusik, Urban (Tarasiewicz 70), Furtok, Warzycha K., Lesniak (Kosecki 58)

	P	W	D	L	F	A	Pts
England	4	3	1	0	10	0	7
Sweden	3	2	1	0	4	2	5
Poland	3	1	0	2	2	5	2
Albania	4	0	0	4	1	10	0

Remaining fixtures: 6.9.89 Sweden v England; 8.10.89 Sweden v Albania; 11.10.89 Poland v England; 25.10.89 Poland v Sweden; 15.11.89 Albania v Poland

Group 3 *(USSR, East Germany, Austria, Iceland, Turkey)*

31 August, Reykjavik, att. 8,300
ICELAND (1) 1 *(Gretarsson 11)*
USSR (0) 1 *(Litovchenko 75)*
Iceland: Sigurdsson; Bergsson, Saevar Jonsson, Edvaldsson, Thordarsson, Gislason, Ormslev, Siggi Jonsson, Sigurvinsson, Gudjohnsen, Gretarsson (Torfasson G. 82)
USSR: Dasayev; Bessonov (Dobrovolski 65), Khidiatulin, Kuznetsov, Demianenko, Aleinikov, Litovchenko, Zavarov, Rats, Protasov, Mikhailichenko

12 October, Istanbul, att. 25,680
TURKEY (0) 1 *(Onal 73)*
ICELAND (0) 1 *(Torfasson O. 62)*
Turkey: Fatih; Recep (Feyyaz 57), Semih, Cuneyt, Mucahit, Gokhan G., Oguz, Ridvan, Onal, Tanju, Savas K.
Iceland: Fridriksson; Gislason, Edvaldsson, Arnthorsson (Askelsson 79), Bergsson, Siggi Jonsson, Margeirsson, Torfasson O., Torfasson G., Gudjohnsen, Thordarsson

19 October, East Berlin, att. 12,000
EAST GERMANY (1) 2 *(Thom 34, 88)*
ICELAND (0) 0
East Germany: Weissflog; Kreer, Schossler, Stahmann, Lindner, Doschner, Raab, Ernst, Stubner (Sammer 34), Kirsten, Thom
Iceland: Sigurdsson; Saevar Jonsson, Bergsson, Edvaldsson, Gislason, Thordarsson, Torfasson O., Gudjohnsen, Sigurvinsson, Gretarsson, Torfasson G. (Margeirsson 77)

19 October, Kiev, att. 100,000
USSR (0) 2 *(Mikhailichenko 47, Zavarov 69)*
AUSTRIA (0) 0
USSR: Dasayev; Ivanauskas (Gorlukovich), Khidiatulin, Zigmantovich, Demianenko, Aleinikov, Litovchenko, Zavarov, Rats, Mikhailichenko, Protasov (Savichev 83)
Austria: Lindenberger; Russ, Degeorgi, Pfeffer, Weber H., Zsak, Keglevits, Artner, Polster, Hormann (Herzog 63), Willfurth

2 November, Vienna, att. 25,000
AUSTRIA (2) 3 *(Polster 38, Herzog 42, 54)*
TURKEY (0) 2 *(Feyyaz 61, Tanju 81)*
Austria: Lindenberger, Weber G., Russ, Pfeffer, Artner, Willfurth (Pacult 55), Prohaska, Herzog (Glatzmayer 68), Degeorgi, Ogris, Polster
Turkey: Fatih; Cuneyt, Recep, Gokhan G. (Savas K.), Semih, Mustafa, Unal, Oguz, Gokhan K., Ridvan, Feyyaz (Tanju)

30 November, Istanbul, att. 39,000
TURKEY (1) 3 *(Tanju 23, 63, Oguz 69)*
EAST GERMANY (0) 1 *(Thom 75)*
Turkey: Fatih; Recep, Semih, Cuneyt, Gokhan G., Onal, Ugur, Tutuneker, Ridvan, Oguz (Hassan 88), Tanju (Metin 78), Feyyaz
East Germany: Weissflog; Kreer (Schossler 66), Stahmann, Lindner, Doschner, Pilz, Stubner, Steinmann, Kirsten, Ernst (Doll 46), Thom

12 April, Magdeburg, att. 23,000
EAST GERMANY (0) 0
TURKEY (1) 2 *(Tanju 21, Ridvan 88)*
East Germany: Muller; Hauptmann, Rohde, Trautmann, Lindner, Stubner (Wuckel 64), Sammer, Pilz (Doll 19), Kirsten, Minge, Thom
Turkey: Engin; Recep, Cuneyt, Gokhan B., Semih, Yusuf, Ugur (Erdal 65), Oguz (Gokhan G. 80), Unal, Ridvan, Tanju

26 April, Kiev, att. 100,000
USSR (3) 3 *(Dobrovolski 3, Litovchenko 22, Protasov 40)*
EAST GERMANY (0) 0
USSR: Dasayev; Luzhny, Gorlukovich, Kuznetsov, Dobrovolski (Savichev 75), Alienikov (Kulkov 80), Litovchenko, Mikhailichenko, Protasov, Rats, Zavarov
East Germany: Weissflog; Hauptmann (Mertz 46), Lieberam, Kohler, Trautmann, Doschner, Sammer, Wosz, Scholz (Kirsten 55), Doll, Thom

10 May, Istanbul, att. 42,500
TURKEY (0) 0
USSR (1) 1 *(Mikhailichenko 40)*
Turkey: Engin; Recep, Cuneyt, Gokhan B., Semih, Yusuf, Ugur (Hasan Vezir 46) (Feyyaz 60), Unal, Mustafa, Ridvan, Tanju
USSR: Dasayev; Luzhny, Gorlukovich, Kuznetsov, Aleinikov (Ketaschvil 89), Rats, Mikhailichenko, Litovchenko, Zavarov, Protasov (Borodyuk 86), Dobrovolski

20 May, Leipzig, att. 22,000
EAST GERMANY (0) 1 *(Kirsten 86)*
AUSTRIA (1) 1 *(Polster 3)*
East Germany: Weissflog; Stahmann, Lindner, Trautmann (Doll 46), Kreer, Rohde, Stubner, Sammer (Weidemann 68), Steinmann, Kirsten, Thom
Austria: Lindenberger; Weber G., Russ, Pfeffer, Pecl, Rodax (Ogris 68), Prohaska, Zsak, Artner, Herzog (Stoger 60), Polster

163

31 MAY, Moscow, att. 50,000
USSR (0) 1 *(Dobrovolski 62)*
ICELAND (0) 1 *(Askelsson 86)*
USSR: Dasayev; Luzhny, Gorlukovich, Kuznetsov, Rats, Aleinikov, Bessonov, (Ketaschvilli 82), Dobrovolski, Litovchenko, Protasov (Savichev 82), Zavarov
Iceland: Sigurdsson; Edvaldsson, Jonsson A., Bergsson, Gislason, Jonsson S., Thordarson, Torfason O. (Kristiansson 82), Arnthorsson, Gretarsson, Torfason G. (Askelsson 69)

14 June, Reykjavik, att. 15,000
ICELAND (0) 0
AUSTRIA (0) 0
Iceland: Sigurdsson; Edvaldsson, Bergsson, Gislason (Thorkelsson 65), Siggi Jonsson, Thordarsson, Saevar Jonsson, Arnthorsson, Sigurvinsson, Gretarsson, Torfason, G.
Austria: Lindenberger; Pecl, Weber, Pfeffer, Hortnagl (Herzog 36), Russ, Zsak, Arnter, Prohaska, Polster, Rodax (Ogris 46)

	P	W	D	L	F	A	Pts
USSR	5	3	2	0	8	2	8
Turkey	5	2	1	2	8	6	5
Austria	4	1	2	1	4	5	4
Iceland	5	0	4	1	3	5	4
East Germany	5	1	1	3	4	9	3

Group 4 *(West Germany, Holland, Wales, Finland)*

31 August, Helsinki, att. 31,693
FINLAND (0) 0
WEST GERMANY (2) 4 *(Voller 6, 15, Matthaus 52, Riedle 86)*
Finland: Laukkanen; Europaeus, Hannikainen (Lipponen 43), Lahtinen, Petaja, Myyry, Pekonen Ukkonen (Alatensio 62), Hjelm, Rantanen, Paatelainen
West Germany: Illgner; Brehme, Gortz, Kohler, Fach, Buchwald (Rolff 26), Littbarski, Hassler, Voller, Matthaus, Eckstein (Riedle 75)

14 September, Amsterdam, att. 58,000
HOLLAND (0) 1 *(Gullit 82)*
WALES (0) 0
Holland: Van Breukelen; Van Aerle, Rijkaard, Koeman R., Van Tiggelen, Vanenburg (Kieft 66), Wouters, Koeman E., Kruzen, Gullit, Van Basten
Wales: Southall; Hall, Blackmore, Williams, Knill, Davies, Horne, Nicholas, Rush, Hughes (Saunders 76), Aizlewood

19 October, Swansea, att. 9,603
WALES (2) 2 *(Saunders (pen) 16, Lahtinen (og) 40)*
FINLAND (2) 2 *(Ukkonen 8, Paatelainen 45)*
Wales: Southall; Hall (Bowen 59), Blackmore, Nicholas, Van Den Hauwe, Ratcliffe, Horne, Saunders, Rush, Hughes, Pascoe
Finland: Huttunen; Pekonen, Lahtinen, Europaeus, Kanerva, Myyry (Lipponen 86), Holmgren, Ukkonen, Petaja (Rantanen 61), Paatelainen, Hjelm

19 October, Munich, att. 73,000
WEST GERMANY (0) 0
HOLLAND (0) 0
West Germany: Illgner; Fach, Kohler, Buchwald, Berthold, Hassler, Matthaus, Thon, Brehme, Klinsmann (Mill 67), Voller
Holland: Van Breukelen; Van Tiggelen, Koeman R., Rijkaard, Vanenburg, Van Aerle (Winter 20), Wouters, Koeman E., Silooy, Van Basten, Bosman

26 April, Rotterdam, att. 53,000
HOLLAND (0) 1 *(Van Basten 87)*
WEST GERMANY (0) 1 *(Riedle 68)*
Holland: Hiele; Van Aerle, Van Tiggelen, Koeman R., Rijkaard, Hofkens (Rutjes 84), Vanenburg, Koeman E., Van Basten, Winter, Huistra (Eykelkamp 75)
West Germany: Illgner; Berthold, Brehme, Kohler (Rolff 75), Reuter, Buchwald, Riedle, Moller, Voller (Klinsmann 33), Matthaus, Hassler

31 May, Cardiff, att. 25,000
WALES (0) 0
WEST GERMANY (0) 0
Wales: Southall; Phillips, Blackmore (Bowen 82), Ratcliffe, Aizlewood, Nicholas, Saunders, Horne, Rush, Hughes, Williams (Pascoe 82)
West Germany: Illgner; Berthold, Reinhardt, Buchwald, Reuter, Fach, Hassler, Moller, Brehme, Riedle (Klinsmann 77), Voller

31 May, Helsinki, att. 48,000
FINLAND (0) 0
HOLLAND (0) 1 *(Kieft 87)*
Finland: Laukkanen; Kanerva, Europacus, Heikkinen, Ikalainen, Holmgren, Ukkonen (Tornvall 68), Hjelm (Petaja 83), Lipponen, Paatelainen, Myyry
Holland: Van Breukelen; Koeman R., Van Tiggelen, Rutjes, Van Aerle, Vanenburg (Huistra 83), Rijkaard, Koeman E., Ellerman (Gullit 66), Van Basten, Kieft

	P	W	D	L	F	A	Pts
Holland	4	2	2	0	3	1	6
West Germany	4	1	3	0	5	1	5
Wales	3	0	2	1	2	3	2
Finland	3	0	1	2	2	7	1

Remaining fixtures: 6.9.89 Finland v Wales; 4.10.89 West Germany v Finland; 11.10.89, Wales v Holland; 15.11.89 West Germany v Wales, Holland v Finland

Group 5 *(France, Scotland, Yugoslavia, Norway, Cyprus)*

14 September, Oslo, att. 22,769
NORWAY (1) 1 *(Fjortoft 44)*
SCOTLAND (1) 2 *(McStay 14, Johnston 62)*
Norway: Thorstvedt; Henriksen, Johnsen, Bratseth, Giske, Osvold, Brandhaug, Lokken, Sorloth, Sundby (Berg 2, Jakobsen 84), Fjortoft
Scotland: Leighton; Nicol, Malpas, Gillespie, McLeish, Miller, Aitken (Durrant 55), McStay, Johnston, McClair, Gallacher

28 September, Paris, att. 25,000
FRANCE (0) 1 *(Papin 84 (pen))*
NORWAY (0) 0
France: Bats; Amoros, Boli (Kastendeuch 63) Casoni, Sonor, Sauzee, Bravo, Dib, Passi (Paille 76), Papin, Xuereb
Norway: Thorstvedt; Henriksen (Halle), Johnsen, Kojedal, Giske, Osvold (Gulbrandsen 81), Brandhaug, Bratseth, Berg, Sorloth, Jakobsen

19 October, Hampden Park, att. 42,771
SCOTLAND (1) 1 *(Johnston 17)*
YUGOSLAVIA (1) 1 *(Katanec 36)*
Scotland: Goram; Gough, Malpas, Nicol, McLeish, Miller, Aitken (Speedie 70), McStay, Johnston, McClair, Bett (McCoist 55)
Yugoslavia: Ivkovic; Stanojkovic, Spasic (Sabanadzovic 83), Jozic, Hadzibegic, Radanovic, Stojkovic, Katanec, Cvetkovic (Jankovic M. 89), Bazdarevic, Zlatko Vujovic

22 October, Nicosia, att. 3,000
CYPRUS (0) 1 *(Pittas(pen) 78)*
FRANCE (1) 1 *(Xuereb 44)*
Cyprus: Pantzarias; Christodolou, Stavru, Miamiliotis, Pittas, Petsas, Yiangudakis, Nicolau, Kantilos, Savva, Christofi (Ioannu 77)
France: Bats; Sonor, Casoni, Boli, Amoros, Bravo (Paille 80), Dib, Sauzee, Passi (Vercruysse 72), Papin, Xuereb

2 November, Limassol, 7,767
CYPRUS (0) 0
NORWAY (0) 3 *(Sorloth 56, 78, Osvold 89)*
Cyprus: Pantzarias; Pittas, Miamiliotis, Christodolou (Kastanis 25), Stavrou, Yiangudakis, Kantilos (Kollandris 31), Savva, Savvides, Nicolau, Christofi
Norway: Thorstvedt; Lokken, Kojedal, Bratseth, Halle, Osvold, Brandhaug, Halvorsen, Gulbrandsen, Sorloth, Agdestein

19 November, Belgrade, att. 16,000
YUGOSLAVIA (1) 3 *(Spasic 11, Susic 76, Stojkovic 82)*
FRANCE (1) 2 *(Perez 3, Sauzee 68)*
Yugoslavia: Ivkovic; Stanojkovic, Spasic (Juric 55), Hadzibegic, Jozic, Stojkovic, Susic, Bazdarevic, Katanec, Cvetkovic (Savicevic 70), Zlatko Vujovic
France: Bats; Roche, Boli, Kastendeuch, Amoros, Ferreri (Papin 78), Dib, Sauzee, Tigana, Paille, Perez (Bravo 69)

11 December, Rijeka, att. 9,000
YUGOSLAVIA (3) 4 *(Savicevic 13, 33, 82, Hadzibegic 44(pen))*
CYPRUS (0) 0
Yugoslavia: Ivkovic; Stanojkovic, Spasic (Juric 46), Brnovic, Hadzibegic, Josic, Stojkovic, Susic, Savicevic, Bazdarevic, Zlatko Vujovic
Cyprus: Pantzarias; Antonionios, Pittas, Papacoats, Stavrou, Yiangudakis, Savva, Nicolau, Christodolou (Kastanas 65), Ioannu (Petsas 77), Tsingis

8 February, Limassol, att. 25,000
CYPRUS (1) 2 *(Kollandris 14, Ioannu 47)*
SCOTLAND (1) 3 *(Johnston 9, Gough 54, 96 – injury time)*
Cyprus: Pantzarias, Pittas, Miamiliotis, Christodolou, Socratous, Yiangudakis, Kollandris, Savva (Petsas 36), Savvides, Nicolau, Ioannu
Scotland: Leighton; Gough, Malpas, Aitken, McLeish, Narey, Nicol (Ferguson I.9), McStay, McClair, Speedie (McInally 68), Johnston

8 March, Hampden Park, att. 65,204
SCOTLAND (1) 2 *(Johnston 28, 52)*
FRANCE (0) 0
Scotland: Leighton; Gough, Malpas, Aitken, McLeish, Gillespie, Nicol, McStay, McCoist (McClair 69), Ferguson (Strachan 56), Johnston
France: Bats; Amoros, Silvestre, Sonor, Battiston, Sauzee, Durand (Paille 57), Laurey, Papin, Blanc, Xuereb (Perez 70)

26 April, Hampden Park, att 50,081
SCOTLAND (1) 2 *(Johnston 26, McCoist 63)*
CYPRUS (0) 1 *(Nicolau 62)*
Scotland: Leighton; Gough, Malpas, Aitken, McLeish, McPherson, Nevin (Nicholas 74), McStay, Johnston, McCoist, Durie (Speedie 59)
Cyprus: Charitou; Castanas, Pittas (Elia 64), Christodolou, Michael, Yiangudakis, Petsas, Nicolau, Savvides, Ioannou Y., Kollandris

29 April, Paris, att. 39,469
FRANCE (0) 0
YUGOSLAVIA (0) 0
France: Bats; Amoros, Sonor, Boli, Battiston, Sauzee, Xuereb (Deschamps 76), Durand (Cocard 46), Paille, Blanc, Perez
Yugoslavia: Ivkovic; Stanojkovic, Spasic, Katanec, Hadzibegic, Josic, Zoran Vujovic, Susic, Bazdarevic, Stojkovic, Zlatko Vujovic (Brnovic 85)

21 May, Oslo, att. 10,273
NORWAY (3) 3 *(Osvold 17, Sorloth 34, Bratseth 35)*
CYPRUS (1) 1 *(Kollandris 44)*
Norway: Thorstvedt; Halle, Kojedal, Bratseth, Giske, Lokken Serkh (Gulbrandsen 82), Osvold, Jakobsen, Sorloth (AGDESTEIN 61), Fjortoft
Cyprus: Charitou; Kastanas, Pittas, Christodolou, Socratous, Yiangudakis, Kollandris (Andrelis 69), Nicolau, Savvides (Orfanides 87), Petsas, Ioannou

14 June, Oslo, att. 22,740
NORWAY (0) 1 *(Fjortoft 90)*
YUGOSLAVIA (1) 2 *(Stojkovic 22, Zlatko Vujovic 88)*
Norway: Ole By Rise; Halle, Bratseth, Kojedal, Giske, Lokken, Berg (Gulbrandsen 83), Osvold, Jakobsen, Sorloth (Agdestein 63), Fjortoft
Yugoslavia: Ivkovic; Spasic, Stanojkovic, Jozic, Katanec, Hadzibegic, Zoran Vujovic, Susic (Vujavic 73), Bazdarevic, Stojkovic, Zlatko Vujovic

	P	W	D	L	F	A	Pts
Scotland	5	4	1	0	10	5	9
Yugoslavia	5	3	2	0	10	4	8
Norway	5	2	0	3	8	6	4
France	5	1	2	2	4	6	4
Cyprus	6	0	1	5	5	16	1

Remaining fixtures: 5.9.89 Norway v France; 6.9.89 Yugoslavia v Scotland; 11.10.89 Yugoslavia v Norway; France v Scotland; 28.10.89 Cyprus v Yugoslavia; 15.11.89 Scotland v Norway; 18.11.89 France v Cyprus

Group 6 *(Spain, Hungary, Northern Ireland, Eire, Malta)*

21 May, Belfast, att. 9,000

NORTHERN IRELAND (3) 3 *(Quinn 14, Penney 23, Clarke 25)*
MALTA (0) 0
Northern Ireland: McKnight; Donaghy, Worthington, McClelland, McDonald, O'Neill, Penney (McNally 81), Wilson D., Clarke, Quinn, Dennison (Black)
Malta: Cluett; Camilleri E. (Refalo 46), Azzopardi, Galea, Brincat, Buttigieg, Busuttil, Scerri, Carabott, Scicluna, De Giorgio (Caruana 60)

14 September, Belfast, att. 19,873
NORTHERN IRELAND (0) 0
EIRE (0) 0
Northern Ireland: McKnight; Donaghy (Rogan), Worthington, McClelland, McDonald, O'Neill, Penney, Wilson D., Clarke, Quinn, Black
Eire: Peyton; Morris, Hughton, McGrath, McCarthy, Moran, Houghton, Whelan, Aldridge, Cascarino, Sheedy

19 October, Budapest, att. 18,000
HUNGARY (0) 1 *(Vincze 84)*
NORTHERN IRELAND (0) 0
Hungary: Disztl P.; Sallai, Nagy, Sass, Meszoly (Dajka 46), Garaba, Kiprich, Kozma, Bognar, Detari, Hajszan (Vincze 81)
Northern Ireland: McKnight; Rogan, Worthington, McClelland, McDonald, Donaghy, Dennison, Wilson D., Clarke (Quinn 81), O'Neill (Wilson K. 58), Black

16 November, Seville, att. 50,000
SPAIN (0) 2 *(Manolo 52, Butragueno 66)*
EIRE (0) 0
Spain: Zubizarreta; Quique Flores (Solana 84), Jimenez, Andrinua, Sanchis, Gorriz, Michel, Roberto, Martin Vazquez, Manolo (Ramon 67) Butragueno
Eire: Bonner; Morris, McCarthy, Staunton, O'Leary, Moran, Houghton, Sheridan (O'Brien 82), Aldridge (Quinn 65), Cascarino, Galvin

11 December, Valletta, att. 12,000
MALTA (0) 2 *(Busuttil 46,90)*
HUNGARY (1) 2 *(Vincze 5, Kiprich 56)*
Malta: Cluett; Camilleri E. (Saliba 53), Azzopardi, Galea, Camilleri S., (Vella S.70), Busuttil, Vella R., Carabott, Gregory, De Giorgio, Woods
Hungary: Disztl P.; Kozma, Disztl L., Keller, Kekesi, Csuhay, Kiprich (Pinter 85), Kovacs, Czucsansky, Vincze (Fischer 70), Balog

21 December, Seville, att. 70,000
SPAIN (1) 4 *(Rogan (og) 30, Butragueno 55, Michel 60 (pen), Roberto 64)*
NORTHERN IRELAND (0) 0
Spain: Quique Flores, Jimenez, Andrinua, Gorriz, Roberto, Manolo (Julio Salinas 78), Michel, Butragueno, Martin Vazquez, Beguiristain (Serna 65)
Northern Ireland: McKnight; Rogan, Worthington, McCreery (Quinn 54), McDonald, McClelland, Donaghy (O'Neill 72), Penney, Clarke, Wilson K., Black

22 January, Valletta, att. 23,000
MALTA (0) 0
SPAIN (1) 2 *(Michel (pen) 16, Beguiristain 51)*
Malta: Cluett; Camilleri S. (Camilleri E. 55), Galea, Buttigieg, Azzopardi, Brincat (Scerri 46), Vella, R., Gregory, Carabott, De Giorgio, Busuttil
Spain: Zubizarreta; Quique Flores, Sanchis, Andrinua, Jimenez, Michel, Roberto, Martin Vazquez, Manolo, Butragueno (Gorriz 76), Beguiristain (Eusebio 66)

8 February, Belfast, att. 20,000
NORTHERN IRELAND (0) 0
SPAIN (1) 2 *(Andrinua 3, Manolo 84)*
Northern Ireland: McKnight; Ramsey, Rogan, Donaghy, McClelland, Wilson D. (Clarke 68), Dennison (O'Neill 63), Sanchez, Quinn, Wilson K., Black
Spain: Zubizarreta; Chendo (Euzebio 44), Jimenez, Andrinua, Serna Sanchis, Gorriz, Bakero (Manolo 75), Michel, Butragueno, Roberto, Martin Vazquez

8 March, Budapest, att. 20,000
HUNGARY (0) 0
EIRE (0) 0
Hungary: Disztl P.; Kozma, Disztl L., Bognar Z., Sass, Kovacs E., Detari, Hajszan, Gregor (Boda 77), Kiprich, Meszaros (Bognar G. 46)
Eire: Bonner; Morris, Hughton, McGrath, McCarthy, Moran, Whelan, Houghton, Aldridge (Brady 80), Cascarino (Quinn 80), Sheedy

23 March, Seville, att. 50,000
SPAIN (1) 4 *(Michel 38, 68 (pen), Manolo 71, 80)*
MALTA (0) 0
Spain: Zubizarreta; Quique Sanchez, Jimenez, Andrinua, Roberto, Sanchis, Michel, Butragueno, Martin Vazquez (Eusebio 68), Beguiristain (Eloy 68), Manolo
Malta: Cluett; Camilleri E., Azzopardi A. (Cauchi 30), Buttigieg, Galea, Vella R., De Giorgio, Scerri C., Carabott, Gregory, Busuttil

168

12 April, Budapest, att. 15,000
HUNGARY (0) 1 *(Boda 49)*
MALTA (1) 1 *(Busuttil 7)*
Hungary: Disztl P.; Kozma (Kiprich 57), Keller, Disztl L., Kovacs E., Bognar Z., Boda, Bognar G., Sass (Fischer 46), Detari. Hajszan
Malta: Cluett; Camilleri E., Azzopardi A., Galea, Cauchi, (Vella S. 46), Buttigieg, Busuttil, Vella R., Carabott, Scerri, Gregory

26 April, Valletta, att. 15,000
MALTA (0) 0
NORTHERN IRELAND (0) 2 *(Clarke 55, O'Neill 73)*
Malta: Cluett; Buttigieg, Camilleri E., Cauchi (Vella S. 62), Gallea, De Giorgio, Scerri, Vella R., Busuttil, Gregory, Carabott (Delia 78)
Northern Ireland: Wright; Donaghy, Worthington (Rogan 86), McCreery, McClelland, Dennison, Wilson D., Quinn, Clarke, Sanchez (O'Neill 70), Wilson K.

26 April, Dublin, att. 49,160
EIRE (1) 1 *(Michel (og) 15)*
SPAIN (0) 0
Eire: Bonner; Hughton, Staunton, McCarthy, Moran, Whelan, McGrath, Houghton, Stapleton (Townsend 69), Cascarino, Sheedy
Spain: Zubizarreta; Quique Sanchez (Eusebio 69), Jimenez, Serna, Gorriz, Manolo, Michel, Butragueno (Julio Salinas 70), Roberto, Martin Vazquez

28 May, Dublin, att. 49,000
EIRE (1) 2 *(Houghton 32, Moran 55)*
MALTA (0) 0
Eire: Bonner; Hughton, Staunton, O'Leary, Moran, Whelan, McGrath, Houghton (Townsend 70), Stapleton (Aldridge 27), Cascarino, Sheedy
Malta: Cluett, Camilleri E., Azzopardi (Carabott 65), Galea, Vella S., Buttigieg, Busuttil, Vella R., Scerri, De Giorgio, Gregory

4 June, Dublin, att. 49,000
EIRE (1) 2 *(McGrath 33, Cascarino 80)*
HUNGARY (0) 0
Eire: Bonner; Hughton, Staunton, O'Leary, McGrath, (Morris 80), Moran, Houghton, Townsend, Aldridge (Brady 74), Cascarino, Sheedy
Hungary: Disztl P., Bognar Z., Fitos, Disztl L., Garaba, Kozma, Meszaros, (Vincze 71) Detari, Czehi (Bognar G. 66), Keller, Boda

	P	W	D	L	F	A	Pts
Spain	6	5	0	1	14	1	10
Eire	6	3	2	1	5	2	8
Northern Ireland	6	2	1	3	5	7	5
Hungary	5	1	3	1	4	5	5
Malta	6	0	2	4	3	14	2

Remaining fixtures: 6.9.89 Northern Ireland v Hungary; 11.10.89 Hungary v Spain, Eire v Northern Ireland; 15.11.89 Spain v Hungary, Malta v Eire

Group 7 *(Belgium, Portugal, Czechoslovakia, Switzerland, Luxembourg)*

21 September, Luxembourg, att. 2,500
LUXEMBOURG (0) 1 *(Langers 80)*
SWITZERLAND (3) 4 *(Sutter A.15, Turkyilmaz 21 (pen), 53, Sutter B. 28)*
Luxembourg: Van Rijswijk; Meunier, Bossi, Weis, Petry, Girres (Scuto 63), Hellers, Jeitz, Scholten, Langers, Krings (Morocutti 73)
Switzerland: Corminboeuf; Geiger, Tschuppert, Weber M., Mottiez, Andermatt (Lei-Ravello 70), Hermann, Favre, Sutter B., Turkyilmaz, Sutter A. (Bonvin 79)

19 October, Brussels, att., 14,450
BELGIUM (1) 1 *(Vervoort 30)*
SWITZERLAND (0) 0
Belgium: Bodart; Grun, Clijsters, Demol, Versavel, Emmers, Van der Elst F., Scifo, Vervoort, Ceulemans, Nilis (Severeyns 76)
Switzerland: Corminboeuf; Mottiez, Geiger, Weber M., Schallibaum, Andermatt (Bonvin 76), Hermann, Favre, Zuffi, Sutter B., Turkyilmaz

18 October, Esch-sur-Alzette, att. 2,500
LUXEMBOURG (0) 0
CZECHOSLOVAKIA (2) 2 *(Hasek 25, Chovanec 35)*
Luxembourg: Van Rijswijk; Meunier, Scheuer, Petry, Bossi, Jeitz (Girres 82), Hellers, Weis, Scholten, Langers, Krings (Morocutti 61)
Czechoslovakia: Stejskal; Bielik, Kadlec, Hasek, Bilek, Nemecek, Fieber, Chovanec, Griga (Danek 81), Skuhravy, Weiss (Hyravy 75)

16 November, Bratislava, att., 48,000
CZECHOSLOVAKIA (0) 0
BELGIUM (0) 0
Czechoslovakia: Stejskal; Bielik, Nemecek, (Danek 87), Chovanec, Kadlec, Vlk, Weiss (Moravcik 80), Hasek, Bilek, Griga, Luhovy
Belgium: Preud'homme; Demol, Gerets, Grun, Albert, Dewolf, Emmers, Veyt, Van der Elst F., Scifo (Van den Linden 75), Christiaens (Nilis 82)

16 November, Oporto, att. 29,000
PORTUGAL (1) 1 *(Gomes 31)*
LUXEMBOURG (0) 0
Portugal: Silvino; Jaime, Sobrinho, Morato, Alvaro, Rui Barros, Vitor Paneira, Nunes, Futre, Jordao (Jaime Magalhaes 46), Gomes
Luxembourg: Van Rijswijk; Meunier, Scheuer, Petry, Bossi, Girres, Jeitz, Weis, Scholten (Thome 82), Krings (Malget 60), Langers

15 February, Lisbon, att. 70,000
PORTUGAL (0) 1 *(Paneira)*
BELGIUM (0) 1 *(Gerets)*
Portugal: Silvino; Joao Pinto, Oliveira, Sobrinho, Veloso, Nunes, Vitor Paneira (Cesar Brito 86), Sousa, Rui Barros, Futre (Pacheco 61) Semedo
Belgium: Preud'homme; Gerets, Grun, De Wolf, Versavel, Emmers, Demol (Van der Linden 77), Scifo, Van der Elst, Ceulemans, Degryse

26 April, Lisbon, att. 15,000
PORTUGAL (0) 3 *(Joao Pinto 48, Frederico 56, Vitor Paneira 69)*
SWITZERLAND (0) 1 *(Zuffi 64)*
Portugal: Silvino; Joao Pinto, Sobrinho, Frederico (Oliveira 87), Veloso, Nunes, Andre, Vitor Paneira, Rui Barros, Sousa (Jorge Silva 46), Cesar Brito
Switzerland: Brunner; Mottiez, Birrel (Ryf 73), Weber M., Koller, Marini, Sutter B., Hermann, Favre, Zuffi, Sutter A. (Turkyilmaz 86)

29 April, Brussels, att. 21,000
BELGIUM (1) 2 *(Degryse 29, 77)*
CZECHOSLOVAKIA (1) 1 *(Luhovy 41)*
Belgium: Preud'homme; Gerets, Demol, Grun, Albert, Versavel, Van der Elst F., Emmers, Ceulemans, Degryse, Nilis (Van der Linden 65)
Czechoslovakia: Stejskal; Bilek (Weiss 85), Chovanec, Kocian, Straka, Kadlec, Moravcik, Vlk (Nemecek 83), Hasek, Griga, Luhovy

9 May, Prague, att. 16,350
CZECHOSLOVAKIA (1) 4 *(Griga 6, Skuhravy 76, 84, Bilek 81)*
LUXEMBOURG (0) 0
Czechoslovakia: Stejskal; Bilek, Kadlec (Bielik 46), Hasek, Kocian, Nemecek (Weiss 71), Straka, Chovanec, Griga, Skuhravy, Moravcik
Luxembourg: Van Rijswijk; Meunier, Scheuer, Petry, Bossi, Girres, Birsens, Weis, Jeitz (Salbene 76), Hellers, Krings (Malget 89)

7 June, Berne, att. 30,000
SWITZERLAND (0) 0
CZECHOSLOVAKIA (1) 1 *(Skuhravy 21)*
Switzerland: Brunner; Koller, Marini, Schepull, Weber, Hermann, Sutter R. (Turkyilmaz 58), Geiger, Sutter A., Sutter B. (Zuffi 71), Halter
Czechoslovakia: Stejskal; Bilik Griga, Kadlec, Kouan, Straka, Hasek, Chovanec (Nemecek 83), Moravcik, Bilek, Skuhravy (Danek 56)

1 June, Lille, att. 10,000
LUXEMBOURG (0) 0
BELGIUM (1) 5 *(Van der Linden 13, 52, 62, (pen), 90, Vervoort 64)*
Luxembourg: Van Rijswijk; Meunier, Scheuer, Petry, Bossi, Girres, Birsens, Jeitz (Salbene 75), Scholten (Malget 83), Langers, Krings
Belgium: Preud'homme; Gerets, Sanders, Versavel, Van der Elst F., (Scifo 73), Emmers, Demol, Vervoort, Degryse, Van der Linden, Ceulemans

	P	W	D	L	F	A	Pts
Belgium	5	3	2	0	9	2	8
Czechoslovakia	5	3	1	1	8	2	7
Portugal	3	2	1	0	5	2	5
Switzerland	4	1	0	3	5	6	2
Luxembourg	5	0	0	5	1	16	0

Remaining fixtures: 6.9.89 Belgium v Portugal; 20.9.89 Switzerland v Portugal; 6.10.89 Czechoslovakia v Portugal; 11.10.89 Switzerland v Belgium, Luxembourg v Portugal; 25.10.89 Czechoslovakia v Switzerland, Belgium v Luxembourg; 15.11.89 Portugal v Czechoslovakia, Switzerland v Luxembourg

SOUTH AMERICA
Group 1
20.8.89 Bolivia v Peru
27.8.89 Peru v Uruguay
3.9.89 Bolivia v Uruguay
10.9.89 Peru v Bolivia
17.9.89 Uruguay v Bolivia
24.9.89 Uruguay v Peru

Group 2
20.8.89 Colombia v Ecuador
27.8.89 Paraguay v Colombia
3.9.89 Ecuador v Colombia
10.9.89 Paraguay v Ecuador
17/24.9.89 Colombia v Paraguay
1.10.89 Ecuador v Paraguay

Group 3
30.7.89 Venezuela v Brazil
6.8.89 Venezuela v Chile
13.8.89 Chile v Brazil
20.8.89 Brazil v Venezuela
27.8.89 Chile v Venezuela
3.9.89 Brazil v Chile

AFRICA
First Round
Group 1
7.8.88 Angola (0) 0 Sudan (0) 0
11.11.88 Sudan (1) 1 Angola (0) 2
(Lesotho withdrew; Zimbabwe walked over; Zambia walked over; Rwanda withdrew)
16.7.88 Uganda (0) 1 Malawi (0) 0
30.7.88 Malawi (2) 3 Uganda (0) 1
Group 2
3.6.88 Libya (3) 3 Burkina Faso (0) 0
3.7.88 Burkina Faso (0) 2 Libya (0) 0
7.8.88 Ghana (0) 0 Liberia (0) 0
21.8.88 Liberia (1) 2 Ghana (0) 0
5.8.88 Tunisia (2) 5 Guinea (0) 0
21.8.88 Guinea (1) 3 Tunisia (0) 0
(Togo withdrew; Gabon walked over)

Second Round
Group A
6.1.89 Algeria (2) 3 Zimbabwe (0) 0
8.1.89 Ivory Coast (0) 1 Libya (0) 0
20.1.89 Libya v Algeria. *(Libya refused to play on the grounds that a state of war existed with
the USA. Algeria were awarded the game 2–0. Libya withdrew.)*
22.1.89 Zimbabwe (0) 0 Ivory Coast (0) 0
11.6.89 Ivory Coast (0) 0 Algeria (0) 0

Group B
6.1.89 Egypt (2) 2 Liberia (0) 0
7.1.89 Kenya (0) 1 Malawi (1) 1
21.1.89 Malawi (0) 1 Egypt (0) 1
22.1.89 Liberia (0) 0 Kenya (0) 0
10.6.89 Kenya (0) 0 Egypt (0) 0
11.6.89 Liberia (1) 1 Malawi (0) 0

Group C
7.1. 89 Nigeria (1) 1 Gabon (0) 0
8.1.89 Cameroon (0) 1 Angola (1) 1
22.1.89 Gabon (1) 1 Cameroon (2) 3
22.1.89 Angola (1) 2 Nigeria (0) 2
10.6.89 Nigeria (1) 2 Cameroon (0) 0
11.6.89 Angola (2) 2 Gabon (0) 0

Group D
8.1.89 Morocco (1) 1 Zambia (0) 0
8.1.89 Zaire (2) 3 Tunisia (1) 1
22.1.89 Tunisia (2) 2 Morocco (1) 1
22.1.89 Zambia (2) 4 Zaire (1) 2
11.6.89 Zaire (0) 0 Morocco (0) 0
11.6.89 Zambia 1 Tunisia (0) 0

OCEANIA
First Round
11.12.88 Chinese Taipei (0) 0 New Zealand (2) 4
15.12.88 New Zealand (3) 4 Chinese Taipei (0) 1
(both matches played in New Zealand)
26.11.88 Fiji (0) 1 Australia (0) 0
3.12.88 Australia (2) 5 Fiji (0) 1

Second Round
5.3.89 Israel (1) 1 New Zealand (0) 0
12.3.89 Australia (2) 4 New Zealand (0) 1
19.3.89 Israel (0) 1 Australia (0) 1
2.4.89 New Zealand (1) 2 Australia (0) 0
9.4.89 New Zealand (2) 2 Israel (2) 2
16.4.89 Australia (0) 1 Israel (1) 1
(Israel qualified for matches against the winner of South American Group 2)

CONCACAF
First Round
17.4.88 Guyana (0) 0 Trinidad/Tobago (2) 4
8.5.88 Trinidad/Tobago (1) 1 Guyana (0) 0
30.4.88 Cuba (0) 0 Guatemala (1) 1
15.5.88 Guatemala (0) 1 Cuba (1) 1
12.5.88 Jamaica (1) 1 Puerto Rico (0) 0
29.5.88 Puerto Rico (0) 1 Jamaica (1) 2
19.6.88 Antigua (0) 0 Netherlands Antilles (0) 1
29.7.88 Netherlands Antilles (0) 0 Antigua (1) 1
(Netherlands Antilles won 3–1 on penalties after extra time)
17.7.88 Costa Rica (1) 1 Panama (1) 1
31.7.88 Panama (0) 0 Costa Rica (1) 2

Second Round
1.10.88 Netherlands Antilles (0) 0 El Salvador (0) 1
16.10.88 El Salvador (2) 5 Netherlands Antilles (0) 0
24.7.88 Jamaica (0) 0 USA (0) 0
13.8.88 USA (1) 5 Jamaica (0) 1
30.10.88 Trinidad/Tobago (0) 0 Honduras (0) 0
13.11.88 Honduras (1) 1 Trinidad/Tobago (0) 1
(Costa Rica walked over; Mexico disqualified)
9.10.88 Guatemala (1) 1 Canada (0) 0
15.10.88 Canada (0) 3 Guatemala (2) 2

Third Round
19.3.89 Guatemala (1) 1 Costa Rica (0) 0
2.4.89 Costa Rica (1) 2 Guatemala (0) 1
16.4.89 Costa Rica (1) 1 USA (0) 0
30.4.89 USA (0) 1 Costa Rica (0) 0
13.5.89 USA (0) 1 Trinidad/Tobago (0) 1
28.5.89 Trinidad/Tobago (0) 1 Costa Rica (0) 1
11.6.89 Costa Rica 1 Trinidad/Tobago 0

ASIA
First Round
Group 1
6.1.89 Qatar (1) 1 Jordan (0) 0
6.1.89 Oman (1) 1 Iraq (1) 1
13.1.89 Oman (0) 0 Qatar (0) 0
13.1.89 Jordan (0) 0 Iraq (0) 1
20.1.89 Jordan (2) 2 Oman (0) 0
20.1.89 Qatar (0) 1 Iraq (0) 0
27.1.89 Jordan (0) 1 Qatar (0) 1
27.1.89 Iraq (1) 3 Oman (0) 1
3.2.89 Qatar (1) 3 Oman (0) 0
3.2.89 Iraq (2) 4 Jordan (0) 0
10.2.89 Oman (0) 0 Jordan (0) 2
10.2.89 Iraq (1) 2 Qatar (1) 2

173

Group 2 *(Bahrain withdrew)*
10.3.89 Yemen AR (0) 0 Syria (1) 1
15.3.89 Saudi Arabia (2) 5 Syria (1) 4
20.3.89 Yemen AR (0) 0 Saudi Arabia (0) 1
25.3.89 Syria (1) 2 Yemen AR (0) 0
30.3.89 Syria (0) 0 Saudi Arabia (0) 0
5.4.89 Saudi Arabia (1) 1 Yemen AR (0) 0

Group 3 *(Yemen PDR withdrew)*
6.1.89 Pakistan (0) 0 Kuwait (0) 1
13.1.89 Kuwait (1) 3 UAE (0) 2
20.1.89 UAE (2) 5 Pakistan (0) 0
27.1.89 Kuwait (1) 2 Pakistan (0) 0
3.2.89 UAE (0) 1 Kuwait (0) 0
10.2.89 Pakistan (0) 1 UAE (3) 4

Group 4 *(India withdrew)*
23.5.89 Malaysia (0) 2 Nepal (0) 0
23.5.89 Singapore (0) 0 Korea Rep (2) 3
25.5.89 Malaysia (0)1 Singapore (0) 0
25.5.89 Nepal (0) 0 Korea Rep (5) 9
27.5.89 Singapore (2) 3 Nepal (0) 0
27.5.89 Korea Rep (1) 3 Malaysia (0) 0
3.6.89 Singapore 0 Malaysia 0
3.6.89 Korea Rep 0 Nepal 0
5.6.89 Malaysia (0) 0 Korea Rep (0) 3
5.6.89 Nepal (0) 0 Singapore (4) 7
7.6.89 Singapore (0) 0 Korea Rep (1) 3
7.6.89 Malaysia 3 Nepal 0

Group 5
19.2.89 Thailand (0) 1 Bangladesh (0) 0
23.2.89 China (0) 2 Bangladesh (0) 0
23.2.89 Thailand (0) 0 Iran (2) 3
27.2.89 Bangladesh (0) 1 Iran (1) 2
28.2.89 Thailand (0) 0 China (0) 3
4.3.89 Bangladesh (0) 0 China (1) 2
8.3.89 Bangladesh (2) 3 Thailand (0) 1
17.3.89 Iran (0) 1 Bangladesh (0) 0
30.5.89 Iran (2) 3 Thailand (0) 0

Group 6
21.5.89 Indonesia (0) 0 Korea DPR (0) 0
22.5.89 Hong Kong (0) 0 Japan (0) 0
27.5.89 Hong Kong (0) 1 Korea DPR (2) 2
28.5.89 Indonesia (0) 0 Japan (0) 0
4.6.89 Hong Kong Indonesia*
4.6.89 Japan Korea DPR*
11.6.89 Korea DPR Hong Kong*
11.6.89 Japan (4) 5 Indonesia (0) 0

* Scores not available

THE WORLD CUP FINALS

Uruguay 1930
URUGUAY 4, ARGENTINA 2 (1–2) *Montevideo*
Uruguay: Ballesteros; Nasazzi (capt), Mascheroni, Andrade, Fernandez, Gestido, Dorado, Scarone, Castro, Cea, Iriarte, **Scorers:** Dorado, Cea, Iriarte, Castro.
Argentina: Botasso; Della Torre, Paternoster, Evaristo, J., Monti, Suarez, Peucelle, Varallo, Stabile, Ferreira (capt), Evaristo, M. **Scorers:** Peucelle, Stabile.
Leading scorer: Stabile (Argentina) 8.

Italy 1934
ITALY 2, CZECHOSLOVAKIA 1 (0–0) (1–1)* *Rome*
Italy: Combi (capt), Monseglio, Allemandi, Ferraris IV, Monti, Bertolini, Guaita, Meazza, Schiavio, Ferrari, Orsi. **Scorers:** Orsi, Schiavio.
Czechoslovakia: Planicka (capt), Zenisek, Ctyroky, Kostalek, Cambal, Krcil, Junek, Svoboda, Sobotka, Nejedly, Puc. **Scorer:** Puc.
Leading scorers: Schiavio (Italy), Nejedly (Czechoslovakia), Conen (Germany) each 4.

France 1938
ITALY 4, HUNGARY 2 (3–1) *Paris*
Italy: Olivieri; Foni, Rava, Serantoni, Andreolo, Locatelli, Biavati, Meazza (capt), Piola, Ferrari, Colaussi. **Scorers:** Colaussi 2, Piola 2.
Hungary: Szabo; Polgar, Biro, Szalay, Szucs, Lazar, Sas, Vincze, Sarosi, (capt.), Szengeller, Titkos. **Scorers:** Titkos, Sarosi.
Leading scorer: Leonidas (Brazil) 8.

Brazil 1950
Final pool *(replaced knock-out system)*

Uruguay 2, Spain 2   Brazil 6, Spain 1
Brazil 7, Sweden 1   Sweden 3, Spain 1
Uruguay 3, Sweden 2   Uruguay 2, Brazil 1

Final positions	*P*	*W*	*D*	*L*	*F*	*A*	*Pts*
Uruguay	3	2	1	0	7	5	5
Brazil	3	2	0	1	14	4	4
Sweden	3	1	0	2	6	11	2
Spain	3	0	1	2	4	11	1

Leading scorers: Ademir (Brazil) 7, Schiaffino (Uruguay), Basora (Spain) 5.

Switzerland 1954
WEST GERMANY 3, HUNGARY 2 *(2–2) Berne*
West Germany: Turek; Posipal, Kohlmeyer, Eckel, Liebrich, Mai, Rahn, Morlock, Walter, O., Walter, F. (capt), Schaefer. **Scorers:** Morlock, Rahn 2.
Hungary: Grosics; Buzansky, Lantos, Bozsik, Lorant, Zakarias, Czibor, Kocsis, Hidegkuti, Puskas (capt), Toth, J. **Scorers:** Puskas, Czibor.
Leading scorer: Kocsis (Hungary) 11.

Sweden 1958
BRAZIL 5, SWEDEN 2 (2–1) *Stockholm*
Brazil: Gilmar; Santos, D., Santos, N., Zito, Bellini, Orlando, Garrincha, Didi, Vavà, Pele, Zagalo. **Scorers:** Vavà 2, Pelé 2, Zagalo.
*Sweden:*Svensson; Bergmark, Axbom, Boerjesson, Gustavsson, Parling, Hamrin, Gren,Simonsson,Liedholm,Skoglund. **Scorers:** Liedholm, Simonsson.
Leading scorer: Fontaine (France) 13 (present record total).

Chile 1962
BRAZIL 3, CZECHOSLOVAKIA 1 (1–1) *Santiago*
Brazil: Gilmar; Santos, D., Mauro, Zozimo, Santos, N., Zito, Didi, Garrincha, Vavà, Amorildo, Zagalo. **Scorers:** Amarildo, Zito, Vavà.
Czechoslovakia: Schroiff; Tichy, Novak, Pluskal, Popluhar, Masopust, Pospichal, Scherer, Kvasniak, Kadraba, Jelinek. **Scorer:** Masopust.
Leading scorer: Jerkovic (Yugoslavia) 5.

England 1966
ENGLAND 4, WEST GERMANY 2 (1–1) (2–2)* *Wembley*
England: Banks; Cohen, Wilson, Stiles, Charlton, J., Moore, Ball, Hurst, Hunt, Charlton, R., Peters. **Scorers:** Hurst 3, Peters.
West Germany: Tilkowski; Hottges, Schulz, Weber, Schnellinger, Haller, Beckenbauer, Overath, Seeler, Held, Emmerich. **Scorers:** Haller, Weber.
Leading scorer: Eusebio (Portugal) 9.

Mexico 1970
BRAZIL 4, ITALY 1 (1–1) *Mexico City*
Brazil: Felix; Carlos Alberto, Brito, Piazza, Everaldo, Gerson, Clodoaldo, Jairzinho, Pelé, Tostão, Rivelino. **Scorers:** Pelé, Gerson, Jairzinho, Carlos Alberto.
Italy: Albertosi; Burgnich, Cera, Rosato, Facchetti, Bertini (Juliano), Riva, Domenghini, Mazzola, De Sisti, Boninsegna (Riveta). **Scorer:** Boninsegna.
Leading scorer: Müller (West Germany) 10.

West Germany 1974
WEST GERMANY 2, HOLLAND 1 (2–1) *Munich*
West Germany: Maier; Vogts, Schwarzenbeck, Beckenbauer, Breitner, Bonhof, Hoeness, Overath, Grabowski, Müller, Holzenbein. **Scorers:** Breitner *(pen)*, Müller.
Holland: Jongbloed; Suurbier, Rijsbergen (De Jong), Haan, Krol, Jansen, Van Hanegem, Neeskens, Rep (Nanninga), Cruyff, Rensenbrink (Van der Kerhof, R.).
Scorer: Nanninga *(pen)*.
Leading scorer: Lato (Poland) 7.

Argentina 1978
ARGENTINA 3, HOLLAND 1 (1–1)* *Buenos Aires*
Argentina: Fillol; Olguin, Passarella, Galvan, Tarantini, Ardiles (Larrosa), Gallego, Ortiz (Houseman), Bertoni, Luque, Kempes. **Scorers:** Kempers 2, Bertoni.
Holland: Jongbloed; Poortvliet, Brandts, Krol, Jansen (Suurbier), Neeskens, Van der Kerkhof, W., Van der Kerkhof, R., Haan, Rep (Nanninga), Rensenbrink. **Scorer:** Nanninga.
Leading scorer: Kempes (Argentina) 6.

Spain 1982
ITALY 3, WEST GERMANY 1 (0–0) *Madrid*
Italy: Zoff; Bergomi, Cabrini, Collovati, Scirea, Gentile, Oriali, Tardelli, Conti, Graziani (Altobelli), Rossi (Causio). **Scorers:** Rossi, Tardelli, Altobelli.
West Germany: Schumacher; Kaltz, Forster, K-H. Stielike, Forster, B. Breitner, Dremmler (Hrubesch), Littbarski, Briegel, Fischer, Rummenigge (Müller). **Scorer:** Breitner.
Leading scorer: Rossi (Italy) 6.

Mexico 1986
ARGENTINA 3, WEST GERMANY 2 (1–0) *Mexico City*
Argentina: Pumpido; Cuciuffo, Olarticoechea, Ruggeri, Brown, Giusti, Burruchaga (Trobbiani), Batista, Valdano, Maradona, Enrique. **Scorers:** Brown, Valdano, Burruchaga.
West Germany: Schumacher; Berthold, Briegel, Jakobs, Forster, Eder, Brehme, Matthaus, Allofs (Voller), Magath (Hoeness), Rummenigge. **Scorers:** Rummenigge, Voller.
Leading scorer: Lineker (England) 6.

*After extra time

WORLD CUP (Under-16)

(in Scotland, 10–24 June)

Group A
Scotland 0, Ghana 0
Cuba 0, Bahrain 3
Scotland 3, Cuba 0
Ghana 0, Bahrain 1
Scotland 1, Bahrain 1
Ghana 2, Cuba 2

Group B
East Germany 1, Australia 0
USA 1, Brazil 0
East Germany 5, USA 2
Australia 1, Brazil 3
Brazil 2, East Germany 1
Australia 2, USA 2

Group C
Argentina 0, China 0
Nigeria 4, Canada 0
Argentina 0, Nigeria 0
China 1, Canada 0
Argentina 4, Canada 1
Nigeria 3, China 0

Group D
Guinea 1, Colombia 1
Saudi Arabia 2, Portugal 2
Guinea 2, Saudi Arabia 2
Colombia 2, Portugal 3
Guinea 1, Portugal 1
Saudi Arabia 1, Colombia 0

Quarter-finals
Scotland 1, East Germany 0
Bahrain 0, Brazil 0
(aet; Bahrain won 4–1 on penalties)
Nigeria 0, Saudi Arabia 0
(aet; Saudi Arabia won 2–0 on penalties)
Portugal 2, Argentina 1

Semi-finals
Saudi Arabia 1, Bahrain 0
Scotland 1, Portugal 0

Final at Hampden Park, 24 June 1989, att. 51,674
Saudi Arabia (0) 2, Scotland (2) 2 *aet*
(Saudi Arabia won 5–4 on penalties)
Scorers: Saudi Arabia: *Al-Reshoudi, Al-Terair*; Scotland: *Downie, Dickov*

EUROPEAN CHAMPIONSHIPS
PAST FINALS

Paris, 10 July 1960 USSR 2, YUGOSLAVIA 1*
Ussr: Yachin; Tchekeli, Kroutikov, Voinov, Maslenkin, Netto, Metreveli, Ivanov, Ponedelnik, Bubukin, Meshki. **Scorers**: Metreveli, Ponedelnik.
Yugoslavia: Vidinic; Durkovic, Jusufi, Zanetic, Miladinovic, Perusic, Sekularac, Jerkovic, Galic, Matus, Kostic. **Scorer**: Netto (og).

Madrid, 21 June 1964 SPAIN 2, USSR 1
Spain; Iribar; Rivilla, Calleja, Fuste, Olivella, Zoco, Amancio, Pereda, Marcellino, Suarez, Lapetra. **Scorers**: Pereda, Marcellino.
USSR: Yachin; Chustikov, Mudrik, Voronin, Shesternjev, Anitchkin, Chislenko, Ivanov, Ponedelnik, Kornaev, Khusainov.**Scorer**: Khusainov.

Rome, 8 June 1968 ITALY 1, YUGOSLAVIA 1
Italy: Zoff; Burgnich, Facchetti, Ferrini, Guarneri, Castano, Domenghini, Juliano, Anatasi, Lodetti, Prati. **Scorer**: Domenghini.
Yugoslavia: Pandelic; Fazlagic, Damjanovic, Pavlovic, Paunovic, Holcer, Petkovic, Acimovic, Musemic, Trivic, Dzajic. **Scorer**: Dzajic.

Replay: Rome, 10 June 1968 ITALY 2, YUGOSLAVIA 0
Italy: Zoff; Burgnich, Facchetti, Rosato, Guarneri, Salvadore, Domenghini, Mazzola, Anastasi, De Sisti, Riva. **Scorers**: Riva, Anastasi.
Yugoslavia: Pantelic; Fazlagic, Damjanovic, Pavlovic, Paunovic, Holcer, Hosic, Acimovic, Meusemic, Trivic, Dzajic.

Brussels, 18 June 1972 WEST GERMANY 3, USSR 0
West Germany: Maier; Hottges, Schwarzenbeck, Beckenbauer, Breitner, Hoeness, Wimmer, Netzer, Heynckes, Muller, Kremers, **Scorers**: Muller 2, Wimmer.
USSR: Rudakov; Dzodzuashvili, Khurtsilava, Kaplichny, Istomin, Troshkin, Kolotov, Baidachni, Konkov (Dolmatov), Banishevski (Konzinkievits), Onishenko.

Belgrade, 20 June 1976 CZECHOSLOVAKIA 2, WEST GERMANY 2*
Czechoslovakia: Viktor; Dobias (Vesely, F.), Pivarnik, Ondrus, Capkovic, Gogh, Moder, Panenka, Svehlik (Jurkemik),Masny, Nehoda. **Scorers**: Svehlik, Dobias.
West Germany: Maier; Vogts, Beckenbauer, Schwarzenbeck, Dietz, Bonhof, Wimmer, (Flohe), Müller, D., Beer (Bongartz), Hoeness, Holzenbein. **Scorers**: Müller, Holzenbein.
Czechoslovakia won 5–3 on penalties.

Rome, 22 June 1980 WEST GERMANY 2, BELGIUM 1
West Germany: Schumacher; Briegel, Forster, K.Dietz, Schuster, Rummenigge, Hrubesch, Müller, Allofs, Stielike,
Kalz. **Scorer**: Hrubesch 2.
Belgium: Pfaff; Gerets, Millecamps, Meeuws, Renquin, Cools, Van der Eycken, Van Moer, Mommens, Van der Elst, Ceulemans. **Scorer**: Van der Eycken.

Paris, 27 June 1984 FRANCE 2, SPAIN 0
France: Bats; Battiston (Amoros), Le Roux, Bossis, Domergue, Giresse, Platini, Tigana, Fernandez, Lacombe (Genghini), Bellone. **Scorers**: Platini, Bellone
Spain: Arconada; Urquiaga, Salva (Roberto), Gallego, Camacho, Francisco, Julio Alberto (Sarabia), Senor, Victor, Carrasco, Santilana.

Munich, 25 June 1988 HOLLAND 2, USSR 0
Holland: Van Breukelen; Van Aerle, Van Tiggelen, Wouters, R. Koeman, Rijkaard, Vanenburg, Gullit, Van Basten, Muhren, E. Koeman. **Scorers: Gullit,** Van Basten.
USSR: Dassayev; Khidiatulin, Aleinikov, Mikhailichenko, Litovchenko, Demianenko, Belanov, Gotsmanov, (Blatcha), Protasov (Pasulko), Zavarov, Rats

*After extra time

SOUTH AMERICAN CHAMPIONSHIP WINNERS

(Copa America)

1916 Uruguay	1935 Uruguay	1957 Argentina
1917 Uruguay	1937 Argentina	1959 Argentina
1919 Brazil	1939 Peru	1959 Uruguay
1920 Uruguay	1941 Argentina	1963 Bolivia
1921 Argentina	1942 Uruguay	1967 Uruguay
1922 Brazil	1945 Argentina	1975 Peru
1923 Uruguay	1946 Argentina	1979 Paraguay
1924 Uruguay	1947 Argentina	1983 Uruguay
1925 Argentina	1949 Brazil	1987 Uruguay
1926 Uruguay	1953 Paraguay	1989 Independiente
1927 Argentina	1955 Argentina	
1929 Argentina	1956 Uruguay	

SOUTH AMERICAN CUP WINNERS

(Copa Libertadores)

1960 Penarol (Uruguay)	1975 Independiente
1961 Penarol	1976 Cruzeiro (Brazil)
1962 Santos (Brazil)	1977 Boca Juniors (Argentina)
1963 Santos	1978 Boca Juniors
1964 Independiente (Argentina)	1979 Olimpia (Paraguay)
1965 Independiente	1980 Nacional
1966 Penarol	1981 Flamengo (Brazil)
1967 Racing Club (Argentina)	1982 Penarol
1968 Estudiantes (Argentina)	1983 Gremio Porto Alegre (Brazil)
1969 Estudiantes	1984 Independiente
1970 Estudiantes	1985 Argentinos Juniors (Argentina)
1971 Nacional (Uruguay)	1986 River Plate (Argentina)
1972 Independiente	1987 Penarol
1973 Independiente	1988 Nacional (Uruguay)
1974 Independiente	1989 Nacional (Colombia)

OLYMPIC FOOTBALL TOURNAMENT, SEOUL 1988

Group A
China 0, West Germany, 3
Sweden 2, Tunisia 2
Tunisia 1, West Germany 4
Sweden 2, China 0
Tunisia 0, China 0
Sweden 2, West Germany 1

Group B
Zambia 2, Iraq 2
Italy 5, Guatemala 2
Iraq 3, Guatemala 0
Zambia 4, Italy 0
Zambia 4, Guatemala 0
Iraq 0, Italy 2

Group C
Korea Rep 0, USSR 0
USA 1, Argentina 1
Korea Rep 0, USA 0
USSR 2, Argentina 1
Korea Rep 1, Argentina 2
USSR 4, USA 2

Group D
Brazil 4, Nigeria 0
Australia 1, Yugoslavia 0
Yugoslavia 3, Nigeria 1
Australia 0, Brazil 3
Yugoslavia 1, Brazil 2
Australia 1, Nigeria 0

Quarter-finals
Sweden 1, Italy 2*
Zambia 0, West Germany 4
USSR 3, Argentina 0
Brazil 1, Argentina 0

Semi-finals
Italy 2, USSR 3*
West Germany 1, Brazil 1*
(*Brazil won 3–2 on penalties*)

Third place
West Germany 3, Italy 0

Final 1 October, att. 74,000
USSR (0)2 (*Dobrovolsky (pen), Savitchev*), Brazil (1)1 (*Romario*)*

After extra time

Football again attracted more spectators in Seoul than any other sport in the Olympic Games. The final attendance figure of 743,000 was below that of the previous two tournaments, partly because smaller capacity stadiums outside the capital were used. In 1984 in Los Angeles the total number of attendances was 1.4 million while in 1980 in Moscow it had reached a record 1.8 million.

The USSR won the gold again 32 years after their first in Melbourne, beating Brazil 2–1 after extra time. West Germany took the ronze with a 3–0 win over Italy in the match for third place.

Previous winners

1896	Athens*	1.	Denmark	1920	Antwerp	1.	Belgium
		2.	Greece			2.	Spain
1900	Paris*	1.	England			3.	Holland
		2.	France	1924	Paris	1.	Uruguay
1904	St Louis**	1.	Canada			2.	Switzerland
		2.	USA			3.	Sweden
1908	London	1.	England	1928	Amsterdam	1.	Uruguay
		2.	Denmark			2.	Argentina
		3.	Holland			3.	Italy
1912	Stockholm	1.	England	1932	Los Angeles		no competition
		2.	Denmark				
		3.	Holland				

1936	Berlin	1. Italy	1968	Mexico City	1. Hungary
		2. Austria			2. Bulgaria
		3. Norway			3. Japan
1948	London	1. Sweden	1972	Munich	1. Poland
		2. Yugoslavia			2. Hungary
		3. Denmark			3. East Germany/
1952	Helsinki	1. Hungary			USSR joint bronze
		2. Yugoslavia	1976	Montreal	1. East Germany
		3. Sweden			2. Poland
1956	Melbourne	1. USSR			3. USSR
		2. Yugoslavia	1980	Moscow	1. Czecholsovakia
		3. Bulgaria			2. East Germany
1960	Rome	1. Yugoslavia			3. USSR
		2. Denmark	1984	Los Angeles	1. France
		3. Hungary			2. Brazil
1964	Tokyo	1. Hungary			3. Yugoslavia
		2. Czechoslovakia			
		3. East Germany			

Official finishing positions 1988:

1. USSR
2. Brazil
3. West Germany
4. Italy
5. Zambia
6. Sweden
7. Australia
8. Argentina
9. Iraq
10. Yugoslavia
11. Korea Rep
12. USA
13. Tunisia
14. China
15. Nigeria
16. Guatemala

*No official tournament **No official tournament, gold medal awarded by IOC.*

OTHER BRITISH AND IRISH INTERNATIONAL MATCHES 1988–89

Wembley, 14 September 1988, att. 25,837
England (1) 1 (*Webb 28*)
Denmark (0) 0
England: Shilton (Woods 46); Stevens, Pearce, Rocastle, Adams (Walker 65), Butcher, Robson, Webb, Harford (Cottee 70), Beardsley (Gascoigne 85), Hodge
Denmark: Rasmussen; Jensen (Heintze 65), Nielsen K., Olsen L., Bartram (Jorgensen 85), Molby, Helt, Hansen, Vilfort (Kristensen 85), Elstrup, Laudrup

Dublin, 19 October, 1988, att. 13,000
Eire (3) 4 (*Cascarino 27, 43, Aldridge 44, Sheedy 87*)
Tunisia (0) 0
Eire: Peyton; Morris (Scully 46), McCarthy, Anderson, Staunton, Houghton (Kelly D.46), O'Brien, Sheedy, Kelly M. Cascarino (De Mange 76), Aldridge (Quinn 76)
Tunisia: Chouchane; Ouachi, Bousina, Ali Mahjoubi, Benyahia, Taoufik, Nabil, Baoueb, Mizouri, Rannane, Yahmadi

Riyadh, 16 November 1988, att. 18,000
Saudi Arabia (1) 1 (*Majid Abdullah 15*)
England (0) 1 (*Adams 54*)
Saudi Arabia: Al Diaye (Al Subiani 44); Saleh, Al Nuaimah, Jameel, Jawad, Al Mutlaq, Al Mussaibeeh, Al Suwayed (Al Thinnayan 75), Majid Abdullah, Mubarak, Al Jamaan (Masa'ad 79)
England: Seaman; Sterland, Pearce, Thomas (Marwood 80), Pallister, Adams, Robson, Rocastle, Beardsley (Smith 68), Lineker, Waddle (Gascoigne 80)

Perugia, 22 December 1988, att. 25,600
Italy (0) 2 (*Giannini 49 (pen), Berti 70*)
Scotland (0) 0
Italy: Zenga (Tacconi 50); Bergomi (Ferrara 50), Maldini, Baresi F., Ferri, Marocchi, Crippa, Berti, Vialli, Giannini, Serena
Scotland: Goram; Gough (Speedie 86), Malpas, Aitken, Narey, McLeish, Ferguson (Durie 75), McStay (McClair 56), MacLeod, Gallacher, Johnston

Dublin, 7 February 1989, att. 22,000
Eire (0) 0
France (0) 0
Eire: Bonner; Morris, Hughton, McCarthy, McGrath, Brady, Whelan, Houghton, Stapleton (Aldridge 76), Cascarino, Townsend
France: Bats; Amoros, Kastendeuch, Sonor, Battiston, Silvestre (Roche 74), Durand, Sauzee, Paille (Toure 46), Papin, Blanc (Vercruysse 68)

Athens, 8 February 1989, att. 6,000
Greece (1) 1 (*Saravakos 2 (pen)*)
England (1) 2 (*Barnes 9, Robson 79*)
Greece: Economopoulos; Hatzithanasiu (Manolas 72), Kutulas, Kalitzakis, Mavridis, Tsalouhides, Saravakos, Lagonidis (Borbokis 39), Samaras (Kalogeropoulos 46), Nioblias, Tsiantakis
England: Shilton; Stevens, Pearce, Webb, Walker, Butcher, Robson, Rocastle, Smith (Beardsley 78), Lineker, Barnes

Tel Aviv, 8 February 1989, att. 6,000
Israel (2) 3 (*Klinger 6, Alon 7, Drieks 73*)
Wales (1) 3 (*Horne 11, Aharoni 57 (og), Allen 87*)
Israel: Gilardi; Amar, Aharoni, Klinger, Davidi, Alon, Sinai, Pizanti, Levin (Atar 79), Rosenthal, Menahem (Drieks 46)
Wales: Dibble; Hall (Slatter 68), Bowen, Nicholas, Ratcliffe, Williams (Allen M.68) Horne, Blackmore, Hughes, Saunders, Pascoe

Wrexham, 26 April 1989, att. 8,000
Wales (0) 0
Sweden (1) 2 (*Schiller 30, Ratcliffe (og) 56*)
Wales: Southall; Phillips, Bowen, Ratcliffe, Van den Hauwe, Nicholas (Aizlewood 67), Saunders, Horne, Rush, Hughes, Williams
Sweden: Ravelli T.; Nilsson R., Lonn, Ljung, Schiller, Limpar, Prytz, Thern, Pettersson, Magnusson (Ekstrom 50), Nilsson B.

Wembley, 23 May 1989, att. 15,628 (Rous Cup)
England (0) 0
Chile (0) 0
England: Shilton; Parker, Pearce, Webb, Walker, Butcher, Robson, Gascoigne, Clough, Fashanu (Cottee 71), Waddle
Chile: Rojas; Reyes, Hurtado (Vera 60), Contreras, Gonzalez, Pizarro, Rubio, Ormeno, Espinoza, Covarrubias (Letelier 46), Astengo

Belfast, 26 May 1989, att. 2,500
Northern Ireland (0) 0
Chile (1) 1 (*Astengo 43*)
Northern Ireland: Wright; Fleming, Rogan, Donaghy, McDonald, McCreery, (O'Neill C.75) Wilson D. (Dennison 75), O'Neill, Clarke, Quinn (Black 64), Wilson K. (Coyle 64)
Chile: Rojas; Astengo (Olmos 46), Espinoza, Gonzalez, Contreras, Reyes, Vera, Pizarro, Hisis, Hurtado (Covarrubias 46), Letelier (Perez 85)

Hampden Park, 27 May 1989, att. 63,282 (Rous Cup)
Scotland (0) 0
England (1) 2 (*Waddle 20, Bull 80*)
Scotland: Leighton; McKimmie, McLeish, McPherson, Malpas, Nevin, Aitken, McStay, Connor (Grant 59), McCoist, Johnston
England: Shilton; Stevens, Pearce, Webb, Walker, Butcher, Robson, Steven, Fashanu (Bull 31), Cottee (Gascoigne 78), Waddle

Hampden Park, 30 May 1989, att. 9,006 (Rous Cup)
Scotland (1) 2 (*McInally 5, MacLeod 53*)
Chile (0) 0
Scotland: Leighton; McKimmie, Malpas, Aitken, McLeish, Gillespie (Whyte 70), Speedie (Johnston 46), Grant, MacLeod, McStay, McInally
Chile: Rojas; Reyes, Contreras, Gonzalez, Pizarro, Covarrubias (Letelier 46), Vera, Olmos, Hisis, Puebla

(*England won Rous Cup*)

POST-WAR INTERNATIONAL APPEARANCES
As at 30 June, 1989

ENGLAND

A'Court, A. (5) (Liverpool) 1957/8, 1958/9.
Adams, T.A. (17) (Arsenal) 1986/7, 1987/8, 1988/9.
Allen, C. (5) (QPR) 1983/4, 1986/7 (Tottenham Hotspur) 1987/8.
Allen, R. (5) (West Bromwich Albion) 1951/2, 1953/4, 1954/5.
Allen, T. (3) (Stoke City) 1959/60.
Anderson, S. (2) (Sunderland) 1961/2.
Anderson, V. (30) (Nottingham Forest) 1978/9, 1979/80, 1980/1, 1981/2, 1983/4, (Arsenal) 1984/5, 1985/6, 1986/7, (Manchester United).
Angus, J. (1) (Burnley) 1960/1.
Armfield, J. (43) (Blackpool) 1958/9, 1959/60, 1960/1, 1961/2, 1962/3, 1963/4, 1965/6.
Armstrong, D. (3) (Middlesbrough) 1979/80, (Southampton) 1982/3, 1983/4.
Armstrong, K. (1) (Chelsea) 1954/5.
Astall, G. (2) (Birmingham) 1955/6.
Astle, J. (5) (West Bromwich Albion) 1968/9, 1969/70.
Aston, J. (17) (Manchester United) 1948/9, 1949/50, 1950/1.
Atyeo, J. (6) (Bristol City) 1955/6, 1956/7.

Bailey, G.R. (2) (Manchester United) 1984/5.
Bailey, M. (2) (Charlton) 1963/4, 1964/5.
Baily, E. (9) (Tottenham Hotspur) 1949/50, 1950/1, 1951/2, 1952/3.
Baker, J. (8) (Hibernian) 1959/60, 1965/6, (Arsenal).
Ball, A. (72) (Blackpool) 1964/5, 1965/6, 1966/7, (Everton) 1967/8, 1968/9, 1969/70, 1970/1, 1971/2 (Arsenal) 1972/3, 1973/4, 1974/5.
Banks, G. (73) (Leicester) 1962/3, 1963/4, 1964/5, 1965/6, 1966/7, 1967/8, (Stoke) 1968/9, 1969/70, 1970/1, 1971/2.
Banks, T. (6) (Bolton Wanderers) 1957/8, 1958/9.
Barham, M. (2) (Norwich City) 1982/3.
Barlow, R. (1) (West Bromwich Albion) 1954/5.
Barnes, J. (47) (Watford) 1982/3, 1983/4, 1984/5, 1985/6, 1986/7, (Liverpool) 1987/8, 1988/9.
Barnes, P. (22) (Manchester City) 1977/8, 1978/9, 1979/80 (West Bromwich Albion) 1980/1, 1981/2 (Leeds United).
Barrass, M. (3) (Bolton Wanderers) 1951/2, 1952/3.
Baynham, R. (3) (Luton Town) 1955/6.
Beardsley P.A. (34) (Newcastle United) 1985/6, 1986/7 (Liverpool) 1987/8., 1988/9.
Beattie, T.K. (9) (Ipswich Town) 1974/5, 1975/6, 1976/7, 1977/8.
Bell, C. (48) (Manchester City) 1967/8, 1968/9, 1969/70, 1971/2, 1972/3, 1973/4, 1974/5, 1975/6.
Bentley, R. (12) (Chelsea) 1948/9, 1949/50, 1952/3, 1954/5.
Berry, J. (4) (Manchester United) 1952/3, 1955/6.
Birtles, G. (3) (Nottingham Forest) 1979/80, 1980/1 (Manchester United).
Blissett, L. (14) (Watford) 1982/3, 1983/4 (AC Milan).
Blockley, J. (1) (Arsenal) 1972/3.
Blunstone, F. (5) (Chelsea) 1954/5, 1956/7.
Bonetti, P. (7) (Chelsea) 1965/6, 1966/7, 1967/8, 1969/70.
Bowles, S. (5) (QPR) 1973/4, 1976/7.
Boyer, P. (1) (Norwich City) 1975/6.
Brabrook, P. (3) (Chelsea) 1957/8, 1959/60.

Bracewell, P.W. (3) (Everton) 1984/5, 1985/6.
Bradford, G. (1) (Bristol Rovers) 1955/6.
Bradley, W. (3) (Manchester United) 1958/9.
Bridges, B. (4) (Chelsea) 1964/5, 1965/6.
Broadbent, P. (7) (Wolverhampton Wanderers) 1957/8, 1958/9, 1959/60.
Broadis, I. (14) (Manchester City) 1951/2, 1952/3 (Newcastle United) 1953/4.
Brooking, T. (47) (West Ham United) 1973/4, 1974/5, 1975/6, 1976/7, 1977/8, 1978/9, 1979/80, 1980/1, 1981/2.
Brooks, J. (3) (Tottenham Hotspur) 1956/7.
Brown, A. (1) (West Bromwich Albion) 1970/1.
Brown, K. (1) (West Ham United) 1959/60.
Bull, S.G. (2) (Wolverhampton Wanderers) 1988/9.
Butcher, T. (63) (Ipswich Town) 1979/80, 1980/1, 1981/2, 1982/3, 1983/4, 1984/5, 1985/6, 1986/7 (Rangers) 1987/8, 1988/9.
Byrne, G. (2) (Liverpool) 1962/3, 1965/6.
Byrne, J. (11) (Crystal Palace) 1961/2, 1962/3, (West Ham United) 1963/4, 1964/5.
Byrne, R. (33) (Manchester United) 1953/4, 1954/5, 1955/6, 1956/7, 1957/8.

Callaghan, I. (4) (Liverpool) 1965/6, 1977/8.
Carter, H. (7) (Derby County) 1946/7.
Chamberlain, M. (8) (Stoke City) 1982/3, 1983/4, 1984/5.
Channon, M. (46) (Southampton) 1972/3, 1973/4, 1974/5, 1975/6, 1976/7, (Manchester City) 1977/8.
Charlton, J. (35) (Leeds United) 1964/5, 1965/6, 1966/7, 1967/8, 1968/9, 1969/70.
Charlton, R. (106) (Manchester United) 1957/8, 1958/9, 1959/60, 1960/1, 1961/2, 1962/3, 1963/4, 1964/5, 1965/6, 1966/7, 1967/8, 1968/9, 1969/70.
Charnley, R. (1) (Blackpool) 1961/2.
Cherry, T. (27) (Leeds United) 1975/6, 1976/7, 1977/8, 1978/9, 1979/80.
Chilton, A. (2) (Manchester United) 1950/1, 1951/2.
Chivers, M. (24) (Tottenham Hotspur) 1970/1, 1971/2, 1972/3, 1973/4.
Clamp, E. (4) (Wolverhampton Wanderers) 1957/8.
Clapton, D. (1) (Arsenal) 1958/9.
Clarke, A. (19) (Leeds United) 1969/70, 1970/1, 1972/3, 1973/4, 1974/5, 1975/6.
Clarke, H. (1) (Tottenham Hotspur) 1953/4.
Clayton, R. (35) (Blackburn Rovers) 1955/6, 1956/7, 1957/8, 1958/9, 1959/60.
Clemence, R. (61) (Liverpool) 1972/3, 1973/4, 1974/5, 1975/6, 1976/7, 1977/8, 1978/9, 1979/80, 1980/1, 1981/2, (Tottenham Hotspur) 1982/3, 1983/4.
Clement, D. (5) (QPR) 1975/6, 1976/7.
Clough, B. (2) (Middlesbrough) 1959/60.
Clough, N.H. (1) (Nottingham Forest) 1988/9.
Coates, R. (4) (Burnley) 1969/70, 1970/1, (Tottenham Hotspur)
Cockburn, H. (13) (Manchester United) 1946/7, 1947/8, 1948/9, 1950/1, 1951/2.
Cohen, G. (37) (Fulham) 1963/4, 1964/5, 1965/6, 1966/7, 1967/8.
Compton, L. (2) (Arsenal) 1950/1.
Connelly J. (20) (Burnley) 1959/60, 1961/2, 1962/3, 1964/5 (Manchester United) 1965/6.
Cooper, T. (20) (Leeds United) 1968/9, 1969/70, 1970/1, 1971/2, 1974/5.
Coppell, S. (42) (Manchester United) 1977/8, 1978/9, 1979/80, 1980/1, 1981/2, 1982/3.
Corrigan J. (9) (Manchester City) 1975/6, 1977/8, 1978/9, 1979/80, 1980/1, 1981/2.
Cottee A.R. (7) (West Ham United) 1986/7, 1987/8, (Everton) 1988/9.
Cowans, G. (9) (Aston Villa) 1982/3, 1985/6 (Bari).
Crawford, R. (2) (Ipswich Town) 1961/2.
Crowe, C. (1) (Wolverhampton Wanderers) 1962/3.

Cunningham, L. (6) (West Bromwich Albion) 1978/9 (Real Madrid) 1979/80, 1980/1.
Currie, A. (17) (Sheffield United) 1971/2, 1972/3, 1973/4, 1975/6 (Leeds United) 1977/8, 1978/9.

Davenport, P. (1) (Nottingham Forest) 1984/5.
Deeley, N. (2) (Wolverhampton Wanderers) 1958/9.
Devonshire, A. (8) (West Ham United) 1979/80, 1981/2, 1982/3, 1983/4.
Dickinson, J. (48) (Portsmouth) 1948/9, 1949/50, 1950/1, 1951/2, 1952/3, 1953/4, 1954/5, 1955/6, 1956/7.
Ditchburn, E. (6) (Tottenham Hotspur) 1948/9, 1952/3, 1956/7.
Dixon, K.M. (8) (Chelsea) 1984/5, 1985/6, 1986/7.
Dobson, M. (5) (Burnley) 1973/4, 1974/5 (Everton).
Douglas, B. (36) (Blackburn Rovers) 1957/8, 1958/9, 1959/60, 1960/1, 1961/2, 1962/3.
Doyle, M. (5) (Manchester City) 1975/6, 1976/7.
Duxbury, M. (10) (Manchester United) 1983/4, 1984/5.

Eastham, G. (19) (Arsenal) 1962/3, 1963/4, 1964/5, 1965/6.
Eckersley, W. (17) (Blackburn Rovers) 1949/50, 1950/1, 1951/2, 1952/3, 1953/4.
Edwards, D. (18) (Manchester United) 1954/5, 1955/6, 1956/7, 1957/8.
Ellerington, W. (2) (Southampton) 1948/9.
Elliott, W.H. (5) (Burnley) 1951/2, 1952/3.

Fantham, J. (1) (Sheffield Wednesday) 1961/2.
Fashanu, J. (2) (Wimbledon) 1988/9.
Fenwick, T. (20) (QPR) 1983/4, 1984/5, 1985/6 (Tottenham Hotspur) 1987/8.
Finney, T. (76) (Preston) 1946/7, 1947/8, 1948/9, 1949/50, 1950/1, 1951/2, 1952/3, 1953/4, 1954/5, 1955/6, 1956/7, 1957/8, 1958/9.
Flowers, R. (49) (Wolverhampton Wanderers) 1954/5, 1958/9, 1959/60, 1960/1, 1961/2, 1962/3, 1963/4, 1964/5, 1965/6.
Foster, S. (3) (Brighton) 1981/2.
Foulkes, W. (1) (Manchester United) 1954/5.
Francis, G. (12) (QPR) 1974/5, 1975/6.
Francis, T. (52) (Birmingham City) 1976/7, 1977/8 (Nottingham Forest) 1978/9, 1979/80, 1980/1, 1981/2 (Manchester City) 1982/3, (Sampdoria) 1983/4, 1984/5, 1985/6.
Franklin, N. (27) (Stoke City) 1946/7, 1947/8, 1948/9, 1949/50.
Froggatt, J. (13) (Portsmouth) 1949/50, 1950/1, 1951/2, 1952/3.
Froggatt, R. (4) (Sheffield Wednesday) 1952/3.

Garrett, T. (3) (Blackpool) 1951/2, 1953/4.
Gascoigne, P.J. (5) (Tottenham Hotspur) 1988/9.
Gates, E. (2) (Ipswich Town) 1980/1.
George, F.C. (1) (Derby County) 1976/7.
Gidman, J. (1) (Aston Villa) 1976/7.
Gillard, I. (3) (QPR) 1974/5, 1975/6.
Goddard, P. (1) (West Ham United) 1981/2.
Grainger, C. (7) (Sheffield United) 1955/6, 1956/7 (Sunderland).
Greaves, J. (57) (Chelsea) 1958/9, 1959/60, 1960/1, 1961/2 (Tottenham Hotspur) 1962/3, 1963/4, 1964/5, 1965/6, 1966/7.
Greenhoff, B. (18) (Manchester United) 1975/6, 1976/7, 1977/8, 1979/80.
Gregory, J. (6) (QPR) 1982/3, 1983/4.

Hagan, J. (1) (Sheffield United) 1948/9.
Haines, J. (1) (West Bromwich Albion) 1948/9.
Hall, J. (17) (Birmingham City) 1955/6, 1956/7.
Hancocks, J. (3) (Wolverhampton Wanderers) 1948/9, 1949/50, 1950/1.
Hardwick, G. (13) (Middlesbrough) 1946/7, 1947/8.
Harford, M.G. (2) (Luton Town) 1987/8, 1988/9.

Harris, G. (1) (Burnley) 1965/6.
Harris, P. (2) (Portsmouth) 1949/50, 1953/4.
Harvey, C. (1) (Everton) 1970/1.
Hassall, H. (5) (Huddersfield Town) 1950/1, 1951/2 (Bolton Wanderers) 1953/4.
Hateley, M. (31) (Portsmouth) 1983/4, 1984/5, (AC Milan) 1985/6, 1986/7, (Monaco) 1987/8.
Haynes, J. (56) (Fulham) 1954/5, 1955/6, 1956/7, 1957/8, 1958/9, 1959/60, 1960/1, 1961/2.
Hector, K. (2) (Derby County) 1973/4.
Hellawell, M. (2) (Birmingham City) 1962/3.
Henry, R. (1) (Tottenham Hotspur) 1962/3.
Hill, F. (2) (Bolton Wanderers) 1962/3.
Hill, G. (6) (Manchester United) 1975/6, 1976/7, 1977/8.
Hill, R. (3) (Luton Town) 1982/3, 1985/6.
Hinton, A. (3) (Wolverhampton W.) 1962/3, 1964/5 (Nottingham Forest).
Hitchens, G. (7) (Aston Villa) 1960/1 (Inter Milan) 1961/2.
Hoddle, G. (53) (Tottenham Hotspur) 1979/80, 1980/1, 1981/2, 1982/3, 1983/4, 1984/5, 1985/6, 1986/7 (Monaco) 1987/8.
Hodge, S.B. (16) (Aston Villa) 1985/6, 1986/7, (Tottenham Hotspur), (Nottingham Forest) 1988/9.
Hodgkinson, A. (5) (Sheffield United) 1956/7, 1960/1.
Holden, D. (5) (Bolton Wanderers) 1958/9.
Holliday, E. (3) (Middlesbrough) 1959/60.
Hollins, J. (1) (Chelsea) 1966/7.
Hopkinson, E. (14) (Bolton Wanderers) 1957/8, 1958/9, 1959/60.
Howe, D. (23) (West Bromwich Albion) 1957/8, 1958/9, 1959/60.
Howe, J. (3) (Derby County) 1947/8, 1948/9.
Hudson, A. (2) (Stoke City) 1974/5.
Hughes, E. (62) (Liverpool) 1969/70, 1970/1, 1971/2, 1972/3, 1973/4, 1974/5, 1976/7, 1977/8, 1978/9 (Wolverhampton Wanderers) 1979/80.
Hughes, L. (3) (Liverpool) 1949/50.
Hunt, R. (34) (Liverpool) 1961/2, 1962/3, 1963/4, 1964/5, 1965/6, 1966/7, 1967/8, 1968/9.
Hunt, S. (2) (West Bromwich Albion) 1983/4.
Hunter, N. (28) (Leeds United) 1965/6, 1966/7, 1967/8, 1968/9, 1969/70, 1970/1, 1971/2, 1972/3, 1973/4, 1974/5.
Hurst, G. (49) (West Ham United) 1965/6, 1966/7, 1967/8, 1968/9, 1969/70, 1970/1, 1971/2.

Jezzard, B. (2) (Fulham) 1953/4, 1955/6.
Johnson, D. (8) (Ipswich Town) 1974/5, 1975/6 (Liverpool) 1979/80.
Johnston, H. (10) (Blackpool) 1946/7, 1950/1, 1952/3, 1953/4.
Jones, M. (3) (Sheffield United) 1964/5 (Leeds United) 1969/70.
Jones, W.H. (2) (Liverpool) 1949/50.

Kay, A. (1) (Everton) 1962/3.
Keegan, K. (63) (Liverpool) 1972/3, 1973/4, 1974/5, 1975/6 1976/7 (SV Hamburg) 1977/8, 1978/9, 1979/80 (Southampton) 1980/1, 1981/2.
Kennedy, A. (2) (Liverpool) 1983/4.
Kennedy, R. (17) (Liverpool) 1975/6, 1977/8, 1979/80.
Kevan, D. (14) (West Bromwich Albion) 1956/7, 1957/8, 1958/9, 1960/1.
Kidd, B. (2) (Manchester United) 1969/70.
Knowles, C. (4) (Tottenham Hotspur) 1967/8.

Labone, B. (26) (Everton) 1962/3, 1966/7, 1967/8, 1968/9, 1969/70.
Lampard, F. (2) (West Ham United) 1972/3, 1979/80.
Langley, J. (3) (Fulham) 1957/8.
Langton, R. (11) (Blackburn Rovers) 1946/7, 1947/8, 1948/9 (Preston North End) 1949/50 (Bolton Wanderers) 1950/1.
Latchford, R. (12) (Everton) 1977/8, 1978/9.
Lawler, C. (4) (Liverpool) 1970/1, 1971/2.

Lawton, T. (15) (Chelsea) 1946/7, 1947/8 (Notts County) 1948/9.
Lee, F. (27) (Manchester City) 1968/9, 1969/70, 1970/1, 1971/2.
Lee, J. (1) (Derby County) 1950/1.
Lee, S. (14) (Liverpool) 1982/3, 1983/4.
Lindsay, A. (4) (Liverpool) 1973/4.
Lineker, G. (42) (Leicester City) 1983/4, 1984/5 (Everton) 1985/6, 1986/7, (Barcelona) 1987/8, 1988/9.
Little, B. (1) (Aston Villa) 1974/5.
Lloyd, L. (4) (Liverpool) 1970/1, 1971/2 (Nottingham Forest) 1979/80.
Lofthouse, N. (33) (Bolton Wanderers) 1950/1, 1951/2, 1952/3, 1953/4, 1954/5, 1955/6, 1958/9.
Lowe, E. (3) (Aston Villa) 1946/7.

Mabbutt, G. (13) (Tottenham Hotspur) 1982/3, 1983/4, 1986/7, 1987/8.
Macdonald, M. (14) (Newcastle United) 1971/2, 1972/3, 1973/4, 1974/5; (Arsenal) 1975/6.
Madeley, P. (24) (Leeds United) 1970/1, 1971/2, 1972/3, 1973/4, 1974/5, 1975/6, 1976/7.
Mannion, W. (26) (Middlesbrough) 1946/7, 1947/8, 1948/9, 1949/50, 1950/1, 1951/2.
Mariner, P. (35) (Ipswich Town) 1976/7, 1977/8, 1979/80, 1980/1, 1981/2, 1982/3, 1983/4, 1984/5 (Arsenal).
Marsh, R. (9) (QPR) 1971/2 (Manchester City) 1972/3.
Martin, A. (17) (West Ham United) 1980/1, 1981/2, 1982/3, 1983/4, 1984/5, 1985/6, 1986/7.
Marwood, B. (1) (Arsenal) 1988/9.
Matthews, R. (5) (Coventry City) 1955/6, 1956/7.
Matthews, S. (37) (Stoke City) 1946/7 (Blackpool) 1947/8, 1948/9, 1949/50, 1950/1, 1953/4, 1954/5, 1955/6, 1956/7.
McDermott, T. (25) (Liverpool) 1977/8, 1978/9, 1979/80, 1980/1, 1981/2.
McDonald, C. (8) (Burnley) 1957/8, 1958/9.
McFarland, R. (28) (Derby County) 1970/1, 1971/2, 1972/3, 1973/4, 1975/6, 1976/7.
McGarry, W. (4) (Huddersfield Town) 1953/4, 1955/6.
McGuinness, W. (2) (Manchester United) 1958/9.
McMahon, S. (5) (Liverpool) 1987/8, 1988/9.
McNab, R. (4) (Arsenal) 1968/9.
McNeil, M. (9) (Middlesbrough) 1960/1, 1961/2.
Meadows, J. (1) (Manchester City) 1954/5.
Medley, L. (Tottenham Hotspur) 1950/1, 1951/2.
Melia, J. (2) (Liverpool) 1962/3.
Merrick, G. (23) (Birmingham City) 1951/2, 1952/3, 1953/4.
Metcalfe, V. (2) (Huddersfield Town) 1950/1.
Milburn, J. (13) (Newcastle United) 1948/9, 1949/50, 1950/1, 1951/2, 1955/6.
Miller, B. (1) (Burnley) 1960/1.
Mills, M. (42) (Ipswich Town) 1972/3, 1975/6, 1976/7, 1977/8, 1978/9, 1979/80, 1980/1, 1981/2.
Milne, G. (14) (Liverpool) 1962/3, 1963/4, 1964/5.
Milton, C.A. (1) (Arsenal) 1951/2.
Moore, R. (108) (West Ham United) 1961/2, 1962/3, 1963/4, 1964/5, 1965/6, 1966/7, 1967/8, 1968/9, 1969/70, 1970/1, 1971/2, 1972/3, 1973/4.
Morley, A. (6) (Aston Villa) 1981/2, 1982/3.
Morris, J. (3) (Derby County) 1948/9, 1949/50.
Mortensen, S. (25) (Blackpool) 1946/7, 1947/8, 1948/9, 1949/50, 1950/1, 1953/4.
Mozley, B. (3) (Derby County) 1949/50.
Mullen, J. (12) (Wolverhampton Wanderers) 1946/7, 1948/9, 1949/50, 1953/4.
Mullery, A. (35) (Tottenham Hotspur) 1964/5, 1966/7, 1967/8, 1968/9, 1969/70, 1970/1, 1971/2.

Neal, P. (50) (Liverpool) 1975/6, 1976/7, 1977/8, 1978/9, 1979/80, 1980/1, 1981/2, 1982/3, 1983/4.
Newton, K. (27) (Blackburn Rovers) 1965/6, 1966/7, 1967/8, 1968/9, 1969/70, (Everton).
Nicholls, J. (2) (West Bromwich Albion) 1953/4.
Nicholson, W. (1) (Tottenham Hotspur) 1950/1.
Nish, D. (5) (Derby County) 1972/3, 1973/4.
Norman, M. (23) (Tottenham Hotspur) 1961/2, 1962/3, 1963/4, 1964/5.

O'Grady, M. (2) (Huddersfield Town) 1962/3, 1968/9 (Leeds United).
Osgood, P. (4) (Chelsea) 1969/70, 1973/4.
Osman, R. (11) (Ipswich Town) 1979/80, 1980/1, 1981/2, 1982/3, 1983/4.
Owen, S. (3) (Luton Town) 1953/4.

Paine, T. (19) (Southampton) 1962/3, 1963/4, 1964/5, 1965/6.
Pallister, G. (2) (Middlesbrough) 1987/8.
Parker, P.A. (3) (QPR) 1988/9.
Parkes, P. (1) (QPR) 1973/4.
Parry, R. (2) (Bolton Wanderers) 1959/60.
Peacock, A. (6) (Middlesbrough) 1961/2, 1962/3, 1965/6 (Leeds United).
Pearce, S. (15) (Nottingham Forest) 1986/7, 1987/8, 1988/9.
Pearson, Stan (8) (Manchester United) 1947/8, 1948/9, 1949/50, 1950/1, 1951/2.
Pearson, Stuart (15) (Manchester United) 1975/6, 1976/7, 1977/8.
Pegg, D. (1) (Manchester United) 1956/7.
Pejic, M. (4) (Stoke City) 1973/4.
Perry, W. (3) (Blackpool) 1955/6.
Perryman, S. (1) (Tottenham Hotspur) 1981/2.
Peters, M. (67) (West Ham United) 1965/6, 1966/7, 1967/8, 1968/9, 1969/70, (Tottenham Hotspur) 1970/1, 1971/2, 1972/3, 1973/4.
Phillips, L. (3) (Portsmouth) 1951/2, 1954/5.
Pickering, F. (3) (Everton) 1963/4, 1964/5.
Pickering, N. (1) (Sunderland) 1982/3.
Pilkington, B. (1) (Burnley) 1954/5.
Pointer, R. (3) (Burnley) 1961/2.
Pye, J. (1) (Wolverhampton Wanderers) 1949/50.

Quixall, A. (5) (Sheffield Wednesday) 1953/4, 1954/5.

Radford, J. (2) (Arsenal) 1968/9, 1971/2.
Ramsey, A. (32) (Southampton) 1948/9, 1949/50, (Tottenham Hotspur) 1950/1, 1951/2, 1952/3, 1953/4.
Reaney, P. (3) (Leeds United) 1968/9, 1969/70, 1970/1.
Reeves, K. (2) (Norwich City) 1979/80.
Regis, C. (5) (West Bromwich Albion) 1981/2, 1982/3, (Coventry).
Reid, P. (13) (Everton) 1984/5, 1985/6, 1986/7.
Revie, D. (6) (Manchester City) 1954/5, 1955/6, 1956/7.
Richards, J. (1) (Wolverhampton Wanderers) 1972/3.
Rickaby, S. (1) (West Bromwich Albion) 1953/4.
Rimmer, J. (1) (Arsenal) 1975/6.
Rix, G. (17) (Arsenal) 1980/1, 1981/2, 1982/3, 1983/4.
Robb, G. (1) (Tottenham Hotspur) 1953/4.
Roberts, G. (6) (Tottenham Hotspur) 1982/3, 1983/4.
Robson, B. (79) (West Bromwich Albion) 1979/80, 1980/1, 1981/2, (Manchester United) 1982/3, 1983/4, 1984/5, 1985/6, 1986/7, 1987/8, 1988/9.
Robson, R. (20) (West Bromwich Albion) 1957/8, 1959/60, 1960/1, 1961/2.
Rocastle, D (7) (Arsenal) 1988/9.
Rowley, J. (6) (Manchester United) 1948/9, 1949/50, 1951/2.
Royle, J. (6) (Everton) 1970/1, 1972/3, (Manchester City) 1975/6, 1976/7.

Sadler, D. (4) (Manchester United) 1967/8, 1969/70, 1970/1.
Sansom, K. (86) (Crystal Palace) 1978/9, 1979/80, 1980/1, (Arsenal) 1981/2, 1982/3, 1983/4, 1984/5, 1985/6, 1986/7, 1987/8.
Scott, L. (17) (Arsenal) 1946/7, 1947/8, 1948/9.
Seaman, D.A. (2) (QPR) 1988/9.
Sewell, J. (6) (Sheffield Wednesday) 1951/2, 1952/3, 1953/4.
Shackleton, L. (5) (Sunderland) 1948/9, 1949/50, 1954/5.
Shaw, G. (5) (Sheffield United) 1958/9, 1962/3.
Shellito, K. (1) (Chelsea) 1962/3.
Shilton, P. (109) (Leicester City) 1970/1, 1971/2, 1972/3, 1973/4, 1974/5, (Stoke City) 1976/7, (Nottingham Forest) 1977/8, 1978/9, 1979/80, 1980/1, 1981/2, (Southampton) 1982/3, 1983/4, 1984/5, 1985/6, 1986/7, (Derby County) 1987/8, 1988/9.
Shimwell, E. (1) (Blackpool) 1948/9.
Sillett, P. (3) (Chelsea) 1954/5.
Slater, W. (12) (Wolverhampton Wanderers) 1954/5, 1957/8, 1958/9, 1959/60.
Smith, A.M. (4) (Arsenal) 1988/9.
Smith, L. (6) (Arsenal) 1950/1, 1951/2, 1952/3.
Smith, R. (15) (Tottenham Hotspur) 1960/1, 1961/2, 1962/3, 1963/4.
Smith, Tom (1) (Liverpool) 1970/1.
Smith, Trevor (2) (Birmingham City) 1959/60.
Spink, N. (1) (Aston Villa) 1982/3.
Springett, R. (33) (Sheffield Wednesday) 1959/60, 1960/1, 1961/2, 1962/3, 1965/6.
Staniforth, R. (8) (Huddersfield Town) 1953/4, 1954/5.
Statham, D. (3) (West Bromwich Albion) 1982/3.
Stein, B. (1) (Luton Town) 1983/4.
Stepney, A. (1) (Manchester United) 1967/8.
Sterland, M. (1) (Sheffield Wednesday) 1988/9.
Steven, T.M. (25) (Everton) 1984/5, 1985/6, 1986/7, 1987/8, 1988/9.
Stevens, G.A. (7) (Tottenham Hotspur) 1984/5, 1985/6.
Stevens, M.G. (33) (Everton) 1984/5, 1985/6, 1986/7, 1987/8, (Rangers) 1988/9.
Stiles, N. (28) (Manchester United) 1964/5, 1965/6, 1966/7, 1967/8, 1968/9, 1969/70.
Storey-Moore, I. (1) (Nottingham Forest) 1969/70.
Storey, P. (19) (Arsenal) 1970/1, 1971/2, 1972/3.
Streten B. (1) (Luton Town) 1949/50.
Summerbee, M. (8) (Manchester City) 1967/8, 1971/2, 1972/3.
Sunderland, A. (1) (Arsenal) 1979/80.
Swan, P. (19) (Sheffield Wednesday) 1959/60, 1960/1, 1961/2.
Swift, F. (19) (Manchester City) 1946/7, 1947/8, 1948/9.

Talbot, B. (6) (Ipswich Town) 1976/7, 1979/80.
Tambling, R. (3) (Chelsea) 1962/3, 1965/6.
Taylor, E. (1) (Blackpool) 1953/4.
Taylor, J. (2) (Fulham) 1950/51.
Taylor, P.H. (3) (Liverpool) 1947/8:.
Taylor, P.J. (4) (Crystal Palace) 1975/6.
Taylor, T. (19) (Manchester United) 1952/3, 1953/4, 1955/6, 1956/7, 1958/9.
Temple, D. (1) (Everton) 1964/5.
Thomas, Danny (2) (Coventry City) 1982/3.
Thomas, Dave. (8) (QPR) 1974/5, 1975/6.
Thomas, M.L. (1) (Arsenal) 1988/9.
Thompson, P.B. (42) (Liverpool) 1975/6, 1976/7, 1978/9, 1979/80, 1980/1, 1981/2, 1982/3.
Thompson, T. (2) (Aston Villa) 1951/2, (Preston) 1956/7.
Thomson, P. (16) (Liverpool) 1963/4, 1964/5 1965/6, 1967/8, 1969/70.
Thomson, R. (8) (Wolverhampton Wanderers) 1963/4, 1964/5.
Todd, C. (27) (Derby County) 1971/2, 1973/4, 1974/5, 1975/6, 1976/7.
Towers, T. (3) (Sunderland) 1975/6.

Tueart, D. (6) (Manchester City) 1974/5, 1976/7.

Ufton, D. (1) (Charlton Athletic) 1953/4.

Venables, T. (2) (Chelsea) 1964/5.
Viljoen, C. (2) (Ipswich Town) 1974/5.
Viollet, D. (2) (Manchester United) 1959/60, 1961/2.

Waddle, C.R. (44) (Newcastle United) 1984/5, (Tottenham Hotspur) 1985/6, 1986/7, 1987/8, 1988/9.
Waiters, A. (5) (Blackpool) 1963/4, 1964/5.
Walker, D.S. (9) (Nottingham Forest) 1988/9.
Wallace, D.L. (1) (Southampton) 1985/6.
Walsh, P. (5) (Luton Town) 1982/3, 1983/4.
Ward, P. (1) (Brighton) 1979/80.
Ward, T. (2) (Derby County) 1947/8, 1948/9.
Watson, D. (12) (Norwich City) 1983/4, 1984/5, 1985/6, 1986/7 (Everton) 1987/8.
Watson, D.V. (65) (Sunderland) 1973/4, 1974/5, 1975/6 (Manchester City) 1976/7, 1977/8 (Southampton) 1978/9 (Werder Bremen) 1979/80, (Southampton) 1980/1, 1981/2 (Stoke City).
Watson, W. (4) (Sunderland) 1949/50, 1950/1.
Webb, N. (18) (Nottingham Forest) 1987/8, 1988/9.
Weller, K. (4) (Leicester City) 1973/4.

West, G. (3) (Everton) 1968/9.
Wheeler, J. (1) (Bolton Wanderers) 1954/5.
Whitworth, S. (7) (Leicester City) 1974/5, 1975/6.
Whymark, T. (1) (Ipswich Town) 1977/8.
Wignall, F. (2) (Nottingham Forest) 1964/5.
Wilkins, R. (84) (Chelsea) 1975/6, 1976/7, 1977/8, 1978/9, (Manchester United) 1979/80, 1980/1, 1981/2, 1982/3, 1983/4, 1984/5, (AC Milan) 1985/6, 1986/7.
Williams, B. (24) (Wolverhampton Wanderers) 1948/9, 1949/50, 1950/1, 1951/2, 1954/5, 1955/6.
Williams, S. (6) (Southampton) 1982/3, 1983/4, 1984/5.
Willis, A. (1) (Tottenham Hotspur) 1951/2.
Wilshaw, D. (12) (Wolverhampton Wanderers) 1953/4, 1954/5, 1955/6, 1956/7.
Wilson, R. (63) (Huddersfield Town) 1959/60, 1961/2, 1962/3, 1963/4, 1964/5, (Everton) 1965/6, 1966/7, 1967/8.
Withe, P. (11) (Aston Villa) 1980/1, 1981/2, 1982/3, 1983/4, 1984/5.
Wood, R. (3) (Manchester United) 1954/5, 1955/6.
Woodcock, A. (42) (Nottingham Forest) 1977/8, 1978/9, 1979/80 (FC Cologne) 1980/1, 1981/2 (Arsenal) 1982/3, 1983/4, 1984/5, 1985/6.
Woods, C.C.E. (14) (Norwich City) 1984/5, 1985/6, 1986/7, (Rangers) 1987/8, 1988/9.
Worthington, F. (8) (Leicester City) 1973/4, 1974/5.
Wright M. (22) (Southampton) 1983/4, 1984/5, 1985/6, 1986/7, (Derby County) 1987/8.
Wright, T. (11) (Everton) 1967/8, 1968/9, 1969/70.
Wright, W. (105) (Wolverhampton Wanderers) 1946/7, 1947/8, 1948/9, 1949/50, 1950/1, 1951/2, 1952/3, 1953/4, 1954/5, 1955/6, 1956/7, 1957/8, 1958/9.

Young, G. (1) (Sheffield Wednesday) 1964/5.

NORTHERN IRELAND

Aherne, T. (4) (Belfast Celtic) 1946/7, 1947/8, 1948/9, 1949/50 (Luton Town).
Anderson, T. (22) (Manchester United) 1972/3, 1973/4, 1974/5, (Swindon Town) 1975/6, 1976/7, 1977/8 (Peterborough United) 1978/9.

Armstrong, G. (63) (Tottenham Hotspur) 1976/7, 1977/8, 1978/9, 1979/80, 1980/1, (Watford) 1981/2, 1982/3, (Real Mallorca) 1983/4, 1984/5, (West Bromwich Albion) 1985/6 (Chesterfield).

Barr, H. (3) (Linfield) 1961/2, 1962/3 (Coventry City).
Best, G. (37) (Manchester United) 1963/4, 1964/5, 1965/6, 1966/7, 1967/8, 1968/9, 1969/70, 1970/1, 1971/2, 1972/3, 1973/4 (Fulham) 1976/7, 1977/8.
Bingham, W. (56) (Sunderland) 1950/1, 1951/2, 1952/3, 1953/4, 1954/5, 1955/6, 1956/7, 1957/8, 1958/9 (Luton Town) 1959/60, 1960/1 (Everton) 1961/2, 1962/3, 1963/4 (Port Vale).
Black, K. (7) (Luton Town) 1987/8, 1988/9.
Blair, R. (5) (Oldham Athletic) 1974/5, 1975/6.
Blanchflower, D. (54) (Barnsley) 1949/50, 1950/1 (Aston Villa) 1951/2, 1952/3, 1953/4, 1954/5 (Tottenham Hotspur) 1955/6, 1956/7, 1957/8, 1958/9, 1959/60, 1960/1, 1961/2, 1962/3.
Blanchflower, J. (12) (Manchester United) 1953/4, 1954/5, 1955/6, 1956/7, 1957/8.
Bowler, G. (3) (Hull City) 1949/50.
Braithwaite, R. (10) (Linfield) 1961/2, 1962/3 (Middlesbrough) 1963/4, 1964/5.
Brennan, R. (5) (Luton Town) 1948/9, 1949/50 (Birmingham City) (Fulham), 1950/1.
Briggs, R. (2) (Manchester United) 1961/2, 1964/5 (Swansea).
Brotherston, N. (27) (Blackburn Rovers) 1979/80, 1980/1, 1981/2, 1982/3, 1983/4, 1984/5.
Bruce, W. (2) (Glentoran) 1960/1, 1966/7.

Campbell, A. (2) (Crusaders) 1962/3, 1964/5.
Campbell, D.A. (10) (Nottingham Forest) 1985/6, 1986/7, 1987/8 (Charlton Athletic).
Campbell, J. (2) (Fulham) 1950/1.
Campbell, R. M. (2) (Bradford City) 1981/2.
Campbell, W. (6) (Dundee) 1967/8, 1968/9, 1969/70.
Carey, J. (7) (Manchester United) 1946/7, 1947/8, 1948/9.
Casey, T. (12) (Newcastle United) 1954/5, 1955/6, 1956/7, 1957/8, 1958/9 (Portsmouth).
Caskey, A. (7) (Derby County) 1978/9, 1979/80, 1981/2 (Tulsa Roughnecks).
Cassidy, T. (24) (Newcastle United) 1970/1, 1971/2, 1973/4, 1974/5, 1975/6, 1976/7, 1979/80 (Burnley) 1980/1, 1981/2.
Caughey, M. (2) (Linfield) 1985/6.
Clarke, C.J. (21) (Bournemouth) 1985/6, 1986/7 (Southampton) 1987/8, 1988/9.
Cleary, J. (5) (Glentoran) 1981/2, 1982/3, 1983/4, 1984/5.
Clements, D. (48) (Coventry City) 1964/5, 1965/6, 1966/7, 1967/8, 1968/9, 1969/70, 1970/1, 1971/2 (Sheffield Wednesday) 1972/3 (Everton) 1973/4, 1974/5, 1975/6 (New York Cosmos).
Cochrane, D. (10) (Leeds United) 1946/7, 1947/8, 1948/9, 1949/50.
Cochrane, T. (26) (Coleraine) 1976, (Burnley) 1977/8, 1978/9, (Middlesbrough) 1979/80, 1980/1, 1981/2, (Gillingham) 1983/4.
Cowan, J. (1) (Newcastle United) 1969/70.
Coyle, F. (4) (Coleraine) 1955/6, 1956/7, 1957/8 (Nottingham Forest).
Coyle, L. (1) (Derry C) 1988/9.
Coyle, R. (5) (Sheffield Wednesday) 1972/3, 1973/4.
Craig, D. (25) (Newcastle United) 1966/7, 1967/8, 1968/9, 1969/70, 1970/1, 1971/2, 1972/3, 1973/4, 1974/5.
Crossan, E. (3) (Blackburn Rovers) 1949/50, 1950/1, 1954/5.
Crossan, J. (23) (Rotterdam Sparta) 1959/60, 1962/3 (Sunderland) 1963/4, 1964/5 (Manchester City) 1965/6, 1966/7, 1967/8 (Middlesbrough).
Cunningham, W. (30) (St Mirren) 1950/1, 1952/3, 1953/4, 1954/5, 1955/6, 1956/7 (Leicester City) 1957/8, 1958/9, 1959/60, 1960/1 (Dunfermline Athletic) 1961/2.
Cush, W. (26) (Glentoran) 1950/1, 1953/4, 1956/7, 1957/8 (Leeds United) 1958/9, 1959/60, 1960/1 (Portadown) 1961/2.

D'Arcy, S. (5) (Chelsea) 1951/2, 1952/3 (Brentford).
Dennison, R. (4) (Wolverhampton Wanderers) 1987/8.
Dickson, D. (4) (Coleraine) 1969/70, 1972/3.
Dickson, T. (1) (Linfield) 1956/7.
Dickson, W. (12) (Chelsea) 1950/1, 1951/2, 1952/3 (Arsenal) 1953/4, 1954/5.
Doherty, L. (2) (Linfield) 1984/5, 1987/8.
Doherty, P. (6) (Derby County) 1946/7 (Huddersfield Town) 1947/8, 1948/9,
(Doncaster Rovers) 1950/1.
Donaghy, M. (62) (Luton Town) 1979/80, 1980/1, 1981/2, 1982/3, 1983/4,
1984/5, 1985/6, 1986/7, 1987/8, (Manchester United) 1988/9.
Dougan, D. (43) (Portsmouth) 1957/8, 1959/60 (Blackburn Rovers) 1960/1,
1962/3 (Aston Villa); 1965/6 (Leicester City); 1966/7 (Wolverhampton
Wanderers) 1967/8, 1968/9, 1969/70, 1970/1, 1971/2, 1972/3.
Douglas, J.P. (1) (Belfast Celtic) 1946/7.
Dowd, H. (3) (Glentoran) 1972/3, 1974/5 (Sheffield Wednesday).
Dunlop, G. (3) (Linfield) 1984/5, 1986/7.

Eglington, T. (6) (Everton) 1946/7, 1947/8, 1948/9.
Elder, A. (40) (Burnley) 1959/60, 1960/1, 1961/2, 1962/3, 1963/4, 1964/5,
1965/6, 1966/7, (Stoke City) 1967/8, 1968/9, 1969/70.

Farrell, P. (7) (Everton) 1946/7, 1947/8, 1948/9.
Feeney, J. (2) (Linfield) 1946/7 (Swansea City) 1949/50.
Feeney, W. (1) (Glentoran) 1975/6.
Ferguson, W. (2) (Linfield) 1965/6, 1966/7.
Ferris, R. (3) (Birmingham City) 1949/50, 1950/1, 1951/2.
Finney, T. (14) (Sunderland) 1974/5, 1975/6 (Cambridge United) 1979/80.
Fleming, J.G. (9) (Nottingham Forest) 1986/7, 1987/8, 1988/9.
Forde, T. (4) (Ards) 1958/9, 1960/1.

Gallogly, C. (2) (Huddersfield Town) 1950/1.
Gaston, R. (1) (Oxford United) 1968/9.
Gorman, W. (4) (Brentford) 1946/7, 1947/8.
Graham, W. (14) (Doncaster Rovers) 1950/1, 1951/2, 1952/3, 1953/4, 1954/5,
1955/6, 1958/9.
Gregg, H. (25) (Doncaster Rovers) 1953/4, 1956/7, 1957/8, (Manchester United)
1958/9, 1959/60, 1960/1, 1961/2, 1963/4.

Hamilton, B. (50) (Linfield) 1968/9, 1970/1, 1971/2 (Ipswich Town) 1972/3,
1973/4, 1974/5, 1975/6 (Everton) 1976/7, 1977/8 (Millwall) 1978/9 (Swindon
Town).
Hamilton, W. (41) (QPR) 1977/8, 1979/80 (Burnley) 1980/1, 1981/2, 1982/3,
1983/4, 1984/5 (Oxford United) 1985/6.
Harkin, T. (5) (Southport) 1967/8, 1968/9 (Shrewsbury Town) 1969/70,
1970/1.
Harvey, M. (34) (Sunderland) 1960/1, 1961/2, 1962/3, 1963/4, 1964/5,
1965/6, 1966/7, 1967/8, 1968/9, 1969/70, 1970/1.
Hatton, S. (2) (Linfield) 1962/3.
Healy, F. (4) (Coleraine) 1981/2 (Glentoran) 1982/3.
Hegan, D. (7) (West Bromwich Albion) 1969/70, 1971/2 (Wolverhampton
Wanderers) 1972/3.
Hill, J. (7) (Norwich City) 1958/9, 1959/60, 1960/1, (Everton) 1961/2, 1963/4.
Hinton, E. (7) (Fulham) 1946/7, 1947/8 (Millwall) 1950/1.
Hughes, P. (3) (Bury) 1986/7.
Hughes, W. (1) (Bolton Wanderers) 1950/1.
Humphries, W. (14) (Ards) 1961/2 (Coventry City) 1962/3, 1963/4, 1964/5
(Swansea Town).
Hunter, A. (53) (Blackburn Rovers) 1969/70, 1970/1, 1971/2 (Ipswich Town)
1972/3, 1973/4, 1974/5, 1975/6, 1976/7, 1977/8, 1978/9, 1979/80.

Irvine, R. (8) (Linfield) 1961/2, 1962/3 (Stoke City) 1964/5.
Irvine, W. (23) (Burnley) 1962/3, 1964/5, 1965/6, 1966/7, 1967/8, 1968/9
(Preston North End) (Brighton & Hove Albion) 1971/2.

Jackson, T. (35) (Everton) 1968/9, 1969/70, 1970/1 (Nottingham Forest)
1971/2, 1972/3, 1973/4, 1974/5 (Manchester United) 1975/6, 1976/7.
Jamison, A. (1) (Glentoran) 1975/6.
Jennings, P. (119) (Watford) 1963/4, 1964/5 (Tottenham Hotspur), 1965/6,
1966/7, 1967/8, 1968/9, 1969/70, 1970/1, 1971/2, 1972/3, 1973/4, 1974/5,
1975/6, 1976/7 (Arsenal) 1977/8, 1978/9, 1979/80, 1980/1, 1981/2,
1982/3, 1983/4, 1984/5, (Tottenham Hotspur) 1985/6.
Johnston, W. (1) (Glentoran) 1961/2, (Oldham Athletic) 1965/6.
Jones, J. (3) (Glenavon) 1955/6, 1956/7.

Keane, T. (1) (Swansea Town) 1948/9.
Keith, R. (23) (Newcastle United) 1957/8, 1958/9, 1959/60, 1960/1, 1961/2.
Kelly, H. (4) (Fulham) 1949/50 (Southampton) 1950/1.
Kelly, P. (1) (Barnsley) 1949/50.

Lawther, I. (4) (Sunderland) 1959/60, 1960/1, 1961/2 (Blackburn Rovers).
Lockhart, N. (8) (Linfield) 1946/7, 1949/50 (Coventry City) 1950/1, 1951/2,
1953/4 (Aston Villa) 1954/5, 1955/6.
Lutton, B. (6) (Wolverhampton Wanderers) 1969/70, 1972/3 (West Ham United)
1973/4.

Magill, E. (26) (Arsenal) 1961/2, 1962/3, 1963/4, 1964/5, 1965/6 (Brighton &
Hove Albion).
Martin, C. (6) (Glentoran) 1946/7, 1947/8 (Leeds United) 1948/9 (Aston Villa)
1949/50.
McAdams, W. (15) (Manchester City) 1953/4, 1954/5, 1956/7, 1957/8, 1960/1
(Bolton Wanderers), 1961/2 (Leeds United).
McAlinden, J. (2) (Portsmouth) 1946/7, 1948/9 (Southend United).
McCabe, J. (6) (Leeds United) 1948/9, 1949/50, 1950/1, 1952/3, 1953/4.
McCavana, T. (3) (Coleraine) 1954/5, 1955/6.
McCleary, J.W. (1) (Cliftonville) 1954/5.
McClelland, J. (6) (Arsenal) 1960/1, 1965/6 (Fulham).
McClelland, J. (52) (Mansfield Town) 1979/80, 1980/1, 1981/2 (Rangers)
1982/3, 1983/4, 1984/5 (Watford) 1985/6, 1986/7, 1987/8, 1988/9.
McCourt, F. (6) (Manchester City) 1951/2, 1952/3.
McCoy, R. (1) (Coleraine) 1986/7.
McCreery, D. (63) (Manchester United) 1975/6, 1976/7, 1977/8, 1978/9,
1979/80 (QPR) 1980/1 (Tulsa Roughnecks) 1981/2, 1982/3 (Newcastle United),
1983/4, 1984/5, 1985/6, 1986/7, 1987/8, 1988/9.
McCrory, S. (1) (Southend United) 1957/8.
McCullough, W. (10) (Arsenal) 1960/1, 1962/3, 1963/4, 1964/5, 1966/7,
(Millwall).
McCurdy, C. (1) (Linfield) 1979/80.
McDonald, A. (22) (QPR) 1985/6, 1986/7, 1987/8, 1988/9.
McElhinney, G. (6) (Bolton Wanderers) 1983/4, 1984/5.
McFaul, I. (6) (Linfield) 1966/7, 1969/70 (Newcastle United) 1970/1, 1971/2,
1972/3, 1973/4.
McGarry, J.K. (3) (Cliftonville) 1950/1.
McGaughey, M. (1) (Linfield) 1984/5.
McGrath, R. (21) (Tottenham Hotspur) 1973/4, 1974/5, 1975/6 (Manchester
United) 1976/7, 1977/8, 1978/9.
McIlroy, J. (55) (Burnley) 1951/2, 1952/3, 1953/4, 1954/5, 1955/6, 1956/7,
1957/8, 1958/9, 1959/60, 1960/1, 1961/2, 1962/3, 1965/6 (Stoke City).
McIlroy, S.B. (88) (Manchester United) 1971/2, 1973/4, 1974/5, 1975/6,
1976/7, 1977/8, 1978/9, 1979/80, 1980/1, 1981/2, (Stoke City) 1982/3,
1983/4, 1984/5, (Manchester City) 1985/6, 1986/7.
McKeag, W. (2) (Glentoran) 1967/8.

McKenna, J. (7) (Huddersfield Town) 1949/50, 1950/1, 1951/2.
McKenzie, R. (1) (Airdrieonians) 1966/7.
McKinney, W. (1) (Falkirk) 1965/6.
McKnight, A. (10) (Celtic) 1987/8, (West Ham United) 1988/9.
McLaughlin, J. (12) (Shrewsbury Town) 1961/2, 1962/3 (Swansea City), 1963/4, 1964/5, 1965/6.
McMichael, A. (39) (Newcastle United) 1949/50, 1950/1, 1951/2, 1952/3, 1953/4, 1954/5, 1955/6, 1956/7, 1957/8, 1958/9, 1959/60.
McMillan, S. (2) (Manchester United) 1962/3.
McMordie, E. (21) (Middlesbrough) 1968/9, 1969/70, 1970/1, 1971/2, 1972/3.
McMorran, E. (15) (Belfast Celtic) 1946/7 (Barnsley) 1950/1, 1951/2, 1952/3, (Doncaster Rovers) 1953/4, 1955/6, 1956/7.
McNally, B.A. (5) (Shrewsbury Town) 1985/6, 1986/7, 1987/8.
McParland, P. (34) (Aston Villa) 1953/4, 1954/5, 1955/6, 1956/7, 1957/8, 1958/9, 1959/60, 1960/1, 1961/2 (Wolverhampton Wanderers).
Montgomery, F.) (Coleraine) 1954/5.
Moore, C. (1) (Glentoran) 1948/9.
Moreland, V. (6) (Derby County) 1978/9, 1979/80.
Morgan, S. (18) (Port Vale) 1971/2, 1972/3, 1973/4 (Aston Villa), 1974/5, 1975/6 (Brighton & Hove Albion) (Sparta Rotterdam) 1978/9.
Mullan, G. (4) (Glentoran) 1982/3.

Napier, R. (1) (Bolton Wanderers) 1965/6.
Neill, T. (59) (Arsenal) 1960/1, 1961/2, 1962/3, 1963/4, 1964/5, 1965/6, 1966/7, 1967/8, 1968/9, 1969/70 (Hull City) 1970/1, 1971/2, 1972/3.
Nelson, S. (51) (Arsenal) 1969/70, 1970/1, 1971/2, 1972/3, 1973/4, 1974/5, 1975/6, 1976/7, 1977/8, 1978/9, 1979/80, 1980/1, 1981/2 (Brighton).
Nicholl, C. (51) (Aston Villa) 1974/5, 1975/6, 1976/7 (Southampton) 1977/8, 1978/9, 1979/80, 1980/1, 1981/2, 1982/3 (Grimsby T.) 1983/4.
Nicholl, J.M. (73) (Manchester United) 1975/6, 1976/7, 1977/8, 1978/9, 1979/80, 1980/1, 1981/2 (Toronto Blizzard) 1982/3 (Sunderland) (Toronto Blizzard) (Rangers) 1983/4 (Toronto Blizzard) 1984/5 (West Bromwich Albion), 1985/6.
Nicholson, J. (41) (Manchester United) 1960/1, 1961/2, 1962/3, 1964/5, (Huddersfield Town) 1965/6, 1966/7, 1967/8, 1968/9, 1969/70, 1970/1, 1971/2.

O'Doherty, A. (2) (Coleraine) 1969/70.
O'Driscoll, J. (3) (Swansea City) 1948/9.
O'Kane, L. (20) (Nottingham Forest) 1969/70, 1970/1, 1971/2, 1972/3, 1973/4, 1974/5.
O'Neill, J. (1) (Sunderland) 1961/2.
O'Neill, J. (39) (Leicester City) 1979/80, 1980/1, 1981/2, 1982/3, 1983/4, 1984/5, 1985/6.
O'Neill, H.M. (64) (Distillery) 1971/2 (Nottingham Forest) 1972/3, 1973/4, 1974/5, 1975/6, 1976/7, 1977/8, 1978/9 1979/80, 1980/1 (Norwich City) 1981/2 (Manchester City) (Norwich City) 1982/3 (Notts County) 1983/4, 1984/5.
O'Neill, M.A. (10) (Newcastle United) 1987/8, 1988/9.

Parke, J. (13) (Linfield) 1963/4 (Hibernian), 1964/5 (Sunderland) 1965/6, 1966/7, 1967/8.
Peacock, R. (31) (Glasgow Celtic) 1951/2, 1952/3, 1953/4, 1954/5, 1955/6, 1956/7, 1957/8, 1958/9, 1959/60, 1960/1 (Coleraine) 1961/2.
Penney, S. (17) (Brighton & Hove Albion) 1984/5, 1985/6, 1986/7, 1987/8, 1988/9.
Platt, J.A. (23) (Middlesbrough) 1975/6, 1977/8, 1979/80, 1980/1, 1981/2, 1982/3 (Ballymena United) 1983/4 (Coleraine) 1985/6.

Quinn, J.M. (25) (Blackburn Rovers) 1984/5, 1985/6, 1986/7, 1987/8, (Leicester) 1988/9 (Bradford City).

Rafferty, P. (1) (Linfield) 1979/80.
Ramsey, P. (14) (Leicester City) 1983/4, 1984/5, 1985/6, 1986/7, 1987/8, 1988/9.
Rice, P. (49) (Arsenal) 1968/9, 1969/70, 1970/1, 1971/2, 1972/3, 1973/4, 1974/5, 1975/6, 1976/7, 1977/8, 1978/9, 1979/80.
Rogan. A. (9) (Celtic) 1987/8, 1988/9.
Ross, E. (1) (Newcastle United) 1968/9.
Russell, A. (1) (Linfield) 1946/7.
Ryan, R. (1) (West Bromwich Albion) 1949/50.

Sanchez, L.P. (3) (Wimbledon) 1986/7, 1988/9.
Scott, J. (2) (Grimsby Town) 1957/8.
Scott, P. (10) (Everton) 1974/5, 1975/6 (York City) 1977/8 (Aldershot) 1978/9.
Sharkey, P. (1) (Ipswich Town) 1975/6.
Shields, J. (1) (Southampton) 1956/7.
Simpson, W. (12) (Glasgow Rangers) 1950/1, 1953/4, 1954/5, 1956/7, 1957/8, 1958/9.
Sloan, D. (2) (Oxford) 1968/9, 1970/1.
Sloan, T. (3) (Manchester United) 1978/9.
Sloan, W. (1) (Arsenal) 1946/7.
Smyth, S. (9) (Wolverhampton Wanderers) 1947/8, 1948/9, 1949/50 (Stoke City) 1951/2.
Smyth, W. (4) (Distillery) 1948/9, 1953/4.
Spence, D. (29) (Bury) 1974/5, 1975/6 (Blackpool) 1976/7, 1978/9, 1979/80, (Southend United) 1980/1, 1981/2.
Stevenson, A. (3) (Everton) 1946/7, 1947/8.
Stewart, A. (7) (Glentoran) 1966/7, 1967/8 (Derby) 1968/9.
Stewart, D. (1) (Hull City) 1977/8.
Stewart, I. (31) (QPR) 1981/2, 1982/3, 1983/4, 1984/5 (Newcastle United) 1985/6, 1986/7.
Stewart, T. (1) (Linfield) 1960/1.

Todd, S. (11) (Burnley) 1965/6, 1966/7, 1967/8, 1968/9, 1969/70 (Sheffield Wednesday) 1970/1.
Trainor, D. (1) (Crusaders) 1966/7
Tulley, C. (10) (Glasgow Celtic) 1948/9, 1949/50, 1951/2, 1952/3, 1953/4, 1955/6, 1958/9.

Uprichard, N. (18) (Swindon Town) 1951/2, 1952/3 (Portsmouth) 1954/5, 1955/6, 1957/8, 1958/9.

Vernon, J. (17) (Belfast Celtic) 1946/7 (West Bromwich Albion) 1947/8, 1948/9, 1949/50, 1950/1, 1951/2.

Walker, J. (1) (Doncaster R) 1954/5.
Walsh, D. (9) (West Bromwich Albion) 1946/7, 1947/8, 1948/9, 1949/50.
Walsh, W. (5) (Manchester City) 1947/8, 1948/9.
Watson, P. (1) (Distillers) 1970/1.
Welsh, S. (4) (Carlisle United) 1965/6, 1966/7.
Whiteside, N. (36) (Manchester United) 1981/2, 1982/3, 1983/4, 1984/5, 1985/6, 1986/7, 1987/8.
Wilson, D.J. (14) (Brighton & Hove Albion) 1986/7 (Luton Town) 1987/8, 1988/9.
Wilson, K.J. (13) (Ipswich Town) 1986/7 (Chelsea) 1987/8, 1988/9.
Wilson, S. (12) (Glenavon) 1961/2, 1963/4 (Falkirk) 1964/5 (Dundee) 1965/6, 1966/7, 1967/8.
Worthington, N. (25) (Sheffield Wednesday) 1983/4, 1984/5, 1985/6, 1986/7, 1987/8, 1988/9.
Wright, T.J. (2) (Newcastle) 1988/9.

SCOTLAND

Aird, J. (4) (Burnley) 1953/4.
Aitken, G.G. (8) (East Fife) 1948/9, 1949/50, 1952/3 (Sunderland) 1953/4.
Aitken, R. (39) (Celtic) 1979/80, 1982/3, 1983/4, 1984/5, 1985/6, 1986/7, 1987/8.
Albiston, A. (14) (Manchester United) 1981/2, 1983/4, 1984/5, 1985/6.
Allan, T. (2) (Dundee) 1973/4.
Anderson, J. (1) (Leicester City) 1953/4
Archibald, S. (27) (Aberdeen) 1979/80 (Tottenham Hotspur) 1980/1, 1981/2, 1982/3, 1983/4, 1984/5 (Barcelona) 1985/6.
Auld, B. (3) (Celtic) 1958/9, 1959/60.

Baird, H. (1) (Airdrieonians) 1955/6.
Baird, S. (7) (Rangers) 1956/7, 1957/8.
Bannon, E. (11) (Dundee United) 1979/80, 1982/3, 1983/4, 1985/6.
Bauld, W. (3) (Heart of Midlothian) 1949/50.
Baxter, J. (34) (Rangers) 1960/1, 1961/2, 1962/3, 1963/4, 1964/5 (Sunderland) 1965/6, 1966/7, 1967/8.
Bell, W. (2) (Leeds United) 1965/6.
Bett, J. (19) (Rangers) 1981/2, 1982/3 (Lokeren) 1983/4, 1984/5 (Aberdeen) 1985/6, 1986/7, 1987/8, 1988/9.
Black, E. (2) (Metz) 1987/8.
Black, I. (1) (Southampton) 1947/8.
Blacklaw, A. (3) (Burnley) 1962/3, 1965/6.
Blackley, J. (7) (Hibernian) 1973/4, 1975/6, 1976/7.
Blair, J. (1) (Blackpool) 1946/7.
Blyth, J. (2) (Coventry City) 1977/8.
Bone, J. (2) (Norwich City) 1971/2, 1972/3.
Brand, R. (8) (Rangers) 1960/1, 1961/2.
Brazil, A. (13) (Ipswich Town) 1979/80, 1981/2, 1982/3 (Tottenham Hotspur).
Bremner, D. (1) (Hibernian) 1975/6.
Bremner, W. (54) (Leeds United) 1964/5, 1965/6, 1966/7, 1967/8, 1968/9, 1969/70, 1970/1, 1971/2, 1972/3, 1973/4, 1974/5, 1975/6.
Brennan, F. (7) (Newcastle United) 1946/7, 1952/3, 1963/4.
Brogan, J. (4) (Celtic) 1970/1.
Brown, A. (14) (East Fife) 1949/50 (Blackpool) 1951/2, 1952/3, 1953/4.
Brown, H. (3) (Partick Thistle) 1946/7.
Brown, J. (1) (Sheffield United) 1974/5.
Brown, R. (3) (Rangers) 1946/7, 1948/9, 1951/2.
Brown, W. (28) (Dundee) 1957/8, 1958/9, 1959/60 (Tottenham Hotspur) 1961/2, 1962/3, 1963/4, 1964/5, 1965/6.
Brownlie, J. (7) (Hibernian) 1970/1, 1971/2, 1972/3, 1975/6.
Buchan, M. (34) (Aberdeen) 1971/2 (Manchester United), 1972/3, 1973/4, 1974/5, 1975/6, 1976/7, 1977/8, 1978/9.
Buckley, P. (3) (Aberdeen) 1953/4, 1954/5.
Burley, G. (11) (Ipswich Town) 1978/9, 1979/80, 1981/2.
Burns, F. (1) (Manchester United) 1969/70.
Burns, K. (20) (Birmingham City) 1973/4, 1974/5, 1976/7 (Nottingham Forest) 1977/8, 1978/9, 1979/80, 1980/1.
Burns, T. (8) (Celtic) 1980/1, 1981/2, 1982/3, 1987/8.

Caldow, E. (40) (Rangers) 1956/7, 1957/8, 1958/9, 1959/60, 1960/1, 1961/2, 1962/3.
Callaghan, W. (2) (Dunfermline) 1969/70.
Campbell, R. (5) (Falkirk) 1946/7 (Chelsea) 1949/50.
Campbell, W. (5) (Morton) 1946/7, 1947/8.
Carr, W. (6) (Coventry City) 1969/70, 1970/1, 1971/2, 1972/3.
Chalmers, S. (5) (Celtic) 1964/5, 1965/6, 1966/7.
Clark, J. (4) (Celtic) 1965/6, 1966/7.
Clark, R. (17) (Aberdeen) 1967/8, 1969/70, 1970/1, 1971/2, 1972/3.

Clarke, S. (5) (Chelsea) 1987/8.
Collins, J. (1) (Hibernian) 1987/8.
Collins, R. (31) (Celtic) 1950/1, 1954/5, 1955/6, 1956/7, 1957/8, 1958/9, (Everton) 1964/5 (Leeds United).
Colquhoun, E. (9) (Sheffield United) 1971/2, 1972/3.
Colquhoun, J. (1) (Hearts) 1987/8.
Combe, R. (3) (Hibernian) 1947/8.
Conn, A. (1) (Heart of Midlothian) 1955/6.
Conn, A. (2) (Tottenham Hotspur) 1974/5.
Connachan, E. (2) (Dunfermline Athletic) 1961/2.
Connelly, G. (2) (Celtic) 1973/4.
Connolly, J. (1) (Everton) 1972/3.
Connor, R. (3) (Dundee) 1985/6 (Aberdeen) 1987/8, 1988/9.
Cooke, C. (16) (Dundee) 1965/6 (Chelsea) 1967/8, 1968/9, 1969/70, 1970/1, 1974/5.
Cooper, D. (20) (Rangers) 1979/80, 1983/4, 1984/5, 1985/6, 1986/7.
Cormack, P. (9) (Hibernian) 1965/6, 1969/70 (Nottingham Forest) 1970/1, 1971/2.
Cowan, J. (25) (Morton) 1947/8, 1948/9, 1949/50, 1950/1, 1951/2.
Cowie, D. (20) (Dundee) 1952/3, 1953/4, 1954/5, 1955/6, 1956/7, 1957/8.
Cox, C. (1) (Hearts) 1947/8.
Cox, S. (25) (Rangers) 1947/8, 1948/9, 1949/50, 1950/1, 1951/2, 1952/3, 1953/4.
Craig, J. (1) (Celtic) 1976/7.
Craig, J.P. (1) (Celtic) 1967/8.
Craig, T. (1) (Newcastle United) 1975/6.
Crerand, P. (16) (Celtic) 1960/1, 1961/2, 1962/3 (Manchester United) 1963/4, 1964/5, 1965/6.
Cropley, A. (2) (Hibernian) 1971/2.
Cruickshank, J. (6) (Heart of Midlothian) 1963/4, 1969/70, 1970/1, 1975/6.
Cullen, M. (1) (Luton Town) 1955/6.
Cumming, J. (9) (Heart of Midlothian) 1954/5, 1959/60.
Cunningham, W. (8) (Preston North End) 1953/4, 1954/5.
Curran, H. (5) (Wolverhampton Wanderers) 1969/70, 1970/1.

Dalglish, K. (102) (Celtic) 1971/2, 1972/3, 1973/4, 1974/5, 1975/6, 1976/7, (Liverpool) 1977/8, 1978/9, 1979/80, 1980/1, 1981/2, 1982/3, 1983/4, 1984/5, 1985/6, 1986/7.
Davidson, J. (8) (Partick Thistle) 1953/4, 1954/5.
Dawson, A. (5) (Rangers) 1979/80, 1982/3.
Deans, D. (2) (Celtic) 1974/5.
Delaney, J. (4) (Manchester United) 1946/7, 1947/8.
Dick, J. (1) (West Ham United) 1958/9.
Dickson, W. (5) (Kilmarnock) 1969/70, 1970/1.
Docherty, T. (25) (Preston North End) 1951/2, 1952/3, 1953/4, 1954/5, 1956/7, 1957/8, 1958/9 (Arsenal).
Dodds, D. (2) (Dundee United) 1983/4.
Donachie, W. (35) (Manchester City) 1971/2, 1972/3, 1973/4, 1975/6, 1976/7, 1977/8, 1978/9.
Dougall, C. (1) (Birmingham City) 1946/7.
Dougan, R. (1) (Heart of Midlothian) 1949/50.
Doyle, J. (1) (Ayr United) 1975/6.
Duncan, A. (6) (Hibernian) 1974/5, 1975/6.
Duncan, D. (3) (East Fife) 1947/8.
Duncanson, J. (1) (Rangers) 1946/7.
Durie, G.S. (3) (Chelsea) 1987/8, 1988/9.
Durrant, I. (5) (Rangers) 1987/8, 1988/9.

Evans, A. (4) (Aston Villa) 1981/2.
Evans, R. (48) (Celtic) 1948/9, 1949/50, 1950/1, 1951/2, 1952/3, 1953/4, 1954/5, 1955/6, 1956/7, 1957/8, 1958/9, 1959/60 (Chelsea).

Ewing, T. (2) (Partick Thistle) 1957/8.

Farm, G. (10) (Blackpool) 1952/3, 1953/4, 1958/9.
Ferguson, D. (2) (Rangers) 1987/8.
Ferguson, I. (3) (Rangers) 1988/9.
Ferguson, R. (7) (Kilmarnock) 1965/6, 1966/7.
Fernie, W. (12) (Celtic) 1953/4, 1954/5, 1956/7, 1957/8.
Flavell, R. (2) (Airdrieonians) 1946/7.
Fleming, C. (1) (East Fife) 1953/4.
Forbes, A. (14) (Sheffield United) 1946/7, 1947/8 (Arsenal) 1949/50, 1950/1, 1951/52.
Ford, D. (3) (Heart of Midlothian) 1973/4.
Forrest, J. (1) (Motherwell) 1957/8.
Forrest, J. (5) (Rangers) 1965/6 (Aberdeen) 1970/1.
Forsyth, A. (10) (Partick Thistle) 1971/2, 1972/3 (Manchester United) 1974/5, 1975/6.
Forsyth, C. (4) (Kilmarnock) 1963/4, 1964/5.
Forsyth, T. (22) (Motherwell) 1970/1 (Rangers) 1973/4, 1975/6, 1976/7, 1977/8.
Fraser, D. (2) (West Bromwich Albion) 1967/8, 1968/9.
Fraser, W. (2) (Sunderland) 1954/5.

Gabriel, J. (2) (Everton) 1960/1, 1961/2.
Gallacher, K.W. (4) (Dundee United) 1987/8, 1988/9.
Gardiner, W. (1) (Motherwell) 1957/8.
Gemmell, T. (2) (St Mirren) 1954/5.
Gemmell, T. (18) (Celtic) 1965/6, 1966/7, 1967/8, 1968/9, 1969/70, 1970/1.
Gemmill, A. (43) (Derby County) 1970/1, 1971/2, 1975/6, 1976/7, 1977/8 (Nottingham Forest) 1978/9 (Birmingham City) 1979/80, 1980/1.
Gibson, D. (7) (Leicester City) 1962/3, 1963/4, 1964/5.
Gillespie, G.T. (6) (Liverpool) 1987/8, 1988/9.
Gilzean, A. (22) (Dundee) 1963/4, 1964/5 (Tottenham Hotspur) 1965/6, 1967/8, 1968/9, 1969/70, 1970/1.
Glavin, R. (1) (Celtic) 1976/7.
Glen, A. (2) (Aberdeen) 1955/6.
Goram, A.L. (6) (Oldham Athletic) 1985/6, 1986/7, (Hibernian) 1988/9.
Gough, C.R. (43) (Dundee United) 1982/3, 1983/4, 1984/5, 1985/6, 1986/7, (Tottenham Hotspur) 1987/8 (Rangers), 1988/9.
Govan, J. (6) (Hibernian) 1947/8, 1948/9.
Graham, A. (10) (Leeds United) 1977/8, 1978/9, 1979/80, 1980/1.
Graham, G. (12) (Arsenal) 1971/2, 1972/3 (Manchester United).
Grant, J. (2) (Hibernian) 1958/9.
Grant, P. (2) (Celtic) 1988/9.
Gray, A. (20) (Aston Villa) 1975/6, 1976/7, 1978/9 (Wolverhampton Wanderers) 1979/80, 1980/1, 1981/2, 1982/3, 1984/5 (Everton).
Gray, E. (12) (Leeds United) 1968/9, 1969/70, 1970/1, 1971/2, 1975/6, 1976/7.
Gray, F. (32) (Leeds United) 1975/6, 1978/9, 1979/80 (Nottingham Forest) 1980/1, (Leeds United) 1981/2, 1982/3.
Green, A. (6) (Blackpool) 1970/1 (Newcastle United) 1971/2.
Greig, J. (44) (Rangers) 1963/4, 1964/5, 1965/6, 1966/7, 1967/8, 1968/9, 1969/70, 1970/1, 1975/6.

Haddock, H. (6) (Clyde) 1954/5, 1957/8.
Haffey, F. (2) (Celtic) 1959/60, 1960/1.
Hamilton, A. (24) (Dundee) 1961/2, 1962/3, 1963/4, 1964/5, 1965/6.
Hamilton, G. (5) (Aberdeen) 1946/7, 1950/1, 1953/4.
Hamilton, W. (1) (Hibernian) 1964/5.
Hansen, A. (26) (Liverpool) 1978/9, 1979/80, 1980/1, 1981/2, 1982/3, 1984/5, 1985/6, 1986/7.
Hansen, J. (2) (Partick Thistle) 1971/2.

Harper, J. (4) (Aberdeen) 1972/3, 1975/6, 1978/9.
Hartford, A. (50) (West Bromwich Albion) 1971/2, 1975/6 (Manchester City) 1976/7, 1977/8, 1978/9, 1979/80 (Everton) 1980/1, 1981/2 (Manchester City).
Harvey, D. (16) (Leeds United) 1972/3, 1973/4, 1974/5, 1975/6, 1976/7.
Haughney, M. (1) (Celtic) 1953/4.
Hay, D. (27) (Celtic) 1969/70, 1970/1, 1971/2, 1972/3, 1973/4.
Hegarty, P. (8) (Dundee United) 1978/9, 1979/80, 1982/3.
Henderson, J. (7) (Portsmouth) 1952/3, 1953/4, 1955/6, 1958/9 (Arsenal).
Henderson, W. (29) (Rangers) 1962/3, 1963/4, 1964/5, 1965/6, 1966/7, 1967/8, 1968/9, 1969/70.
Herd, D. (5) (Arsenal) 1958/9, 1960/1, 1970/1.
Herd, G. (5) (Clyde) 1957/8, 1959/60, 1960/1.
Herriot, J. (8) (Birmingham City) 1968/9, 1969/70.
Hewie, J. (19) (Charlton Athletic) 1955/6, 1956/7, 1957/8, 1958/9, 1959/60.
Holt, D. (5) (Heart of Midlothian) 1962/3, 1963/4.
Holton, J. (15) (Manchester United) 1972/3, 1973/4, 1974/5.
Hope, R. (2) (West Bromwich Albion) 1967/8, 1968/9.
Houliston, W. (3) (Queen of the South) 1948/9.
Houston, S. (1) (Manchester United) 1975/6.
Howie, H. (1) (Hibernian) 1948/9.
Hughes, J. (8) (Celtic) 1964/5, 1965/6, 1967/8, 1968/9, 1969/70.
Hughes, W. (1) (Sunderland) 1974/5.
Humphries, W. (1) (Motherwell) 1951/2.
Hunter, A. (4) (Kilmarnock) 1971/2, 1972/3 (Celtic) 1973/4.
Hunter, W. (3) (Motherwell) 1959/60, 1960/1.
Husband, J. (1) (Partick Thistle) 1946/7.
Hutchison, T. (17) (Coventry City) 1973/4, 1974/5, 1975/6.

Imlach, S. (4) (Nottingham Forest) 1957/8.

Jackson, C. (8) (Rangers) 1974/5, 1975/6.
Jardine, A. (38) (Rangers) 1970/1, 1971/2, 1972/3, 1973/4, 1974/5, 1976/7, 1977/8, 1978/9, 1979/80.
Jarvie, A. (3) (Airdrieonians) 1970/1.
Johnston, M. (28) (Watford) 1983/4, 1984/5 (Celtic) 1985/6, 1986/7, (Nantes) 1987/8, 1988/9.
Johnston, W. (22) (Rangers) 1965/6, 1967/8, 1968/9, 1969/70, 1970/1 (West Bromwich Albion) 1976/7, 1977/8.
Johnstone, D. (14) (Rangers) 1972/3, 1974/5, 1975/6, 1977/8, 1979/80.
Johnstone, J. (23) (Celtic) 1964/5, 1965/6, 1966/7, 1967/8, 1968/9, 1969/70, 1970/1, 1971/2, 1973/4, 1974/5.
Johnstone, L. (2) (Clyde) 1947/8.
Johnstone, R. (17) (Hibernian) 1950/1, 1951/2, 1952/3, 1953/4, 1954/5 (Manchester City) 1955/6.
Jordan, J. (52) (Leeds United) 1972/3, 1973/4, 1974/5, 1975/6, 1976/7, 1977/8, (Manchester United) 1978/9, 1979/80, 1980/1, 1981/2 (AC Milan).

Kelly, H. (1) (Blackpool) 1951/2
Kelly, J. (2) (Barnsley) 1948/9.
Kennedy, J. (6) (Celtic) 1963/4, 1964/5.
Kennedy, S. (8) (Aberdeen) 1977/8, 1978/9, 1981/2.
Kennedy, S. (5) (Rangers) 1974/5.
Kerr, A. (2) (Partick Thistle) 1954/5.

Law, D. (55) (Huddersfield Town) 1958/9, 1959/60 (Manchester City) 1960/1, 1961/2 (Torino) 1962/3 (Manchester United) 1963/4, 1964/5, 1965/6, 1966/7, 1967/8, 1968/9, 1971/2, 1973/4 (Manchester City).
Lawrence, T. (3) (Liverpool) 1962/3, 1968/9.
Leggat, G. (18) (Aberdeen) 1955/6, 1956/7, 1957/8, 1958/9 (Fulham) 1959/60.

Leighton, J. (50) (Aberdeen) 1982/3, 1983/4, 1984/5, 1985/6, 1986/7, 1987/8, (Manchester United), 1988/9.
Lennox, R. (10) (Celtic) 1966/7, 1967/8, 1968/9.
Leslie, L. (5) (Airdrieonians) 1960/1.
Liddell, W. (28) (Liverpool) 1946/7, 1947/8, 1949/50, 1950/1, 1951/2, 1952/3, 1953/4, 1954/5, 1955/6.
Linwood, A. (1) (Clyde) 1949/50.
Little, A. (1) (Rangers) 1952/3.
Logie, J. (1) (Arsenal) 1952/3.
Long, H. (1) (Clyde) 1946/7.
Lorimer, P. (21) (Leeds United) 1969/70, 1970/1, 1971/2, 1972/3, 1973/4, 1974/5, 1975/6.

Macari, L. (24) (Celtic) 1971/2, 1972/3 (Manchester United) 1974/5, 1976/7, 1977/8, 1978/9.
Macaulay, A. (7) (Brentford) 1946/7 (Arsenal) 1947/8.
Macdougall, E. (7) (Norwich City) 1974/5, 1975/6.
Mackay, D. (22) (Heart of Midlothian) 1956/7, 1957/8, 1958/9 (Tottenham Hotspur) 1959/60, 1960/1, 1962/3, 1963/4, 1965/6.
Mackay, G. (4) (Heart of Midlothian) 1987/8.
Malpas, M. (28) (Dundee United) 1983/4, 1984/5, 1985/6, 1986/7, 1987/8, 1988/9.
Martin, F. (6) (Aberdeen) 1953/4, 1954/5.
Martin, N. (3) (Hibernian) 1964/5, 1965/6 (Sunderland).
Martis, J. (1) (Motherwell) 1960/1.
Mason, J. (7) (Third Lanark) 1948/9, 1949/50, 1950/1.
Masson, D. (17) (QPR) 1975/6, 1976/7, 1977/8 (Derby County) 1978/9.
Mathers, D. (1) (Partick Thistle) 1953/4.
McAvennie, F. (5) (West Ham United) 1985/6 (Celtic) 1987/8.
McBride, J. (2) (Celtic) 1966/7.
McCalliog, J. (5) (Sheffield Wednesday) 1966/7, 1967/8, 1968/9, 1970/1 (Wolverhampton Wanderers).
McCann, R. (5) (Motherwell) 1958/9, 1959/60, 1960/1.
McClair, B. (12) (Celtic) 1986/7 (Manchester United) 1987/8, 1988/9.
McCloy, P. (4) (Rangers) 1972/3.
McCoist, A. (16) (Rangers) 1985/6, 1986/7, 1987/8, 1988/9.
McColl, I. (14) (Rangers) 1949/50, 1950/1, 1956/7, 1957/8.
McCreadie, E. (23) (Chelsea) 1964/5, 1965/6, 1966/7, 1967/8, 1968/9.
MacDonald, A. (1) (Rangers) 1975/6.
MacDonald, J. (2) (Sunderland) 1955/6.
McFarlane, W. (1) (Heart of Midlothian) 1946/7.
McGarr, E. (2) (Aberdeen) 1969/70.
McGarvey, F. (7) (Liverpool) 1978/79 (Celtic) 1983/4.
McGhee, M. (4) (Aberdeen) 1982/3, 1983/4.
McGrain, D. (62) (Celtic) 1972/3, 1973/4, 1974/5, 1975/6, 1976/7, 1977/8, 1979/80, 1980/1, 1981/2.
McGrory, J. (3) (Kilmarnock) 1964/5, 1965/6.
McInally, A. (2) (Aston Villa) 1988/9.
McInally, J. (3) (Dundee United) 1986/7, 1987/8.
McKay, D. (14) (Celtic) 1958/9, 1959/60, 1960/1, 1961/2.
McKean, R. (1) (Rangers) 1975/6.
McKenzie, J. (9) (Partick Thistle) 1953/4, 1954/5, 1955/6.
McKimmie, S. (2) (Aberdeen) 1988/9.
McKinnon, R. (28) (Rangers) 1965/6, 1966/7, 1967/8, 1968/9, 1969/70, 1970/1.
McLaren, A. (4) (Preston North End) 1946/7, 1947/8.
McLean, G. (1) (Dundee) 1967/8.
McLean, T. (6) (Kilmarnock) 1968/9, 1969/70, 1970/1.
McLeish, A. (63) (Aberdeen) 1979/80, 1980/1, 1981/2, 1982/3, 1983/4, 1984/5, 1985/6, 1986/7, 1987/8, 1988/9.
McLeod, J. (4) (Hibernian) 1960/1.

MacLeod, M. (9) (Celtic) 1984/5, 1986/7 (Borussia Dortmund) 1987/8, 1988/9.
McLintock, F. (9) (Leicester City) 1962/3, 1964/5 (Arsenal) 1966/7, 1969/70, 1970/1.
McMillan, I. (6) (Airdrieonians) 1951/2, 1954/5, 1955/6 (Rangers) 1960/1.
McNaught, W. (5) (Raith Rovers) 1950/1, 1951/2, 1954/5.
McNeill, W. (29) (Celtic) 1960/1, 1961/2, 1962/3, 1963/4, 1964/5, 1965/6, 1966/7, 1967/8, 1968/9, 1969/70, 1971/2.
McPhail, J. (5) (Celtic) 1949/50, 1950/1, 1953/4
McPherson, D. (2) (Hearts) 1988/9.
McQueen, G. (30) (Leeds United) 1973/4, 1974/5, 1975/6, 1976/7, 1977/8, (Manchester United) 1978/9, 1979/80, 1980/1.
McStay, P. (37) (Celtic) 1983/4, 1984/5, 1985/6, 1986/7, 1987/8, 1988/9.
Millar, J. (2) (Rangers) 1962/3.
Miller, W. (6) (Celtic) 1946/7, 1947/8.
Miller, W. (63) (Aberdeen) 1974/5, 1977/8, 1979/80, 1980/1 1981/2, 1982/3, 1983/4, 1984/5, 1985/6, 1986/7, 1987/8, 1988/9.
Mitchell, R. (2) (Newcastle United) 1950/1.
Mochan, N. (3) (Celtic) 1953/4.
Moir, W. (1) (Bolton Wanderers) 1949/50.
Moncur, R. (16) (Newcastle United) 1967/8, 1969/70, 1970/1, 1971/2.
Morgan, W. (21) (Burnley) 1967/8 (Manchester United) 1971/2, 1972/3, 1973/4.
Morris, H. (1) (East Fife) 1949/50.
Mudie, J. (17) (Blackpool) 1956/7, 1957/8.
Mulhall, G. (3) (Aberdeen) 1959/60, 1962/3 (Sunderland) 1963/4.
Munro, F. (9) (Wolverhampton Wanderers) 1970/1, 1974/5.
Munro, I. (7) (St Mirren) 1978/9, 1979/80.
Murdoch, R. (12) (Celtic) 1965/6, 1966/7, 1967/8, 1968/9, 1969/70.
Murray, J. (5) (Heart of Midlothian) 1957/8.
Murray, S. (1) (Aberdeen) 1971/2.

Narey, D. (35) (Dundee United) 1976/7, 1978/9, 1979/80, 1980/1, 1981/2, 1982/3, 1985/6, 1986/7, 1988/9.
Nevin, P.K.F. (8) (Chelsea) 1985/6, 1986/7, 1987/8, (Everton) 1988/9.
Nicholas, C. (20) (Celtic) 1982/3 (Arsenal) 1983/4, 1984/5, 1985/6, 1986/7, (Aberdeen) 1988/9.
Nicol, S. (21) (Liverpool) 1984/5, 1985/6, 1987/8, 1988/9.

O'Hare, J. (13) (Derby County) 1969/70, 1970/1, 1971/2.
Ormond, W. (6) (Hibernian) 1953/4, 1958/9.
Orr, T. (2) (Morton) 1951/2.

Parker, A. (15) (Falkirk) 1954/5, 1955/6, 1956/7, 1957/8.
Parlane, D. (12) (Rangers) 1972/3, 1974/5, 1975/6, 1976/7.
Paton, A. (2) (Motherwell) 1951/2.
Pearson, T. (2) (Newcastle United) 1946/7.
Penman, A. (1) (Dundee) 1965/6.
Pettigrew, W. (5) (Motherwell) 1975/6, 1976/7.
Plenderleith, J. (1) (Manchester City) 1960/1.
Provan, D. (5) (Rangers) 1963/4, 1965/6.
Provan, D. (10) (Celtic) 1979/80, 1980/1, 1981/2.

Quinn, P. (4) (Motherwell) 1960/1, 1961/2.

Redpath, W. (9) (Motherwell) 1948/9, 1950/1, 1951/2.
Reilly, L. (38) (Hibernian) 1948/9, 1949/50, 1950/1, 1951/2, 1952/3, 1953/4, 1954/5, 1955/6, 1956/7.
Ring, T. (12) (Clydebank) 1952/3, 1954/5, 1956/7, 1957/8.

Rioch, B. (24) (Derby County) 1974/5, 1975/6, 1976/7 (Everton) 1977/8 (Derby County) 1978/9.
Robb, D. (5) (Aberdeen) 1970/1.
Robertson, A. (5) (Clyde) 1954/5, 1957/8.
Robertson, H. (1) (Dundee) 1961/2.
Robertson, J. (1) (Tottenham Hotspur) 1964/5.
Robertson, J. (28) (Nottingham Forest) 1977/8, 1978/9, 1979/80, 1980/1, 1981/2, 1982/3 (Derby County) 1983/4.
Robinson, B. (4) (Dundee) 1973/4, 1974/5.
Rough, A. (53) (Partick Thistle) 1975/6, 1976/7, 1977/8, 1978/9, 1979/80, 1980/1, 1981/2 (Hibernian) 1985/6.
Rougvie, D. (1) (Aberdeen) 1983/4.
Rutherford, E. (1) (Rangers) 1947/8.

St John, I. (21) (Motherwell) 1958/9, 1959/60, 1960/1, 1961/2 (Liverpool) 1962/3, 1963/4, 1964/5.
Schaedler, E. (1) (Hibernian) 1973/4.
Scott, A. (16) (Rangers) 1956/7, 1957/8, 1958/9, 1961/2 (Everton) 1963/4, 1964/5, 1965/6.
Scott, J. (1) (Hibernian) 1965/6.
Scott, J. (2) (Dundee) 1970/1.
Scoular, J. (9) (Portsmouth) 1950/1, 1951/2, 1952/3.
Sharp, G.M. (12) (Everton) 1984/5, 1985/6, 1986/7, 1987/8.
Shaw, D. (8) (Hibernian) 1946/7, 1947/8, 1948/9.
Shaw, J. (4) (Rangers) 1946/7, 1947/8.
Shearer, R. (4) (Rangers) 1960/1.
Simpson, N. (4) (Aberdeen) 1982/3, 1983/4, 1986/7, 1987/8.
Simpson, R. (5) (Celtic) 1966/7, 1967/8, 1968/9.
Sinclair, J. (1) (Leicester City) 1965/6.
Smith, D. (2) (Aberdeen) 1965/6, 1967/8 (Rangers).
Smith, E. (2) (Celtic) 1958/9.
Smith, G. (18) (Hibernian) 1946/7, 1947/8, 1951/2, 1954/5, 1955/6, 1956/7.
Smith, H.G. (1) (Heart of Midlothian) 1987/8.
Smith, J. (4) (Aberdeen) 1967/8, 1973/4 (Newcastle United).
Souness, G. (54) (Middlesbrough) 1974/5 (Liverpool) 1977/8, 1978/9, 1979/80, 1980/1, 1981/2, 1982/3, 1983/4 (Sampdoria) 1984/5, 1985/6.
Speedie, D.R. (10) (Chelsea) 1984/5, 1985/6, (Coventry City) 1988/9.
Stanton, P. (16) (Hibernian) 1965/6, 1968/9, 1969/70, 1970/1, 1971/2, 1972/3, 1973/4.
Steel, W. (30) (Morton) 1946/7, 1947/8 (Derby County) 1948/9, 1949/50, (Dundee) 1950/1, 1951/2, 1952/3.
Stein, C. (21) (Rangers) 1968/9, 1969/70, 1970/1, 1971/2 (Coventry City).
Stephen, J. (2) (Bradford City) 1946/7, 1947/8.
Stewart, D. (1) (Leeds United) 1977/8.
Stewart, J. (2) (Kilmarnock) 1976/7 (Middlesbrough) 1978/9.
Stewart, R. (10) (West Ham United) 1980/1, 1981/2, 1983/4, 1986/7.
Strachan, G. (42) (Aberdeen) 1979/80, 1980/1, 1981/2, 1982/3, 1983/4 (Manchester United) 1984/5, 1985/6, 1986/7, 1987/8, 1988/9.
Sturrock, P. (20) (Dundee United) 1980/1, 1981/2, 1982/3, 1983/4, 1984/5, 1985/6, 1986/7.

Telfer, W. (1) (St Mirren) 1953/4.
Thomson, W. (7) (St Mirren) 1979/80, 1980/1, 1981/2, 1982/3, 1983/4.
Thornton, W. (7) (Rangers) 1946/7, 1947/8, 1948/9, 1951/2.
Toner, W. (2) (Kilmarnock) 1958/9.
Turnbull, E. (8) (Hibernian) 1957/8, 1950/1, 1957/8.

Ure, I. (11) (Dundee) 1961/2, 1962/3 (Arsenal) 1963/4, 1967/8.

Waddell, W. (17) (Rangers) 1946/7, 1948/9, 1949/50, 1950/1, 1951/2, 1953/4, 1954/5.

Walker, A. (1) (Celtic) 1987/8.
Wallace, I.A. (3) (Coventry City) 1977/8, 1978/9.
Wallace, W.S.B. (7) (Heart of Midlothian) 1964/5, 1965/6, 1966/7 (Celtic) 1967/8, 1968/9.
Wardhaugh, J. (2) (Heart of Midlothian) 1954/5, 1956/7.
Wark, J. (29) (Ipswich Town) 1978/9, 1979/80, 1980/1, 1981/2, 1982/3, 1983/4 (Liverpool) 1984/5.
Watson, J. (2) (Motherwell) 1947/8 (Huddersfield Town) 1953/4.
Watson, R. (1) (Motherwell) 1970/1.
Weir, A. (6) (Motherwell) 1958/9, 1959/60.
Weir, P. (6) (St Mirren) 1979/80, 1982/3 (Aberdeen) 1983/4.
White, J. (22) (Falkirk) 1958/9, 1959/60 (Tottenham Hotspur) 1960/1, 1961/2, 1962/3, 1963/4.
Whyte, D. (3) (Celtic) 1987/8, 1988/9.
Wilson, A. (1) (Portsmouth) 1953/4.
Wilson, D. (22) (Rangers) 1960/1, 1961/2, 1962/3, 1963/4, 1964/5.
Wilson, I.A. (5) (Leicester City) 1986/7 (Everton) 1987/8.
Wilson, P. (1) (Celtic) 1974/5.
Wilson, R. (2) (Arsenal) 1971/2.
Wood, G. (4) (Everton) 1978/9, 1981/2 (Arsenal).
Woodburn, W. (24) (Rangers) 1946/7, 1947/8, 1948/9, 1949/50, 1950/1, 1951/2.
Wright, T. (3) (Sunderland) 1952/3.

Yeats, R. (2) (Liverpool) 1964/5, 1965/6.
Yorston, H. (1) (Aberdeen) 1954/5.
Young, A. (9) (Heart of Midlothian) 1959/60, 1960/1 (Everton) 1965/6.
Young, G. (53) (Rangers) 1946/7, 1947/8, 1948/9, 1949/50, 1950/1, 1951/2, 1952/3, 1953/4, 1954/5, 1955/6, 1956/7.
Younger, T. (24) (Hibernian) 1954/5, 1955/6, 1956/7 (Liverpool) 1957/8.

WALES

Aizlewood, M. (13) (Charlton Athletic) 1985/6, 1986/7 (Leeds United) 1987/8, 1988/9.
Allchurch, I. (68) (Swansea City) 1950/1, 1951/2, 1952/3, 1953/4, 1954/5, 1955/6, 1956/7, 1957/8, 1958/9 (Newcastle United) 1959/60, 1960/1, 1961/2, 1962/3 (Cardiff City) 1963/4, 1964/5 1965/6 (Swansea City).
Allchurch, L. (11) (Swansea City) 1954/5, 1955/6, 1957/8, 1958/9 1961/2, (Sheffield United) 1963/4.
Allen, B. (2) (Coventry City) 1950/1.
Allen, M. (4) (Watford) 1985/6, (Norwich City) 1988/9.

Baker, C. (7) (Cardiff City) 1957/8, 1959/60, 1960/1, 1961/2.
Baker, W. (1) (Cardiff City) 1947/8.
Barnes, W. (22) (Arsenal) 1947/8, 1948/9, 1949/50, 1950/1, 1951/2, 1953/4, 1954/5.
Berry, G. (5) (Wolverhampton Wanderers) 1978/9, 1979/80, 1982/3,(Stoke City).
Blackmore, C.G. (21) (Manchester United) 1984/5, 1985/6, 1986/7, 1987/8, 1988/9.
Bowen, D. (19) (Arsenal) 1954/5, 1956/7, 1957/8, 1958/9.
Bowen, M.R. (7) (Tottenham Hotspur) 1985/6 (Norwich City) 1987/8, 1988/9.
Boyle, T. (2) (Crystal Palace) 1980/1.
Burgess, R. (32) (Tottenham Hotspur) 1946/7, 1947/8, 1948/9, 1949/50, 1950/1, 1951/2, 1952/3, 1953/4.
Burton, O. (9) (Norwich City) 1962/3 (Newcastle United) 1963/4, 1968/9, 1971/2.

Cartwright, L. (7) (Coventry City) 1973/4, 1975/6, 1976/7 (Wrexham) 1977/8, 1978/9.
Charles, J. (38) (Leeds United) 1949/50, 1950/1, 1952/3, 1953/4, 1954/5, 1955/6, 1956/7 (Juventus Turin) 1957/8, 1959/60, 1961/2, 1962/3 (Leeds United) (Cardiff City) 1963/4, 1964/5.
Charles, J.M. (19) (Swansea City) 1980/1, 1981/2, 1982/3, 1983/4 (QPR), (Oxford United) 1984/5, 1985/6, 1986/7.
Charles, M. (31) (Swansea City) 1954/5, 1955/6, 1956/7, 1957/8, 1958/9 (Arsenal) 1960/1, 1961/2 (Cardiff City) 1962/3.
Clarke, R. (22) (Manchester City) 1948/9, 1949/50, 1950/1, 1951/2 1952/3, 1953/4, 1954/5, 1955/6.
Crowe, V. (16) (Aston Villa) 1958/9, 1959/60, 1960/1, 1961/2, 1962/3.
Curtis, A. (35) (Swansea City) 1975/6, 1976/7, 1977/8, 1978/9, 1979/80, 1981/2, 1982/3, 1983/4 (Southampton) 1984/5, 1985/6, 1986/7 (Cardiff City).

Daniel, R. (21) (Arsenal) 1950/1, 1951/2, 1952/3, 1953/4 (Sunderland) 1954/5, 1956/7.
Davies, A. (9) (Manchester United) 1982/3, 1983/4, 1984/5 (Newcastle United) 1985/6 (Swansea City) 1987/8, 1988/9.
Davies, D. (52) (Everton) 1974/5, 1975/6, 1976/7, 1977/8, (Wrexham) 1978/9, 1979/80, 1980/1 (Swansea City) 1981/2, 1982/3.
Davies, G. (18) (Fulham) 1979/80, 1981/2, 1982/3, 1983/4, 1984/5 (Chelsea), (Manchester City) 1985/6.
Davies, R. Wyn (34) (Bolton Wanderers) 1963/4, 1964/5, 1965/6, 1966/7 (Newcastle United) 1967/8, 1968/9, 1969/70, 1970/1, 1971/2 (Manchester City), (Blackpool) 1972/3 (Manchester United) 1973/4.
Davies, Reg (6) (Newcastle United) 1952/3, 1953/4, 1957/8.
Davies, Ron (29) (Norwich City) 1963/4, 1964/5, 1965/6, 1966/7, (Southampton) 1967/8, 1968/9, 1969/70, 1970/1, 1971/2, 1973/4 (Portsmouth).
Davis, C. (1) (Charlton Athletic) 1971/2.
Davis, G. (4) (Wrexham) 1977/8.
Deacy, N. (11) (PSV Eindhoven) 1976/7, 1977/8 (Beringen) 1978/9.
Derrett, S. (4) (Cardiff City) 1968/9, 1969/70, 1970/1.
Dibble, A. (3) (Luton Town) 1985/6, (Manchester City) 1988/9.
Durban, A. (27) (Derby County) 1965/6, 1966/7, 1967/8, 1968/9, 1969/70, 1970/1, 1971/2.
Dwyer, P. (10) (Cardiff City) 1977/8, 1978/9, 1979/80.

Edwards, I. (4) (Chester) 1977/8, 1978/9, 1979/80.
Edwards, G. (12) (Birmingham City) 1946/7, 1947/8 (Cardiff City) 1948/9, 1949/50.
Edwards, T. (2) (Charlton Athletic) 1956/7.
Emanuel, J. (2) (Bristol City) 1972/3.
England, M. (44) (Blackburn Rovers) 1961/2, 1962/3, 1963/4, 1964/5, 1965/6, 1966/7 (Tottenham Hotspur) 1967/8, 1968/9, 1969/70, 1970/1, 1971/2, 1972/3, 1973/4, 1974/5.
Evans, B. (7) (Swansea City) 1971/2, 1972/3 (Hereford United) 1973/4.
Evans, I. (13) (Crystal Palace) 1975/6, 1976/7, 1977/8.
Evans, R. (1) (Swansea City) 1963/4.

Felgate D. (1) (Lincoln City) 1983/4.
Flynn, B. (66) (Burnley) 1974/5, 1975/6, 1976/7, 1977/8 (Leeds United) 1978/9, 1979/80, 1980/1, 1981/2, 1982/3 (Burnley) 1983/4.
Ford, T. (38) (Swansea City) 1946/7 (Aston Villa) 1947/8, 1948/9, 1949/50, 1950/1 (Sunderland) 1951/2, 1952/3 (Cardiff City) 1953/4, 1954/5, 1955/6, 1956/7.
Foulkes, W. (11) (Newcastle United) 1951/2, 1952/3, 1953/4.

Giles, D. (12) (Swansea City) 1979/80, 1980/1, 1981/2 (Crystal Palace) 1982/3.

Godfrey, B. (3) (Preston North End) 1963/4, 1964/5.
Green, C. (15) (Birmingham City) 1964/5, 1965/6, 1966/7, 1967/8, 1968/9.
Griffiths, A. (17) (Wrexham) 1970/1, 1974/5, 1975/6, 1976/7.
Griffiths, H. (1) (Swansea City) 1952/3.
Griffiths, M. (11) (Leicester City) 1946/7, 1948/9, 1949/50, 1950/1, 1953/4.

Hall, G.D. (6) (Chelsea) 1987/8, 1988/9.
Harrington, A. (11) (Cardiff City) 1955/6, 1956/7, 1957/8, 1960/1, 1961/2.
Harris, C. (24) (Leeds United) 1975/6, 1977/8, 1978/9, 1979/80, 1980/1, 1981/2.
Harris, W. (6) (Middlesbrough) 1953/4, 1956/7, 1957/8.
Hennessey, T. (39) (Birmingham City) 1961/2, 1962/3, 1963/4, 1964/5, 1965/6, (Nottingham Forest) 1966/7, 1967/8, 1968/9, 1969/70 (Derby County) 1971/2, 1972/3.
Hewitt, R. (5) (Cardiff City) 1957/8.
Hill, M. (2) (Ipswich Town) 1971/2.
Hockey, T. (9) (Sheffield United) 1971/2, 1972/3 (Norwich City) 1973/4, (Aston Villa).
Hodges, G. (11) (Wimbledon) 1983/4, 1986/7 (Newcastle United) 1987/8, (Watford).
Holden, A. (1) (Chester City) 1983/4.
Hole, B. (30) (Cardiff City) 1962/3, 1963/4, 1964/5, 1965/6, 1966/7, (Blackburn Rovers) 1967/8, 1968/9 (Aston Villa) 1969/70 (Swansea City) 1970/71.
Hollins, D. (11) (Newcastle United) 1961/2, 1962/3, 1963/4, 1964/5, 1965/6.
Hopkins, J. (14) (Fulham) 1982/3, 1983/4, 1984/5.
Hopkins, M. (34) (Tottenham Hotspur) 1955/6, 1956/7, 1957/8, 1958/9, 1959/60, 1960/1, 1961/2, 1962/3.
Horne, B. (10) (Portsmouth) 1987/8, (Southampton) 1988/9.
Howells, R. (2) (Cardiff City) 1953/4.
Hughes, I. (4) (Luton Town) 1950/1.
Hughes, L.M. (25) (Manchester United) 1983/4, 1984/5, 1985/6, 1986/7, (Barcelona) 1987/8, 1988/9 (Manchester United).
Hughes, W. (3) (Birmingham City) 1946/7.
Hughes, W.A. (5) (Blackburn Rovers) 1948/9.
Humphreys, J. (1) (Everton) 1946/7.

Jackett, K. (31) (Watford) 1982/3, 1983/4, 1984/5, 1985/6, 1986/7, 1987/8.
James, G. (9) (Blackpool) 1965/6, 1966/7, 1967/8, 1970/1.
James, L. (54) (Burnley) 1971/2, 1972/3, 1973/4, 1974/5, 1975/6 (Derby County) 1976/7, 1977/8 (QPR) (Burnley) 1978/9, 1979/80 (Swansea City) 1980/1, 1981/2 (Sunderland) 1982/3.
James, R.M. (47) (Swansea City) 1978/9, 1979/80, 1981/2, 1982/3 (Stoke City) 1983/4, 1984/5 (QPR) 1985/6, 1986/7 (Leicester City) 1987/8 (Swansea City).
Jarvis, A. (3) (Hull City) 1966/7.
Johnson, M. (1) (Swansea City) 1963/4.
Jones, A. (5) (Port Vale) 1986/7, 1987/8 (Charlton Athletic).
Jones, Barrie. (15) (Swansea City) 1962/3, 1963/4, 1964/5 (Plymouth Argyle) 1968/9 (Cardiff City).
Jones, Bryn. (4) (Arsenal) 1946/7, 1947/8, 1948/9.
Jones, C. (59) (Swansea City) 1953/4, 1955/6, 1956/7, 1957/8 (Tottenham Hotspur) 1958/9, 1959/60, 1960/1, 1961/2, 1962/3, 1963/4, 1964/5, 1966/7, 1967/8, 1968/9 (Fulham) 1969/70.
Jones, D. (8) (Norwich City) 1975/6, 1977/8, 1979/80.
Jones, E. (4) (Swansea City) 1947/8 (Tottenham Hotspur) 1948/9.
Jones, J. (72) (Liverpool) 1975/6, 1976/7, 1977/8 (Wrexham) 1978/9, 1979/80, 1980/1, 1981/2, 1982/3 (Chelsea) 1983/4, 1984/5 (Huddersfield Town) 1985/6.
Jones, K. (1) (Aston Villa) 1949/50.
Jones, T.G. (13) (Everton) 1946/7, 1947/8, 1948/9, 1949/50.
Jones, W. (1) (Bristol Rovers) 1970/1.

Kelsey, J. (41) (Arsenal) 1953/4, 1954/5, 1955/6, 1956/7, 1957/8, 1958/9, 1959/60, 1960/1, 1961/2.
King, J. (1) (Swansea City) 1954/5.
Kinsey, N. (7) (Norwich City) 1950/1, 1951/2, 1953/4 (Birmingham City) 1955/6.
Knill, A.R. (1) (Swansea City) 1988/9.
Krzywicki, R. (8) (West Bromwich Albion) 1969/70 (Huddersfield Town) 1970/1, 1971/2.

Lambert, R. (5) (Liverpool) 1946/7, 1947/8, 1948/9.
Lea, C. (2) (Ipswich Town) 1964/5.
Leek, K. (13) (Leicester City) 1960/1, 1961/2 (Newcastle United) (Birmingham City) 1962/3, 1964/5.
Lever, A. (1) (Leicester City) 1952/3.
Lewis, D. (1) (Swansea City) 1982/3.
Lloyd, B. (3) (Wrexham) 1975/6.
Lovell, S. (6) (Crystal Palace) 1981/2 (Millwall) 1984/5, 1985/6.
Lowndes, S. (10) (Newport County) 1982/3 (Millwall) 1984/5, 1985/6, 1986/7, (Barnsley) 1987/8.
Lowrie, G. (4) (Coventry City) 1947/8, 1948/9 (Newcastle United).
Lucas, M. (4) (Leyton Orient) 1961/2, 1962/3.
Lucas, W. (7) (Swansea City) 1948/9, 1949/50, 1950/1.

Mahoney, J. (51) (Stoke City) 1967/8, 1968/9, 1970/1, 1972/3, 1973/4, 1974/5, 1975/6, 1976/7 (Middlesbrough) 1977/8, 1978/9 (Swansea City) 1979/80, 1981/2, 1982/3.
Marustik, C. (6) (Swansea City) 1981/2, 1982/3.
Medwin, T. (30) (Swansea City) 1952/3, 1956/7 (Tottenham Hotspur) 1957/8, 1958/9, 1959/60, 1960/1, 1962/3.
Mielczarek, R. (1) (Rotherham United) 1970/1.
Millington, A. (21) (West Bromwich Albion) 1962/3, 1964/5 (Crystal Palace) 1965/6 (Peterborough United) 1966/7, 1967/8, 1968/9, 1969/70 (Swansea City) 1970/1, 1971/2.
Moore, G. (21) (Cardiff City) 1959/60, 1960/1, 1961/2 (Chelsea) 1962/3, (Manchester United) 1963/4 (Northampton Town) 1965/6, 1968/9 (Charlton Athletic) 1969/70, 1970/1.
Morris, W. (5) (Burnley) 1946/7, 1948/9, 1951/2.

Nardiello, D. (2) (Coventry City) 1977/8.
Nicholas, P. (59) (Crystal Palace) 1978/9, 1979/80, 1980/1 (Arsenal) 1981/2, 1982/3, 1983/4 (Crystal Palace) 1984/5 (Luton Town) 1985/6, 1986/7, 1987/8 (Aberdeen), (Chelsea) 1988/9.
Niedzwiecki, E.A. (2) (Chelsea) 1984/5, 1987/8.
Norman, A.J. (5) (Hull City) 1985/6, 1987/8.
Nurse, M. (12) (Swansea City) 1959/60, 1960/1, 1962/3 (Middlesbrough) 1963/4.

O'Sullivan, P. (3) (Brighton & Hove Albion) 1972/3, 1975/6, 1978/9.

Page, M. (28) (Birmingham City) 1970/1, 1971/2, 1972/3, 1973/4, 1974/5, 1975/6, 1976/7, 1977/8, 1978/9.
Palmer, D. (3) (Swansea City) 1956/7, 1957/8.
Parry, J. (1) (Swansea City) 1950/1.
Pascoe, C. (5) (Swansea City) 1983/4, (Sunderland) 1988/9.
Paul, R. (33) (Swansea City) 1948/9, 1949/50 (Manchester City) 1950/1, 1951/2, 1952/3, 1953/4, 1954/5, 1955/6.
Phillips, D. (22) (Plymouth Argyle) 1983/4 (Manchester City) 1984/5, 1985/6, 1986/7 (Coventry City) 1987/8, 1988/9.
Phillips, J. (4) (Chelsea) 1972/3, 1973/4, 1974/5, 1977/8.

Phillips, L. (58) (Cardiff City) 1970/1, 1971/2, 1972/3, 1973/4, 1974/5, (Aston Villa) 1975/6, 1976/7, 1977/8, 1978/9 (Swansea City) 1979/80, 1980/1, 1981/2 (Charlton Athletic).
Pontin, K. (2) (Cardiff City) 1979/80.
Powell, A. (8) (Leeds United) 1946/7, 1947/8, 1948/9 (Everton) 1949/50, 1950/1 (Birmingham City).
Powell, D. (11) (Wrexham) 1967/8, 1968/9 (Sheffield United) 1969/70, 1970/1.
Powell, I. (8) (QPR) 1946/7, 1947/8, 1948/9 (Aston Villa) 1949/50, 1950/1.
Price, P. (25) (Luton Town) 1979/80, 1980/1, 1981/2 (Tottenham Hotspur) 1982/3, 1983/4.
Pring, K. (3) (Rotherham United) 1965/6, 1966/7.
Pritchard, H.K. (1) (Bristol City) 1984/5.

Rankmore, F. (1) (Peterborough United) 1965/6.
Ratcliffe, K. (47) (Everton) 1980/1, 1981/2, 1982/3, 1983/4, 1984/5, 1985/6, 1986/7, 1987/8, 1988/9.
Reece, G. (29) (Sheffield United) 1965/6, 1966/7, 1969/70, 1970/1, 1971/2, (Cardiff City) 1972/3, 1973/4, 1974/5.
Reed, W. (2) (Ipswich Town) 1954/5.
Rees, A. (1) (Birmingham City) 1983/4.
Rees, R. (39) (Coventry City) 1964/5, 1965/6, 1966/7, 1967/8 (West Bromwich Albion) 1968/9 (Nottingham Forest) 1969/70, 1970/1, 1971/2.
Rees, W. (4) (Cardiff City) 1948/9 (Tottenham Hotspur) 1949/50.
Richards, S. (1) (Cardiff City) 1946/7.
Roberts, D. (17) (Oxford United) 1972/3, 1973/4, 1974/5 (Hull City) 1975/6, 1976/7, 1977/8.
Roberts, J.G. (22) (Arsenal) 1970/1, 1971/2, 1972/3,(Birmingham City) 1973/4, 1974/5, 1975/6.
Roberts, J.H. (1) (Bolton Wanderers) 1948/9.
Roberts, P. (4) (Portsmouth) 1973/4, 1974/5.
Rodrigues, P. (40) (Cardiff City) 1964/5, 1965/6 (Leicester City) 1966/7, 1967/8, 1968/9, 1969/70 (Sheffield Wednesday) 1970/1, 1971/2, 1972/3, 1973/4.
Rouse, V. (1) (Crystal Palace) 1958/9.
Rowley, T. (1) (Tranmere Rovers) 1958/9.
Rush, I. (42) (Liverpool) 1979/80, 1980/1, 1981/2, 1982/3, 1983/4, 1984/5, 1985/6, 1986/7 (Juventus) 1987/8, (Liverpool) 1988/9.

Saunders, D. (14) (Brighton & Hove Albion) 1985/6, 1986/7 (Oxford United) 1987/8, (Derby County) 1988/9.
Sayer, P. (7) (Cardiff City) 1976/7, 1977/8.
Scrine, F. (2) (Swansea City) 1949/50.
Sear, C. (1) (Manchester City) 1962/3.
Sherwood, A. (41) (Cardiff City) 1946/7, 1947/8, 1948/9, 1949/50, 1950/1, 1951/2, 1952/3, 1953/4, 1954/5, 1955/6, 1956/7 (Newport County).
Shortt, W. (12) (Plymouth Argyle) 1946/7, 1949/50, 1951/2, 1952/3.
Showers, D. (2) (Cardiff City) 1974/5.
Sidlow, C. (7) (Liverpool) 1946/7, 1947/8, 1948/9, 1949/50.
Slatter, N. (22) (Bristol Rovers) 1982/3, 1983/4, 1984/5 (Oxford United) 1985/6, 1986/7, 1987/8, 1988/9.
Smallman, D. (7) (Wrexham) 1973/4 (Everton) 1974/5, 1975/6.
Southall, N. (38) (Everton) 1981/2, 1982/3, 1983/4, 1984/5, 1985/6, 1986/7, 1987/8, 1988/9.
Sprake, G. (37) (Leeds United) 1963/4, 1964/5, 1965/6, 1966/7, 1967/8, 1968/9, 1969/70, 1970/1, 1971/2, 1972/3, 1973/4 (Birmingham City) 1974/5.
Stansfield, F. (1) (Cardiff City) 1948/9.
Stevenson, B. (15) (Leeds United) 1977/8, 1978/9, 1979/80, 1981/2 (Birmingham City).
Stevenson, N. (4) (Swansea City) 1981/2, 1982/3.
Stitfall, R. (2) (Cardiff City) 1952/3, 1956/7.

Sullivan, D. (17) (Cardiff City) 1952/3, 1953/4, 1954/5, 1956/7, 1957/8, 1958/9, 1959/60.

Tapscott, D. (14) (Arsenal) 1953/4, 1954/5, 1955/6, 1956/7, 1958/9 (Cardiff City).
Thomas, D. (2) (Swansea City) 1956/7, 1957/8.
Thomas, M. (51) (Wrexham) 1976/7, 1977/8, 1978/9 (Manchester United) 1979/80, 1980/1, 1981/2 (Everton) (Brighton) 1982/3 (Stoke City) 1983/4, (Chelsea) 1984/5, 1985/6 (West Bromwich Albion).
Thomas, M.R. (1) (Newcastle United) 1986/7.
Thomas, R. (50) (Swindon Town) 1966/7, 1967/8, 1968/9, 1969/70, 1970/1, 1971/2, 1972/3, 1973/4 (Derby County) 1974/5, 1975/6, 1976/7, 1977/8 (Cardiff City).
Thomas, S. (4) (Fulham) 1947/8, 1948/9.
Toshack, J. (40) (Cardiff City) 1968/9, 1969/70 (Liverpool) 1970/1, 1971/2, 1972/3, 1974/5, 1975/6, 1976/7, 1977/8 (Swansea City) 1978/9, 1979/80.

Van den Hauwe, P.W.R. (13) (Everton) 1984/5, 1985/6, 1986/7, 1987/8, 1988/9.
Vaughan, N. (10) (Newport County) 1982/3, 1983/4 (Cardiff City) 1984/5.
Vearncombe, G. (2) (Cardiff City) 1957/8, 1960/1.
Vernon, R. (32) (Blackburn Rovers) 1956/7, 1957/8, 1958/9, 1959/60 (Everton) 1960/1, 1961/2, 1962/3, 1963/4, 1964/5 (Stoke City) 1965/6, 1966/7, 1967/8.
Villars, A. (3) (Cardiff City) 1973/4.

Walley, T. (1) (Watford) 1970/1.
Walsh, I. (18) (Crystal Palace) 1979/80, 1980/1, 1981/2 (Swansea City).
Ward, D. (2) (Bristol Rovers) 1958/9, 1961/2 (Cardiff City).
Webster, C. (4) (Manchester United) 1956/7, 1957/8.
Williams, D.G. (9) 1987/8, (Derby County) 1988/9.
Williams, D.M. (5) (Norwich City) 1985/6, 1986/7.
Williams, G. (1) (Cardiff City) 1950/1.
Williams, G.E. (26) (West Bromwich Albion) 1959/60, 1960/1, 1962/3, 1963/4, 1964/5, 1965/6, 1966/7, 1967/8, 1968/9.
Williams, G.G. (5) (Swansea City) 1960/1, 1961/2.
Williams, H. (4) (Newport County) 1948/9 (Leeds United) 1949/50, 1950/1.
Williams, Herbert (3) (Swansea City) 1964/5, 1970/1.
Williams, S. (43) (West Bromwich Albion) 1953/4, 1954/5, 1955/6, 1957/8, 1958/9, 1959/60, 1960/1, 1961/2, 1962/3 (Southampton) 1963/4, 1964/5, 1965/6.
Witcomb, D. (3) (West Bromwich Albion) 1946/7 (Sheffield Wednesday).
Woosnam, P. (17) (Leyton Orient) 1958/9 (West Ham United) 1959/60, 1960/1, 1961/2, 1962/3 (Aston Villa).

Yorath, T. (59) (Leeds United) 1969/70, 1970/1, 1971/2, 1972/3, 1973/4, 1974/5, 1975/6 (Coventry City) 1976/7, 1977/8, 1978/9 (Tottenham Hotspur) 1979/80, 1980/1.

EIRE

Aherne, T. (16) (Belfast Celtic) 1945/6 (Luton Town) 1949/50, 1950/1, 1951/2, 1952/3, 1953/4.
Aldridge, J.W. (25) (Oxford United) 1985/6, 1986/7 (Liverpool) 1987/8, 1988/9.
Ambrose, P. (5) (Shamrock Rovers) 1954/5, 1963/4.
Anderson, J. (16) (Preston North End) 1979/80, 1981/2 (Newcastle United) 1983/4, 1985/6, 1986/7, 1987/8, 1988/9.

Bailham, E. (1) (Shamrock Rovers) 1963/4.
Barber, E. (2) (Shelbourne) 1965/6 (Birmingham City) 1965/6.
Beglin, J. (15) (Liverpool) 1983/4, 1984/5, 1985/6, 1986/7.
Bonner, P. (32) (Celtic) 1980/1, 1981/2, 1983/4, 1984/5, 1985/6, 1986/7, 1987/8, 1988/9.
Braddish, S. (1) (Dundalk) 1977/8.
Brady, T.R. (6) (QPR) 1963/4.
Brady, W.L. (70) (Arsenal) 1974/5, 1975/6, 1976/7, 1977/8, 1978/9, 1979/80, (Juventus) 1980/1, 1981/2 (Sampdoria) 1982/3, 1983/4 (Internazionale) 1984/5, 1985/6 (Ascoli) 1986/7 (West Ham United) 1987/8, 1988/9.
Breen, T. (3) (Shamrock Rovers) 1946/7.
Brennan, F. (1) (Drumcondra) 1964/5.
Brennan, S.A. (19) (Manchester United) 1964/5, 1965/6, 1966/7, 1968/9, 1969/70 (Waterford) 1970/1.
Browne, W. (3) (Bohemians) 1963/4.
Buckley, L. (2) (Shamrock Rovers) 1983/4 (Waregem) 1984/5.
Burke, F. (1) (Cork Athletic) 1951/2.
Byrne, A.B. (14) (Southampton) 1969/70, 1970/1, 1972/3, 1973/4.
Byrne, J. (14) (QPR) 1984/5, 1986/7, 1987/8.
Byrne, P. (9) (Shamrock Rovers) 1983/4, 1984/5, 1985/6.

Campbell, A. (3) (Santander) 1984/5.
Campbell, N. (11) (St Patrick's Athletic) 1970/1 (Fortuna Cologne) 1971/2, 1972/3, 1974/5, 1975/6.
Cantwell, N. (36) (West Ham United) 1953/4, 1955/6, 1956/7, 1957/8, 1958/9, 1959/60, 1960/1 (Manchester Untied) 1960/1, 1961/2, 1962/3, 1963/4, 1964/5, 1965/6, 1966/7.
Carey, J.J. (21) (Manchester United) 1945/6, 1946/7, 1947/8, 1948/9, 1949/50, 1950/1, 1952/3.
Carolan, J. (2) (Manchester United) 1959/60.
Carroll, B. (2) (Shelbourne) 1948/9, 1949/50.
Carroll, T.R. (17) (Ipswich Town) 1967/8, 1968/9, 1969/70, 1970/1 (Birmingham City) 1971/2, 1972/3.
Cascarino, A.G. (15) (Gillingham) 1985/6 (Millwall) 1987/8, 1988/9.
Chandler, J. (2) (Leeds United) 1979/80.
Clarke, J. (1) (Drogheda United) 1977/8.
Clarke, K. (2) (Drumcondra) 1947/8.
Clarke, M. (1) (Shamrock Rovers) 1949/50.
Clinton, T.J. (3) (Everton) 1950/1, 1953/4.
Coad, P. (11) (Shamrock Rovers) 1946/7, 1947/8, 1948/9, 1950/1, 1951/2.
Coffey, T. (1) (Drumcondra) 1949/50.
Colfer, M.D. (2) (Shelbourne) 1949/50, 1950/1.
Conmy, O.M. (5) (Peterborough United) 1964/5, 1966/7, 1967/8, 1969/70.
Conroy, G.A. (27) (Stoke City) 1969/70, 1970/1, 1972/3, 1973/4, 1974/5, 1975/6, 1976/7.
Conway, J.P. (20) (Fulham) 1966/7, 1967/8, 1968/9, 1969/70, 1970/1, 1973/4, 1974/5, 1975/6 (Manchester City) 1976/7.
Corr, P.J. (4) (Everton) 1948/9.
Courtney, E. (1) (Cork United) 1945/6.
Cummins, G.P. (19) (Luton Town) 1953/4, 1954/5, 1955/6, 1957/8, 1958/9, 1959/60, 1960/1.
Cuneen, T. (1) (Limerick) 1950/1.
Curtis, D.P. (17) (Shelbourne) 1956/7 (Bristol City) 1956/7, 1957/8, (Ipswich Town) 1958/9, 1959/60, 1960/1, 1961/2, 1962/3 (Exeter City) 1963/4.
Cusack, S. (1) (Limerick) 1952/3.

Daly, G.A. (47) (Manchester United) 1972/3, 1973/4, 1974/5, 1976/7 (Derby County) 1977/8, 1978/9, 1979/80 (Coventry City) 1980/1, 1981/2, 1982/3, 1983/4 (Birmingham City) 1984/5, 1985/6 (Shrewsbury Town) 1986/7.
Daly, M. (2) (Wolverhampton Wanderers) 1977/8.

Daly. P. (1) (Shamrock Rovers) 1949/50.
De Mange, K.J.P.P. (2) (Liverpool) 1986/7, (Hull City) 1988/9.
Deacy, E. (4) (Aston Villa) 1981/2.
Dempsey, J.T. (19) (Fulham) 1966/7, 1967/8, 1968/9 (Chelsea) 1968/9,
1969/70, 1970/1, 1971/2.
Dennehy, J. (11) (Cork Hibernian) 1971/2 (Nottingham Forest) 1972/3, 1973/4,
1974/5 (Walsall) 1975/6, 1976/7.
Desmond, P. (4) (Middlesbrough) 1949/50.
Devine, J. (12) (Arsenal) 1979/80, 1980/1, 1981/2, 1982/3 (Norwich City)
1983/4, 1984/5.
Donovan, D.C. (5) (Everton) 1954/5, 1956/7.
Donovan, T. (1) (Aston Villa) 1979/80.
Doyle, C. (1) (Shelbourne) 1958/9.
Duffy, B. (1) (Shamrock Rovers) 1949/50.
Dunne, A.P. (33) (Manchester United) 1961/2, 1962/3, 1963/4, 1964/5,
1965/6, 1966/7, 1968/9, 1969/70, 1970/1 (Bolton Wanderers) 1973/4,
1974/5, 1975/6.
Dunne, J.C. (1) (Fulham) 1970/1.
Dunne, P.A.J. (5) (Manchester United) 1964/5, 1965/6, 1966/7.
Dunne, S. (15) (Luton Town) 1952/3, 1953/4, 1955/6, 1956/7, 1957/8,
1958/9, 1959/60.
Dunne, T. (3) (St Patrick's Athletic) 1955/6, 1956/7.
Dunning, P. (2) (Shelbourne) 1970/1.
Dunphy, E.M. (23) (York City) 1965/6 (Millwall) 1965/6, 1966/7, 1967/8,
1968/9, 1969/70, 1970/1.
Dwyer, N.M. (14) (West Ham United) 1959/60 (Swansea Town) 1960/1, 1961/2,
1963/4, 1964/5.

Eccles, P. (1) (Shamrock Rovers) 1985/6.
Eglington, T.J. (24) (Shamrock Rovers) 1945/6 (Everton) 1946/7, 1947/8,
1948/9, 1950/1, 1951/2, 1952/3, 1953/4, 1954/5, 1955/6.

Fagan, E. (1) (Shamrock Rovers) 1972/3.
Fagan, F. (8) (Manchester City) 1954/5, 1959/60 (Derby County) 1959/60,
1960/1.
Fairclough, M. (2) (Dundalk) 1981/2.
Fallon, S. (8) (Celtic) 1950/1, 1951/2, 1952/3, 1954/5.
Farrell, P.D. (28) (Shamrock Rovers) 1945/6 (Everton) 1946/7, 1947/8, 1948/9,
1949/50, 1950/1, 1951/2, 1952/3, 1953/4, 1954/5, 1955/6, 1956/7.
Finucane, A. (11) (Limerick) 1966/7, 1968/9, 1969/70, 1970/1, 1971/2.
Fitzgerald, F.J. (2) (Waterford) 1954/5, 1955/6.
Fitzgerald, P.J. (5) (Leeds United) 1960/1, 1961/2.
Fitzpatrick, K. (1) (Limerick) 1969/70.
Fitzsimons, A.G. (26) (Middlesbrough) 1949/50, 1951/2, 1952/3, 1953/4,
1954/5, 1955/6, 1956/7, 1957/8, 1958/9 (Lincoln City) 1958/9.
Fogarty, A. (11) (Sunderland) 1959/60, 1960/1, 1961/2, 1962/3, 1963/4,
(Hartlepool United) 1963/4.
Foley, T.C. (9) (Northampton Town) 1963/4, 1964/5, 1965/6, 1966/7.
Fullam, J. (11) (Preston North End) 1960/1 (Shamrock Rovers) 1963/4, 1965/6,
1967/8, 1968/9, 1969/70.

Gallagher, C. (2) (Celtic) 1966/7.
Gallagher, M. (1) (Hibernian) 1953/4.
Galvin, A. (28) (Tottenham Hotspur) 1982/3, 1983/4, 1984/5, 1985/6, 1986/7,
(Sheffield Wednesday) 1987/8, 1988/9.
Gannon, E. (14) (Notts County) 1948/9 (Sheffield Wednesday) 1948/9, 1949/50,
1950/1, 1951/2, 1953/4, 1954/5 (Shelbourne) 1954/5.
Gannon, M. (1) (Shelbourne) 1971/2.
Gavin, J.T. (7) (Norwich City) 1949/50, 1952/3, 1953/4 (Tottenham Hotspur)
1954/5 (Norwich City) 1956/7.
Gibbons, A. (4) (St Patrick's Athletic) 1951/2, 1953/4, 1955/6.

Gilbert, R. (1) (Shamrock Rovers) 1965/6.
Giles, C. (1) (Doncaster Rovers) 1950/1.
Giles, M.J. (60) (Manchester United) 1959/60, 1960/1, 1961/2, 1962/3 (Leeds United) 1963/4, 1964/5, 1965/6, 1966/7, 1968/9, 1969/70, 1970/1, 1972/3, 1973/4, 1974/5 (West Bromwich Albion) 1975/6, 1976/7 (Shamrock Rovers) 1977/8, 1978/9.
Givens, D.J. (56) (Manchester United) 1968/9, 1969/70 (Luton Town) 1969/70, 1970/1, 1971/2 (QPR) 1972/3, 1973/4, 1974/5, 1975/6, 1976/7, 1977/8 (Birmingham City) 1978/9, 1979/80, 1980/1 (Neuchatel Xamax) 1981/2.
Glynn, D. (2) (Drumcondra) 1951/2, 1954/5.
Godwin, T.F. (13) (Shamrock Rovers) 1948/9, 1949/50 (Leicester City) 1949/50, 1950/1 (Bournemouth) 1955/6, 1956/7, 1957/8.
Gorman, W.C. (2) (Brentford) 1946/7.
Grealish, A. (44) (Orient) 1975/6, 1978/9 (Luton Town) 1979/80, 1980/1, (Brighton & Hove Albion) 1981/2, 1982/3, 1983/4 (West Bromwich Albion) 1984/5, 1985/6.
Gregg, E. (9) (Bohemians) 1977/8, 1978/9, 1979/80.
Grimes, A.A. (17) (Manchester United) 1977/8, 1979/80, 1980/1, 1981/2, 1982/3 (Coventry City) 1983/4 (Luton Town) 1987/8.

Hale, A. (13) (Aston Villa) 1961/2 (Doncaster Rovers) 1962/3, 1963/4, (Waterford) 1966/7, 1967/8, 1968/9, 1969/70, 1970/1, 1971/2.
Hamilton, T. (2) (Shamrock Rovers) 1958/9.
Hand, E.K. (20) (Portsmouth) 1968/9, 1969/70, 1970/1, 1972/3, 1973/4, 1974/5, 1975/6.
Hartnett, J.B. (2) (Middlesbrough) 1948/9, 1953/4.
Haverty, J. (32) (Arsenal) 1955/6, 1956/7, 1957/8, 1958/9, 1959/60, 1960/1, (Blackburn Rovers) 1961/2 (Millwall) 1962/3, 1963/4 (Celtic) 1964/5 (Bristol Rovers) 1964/5 (Shelbourne) 1965/6, 1966/7.
Hayes, A.W.P. (1) (Southampton) 1978/9.
Hayes, W.E. (2) (Huddersfield Town) 1946/7.
Hayes, W.J. (1) (Limerick) 1948/9.
Healey, R. (2) (Cardiff City) 1976/7, 1979/80.
Heighway, S.D. (34) (Liverpool) 1970/1, 1972/3, 1974/5, 1975/6, 1976/7, 1977/8, 1978/9, 1979/80, 1980/1 (Minnesota Kicks) 1981/2.
Henderson, B. (2) (Drumcondra) 1947/8.
Hennessy, J. (5) (Shelbourne) 1955/6, 1965/6 (St Patrick's Athletic) 1968/9.
Herrick, J. (3) (Cork Hibernians) 1971/2 (Shamrock Rovers) 1972/3.
Higgins, J. (1) (Birmingham City) 1950/1.
Holmes, J. (30) (Coventry City) 1970/1, 1972/3, 1973/4, 1974/5, 1975/6, 1976/7 (Tottenham Hotspur) 1977/8, 1978/9, 1980/1 (Vancouver Whitecaps) 1980/1.
Houghton, R.J. (26) (Oxford United) 1985/6, 1986/7, 1987/8 (Liverpool) 1987/8, 1988/9.
Howlett, G. (1) (Brighton & Hove Albion) 1983/4.
Hughton, C. (45) (Tottenham Hotspur) 1979/80, 1980/1, 1981/2, 1982/3, 1983/4, 1984/5, 1985/6, 1986/7, 1987/8, 1988/9.
Hurley, C.J. (40) (Millwall) 1956/7, 1957/8 (Sunderland) 1958/9, 1959/60, 1960/1, 1961/2, 1962/3, 1963/4, 1964/5, 1965/6, 1966/7, 1967/8 (Bolton Wanderers) 1968/9.

Keane, T.R. (4) (Swansea Town) 1948/9.
Kearin, M. (1) (Shamrock Rovers) 1971/2.
Kearns, F.T. (1) (West Ham United) 1953/4.
Kearns, M. (18) (Oxford United) 1969/70 (Walsall) 1973/4, 1975/6, 1976/7, 1977/8, 1978/9 (Wolverhampton Wanderers) 1979/80.
Kelly, D.T. (4) (Walsall) 1987/8, (West Ham United) 1988/9.
Kelly, J.A. (47) (Drumcondra) 1956/7 (Preston North End) 1961/2, 1962/3, 1963/4, 1964/5, 1965/6, 1966/7, 1967/8, 1969/70, 1970/1, 1971/2, 1972/3.
Kelly, J.P.V. (5) (Wolverhampton Wanderers) 1960/1, 1961/2.
Kelly, M.J. (3) (Portsmouth) 1987/8, 1988/9.

Kelly, N. (1) (Nottingham Forest) 1953/4.
Kennedy, M.F. (2) (Portsmouth) 1985/6.
Keogh, J. (1) (Shamrock Rovers) 1965/6.
Keogh, S. (1) (Shamrock Rovers) 1958/9.
Kiernan, F.W. (5) (Shamrock Rovers) 1950/1 (Southampton) 1951/2.
Kinnear, J.P. (26) (Tottenham Hotspur) 1966/7, 1967/8, 1968/9, 1969/70, 1970/1, 1971/2, 1972/3, 1973/4, 1974/5 (Brighton & Hove Albion) 1975/6.

Langan, D. (25) (Derby County) 1977/8, 1979/80 (Birmingham City) 1980/1, 1981/2 (Oxford United) 1984/5, 1985/6, 1986/7, 1987/8.
Lawler, J.F. (8) (Fulham) 1952/3, 1953/4, 1954/5, 1955/6.
Lawlor, J.C. (3) (Drumcondra) 1948/9 (Doncaster Rovers) 1950/1.
Lawlor, M. (5) (Shamrock Rovers) 1970/1, 1972/3.
Lawrenson, M. (38) (Preston North End) 1976/7 (Brighton & Hove Albion) 1977/8, 1978/9, 1979/80, 1980/1 (Liverpool) 1981/2, 1982/3, 1983/4, 1984/5, 1985/6, 1986/7, 1987/8.
Leech, M. (8) (Shamrock Rovers) 1968/9, 1971/2, 1972/3.
Lowry, D. (1) (St Patrick's Athletic) 1961/2.

McAlinden, J. (2) (Portsmouth) 1945/6.
McCann, J. (1) (Shamrock Rovers) 1956/7.
McCarthy, M. (36) (Manchester City) 1983/4, 1984/5, 1985/6, 1986/7 (Celtic) 1987/8, 1988/9.
McConville, T. (6) (Dundalk) 1971/2 (Waterford) 1972/3.
McDonagh, J. (24) (Everton) 1980/1 (Bolton Wanderers) 1981/2, 1982/3, (Notts County) 1983/4, 1984/5, 1985/6.
McDonagh, Joe (3) (Shamrock Rovers) 1983/4, 1984/5.
McEvoy, M.A. (17) (Blackburn Rovers) 1960/1, 1962/3, 1963/4, 1964/5, 1965/6, 1966/7.
McGee, P. (15) (QPR) 1977/8, 1978/9, 1979/80 (Preston North End) 1980/1.
McGowan, D. (3) (West Ham United) 1948/9.
McGowan, J. (1) (Cork United) 1946/7.
McGrath, M. (22) (Blackburn Rovers) 1957/8, 1958/9, 1959/60, 1960/1, 1961/2, 1962/3, 1963/4, 1964/5, 1965/6 (Bradford Park Avenue) 1965/6, 1966/7.
McGrath, P. (31) (Manchester United) 1984/5, 1985/6, 1986/7, 1987/8, 1988/9.
Macken, A. (1) (Derby County) 1976/7.
Mackey, G. (3) (Shamrock Rovers) 1956/7.
McMillan, W. (2) (Belfast Celtic) 1945/6.
McNally, J.B. (3) (Luton Town) 1958/9, 1960/1, 1962/3.
Malone, G. (1) (Shelbourne) 1948/9.
Mancini, T.J. (5) (QPR) 1973/4 (Arsenal) 1974/5.
Martin, C.J. (30) (Glentoran) 1945/6, 1946/7 (Leeds United) 1946/7, 1947/8, (Aston Villa) 1948/9, 1949/50, 1950/1, 1951/2, 1953/4, 1954/5, 1955/6.
Martin, M.P. (51) (Bohemians) 1971/2, 1972/3 (Manchester United) 1972/3, 1973/4, 1974/5 (West Bromwich Albion) 1975/6, 1976/7 (Newcastle United) 1978/9, 1979/80, 1980/1, 1981/2, 1982/3.
Meagan, M.K. (17) (Everton) 1960/1, 1961/2, 1962/3, 1963/4 (Huddersfield Town) 1964/5, 1965/6, 1966/7, 1967/8 (Drogheda) 1969/70.
Mooney, J. (2) (Shamrock Rovers) 1964/5.
Moran, K. (44) (Manchester United) 1979/80, 1980/1, 1981/2, 1982/3, 1983/4, 1984/5, 1985/6, 1986/7, 1987/8, (Sporting Gijon) 1988/9.
Moroney, T. (12) (West Ham United) 1947/8, 1948/9, 1949/50, 1950/1, 1951/2, 1953/4.
Morris, C.B. (14) (Celtic) 1987/8, 1988/9.
Moulson, G.B. (3) (Lincoln City) 1947/8, 1948/9.
Mucklan, C. (1) (Drogheda) 1977/8.
Mulligan, P.M. (50) (Shamrock Rovers) 1968/9, 1969/70 (Chelsea) 1969/70, 1970/1, 1971/2 (Crystal Palace) 1972/3, 1973/4, 1974/5 (West Bromwich Albion) 1975/6, 1976/7, 1977/8, 1978/9 (Shamrock Rovers) 1979/80.

Munroe, L. (1) (Shamrock Rovers) 1953/4.
Murphy, A. (1) (Clyde) 1955/6.
Murphy, B. (1) (Bohemians) 1985/6.
Murphy, J. (3) (Crystal Palace) 1979/80.
Murray, T. (1) (Dundalk) 1949/50.

Newman, W. (1) (Shelbourne) 1968/9.
Nolan, R. (10) (Shamrock Rovers) 1956/7, 1957/8, 1959/60, 1961/2, 1962/3.

O'Brien, F. (4) (Philadelphia Fury) 1979/80
O'Brien, L. (8) (Shamrock Rovers) 1985/6 (Manchester United) 1986/7, 1987/8, (Newcastle United) 1988/9.
O'Brien, R. (4) (Notts County) 1975/6, 1976/7.
O'Byrne, L.B. (1) (Shamrock Rovers) 1948/9.
O'Callaghan, B.R. (6) (Stoke City) 1978/9, 1979/80, 1980/1, 1981/2.
O'Callaghan, K. (20) (Ipswich Town) 1980/1, 1981/2, 1982/3, 1983/4, 1984/5, (Portsmouth) 1985/6, 1986/7.
O'Connell, A. (2) (Dundalk) 1966/7 (Bohemians) 1970/1.
O'Connor, T. (4) (Shamrock Rovers) 1949/50.
O'Connor, T. (7) (Fulham) 1967/8 (Dundalk) 1971/2 (Bohemians) 1972/3.
O'Driscoll, J.F. (3) (Swansea Town) 1948/9.
O'Driscoll, S. (3) (Fulham) 1981/2.
O'Farrell, F. (9) (West Ham United) 1951/2, 1952/3, 1953/4, 1954/5, 1955/6, (Preston North End) 1957/8, 1958/9.
O'Flanagan, K.P. (3) (Arsenal) 1946/7.
O'Flanagan, M. (1) (Bohemians) 1946/7.
O'Hanlon, K.G. (1) (Rotherham United) 1987/8.
O'Keefe, E. (5) (Everton) 1980/1 (Port Vale) 1983/4.
O'Leary, D. (42) (Arsenal) 1976/7, 1977/8, 1978/9, 1979/80, 1980/1, 1981/2, 1982/3, 1983/4, 1984/5, 1985/6, 1988/9.
O'Leary, P. (7) (Shamrock Rovers) 1979/80, 1980/1.
O'Neill, F.S. (20) (Shamrock Rovers) 1961/2, 1964/5, 1965/6, 1966/7, 1968/9, 1971/2.
O'Neill, J. (17) (Everton) 1951/2, 1952/3, 1953/4, 1954/5, 1955/6, 1956/7, 1957/8, 1958/9.
O'Neill, J. (1) (Preston North End) 1960/1.
O'Regan, K. (4) (Brighton & Hove Albion) 1983/4, 1984/5.
O'Reilly, J. (2) (Cork United) 1945/6.

Peyton, G. (26) (Fulham) 1976/7, 1977/8, 1978/9, 1979/80, 1980/1, 1981/2, 1984/5, 1985/6 (Bournemouth) 1987/8, 1988/9.
Peyton, N. (6) (Shamrock Rovers) 1956/7 (Leeds United) 1959/60, 1960/1, 1962/3.

Quinn, N.J. (12) (Arsenal) 1985/6, 1986/7, 1987/8, 1988/9.

Richardson, D.J. (3) (Shamrock Rovers) 1971/2 (Gillingham) 1972/3, 1979/80.
Ringstead, A. (20) (Sheffield United) 1950/1, 1951/2, 1952/3, 1953/4, 1954/5, 1955/6, 1956/7, 1957/8, 1958/9.
Robinson, M. (23) (Brighton & Hove Albion) 1980/1, 1981/2, 1982/3, (Liverpool) 1983/4, 1984/5 (QPR) 1985/6.
Roche, P.J. (8) (Shelbourne) 1971/2 (Manchester United) 1974/5, 1975/6.
Rogers, E. (19) (Blackburn Rovers) 1967/8, 1968/9, 1969/70, 1970/1, (Charlton Athletic) 1971/2, 1972/3.
Ryan, G. (16) (Derby County) 1977/8 (Brighton & Hove Albion) 1978/9, 1979/80, 1980/1, 1981/2, 1983/4, 1984/5.
Ryan R.A. (16) (West Bromwich Albion) 1949/50, 1950/1, 1951/2, 1952/3, 1953/4, 1954/5 (Derby County) 1955/6.

Saward, P. (18) (Millwall) 1953/4 (Aston Villa) 1956/7, 1957/8, 1958/9, 1959/60, 1960/1 (Huddersfield Town) 1960/1, 1961/2, 1962/3.

Scannell, T. (1) (Southend United) 1953/4.
Scully, P.J. (1) (Arsenal) 1988/9.
Sheedy, K. (21) (Everton) 1983/4, 1984/5, 1985/6, 1986/7, 1987/8, 1988/9.
Sheridan, J.J. (5) (Leeds United) 1987/8, 1988/9.
Sloan, J.W. (2) (Arsenal) 1945/6.
Smyth, M. (1) (Shamrock Rovers) 1968/9.
Stapleton, F. (68) (Arsenal) 1976/7, 1977/8, 1978/9, 1979/80, 1980/1
(Manchester United) 1981/2, 1982/3, 1983/4, 1984/5, 1985/6, 1986/7 (Ajax)
1987/8 (Derby County) 1987/8, (Le Havre) 1988/9.
Staunton, S. (5) (Liverpool) 1988/9.
Stevenson, A.E. (6) (Everton) 1946/7, 1947/8, 1948/9.
Strahan, F. (5) (Shelbourne) 1963/4, 1964/5, 1965/6.
Swan, M.M.G. (1) (Drumcondra) 1959/60.
Synott, N. (3) (Shamrock Rovers) 1977/8, 1978/9.

Thomas, P. (2) (Waterford) 1973/4.
Townsend, A.D. (4) (Norwich City) 1988/9.
Traynor, T.J. (8) (Southampton) 1953/4, 1961/2, 1962/3, 1963/4.
Treacy, R.C.P. (43) (West Bromwich Albion) 1965/6, 1966/7, 1967/8 (Charlton
Athletic) 1967/8, 1968/9, 1969/70, 1970/1 (Swindon Town) 1971/2, 1972/3,
1973/4 (Preston North End) 1973/4, 1974/5, 1975/6 (West Bromwich Albion)
1976/7, 1977/8 (Shamrock Rovers) 1979/80.
Tuohy, L. (8) (Shamrock Rovers) 1955/6, 1958/9 (Newcastle United) 1961/2,
1962/3 (Shamrock Rovers) 1963/4, 1964/5.
Turner, A. (2) (Celtic) 1962/3, 1963/4.

Vernon, J. (2) (Belfast Celtic) 1945/6.

Waddock, G. (18) (QPR) 1979/80, 1980/1, 1981/2, 1982/3, 1983/4, 1984/5,
1985/6.
Walsh, D.J. (20) (West Bromwich Albion) 1945/6, 1946/7, 1947/8, 1948/9,
1949/50, 1950/1 (Aston Villa) 1951/2, 1952/3, 1953/4.
Walsh, J. (1) (Limerick) 1981/2.
Walsh, M. (22) (Blackpool) 1975/6, 1976/7 (Everton) 1978/9 (QPR) 1978/9
(Porto) 1980/1, 1981/2, 1982/3, 1983/4, 1984/5.
Walsh, M. (5) (Everton) 1981/2, 1982/3 (Norwich City) 1982/3.
Walsh, W. (9) (Manchester City) 1946/7, 1947/8, 1948/9, 1949/50.
Waters, J. (2) (Grimsby Town) 1976/7, 1979/80.
Whelan, R. (2) (St Patrick's Athletic) 1963/4.
Whelan, R. (34) (Liverpool) 1980/1, 1981/2, 1982/3, 1983/4, 1984/5, 1985/6,
1986/7, 1987/8, 1988/9.
Whelan, W. (4) (Manchester United) 1955/6, 1956/7.
Whittaker, R. (1) (Chelsea) 1958/9.

BRITISH ISLES INTERNATIONAL GOALSCORERS SINCE 1946

ENGLAND

A'Court, A 1
Adams, T.A 4
Allen, R 2
Anderson, V 2
Astall, G 1
Atyeo, P.J.W 5

Baily, E.F. 5
Baker, J.H 3
Ball, A.J 8
Barnes, J 9
Barnes, P.S 4
Beardsley, P.A 7
Beattie, T.K 1
Bell, C 9
Bentley, R.T.F 9
Blissett, L 3
Bowles, S 1
Bradford, G.R.W 1
Bradley, W 2
Bridges, B.J 1
Broadbent, P.F 2
Broadis, I.A 8
Brooking, T.D 5
Brooks, J 2
Bull, S 1
Butcher, T 3
Byrne, J.J 8

Carter, H.S 7
(inc. 2 scored pre-war)
Chamberlain, M 1
Channon, M.R 21
Charlton, J 6
Charlton, R 49
Chivers, M 13
Clarke, A.J 10
Connelly, J.M 7
Coppell, S.J 7
Cowans, G 2
Crawford, R 1
Currie, A.W 3

Dixon, K.M 4
Douglas, B 11

Eastham, G 2
Edwards, D 5
Elliot, W.H 3

Finney, T 30
Flowers, R 10
Francis, G.C.J 3
Francis, T 12
Froggatt, J 2
Froggatt, R 2

Gascoigne, P 1
Goddard, P 1
Grainger, C 3
Greaves, J 44

Haines, J.T.W 2
Hancocks, J 2
Hassall, H.W 4
Hateley, M 9
Haynes, J.N 18
Hitchens, G.A 5
Hoddle, G 8
Hughes, E.W 1
Hunt, R 18
Hunter, N 2
Hurst, G.C 24

Johnson, D.E 6

Kay, A.H 1
Keegan, J.K 21
Kennedy, R 3
Kevan, D.T 8
Kidd, B 1

Langton, R 1
Latchford, R.D 5
Lawler, C 1
Lawler, T 22
(inc. 6 scored pre-war)
Lee, F 10
Lee, J 1
Lee, S 2
Lineker, G 29
Lofthouse, N 30

Mabbutt, G 1
McDermott, T 3
Macdonald, M 6
Mannion, W.J 11
Mariner, P 13
Marsh, R.W 1

216

Matthews, S 11
(inc. 8 scored pre-war)
Medley, L.D 1
Melia, J........................1
Milburn, J.E.T 10
Moore, R.F.....................2
Morris, J 3
Mortensen, S.H 23
Mullen, J......................6
Mullery, A.P 1

Neal, P.G 5
Nicholls, J.....................1
Nicholson, W.E 1

O'Grady, M 3
Own goals....................15

Paine, T.L 7
Parry, R.A.....................1
Peacock, A 3
Pearson, J.S 5
Pearson, S.C 5
Perry, W 2
Peters, M.....................20
Pickering, F 5
Pointer, R.....................2

Ramsey, A.E 3
Revie, D.G 4
Robson, B 24
Robson, R 4
Rowley, J.F 6
Royle, J 2

Sansom, K 1
Sewell, J.......................3
Shackleton, L.F 1
Smith, R......................13
Steven, T.M....................3
Stiles, N.P 13
Summerbee, M.G 1

Tambling, R.V 1
Taylor, P.J.....................2
Taylor, T......................16
Thompson, P.B 1
Tueart, D 2

Viollet, D.S 1

Waddle, C.R...................6
Wallace, D.L 1
Walsh, P.......................1
Watson, D.V...................4
Webb, N 3
Weller, K 1

Wignall, F......................2
Wilkins, R.G...................3
Wilshaw, D.J 10
Withe, P.......................1
Woodcock, T 16
Worthington, F.S 2
Wright, W.A 3

SCOTLAND

Aitken, R 1
Archibald, S...................4

Baird, S.......................2
Bannon, E 1
Bauld, W 2
Baxter, J.C 3
Bett, J..........................1
Bone, J 1
Brand, R 8
Brazil, A 1
Bremner, W.J 3
Brown, A.D....................6
Buckley, P 1
Burns, K 1

Caldow, E 4
Campbell, R 1
Chalmers, S 3
Collins, J.......................1
Collins, R.V...................10
Combe, J.R 1
Conn, A 1
Cooper, D 6
Craig, J 1
Curran, H.P....................1

Dalglish, K 30
Davidson, J.A 1
Docherty, T.H.................1
Dodds, D 1
Duncan, D.M...................1

Fernie, W 1
Flavell, R 2
Fleming, C 2

Gemmell, T. *(St Mirren)* ...1
Gemmell, T. *(Celtic)*.........1
Gemmill, A.....................8
Gibson, D.W 3
Gilzean, A.J 10
Gough, C.R 5
Graham, A 2
Graham, G 3

WALES

NORTHERN IRELAND

Doherty, L.........................1
Doherty, P.D 3
(inc. 1 scored pre-war)
Dougan, A.D 8

Elder, A.R 1

Ferguson, W 1
Ferris, R.O 1
Finney, T.........................2

Hamilton, B 4
Hamilton, W 5
Harkin, J.T.......................2
Harvey, M........................3
Hughes, L.M.....................1
Humphries, W 1
Hunter, A.........................1

Irvine, W.J 8

Johnston, W.C 1
Jones, J............................1

Lockhart, N 3

McAdams, W.J..................7
McClelland, J 1
McCrory, S 1
McCurdy, C 1
McDonald, A 1
McGarry, J.K....................1
McGrath, R.C 4
McIlroy, J.......................10
McIlroy, S.B 5
McLaughlin, J.C 6
McMordie, A.S 3
McMorran, E.J 4
McParland, P.J 10
Moreland, V 1
Morgan, S.........................3

Neill, W.J.T 2
Nelson, S..........................1
Nicholl, C.J......................3
Nicholl, J.M.....................2
Nicholson, J.J...................6

O'Kane, W.J.....................1
O'Neill, J..........................1
O'Neill, M 1
O'Neill, M.H 8
Own goals.........................4

Peacock, R 2
Penney, S 2

Quinn, J.M.......................5

Simpson, W.J 5
Smyth, S...........................5
Spence, D.W.....................3
Stewart, I 2

Tully, C.P........................3

Walker, J..........................1
Walsh, D.J........................5
Welsh, E 1
Whiteside, N 8
Wilson, D..........................1
Wilson, S.J 7

EIRE

Aldridge, J........................1
Ambrose, P.......................1
Anderson, J 1

Bermingham, P.................1
Bradshaw, P.....................4
Brady, L............................9
Brown, D 1
Byrne, J. (Bray) 1
Byrne, J. (QPR) 2

Cantwell, J......................14
Carey, J 3
Carroll, T 1
Cascarino, A 4
Coad, P.............................3
Conroy, T.........................2
Conway, J.........................3
Cummings, G 5
Curtis, D 8

Daly, G............................13
Davis, T 4
Dempsey, J.......................1
Dennehy, M......................2
Donnelly, J 3
Donnelly, T 1
Duffy, B............................1
Duggan, H........................1
Dunne, J 12
Dunne, L...........................1

Eglinton, T 2
Ellis, P 1

Fagan, F............................5
Fallon, S............................2
Fallon W 2
Farrell, P...........................3
Fitzgerald, P 2
Fitzgerald, J 1

7th UEFA UNDER-21 TOURNAMENT 1988–90

Group 1 (*Bulgaria, Denmark, Greece, Rumania*)
Greece (1) 2, Denmark (1) 2; Bulgaria (1) 2, Rumania (1) 1; Denmark (0) 1, Bulgaria (0) 3; Rumania (1) 2, Greece (0) 0; Bulgaria (2) 6, Denmark (0) 0; Greece (0) 1, Rumania (0) 0; Denmark (0) 3, Greece (0) 0; Rumania (2) 2, Bulgaria (1) 1.
Remaining fixtures: 10.10.89 Denmark v Rumania, Bulgaria v Greece; 14.11.89 Rumania v Denmark, Greece v Bulgaria.

Group 2 (*Albania, England, Poland, Sweden*)
England (1) 1, Sweden (0) 1; Poland (0) 0, Albania (0) 0; Albania (0) 0, Sweden (1) 2; Albania (1) 1, England (0) 2; England (1) 2, Albania (0) 0; Sweden (1) 4, Poland (0) 0; England (2) 2, Poland (0) 1.
Remaining fixtures: 5.9.89 Sweden v England; 7.10.89 Sweden v Albania; 10.10.89 Poland v England; 24.10.89 Poland v Sweden; 14.11.89 Albania v Poland.

Group 3 (*Austria, East Germany, Turkey, USSR*)
USSR (1) 2, Austria (2) 2; Austria (2) 3, Turkey (0) 0; Turkey (2) 3, East Germany (2) 2; East Germany (0) 0, Turkey (0) 0; USSR (0) 1, East Germany (0) 0; Turkey (0) 0, USSR (2) 3; East Germany (0) 2; Austria (0) 0.
Remaining fixtures: 5.9.89 Austria v USSR; 6.10.89 East Germany v USSR; 24.10.89 Turkey v Austria; 7.11.89 USSR v Turkey; 14.11.89 Austria v East Germany.

Group 4 (*Finland, Holland, Iceland, West Germany*)
Finland (0) 0, West Germany (2) 3; Iceland (0) 1, Holland (1) 1; Finland (0) 2, Iceland (1) 1; West Germany (0) 2, Holland (0) 0; Holland (0) 0, West Germany (1) 1; Finland (1) 1, Holland (1) 1; Iceland (0) 1, West Germany (0) 1.
Remaining fixtures: 5.9.89 Iceland v Finland; 3.10.89 West Germany v Finland; 10.10.89 Holland v Iceland; 25.10.89 West Germany v Iceland; 14.11.89 Holland v Finland.

Group 5 (*France, Norway, Scotland, Yugoslavia*)
Norway (0) 1, Scotland (1) 1; France (1) 2, Norway (0) 0; Scotland (0) 0, Yugoslavia (0) 2; Yugoslavia (1) 2, France (1) 2; Scotland (1) 2, France (0) 3; France (0) 0, Yugoslavia (0) 1; Norway (0) 0, Yugoslavia (0) 1.
Remaining fixtures: 5.9.89 Norway v France, Yugoslavia v Scotland; 10.10.89 Yugoslavia v Norway, France v Scotland; 14.11.89 Scotland v Norway.

Group 6 (*Cyprus, Hungary, Spain*)
Cyprus (0) 0, Hungary (0) 0; Cyprus (0) 0, Spain (0) 1; Hungary (1) 1, Cyprus (0) 0; Spain (0) 1, Cyprus (0).
Remaining fixtures: 10.10.89 Hungary v Spain; 14.11.89 Spain v Hungary.

Group 7 (*Belgium, Czechoslovakia, Luxembourg, Portugal*)
Czechoslovakia (0) 0, Belgium (2) 3; Portugal (0) 1, Belgium (1) 1; Czechoslovakia (2) 4, Luxembourg (0) 0; Portugal (0) 1, Luxembourg (0) 0; Belgium (1) 1, Czechoslovakia (0) 1; Luxembourg (0) 0, Belgium (0) 0.
Remaining fixtures: 5.9.89 Belgium v Portugal; 5.10.89 Czechoslovakia v Portugal; 9.10.89 Luxembourg v Portugal; 24.10.89 Belgium v Luxembourg; 14.11.89 Portugal v Czechoslovakia; 29.11.89 Luxembourg v Czechoslovakia.

Group 8 (*Italy, San Marino, Switzerland*)
Switzerland (0) 0, Italy (0) 0; San Marino (0) 0, Switzerland (2) 5.
Remaining fixtures: 4.10.89 San Marino v Italy; 25.10.89 Italy v Switzerland; 14.11.89 Switzerland v San Marino; 29.11.89 Italy v San Marino.

6th UEFA Under-21 Tournament
Final (*second leg*)
France (1) 3, Greece (0) 0
(*France won 3–0 on aggregate*)

7th UEFA UNDER-18 CHAMPIONSHIP 1988–90

Group 1 (*Poland, Scotland, Sweden, West Germany*)
Scotland (0) 0, Sweden (0) 0; Scotland (0) 1, Poland (2) 2; West Germany (0) 0, Poland (0) 0; West Germany 0, Scotland 0; Sweden 0, West Germany 0; Sweden 0, Poland 0.
Remaining fixtures: 30.8.89 Poland v Scotland; 20.9.89 Sweden v Scotland; 27.9.89 Poland v West Germany; 17.10.89 Poland v Sweden 18.10.89 Scotland v West Germany; 1.11.89 West Germany v Sweden.

Group 2 (*Cyprus, Holland, Norway, USSR*)
Norway (1) 2, Holland (0) 2; Cyprus (0) 0, Norway (0) 0; Holland (2) 2, Cyprus (0) 1; USSR 0, Cyprus 0; Norway 0, Cyprus 0; Norway 0, USSR 0.
Remaining fixtures: 6.9.89 USSR v Norway; 4.10.89 Holland v Norway; 25.10.89 Holland v USSR; 19.11.89 Cyprus v USSR; 29.11.89 USSR v Holland; 6.12.89 Cyprus v Holland.

Group 3 (*Czechoslovakia, England, France, Greece*)
England (1) 5, Greece (0) 0; England (0) 1, France (1) 1; Greece (1) 2, France (3) 3; Greece (0) 0, England (2) 3; Czechoslovakia (0) 0, Greece (0) 0; Czechoslovakia 0, England 0; France 0, Czechoslovakia 0.
Remaining fixtures: 11.10.89 France v England; Greece v Czechoslovakia; 28.10.89 Czechoslovakia v France; 14.11.89 England v Czechoslovakia; 29.11.89 France v Greece.

Group 4 (*Albania, Italy, Portugal, Switzerland*)
Albania (0) 4, Switzerland (0) 0; Portugal (2) 2, Albania (0) 1; Albania (0) 1, Italy (2) 2; Switzerland (0) 0, Portugal (3) 3; Albania (0) 0, Portugal (1) 2; Switzerland 0, Italy 0.
Remaining fixtures: 11.10.89 Portugal v Switzerland, Italy v Albania; 1.11.89 Italy v Portugal; 7.11.89 Switzerland v Albania; 22.11.89. Italy v Switzerland; 6.12 89 Portugal v Italy.

Group 5 (*Belgium, Wales, East Germany, Yugoslavia*)
East Germany (0) 0, Yugoslavia (1) 1; Belgium (1) 1, East Germany (1) 1; Yugoslavia (2) 4, Wales (1) 1; Wales (0) 2, Belgium (0) 0; Belgium (2) 2, Yugoslavia (0) 1; Wales (0) 0, East Germany (0) 0; East Germany 0, Belgium 0.
Remaining fixtures: 20.9.89 Yugoslavia v East Germany; 4.10.89 Yugoslavia v Belgium; 17.10.89 Belgium v Wales; 19.10.89 East Germany v Wales; 8.11.89 Wales v Yugoslavia.

Group 6 *(Bulgaria, Eire, Malta, Iceland (withdrew))*
Malta (1) 1, Bulgaria (1) 2; Eire 0, Malta 0.
Remaining fixtures: 4.10.89 Bulgaria v Malta; 31.10.89 Eire v Bulgaria; 14.11.89 Malta
v Eire; 28.11.89 Bulgaria v Eire.

Group 7 *(Austria, Denmark, Rumania, Spain)*
Spain (1) 4, Denmark (0) 2; Austria (0) 1, Spain (0) 2; Austria 0, Rumania 0; Denmark
0, Spain 0; Rumania 0, Spain 0.
Remaining fixtures: 6.9.89 Denmark v Rumania; 20.9.89 Denmark v Austria; 4.10.89
Spain v Rumania; 18.10.89 Austria v Denmark; 1.11.89 Rumania v Austria; 14.11.89
Rumania v Denmark; 22.11.89 Spain v Austria.

Group 8 *(Finland, Hungary, Luxembourg, Turkey)*
Finland (0) 0, Hungary (0) 1; Luxembourg (0) 0, Finland (3) 5; Turkey (2) 3, Luxem-
bourg (0) 1; Hungary 0, Luxembourg 0; Hungary 0, Finland 0; Finland 0, Turkey 0.
Remaining fixtures: 3.9.89 Turkey v Finland; 4.10.89 Finland v Luxembourg; 7.10.89
Hungary v Turkey; 18.10.89 Luxembourg v Hungary; 5.11.89 Turkey v Hungary;
29.11.89 Luxembourg v Turkey.

6th UEFA Under-18 Championship
(final stages in Czechoslovakia July 1988)
Quarter-finals: Spain 1, Czechoslovakia 0; East Germany 2, Denmark 0; Portugal 3,
Holland 0; USSR 4, Norway 2.

Semi-finals: USSR 3, East Germany 0; Portugal 2, Spain 0.

Final: USSR 3, Portugal 1 aet

Third place: East Germany 2, Spain 0

Fifth place: Czechoslovakia 1, Holland 0; Norway 1, Denmark 1 *(Norway won 5–4 on
penalties)*.

Final placings: 1. USSR 2. Portugal 3. East Germany 4. Spain 5. Czechoslovakia and
Norway 7. Denmark and Holland

Two penetrating studies of the world of football from Queen Anne Press:

THE FOOTBALL MANAGERS

Johnny Rogan's provocative book looks at the development of football management since the War, concentrating on ten of the most successful managers of the period and analysing the way they excelled where so many others have failed.
On sale from 7 September at £11.95

THE SECRET LIFE OF FOOTBALL

What are the main reasons for falling standards and declining attendances in English soccer – is it the failure of the footballing authorities and administrators to react to the changes in the game? In *The Secret Life of Football* Alex Fynn and Lynton Guest reveal how England is in danger of becoming a footballing backwater if the lessons learned by the rest of the world are not heeded.
On sale from 9 November at £11.95

Available through bookshops or in case of difficulty direct from Sale Administration Dept, Queen Anne Press, Headway House, 66-73 Shoe Lane, London EC4P 4AB. Allow £2.20 p&p per copy and 28 days for delivery.

Macdonald Queen Anne Press

a member of Maxwell Pergamon Publishing Corporation plc

GM VAUXHALL CONFERENCE

	Altrincham	Aylesbury U	Barnet	Boston U	Cheltenham T	Chorley	Enfield	Fisher Ath	Kettering T	Kidderminster H	Macclesfield T	Maidstone U	Northwich Vic	Runcorn	Stafford Rangers	Sutton U	Telford U	Welling U	Weymouth	Wycombe W	Yeovil T
Altrincham	—	1-0	1-1	0-0	0-1	1-2	1-1	1-1	1-2	3-1	1-2	0-1	2-2	1-2	2-1	1-0	0-2	3-0	2-1	2-2	2-2
Aylesbury U	1-2	—	1-3	0-2	0-3	4-3	1-1	1-1	2-1	1-5	1-2	1-2	2-0	1-2	1-1	1-1	2-2	0-3	1-4	2-2	3-2
Barnet	3-0	2-0	—	1-1	0-1	2-4	2-3	2-4	2-3	0-2	1-3	1-1	2-2	1-3	1-2	1-1	1-2	2-2	4-1	0-1	2-0
Boston U	3-1	0-0	5-0	—	1-1	2-2	2-2	2-2	2-2	2-1	1-0	2-3	1-1	2-2	1-2	2-3	1-0	2-3	1-0	0-1	1-1
Cheltenham T	2-1	2-2	2-3	1-2	—	2-2	2-1	2-1	1-0	2-1	3-0	4-1	1-4	0-3	3-4	2-3	1-1	1-1	1-0	3-1	1-2
Chorley	1-0	4-3	4-2	1-1	3-4	—	1-2	2-2	2-1	0-4	3-0	1-2	2-1	0-3	4-1	1-1	2-1	1-1	3-1	3-1	2-3
Enfield	2-1	1-1	3-1	2-2	1-2	2-2	—	2-1	1-1	2-2	2-1	2-1	2-1	2-1	0-1	1-1	3-1	1-2	3-0	3-0	4-2
Fisher Ath	1-1	0-2	2-1	0-1	1-3	0-2	2-2	—	0-3	1-1	3-1	2-0	1-2	3-2	2-1	1-1	1-2	1-1	1-0	0-3	0-1
Kettering T	0-1	5-2	1-0	1-2	4-0	0-3	2-0	2-2	—	1-2	3-0	3-1	2-1	2-2	2-1	1-1	4-1	0-1	2-1	3-0	1-2
Kidderminster H	2-3	4-3	2-2	3-2	2-2	0-2	1-3	2-0	1-3	—	1-3	2-2	3-1	2-0	3-1	1-1	0-1	1-0	1-1	3-0	1-3
Macclesfield T	1-0	3-1	2-1	2-1	3-2	0-1	2-2	2-1	0-1	2-1	—	3-2	2-2	1-2	1-2	1-0	2-1	2-0	0-2	1-1	2-0
Maidstone U	7-2	1-1	3-3	0-1	0-1	2-2	3-3	3-0	4-3	0-2	0-1	—	2-0	1-2	1-2	2-1	0-0	3-1	3-1	2-3	1-2
Northwich Vic	4-3	5-0	4-1	2-2	1-1	2-2	2-1	2-2	1-0	3-3	1-1	4-3	—	1-1	2-1	2-0	2-1	2-0	0-0	2-2	2-1
Runcorn	3-0	3-1	1-2	3-6	0-4	1-3	0-3	2-1	2-2	2-2	0-1	0-4	3-1	—	1-0	4-1	1-0	4-1	1-3	3-3	2-2
Stafford Rangers	0-2	2-1	1-1	2-2	1-2	4-3	0-1	3-2	2-3	0-1	1-1	4-1	2-1	—	0-2	2-2	3-0	1-0	6-1	2-0	—
Sutton U	3-2	5-2	1-1	1-2	3-1	1-1	0-2	1-1	1-0	1-2	1-1	2-1	4-1	2-1	—	0-1	2-2	2-0	0-0	—	—
Telford U	0-1	3-1	0-3	0-1	2-2	2-1	1-0	2-1	1-1	0-3	3-2	1-2	1-0	3-1	1-0	—	1-0	3-0	1-0	2-2	0-1
Welling U	0-0	5-0	1-0	1-2	1-1	1-2	3-1	2-0	1-2	1-1	1-0	0-0	3-3	4-1	2-2	2-2	—	2-0	—	0-2	4-0
Weymouth	1-3	0-0	2-3	2-1	1-1	2-3	0-1	1-1	2-1	0-1	0-1	1-0	1-0	3-2	2-3	1-1	1-0	—	—	0-3	2-3
Wycombe W	2-1	1-0	1-1	2-1	1-1	2-2	2-0	2-2	2-0	1-3	1-3	3-2	1-0	0-4	2-2	2-2	0-1	1-0	—	—	1-1
Yeovil T	2-3	3-0	2-1	1-1	2-3	4-2	1-0	2-2	2-3	3-0	2-1	2-6	5-2	0-2	2-2	0-0	1-1	4-0	2-3	1-1	—

RESULTS 1988–89
Final Table for Season 1988–89

	P	W	D	L	F	A	W	D	L	F	A	Pts
			Home						Away			
Maidstone U	40	12	5	3	48	22	13	4	3	44	24	84
Kettering T	40	16	1	3	35	15	7	6	7	21	24	76
Boston U	40	12	3	5	36	28	10	5	5	25	23	74
Wycombe W	40	9	7	4	34	25	11	4	5	34	27	71
Kidderminster H	40	10	4	6	32	32	11	2	7	36	25	69
Runcorn	40	11	3	6	39	22	8	5	7	38	31	65
Macclesfield T	40	9	5	6	31	26	8	5	7	32	31	61
Barnet	40	11	2	7	36	30	7	5	8	28	39	61
Yeovil T	40	8	5	7	34	30	7	6	7	34	37	56
Northwich Vic	40	8	5	7	31	30	6	6	8	33	35	53
Welling U	40	8	6	6	27	16	6	5	9	18	30	53
Sutton U	40	10	5	5	43	26	2	10	8	21	28	51
Enfield	40	7	4	9	33	32	7	4	9	29	35	50
Altrincham	40	6	8	6	24	23	7	2	11	27	38	49
Cheltenham T	40	7	7	6	32	29	5	5	10	23	29	48
Telford U	40	5	5	10	17	24	8	4	8	20	19	48
Chorley	40	6	4	10	26	32	7	2	11	31	39	45
Fisher Ath	40	6	4	10	31	32	4	7	9	24	33	41
Stafford Rangers	40	7	4	9	27	32	4	3	13	22	42	40
Aylesbury U	40	7	4	9	27	30	2	5	13	16	41	36
Weymouth	40	6	7	7	27	30	1	3	16	10	40	31

Following Newport County's expulsion only two clubs will be relegated from the GM Vauxhall Conference this season

Leading Goalscorers

League goals

		Cup goals			
		FA	Trophy	Club	
26	Steve Butler (Maidstone U)	+	–	–	1
	Mark Gall (Maidstone U)	+	2	–	1
23	Chris Camden (Stafford Rangers)	+	9	–	2
	Mark Carter (Runcorn)	+	–	–	1
22	Ken Charlery (Maidstone U)	+	4	–	–
21	Steve Burr (Macclesfield T)	+	–	5	–
	Don Page (Ex-Runcorn)	+	1	–	3
20	Paul Davies (Kidderminster H)	+	1	–	4
	Lenny Dennis (Sutton U)	+	3	1	5
	Mark West (Wycombe W)	+	4	2	–
18	Ronnie Ellis (Altrincham)	+	2	–	–
	Derrick Parker (Northwich Vic)	+	2	2	–
16	Phil Power (Chorley)	+	1	–	–
	Guy Whittingham (Yeovil T)	+	–	–	–
15	Chris Cook (Boston U)	+	6	1	1
	Dean Neal (Fisher Ath)	+	6	–	–
	Paul Wilson (Boston U)	+	5	1	–
14	Malcolm O'Connor (Northwich Vic)	+	6	1	1
13	Gary Abbott (Enfield)	+	4	1	–
	Phil Derbyshire (Macclesfield T)	+	–	–	1
	Ernie Moss (Kettering T)	+	1	3	–
	Frank Murphy (Barnet)	+	2	–	2

HFS LOANS LEAGUE (PREMIER

(*formerly Northern Premier League*)

	Bangor C	Barrow	Buxton	Caernarfon	Fleetwood T	Frickley Ath	Gainsbro	Gateshead	Goole T	Horwich	Hyde U	Marine	Matlock T	Morecambe	Mossley	Rhyl	Shepshed Ch	S. L'pool	Southport	Stalybridge	Witton Albion	Worksop T
Bangor C	—	1-2	0-1	1-1	2-0	1-2	1-0	1-0	2-3	3-2	1-2	3-2	2-0	3-0	3-2	3-1	1-0	2-2	3-0	3-1	2-3	2-1
Barrow	1-0	—	1-0	1-0	2-3	1-2	0-3	0-3	0-2	0-0	3-1	0-2	4-0	3-1	0-1	0-2	1-2	0-3	3-1	4-0	3-0	1-0
Buxton	1-1	5-2	—	1-0	2-2	0-3	3-0	2-0	0-1	2-2	1-2	1-1	0-0	0-3	0-2	0-1	1-0	1-2	1-1	2-0	0-0	1-1
Caernarfon	0-1	0-1	1-0	—	2-2	1-0	1-0	1-1	0-1	2-2	0-2	2-3	2-0	1-0	1-0	0-3	1-1	1-1	0-0	3-0	0-1	1-1
FleetwoodT	2-0	2-1	1-2	2-2	—	1-1	1-0	4-1	1-3	2-0	0-2	1-2	2-1	1-0	5-0	6-1	3-1	0-4	1-2	1-1	3-3	2-1
Frickley Ath	0-4	1-2	0-3	1-0	1-1	—	1-1	4-2	1-3	3-3	2-0	2-4	2-1	2-3	1-3	1-3	0-2	1-2	2-5	1-1	0-1	1-3
Gainsbro	2-2	0-3	3-0	1-0	1-0	1-1	—	1-1	2-3	1-0	2-0	1-1	0-1	1-0	0-1	2-1	1-0	1-2	2-2	2-1	3-0	1-2
Gateshead	0-0	0-3	2-0	1-1	4-1	4-2	1-1	—	4-2	3-1	5-0	1-0	1-1	2-3	0-1	2-2	1-0	1-0	2-5	3-1	2-2	1-0
Goole T	3-1	0-2	0-1	0-1	1-3	1-3	2-3	4-2	—	3-1	4-0	4-1	1-1	1-0	3-1	2-0	5-2	1-0	2-2	3-0	2-0	1-0
Horwich	0-3	0-0	3-2	2-2	2-0	3-1	0-4	1-1	3-1	—	0-2	2-1	3-1	2-2	2-0	3-1	2-1	2-2	2-0	1-3	2-0	0-1
Hyde U	2-1	3-1	0-2	0-2	0-2	0-1	2-0	5-0	2-1	0-0	—	2-4	1-2	1-0	3-3	2-1	6-1	1-0	0-2	2-1	0-1	6-1
Marine	1-2	0-2	1-1	2-3	2-3	2-4	2-2	1-0	1-1	2-2	3-1	—	2-0	3-1	4-0	0-1	4-1	2-2	1-0	3-0	1-1	3-1
Matlock T	4-2	1-1	5-4	2-0	2-1	1-2	5-2	3-0	2-0	1-0	2-1	1-1	—	1-1	2-1	3-1	1-1	4-3	2-0	2-0	2-0	2-1
Morecambe	1-2	1-2	1-0	1-0	0-1	2-3	2-1	0-1	0-1	2-1	2-1	0-2	2-0	—	0-2	2-0	0-3	1-0	1-2	4-3	1-1	2-1
Mossley	1-2	1-1	1-1	1-1	1-1	1-3	3-0	3-0	0-2	6-1	2-1	1-0	2-0	2-1	—	1-1	2-0	2-2	0-2	1-0	0-1	2-1
Rhyl	2-2	1-1	0-1	0-3	0-1	2-1	4-1	1-1	3-0	1-2	1-2	1-2	1-0	2-2	4-0	—	3-0	2-2	0-1	1-3	0-1	1-1
Shepshed Ch	1-1	1-1	1-1	1-0	1-2	3-3	2-1	1-1	0-1	4-2	0-3	1-0	4-0	1-1	4-1	1-1	—	1-2	2-0	4-3	1-1	5-1
S. L'pool	1-3	1-2	2-3	2-1	0-2	2-0	2-1	1-1	4-5	1-1	1-2	2-0	1-3	1-1	0-3	1-3	4-1	—	2-1	4-3	1-5	3-1
Southport	0-2	0-4	2-3	1-1	1-1	0-1	4-1	7-0	0-0	0-2	0-1	1-2	1-4	1-1	1-0	0-1	0-3	2-2	—	0-1	0-1	2-1
Stalybridge	2-2	0-0	1-1	2-0	2-1	3-1	0-0	2-2	1-1	1-1	1-2	1-0	0-1	1-1	1-0	2-3	2-0	1-0	1-0	—	1-0	1-0
Witton Albion	0-1	0-0	3-0	0-1	1-1	1-1	4-0	2-0	3-0	2-1	2-2	1-0	1-0	3-1	1-0	0-1	2-0	1-0	1-0	1-5	—	3-1
Worksop T	0-5	0-1	3-0	1-1	1-2	1-3	1-2	1-0	1-0	6-1	3-1	1-3	1-4	2-1	1-5	0-4	1-2	1-1	0-5	4-3	1-0	—

228

DIVISION) RESULTS 1988–89

Final table for season 1988–89

			Home				Away				
	P	W	D	L	F	A	W	D	L	F	A	Pts
Barrow	42	15	2	4	38	17	10	7	3	31	18	87
Hyde U	42	14	4	3	49	17	10	4	7	28	27	80
Witton Albion	42	13	5	3	40	16	9	8	4	27	23	79
Bangor C	42	12	4	5	40	24	10	6	5	37	24	76
Marine	42	12	5	4	39	21	11	2	8	30	27	76
Goole T	42	14	2	5	49	31	8	5	8	26	29	73
Fleetwood T	42	12	6	3	28	16	7	10	4	30	28	73
Rhyl	42	10	6	5	43	30	8	4	9	32	35	64
Frickley Ath	42	11	5	5	38	25	6	5	10	26	28	61
Mossley	42	9	6	6	24	19	8	3	10	32	39	60
S. L'pool	42	8	7	6	36	29	7	6	8	29	28	58
Caernarfon T	42	8	6	7	21	20	7	4	10	28	43	55
Matlock T	42	12	4	5	47	32	4	1	16	18	41	53
Southport	42	7	6	8	36	22	6	6	9	30	30	51
Buxton	42	6	9	6	35	30	6	5	10	26	33	50
*1 Morecambe	42	9	6	6	35	25	4	3	14	20	35	47
Gainsborough T	42	7	5	9	33	35	5	6	10	23	38	47
*6 Shepshed Ch	42	8	5	8	27	21	6	3	12	22	39	44
Stalybridge C	42	3	8	10	20	35	6	5	10	26	46	40
Horwich	42	4	6	11	19	35	3	8	10	23	35	35
Gateshead	42	6	5	10	18	24	1	8	12	18	46	34
Worksop T	42	4	1	16	22	58	2	4	15	20	45	23

pts deducted for breaches of rules

Leading goalscorers (*HFS Loans League and HFS cups only*)

26 Graham Hoyland (Gainsborough Trinity)
25 Mark Edwards (Witton Albion), Ian Cain (Fleetwood T)
22 Colin Cowperthwaite (Barrow), Jim McCluskie (Mossley)
21 David Eyres (Rhyl)
20 Karl Thomas (S. L'pool)
19 Graham Bennett (Marine), Paul Crooks (Bangor C, 12 with Rhyl)
18 Bob Gauden (Goole T), Malcolm Wagstaffe (Stalybridge Celtic)
17 John Sheppard (Matlock T)
16 Clint Neysmith (Southport), Mike Lutkevitch (Hyde U)
15 Mark Ferguson (ex-Bangor City, now Runcorn), Michael Downing (Frickley Athletic)
13 Barry Diamond (Hyde U), Malcolm Poskett (Morecambe)

Cup Honours – 1988–89
HFS Challenge Cup winners Mossley; runners-up Fleetwood Town
HFS President's Cup winners Bangor City; runners-up South Liverpool

BEAZER HOMES LEAGUE
(*Formerly Southern League*)

	Alvechurch	Ashford T	Bath C	Bedworth U	Bromsgrove R	Burton Albion	Cambridge C	Corby T	Crawley T	Dartford	Dorchester T	Dover Ath	Fareham T	Gosport Borough	Leicester U	Merthyr Tydfil	Moor Green	Redditch U	V.S. Rugby	Waterlooville	Wealdstone	Worcester C
Alvechurch	—	0-0	1-0	3-0	2-1	3-4	1-1	0-1	2-2	1-0	2-1	0-1	3-4	2-0	2-1	4-3	1-0	3-1	1-2	2-1	2-1	0-2
Ashford T	0-1	—	2-1	4-0	0-2	1-3	1-1	2-0	2-0	0-9	1-0	2-1	1-0	5-1	4-0	6-1	1-2	1-5	0-1	1-3	3-2	1-2
Bath C	1-0	4-3	—	1-0	0-1	1-3	3-1	1-1	2-0	0-2	1-0	2-1	3-3	1-1	1-3	3-0	2-3	4-1	1-5	3-2	1-0	0-1
Bedworth U	1-1	0-3	3-1	—	0-1	1-7	1-2	1-1	0-1	4-6	3-0	2-2	1-0	2-3	1-3	2-1	0-3	4-2	1-5	2-0	0-1	2-2
Bromsgrove R	2-4	2-2	1-1	3-0	—	2-3	0-2	3-0	0-1	0-2	3-0	3-3	4-0	7-1	4-0	1-1	5-1	5-0	3-2	0-0	2-2	3-0
Burton Albion	3-1	1-3	1-1	3-2	0-4	—	1-0	0-3	2-0	0-1	1-0	2-0	1-2	3-3	1-0	1-1	2-0	2-0	3-2	2-1	1-1	0-2
Cambridge C	4-2	1-3	1-0	1-2	0-1	2-2	—	2-0	1-0	0-4	1-1	2-0	2-4	3-3	3-0	4-2	3-1	2-0	2-4	3-1	2-0	2-0
Corby T	2-1	1-0	1-1	2-2	1-3	0-1	1-0	—	2-3	1-3	1-0	1-1	0-1	4-2	2-1	2-1	5-1	2-0	1-0	1-1	2-1	3-3
Crawley T	2-1	1-1	1-0	4-2	0-1	1-3	2-2	1-0	—	1-3	4-0	2-2	3-2	3-2	3-0	1-0	3-1	4-3	1-0	1-1	2-2	2-1
Dartford	1-0	2-1	2-1	3-0	1-0	3-0	1-0	2-3	1-1	—	4-0	1-1	3-0	3-2	3-0	1-2	1-0	3-0	2-0	3-1	2-1	1-1
Dorchester T	2-0	1-1	1-1	3-0	0-1	3-1	1-3	0-0	0-2	2-1	—	1-1	0-1	0-1	1-0	0-3	1-1	1-2	0-1	1-2	0-0	1-1
Dover Ath	1-0	2-1	0-2	4-2	1-1	0-1	2-0	2-0	0-1	0-1	4-0	—	0-1	2-2	2-1	2-0	1-0	2-0	1-0	1-1	1-1	2-0
Fareham T	3-4	5-1	1-1	3-0	1-1	3-1	1-1	0-3	2-2	1-0	3-0	2-1	—	0-1	1-1	2-1	1-1	0-1	2-0	5-0	1-1	2-1
Gosport Borough	2-0	4-0	4-0	1-0	0-1	2-0	0-2	0-3	0-1	1-2	2-0	0-6	1-2	—	0-1	2-1	0-2	2-0	1-0	0-4	2-2	1-1
Leicester U	1-1	6-1	2-1	1-0	1-4	0-4	1-3	0-3	2-1	3-3	1-0	1-0	1-5	1-0	—	2-1	2-1	0-2	1-0	1-2	1-1	1-3
Merthyr Tydfil	2-1	2-2	1-1	3-1	2-2	1-1	2-1	0-1	0-3	1-0	2-1	0-1	3-1	0-1	2-1	—	1-0	1-2	2-1	1-1	2-2	1-1
Moor Green	1-2	1-3	0-6	0-2	1-1	1-1	1-5	3-0	2-1	1-2	3-1	2-0	1-1	0-2	2-2	1-2	—	1-3	0-1	1-2	2-0	0-1
Redditch U	1-1	2-1	0-2	3-1	1-1	2-1	2-1	3-1	1-2	0-2	1-0	0-6	2-0	1-1	2-2	2-1	3-0	—	2-3	2-2	3-1	1-1
V.S. Rugby	2-1	1-1	2-0	0-2	1-1	2-2	1-5	1-1	2-1	2-1	3-1	1-0	0-0	0-2	3-1	0-1	2-2	4-2	—	0-2	0-2	1-1
Waterlooville	0-1	1-3	3-2	3-1	2-5	2-1	0-1	2-3	1-3	1-0	0-1	1-0	3-3	0-4	0-1	4-1	2-2	1-2	0-2	—	2-0	1-2
Wealdstone	2-0	4-1	1-2	3-1	3-3	2-1	0-1	2-1	1-3	1-1	3-1	1-1	3-0	3-0	5-0	0-3	2-2	4-0	0-2	2-0	—	1-1
Worcester C	1-0	6-0	1-1	1-3	1-0	3-2	0-1	3-1	1-3	1-0	1-1	0-5	5-1	2-2	5-0	3-1	2-1	3-0	0-1	2-0	1-1	—

230

PREMIER DIVISION 1988–89

Final table for season 1988–89

	P	W	D	L	F	A	W	D	L	F	A	Pts
			Home						Away			
Merthyr Tydfil	42	16	3	2	62	22	10	4	7	42	36	85
Dartford	42	15	3	3	37	10	10	4	7	42	23	82
V.S. Rugby	42	11	5	5	30	20	13	2	6	34	23	79
Worcester C	42	12	5	4	42	22	8	8	5	30	27	73
Cambridge C	42	12	3	6	41	21	8	7	6	31	30	70
Dover Ath	42	12	5	4	34	21	7	7	7	31	26	69
Gosport Borough	42	13	3	5	43	18	5	9	7	30	39	66
Burton Albion	42	12	5	4	41	26	6	5	10	38	42	64
Bath C	42	9	8	4	38	20	6	5	10	28	31	58
Bromsgrove R	42	10	7	4	42	26	4	9	8	26	30	58
Wealdstone	42	12	4	5	38	21	4	6	11	22	32	58
Crawley T	42	8	7	6	34	31	6	9	6	27	25	58
Dorchester T	42	8	9	4	38	34	6	7	8	18	27	58
Alvechurch	42	11	3	7	32	26	5	5	11	24	33	56
Moor Green	42	9	8	4	33	28	5	5	11	25	42	55
Corby T	42	8	7	6	32	32	6	4	11	23	27	53
Waterlooville	42	8	7	6	36	32	5	6	10	25	31	52
Ashford T	42	7	8	6	28	29	6	5	10	31	47	52
Fareham T	42	9	3	9	21	26	6	3	12	22	42	51
Leicester U	42	4	7	10	26	39	2	4	15	20	45	29
Redditch U	42	4	4	13	20	49	1	3	17	16	56	22
Bedworth U	42	2	5	14	18	50	2	2	17	18	52	19

Leading goalscorers

M. Whitehouse (Burton Albion)	42
D. Webley (Merthyr Tydfil)	37
C. Hanks (Bromsgrove R)	25
K. Wilkin (Cambridge C)	25
A. Canning (Burton Albion)	23
S. Cotterill (Burton Albion)	23
P. Taylor (Dartford)	22
L. Lee (Dover Ath)	22
D. Arter (Ashford T)	21
L. Maddocks (Fareham T)	20

Westgate Insurance Cup final

Dartford 1,2; Burton Albion 1,0
Dartford won 3–1 on aggregate

BEAZER HOMES LEAGUE

	Andover	Baldock T	Buckingham T	Burnham	Bury T	Canterbury C	Chelmsford C	Corinthian	Dunstable	Erith & Belvedere	Folkestone	Gravesend & Northfleet	Hastings T	Hounslow	Poole T	Ruislip	Salisbury	Sheppey U	Thanet U	Tonbridge AFC	Trowbridge T	Witney T
Andover	—																					
Baldock T	0-1	—																				
Buckingham T	1-2		—																			
Burnham	2-2			—																		
Bury T	2-0				—																	
Canterbury C	3-2					—																
Chelmsford C	2-0						—															
Corinthian	5-1							—														
Dunstable	3-2								—													
Erith & Belvedere	0-1									—												
Folkestone	2-0										—											
Gravesend & Northfleet	3-1											—										
Hastings T	1-2												—									
Hounslow	7-0													—								
Poole T															—							
Ruislip	4-2															—						
Salisbury	1-1																—					
Sheppey U	1-3																	—				
Thanet U	0-4																		—			
Tonbridge AFC	6-2																			—		
Trowbridge T	4-3																				—	
Witney T	1-2																					—

SOUTHERN DIVISION 1988–89

Final Table for Season 1988–89

	P	Home W	D	L	F	A	Away W	D	L	F	A	Pts
Chelmsford C	42	17	1	3	58	18	13	4	4	48	20	95
Gravesend & Northfleet	42	13	2	6	33	18	14	4	3	37	22	87
Poole T	42	13	6	2	56	27	11	5	5	42	21	83
Bury T	42	15	2	4	43	8	10	5	6	32	26	82
Burnham	42	10	8	3	42	22	12	5	4	36	25	79
Baldock T	42	12	2	7	34	17	11	3	7	35	23	74
Hastings T	42	11	5	5	43	28	10	6	5	32	20	74
Hounslow	42	11	4	6	40	24	10	2	9	35	36	69
Salisbury	42	12	2	7	48	25	8	3	10	31	33	65
Trowbridge T	42	10	6	5	39	23	9	1	11	20	29	64
Folkstone	42	10	4	7	32	27	7	4	10	30	38	59
Corinthian	42	6	4	11	32	42	7	9	5	27	27	52
Canterbury C	42	7	4	10	28	23	7	4	10	24	37	50
Witney T	42	8	5	8	36	32	5	6	10	25	39	50
Dunstable	42	6	9	6	25	28	5	5	11	17	29	47
Buckingham T	42	4	8	9	23	34	8	2	11	33	45	46
Erith & Belvedere	42	8	3	10	33	28	3	7	11	15	35	43
Andover	42	4	6	11	24	41	7	3	11	32	49	42
Sheppey U	42	5	5	11	27	36	5	3	13	23	54	38
Thanet U	42	5	5	11	22	37	2	10	9	25	58	36
Tonbridge AFC	42	6	1	14	32	45	1	5	15	18	53	27
Ruislip	42	2	6	13	24	57	4	2	15	23	55	26

Leading goalscorers

G. Manson (Poole T) 29
T. Funnell (Poole T) 25
M. Springett (Chelmsford C) 23
D. Lansley (Burnham) 20
I. Pickering (Folkestone) 20
D. Platt (Salisbury) 19
I. Chalk (Salisbury) 18
V. Schwartz (Hounslow) 18
K. Alexander (Erith & Belvedere) 17
A. Douglas (Gravesend & Northfleet) 17
M. Freeman (Corinthian) 17

Merit Cup winners (most goals): Chelmsford City

BEAZER HOMES LEAGUE

(*Formerly Southern League*)

	Willenhall T	Wellingborough	Tamworth	Sutton Coldfield	Stourbridge	Spalding	Rushden T	Nuneaton Borough	Mile Oak R	Kings Lynn	Hednesford T	Halesowen T	Grantham	Gloucester C	Forest Green R	Dudley T	Coventry Sporting	Bridgnorth T	Bilston T	Banbury U	Atherstone U	Ashtree Highfield
Ashtree Highfield	3-2	0-0	3-3	5-1	2-1	0-2	1-2	3-1	3-1	0-1	1-9	0-3	2-1	0-0	1-2	3-4	2-0	2-1	1-2	1-1	0-0	—
Atherstone U	3-0	0-0	0-2	2-1	2-1	1-1	5-0	1-1	3-2	1-3	4-0	0-3	1-1	1-1	4-1	6-1	1-4	1-1	1-3	3-1	—	2-2
Banbury U	1-1	1-0	0-2	3-1	4-1	1-1	1-0	0-1	3-2	2-0	6-1	1-1	0-1	1-1	2-0	0-0	2-2	5-2	1-3	—	0-1	0-4
Bilston T	2-3	4-2	0-1	3-1	0-0	3-2	0-1	0-0	4-2	3-0	6-3	2-5	2-3	3-2	4-0	1-3	2-0	2-6	—	3-1	0-3	0-2
Bridgnorth T	0-2	1-1	3-1	1-1	0-0	1-3	2-4	0-0	1-2	0-1	0-3	0-2	0-0	2-4	1-0	1-1	5-1	—	2-6	3-1	0-2	1-1
Coventry Sporting	2-1	1-1	2-2	3-3	2-0	0-2	1-1	4-2	0-2	1-1	4-4	1-5	0-1	0-2	2-1	1-1	—	1-1	3-2	2-4	3-2	2-0
Dudley T	1-1	1-1	0-4	1-1	2-1	1-0	1-0	1-2	1-0	1-1	2-1	2-1	5-1	0-1	5-1	—	1-1	0-0	0-0	3-1	2-2	1-0
Forest Green R	2-2	1-1	1-1	3-1	6-1	2-2	2-0	2-0	3-0	0-1	4-0	2-1	2-0	1-0	—	7-0	1-0	1-2	2-1	1-0	1-1	1-1
Gloucester C	2-0	3-0	1-1	0-0	0-2	1-0	1-2	2-0	2-1	6-3	2-2	0-1	1-0	—	0-0	0-0	2-3	1-4	1-3	1-0	1-0	2-1
Grantham	3-1	0-0	0-1	3-1	2-1	2-2	3-0	4-2	8-0	6-3	3-1	1-0	—	1-0	0-0	3-0	2-1	4-3	4-1	4-0	0-1	3-1
Halesowen T	4-4	2-0	0-1	0-1	1-1	3-0	0-1	1-0	2-1	—	2-1	—	2-3	2-3	1-3	3-0	1-1	4-3	4-1	0-1	0-1	2-1
Hednesford T	2-3	1-1	2-2	0-1	3-1	3-0	2-2	1-0	3-0	1-0	—	2-2	2-0	2-3	1-2	1-1	3-1	3-1	3-1	1-0	0-4	3-1
Kings Lynn	3-0	1-1	2-2	0-1	1-1	1-0	7-0	1-1	5-0	—	2-1	2-0	0-3	2-3	4-2	3-0	4-0	1-3	0-0	2-0	1-1	0-3
Mile Oak R	0-1	1-1	1-2	0-1	3-1	3-0	0-0	0-1	—	0-0	3-3	0-1	5-0	1-4	2-7	3-0	5-1	1-3	3-2	3-2	1-0	3-2
Nuneaton Borough	2-1	1-0	2-2	0-1	3-1	3-0	0-1	—	2-2	1-3	2-0	2-2	1-1	2-2	2-7	3-0	1-1	2-0	0-0	1-0	1-1	2-0
Rushden T	1-0	1-1	0-0	1-1	3-1	0-3	—	1-2	2-1	6-0	1-2	0-2	0-2	0-0	0-1	1-3	4-0	4-0	4-1	1-1	1-0	2-0
Spalding	3-0	1-1	2-2	0-3	1-1	—	3-0	1-0	3-0	1-0	0-0	2-3	0-0	2-3	1-2	3-0	1-0	2-1	3-1	0-3	1-0	3-0
Stourbridge	0-3	0-0	0-0	0-2	—	2-1	2-2	4-2	1-0	4-1	2-1	2-2	1-2	1-2	2-1	0-1	2-0	4-3	3-1	1-0	1-2	1-1
Sutton Coldfield	1-0	1-0	0-1	—	0-2	0-0	2-0	0-0	4-2	2-2	4-3	1-2	3-3	2-3	0-0	2-1	5-1	2-4	2-0	2-2	0-1	2-0
Tamworth	3-0	1-0	—	0-2	4-0	3-1	3-1	1-0	3-1	3-0	2-0	3-0	1-3	1-4	1-1	0-3	2-0	0-2	3-0	1-0	0-2	2-2
Wellingborough	0-1	—	1-2	2-1	0-1	3-1	3-1	2-1	1-1	0-2	0-1	4-0	2-1	1-2	1-1	0-3	1-1	0-1	0-2	0-3	0-1	1-0
Willenhall T	—	2-1	1-0	3-2	3-1	4-1	1-0	1-3	4-2	1-0	1-1	1-0	0-2	2-1	1-1	1-1	1-1	0-5	1-2	0-0	0-2	5-4

234

MIDLAND DIVISION 1988–9

Final table for season 1988–89

		Home					Away				
	P	W	D	L	F	A	W	D	L	F	A	Pts
Gloucester C	42	14	3	4	55	20	14	5	2	40	17	92
Atherstone U	42	15	5	1	48	19	11	4	6	37	19	87
Tamworth	42	15	2	4	44	20	11	7	3	41	25	87
Halesowen T	42	11	8	2	50	23	14	2	5	35	19	85
Grantham T	42	12	7	2	32	10	11	4	6	34	27	80
Nuneaton Borough	42	12	3	6	44	28	7	6	8	27	30	66
Rushden T	42	13	3	5	49	26	6	5	10	22	24	65
Spalding U	42	10	6	6	40	31	7	7	7	32	33	64
Dudley T	42	9	4	8	37	32	7	9	5	36	30	61
Sutton Coldfield T	42	11	4	6	32	26	7	3	11	24	30	61
Willenhall T	42	11	4	6	32	30	5	8	8	33	41	60
Forest Green R	42	7	8	6	39	32	5	8	8	25	35	52
Bilston T	42	11	3	7	42	33	4	4	13	21	38	52
Ashtree Highfield	42	9	7	5	34	27	3	8	10	23	35	51
Hednesford T	42	7	8	6	23	20	5	7	9	26	37	51
Banbury U	42	8	7	6	31	27	2	7	12	22	47	44
Bridgnorth T	42	9	4	8	29	29	3	3	15	30	48	43
Stourbridge	42	6	7	8	17	25	5	3	13	20	40	43
Kings Lynn	42	7	9	5	20	19	0	4	17	11	48	34
Coventry Sporting	42	6	4	11	25	41	0	9	12	14	50	31
Wellingborough T	42	4	8	9	20	29	1	7	13	19	43	30
Mile Oak R	42	4	8	9	29	42	1	2	18	17	56	25

Leading goalscorers

C Townsend (Gloucester C)	30
J. Muir (Dudley T)	30
A. Rammell (Atherstone U)	28
P. Joinson (Halesowen T)	27
S. Penney (Gloucester C)	26
T. Shrieves (Rushden T)	26
N. Civil (Ashtree Highfield)	23
M. Stanton (Tamworth)	23
M. Richards (Bilston T)	21
M. Devaney (Tamworth)	20

FA Vase winners: Tamworth

VAUXHALL OPEL LEAGUE PREMIER

	Barking	Bishops Stortford	Bognor Regis	Bromley	Carshalton Ath	Croydon	Dagenham	Dulwich Hamlet	Farnborough T	Grays Ath	Harrow Borough	Hayes	Hendon	Kingstonian	Leytonstone-Ilford	Leyton-Wingate	Marlow	St Albans C	Slough T	Tooting & Mitcham U	Windsor & Eton	Wokingham T
Barking	—	4-0	0-0	2-2	0-1	1-1	0-1	0-0	2-2	1-0	3-1	2-2	0-1	0-1	0-1	1-0	0-1	1-0	1-0	2-1	2-3	1-0
Bishops Stortford	—	—	1-2	2-2	1-3	3-3	3-3	2-2	4-3	1-1	1-1	2-1	3-2	0-1	3-2	1-2	1-1	0-2	4-1	2-1	4-1	1-2
Bognor Regis	1-0	0-4	—	0-3	0-0	1-0	3-1	2-2	1-2	5-0	2-1	2-0	2-0	0-1	0-0	2-0	1-2	1-1	0-1	2-1	0-0	1-2
Bromley	1-2	2-0	0-3	—	1-1	3-2	3-3	2-2	1-2	4-0	2-1	2-1	2-0	0-3	0-2	1-1	0-1	5-1	0-0	3-0	0-3	2-1
Carshalton Ath	0-1	1-2	2-1	1-1	—	1-0	3-1	1-0	4-4	0-4	0-0	0-2	1-1	3-3	0-3	0-0	3-0	0-1	0-2	1-3	0-3	2-1
Croydon	1-2	0-3	0-0	3-2	1-0	—	5-2	2-1	2-1	5-1	0-1	1-2	1-2	0-3	0-3	1-0	0-3	1-0	0-1	2-1	1-0	3-0
Dagenham	1-2	0-2	2-2	3-1	0-4	1-1	—	1-1	1-2	4-1	2-2	0-0	1-2	3-1	1-4	0-1	1-2	1-1	2-6	1-1	0-1	5-1
Dulwich Hamlet	1-1	1-3	2-2	3-3	1-2	2-1	1-2	—	2-4	2-2	2-2	0-0	4-2	0-3	0-2	1-2	1-2	2-1	1-2	2-1	0-3	3-1
Farnborough T	1-0	2-2	3-0	1-1	2-1	1-0	1-2	1-2	—	3-0	2-0	0-0	2-1	0-3	2-1	3-2	2-0	2-1	2-6	2-1	3-0	3-1
Grays Ath	2-3	4-3	4-0	2-2	2-0	4-1	4-1	2-1	3-0	—	5-0	4-1	4-2	0-3	0-2	3-2	4-4	2-1	2-6	2-1	2-2	3-1
Harrow Borough	3-1	1-2	2-0	1-0	2-0	2-0	2-2	1-1	3-1	5-0	—	2-0	0-3	1-0	2-1	3-1	3-1	3-0	1-1	2-2	2-3	2-2
Hayes	2-2	1-0	1-1	0-2	0-0	4-1	1-2	1-2	1-1	3-0	1-3	—	7-0	1-3	2-1	2-2	0-4	2-2	1-0	2-1	1-0	1-0
Hendon	0-1	2-0	2-0	0-0	1-1	2-0	4-2	0-2	1-2	0-0	7-0	—	2-0	2-2	1-4	2-2	1-1	3-0	1-0	1-2	1-0	2-2
Kingstonian	0-1	0-1	0-1	1-1	3-3	3-3	3-2	1-1	1-2	3-0	2-0	0-1	—	2-0	2-2	3-0	2-0	2-1	0-1	1-0	1-0	2-1
Leytonstone-Ilford	0-1	1-2	0-0	0-2	0-0	2-3	0-3	0-0	2-2	2-2	0-1	2-0	4-1	—	2-1	2-0	2-1	1-1	0-3	2-0	1-0	0-1
Leyton-Wingate	1-0	0-1	2-0	1-1	0-0	1-0	3-0	3-2	2-2	3-0	1-1	0-2	1-2	2-1	—	3-1	2-4	3-0	1-3	2-0	1-0	1-1
Marlow	0-1	1-2	6-0	3-0	0-2	1-2	4-1	3-2	0-2	4-1	2-0	1-0	4-2	1-0	2-1	1-1	—	4-0	3-2	1-3	0-1	2-0
St Albans C	1-0	1-1	1-1	3-1	5-1	1-0	1-1	2-1	2-1	2-1	1-0	2-1	1-1	0-1	1-1	0-1	1-0	—	4-3	1-0	3-2	0-2
Slough T	1-0	0-2	3-0	0-0	0-2	0-1	1-2	2-6	2-1	1-1	1-1	1-0	1-0	1-2	1-1	2-1	1-1	0-1	—	2-3	3-2	1-1
Bognor — see above																						
Tooting & Mitcham U	2-3	1-2	0-1	0-3	3-1	1-1	2-1	1-0	3-3	2-2	2-1	0-2	1-1	2-2	1-4	3-2	4-0	1-2	0-2	—	1-0	2-1
Windsor & Eton	2-3	1-2	0-1	1-1	0-3	1-1	2-1	1-0	3-3	2-1	1-1	0-3	2-0	0-1	0-3	2-0	1-3	3-2	0-1	5-0	—	1-1
Wokingham T	1-0	1-2	1-2	2-1	1-0	3-0	5-1	3-1	1-2	2-2	0-3	1-2	2-2	0-1	2-2	1-2	3-0	1-3	1-1	7-0	2-0	—

DIVISION RESULTS 1988–89

Final table for season 1988–89

		Home					Away					
	P	W	D	L	F	A	W	D	L	F	A	Pts
Leytonstone Ilford	42	15	5	1	45	21	11	6	4	31	15	89
Farnborough T	42	14	2	5	48	29	10	7	4	37	32	81
Slough T	42	14	2	5	43	20	10	4	7	29	22	78
Carshalton Ath	42	11	6	4	26	12	8	9	4	33	24	72
Grays Ath	42	11	6	4	42	26	8	7	6	20	21	70
Kingstonian	42	11	3	7	33	20	8	8	5	21	17	68
Bishops Stortford	42	11	3	7	34	23	9	3	9	36	33	66
Hayes	42	11	5	5	34	24	7	7	7	27	23	66
Bognor Regis T	42	10	5	6	21	20	7	6	8	17	29	62
Barking	42	8	8	5	23	16	8	5	8	26	29	61
Wokingham T	42	7	7	7	31	19	8	4	9	29	35	56
Hendon	42	5	13	3	26	25	8	4	9	25	43	56
Windsor & Eton	42	8	5	8	30	27	6	8	7	22	23	55
Bromley	42	6	8	7	32	24	7	7	7	29	24	54
Leyton-Wingate	42	7	9	5	32	25	6	6	9	23	31	54
Dulwich Hamlet	42	7	7	7	32	29	5	5	11	26	28	48
St Albans C	42	7	7	7	31	27	5	2	14	20	32	45
Dagenham	42	5	5	11	24	33	6	7	8	29	35	45
Harrow Borough	42	7	3	11	30	36	2	10	9	23	39	40
Marlow	42	3	8	10	26	38	6	3	12	22	45	38
Tooting & Mitcham U	42	8	3	10	25	35	2	3	16	16	46	36
Croydon	42	3	5	13	8	31	1	4	16	19	50	21

Leading goalscorers

		LGE	AC	CC
41	Simon Read (Farnborough T.)	34	7	0
26	Tom English (Bishops Stortford)	18	2	6
24	Neal Stanley (Slough T.)	23	0	1
21	Carl Zachhau (Bishops Stortford)	12	4	5
20	Graham Westley (Kingstonian)	17	3	0
19	Steve Thompson (Slough T.)	18	0	1
18	Dave Pearce (Wokingham T.)	17	1	0
	Jimmy Bolton (Harrow Borough)	17	1	0
	Andy Weddell (Bishops Stortford)	14	2	2

Top attendances

1763	Slough T	v	Farnborough T
1347	Farnborough T	v	Leytonstone-Ilford
1046	Windsor & Eton	v	Slough T
645	Grays Ath	v	Slough T
608	Barking	v	Dagenham
596	Marlow	v	Carshalton Ath

VAUXHALL OPEL LEAGUE FIRST

	Basildon U	Basingstoke T	Boreham Wood	Bracknell T	Chalfont St Peter	Chesham U	Collier Row	Hampton	Hitchin T	Kingsbury T	Leatherhead	Lewes	Metropolitan Police	Southwick	Staines T	Uxbridge	Walton & Hersham	Wembley	Wivenhoe T	Woking	Worthing
Basildon U	—	0-2	2-0	1-1	2-0	1-0	1-0	0-0	0-3	1-2	1-2	2-1	3-0	4-2	0-0	4-2	2-0	5-1	0-2	1-0	2-3
Basingstoke T	3-0	—	2-2	3-1	1-4	0-3	4-1	1-2	0-3	4-0	0-1	1-2	1-3	2-1	0-3	1-1	2-1	3-0	3-2	1-1	1-1
Boreham Wood	2-0	2-0	—	5-0	3-2	7-0	5-0	4-1	1-2	2-0	2-1	1-2	3-2	1-3	0-1	2-1	2-0	0-1	1-0	2-3	2-1
Bracknell T	1-1	0-2	1-0	—	4-1	1-0	2-2	3-1	1-2	2-0	0-1	4-0	2-3	1-0	0-3	2-4	3-1	3-1	0-1	1-3	5-1
Chalfont St Peter	2-0	1-4	3-2	4-1	—	2-1	0-3	3-0	0-2	1-1	1-0	2-1	1-1	0-0	0-2	0-1	1-2	2-3	2-2	0-3	1-1
Chesham U	1-0	0-3	2-2	1-0	4-1	—	1-3	3-2	0-1	1-2	6-4	1-1	3-0	5-2	1-2	3-2	0-2	1-0	1-3	1-3	1-1
Collier Row	1-0	0-0	2-0	1-0	0-1	2-1	—	1-1	6-1	1-2	1-3	0-1	1-1	0-0	1-0	6-0	2-0	2-0	2-0	0-1	1-0
Hampton	0-0	3-2	2-0	1-1	3-2	0-3	2-1	—	3-1	1-1	3-3	1-1	3-1	2-1	3-1	1-1	1-1	2-2	0-3	2-1	1-2
Hitchin T	0-3	0-0	2-1	0-2	1-5	2-0	0-2	3-1	—	2-1	3-0	1-0	1-0	1-0	1-1	3-1	2-2	1-1	0-0	0-1	1-0
Kingsbury T	1-2	3-0	0-0	2-0	2-2	3-1	0-2	1-1	2-0	—	3-0	2-2	4-0	3-1	2-1	1-2	2-3	0-1	1-3	0-2	1-0
Leatherhead	1-2	2-1	3-1	3-0	3-0	6-4	6-0	3-1	1-0	1-2	—	2-2	3-0	2-0	0-1	2-1	1-2	4-1	1-3	0-3	3-1
Lewes	2-1	0-0	0-1	1-1	1-2	2-2	0-1	3-1	1-0	2-4	3-0	—	2-0	0-2	1-0	2-1	1-0	2-3	3-3	0-2	1-0
Metropolitan Police	3-0	0-3	0-1	1-1	2-1	0-1	0-1	3-2	1-0	2-0	0-0	2-0	—	1-2	3-0	1-0	1-1	2-3	1-3	0-2	3-0
Southwick	4-2	2-1	2-1	3-0	1-2	0-1	6-0	1-1	2-2	1-3	0-0	2-0	3-0	—	1-1	3-2	1-1	5-2	0-1	0-3	0-0
Staines T	0-0	0-3	3-0	3-0	0-0	1-1	0-1	3-1	1-1	1-0	3-0	1-0	2-0	3-0	—	1-1	0-0	0-1	1-3	0-0	1-1
Uxbridge	2-0	2-1	2-0	2-3	0-2	1-0	1-1	1-1	1-0	2-1	2-0	3-3	1-0	2-0	2-2	—	1-2	0-0	1-3	1-0	3-0
Walton & Hersham	2-0	1-2	2-0	1-0	3-1	2-0	2-0	0-1	3-1	2-1	2-1	0-1	3-0	1-1	0-2	2-3	—	2-0	1-0	0-1	4-5
Wembley	0-2	4-2	2-2	2-2	1-2	1-1	3-1	1-0	2-0	0-2	3-0	0-1	1-2	1-1	5-1	1-2	2-0	—	1-2	1-2	3-1
Wivenhoe T	0-2	1-0	3-0	3-1	1-2	2-0	2-0	1-1	0-0	3-0	2-0	3-1	4-0	1-3	1-3	2-1	2-3	0-1	—	2-0	1-1
Woking	1-0	3-0	4-1	1-2	2-2	0-2	3-1	1-1	2-1	1-0	2-1	2-2	1-1	1-1	1-1	2-3	1-0	5-0	2-0	—	3-1
Worthing	2-3	0-2	0-1	1-0	1-1	0-2	1-0	3-1	1-0	0-3	1-4	4-3	1-2	0-0	2-1	1-2	2-0	1-2	0-2	1-1	—

DIVISION RESULTS 1988–89

Final table for season 1988–89

		Home					Away					
	P	W	D	L	F	A	W	D	L	F	A	Pts
Staines T	40	14	5	1	45	13	12	4	4	34	16	87
Basingstoke T	40	14	4	2	47	15	11	4	5	38	21	83
Woking	40	9	6	5	29	20	15	4	1	43	10	82
Hitchin T	40	13	4	3	35	17	8	7	5	25	15	74
Wivenhoe T	40	11	3	6	34	26	11	3	6	28	18	72
Lewes	40	13	2	5	40	23	8	6	6	32	31	71
Walton & Hersham	40	10	4	6	30	17	11	3	6	26	19	70
Kingsbury T	40	12	2	6	37	21	8	5	7	28	20	67
Uxbridge	40	8	6	6	27	25	11	1	8	33	29	64
Wembley	40	8	5	7	22	29	10	1	9	23	29	60
Boreham Wood	40	8	5	7	36	28	8	4	8	21	24	57
Leatherhead	40	7	5	8	35	29	7	3	10	21	29	50
Metropolitan Police	40	8	4	8	31	34	5	5	10	21	34	48
Chesham U	40	7	5	8	28	28	5	4	11	26	39	45
Southwick	40	6	5	9	20	25	3	10	7	24	33	42
Chalfont St Peter	40	7	4	9	33	37	4	5	11	23	45	42
Hampton	40	5	6	9	16	28	2	8	10	21	34	35
Worthing	40	5	5	10	20	31	3	5	12	29	49	32*
Collier Row	40	5	5	10	23	33	3	2	15	14	49	31
Bracknell T	40	6	2	12	18	27	2	4	14	15	43	30
Basildon U	40	2	4	14	18	35	4	3	13	16	42	25

* 2 pts deducted

Leading goalscorers

		LGE+CUP
23	Paul Harrison (Wivenhoe T)	23
21	Mark Deacon (Basingstoke T)	20+1
	Pip Parris (Lewes)	20+1
	Steve Wallace (Chesham U)	21
	(includes 6 League goals for Borehamwood)	
20	Mark Dawber (Staines T)	17+3
19	Mark Reed (Lewes)	18+1

Top attendances

1432	Woking	v	Lewes
1122	Staines T	v	Woking
753	Basingstoke T	v	Woking
			Staines T
459	Hitchin T	v	Wembley
442	Chalfont St Peter	v	Woking
427	Wivenhoe T	v	Wembley

VAUXHALL OPEL LEAGUE SECOND

	Aveley	Barton Rovers	Berkhamsted T	Billericay T	Clapton	Harlow T	Hemel Hempstead	Hertford T	Heybridge Swifts	Hornchurch	Letchworth Garden C	Purfleet	Rainham T	Royston T	Saffron Walden T	Stevenage Borough	Tilbury	Tring T	Vauxhall Motors	Ware	Witham T	Wolverton T
Aveley	—	2-1	2-0	0-1	3-1	3-0	2-0	2-1	2-1	1-1	1-1	1-2	2-1	3-2	1-0	0-1	1-0	1-0	2-0	1-0	1-0	1-1
Barton Rovers	3-1	—	1-2	3-0	2-2	4-1	1-0	2-1	1-3	2-0	1-1	2-3	2-1	3-1	2-0	1-1	1-0	1-1	0-1	2-3	2-1	2-1
Berkhamsted T	2-0	1-2	—	0-1	3-3	1-2	2-3	2-1	1-3	2-0	2-0	4-2	2-4	3-1	0-3	3-1	2-1	3-2	3-1	2-1	1-1	2-4
Billericay T	1-2	1-2	6-1	—	3-3	1-2	2-1	1-2	2-1	2-0	1-0	1-0	4-3	3-1	2-0	3-1	3-2	2-2	0-1	1-1	1-1	3-2
Clapton	0-1	1-0	1-1	1-2	—	2-2	2-1	1-0	1-1	3-3	2-2	3-0	0-0	0-2	2-0	3-1	2-0	0-2	3-1	1-1	0-3	0-0
Harlow T	3-0	4-1	1-2	1-0	3-0	—	2-0	0-0	3-1	3-0	2-2	1-4	0-0	2-1	2-0	2-1	1-1	0-2	3-1	1-3	0-3	1-0
Hemel Hempstead	2-0	1-0	1-0	2-0	1-1	1-0	—	2-0	1-2	2-2	0-0	1-1	3-0	2-3	1-1	2-0	2-1	0-1	1-2	6-1	0-3	2-0
Hertford T	0-2	3-0	0-1	1-1	1-2	2-1	0-3	—	2-0	1-1	3-0	3-0	0-0	3-3	0-2	1-2	2-2	0-0	1-3	2-0	0-3	2-1
Heybridge Swifts	2-0	2-0	0-1	2-0	1-2	0-1	0-3	2-0	—	1-1	0-0	1-3	0-1	2-2	2-1	1-2	2-2	2-1	1-2	1-2	0-3	1-1
Hornchurch	1-1	1-1	0-0	3-3	2-6	0-1	0-1	1-1	2-0	—	1-1	2-3	0-1	2-1	1-1	2-3	1-1	1-0	1-1	1-3	2-1	0-3
Letchworth Garden C	0-1	0-0	0-1	2-1	2-1	1-5	1-2	2-1	0-0	3-0	—	1-0	0-2	0-3	1-4	0-0	1-1	0-2	2-1	2-1	2-1	2-1
Purfleet	2-0	1-3	2-1	6-1	2-1	2-0	1-2	2-1	3-2	2-4	0-3	—	1-0	0-1	1-0	0-3	3-0	2-4	3-1	1-1	0-1	4-0
Rainham T	2-3	1-3	0-3	0-2	1-1	1-0	1-1	0-4	2-2	1-3	1-1	1-3	—	3-3	2-0	1-2	3-1	1-2	1-2	2-2	1-0	2-3
Royston T	0-1	2-1	2-1	3-2	0-0	2-3	0-1	2-2	0-2	1-0	0-1	2-3	3-3	—	3-0	1-3	3-1	3-1	2-0	2-0	0-1	3-1
Saffron Walden T	1-1	1-3	2-1	1-1	0-0	2-3	2-1	1-2	0-0	1-1	1-1	2-3	1-2	1-1	—	2-0	2-0	1-0	1-0	1-3	2-0	2-0
Stevenage Borough	3-0	3-3	2-1	6-0	1-0	2-0	2-0	3-5	2-2	1-3	2-1	0-0	1-1	3-0	3-4	—	2-3	1-1	4-0	3-2	1-0	4-1
Tilbury	2-3	0-0	0-1	1-0	0-0	1-1	2-1	3-2	2-0	1-2	3-0	1-1	1-1	3-0	0-0	3-1	—	1-2	1-2	0-2	3-0	3-0
Tring T	0-0	3-1	3-1	3-1	1-1	2-1	2-1	0-0	1-1	0-1	0-1	1-0	2-2	0-1	2-1	1-3	1-2	—	4-0	0-0	1-1	3-0
Vauxhall Motors	2-1	0-1	0-2	3-1	0-0	2-1	0-1	0-2	2-2	0-3	3-3	2-3	1-0	3-0	2-0	2-1	3-0	1-2	—	1-1	2-2	1-1
Ware	2-1	3-1	0-1	1-1	1-0	3-1	2-1	3-5	2-0	1-1	2-3	0-1	1-0	2-1	2-0	1-2	2-2	3-2	3-2	—	1-1	0-1
Witham T	4-3	2-1	3-1	2-2	3-0	3-0	2-1	1-4	0-0	0-1	2-3	3-1	1-0	0-1	1-1	2-0	2-6	1-1	0-2	3-1	—	1-2
Wolverton T	0-4	2-3	3-0	1-1	0-1	1-2	2-2	1-4	0-2	2-2	0-0	1-2	1-3	3-2	0-2	0-4	0-2	2-1	1-1	0-1	1-2	—

240

DIVISION NORTH RESULTS 1988–89

Final table for season 1988–89

	P	W	D	L	F	A	Pts
Harlow T	42	27	9	6	83	38	90
Purfleet	42	22	12	8	60	42	78
Tring T	42	22	10	10	65	44	76
Stevenage Borough	42	20	13	9	84	55	73
Heybridge Swifts	42	21	9	12	64	43	72
Billericay T	42	19	11	12	65	52	68
Clapton	42	18	11	13	65	56	65
Barton Rovers	42	18	11	13	58	50	65
Aveley	42	18	10	14	54	52	64
Hertford T	42	16	13	13	62	49	59*
Ware	42	17	8	17	60	65	59
Hemel Hempstead	42	16	10	16	55	58	58
Witham T	42	16	7	19	69	67	55
Vauxhall Motors	42	15	9	18	53	57	54
Berkhamsted T	42	14	10	18	57	70	52
Hornchurch	42	11	16	15	59	61	49
Tilbury	42	13	10	19	53	60	49
Royston T	42	12	7	23	46	72	43
Rainham T	42	8	15	18	49	62	42
Saffron Walden T	42	8	16	18	54	72	40
Letchworth Garden C	42	4	18	20	34	71	30
Wolverton T	24	5	7	30	42	95	13**

*2 pts deducted by League ** 9 pts deducted by League*

Leading goalscorers

		LGE+CUP
30	Jeff Wood (Harlow T)	28+2
27	Mark Watkins (Tring T)	27
20	Martin Gitings (Harlow T)	20
	(includes 18 League goals for Stevenage Borough)	
	Bobby Moyce (Aveley)	20
	(includes 4 League goals for Rainham T)	
	Jason Spiteri (Clapton)	20
19	Cliff Campbell (Barton Rovers)	18+1

Top attendances

512	Stevenage Borough	v	Harlow T
443	Billericay T	v	Harlow T
379	Aveley	v	Tilbury
316	Ware	v	Stevenage Borough
289	Tring T	v	Harlow T
281	Royston T	v	Stevenage Borough

VAUXHALL OPEL LEAGUE SECOND

	Banstead Ath	Camberley T	Chertsey T	Dorking	Eastbourne U	Egham T	Epsom & Ewell	Feltham	Finchley	Flackwell Heath	Harefield U	Horsham	Hungerford T	Maidenhead U	Molesey	Newbury T	Petersfield U	Ruislip Manor	Southall	Whyteleafe	Yeading
Banstead Ath	—	2-3	2-3	0-2	0-2	1-0	3-0	3-0	1-2	1-1	1-2	0-2	0-0	1-2	0-0	1-0	3-0	2-0	0-0	2-4	0-0
Camberley T	0-3	—	0-4	2-3	1-3	2-1	2-0	2-1	1-2	0-1	2-4	0-1	2-2	2-2	1-2	3-1	2-0	0-2	0-5	0-3	1-1
Chertsey T	2-0	0-3	—	1-2	1-1	2-3	1-0	1-2	2-2	0-2	1-1	3-1	1-0	4-1	0-0	4-2	0-0	1-1	1-0	1-6	3-2
Dorking	8-1	5-0	4-2	—	1-1	4-2	3-2	0-2	3-1	1-2	2-1	3-1	1-1	3-0	2-0	4-2	0-3	1-3	5-0	2-4	3-0
Eastbourne U	0-2	2-0	1-3	2-4	—	1-3	5-2	4-1	3-0	0-1	0-3	1-1	3-2	0-0	1-0	3-1	5-2	2-1	0-3	0-1	1-2
Egham T	1-0	1-2	2-1	1-3	2-1	—	1-2	3-1	1-2	0-0	3-0	1-1	3-2	0-0	3-0	2-3	3-0	2-1	2-3	1-3	1-2
Epsom & Ewell	3-0	3-1	3-0	1-3	2-2	2-1	—	4-0	0-0	5-1	1-0	4-1	1-3	2-3	1-1	0-3	2-1	2-1	2-1	0-0	1-0
Feltham	3-0	0-1	1-3	0-3	2-1	0-3	1-1	—	1-1	5-2	0-4	3-0	4-1	2-0	1-1	3-0	3-3	1-3	2-3	2-2	3-1
Finchley	2-0	1-1	1-2	1-3	1-0	0-3	3-1	2-1	—	2-1	2-1	1-0	2-2	2-2	0-1	1-3	2-1	1-2	2-1	2-2	1-0
Flackwell Heath	1-1	0-1	2-3	0-2	3-1	2-4	3-1	0-0	0-0	—	2-2	1-1	4-2	1-0	1-1	0-3	2-2	2-3	2-1	0-0	3-1
Harefield U	1-2	2-4	1-1	1-4	4-0	1-1	1-3	1-1	2-4	1-2	—	1-2	0-2	1-0	1-0	0-3	2-2	2-0	0-1	2-2	0-1
Horsham	0-2	0-0	4-1	1-2	0-0	3-0	3-0	2-1	0-3	3-0	3-1	—	2-0	4-0	1-0	4-1	1-0	1-1	3-1	1-1	2-0
Hungerford T	0-0	0-1	0-0	0-4	3-3	1-2	2-2	1-1	0-1	5-1	1-1	0-1	—	0-2	4-0	3-0	1-1	0-1	1-1	3-2	0-0
Maidenhead U	1-2	0-1	1-1	0-2	0-0	1-2	3-0	3-2	1-1	2-3	1-0	2-0	1-0	—	2-1	2-0	0-2	1-0	2-0	2-2	2-1
Molesey	1-0	2-0	2-0	0-3	1-0	2-1	3-1	4-0	1-1	0-0	0-1	0-0	0-0	0-1	—	0-3	2-3	1-1	1-1	1-3	4-1
Newbury T	2-2	0-3	4-1	1-0	3-3	1-0	2-2	1-0	3-3	1-3	0-3	4-0	0-1	2-0	3-0	—	1-4	2-1	2-1	2-1	2-0
Petersfield U	2-1	2-0	1-1	0-4	3-2	1-3	3-0	0-3	0-0	0-4	0-1	0-0	0-3	0-3	2-3	3-1	—	2-1	3-1	3-2	3-1
Ruislip Manor	2-1	2-0	0-0	1-0	0-1	3-0	2-1	1-1	0-4	1-0	2-1	2-0	4-0	1-0	1-2	2-1	6-2	—	2-0	2-0	2-0
Southall	0-2	0-2	0-1	0-0	1-1	0-1	1-2	3-0	0-3	1-3	0-1	2-0	0-1	2-0	4-0	2-0	4-0	2-1	—	4-0	6-1
Whyteleafe	3-2	5-2	1-1	0-1	3-1	1-0	1-1	1-0	3-2	0-2	2-1	4-0	3-3	3-1	3-1	0-1	2-1	2-1	2-1	—	1-3
Yeading	2-2	3-2	2-2	0-2	0-1	1-2	1-3	0-0	0-6	3-1	0-2	1-1	3-0	1-1	4-1	2-0	1-0	3-2	1-1	1-3	—

DIVISION SOUTH RESULTS 1988–89

Final table for season 1988–89

	P	W	D	L	F	A	Pts
Dorking	40	32	4	4	109	35	100
Whytcleafe	40	25	9	6	86	41	84
Finchley	40	21	9	10	70	45	72
Molesey	40	19	13	8	58	42	70
Harefield U	40	19	7	14	56	45	64
Hungerford T	40	17	13	10	55	45	64
Ruislip Manor	40	16	9	15	56	43	57
Feltham	40	16	9	15	58	43	57
Epsom & Ewell	40	16	8	16	55	55	56
Egham T	40	16	7	17	54	58	55
Eastbourne U	40	15	9	16	68	61	54
Chertsey T	40	13	14	13	55	58	53
Flackwell Heath	40	13	11	16	51	49	50
Camberley T	40	15	5	20	51	71	50
Yeading	40	13	9	18	47	63	46*
Banstead Ath	40	12	8	20	50	65	44
Maidenhead U	40	10	13	17	44	61	43
Southall	40	11	10	19	41	73	43
Newbury T	40	11	8	21	47	65	41
Horsham	40	7	14	19	36	68	35
Petersfield U	40	5	7	28	36	87	22

* 2 pts deducted by League

Leading goalscorers

		LGE+CUP
32	Andy Bushnell (Dorking)	32
28	Steve Milton (Whyteleafe)	27+1
25	John Daubney (Eastbourne U)	25
21	Paul Grainger (Dorking)	16+5
	Glen Price (Camberley T)	21
20	Lee Mooney (Feltham)	18+2

Top attendances

365	Whyteleafe	v	Dorking
315	Dorking	v	Eastbourne U
258	Epsom & Ewell	v	Dorking
236	Ruislip Manor	v	Yeading
235	Egham T	v	Southall
225	Horsham	v	Dorking

OTHER LEAGUE TABLES 1988–89

Bass North West Counties League – First Division

	P	W	D	L	F	A	Pts
Rossendale U	34	24	8	2	84	27	56
Knowsley U	34	21	8	5	85	43	50
—St Helens T	34	20	8	6	60	25	48
Colwyn Bay	34	19	9	6	77	45	47
Darwen	34	19	9	6	64	36	47
Warrington T	34	16	10	8	47	37	42
Flixton	34	15	8	11	61	44	38
Leyland Motors	34	15	8	11	53	44	38
Bootle	34	14	4	16	49	54	32
Burscough	34	11	10	13	40	51	32
Ellesmere Port	34	9	12	13	36	42	30
Clitheroe	34	8	12	14	38	41	28
Skelmersdale U	34	8	9	17	39	68	25
Atherton L.R.	34	9	6	19	47	74	24
Prescot Cables	34	7	9	18	36	60	23
Salford	34	7	8	19	33	70	22
Ashton U	34	7	6	21	37	72	18*
Formby	34	3	4	27	24	77	10

*pts deducted for breach of rule

Highland League

	P	W	D	L	F	A	Pts
Peterhead	34	22	7	5	79	38	73
Cove Rangers	34	21	6	7	71	38	69
Huntly	34	20	6	8	82	40	66
Inverness Th	34	19	9	6	70	29	66
Elgin C	34	19	9	6	73	37	66
Keith	34	19	8	7	61	32	65
Forres Mechanics	34	18	9	7	63	34	63
Ross Co	34	18	3	13	61	51	57
Buckie Th	34	16	6	12	66	53	54
Caledonian	34	14	11	9	70	42	53
Fraserburgh	34	15	8	11	52	43	53
Lossiemouth	34	11	7	16	57	66	40
Deveronvale C	34	8	7	19	44	80	31
Brora Rangers	34	8	2	24	42	67	26
Clachnacuddin	34	6	6	22	34	83	24
Nairn Co	34	5	8	21	49	102	23
Rothes	34	4	4	26	41	104	16
Fort William	34	3	4	27	24	100	13

Central League – First Division

	P	W	D	L	F	A	Pts
Nottingham F	34	20	6	8	83	45	66
• Everton	34	19	7	8	70	35	64
Aston Villa	34	18	7	9	73	50	61
Liverpool	34	16	9	9	64	40	57
Coventry C	34	17	6	11	66	52	57
Derby C	34	15	11	8	44	33	56
Sheffield U	34	14	9	11	67	74	51
Huddersfield T	34	12	12	10	51	54	48
Leeds U	34	13	7	14	59	59	46
Leicester C	34	13	6	15	65	63	45
Manchester C	34	12	9	13	64	65	45
Blackburn R	34	13	2	19	55	62	41
Manchester U	34	10	10	14	61	62	40
Newcastle U	34	10	10	14	51	58	40
WBA	34	10	8	16	55	76	38
Barnsley	34	8	9	17	46	80	33
Sheffield W	34	8	8	18	40	70	32
Sunderland	34	6	8	20	40	76	26

Central League – Second Division

	P	W	D	L	F	A	Pts
Hull C	34	25	3	6	82	38	78
Notts C	34	20	8	6	77	48	68
Bradford C	34	19	7	8	78	53	64
Oldham Ath	34	18	8	8	67	39	62
Bolton W	34	18	8	8	77	52	62
Stoke C	34	17	10	7	60	38	61
Middlesbrough	34	15	7	12	78	61	52
Darlington	34	13	7	14	50	60	46
Rotherham U	34	12	6	16	60	64	42
Grimsby T	34	12	5	17	47	61	41
Blackpool	34	12	5	17	52	78	41
Preston NE	34	12	4	18	56	63	40
Port Vale	34	11	6	17	44	58	39
York C	34	10	8	16	52	58	38
Mansfield T	34	9	11	14	59	68	38
Wigan Ath	34	7	11	16	44	60	32
Scunthorpe U	34	8	7	19	39	68	31
Doncaster R	34	4	7	23	31	86	19

Midland Football Combination – Premier Division

	P	W	D	L	F	A	Pts
Boldmere St Michaels	34	23	9	2	76	22	55
Racing Club Warwick	34	22	8	4	77	31	52
Evesham U	34	21	7	6	82	30	49
Princes End U	34	17	9	8	58	37	43
West Midlands Police........	34	18	6	10	66	41	42
Northfield T	34	15	10	9	55	43	40
Stratford T	34	14	10	10	60	44	38
Walsall Wood	34	13	10	11	49	52	36
Hinckley	34	12	11	11	49	55	35
Highgate........................	34	9	15	10	60	61	33
Bolehall Swifts.................	34	12	8	14	44	55	32
Kings Heath	34	9	11	14	42	52	29
Chelmsley T	34	10	7	17	37	65	27
Knowle...........................	34	8	10	16	34	58	26
Polesworth North Warwick	34	4	14	16	37	62	22
Coleshill T	34	8	6	20	46	73	22
Solihull Borough	34	7	6	21	41	72	20
Shirley T........................	34	4	3	27	20	80	11

Skol Northern League – First Division

	P	W	D	L	F	A	Pts
Billingham Synthonia	38	26	6	6	83	34	84
Tow Law T	38	23	8	7	74	45	77
Gretna	38	22	7	9	80	37	73
Guisborough T	38	21	9	8	74	37	72
Billingham T	38	20	4	14	59	47	64
Newcastle Blue Star..........	38	17	10	11	61	38	61
Brandon U......................	38	15	8	15	50	60	53
Ferryhill Ath	38	15	7	16	72	65	52
Blyth Spartans	38	13	13	12	51	50	52
Stockton	38	15	7	16	58	63	52
Spennymoor U	38	14	9	15	47	60	51
Whitby T	38	13	9	16	56	52	48
Easington Colliery............	38	12	11	15	51	57	47
Durham C	38	11	13	14	41	42	46
South Bank	38	12	10	16	46	58	46
Seaham Red Star	38	12	8	18	50	67	44
Shildon..........................	38	9	11	18	50	88	38
North Shields	38	10	6	22	56	77	36
Chester-le-Street T	38	6	14	18	35	60	32
Crook T	38	5	8	25	32	89	20*

*3pts deducted

Banks's Brewery West Midland (Regional) League – Premier Division

	P	W	D	L	F	A	Pts
Blakenall	40	25	11	4	81	31	86
Gresley	40	24	13	3	100	30	85
Halesowen Harriers	40	23	9	8	74	43	78
Paget Rangers	40	23	8	9	91	41	77
Rushall Olympic	40	22	11	7	73	39	77
Oldbury U	40	22	10	8	89	49	76
Hinckley T	40	23	6	11	96	38	75
Lye T	40	20	7	13	61	42	67
Chasetown	40	19	9	12	54	48	66
Malvern T	40	17	12	11	81	47	63
Rocester	40	14	15	11	67	49	57
Harrisons	40	12	10	18	50	71	46
Tividale	40	10	9	21	65	84	39
Hinckley Ath	40	9	12	19	50	76	39
Wolverhampton Casuals	40	8	13	19	49	86	37
Wednesfield Social	40	9	8	23	33	82	35
Westfields	40	8	9	23	43	97	33
Millfields	40	9	5	26	42	85	32
Oldswinford	40	8	8	24	42	98	32
Tipton T	40	8	6	26	30	86	30
Stourport Swifts	40	6	11	23	45	94	29

Great Mills League – Premier Division

	P	W	D	L	F	A	Pts
Saltash U	40	26	10	4	90	35	62
Exmouth T	40	29	4	7	79	43	62
Taunton T	40	23	10	7	95	41	56
Liskeard Ath	40	20	12	8	46	25	52
Plymouth Argyle	40	19	13	8	84	39	51
Bristol Manor Farm	40	20	7	13	72	49	47
Weston-super-Mare	40	17	8	15	73	52	42
Paulton Rovers	40	14	14	12	60	53	42
Barnstaple T	40	17	7	16	61	54	41
Swanage & Herston	40	15	10	15	71	73	40
Clevedon T	40	16	7	17	63	70	39
Chippenham T	40	11	14	15	48	52	36
Welton Rovers	40	13	10	17	50	57	36
Radstock T	40	9	18	13	38	65	36
Chard T	40	12	11	17	49	78	35
Bideford	40	12	9	19	49	72	33
Frome T	40	11	10	19	54	80	32
Mangotsfield U	40	10	9	21	53	74	29
Dawlish T	40	11	7	22	48	69	29
Torrington	40	7	12	21	46	84	26
Minehead	40	5	4	31	30	94	14

Nene Group United Counties League – Premier Division

	P	W	D	L	F	A	Pts
Potton	38	24	6	8	70	37	78
Brackley	38	20	8	10	71	33	68
Holbeach	38	18	10	10	70	46	64
Irthlingborough	38	17	13	8	56	37	64
Rothwell	38	18	8	12	63	55	62
Raunds	38	18	8	12	54	47	62
Stamford	38	17	10	11	55	51	61
Wootton	38	17	8	13	50	46	59
Long Buckby	38	15	8	15	60	55	53
Stotfold	38	14	10	14	59	55	52
Desborough	38	13	10	15	58	65	49
Eynesbury	38	12	12	14	47	44	48
N'ton Spencer	38	13	8	17	56	55	47
Arlesey	38	14	5	19	40	66	47
S & L Corby	38	12	8	18	57	68	44
Cogenhoe	38	12	8	18	53	71	44
Baker Perkins	38	10	11	17	43	62	41
M Blackstone	38	10	8	20	43	58	38
Kempston	38	8	11	19	46	67	35
Bourne	38	8	10	20	39	72	34

Ovenden Papers Combination

	P	W	D	L	F	A	Pts
Tottenham H	38	23	10	5	90	37	56
Arsenal	38	20	12	6	83	44	52
Wimbledon	38	22	7	9	77	39	51
Watford	38	20	9	9	90	60	49
Chelsea	38	20	9	9	74	52	49
Millwall	38	19	10	9	79	46	48
Luton T	38	18	10	10	90	55	46
Swindon T	38	20	5	13	70	62	45
Oxford U	38	18	7	13	82	66	43
Crystal Palace	38	16	9	13	55	44	41
Ipswich T	38	18	5	15	63	62	41
Norwich C	38	16	8	14	64	63	40
Southampton	38	15	7	16	66	67	37
West Ham U	38	9	10	19	53	72	28
Brighton & H A	38	7	13	18	43	81	27
Fulham	38	10	7	21	49	96	27
Charlton Ath	38	8	9	21	59	80	25
Portsmouth	38	8	6	24	33	88	22
QPR	38	6	5	27	36	79	17
Reading	38	5	6	27	38	101	16

FA CHALLENGE VASE 1988–89

Third Round

Harrogate RA	6	Borrowash Vic	3
Whickham	3	Dunston FB	0
Ossett T	2 1	Bridlington T	2 0
Emley	4	Guiseley	0
Garforrth T	1	Rossendale U	4
North Ferriby U	3	Murton	0
Ilkeston T	4	Northfield T	2
Paget Rangers	3	Louth U	1
Halesowen Harriers	0	Heanor T	1
Gresley Rovers	1	Tamworth	3
Eastwood Hanley	3	Poulton Vic	1
Vauxhall GM (Cheshire)	1	Holbeach U	2
Brigg T	2 1	Boldmere St Michaels	2 0
Braintree T	0 2	Finchley	0 0
Cheshunt	1	Bury T	3
Berkhamsted T	2	Wisbech T	4
Harlow T	3	Tilbury	3

(tie awarded to Tilbury as Harlow T failed to fulfil the replay fixture)

East Thurrock U	3	Great Yarmouth T	0
Burnham Ramblers	6	Haverhill Rovers	0
March Town U	1	Sudbury T	2
Hailsham T	1	Darenth Heathside	0
Burgess Hill T	1 1	Chertsey T	1 3
Hungerford T	5	Eastbourne T	1
Wick	1 2	Epsom & Ewell	1 4
Hounslow	2	Corinthian	0
Havant T	1	Camberley T	7
Abingdon U	0	Thatcham T	1
Bashley	4	Moreton T	1
Paulton Rovers	4	Devizes T	3
Welton Rovers	5	Yate T	1
Romsey T	1	Bridport	2
Tiverton T	3	Chippenham T	0

Fourth Round

Ossett T	1	Whickham	0
Rossendale U	3	Emley	1
Heanor T	1 1	Eastwood Hanley	1 2
North Ferriby U	2 3	Harrogate RA	2 1
Ilkeston T	1	Tamworth	2
Brigg T	3	Holbeach U	5
Braintree T	0 1	Bury T	0 2
Wisbech T	1	Paget Rangers	0
East Thurrock U	2	Chertsey T	0
Hounslow	0	Sudbury U	1
Epsom & Ewell	1	Hailsham T	2
Tilbury	0	Burnham Ramblers	1
Camberley T	0	Hungerford T	1
Bridport	3	Welton Rovers	0
Tiverton T	1	Thatcham T	2
Paulton Rovers	1	Bashley	3

Ossett T	1	North Ferriby U	2
Eastwood Hanley	0	Tamworth	1
Holbeach U	2	Wisbech T	4
Rossendale U	0	Sudbury T	1
Bury T	2	Burnham Ramblers	0
Hailsham T	2	Hungerford T	3
Bridport	0	Thatcham T	2
East Thurrock U	1	Bashley	4

Quarter-finals

Bury T	1	North Ferriby U	2
Sudbury T	2	Bashley	0
Tamworth	1	Wisbech T	0
Hungerford T	2	Thatcham T	0

Semi-finals *(2 legs)*

Tamworth	1 3	North Ferriby U	2 1
Hungerford T	0 0	Sudbury T	0 6

Final at Wembley, 6 May 1989, att. 26,487
Sudbury T .... (1)1 *(Hubbick)*   Tamworth .... (0)1 *(Devaney)*
Replay at Peterborough, 10 May 1989, att. 11, 201
Tamworth (1)3 *(Stanton 2, Moores)*   Sudbury Town .... (0)0

FA CHALLENGE TROPHY 1988–89

First Round

Bangor C	2	South Bank	3
Matlock T	2	Northwich Vic	6
Boston U	2	Stafford Rangers	0
Stockton	1	Hyde U	4
Telford U	3	Witton Albion	0
Burton Albion	4	Chorley	1
Colwyn Bay	1 0	Frickley Ath	1 3
Marine	2 1	Macclesfield T	2 4
Buxton	0	Altrincham	2
Leicester U	3	Blyth Spartans	0
Runcorn	2	Gretna	3
Newcastle Blue Star	1	S. L'pool	0
Fleetwood T	0 1	Bishop Auckland	0 5
Atherstone U	1	Barrow	4
Fisher Ath	0	Cheltenham T	1
Dover Ath	3	Worcester C	1
Bromsgrove Rovers	2	Woking	3
Fareham T	1	Yeovil T	0
Windsor & Eton	2	Gosport Borough	0
Enfield	4	Hendon	1
Barnet	1 1	Gravesend & Northfleet	1 2
Sutton U	1	Kingstonian	0
Kidderminster Harriers	2	Maidstone U	0
Bath C	0 0	Wycombe Wanderers	0 4

Dagenham	2 0	Aylesbury U	2 4
Uxbridge	1 2	Carshalton Ath	1 5
Wokingham T	2 0	Merthyr Tydfil	2 1
Dartford	4	Dorchester T	0
Weymouth	2	Newport Co	1
Welling U	4	Slough T	0
Basingstoke T	1 3	Kettering T	1 5
Bromley	1	Wealdstone	2

Second Round

Boston U	3	Northwich Vic	2
Gravesend & Northfleet	1 2	Kettering T	1 1
Kidderminster Harriers	1 1	Burton Albion	1 0
Aylesbury U	1	Merthyr Tydfil	3
Sutton U	1 1	Bishop Auckland	1 2
Wealdstone	0	Wycombe Wanderers	1
Cheltenham T	0 0 0	Barrow	0 0 1
Altrincham	2	Carshalton Ath	0
Windsor & Eton	1	Enfield	0
Woking	2	Weymouth	1
South Bank	0	Macclesfield T	3
Hyde United	1 3	Gretna	1 2
Newcastle Blue Star	3	Frickley Ath	1
Dover Ath	0 0	Dartford	0 2
Yeovil T	1	Telford U	4
Leicester U	1	Welling U	3

Third Round

Dartford	2	Bishop Auckland	0
Newcastle Blue Star	2	Woking	0
Windsor & Eton	2 0	Hyde U	2 2
Kidderminster Harriers	1 0	Telford U	1 2
Welling U	0 1	Boston U	0 0
Wycombe Wanderers	2	Merthyr Tydfil	0
Altrincham	5	Barrow	3
Macclesfield T	2	Gravesend & Northfleet	0

Quarter-finals

Macclesfield T	1	Welling U	0
Newcastle Blue Star	1	Telford U	4
Hyde U	1	Wycombe Wanderers	0
Dartford	1	Altrincham	0

Semi-finals *(2 legs)*

Dartford	0 1	Macclesfield T	0 4
Hyde U	0 0	Telford U	1 3

Final at Wembley, 13 May 1989, att. 18,106
Macclesfield T .... (0)0   Telford U .... (0)1 (*Crawley*) aet.

FA YOUTH CUP 1988–89

Second Round

Bradford C	2	Port Vale	1
Liverpool	3	Carlisle U	0
Burnley	1	Leeds U	2
Blackpool	1	Newcastle U	2
Darlington	2	Manchester U	5
Doncaster Rovers	1 1	←Everton	1 4
Middlesbrough	2 0	Sheffield Wednesday	2 2
Oldham Ath	1	Sheffield U	2
Mansfield T	0	Manchester C	1
Crewe Alex	1	Hull C	4
Hednesford T	0	Birmingham C	5
Leicester C	2	Nottingham F	1
Aston Villa	1	Luton T	3
Northampton T	0	Walsall	3
Colchester U	2	Southend U	3
Derby Co	1 1	Coventry C	1 3
West Bromwich Albion	3	West Ham U	1
Notts Co	2 1	Ipswich T	2 4
Watford	1 0 2	Leyton Orient	1 0 1
Cambridge U	2 1	Stoke C	2 6
Tottenham H	7	Peterborough U	1
Epson & Ewell	0	Arsenal	11
Crystal Palace	2	Southampton	1
Queen's Park Rangers	3	Fulham	1
(at Yeading FC)			
Whyteleafe	1	Reading	5
Newbury Town	0	Cardiff City	3
Brighton & H A	1	Charlton Ath	7
Millwall	2	Hereford U	0
Wimbledon	0	Chelsea	4
Bristol C	2	Plymouth Argyle	3
AFC Bournemouth	2	Brentford	3
Portsmouth	1	Gillingham	0

Third Round

←Everton	0 1	Leicester C	0 4
Newcastle U	4	Walsall	3
Coventry C	2	Liverpool	4
Leeds U	0 1 2	Birmingham C	0 1 4
Sheffield U	0 0	Bradford C	0 1
Manchester C	1	Hull C	0
Sheffield Wednesday	0 0	Manchester U	0 2
Chelsea	2 1	Ipswich T	2 2
Millwall	4	Reading	2
Plymouth Argyle	0	Portsmouth	6
Charlton Ath	2 0	Tottenham H	2 2

Cardiff C 0	Stoke C 1
Brentford 1	Crystal Palace 0
Watford 2 2	Queens Park Rangers...............2 0
West Bromwich Albion 3	Southend U 2
Arsenal.....................................3	Luton T 2

Fourth Round

Brentford...............................1 2	Stoke C 1 1
Millwall 0	Liverpool 1
Manchester U 4	Ipswich T 1
Bradford C................................0	Manchester C 5
Leicester C................................1	Newcastle U 3
Portsmouth.............................1 2	Watford 1 5
Arsenal.....................................2	West Bromwich Albion 0
Tottenham H.............................2	Birmingham C 1

Quarter-finals

Tottenham H.............................0	Manchester C 2
Newcastle U 1	Arsenal.....................................0
Watford 3	Liverpool 0
Brentford..................................2	Manchester U 1

Semi-finals *(2 legs)*

Watford 2 2	Brentford...............................1 2
Manchester C 2 1	Newcastle U 1 0

Final *(2 legs)*

Manchester C ....(1)1 (*Wallace*)	Watford ....(0)0 att. 4900
Watford ....(0)2 (*Gunn, Thomas*)	Manchester C (0)0 aet. att. 5442

FA SUNDAY CUP 1988–89

Second Round

Oakenshaw................................1	Blackhall WMC..........................5
Nenthead 1 0	Sunderland Humbledon Plains ... 1 3
Almethak...................................2	Eagle...1
Morrison Sports 2	Lynemouth Inn 0
East Bowling Unity.....................2	Cleator Moor WMC.....................5
Boundary...................................1	Croxtoth & Gillmoss RDL 3
Northwood.................................3	Whetley Lane WMC 0
Deborah United..........................1	Woodpecker 4
East Levenshulme 3	Nicosia 2
Hoval Farrar..............................5	Railway Hotel............................1
Fantail......................................0	Lodge Cottrell 2
Avenue Victoria Lodge 1 2	FC Coachman 1 1
Iron Bridge 0	Slade Celtic 1
Chuckery WMC 2	Brereton Town............................3
Greenleys..................................	Lion Rangers..............................
(walkover for Greenleys)	
FC Nirvana 1	Birmingham Celtic......................0
Veralum Arms Ath......................4	Sandwell 3
Girton Eagles 3	Dereham Hobbies U....................1
Grosvenor Park..........................5	Kettering Odyssey 1

Hazel Tennants	2	Leyton Argyle	1
Halesowen Harriers	4	Brimsdown Rovers	0
Newey Goodman	1	Leggatts Ath	0
Inter Volante	3	HSC	2
Ford Basildon	3	Colne Hammers	1
Sheffield House Rangers	2	Santogee 66	3
Nexday	1	Rolls Royce Sunday	0
Hallen Sunday	5	St Josephs (South Oxhey)	4
Oxford Road Social	0	Lee Chapel North	2
Artois U	0	Chequers	1
Cabot Towers	4	Horndean	1
Broad Plain House	1	Ranelagh Sports	0
Sartan U	2 2	Watford Labour Club	2 1

Third Round

Woodpecker	3	Cleator Moor WMC	0
Avenue Vitoria Lodge	5	Morrison Sports	1
Blackhall WMC	3	Croxteth & Gillmoss RBL	1

(Blackhall subsequently disqualified following misconduct by their supporters. Croxteth were not awarded the tie following misconduct by their players)

Almethak	2	Northwood	0
Sunderland Humbledon Plains	0	East Levenshulme	2
Hoval Farrar	0	Slade Celtic	3
Girton Eagles	4	FC Nirvana	1
Lodge Cottrell	1	Verulam Arms Ath	0
Hazel Tennants	4	Brereton T	2
Grosvenor Park	0	Greenleys	1
Halesowen Harriers	0	Broad Plain House	8
Newey Goodman	2	Hallen Sunday	0
Chequers	0	Nexday	4
Cabot Towers	2 1	Inter Volante	2 4
Ford Basildon	4	Santogee 66	1
Sartan United	0	Lee Chapel North	2

Fourth Round

East Levenshulme	3	Avenue Victoria Lodge	2
Blackhall WMC		Woodpecker	
(walkover for Woodpecker)			
Almethak	3	Slade Celtic	0
Ford Basildon	5	Hazel Tennants	1
Nexday	4	Girton Eagles	0
Greenleys	0	Lodge Cottrell	3
Lee Chapel North	2	Broad Plain House	0
Inter Volante	2 1	Newey Goodman	2 2

Quarter-finals

Almethak	2	Newey Goodman	1
Woodpecker	0	East Levenshulme	3
Lee Chapel North	2	Lodge Cottrell	3
Nexday	3	Ford Basildon	2

Semi-finals

East Levenshulme	4	Lodge Cottrell	1
(at Warrington T FC)			

Nexday 0   Almethak 1
(at Irthlingborough Diamonds FC)

Final: East Levenshulme 1   Almethak 3

LEAGUE REFEREES FOR SEASON 1989–90

ALCOCK, P.E. (S. Merstham Surrey)
ALLISON, D.B. (Lancaster)
APLIN, G. (Kendal)
ASHBY, G.R. (Worcester)
ASHWORTH, J. (Luffenham, Leics.)
AXCELL, D.J. (Southend)
BAILEY, M.C. (Impington, Cambridge)
BARRATT, K.P. (Coventry)
BELL, S.D. (Huddersfield)
BENNETT, A. (Chesterfield)
BIGGER, R.L. (Croydon)
BODENHAM, M.J. (Looe, Cornwall)
BORRETT, I.J. (Harleston, Norfolk)
BREEN, K.J. (Liverpool)
BUKSH, A.N. (London)
BURGE, W.K. (Tonypandy)
BURNS, W.C. (Scarborough)
BUTLER, N.S. (E. Grinstead, W. Sussex)
CALLOW, V.G. (Solihull)
CARTER, J.M. (Christchurch)
COOPER, K. (Pontypridd)
COOPER, K.A. (Swindon)
COURTNEY, G. (Spennymoor)
CRUIKSHANKS, I.G. (Hartlepool)
DANSON, P.S. (Leicester)
DAWSON, A. (Jarrow)
DEAKIN, J.C. (Llantwit Major, S. Glam.)
DILKES, L.R. (Mossley, Lancs.)
DON, P. (Hanworth Park, Middlesex)
DURKIN, P.A. (Portland, Dorset)
ELLERAY, D.R. (Harrow)
FITZHARRIS, T. (Bolton)
FLOOD, W.A. (Stockport)
FOAKES, P.L. (Clacton-on-Sea)
GIFFORD, R.B. (Llanbradach, Mid Glam.)
GROVES, R.G. (Weston-super-Mare)
GUNN, A. (South Chailey, Sussex)
HACKETT, K.S. (Sheffield)
HAMER, R.L. (Bristol)
HARRISON, P.W. (Oldham)
HART, R.A. (Darlington)
HEDGES, D.A. (Oxford)
HEMLEY, I.S. (Ampthill, Beds.)
HENDRICK, I.A. (Preston)
HILL, B. (Kettering)
HOLBROOK, T.J. (Walsall)
HUTCHINSON, D. (Marcham, Oxford)
JAMES, M.L. (Horsham)

JONES, P. (Loughborough)
KEY, J.M. (Sheffield)
KING, H.W. (Merthyr Tydfill)
KIRKBY, J.A. (Sheffield)
LEWIS, R.S. (Gt. Bookham, Surrey)
LLOYD, J.W. (Wrexham)
LODGE, S.J. (Barnsley)
LUNT, T. (Ashton-in-Makerfield, Lancs.)
LUPTON, K.A. (Stockton-on-Tees)
MARTIN, J.E. (Nr. Alton, Hants.)
MIDGLEY, N. (Bolton)
MILFORD, R.G. (Bristol)
MILLS, T. (Barnsley)
MORTON, K. (Bury St Edmunds)
MOULES, J.A. (Erith, Kent)
NIXON, R.F. (West Kirby, Wirral)
PARKER, E.J. (Preston)
PAWLEY, R.K. (Cambridge)
PECK, M.G. (Kendal)
PHILLIPS, D.T. (Barnsley)
PIERCE, M.E. (Portsmouth)
POOLEY, G.R. (Bishops Stortford)
REDFERN, K.A. (Whitley Bay)
REED, M.D. (Birmingham)
ROBERTS, F. (Prestatyn)
RUSHTON, J. (Stoke-on-Trent)
SCOTT, D. (Burnley)
SEVILLE, A. (Birmingham)
SHAPTER, L.C. (Torquay)
SIMMONS, A.F. (Cheadle Hulme, Cheshire)
SIMPSON, T. (Sowerby Bridge, W. Yorks.)
SINGH, G (Wolverhampton)
SMITH A.W. (Rubery, Birmingham)
STEVENS, B.T. (Stonehouse, Glos.)
TRUSSELL, C.C. (Liverpool)
TYLDESLEY, P.A. (Stockport)
TYSON, G.M. (Sunderland)
VANES, P.W. (Warley, W. Midlands)
VICKERS, D.S. (Ilford, Essex)
WARD, A.W. (London)
WATSON, J.L. (Whitley Bay)
WEST, T.E. (Hull)
WILKIE, A.B. (Chester-le-Street)
WISEMAN, R.M. (Borehamwood, Herts.)
WORRALL, J.B. (Warrington)
WRIGHT, P.L. (Northwich)

FOOTBALL AWARDS 1988–89
Footballer of the Year

The Football Writers' Association this year voted the Liverpool and Scotland player Steve Nichol Footballer of the Year.

Past winners: 1947–8 Stanley Matthews (Blackpool), 1948–9 Johnnie Carey (Manchester U), 1949–50 Joe Mercer (Arsenal), 1950–1 Harry Johnston (Blackpool), 1951–2 Billy Wright (Wolverhampton W), 1952–3 Nat Lofthouse (Bolton W), 1953–4 Tom Finney (Preston NE), 1954–5 Don Revie (Manchester C), 1955–6 Bert Trautmann (Manchester C), 1956–7 Tom Finney (Preston NE), 1957–8 Danny Blanchflower (Tottenham H), 1958–9 Sid Owen (Luton T), 1959–60 Bill Slater (Wolverhampton W), 1960–1 Danny Blanchflower (Tottenham H), 1961–2 Jimmy Adamson (Burnley), 1962–3 Stanley Matthews (Stoke C), 1963–4 Bobby Moore (West Ham U), 1964–5 Bobby Collins (Leeds U), 1965–6 Bobby Charlton (Manchester U), 1966–7 Jackie Charlton (Leeds U), 1967–8 George Best (Manchester U), 1968–9 Dave MacKay (Derby Co), Tony Book (Manchester C), 1969–70 Billy Bremner (Leeds U), 1970–1 Frank McLintock (Arsenal), 1971–2 Gordon Banks (Stoke C), 1972–3 Pat Jennings (Tottenham H), 1973–4 Ian Callaghan (Liverpool), 1974–5 Alan Mullery (Fulham), 1975–6 Kevin Keegan (Liverpool), 1976–7 Emlyn Hughes (Liverpool), 1977–8 Kenny Burns (Nottingham F), 1978–9 Kenny Dalglish (Liverpool), 1979–80 Terry McDermott (Liverpool), 1980–1 Frans Thijssen (Ipswich T), 1981–2 Steve Perryman (Tottenham H), 1982–3 Kenny Dalglish (Liverpool), 1983–4 Ian Rush (Liverpool), 1984–5 Neville Southall (Everton), 1985–6 Gary Lineker (Everton), 1986–7 Clive Allen (Tottenham H), 1987–8 John Barnes (Liverpool).

PFA Player of the Year
The Professional Footballers' Association chose Mark Hughes of Manchester United as their Player of the Year.

Past winners: 1974 Norman Hunter (Leeds U), 1975 Colin Todd (Derby Co), 1976 Pat Jennings (Tottenham H), 1977 Andy Gray (Aston Villa), 1978 Peter Shilton (Nottingham F), 1979 Liam Brady (Arsenal), 1980 Terry McDermott (Liverpool), 1981 John Wark (Ipswich T), 1982 Kevin Keegan OBE (Southampton), 1983 Kenny Dalglish (Liverpool), 1984 Ian Rush (Liverpool), 1985 Peter Reid (Everton), 1986 Gary Lineker (Everton), 1987 Clive Allen (Tottenham H), 1988 John Barnes (Liverpool).

PFA Young Player of the Year 1988–89: Paul Merson (Arsenal).

Barclays Manager of the Year 1988–89: George Graham (Arsenal).

Scottish Football Writers' Association Player of the Year 1989: Richard Gough (Rangers).

Past winners: 1965 Billy McNeill (Celtic), 1966 John Greig (Rangers), 1967 Ronnie Simpson (Celtic), 1968 Gordon Wallace (Raith R), 1969 Bobby Murdoch (Celtic) 1970 Pat Stanton (Hibernian), 1971 Martin Buchan (Aberdeen), 1972 Dave Smith (Rangers), 1973 George Connelly (Celtic), 1974 Scotland's World Cup Squad, 1975 Sandy Jardine (Rangers), 1976 John Greig (Rangers), 1977 Danny McGrain (Celtic), 1978 Derek Johnstone (Rangers), 1979 Andy Ritchie (Morton), 1980 Gordon Strachan (Aberdeen), 1981 Alan Rough (Partick Th), 1982 Paul Sturrock (Dundee U), 1983 Charlie Nicholas (Celtic), 1984 Willie Miller (Aberdeen), 1985 Hamish McAlpine (Dundee U), 1986 Sandy Jardine (Hearts), 1987 Brian McClair (Celtic), 1988 Paul McStay (Celtic).

Scottish PFA Player of the Year 1988–89: Theo Snelders (Aberdeen).

Past winners: 1978 Derek Johnstone (Rangers), 1979 Paul Hegarty (Dundee U), 1980 Davie Provan (Celtic), 1981 Sandy Clark (Airdrieonians), 1982 Mark McGhee (Aberdeen), 1983 Charlie Nicholas (Celtic), 1984 Willie Miller (Aberdeen), 1985 Jim Duffy (Morton), 1986 Richard Gough (Dundee U), 1987 Brian McClair (Celtic), 1988 Paul McStay (Celtic).

Scottish PFA Young Player of the Year 1988–89: Billy McKinlay (Dundee U).

European Footballer of the Year 1988: Marco van Basten (AC Milan).

Previous winners
1956 Stanley Matthews (Blackpool), 1957 Alfredo Di Stefano (Real Madrid), 1958 Raymond Kopa (Real Madrid), 1959 Alfredo Di Stefano (Real Madrid), 1960 Luis Suarez (Barcelona), 1961 Omar Sivori (Juventus), 1962 Josef Masopust (Dukla Prague), 1963 Lev Yashin (Moscow Dynamo), 1964 Denis Law (Manchester United), 1965 Eusebio (Benfica), 1966 Bobby Charlton (Manchester United), 1967 Florian Albert (Ferencvaros), 1968 George Best (Manchester United), 1969 Gianni Rivera (AC Milan), 1970 Gerd Muller (Bayern Munich), 1971 Johan Cruyff (Ajax), 1972 Franz Beckenbauer (Bayern Munich), 1973 Johan Cruyff (Barcelona), 1974 Johan Cruyff (Barcelona), 1975 Oleg Blokhin (Dynamo Kiev), 1976 Franz Beckenbauer (Bayern Munich), 1977 Allan Simonsen (Moenchengladbach), 1978 Kevin Keegan (SV Hamburg), 1979 Kevin Keegan (SV Hamburg), 1980 Karl-Heinz Rummenigge (Bayern Munich), 1981 Karl-Heinz Rummenigge (Bayern Munich), 1982 Paolo Rossi (Juventus), 1983 Michel Platini (Juventus), 1984 Michel Platini (Juventus), 1985 Michel Platini (Juventus), 1986 Igor Belanov (Dynamo Kiev), 1987 Ruud Gullit (AC Milan).

BRITISH FOOTBALL RECORDS

HIGHEST SCORES
First class match
Arbroath 36 Bon Accord 0 *Scottish Cup 1st Rd, 12.9.1985*
International match
England 13 Ireland 0 *Belfast, 18.2.1882*
Football League Tranmere R 13, Oldham Ath 4, *Division 3 (N) 26.12.1935*
FA Cup
Preston NE 26 Hyde U 0 *1st Rd, 15.10.1887*
League Cup
West Ham U 10 Bury 0 *2nd Rd, 2nd leg, 25.10.1983*
Liverpool 10 Fulham 0 *2nd Rd, 1st leg, 23.9.1986*
Scottish League
East Fife 13 Edinburg C 2 *Division 2, 11.12.1937*

MOST GOALS IN A SEASON
Football League
128 in 42 games, Aston Villa *Division 1, 1930–31*
128 in 42 games, Bradford C *Division 3 (N), 1928–29*
134 in 46 games, Peterborough U *Division 4, 1960–61*
Scottish League
142 in 34 games, Raith R *Division 2, 1937–38*

FEWEST GOALS IN A SEASON
Football League (*minimum 42 games*)
24 in 42 games, Stoke C *Division 1, 1984–85*
24 in 42 games, Watford *Division 2, 1971–72*
27 in 46 games, Stockport Co *Division 3, 1969–70*
Scottish League (*minimum 30 games*)
18 in 39 games, Stirling A *Division 1, 1980–81*

MOST GOALS AGAINST IN A SEASON
Football League
141 in 34 games, Darwen *Division 2, 1898–99*
Scottish League
146 in 38 games, Edinburgh C *Division 2, 1931–32*

FEWEST GOALS AGAINST IN A SEASON
Football League (*minimum 42 games*)
16 in 42 games, Liverpool *Division 1, 1978–79*
21 in 46 games, Port Vale *Division 3 (N), 1953–54*
Scottish League (*minimum 30 games*)
14 in 38 games, Celtic *Division 1, 1913–14*

MOST POINTS IN A SEASON
Football League (*2 points for a win*)
72 in 42 games, Doncaster R *Division 3 (N), 1946–47*
74 in 46 games, Lincoln C *Division 4, 1975–76*
Football League (*3 points for a win*)
76 in 38 games, Arsenal *Division 1, 1988–89*
76 in 38 games, Liverpool *Division 1, 1988–89*
90 in 40 games, Liverpool *Division 1, 1987–88*
90 in 42 games, Everton *Division 1, 1984–85*
102 in 46 games, Swindon T *Division 4, 1985–86*
Scottish League
72 in 44 games, Celtic *Premier Division, 1987–88*
69 in 38 games, Morton *Division 2, 1966–67*
76 in 42 games, Rangers *Division 1, 1920–21*

FEWEST POINTS IN A SEASON
Football League (*minimum 34 games*)
8 in 34 games, Doncaster R *Division 2, 1904–05*
8 in 34 games, Loughborough T *Division 2, 1899–1900*
11 in 40 games, Rochdale *Division 3 (N), 1931–32*
17 in 42 games, Stoke C *Division 1, 1984–85*
19 in 46 games, Workington *Division 4, 1976–77*
Scottish League (*minimum 30 games*)
6 in 30 games, Stirling A *Division 1, 1954–55*
7 in 34 games, Edinburgh C *Division 2, 1936–37*
11 in 36 games, St Johnstone *Premier Division, 1975–76*

MOST WINS IN A SEASON
Football League
33 in 42 games, Doncaster R *Division 3 (N), 1946–47*
Scottish League
27 in 36 games, Aberdeen *Premier Division, 1984–85*
33 in 38 games, Morton *Division 2, 1966–67*
35 in 42 games, Rangers *Division 1, 1920–21*
Home
Brentford won all 21 games in Division 3(S) in 1929–30
Away
Doncaster R won 18 out of 21 games in Division 3(N) in 1946–47

FEWEST WINS IN A SEASON
Football League *(minimum 34 games)*
1 in 34 games, Loughborough T *Division 2, 1899–1900*
2 in 46 games, Rochdale *Division 3, 1973–74*
Scottish League *(minimum 22 games)*
0 in 22 games, Vale of Leven *Division 1, 1891–92*
1 in 38 games, Forfar Ath *Division 2, 1974–75*

MOST DEFEATS IN A SEASON
Football League
33 in 40 games, Rochdale *Division 3(N), 1931–32*
Scottish League
30 in 36 games, Brechin C *Division 2, 1962–63*
31 in 42 games, St Mirren *Division 1, 1920–21*

FEWEST DEFEATS IN A SEASON
Football League *(minimum 20 games)*
0 in 22 games, Preston NE *Division 1, 1888–89*
0 in 28 games, Liverpool *Division 2, 1893–94*
2 in 40 games, Liverpool *Division 1, 1987–88*
2 in 42 games, Leeds U *Division 1, 1968–69*
3 in 46 games, Port Vale *Division 3(N), 1953–54*
Scottish League *(minimum 20 games)*
1 in 42 games, Rangers *Division 1, 1920–21*

MOST DRAWS IN A SEASON
Football League
23 in 42 games, Norwich C *Division 1, 1978–79*
23 in 46 games, Exeter C, *Division 4, 1986–87*
Scottish League
19 in 44 games, Hibernian *Premier Division, 1987–88*
21 in 44 games, East Fife *Division 1, 1986–87*

MOST GOALS IN A GAME
Football League
10, Joe Payne, for Luton T v Bristol R *Division 3(S), 13.4.1936*
Scottish League
8, Jimmy McGrory, for Celtic v Dunfermline Ath *Division 1, 14.9.1928*
8, Owen McNally, for Arthurlie v Armadale *Division 2, 1.10.1927*
8, Jim Dyet, for King's Park v Forfar Ath *Division 2, 2.1.1930*
8, John Calder, for Morton v Raith R *Division 2, 18.4.1936*
FA Cup
9, Ted MacDougall, for Bournemouth v Margate *1st Rd, 20.11.1971*
Scottish Cup
13, John Petrie, for Arbroath v Bon Accord *1st Rd, 12.9.1885*

MOST LEAGUE GOALS IN A SEASON
Football League
60 in 39 games, W.R. "Dixie" Dean (Everton) *Division 1, 1927–28*
59 in 37 games, George Camsell (Middlesbrough) *Division 2, 1926–27*
Scottish League
66 in 38 games, Jim Smith (Ayr U) *Division 2, 1927–28*
52 in 34 games, William McFadyen (Motherwell) *Division 1, 1931–32*

MOST LEAGUE GOALS IN A CAREER
Football League
434 in 619 games, Arthur Rowley *(WBA, Fulham, Leicester C, Shrewsbury T, 1946–65)*
Scottish League
410 in 408 games, Jimmy McGrory *(Celtic, Clydebank, Celtic, 1922–38)*

MOST CUP WINNERS' MEDALS
FA Cup
5, James Forrest (Blackburn R) *1884, 1885, 1886, 1890, 1891*
5, Hon. A.F. Kinnaird (Wanderers) *1873, 1877, 1878,* (Old Etonians) *1879, 1882*
5, C.H.R. Wollaston (Wanderers) *1872, 1873, 1876, 1877, 1878*
Scottish Cup
7, Jimmy McMenemy (Celtic) *1904, 1907, 1908, 1911, 1912, 1914,* (Partick Th) *1921*
7, Bob McPhail (Airdrieonians) *1924,* (Rangers) *1928, 1930, 1932, 1934, 1935, 1936*
7, Billy McNeill (Celtic) *1965, 1967, 1969, 1971, 1972, 1974, 1975*

RECORD ATTENDANCES
Football League
83,260, Manchester U v Arsenal, Maine Road, 17.1.1948
Scottish League
118,567, Rangers v Celtic, Ibrox Stadium, 2.1.1939
FA Cup-tie (other than the final)
84,569, Manchester C v Stoke C, 6th Rd at Maine Road, 3.3.1934 *(a British record for any game outside London or Glasgow)*
FA Cup final
126,047*, Bolton W v West Ham U, Wembley, 28.4.1923 *The figure stated is the official one. Perhaps as many as 70,000 more got in without paying.*
European Cup
135,826, Celtic v Leeds U, semi-final at Hampden Park, 15.4.1970

TRANSFER MILESTONES
First four-figure transaction
Alf Common: Sunderland to Middlesbrough £1,000, February 1905.
First five-figure transaction
David Jack: Bolton W to Arsenal £10,340, October 1928.
First six-figure transaction:
Alan Ball: Blackpool to Everton £112,000, August 1966.
First £200,000 transaction
Martin Peters: West Ham U to Tottenham H £200,000, March 1970.
First seven-figure transaction
Trevor Francis: Birmingham C to Nottingham F £1,000,000, February 1979.
First £2,000,000 transaction (record)
Paul Gascoigne: Newcastle U to Tottenham H £2,000,000, July 1988.
Highest British transaction
Chris Waddle: Tottenham H to Marseille £4.25 million July 1989.

MOST GOALS IN AN INTERNATIONAL MATCH
England
5, Malcolm Macdonald (Newcastle U) v Cyprus, Wembley, 16.4.1975
5, Willie Hall (Tottenham H) v Ireland, Old Trafford, 16.11.1938
5, G.O. Smith (Corinthians) v Ireland, Sunderland, 18.2.1899
5*, Steve Bloomer (Derby Co) v Wales, Cardiff, 16.3.1896 *(*one of which was credited to him in only some sources)*
5, Oliver Vaughton (Aston Villa) v Ireland, Belfast 18.2.1882
Scotland
5, Charles Heggie (Rangers) v Ireland, Belfast, 20.3.1886
Ireland
6, Joe Bambrick (Linfield) v Wales, Belfast, 1.2.1930
Wales
4, James Price (Wrexham) v Ireland, Wrexham, 25.2.1882
4, Mel Charles (Cardiff C) v N. Ireland, Cardiff, 11.4.1962
4, Ian Edwards (Chester) v Malta, Wrexham, 25.10.1978

MOST GOALS IN AN INTERNATIONAL CAREER
England
49 in 106 games, Bobby Charlton *(Manchester U)*
Scotland
30 in 55 games, Denis Law *(Huddersfield T, Manchester C, Torino, Manchester U)*
30 in 102 games, Kenny Dalglish *(Celtic, Liverpool)*
Ireland
12 in 25 games, Billy Gillespie *(Sheffield U)*
12 in 63 games, Gerry Armstrong *(Tottenham H, Watford, Real Mallorca, WBA, Chesterfield)*
12 in 11 games, Joe Bambrick *(Linfield, Chelsea)*
Wales
23 in 38 games, Trevor Ford *(Swansea T, Aston Villa, Sunderland, Cardiff C)*
23 in 68 games, Ivor Allchurch *(Swansea T, Newcastle U, Cardiff C)*
Republic of Ireland
19 in 56 games, Don Givens *(Manchester U, Luton T, QPR, Birmingham C, Neuchatel Xamax)*

HIGHEST INTERNATIONAL SCORES
World Cup Match: New Zealand 13, Fiji 0, 1981
Olympic Games: Denmark 17, France 1, 1908; Germany 16, USSR 0, 1912
Friendlies: Germany 13, Finland 0, 1940; Spain 13, Bulgaria 0, 1933
European Cup: Feyenoord 12, Reykjavik 2, 1969
Cup Winners' Cup: Sporting Lisbon 16, Apoel Nicosia 1, 1963
Fairs/UEFA Cup: IFC Cologne 13, Union Luxembourg 0, 1965

BARCLAYS LEAGUE DIVISION ONE

The copyrights in the League Fixtures Lists are owned by The Football League Limited
© *The Football League Limited 1989. Subject to alteration.*

	Arsenal	Aston Villa	Charlton Ath	Chelsea	Coventry C	Crystal Palace	Derby Co	Everton	Liverpool
Arsenal	–	7–4	23–9	17–3	22–8	1–1	28–10	31–3	24–2
Aston Villa	30–12	–	26–8	14–4	18–11	28–10	30–9	4–11	23–8
Charlton Ath	3–2	13–1	–	29–8	28–10	16–12	19–8	16–9	7–4
Chelsea	30–9	1–1	20–1	–	23–9	16–4	31–3	28–4	16–12
Coventry C	9–12	3–3	24–3	3–2	–	13–1	7–4	19–8	5–5
Crystal Palace....	14–4	24–3	21–4	26–12	26–8	–	10–3	30–9	20–1
Derby Co	24–3	17–3	2–12	21–10	30–12	14–10	–	26–12	9–9
Everton	21–10	5–5	10–2	11–11	2–12	17–3	16–4	–	23–9
Liverpool	25–11	9–12	30–12	21–4	4–11	30–8	17–2	3–2	–
Luton T...........	21–4	14–10	9–9	30–12	10–2	28–4	4–11	14–4	26–8
Manchester C ...	10–3	21–10	24–2	24–3	20–1	4–11	28–4	21–4	2–12
Manchester U ...	19–8	17–4	5–5	25–11	31–3	9–12	13–1	17–2	17–3
Millwall	11–11	16–12	22–8	5–5	9–9	31–3	1–1	10–3	18–11
Norwich C	5–5	11–11	18–11	14–10	24–2	7–4	16–12	28–10	10–2
Nottingham F ...	16–9	19–8	30–9	17–1	10–3	3–2	30–8	25–11	1–1
QPR	3–3	3–2	21–10	9–12	26–12	19–8	16–9	30–12	11–11
Sheffield W	17–2	16–9	11–11	13–1	30–9	25–11	3–3	30–8	29–11
Southampton	26–12	29–8	14–4	3–3	28–4	16–9	3–2	13–1	21–10
Tottenham H....	18–10	17–2	10–3	16–9	14–4	3–3	25–11	9–12	24–3
Wimbledon	13–1	25–11	26–12	19–8	21–4	17–2	9–12	3–3	14–10

FIXTURES 1989–90

and have been reproduced with their permission under Licence.

Luton T	Manchester C	Manchester U	Millwall	Norwich C	Nottingham F	QPR	Sheffield W	Southampton	Tottenham H	Wimbledon
16–12	14–10	2–12	28–4	4–11	10–2	18–11	9–9	16–4	20–1	26–8
10–3	31–3	26–12	21–4	28–4	2–12	23–9	10–2	20–1	9–9	24–2
17–2	25–11	4–11	9–12	3–3	17–3	31–3	28–4	1–1	14–10	16–4
7–4	28–10	24–2	4–11	10–3	9–9	22–8	26–8	18–11	10–2	2–12
16–9	30–8	21–10	17–2	25–11	14–10	16–4	17–3	11–11	1–1	16–12
11–11	5–5	22–8	21–10	30–12	23–9	2–12	24–2	10–2	18–11	9–9
5–5	11–11	26–8	14–4	21–4	20–1	10–2	18–11	23–9	24–2	23–8
1–1	16–12	9–9	14–10	24–3	24–2	7–4	20–1	26–8	22–8	18–11
13–1	19–8	30–9	3–3	16–9	14–4	28–4	26–12	13–3	28–10	10–3
–	17–3	18–11	24–3	21–10	26–12	20–1	22–8	24–2	2–12	23–9
30–9	–	23–9	30–12	26–12	18–11	9–9	14–4	23–8	26–8	10–2
3–3	3–2	–	16–9	30–8	11–11	1–1	14–10	28–10	16–12	7–4
28–10	7–4	10–2	–	30–9	26–8	24–2	23–9	2–12	16–4	20–1
31–3	16–4	20–1	17–3	–	23–8	26–8	2–12	9–9	23–9	1–1
16–4	3–3	28–4	13–1	9–12	–	28–10	4–11	17–12	7–4	31–3
30–8	17–2	14–4	25–11	13–1	24–3	–	21–4	14–10	17–3	5–5
9–12	1–1	10–3	3–1	19–8	5–5	16–12	–	7–4	31–3	28–10
25–11	9–12	24–3	19–8	17–2	21–4	10–3	30–12	—	4–11	30–9
19–8	13–1	21–4	26–12	3–2	30–12	30–9	21–10	5–5	–	11–11
3–2	16–9	30–12	29–8	14–4	21–10	4–11	24–3	17–3	28–4	–

BARCLAYS LEAGUE DIVISION TWO

The copyrights in the League Fixtures Lists are owned by The Football League Limited © The Football League Limited 1989. Subject to alteration.

	Barnsley	Blackburn R	Bournemouth	Bradford C	Brighton & HA	Hull C	Ipswich T	Leeds U	Leicester C	Middlesbrough
Barnsley	–	6–3	21–4	23–9	26–8	24–2	2–12	30–12	28–10	9–9
Blackburn R	30–9	–	3–2	1–1	5–5	31–10	11–11	13–1	9–12	7–10
Bournemouth	16–12	23–9	–	24–2	2–12	26–8	20–1	5–5	17–4	10–2
Bradford C	3–2	14–4	25–11	–	7–10	11–11	18–10	28–10	16–9	26–12
Brighton & HA	13–1	4–11	19–8	17–3	–	6–4	27–9	21–4	3–2	24–3
Hull C	25–11	10–4	13–1	28–4	28–10	–	16–12	16–9	19–8	10–3
Ipswich T	19–8	28–4	2–9	24–3	10–3	21–4	–	17–2	3–3	30–12
Leeds U	25–4	26–8	4–11	7–4	16–12	10–2	9–9	–	28–4	23–8
Leicester C	7–4	23–8	26–12	10–2	23–9	2–12	18–11	11–11	–	21–4
Middlesbrough	17–2	17–3	16–9	16–4	18–10	27–9	25–4	9–12	16–12	–
Newcastle U	3–3	18–10	17–2	14–10	31–3	7–3	17–3	19–8	13–1	4–11
Oldham Ath	7–10	1–12	20–3	31–10	18–11	24–3	24–2	13–4	30–9	21–10
Oxford U	21–10	20–1	30–9	9–9	25–4	18–11	23–9	10–3	21–3	24–2
Plymouth Arg	2–9	28–10	14–4	4–11	30–9	29–12	31–3	10–4	17–10	20–3
Portsmouth	5–5	14–10	31–3	20–1	16–4	9–9	28–10	17–10	1–1	23–9
Port Vale	19–8	9–9	10–3	2–12	20–1	12–9	1–1	30–9	7–10	30–10
Sheffield U	24–3	30–12	28–4	18–11	9–9	23–9	26–8	26–12	4–11	20–1
Stoke C	9–12	21–4	3–3	26–9	11–11	14–10	6–3	2–9	25–11	14–4
Sunderland	31–10	10–2	7–10	21–10	24–2	14–4	22–8	20–3	10–3	26–8
Swindon T	16–9	26–12	28–10	6–3	10–4	17–3	14–10	4–2	31–3	28–4
Watford	17–4	31–3	17–10	16–12	20–3	5–5	7–4	3–3	2–9	30–9
WBA	11–11	27–9	9–12	25–4	1–1	21–10	5–5	25–11	17–2	7–4
West Ham U	1–1	24–2	11–4	23–8	10–2	20–1	17–4	7–10	25–4	18–11
Wolverhampton W	10–3	18–11	30–12	26–8	12–9	26–12	10–2	31–3	10–4	2–12

FIXTURES 1989–90

and have been reproduced with their permission under Licence.

Newcastle U	Oldham Ath	Oxford U	Plymouth Arg	Portsmouth	Port Vale	Sheffield U	Stoke C	Sunderland	Swindon T	Watford	WBA	West Ham U	Wolverhampton W
18-11	17-3	31-3	20-1	4-11	14-10	17-10	22-8	10-4	10-2	26-12	28-4	14-4	26-9
24-3	19-8	2-9	7-4	20-3	17-2	24-4	16-12	16-9	16-4	21-10	10-3	25-11	3-3
9-9	14-10	6-3	1-1	21-10	26-9	11-11	18-11	17-3	7-4	24-3	22-8	31-10	24-4
21-3	10-4	17-2	5-5	2-9	19-8	3-3	10-3	31-3	30-9	21-4	30-12	9-12	13-1
21-10	3-3	30-12	7-3	26-12	2-9	17-2	28-4	25-11	1-11	14-10	14-4	16-9	9-12
30-9	7-10	3-3	24-4	17-2	9-12	3-2	20-3	1-1	7-10	4-11	31-3	2-9	16-4
7-10	25-11	3-2	21-10	10-4	14-4	13-1	30-9	9-12	20-3	31-10	4-11	26-12	16-9
2-12	1-1	27-9	1-11	24-3	7-3	16-4	20-1	14-10	23-9	18-11	24-2	17-3	21-10
26-8	7-3	14-10	24-3	14-4	17-3	5-5	24-2	27-9	21-10	20-1	9-9	30-12	1-11
5-5	31-3	25-11	14-10	3-2	11-4	2-9	1-1	13-1	11-11	7-3	28-10	3-3	19-8
–	2-9	9-12	16-12	16-9	28-10	25-11	16-4	3-2	25-4	27-9	11-4	28-4	1-1
20-1	–	28-4	9-9	30-12	26-12	10-3	10-2	4-11	26-8	22-8	23-9	21-4	6-4
13-9	11-11	–	2-12	7-10	5-5	1-1	1-11	16-4	24-3	26-8	10-2	7-4	16-12
21-4	17-2	19-8	–	10-12	25-11	16-9	7-10	3-3	10-3	28-4	26-12	13-1	3-2
10-2	24-4	17-3	12-9	–	11-11	7-4	26-8	16-12	24-2	2-12	18-11	26-9	6-3
7-4	16-4	4-11	24-2	28-4	–	16-12	23-9		18-11	10-2	26-8	21-10	24-3
24-2	26-9	14-4	10-2	31-10	21-4	–	21-10	6-3	12-9	10-4	2-12	14-10	17-3
26-12	16-9	10-4	17-3	13-1	3-2	31-3	–	28-10	5-5	30-12	17-10	19-8	17-2
23-9	5-5	26-12	18-11	21-4	30-12	30-9	7-4	–	2-12	9-9	20-1	24-3	11-11
30-12	13-1	17-10	26-9	26-11	3-3	10-12	4-11	19-8	–	14-4	21-4	17-2	3-9
10-3	9-12	13-1	11-11	19-8	16-9	28-10	24-4	17-2	1-1	–	7-10	3-2	25-11
1-11	3-2	16-9	16-4	3-3	13-1	19-8	24-3	2-9	17-12	17-3	–	7-3	14-10
11-11	16-12	28-10	26-8	10-3	31-3	21-3	2-12	18-10	9-9	23-9	30-9	–	5-5
14-4	28-10	21-4	23-9	30-9	17-10	7-10	9-9	28-4	20-1	24-2	20-3	4-11	–

BARCLAYS LEAGUE DIVISION

The copyrights in the League Fixtures Lists are owned by The Football League © The Football League Limited 1989. Subject to alteration.

	Birmingham C	Blackpool	Bolton W	Brentford	Bristol C	Bristol R	Bury	Cardiff C	Chester C	Crewe Alex	Fulham
Birmingham C....	–	6–3	25–11	3–2	13–1	16–4	7–4	31–10	24–3	19–8	1–1
Blackpool	30–9	–	16–4	11–11	27–1	5–5	31–10	21–10	24–4	16–9	16–12
Bolton W...........	24–2	26–12	–	24–3	28–4	9–9	30–12	20–1	21–10	20–3	26–8
Brentford...........	23–9	28–4	17–10	–	7–10	20–1	9–9	13–2	26–8	10–3	28–10
Bristol C.............	26–8	9–9	11–11	17–3	–	23–9	20–1	10–2	6–1	10–4	16–4
Bristol R	26–12	4–11	27–1	19–8	3–2	–	21–3	24–3	7–4	21–4	7–10
Bury	28–10	10–4	24–4	27–1	19–8	14–10	–	5–5	17–3	25–11	31–3
Cardiff C	10–4	31–3	19–8	2–9	16–9	17–10	3–11	–	14–10	17–2	28–4
Chester C	17–10	30–12	31–3	12–1	3–3	28–10	7–10	20–3	–	2–9	30–9
Crewe Alex........	20–1	10–2	14–10	26–9	31–10	16–12	24–2	2–12	13–2	–	9–9
Fulham..............	14–4	21–4	13–1	10–4	26–12	17–3	21–10	11–11	6–3	27–1	–
Huddersfield T ...	31–3	14–4	2–9	16–9	30–12	10–4	26–12	7–10	5–5	3–3	10–3
Leyton Orient.....	28–4	14–10	3–2	17–2	21–4	26–9	14–4	7–4	31–10	30–12	4–11
Mansfield T........	6–1	23–9	6–3	21–4	21–10	26–8	10–2	9–9	20–1	28–4	13–2
Northampton T.	20–3	17–10	17–2	25–11	2–9	31–3	30–9	10–3	1–1	3–2	7–4
Notts Co.............	30–12	26–8	26–9	31–10	24–3	13–2	6–1	21–4	10–2	14–4	2–12
Preston NE	21–4	26–9	28–10	14–10	14–4	10–2	26–8	24–2	23–9	17–10	6–1
Reading.............	4–11	17–3	3–3	26–12	25–11	6–3	28–4	14–4	26–9	13–1	17–10
Rotherham U.	7–10	28–10	16–9	3–3	17–2	1–1	10–3	30–9	11–11	31–3	20–3
Shrewsbury T	9–9	13–2	16–12	21–10	10–3	11–11	23–9	6–1	2–12	30–9	24–4
Swansea C	13–2	2–12	5–5	30–12	20–3	24–2	23–3	26–12	9–9	7–10	10–2
Tranmere R	9–2	23–2	1–1	5–5	29–9	23–4	2–12	26–8	15–12	27–10	19–1
Walsall..............	10–3	6–1	10–4	14–4	4–11	2–12	21–4	30–12	24–2	26–12	23–9
Wigan Ath.........	1–12	20–10	16–3	6–3	7–4	6–1	13–2	23–9	16–4	4–11	24–2

THREE FIXTURES 1989–90

Limited and have been reproduced with their permission under Licence.

Huddersfield T	Leyton Orient	Mansfield T	Northampton T	Notts Co	Preston NE	Reading	Rotherham U	Shrewsbury T	Swansea C	Tranmere R	Walsall	Wigan Ath
21–10	11–11	3–3	14–10	24–4	16–12	5–5	17–3	27–1	2–9	16–9	26–9	17–2
1–1	20–3	3–2	24–3	13–1	10–3	6–10	7–4	2–9	17–2	25–11	3–3	19–8
13–2	23–9	30–9	2–12	10–3	7–4	6–1	10–2	21–4	4–11	14–4	31–10	7–10
10–2	3–12	17–12	25–2	7–4	20–3	16–4	6–1	31–3	24–4	4–11	1–1	30–9
24–4	16–12	31–3	13–2	17–10	1–1	24–2	2–12	26–9	14–10	6–3	5–5	28–10
1–11	10–3	13–1	21–10	2–9	16–9	30–9	14–4	28–4	25–11	30–12	17–2	3–3
16–4	1–1	16–9	6–3	3–3	13–1	11–11	26–9	3–2	17–10	17–2	16–12	2–9
17–3	28–10	27–1	26–9	16–12	25–11	1–1	6–3	2–3	16–4	13–1	24–4	3–2
4–11	10–4	19–8	14–4	15–9	3–2	9–3	28–4	17–2	26–1	20–4	24–11	26–12
6–1	24–4	10–11	23–9	1–1	24–3	25–8	21–10	6–3	17–3	6–4	16–4	5–5
26–9	5–5	2–9	31–10	17–2	3–3	24–3	14–10	30–12	16–9	19–8	3–2	25–11
–	30–9	17–2	11–11	25–11	27–1	20–3	21–4	28–10	19–8	3–2	13–1	17–10
6–3	–	25–11	26–12	19–8	2–9	21–10	24–3	13–1	3–3	17–3	27–1	16–9
2–12	24–2	–	30–12	4–11	31–10	7–4	26–12	17–3	24–10	24–3	14–10	14–4
28–4	16–4	24–4	–	28–10	7–10	17–12	4–11	16–9	14–1	3–3	20–2	28–1
24–2	20–1	5–5	10–4	–	21–10	9–9	23–9	26–12	6–3	14–10	17–3	11–11
9–9	13–2	10–4	17–3	31–3	–	2–12	20–1	4–11	28–4	26–12	6–3	30–12
14–10	31–3	28–10	21–4	27–1	17–2	–	30–12	19–8	3–2	2–9	16–9	10–4
16–12	17–10	16–4	5–5	3–2	19–8	24–4	–	25–11	10–4	27–1	2–9	13–1
7–4	26–8	7–10	10–2	17–4	5–5	20–1	24–2	–	1–1	31–10	24–3	20–3
21–1	6–1	10–3	26–8	30–9	11–11	23–9	31–10	14–4	–	20–10	7–4	21–4
22–9	6–10	16–10	5–1	19–3	16–4	12–2	9–9	9–4	30–3	–	10–11	9–3
26–8	9–9	20–3	19–8	7–10	30–9	10–2	13–2	17–10	28–10	28–4	–	31–3
24–3	10–2	1–1	9–9	28–4	24–4	31–10	26–8	14–10	16–12	26–9	21–10	–

BARCLAYS LEAGUE DIVISION FOUR

The copyrights in the League Fixtures Lists are owned by The Football League Limited
© The Football League Limited 1989. Subject to alteration.

	Aldershot	Burnley	Cambridge U	Carlisle U	Chesterfield	Colchester U	Doncaster R	Exeter C	Gillingham	Grimsby T	Halifax T
Aldershot	—	6–4	5–5	31–10	10–2	7–10	10–3	26–12	20–1	24–2	2–12
Burnley	28–10	—	14–4	26–12	13–2	4–11	31–3	9–9	10–2	2–12	30–12
Cambridge U	4–11	1–1	—	26–9	9–9	29–4	17–10	10–2	6–1	20–1	22–9
Carlisle U	10–4	16–4	10–3	—	26–8	30–9	20–3	13–2	23–9	9–9	10–2
Chesterfield	16–9	2–9	27–1	13–1	—	19–8	1–1	20–3	31–3	5–5	17–10
Colchester U	17–3	5–5	10–11	6–3	20–1	—	24–4	10–4	23–2	13–2	26–8
Doncaster R	26–9	21–10	25–3	14–10	14–4	30–12	—	20–1	26–8	6–1	21–4
Exeter C	16–4	27–1	16–9	2–9	14–10	1–11	19–8	—	16–12	27–9	7–3
Gillingham	19–8	16–9	3–3	3–2	21–10	24–11	13–1	21–4	—	24–3	16–3
Grimsby T	25–11	17–2	19–8	27–1	4–11	2–9	3–3	10–3	17–10	—	28–10
Halifax T	17–2	24–4	2–2	15–9	24–3	12–1	15–12	30–9	6–10	7–4	—
Hartlepool U	28–4	20–3	31–10	7–4	24–2	14–4	30–9	26–8	9–9	30–12	20–1
Hereford U	3–3	3–2	13–1	19–8	27–9	27–1	25–11	31–3	1–1	7–3	11–4
Lincoln C	13–1	25–11	26–12	30–12	17–3	17–2	2–9	5–5	11–11	21–10	14–10
Maidstone U	1–1	7–10	30–9	5–5	23–9	10–3	11–4	2–12	16–4	10–2	24–2
Peterborough U	2–9	24–3	21–4	17–2	26–12	7–4	27–1	7–10	30–9	1–11	14–4
Rochdale	24–4	19–8	17–2	25–11	6–3	16–9	11–11	17–10	10–4	17–3	31–3
Scarborough	16–12	3–3	2–9	21–10	1–11	3–2	16–9	11–11	5–5	14–10	27–9
Scunthorpe U	6–3	11–11	7–4	24–3	30–12	21–10	5–5	23–9	13–2	26–12	6–1
Southend U	27–1	31–10	24–11	3–3	7–4	26–12	2–2	30–12	9–3	20–4	27–4
Stockport Co	3–2	13–1	29–12	20–4	28–4	2–3	16–2	28–10	19–3	14–4	3–11
Torquay U	31–3	30–9	20–3	11–11	6–1	21–4	7–10	14–4	28–10	26–8	13–2
Wrexham	14–10	16–12	21–10	17–3	2–12	24–3	16–4	24–2	24–4	11–11	9–9
York C	17–10	10–3	7–10	14–4	21–4	20–3	28–10	6–1	2–12	23–9	26–12

FIXTURES 1989–90
and have been reproduced with their permission under Licence.

Hartlepool U	Hereford U	Lincoln C	Maidstone U	Peterborough U	Rochdale	Scarborough	Scunthorpe U	Southend U	Stockport Co	Torquay U	Wrexham	York C
11–11	6–1	26–8	14–4	13–2	30–12	21–4	30–9	9–9	23–9	21–10	20–3	24–3
14–10	23–9	24–2	17–3	17–10	20–1	6–1	28–4	10–4	26–8	6–3	21–4	26–9
10–4	26–8	17–4	6–3	17–12	2–12	13–2	28–10	25–2	24–4	13–10	30–3	16–3
28–10	20–1	24–4	4–11	2–12	24–2	31–3	17–10	6–1	17–12	28–4	7–10	1–1
25–11	10–3	7–10	3–2	16–4	30–9	10–4	24–4	28–10	11–11	3–3	17–2	16–12
1–1	8–9	2–12	26–9	28–10	10–2	23–9	31–3	16–4	5–1	16–12	17–10	13–10
6–3	25–2	13–2	31–10	9–9	28–4	10–2	4–11	22–9	2–12	17–3	26–12	7–4
13–1	21–10	4–11	17–2	17–3	24–3	28–4	3–2	25–4	7–4	1–1	25–11	3–3
27–1	14–4	28–4	26–12	6–3	31–10	4–11	2–9	26–9	14–10	7–4	30–12	17–2
24–4	30–9	31–3	16–9	10–4	7–10	20–3	16–4	16–12	1–1	13–1	28–4	3–2
19–8	31–10	20–3	25–11	1–1	21–10	10–3	3–3	10–11	5–5	2–9	26–1	16–4
—	2–12	6–1	21–4	23–9	10–3	26–12	7–10	13–2	10–2	24–3	4–11	21–10
17–2	—	28–10	2–9	28–4	4–11	18–10	16–12	14–10	17–3	16–4	16–9	25–4
3–3	7–4	—	25–3	27–9	21–4	14–4	19–8	7–3	1–11	27–1	3–2	16–9
16–12	14–12	18–10	—	20–1	6–1	26–8	21–3	31–3	9–9	25–4	28–10	11–11
3–2	11–11	10–3	19–8	—	21–3	30–12	16–9	5–5	21–10	25–11	3–3	13–1
26–9	5–5	16–12	3–3	14–10	—	28–10	13–1	1–1	16–4	3–2	2–9	27–1
16–4	24–3	1–1	13–1	25–4	7–4	—	27–1	17–3	7–3	17–2	19–8	24–11
17–3	21–4	20–1	14–10	10–2	26–8	9–9	—	2–12	24–2	26–9	14–4	31–10
1–9	20–3	30–9	21–10	4–11	14–4	7–10	17–2	—	23–3	15–9	12–1	19–8
15–9	7–10	9–4	27–1	30–3	26–12	30–9	25–11	16–10	—	19–8	9–3	1–9
17–10	26–12	9–9	30–12	24–2	23–9	2–12	10–3	10–2	20–1	—	10–4	5–5
5–5	10–2	23–9	7–4	6–1	13–2	20–1	1–1	26–8	26–9	31–10	—	6–3
31–3	30–12	10–2	28–4	26–8	9–9	24–2	10–4	20–1	13–2	4–11	30–9	—

GM VAUXHALL CONFERENCE FIXTURES 1989–90

© These fixtures are the copyright of the GM Vauxhall Conference and must not be reproduced without prior permission. Subject to alterations.

Saturday 26 August
Altrincham v Barnet
Boston U v Farnborough T
Cheltenham T v Fisher Ath
Chorley v Telford U
Darlington v Kidderminster
  Harriers
Enfield v Barrow
Kettering T v Runcorn
Macclesfield v Welling U
Northwich Vic v Wycombe W
Stafford Rangers v Yeovil T
Sutton U v Merthyr Tydfil

Monday 28 August (*Bank Holiday*)
Barnet v Cheltenham T
Barrow v Runcorn
Darlington v Northwich Vic
Farnborough T v Welling U
Kettering T v Kidderminster
  Harriers (7.30pm.)
Macclesfield T v Enfield
Stafford Rangers v Chorley
Telford U v Fisher Ath
Wycombe W v Altrincham
Yeovil T v Sutton U
Championship match: Merthyr
  Tydfil
No fixture: Boston U

Saturday 2 September
Altrincham v Sutton U
Barnet v Chorley
Barrow v Boston U
Farnborough T v Stafford Rangers
Fisher Ath v Macclesfield T
Kidderminster Harriers v Enfield
Runcorn v Cheltenham T
Telford U v Merthyr Tydfil
Welling U v Kettering T
Wycombe W v Darlington
Yeovil T v Northwich Vic

Monday 4 September
Fisher Ath v Farnborough T
Kidderminster Harriers v
  Macclesfield T
Northwich Vic v Barrow

Tuesday 5 September
Chorley v Altrincham
Enfield v Kettering T
Merthyr Tydfil v Yeovil T
Runcorn v Telford U
Sutton U v Barnet

Wednesday 6 September
Boston U v Darlington
Cheltenham T v Stafford Rangers
Welling U v Wycombe W

Saturday 9 September
Boston U v Yeovil T
Cheltenham T v Barrow
Chorley v Welling U
Darlington v Telford U
Enfield v Runcorn
Kettering T v Altrincham
Macclesfield T v Farnborough T
Merthyr Tydfil v Barnet
Northwich Vic v Fisher Ath
Stafford Rangers v Wycombe W
Sutton U v Kidderminster Harriers

Monday 11 September
Fisher Ath v Enfield

Tuesday 12 September
Altrincham v Kidderminster
  Harriers
Barnet v Boston U
Barrow v Chorley
Darlington v Runcorn
Kettering T v Stafford Rangers
Macclesfield T v Northwich Vic
Telford U v Cheltenham T
Wycombe W v Merthyr Tydfil

Wednesday 13 September
Farnborough T v Sutton U
Yeovil T v Welling U

Saturday 16 September (*FA Cup 1st qualifying round*)
Chorley v Sutton U
Farnborough T v Enfield
Kidderminster Harriers v
  Northwich Vic
Runcorn v Merthyr Tydfil
Telford U v Kettering T
Welling U v Altrincham
Yeovil T v Darlington
No fixture: Macclesfield Town
Teams engaged in FA Cup: Barnet,
  Boston U, Barrow, Cheltenham
  T, Fisher Ath, Stafford Rangers,
  Wycombe W.

Monday 18 September
*Fisher Ath v Barnet
Chorley v Northwich Vic

Tuesday 19 September
*Enfield v Wycombe W
Merthyr Tydfil v Kettering Town
Runcorn v Macclesfield Town
Stafford Rangers v Barrow
Sutton United v Farnborough Town

Wednesday 20 September
*Cheltenham T v Yeovil T
*Welling U v Boston U
 subject to FA Cup replays

Saturday 23 September
Altrincham v Cheltenham T
Barnet v Runcorn
Barrow v Welling U
Chorley v Yeovil T
Darlington v Stafford Rangers
Enfield v Telford U
Kettering T v Fisher Ath
Macclesfield T v Sutton U
Merthyr Tydfil v Boston U
Northwich Vic v Farnborough T
Wycombe W v Kidderminster
  Harriers

Tuesday 26 September
Altrincham v Barrow
Barnet v Welling U
Chorley v Darlington
Macclesfield T v Cheltenham T
Stafford Rangers v Runcorn
Telford U v Northwich Vic
Wycombe W v Fisher Ath

Wednesday 27 September
Boston U v Enfield
Farnborough T v Merthyr Tydfil
Yeovil T v Kidderminster Harriers

Saturday 30 September (*FA Cup 2nd qualifying round*)
Darlington v Kettering T
Kidderminster Harriers v Chorley
Merthyr Tydfil v Macclesfield T
Sutton U v Northwich Vic
Telford U v Farnborough T
Welling U v Enfield
Yeovil T v Altrincham
No fixture: Runcorn
Teams engaged in FA Cup: Barnet,
  Barrow, Boston U, Cheltenham
  T, Fisher Ath, Stafford Rangers,
  Wycombe W.

Monday 2 October
*Fisher Ath v Boston U
*Kidderminster Harriers v Stafford
  Rangers

Tuesday 3 October
*Barrow v Macclesfield T
*Kettering T v Wycombe W
 Runcorn v Altrincham

Wednesday 4 October
*Farnborough T v Barnet
 subject to FA Cup replays

Saturday 7 October
Altrincham v Farnborough T
Barnet v Telford U
Barrow v Sutton U
Boston U v Kidderminster Harriers
Cheltenham T v Welling U
Enfield v Darlington
Fisher Ath v Chorley
Macclesfield T v Yeovil T
Northwich Vic v Kettering T
Stafford Rangers v Merthyr Tydfil
Wycombe W v Runcorn

Tuesday 10 October
**Bob Lord Challenge Trophy 1st
 round 1st leg**
Chorley v Barrow
Enfield v Fisher Ath
Stafford Rangers v Altrincham
Sutton U v Welling U

Wednesday 11 October
**Bob Lord Challenge Trophy 1st
 round 1st leg**
Cheltenham T v Telford U
Farnborough T v Merthyr Tydfil
League match
Boston U v Barnet

Saturday 14 October, (*FA Cup 3rd
 qualifying round*)
Chorley v Enfield
Farnborough T v Wycombe W
Kettering T v Cheltenham T
Macclesfield T v Stafford Rangers
Merthyr Tydfil v Darlington
Runcorn v Kidderminster Harriers
Sutton U v Fisher Ath
Telford U v Altrincham
Welling U v Northwich Vic
Yeovil T v Barnet
Teams engaged in FA Cup: Barrow,
 Boston U

Tuesday 17 October
*Enfield v Boston U
**Kettering T v Cheltenham T
*Runcorn v Stafford Rangers
**Sutton U v Fisher Ath

Wednesday 18 October
**Farnborough T v Wycombe W

***These games played mid-week if
 due to FA Cup 2nd qualifying
 round results they cannot be
 played on Saturday 14 October.*
* *Subject to FA Cup replays*

Saturday 21 October
Altrincham v Boston U
Barnet v Macclesfield T
Barrow v Yeovil T
Cheltenham T v Chorley
Darlington v Sutton U
Fisher Ath v Runcorn
Kettering T v Merthyr Tydfil
Kidderminster Harriers v
 Farnborough T
Northwich Vic v Enfield
Stafford Rangers v Welling U
Wycombe W v Telford U

Saturday 28 October (*FA Cup 4th
 qualifying round*)
Macclesfield T v Kettering T
Sutton U v Telford U

Tuesday 31 October
**Bob Lord Challenge Trophy 1st
 round 2nd leg**
Telford U v Cheltenham T
League matches
Barnet v Wycombe W
Merthyr Tydfil v Kidderminster
 Harriers
Stafford Rangers v Boston U

Saturday 4 November
Altrincham v Merthyr Tydfil
Barrow v Telford U
Boston U v Northwich Vic
Chorley v Wycombe W
Darlington v Barnet
Enfield v Cheltenham T
Farnborough T v Kettering T
Fisher Ath v Stafford Rangers
Runcorn v Sutton U
Welling U v Kidderminster Harriers
Yeovil T v Macclesfield T

Monday 6 November
**Bob Lord Challenge Trophy 1st
 round 2nd leg**
Fisher Ath v Enfield

Tuesday 7 November
**Bob Lord Challenge Trophy 1st
 round 2nd leg**
Altrincham v Stafford Rangers
Barrow v Chorley
Merthyr Tydfil v Farnborough T

League Match
Wycombe W v Yeovil T

Wednesday 8 November
Bob Lord Challenge Trophy 1st round 2nd leg
Welling U v Sutton U

Saturday 11 November
Barnet v Barrow
Cheltenham T v Altrincham
Farnborough T v Runcorn
Kettering T v Yeovil T
Kidderminster Harriers v Fisher Ath
Macclesfield T v Darlington
Northwich V v Merthyr Tydfil
Stafford Rangers v Enfield
Sutton U v Chorley
Telford U v Welling U
Wycombe W v Boston U

Saturday 18 November (*FA Cup 1st round*)
Boston U v Welling U
Farnborough T v Barrow
Runcorn v Fisher Ath
Stafford Rangers v Cheltenham T

Saturday 25 November
Barnet v Stafford Rangers
Barrow v Kettering T
Chorley v Boston U
Enfield v Altrincham
Farnborough T v Darlington
Fisher Ath v Telford U
Kidderminster Harriers v Sutton U
Merthyr Tydfil v Runcorn
Northwich Vic v Cheltenham T
Welling U v Macclesfield T
Yeovil T v Wycombe W

Saturday 2 December (*FA Trophy 3rd qualifying round*)
Altrincham v Fisher Ath
Boston U v Runcorn
Cheltenham T v Farnborough T
Darlington v Welling U
Enfield v Kidderminster Harriers
Kettering T v Barnet
Macclesfield T v Telford U

Merthyr Tydfil v Barrow
Sutton U v Yeovil T
FA Trophy: Chorley, Stafford Rangers
No fixture: Northwich Vic, Wycombe W

Saturday 9 December (*FA Cup 2nd round*)
Barnet v Farnborough T
Barrow v Kidderminster Harriers
Boston U v Wycombe W
Fisher Ath v Cheltenham T
Kettering T v Enfield
Northwich Vic v Altrincham
Runcorn v Darlington
Stafford Rangers v Macclesfield T
Sutton U v Welling U
Telford U v Chorley
Yeovil T v Merthyr Tydfil

Saturday 16 December
Altrincham v Stafford Rangers
Cheltenham T v Darlington
Enfield v Sutton U
Farnborough T v Chorley
Fisher Ath v Barrow
Kidderminster Harriers v Kettering T
Macclesfield T v Merthyr Tydfil
Runcorn v Northwich Vic
Telford U v Boston U
Welling U v Yeovil T
Wycombe W v Barnet

Tuesday 19 December
Chorley v Barrow

Wednesday 20 December
Farnborough T v Fisher Ath

Tuesday 26 December (*Boxing Day*)
Altrincham v Macclesfield T
Barnet v Enfield
Boston U v Kettering T
Chorley v Runcorn
Darlington v Barrow
Kidderminster Harriers v Telford U
Merthyr Tydfil v Cheltenham T
Stafford Rangers v Northwich Vic
Sutton U v Wycombe W
Welling U v Fisher Ath
Yeovil T v Farnborough T

Saturday 30 December
Barnet v Sutton U
Barrow v Altrincham
Boston U v Stafford Rangers
Darlington v Chorley
Enfield v Welling U
Fisher Ath v Yeovil T
Kettering T v Farnborough T
Macclesfield T v Runcorn
Merthyr Tydfil v Telford U
Northwich Vic v Kidderminster
  Harriers
Wycombe W v Cheltenham T

Monday 1 January 1990
Barrow v Darlington
Cheltenham T v Merthyr Tydfil
Enfield v Barnet
Farnborough T v Yeovil T
Fisher Ath v Welling U
Kettering T v Boston U
Macclesfield T v Altrincham
Northwich Vic v Stafford Rangers
Runcorn v Chorley
Telford U v Kidderminster Harriers
Wycombe W v Sutton U

Saturday 6 January (*FA Cup 3rd
  round*)
Altrincham v Darlington
Cheltenham T v Boston U
Chorley v Macclesfield T
Kidderminster Harriers v Barnet
Merthyr Tydfil v Northwich Vic
Runcorn v Barrow
Stafford Rangers v Fisher Ath
Sutton U v Kettering T
Telford U v Wycombe W
Welling U v Farnborough T
Yeovil T v Enfield

Saturday 13 January (*FA Trophy 1st
  round*)
No matches arranged

Saturday 20th January
Barnet v Merthyr Tydfil
Barrow v Wycombe W
Boston U v Altrincham
Chorley v Cheltenham T
Darlington v Fisher Ath
Enfield v Farnborough T
Kettering T v Telford U

Macclesfield T v Kidderminster
  Harriers
Northwich Vic v Welling U
Stafford Rangers v Sutton U
Yeovil T v Runcorn

Saturday 27 January
Altrincham v Yeovil T
Cheltenham T v Barnet
Darlington v Enfield
Farnborough T v Telford U
Fisher Ath v Northwich Vic
Kidderminster Harriers v Barrow
Merthyr Tydfil v Chorley
Runcorn v Kettering T
Sutton U v Boston U
Welling U v Stafford Rangers
Wycombe W v Macclesfield T

Saturday 3 February (*FA Trophy
  2nd round*)
Cheltenham T v Northwich Vic
Darlington v Boston U
Fisher Ath v Wycombe W
Kettering T v Chorley
Kidderminster Harriers v Yeovil T
Merthyr Tydfil v Altrincham
Telford U v Enfield
Welling U v Barrow

Tuesday 6 February
Chorley v Stafford Rangers

Saturday 10 February (*Welsh Cup*)
Barrow v Farnborough T
Boston U v Fisher Ath
Chorley v Kidderminster Harriers
Enfield v Macclesfield T
Kettering T v Darlington
Merthyr Tydfil v Wycombe W
Northwich Vic v Barnet
Stafford Rangers v Altrincham
Telford U v Sutton U
Welling U v Runcorn
Yeovil T v Cheltenham T

Saturday 17 February (*Cheshire
  Cup*)
Altrincham v Telford U
Barnet v Kettering T
Cheltenham T v Enfield
Fisher Ath v Merthyr Tydfil
Kidderminster Harriers v Runcorn

Macclesfield T v Barrow
Northwich Vic v Boston U
Sutton U v Darlington
Wycombe W v Welling U
Yeovil T v Stafford Rangers
No fixture: Chorley, Farnborough T

Monday 19 February
Kidderminster Harriers v Merthyr
  Tydfil

Tuesday 20 February
Barnet v Fisher Ath
Darlington v Altrincham
Wycombe W v Kettering T

Wednesday 21 February
Boston U v Macclesfield T
Farnborough T v Cheltenham T

Saturday 24 February (*FA Trophy
  3rd round*)
Altrincham v Chorley
Barrow v Stafford Rangers
Boston U v Sutton U
Cheltenham T v Kidderminster
  Harriers
Darlington v Macclesfield T
Enfield v Fisher Ath
Kettering T v Northwich Vic
Merthyr Tydfil v Farnborough T
Runcorn v Wycombe W
Telford U v Yeovil T
Welling U v Barnet

Tuesday 27 February
Macclesfield T v Barnet

Saturday 3 March
Barnet v Northwich Vic
Chorley v Kettering T
Farnborough T v Altrincham
Fisher Ath v Darlington
Kidderminster Harriers v Boston U
Macclesfield T v Wycombe W
Runcorn v Enfield
Stafford Rangers v Telford U
Sutton U v Cheltenham T
Welling U v Merthyr Tydfil
Yeovil T v Barrow

Monday 5 March
Northwich Vic v Darlington

Saturday 10 March
Altrincham v Welling U
Barnet v Kidderminster Harriers
Barrow v Fisher Ath
Boston U v Telford U
Cheltenham T v Macclesfield T
Chorley v Farnborough T
Darlington v Yeovil T
Merthyr Tydfil v Sutton U
Stafford Rangers v Kettering T
Wycombe W v Enfield
No fixture: Northwich Vic, Runcorn

Tuesday 13 March
Altrincham v Northwich Vic

Saturday 17 March (*FA Trophy 4th
  round*)
Barrow v Merthyr Tydfil
Cheltenham T v Wycombe W
Enfield v Chorley
Farnborough T v Boston U
Fisher Ath v Altrincham
Kettering T v Welling U
Kidderminster Harriers v
  Darlington
Northwich Vic v Yeovil T
Runcorn v Barnet
Sutton U v Macclesfield T
Telford U v Stafford Rangers

Saturday 24 March (*Cheshire Cup*)
Darlington v Merthyr Tydfil
Enfield v Northwich Vic
Kettering T v Barrow
Macclesfield T v Fisher Ath
Runcorn v Farnborough T
Stafford Rangers v Kidderminster
  Harriers
Sutton U v Altrincham
Telford U v Barnet
Welling U v Cheltenham T
Wycombe W v Chorley
Yeovil T v Boston U

Tuesday 27 March
Barrow v Northwich Vic

Wednesday 28 March
Cheltenham T v Sutton U

Saturday 31 March
Altrincham v Enfield
Barnet v Darlington
Boston U v Barrow
Cheltenham T v Runcorn
Chorley v Fisher Ath
Farnborough T v Macclesfield T
Kidderminster Harriers v
  Wycombe W
Merthyr Tydfil v Stafford Rangers
Northwich Vic v Telford U
Welling U v Sutton U
Yeovil T v Kettering T

Saturday 7 April (*FA Trophy
  semi-final 1st leg*)
Altrincham v Kettering T
Barnet v Yeovil T
Boston U v Cheltenham T
Darlington v Farnborough T
Fisher Ath v Kidderminster
  Harriers
Macclesfield T v Chorley
Merthyr Tydfil v Welling U
Sutton U v Runcorn
Telford U v Barrow
Wycombe W v Stafford Rangers
No fixture: Enfield, Northwich Vic

Tuesday 10 April
Sutton U v Enfield

Saturday 14 April (*FA Trophy
  semi-final 2nd leg*)
Barrow v Cheltenham T
Chorley v Merthyr Tydfil
Darlington v Wycombe W
Enfield v Yeovil T
Farnborough T v Northwich Vic
Fisher Ath v Sutton U
Kettering T v Macclesfield U
Kidderminster Harriers v
  Altrincham
Runcorn v Boston U
Stafford Rangers v Barnet
Welling U v Telford U

Monday 16 April (*Easter*)
Altrincham v Runcorn
Cheltenham T v Kettering T
Enfield v Merthyr Tydfil
Northwich Vic v Macclesfield T
Kidderminster Harriers v Welling U
Sutton U v Stafford Rangers
Telford U v Darlington
Wycombe W v Barrow

Yeovil T v Chorley
No fixture: Barnet, Boston U,
  Farnborough T, Fisher Ath

Saturday 21 April
Barrow v Barnet
Boston U v Chorley
Cheltenham T v Telford U
Merthyr Tydfil v Enfield
Northwich Vic v Sutton U
Runcorn v Welling U
Stafford Rangers v Darlington
Wycombe W v Farnborough T
Yeovil T v Fisher Ath
No fixture: Altrincham, Kettering
  T, Kidderminster H,
  Macclesfield T

Tuesday 24 April
Chorley v Northwich Vic
Telford U v Runcorn

Saturday 28 April
Barnet v Altrincham
Boston U v Merthyr Tydfil
Darlington v Cheltenham T
Enfield v Stafford Rangers
Farnborough T v Kidderminster H
Fisher Ath v Kettering T
Runcorn v Yeovil T
Sutton U v Barrow
Telford U v Macclesfield T
Welling U v Chorley
Wycombe W v Northwich Vic

Saturday 5 May
Altrincham v Wycombe W
Barrow v Enfield
Chorley v Barnet
Kettering T v Sutton U
Kidderminster Harriers v
  Cheltenham T
Macclesfield T v Boston U
Merthyr Tydfil v Fisher Ath
Northwich Vic v Runcorn
Stafford Rangers v Farnborough T
Welling U v Darlington
Yeovil T v Telford U

Saturday 19 May
FA Trophy Final Tie

Saturday 12 May
FA Cup Final Tie

INTERNATIONAL AND CUP
FIXTURES 1989–90
(Subject to alteration)

P – Preliminary round; WC – World Cup; EP – Extra preliminary round; IQ – First quali-fying round; F – Friendly; QF – Quarter-final; SF – Semi-final; *closing date for round

August 1989
Sat 5	Official opening of season
Sat 12	FA Charity Shield
Sat 19	Football League season starts
Wed 23	Littlewoods Cup (1) 1st leg
Wed 30	Littlewoods Cup (1) 2nd leg

September 1989
Sat 2	FA Cup (P)
Wed 6	Sweden v England (WC)
	Finland v Wales (WC)
	Yugoslavia v Scotland (WC)
Sat 9	FA Vase (EP)
	FA Youth Cup (P)*
Wed 13	European Cups (1) 1st leg
Sat 16	FA Cup (1Q)
Wed 20	Littlewoods Cup (2) 1st leg
Sat 23	FA Trophy (1Q)
Wed 27	European Cups (1) 2nd leg
Sat 30	FA Cup (2Q)
	FA Youth Cup (1Q)*

October 1989
Wed 4	Littlewoods Cup (2) 2nd leg
Sat 7	FA Vase (P)
Sun 8	FA Sunday Cup (1)
Wed 11	Poland v England (WC)
	Wales v Holland (WC)
	France v Scotland (WC)
	Rep. of Ireland v N. Ireland (WC)
Sat 14	FA Cup (3Q)
	FA Youth Cup (2Q)*
Wed 18	European Cups (2) 1st leg
Sat 21	FA Trophy (2Q)
	FA County Youth Cup (1)*
Wed 25	Littlewoods Cup (3)
Sat 28	FA Cup (4Q)

November 1989
Wed 1	European Cups (2) 2nd leg
Sat 4	FA Vase (1)
Sat 11	FA Youth Cup (1)*
Sun 12	FA Sunday Cup (2)

Wed 15	England v Italy (F)
	West Germany v Wales (WC)
	Scotland v Norway (WC)
Sat 18	FA Cup (1)
Wed 22	UEFA Cup (3) 1st leg
Sat 25	FA Vase (2)
Wed 29	Littlewoods Cup (4)

December 1989
Sat 2	FA Trophy (3Q)
	FA County Youth Cup (2)*
Wed 6	UEFA Cup (3) 2nd leg
Sat 9	FA Cup (2)
	FA Youth Cup (2)*
Sun 10	FA Sunday Cup (3)
Sat 16	FA Vase (3)

January 1990
Sat 6	FA Cup (3)
Sat 13	FA Trophy (1)
	FA Youth Cup (3)*
Wed 17	Littlewoods Cup (5)
Sat 20	FA Vase (4)
	FA County Youth Cup (3)*
Sun 21	FA Sunday Cup (4)
Sat 27	FA Cup (4)

February 1990
Sat 3	FA Trophy (2)
Sat 10	FA Vase (5)
	FA Youth Cup (4)*
Wed 14	Littlewoods Cup (SF) 1st leg
Sat 17	FA Cup (5)
Sun 18	FA Sunday Cup (5)
Sat 24	FA Trophy (3)
	FA County Youth Cup (4)*
Wed 28	Littlewoods Cup (SF) 2nd leg

March 1990
Sat 3	FA Vase (6)
	FA Youth Cup (5)*
Wed 7	European Cups (QF) 1st leg

Sat 10	FA Cup (6)
	England v France (Schoolboys)
Sat 17	FA Trophy (4)
Sun 18	FA Sunday Cup (SF)
Wed 21	European Cups (QF) 2nd leg
Sat 24	FA Vase (SF) 1st leg
	FA County Youth Cup (SF)*
Wed 28	International date
Sat 31	FA Vase (SF) 2nd leg
	FA Youth Cup (SF)*

April 1990

Wed 4	European Cups (SF) 1st leg
Sat 7	FA Cup (SF)
	FA Trophy (SF) 1st leg
Sat 14	FA Trophy (SF) 2nd leg
Wed 18	European Cups (SF) 2nd leg
Wed 25	International date
Sat 28	FA County Youth Cup final
Sun 29	Littlewoods Cup final
	FA Sunday Cup final

May 1990

Wed 2	UEFA Cup final 1st leg
Sat 5	FA Vase final
	FA Youth Cup final *
Wed 9	European Cup Winners' Cup final
Sat 12	FA Cup final
Wed 16	UEFA Cup final 2nd leg
Sat 19	FA Trophy final
Wed 23	European Champion Clubs' Cup final

June 1990

| Sat 2 | England v Holland (Schoolboys) |
| Fri 8 | World Cup finals (end 8 July) |

USEFUL ADDRESSES

Football Association: R.H.G. Kelly, FCIS, 16 Lancaster Gate, London W2 3LW.
Scottish FA: E. Walker, 6 Park Gardens, Glasgow G3 7YF.
Irish FA: D. Bowen, 20 Windsor Avenue, Belfast BT9 6EG.
Welsh FA: A.E. Evans B.Sc., 3 Westgate Street, Cardiff CF1 1JF.
FA of Ireland (Eire): Dr T. O'Neill, 80 Merrion Square South, Dublin 2.
League of Ireland: E. Morris, 80 Merrion Square, Dublin 2.
Fedération Internationale de Football Association (FIFA): J. Blatter, FIFA House, 11 Hitzigweg, CH-8032 Zurich, Switzerland.
Union des Associations Européenes de Football (UEFA): G. Aigner, Jupiterstrasse 33 PO Box 16, CH-3000 Berne 15, Switzerland.
Football League: J.D. Dent, Lytham St Annes, Lancashire FY8 1JG.
Scottish League: J. Farry, 188 West Regent Street, Glasgow G2 4RY.
Irish League: M. Brown, 87 University Street, Belfast BT7 1HP.
Welsh League: W.T. Williams, 39 Ty Newydd, Whitchurch, Cardiff, CF4 1NQ.
GM Vauxhall Conference: P.D. Hunter, 24 Barnehurst Road, Bexley Heath, Kent DA7 6EZ.
Beazer Homes League: D.J. Strudwick, 42 Cotswold Court, Burford Road, Horsham, West Sussex RH13 5ST.
Northern Premier League: R.D. Bayley, 22 Woburn Drive, Hale, Altrincham, Cheshire WA15 8LZ.
Vauxhaull League: N. Robinson, 226 Rye Lane, Peckham, London SE15 4NL.
The Association of Football League Referees and Linesmen: J.B. Goggins, 1 Tewkesbury Drive, Lytham St Annes, Lancs FY8 4LN.
Football League Managers and Secretaries Association: K. Friar, c/o Arsenal FC, Arsenal Stadium, Highbury, London N5.
Women's Football Association: Miss L. Whitehead, 448/450, Hanging Ditch, The Corn Exchange, Manchester M4 3ES.
Universities Athletic Union: I. Grant, 28 Woburn Square, London WC1.
English Schools FA: C.S. Allatt, 4a Eastgate Street, Stafford ST16 2NN.
Professional Footballers' Association: G. Taylor, 2 Oxford Court, Bishopsgate, off Lower Mosley Street, Manchester, M2 3W2.
The Association of Football Statisticians: R.J. Spiller, 22 Bretons, Basildon, Essex.
England Supporters' Association: David Stacey, 66 Southend Road, Wickford, Essex SS11 8EN.
The Football Programme Directory: Editor, David Stacey, 66 Southend Road, Wickford, Essex SS11 8EN.
National Federation of Football Supporters' Clubs: Chairman, A.M. Kershaw, 87 Brookfield Avenue, Loughborough, Leicestershire LE11 3LN (0509 267643)
Football Trust Second Floor, Walkden House, 10 Melton Street, London NW1 2EJ.